Marketing Research
An Applied Approach

Jay Switzer

672-6084

192-196
702-710
212
215-28
225-236
ch. 11

measurement scale 280

sampling techniques 257

McGraw-Hill Series in Marketing

CONSULTING EDITOR

Charles Schewe *University of Massachusetts*

Marketing Research

An Applied Approach

Thomas C. Kinnear
Associate Professor of Marketing

James R. Taylor
*Sebastian S. Kresge
Professor of Marketing*

*Both at the
Graduate School of Business Administration
University of Michigan*

McGraw-Hill Book Company

New York St. Louis San Francisco Auckland Bogotá Düsseldorf
Johannesburg London Madrid Mexico Montreal New Delhi
Panama Paris São Paulo Singapore Sydney Tokyo Toronto

MARKETING RESEARCH:
An Applied Approach

4 5 6 7 8 9 0 DODO   8 3 2 1

Library of Congress Cataloging in Publication Data

Kinnear, Thomas C date
  Marketing research.

  (McGraw-Hill series in marketing)
  Includes bibliographies and index.
  1. Marketing research. 2. Marketing management.
I. Taylor, James Ronald, date   joint author.
II. Title.
HF5415.2.K53   658.8'3   78-12770
ISBN 0-07-034741-7

This book was set in Times Roman by Monotype Composition Company, Inc.
The editors were John F. Carleo, William J. Kane, and James B. Armstrong;
the cover was designed by Albert M. Cetta;
the production supervisor was Charles Hess.
The drawings were done by ANCO/Boston.
R. R. Donnelley & Sons Company was printer and binder.

Contents

2

EARLY STAGES OF THE RESEARCH PROCESS

3

SAMPLING

4

MEASUREMENT

5

EXPERIMENTATION AND TEST MARKETING

6

OBTAINING INFORMATION FROM RESPONDENTS

7

FINAL STAGES OF THE RESEARCH PROCESS

8

ADVANCED TOPICS

Preface

The quality of marketing decisions is to a great extent dependent on the information available to the marketing decision maker. It is the function of marketing research to provide information for this decision making. A marketing manager who does not know how to use or evaluate marketing research is much like a general manager who does not understand the income statement for the company. Both individuals are severely limited in their ability to effectively perform their jobs.

OBJECTIVES

The main purpose of this book is to provide the prospective marketing manager with an understanding of marketing research. It may also serve as a first book for people with career objectives in the field of marketing research. The book is designed for use either in junior or senior undergraduate courses in marketing research or in a first graduate course in marketing research.

UNIQUE FEATURES

There are certain attributes of this book that define its competitive positioning. These are:

    1 It is designed to be easily read and understood. Great care has been taken to explain the basic technical issues in a step-by-step fashion.

    2 It presents marketing research as a managerially and decision-making–oriented subject.

    3 It presents marketing research in a pragmatic, "here's how to do it" fashion.

    4 Advanced quantitative procedures are not dealt with in detail. It is not a text on quantitative techniques in marketing research.

    5 It contains 14 real cases that are designed to allow students to apply material presented in the chapters.

    6 Its accompanying volume, *Exercise in Marketing Research,* is designed to allow for the actual undertaking of certain parts of the research process described in the text. Thus, learning by doing is encouraged.

    7 It contains one whole chapter that presents an actual research project from beginning stages to completion. Managerial interactions are described along with study objectives and some results.

    8 It has been designed for flexibility of use; the more complex chapters may be skipped without disrupting the flow of the book.

    9 It contains a glossary of important marketing research terms.

    10 Each chapter is concluded with a point-by-point summary.

    11 Each chapter includes a list of additional readings.

    12 Each chapter has questions and/or problems for student discussion.

ORGANIZATION OF THE BOOK

The book is organized around the steps one would actually take in conducting a marketing research project. Part One presents an overview of marketing research. Chapters 1 and 2 define marketing research and positions it within marketing management. Chapter 3 presents a detailed example of a real marketing research project, while Chapter 4 describes a number of aspects about the business of marketing research, including types of institutions, jobs, use of outside suppliers, and ethics.

    Part Two consists of three chapters that examine issues that are usually dealt with early in the process of marketing research. Chapter 5 discusses when marketing research should be undertaken and includes a discussion of problem definition and an nonquantitative discussion regarding the cost and value of information. (A quantitative discussion of the latter topic appears in Chapter 27.) Alternative research designs and data sources, including syndicated sources, are the subject of Chapter 6. Chapter 7 presents a detailed review of available secondary data, including census and library data.

    Part Three considers various aspects of sampling. Chapter 8 presents an overview of sampling and a discussion of nonprobability sampling procedures. Chapter 9 discusses the most straightforward type of probability sampling, simple random sampling. Statistical concepts are reviewed as they apply to marketing research, with the emphasis on usefulness, not theory. In Chapter 10 more complex but more useful sampling procedures are discussed, including stratified sampling and cluster sampling. In Chapter 11 the question of sample size is addressed along with the types and effects of nonsampling errors that can confound marketing research results.

In Part Four the question of measurement in marketing research is dealt with. Chapter 12 discusses how numbers can properly be assigned to the types of variables one attempts to measure in marketing research. This is a necessary step in quantitative analysis of marketing data. Chapter 13 covers in detail one area of measurement that is extremely important in marketing research: attitude measurement. Different attitude scaling techniques are discussed.

Part Five examines the use of experimental procedures in marketing research. Chapter 14 outlines the preconditions necessary for one to be able to infer causality in marketing situations and discusses certain research designs that aid this process. Chapters 15 and 16 describe statistically the design and analysis of different types of experiments. Chapter 17 covers the uses and practical aspects of test marketing.

In Part Six the steps necessary for actually collecting information from respondents are discussed. Chapter 18 reviews the different types of procedures available, including mail, phone, and in-person interviews, and examines focus-group interviews and other qualitative procedures. Chapter 19 presents a discussion of how to design effective data collection forms, including questionnaires. In Chapter 20 the interviewing process and the control of the actual interviews in the field are examined.

Once the research has been designed, the sample drawn, and the field work completed, the data must be analyzed and reported. The four chapters that make up Part Seven deal with this area. Chapter 21 describes how data on data collection instruments can be converted into computer readable form. Chapter 22 presents data analysis techniques of the simplest type—those for analyzing only one variable at a time. Data analysis involving two variables at a time is discussed in Chapter 23. The emphasis is on the pragmatics of data analysis. (More complex data analysis procedures are presented in Part Eight.) Chapter 24 discusses reporting research findings both orally and in written form.

More advanced topics in the field of marketing research are presented in Part Eight. They are not examined in the detail in which other material in the book is presented, however. Our objective is to acquaint readers with this material so that they are familiar with the terms and concepts and have some understanding of how these procedures might be used. Chapters 25 and 26 offer an overview of data analysis procedures that analyze more than two variables at a time. Specifically, Chapter 25 discusses factor analysis, cluster analysis, and multidimensional scaling, while Chapter 26 examines such procedures as multiple regression, discriminant analysis, analysis of covariance, conjoint measurement, and AID. Chapter 27 presents a Bayesian, or decision-theory-based, approach to the quantification of the cost and value of marketing research information.

CASES AND EXERCISES

Throughout the book, the thrust is pragmatic in terms of showing what it is like to actually do a marketing research project in the context of providing the decision maker with relevant information. This approach is aided by 14 real cases and by the companion volume, *Exercises In Marketing Research*. These cases and exercises allow the student to actually do the things presented in the chapters.

ALTERNATIVE USAGE PATTERNS

The book is designed for flexibility of use. We have opted for a large number of relatively short chapters to accomplish this. More complex material can easily be skipped without disrupting the flow of the book. We have employed this approach in order to use this text at both the undergraduate and graduate levels. Some possible usage patterns might be:

    1 A course designed to provide a managerial overview with little quantitative material (Chapters 1–8, 11, 17–24).

    2 A course designed to provide both a managerial overview and a good understanding of the basic quantitative concepts (Chapter 1–14, 17–24).

    3 A course designed to provide a managerial overview and a somewhat detailed understanding of quantitative material (Chapters 1–27).

ACKNOWLEDGMENTS

We owe a great deal of thanks to many people in preparing this manuscript. Specifically, our McGraw-Hill editor, William J. Kane, and consulting editor, Charles D. Schewe (University of Massachusetts, Amherst), provided most insightful guidance. Helpful reviewer comments were provided by Gerald Albaum (University of Oregon, Eugene), Robert H. Collins (Oregon State University, Corvallis), Robert Small (Fairleigh Dickinson University), and Joseph J. Vidali (San Diego State University). In addition, we would like to acknowledge the special assistance of Phillip E. Hendrix, Duncan G. LaBay, Lawrence A. Crosby, Cynthia J. Frey, and the many Michigan students who made discerning comments regarding the early drafts of the chapters, cases, and exercises. Finally, we wish to thank Mrs. Sandra Laurie for her assistance in typing the manuscript. We are grateful to the Literary Executor of the late Sir Ronald A. Fisher, F.R.S.; to Dr. Frank Yates, F.R.S.; and to Longman Group Ltd., London, for permission to reprint Table III from their book *Statistical Tables for Biological, Agricultural and Medical Research* (6th ed., 1974).

    In closing, we owe a special thanks to our families for pushing us "to get that book finished." Naturally, the book is dedicated to them: Connie, Maggie, and Jamie; Bobbie, Pam, and Sandy.

Thomas C. Kinnear
James R. Taylor

Part One

Introduction

Chapter 1

The Nature and Role of Marketing Research

Consumers, perplexing creatures, appear to have ever-expanding needs and wants.[1] They purchase textbooks, golf lessons, homes, deodorant, life insurance, ice cream cones, vacations, dental care, and a seemingly perpetual array of other modern-day necessities and luxuries. In the modern democracies, the marketing system is designed to be highly responsive to these expanding and ever-changing needs. This is reflected in the growing acceptance of the marketing concept by many diverse organizations. The marketing concept suggests that the resources and activities of the organization be focused in an integrated way on the *needs and wants of the consumer* as opposed to the needs and wants of the organization.[2] The central problem confronting these organizations is how to monitor the needs of the marketplace and anticipate the future. In response to this situation, the concept of a formalized system for acquiring information to assist in understanding the marketplace and to facilitate the decision-making process has emerged. This system is called a *marketing information system*

---

[1] George Katona, *Psychological Economics* (New York: Elsevier, 1975), p.15.
[2] See J. B. McKitterick, "What Is the Marketing Management Concept?" in Frank M. Bass (ed.), *The Frontiers of Marketing Thought and Action* (Chicago: American Marketing Association, 1957), pp. 71–82.

3

(MIS).[3] The objective of an MIS is to integrate marketing data sources (internal accounting data, salespeople's reports, marketing services data, marketing research studies, and so on) into a continuous information flow for marketing decision making. The cornerstone of an MIS is marketing research, the topic of this book.

The marketing concept has expanded to many types of organizations. Producers and distributors of consumer and industrial goods were the first to formalize and implement the marketing concept, but this consumer-oriented philosophy has now been extended to service and nonprofit organizations such as financial institutions, the entertainment industry, hospitals, universities, churches, fund-raising groups, museums, and government agencies.[4] Nations are beginning to adopt the marketing concept in their efforts to sell goods and services in the world's markets. As we see the marketing concept adopted by more and more organizations, the need for understanding the nature and role of marketing research has expanded. This textbook is designed to serve the needs of students training for, and practitioners serving in, these organizations.

It is tempting to turn immediately to a discussion of contemporary research techniques and methodology. But this would be hasty; several introductory concepts and issues must be discussed first. In particular, we must address the following questions:

1   What is the character of marketing activity?
2   What is the task of marketing management?
3   What type of information is needed by marketing management?
4   What are the sources of information for marketing decision making?
5   What is the role of marketing research in the marketing system?

THE MARKETING SYSTEM

To facilitate our understanding of the nature and role of marketing research, we must first characterize the marketing system of which it is a part. Figure 1-1 presents a diagrammatic model of this system. This conceptual scheme depicts the marketing system from the perspective of the selling organization. The model specifies a performance measure(s) for the organization, identifies relevant variables in the process, and classifies the variables as independent or dependent.

Marketing Mix

By *variable* we mean a property that takes on different values at different times. For example, an organization may vary its advertising budget or change its

---

[3] Chapter 2 introduces the concept of a *marketing research system.* The marketing research system is viewed as the intermediate stage in the transition from the traditional view of marketing research as a series of ad hoc surveys to the more idealized concept of a marketing information system. The marketing research system includes many of the diverse data sources found in a marketing information system but does not have the degree of structure and interactive people-machine concepts found in a marketing information system. Chapter 6 discusses this area in more detail.

[4] Philip Kotler, *Marketing Management,* 3d ed. (Englewood Cliffs, N.J.: Prentice-Hall, 1976), p. 1.

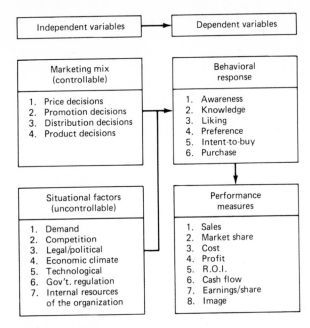

Figure 1-1   Model of the marketing system.

selling price. An *independent variable* is the presumed cause of the dependent variable, which is the presumed effect.[5] The independent variables are classified as to whether they can be manipulated or controlled by the selling organization. Those variables that can be controlled are identified as the marketing mix components of *product, price, place,* and *promotion.*[6] Different levels of these variables can be combined to form alternative marketing programs or courses of action.

Situational Factors

The situational variables represent independent variables that are not under the control of the selling organization. These variables make up the state of nature which the selling organization must adapt to in formulating and implementing a marketing program. The state of nature consists of factors such as the energy crisis, competitive actions, economic climate, market trends, and government regulation.

Behavioral Response

Both sets of independent variables, marketing mix and situational factors, combine to influence a behavioral response such as purchase, buying intentions,

[5] Fred N. Kerlinger, *Foundations of Behavioral Research,* 2d ed. (New York: Holt, Rinehart, 1973), p. 35.
[6] E. Jerome McCarthy, *Basic Marketing: A Managerial Approach,* 4th ed. (Homewood, Ill.: Richard D. Irwin, 1971), p. 44.

preference, attitudes, and so on. This behavioral response is the dependent variable, or the presumed effect. A complicating factor is that the behavioral response is also influenced by the consequences of past behavior in addition to the immediate influence of the independent variables.[7] Consequently, developing an effective marketing program is a challenging and complicated process involving a dynamic set of variables and a behavioral response which changes as a result of learning. This situation requires skilled managers who can give proper perspective to past experience and effectively use marketing research information in their decision making.

Formally identifying the functional relationships among the independent and dependent variables is obviously a difficult assignment. Regardless of how difficult, it is important to recognize that the nature of these relationships is *implicit* to the manager's choice of alternative courses of action. In attempting to use marketing research to formalize these relationships, the manager must consider the cost of gathering the information relative to the level of confidence gained in selecting the optimum course of action.[8] In practice, management experience and judgment, combined with information from the marketing research system, form the basis for management decision making.

It should be clearly understood that a manager can make decisions without using marketing research. These decisions may be very sound if the manager's experience is relevant and judgment good. The idea is to make a wise decision, not to spend money on marketing research that will not be used to aid a decision. It is when the decision maker needs additional information to decrease the uncertainty associated with a decision that marketing research is used.

Performance Measures

The behavior responses form the basis for the organization's monetary and nonmonetary performance measures. Monetary measures are sales, market share, profit, internal rate of return, and so on. Nonmonetary measures are the organization's image, consumer attitudes toward the organization, and so on. Developing valid performance measures is central to the effective management of the marketing system. Marketing research plays an important role in supplying the tools and data sources for performance measurement.

THE MARKETING MANAGEMENT PROCESS

What do marketing managers do? Figure 1-2 illustrates the four main components of the marketing management process. The activities of marketing management are typically identified by (1) the functions performed and (2) the decision-making process. Marketing managers are decision makers who perform the management functions of *planning, control, organizing, directing,* and *staffing* in the context of the marketing system. Fundamental to the decision-making process is information. Marketing managers rely on two information inputs, namely their own

---

[7] See B. F. Skinner, *Science and Human Behavior* (New York: The Free Press, 1953).
[8] The cost and value of information will be discussed more fully in Chapters 5 and 27.

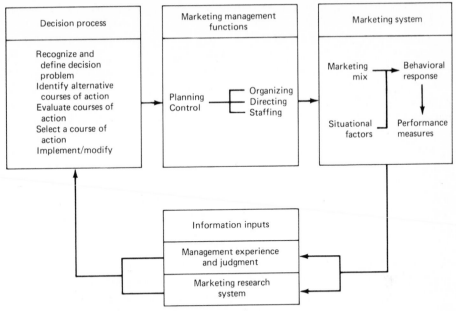

Figure 1-2 The marketing management process.

experience and judgment and the more formalized information available from the marketing research system. Let's discuss the components of the marketing management process in more detail.

The Decision-making Process

A characteristic of fundamental importance to the marketing management process is decision making. The decision-making process permeates the management process, and the two terms are often considered synonymous.[9]

The organization's well-being is dependent on the wisdom of the decisions made by its managers. The vast majority of decisions made by managers are *programmed*.[10] These day-to-day decisions concern routine situations which they have dealt with previously. Programmed decisions involve practically no uncertainty and have a low potential for surprise. Managers rely heavily, if not exclusively, on their experience and judgment in making such decisions.

A second type of decision involves situations where past experience and judgment are less relevant. The problem is new or the situation is unique in some way so that the manager's normal decision-making approach does not fit neatly into the new setting. Confronted with this *unprogrammed* decision situation, the manager would follow a more formal approach which we will call the decision-making process.

[9] Herbert A. Simon, *The New Science of Management Decision* (New York: Harper & Row, 1960), p. 1.

[10] David J. Luck, Hugh G. Wales, and Donald A. Taylor, *Marketing Research*, 4th ed. (Englewood Cliffs, N.J.: Prentice-Hall, 1974), p. 15.

The decision-making process may be thought of as involving a series of steps (see Figure 1-3). *The first step is the recognition that a unique marketing problem exists or that an opportunity is present.* Marketing problems and opportunities result from the dynamic nature of the situational factors and/or the implementation of the marketing program. Performance measures often signal the presence of problems, while the monitoring of the situational factors can signal the presence of both problems and opportunities. For example, the manager may be informed that a product's market share has declined, or that a competitor will be introducing a new product, or that primary demand for a product has risen faster than anticipated, or that government action has negatively influenced the sale of a competitor's product, and so on. Consequently, managers make decisions to solve problems or to capitalize on opportunities.

The word "problem" carries a connotation of trouble. Something is not working right or needs attention. Typical situations would be where the marketing program is inefficient or where the situational factors have changed and require adjustments in the marketing program. This could range from minor changes in existing programs to developing new programs for new markets. Opportunities differ from problems in that the manager may not be required to do anything about them. In fact, they may not even be recognized. Most opportunities do not force themselves on managers in the same way that problems do. The reason is that most firms have formal methods for detecting the presence of problems via their performance measures but less formal methods for monitoring the opportunities.

The second step in the decision process is the definition of the decision problem. The manager needs to define and clarify the main issues and causal factors operating in the decision situation. It is not always easy to identify what fundamental variables are causing trouble and what needs correcting. Marketing research personnel and techniques play an important role in this regard. By involving the research function in this early phase of the decision-making process,

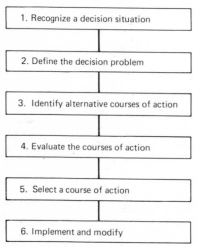

1. Recognize a decision situation

2. Define the decision problem

3. Identify alternative courses of action

4. Evaluate the courses of action

5. Select a course of action

6. Implement and modify

Figure 1-3   Steps in the decision-making process.

the marketing manager can benefit from more effective formulation of problems and opportunities, while at the same time assuring more effective use of marketing research in later stages of the decision process.

The third step in the decision process is the identification of alternative courses of action. In marketing, a course of action involves the specification of some combination of the marketing mix variables. "Do nothing new" or "maintain the status quo" is just as much a course of action as one denoting a change in marketing activities.

The effectiveness of management decision making is constrained by the quality of the alternatives considered. Consequently, it is critical that the "best" alternative be identified. The process of identifying courses of action is a *creative process* similar to the first stage of the decision-making process. The manager and marketing researcher have to search for new ideas, which come from creative thinking and imagination. Various marketing research approaches are available that can stimulate the manager's creative process and broaden the domain of alternatives identified.

The fourth and fifth steps in the decision process include the evaluation of alternatives and the selection of a course of action. In order that a decision can be made, there must be at least two courses of action identified and uncertainty as to which course of action will maximize the attainment of management objectives. If the decision maker is faced with a situation where there is only one realistic course of action, and that is to "do nothing," then there is no decision involved, even though the problem or opportunity confronting the management has significant consequences for the organization.

Marketing research is a valuable tool in the evaluation of alternative courses of action. Often, unprogrammed decision situations involve substantial uncertainty and risk. The manager is interested in marketing research information as a way to reduce the uncertainty inherent in the selection of a course of action.

The final step in the decision-making process is the implementation of the selected course of action. Again, marketing research supplies the means for monitoring the effectiveness of the action selected and the situational variables that influence the program's performance.

Decision making involving unprogrammed decision situations can never be as well done as managers would like. This is caused partly by the uncertainty regarding the future state of the situational factors, partly by the limitations of gathering clear and precise information regarding the outcomes of the alternatives considered, and partly by the fact that decision making is a human process. The long time span between making decisions and receiving definite feedback plus the uncertainty regarding the nature of the cause-and-effect relations in the marketing system contribute substantially to this situation.

Marketing Management Functions

Marketing management is the process of making decisions while performing various functions for the purpose of developing and implementing effective marketing programs to accomplish organizational objectives. The functions performed by management are typically classified as *planning, control, organizing, directing,* and *staffing.*[11] Marketing research can provide information to facilitate the decision-making process for each of these functions. In recent years, formalized marketing planning and more effective control procedures have been receiving increased emphasis in both consumer and industrial marketing management.[12]

Planning and Control

Planning involves making decisions today regarding what marketing action to take in the future. It is the process whereby the organization must reconcile its ability to develop and implement a marketing program with the problems and opportunities presented by the situational factors in order to accomplish objectives. All managers do planning. The process of deciding what to do next week or next year is planning. Decisions regarding future advertising appropriations, price changes, dealer margins, and so on represent planning.

While all organizations have managers who plan, they differ considerably in how formally it is done. This ranges from managers who are preoccupied with current operations and what will happen tomorrow to managers and staff groups who are committed to extensive formal planning procedures and produce written annual plans, profit plans, five-year plans, and so on.

The three main questions in the formal planning process are typically stated as "Where are we now?" (situational analysis), "Where do we want to go?" (objectives), and "How do we get there?" (programming).[13]

Situational Analysis   The formal planning process of most organizations begins with a review of the past five years' activities. This includes areas such as the performance of marketing activities, trends in markets and segments, nature of the competitive environment, role of government regulation, and limitations of the organization's resources. The purpose of this section is not merely description but rather the diagnosis of the marketing program's performance and the influencing variables. The next section involves a detailed forecasting of situational factors and their influence. This should be concluded with a statement of key problems and opportunities confronting the organization.

Objectives   Establishing objectives is a critical aspect of planning. As is often stated, "If you don't know where you want to go, any road will take you there." Marketing objectives are guided by the organization's "charter" or "primary mission."[14] This is often characterized by the question "What business

    [11] H. Koontz and C. O'Donnell, *Principles of Management,* 5th ed. (New York: McGraw-Hill, 1972), p. 46.
    [12] Elmer P. Lotshaw, "Industrial Marketing: Trends and Challenges," *Journal of Marketing,* January 1970, p. 22.
    [13] David S. Hopkins, *The Short Term Marketing Plan* (New York: The Conference Board, Research Report 565, 1975), p. 11.
    [14] Ibid., p. 13.

are we in?'' The charter provides guidelines as to the limits of the organization's marketing activities.

Marketing decisions are made to achieve some objective. This typically involves achieving a particular level of behavioral response in the market place, i.e., purchases, awareness, and so on. This response can be translated into more specific statements of monetary and/or nonmonetary performance measures. For example, the objectives set for a new-product introduction could be to achieve 50 percent trial rate and a market share of 15 percent within the first year of national introduction.

Overall marketing program objectives are typically broken down into more specific objectives regarding the components of the marketing mix. Consequently, a marketing plan may include subobjectives for the sales force, advertising, sales promotion, pricing, and many other areas.

Programming   Developing effective marketing programs to achieve objectives is the heart of the marketing manager's job. This involves formulating a marketing strategy and specifying the tactical plans for implementing the marketing program.

Strategy specifies the broad principles according to which the marketing program will operate in achieving objectives. It is an attempt to answer in a fundamental way the "How do we get there?" question. The actual carrying out of the strategy involves action-oriented programs regarding the marketing mix elements of product, place, promotion, and price. This section involves the "tactics" of the marketing program.

Planning includes formulating and implementing marketing programs based on a set of premises regarding the effectiveness of the marketing program and the influence of the situational factors. The validity of these assumptions will be revealed through the course of time. Modern marketing management requires a control mechanism to monitor the effectiveness of the marketing program and detect changes in the situational factors. Control involves (1) setting standards of performance in order to reach objectives, (2) measuring actual performance against these standards, and (3) taking action to correct deviations in performance.[15]

Contingency planning is a way for the organization to react quickly and effectively to deviations in performance. It involves specifying alternative courses of action to meet invalid planning assumptions or unanticipated changes in the situational factors. For example, an advertising program is found to be ineffective, or a major competitor lowers its price. Planning should not be considered as a constraint on future marketing action. Rather, effective planning demands a continual rethinking and replanning in order to accomplish objectives.

---

[15] R. G. Murdick and J. E. Ross, *Information Systems for Modern Management* (Englewood Cliffs, N.J.: Prentice-Hall, 1971), p. 49.

Information Needs

There are certain essential groups of information required by the marketing manager for planning and control purposes.[16] Exhibit 1-1 illustrates this type of information. While this listing is not intended to be complete, it does indicate that information is needed regarding the controllable and uncontrollable variables in the marketing system plus the measurement of their influence on the behavioral response.

Exhibit 1-1   Types of Information Needed for Planning and Control

I Situational analysis
  A Demand analysis
    1 Buyer behavior and characteristics:
      a What do they buy?
      b Who buys?
      c Where do they buy?
      d Why do they buy?
      e How do they buy?
      f When do they buy?
      g How much do they buy?
      h How will buyer behavior and characteristics change in the future?
    2 Market characteristics:
      a Market size/potential
      b Segments
      c Selective demand
      d Future market trends
  B Competition
    1 Who are competitors?
    2 Competitor characteristics:
      a Marketing programs
      b Competitive behavior
      c Resources
    3 Major strengths and weaknesses
    4 Future competitive environment
  C General environment
    1 Economic conditions and trends
    2 Government regulation and trends
    3 Pollution, safety, consumerism concerns
    4 Technological trends
    5 Political climate
  D Internal environment
    1 Marketing resources/skills
    2 Production resources/skills
    3 Financial resources/skills
    4 Technological resources/skills
    5 Future trends in internal environment

[16] The discussion that follows is based on Murray A. Cayley, "Marketing Research Planning and Evaluation," *The Business Quarterly,* Spring 1975.

Exhibit 1-1 (*Continued*)

II Marketing mix
  A Product
    1 What product attributes/benefits are important?
    2 How should the product be differentiated?
    3 What segments will be attracted?
    4 How important is service, warranty, and so on?
    5 Is there a need for product variation/product line?
    6 How important is packaging?
    7 How is the product perceived relative to competitive offerings?
  B Place
    1 What types of distributors should handle the product?
    2 What are the channel attitudes and motivations for handling the product?
    3 What intensity of wholesale/retail coverage is needed?
    4 What margins are appropriate?
    5 What forms of physical distribution are needed?
  C Price
    1 What is the elasticity of demand?
    2 What pricing policies are appropriate?
    3 How should the product line be priced?
    4 How do we establish price variations for a product?
    5 How should we react to a competitive price threat?
    6 How important is price to the buyer?
  D Promotion
    1 What is the optimal promotional budget?
    2 How important is sales promotion, advertising, personal selling in stimulating demand?
    3 What is the proper promotion mix?
    4 How do you measure the effectiveness of the promotion tools?
    5 What copy is most effective?
    6 What media are most effective?

III Performance measures
    1 What are current sales by product line?
    2 What are current market shares by product line?
    3 What are current sales/market share by customer types, sales region, so on?
    4 What is our product/company image among customers, distributors, public?
    5 What is the awareness level to our promotion?
    6 What is the recall level of our brand name?
    7 What percentage distributorship do we have in large retailers, medium, small? By geography, customer type?
    8 What percentage of the channel is selling below suggested retail price? What is the average retail price of our product?

Marketing research plays a central role in supplying information for the planning and control functions. It is in response to the need for formal planning and control that research is able to develop a systematic approach to the information needs of management. The activities of research can be built to a large extent around the needs of the planning process. The responsibility of research is not only to have such information on hand but to organize and present it in a manner that contributes to the organization's planning and control activities. With a continually updated library of information available to facilitate decision making, the manager should be able to do an effective job of (1) developing the objectives, (2) allocating marketing resources, and (3) auditing performance. The balance of the research activities will arise ad hoc as problems and opportunities develop in the course of implementing the marketing plan.

What types of information do organizations collect for planning and control purposes? Who collects the information? Table 1-1 presents the findings of a survey conducted by the American Marketing Association to answer these questions.[17]

Companies collect information on all aspects of the marketing system, i.e., situational variables, marketing mix variables, and performance measures. Over 60 percent of the companies surveyed conducted research on the situational variables. This included research on demand (market characteristics, market potential, short- and long-range forecasting), competitive research studies, and research on business trends. Over 50 percent did studies on the marketing mix variables of product (new products, existing products, acquisition studies, and product mix studies) and price. Over 60 percent of the companies collected performance information (market share and sales analysis).

The vast majority of these studies were conducted by the companies' own marketing research departments. Of the studies not done by the marketing research department, the bulk were conducted by another department within the organization. Only a few studies (media research, copy research, ad effectiveness research, and motivation research) tend to be conducted by an outside firm.

Information Inputs

Marketing decision making draws upon two information inputs: (1) information from the manager's experience and judgment, and (2) information from the marketing research system. The relative importance of these two inputs to decision making varies according to the receptivity and skills of the manager in using the marketing research system and according to the nature of the decision situation.

Many marketing decisions involve limited input from the marketing research system. These decisions are often repetitive in nature, and the manager's experience and judgment provide adequate information for sound decisions. In many programmed decision situations the delay and costs involved in collecting new information are typically outweighed by the immediacy of the situation, the adequacy of current information, and the high degree of confidence the manager has regarding the correct course of action. We should avoid downgrading the importance of experience and judgment in decision making. A characteristic of professional management is the ability to respond quickly to problems and opportunities by taking action in an effective and efficient manner.

---

[17] Dik Warren Twedt, *1973 Survey of Marketing Research* (Chicago: American Marketing Association, 1973). This survey, the fifth in a series begun in 1947, was sent to 3432 companies, and the tabulation in Exhibit 1-1 is based on the returns from the 1322 usable questionnaires.

Table 1-1 Types of Research Activity Conducted by Companies

	Percentage doing	Done by marketing research department	Done by another department	Done by outside firm
I Situational research				
A Demand research				
1 Determination of market characteristics	68	61*	6*	6*
2 Measurement of market potential	68	60	8	6
3 Short-range forecasting (up to one year)	63	43	23	1
4 Long-range forecasting (over one year)	61	42	22	2
5 Export and international studies	41	19	22	3
6 Motivation research	33	18	2	16
B Competition research				
1 Competitive product studies	64	52	11	6
C General environment research				
1 Studies of business trends	61	46	16	3
2 Studies of legal constraints on advertising and promotion	38	7	28	5
3 Ecological impact studies	27	8	16	5
4 Social values and policies studies	25	11	12	4
5 Consumers' "right to know" studies	18	9	7	4
6 Other	2	1	1	—
D Internal environment research				
1 Internal company employee studies (attitudes, communication, etc.)	45	13	29	6
II Marketing mix research				
A Product research				
1 New product acceptance and potential	63	51	9	8
2 Testing of existing products	57	35	20	7
3 Acquisition studies	53	25	30	3
4 Product mix studies	51	36	16	2
5 Packaging research	44	23	17	9
6 Other	3	2	1	1
B Place research				
1 Distribution channel studies	48	30	19	3
2 Plant and warehouse location	47	18	28	3
C Price research	56	33	25	2
D Promotion research				
1 Studies of ad effectiveness	49	26	7	21
2 Sales compensation studies	45	11	33	2

Table 1-1 *(Continued)*

		Percentage doing	Done by marketing research department	Done by another department	Done by outside firm
3	Media research	44	16	10	21
4	Promotional studies of premiums, coupons, sampling, deals, etc.	39	25	13	6
5	Copy research	37	17	6	18
6	Other	7	5	–	2
III	Performance research				
1	Market share analysis	67	58	9	5
2	Sales analysis	65	46	23	2
3	Establishment of sales quotas, territories	57	23	35	1
4	Test markets, store audits	38	28	6	9
5	Consumer panel operations	33	21	3	12

*The total of the percentages "done by market research department," "done by other departments," "done by outside firm" is greater than "percentage of companies doing" because some firms have studies done by both inside departments and outside firms.

Source: D. W. Twedt, *1973 Survey of Marketing Research* (Chicago: American Marketing Association, 1973).

While experience and judgment are the major inputs to *programmed* decision making, marketing research information is typically the main input to *nonprogrammed* decision situations. Here, the manager is confronted with a situation where past experience and judgment cannot adequately be generalized to fit this new setting. Consequently, the level of uncertainty regarding the correct course of action is much higher. The successful manager is one who can recognize the varying role of experience and judgment in decision making and is skillful in using marketing research to decrease the level of uncertainty regarding the decision situation.

It is useful to make a distinction between the terms "information" and "data." *Data* are observations and evidence regarding some aspect of the marketing system. *Information* refers to data which reduce the uncertainty in a decision situation. This definition makes the use of the term "information" dependent upon the manager and the decision-making situation. An example will clarify this distinction. A ship's captain is confronted with the problem of piloting his ship into a treacherous harbor at night. To aid the decision-making process, the captain is radioed the following data: (1) channel depth, (2) wind speed and direction, (3) score of the local baseball game, (4) tide speed and direction. Given the captain's problem, which data could be labeled information? Most readers, it is hoped, will find this distinction fairly easy, but given a typical marketing decision-making situation, distinguishing between data and information becomes substantially more challenging.

An advantage which experience and judgment have over marketing research is that with experience and judgment the decision maker is the person who distinguishes information from data. With marketing research, this task is often the responsibility of the researcher. Unless the researcher is thoroughly immersed in the decision situation, it is difficult for him or her to make this distinction adequately. Consequently, one often hears managers complain that they are presented with too much data and not enough information. It is not surprising to hear researchers complain that the reason for this situation is that they have not been included in the decision-making process. More will be said on this matter later.

SUMMARY

1 The need for marketing research parallels acceptance of the marketing concept. Organizations of all types are integrating and directing their activities to meet the needs of the marketplace. The growing acceptance of the marketing concept has increased the need for a formal process of acquiring information, namely, marketing research.

2 Marketing research can supply information regarding many aspects of the marketing system. This domain ranges from monitoring and describing situational factors to evaluating marketing programs and measuring the performance of these programs.

3 The primary purpose of marketing research is to provide information for decision making. Marketing research information can be useful in all stages of the decision-making process. This ranges from information to aid in recognizing that a decision situation is present to information that will guide the selection of a course of action.

4 Marketing management's increased emphasis on the planning and control functions has influenced the nature of marketing research activity. A more systematic and continuous flow of information is required. The activities of marketing research must be designed in accord with the requirements of the planning and control process. Marketing research is required to have available a continually updated library of information to facilitate the decision-making process.

5 Most marketing decisions involve limited marketing research input. These decisions are repetitive in nature, and the manager's experience and judgment provide adequate information for sound decisions. Marketing information is typically the main input to nonrepetitive decision situations.

DISCUSSION QUESTIONS

1 What effect has the increasing adoption of the marketing concept by organizations had on marketing research?

2 Present the four essential components of the marketing system and examples of each.

3 In what aspects of the marketing system is marketing research of limited applicability?

4 Why must an organization monitor situational variables?

5 What is marketing management?

6 Outline the steps involved in the decision-making process.

7   What factors determine the relative importance of managerial experience versus marketing research in a given situation?
8   What is the difference between "data" and "information"?

SUGGESTED READING

Alderson, Wroe, and Paul E. Green, *Planning and Problem Solving in Marketing* (Homewood, Ill.: Richard D. Irwin, Inc., 1964). This book contains an excellent discussion of marketing decision making.

Drucker, Peter, *Managing for Results* (New York: Harper and Row, 1969). An excellent explanation of the nature and scope of the manager's job and the role of the marketing function in the organization.

Kotler, Philip, *Marketing Management: Analysis, Planning and Control* (Englewood Cliffs, N.J.: Prentice-Hall, 1976). A leading text on marketing management.

Newman, Joseph W., "Put Research into Marketing Decisions," *Harvard Business Review*, vol. 40, no. 2, pp. 105–112, March–April 1962. This article discusses the manager/researcher relationship and the organizational issues involved.

Simon, Herbert A., *The New Science of Management Decision* (New York: Harper and Row, 1960). This book presents a thorough discussion of the decision-making process. The distinction between programmed and unprogrammed decision situations was first introduced in this text.

Chapter 2

The Marketing Research System

While the importance of marketing research has grown rapidly during the last three decades, organizations vary substantially as to the role and responsibility assigned marketing research. Some, for example, view research as mainly an ad hoc data gathering and analysis function, while others broadly define the role and responsibility of research and view the marketing research department as an information center for decision making. This latter view of research is what we refer to as a *marketing research system*.

The concept of a marketing research system implies a deeply involved role for research in the marketing management process. This includes the active participation of research in the decision-making process, with particular emphasis on the provision of meaningful information for the planning and control functions. The purpose of this information input is to narrow decision-making error and broaden the decision-making perspective. Better decisions should result from better information inputs.

Organizations which embrace the marketing concept tend to view marketing research as a research system. As an organization adopts the marketing concept, marketing research is seen as a way to integrate the organization's activities and focus them on the needs of the marketplace. The growing acceptance of the marketing concept implies a more important role for marketing research in the marketing management process.

MARKETING RESEARCH DEFINED

What is marketing research? There are many excellent definitions.[1] For our purposes, there are four terms that need to be included in such a definition. These are (1) systematic, (2) objective, (3) information, and (4) decision making. Consequently, we define marketing research as the systematic and objective approach to the development and provision of information for the marketing management decision-making process.

A few comments are in order regarding this definition. "Systematic" refers to the requirement that the research project should be well organized and planned: the strategic and tactical aspects of the research design must be detailed in advance, and the nature of the data to be gathered and the mode of analysis to be employed must be anticipated. "Objectivity" implies that marketing research strives to be unbiased and unemotional in performing its responsibilities. One often hears that marketing research is "the application of the scientific method to marketing." The hallmark of the scientific method is the objective gathering, analysis, and interpretation of data. While one may learn of a scientist who violates the rule of objectivity, this is rare and often results in sanctions by the scientific community. While marketing research operates in a different setting from those of the physical, social, and medical sciences, it shares their common standard of objectivity.

The remaining two elements of this definition, information and the decision-making process, have been discussed previously. It is important to recognize that these are the two elements that differentiate marketing research from research in other fields. The primary purpose of marketing research is to provide information, not data, for the management decision-making process.

Does the definition of marketing research apply to experience and judgment? The answer is—not completely. The definition's two elements of information and the management decision-making process are characteristics of experience and judgment. As discussed previously, the latter qualities even have an advantage over marketing research in that they are almost always in the form of information rather than data.

It is in regard to the remaining elements, being objective and systematic, that experience and judgment fail to fit this definition. "Systematic" refers to being well organized in the collecting and processing of data. Since experience and judgment involve the acquisition of knowledge about the marketing system through personal observations and experiences, they are subject to the bias and frailty resulting from this rather casual approach to data collection. The element of objectivity involves the unemotional and unbiased description of reality. Knowledge gained through personal experience and observation is subject to being biased through selective perception of reality, the distorting of facts for the benefit of personal objectives and to conform with existing attitudes regarding the marketing system.

[1] A very popular definition is "the systematic gathering, recording, and analyzing of data about problems relating to the marketing of goods and services" (report of the Definitions Committee of the American Marketing Association, Chicago, 1961).

Biases of this nature are likely to be minimized in programmed decision situations because of the feedback regarding the accuracy of decision making in previous similar decision situations. Here, effective decision making can result from information inputs based on experience and judgment. However, with unprogrammed decision situations, these biases can be serious and may result in a conflict with information emanating from the marketing research system. A skilled manager recognizes and attempts to control such biases in executing the decision-making process.

BASIC AND APPLIED RESEARCH

Marketing research studies can be classified as being basic or applied in nature. *Basic* (pure or fundamental) *research* seeks to extend the boundaries of knowledge regarding some aspect of the marketing system. There is little concern with how this knowledge can be used in the marketing management process. In contrast, *applied research* studies or investigations are concerned with assisting managers in making better decisions. These studies are directed toward the organization's specific situation and guided by the requirements of the decision-making process. Basic research studies tend to be less organization-specific, broader in purpose, and guided by marketing hypotheses and theory.

The character of basic research studies involves hypothesis testing, and the results focus on the acceptance or rejection of the hypotheses. Concern is with the replication of research findings and development of a body of knowledge composed of marketing principles and a theoretical structure regarding the behavior of the marketing system. Researchers in the marketing field's academic community are guided by this philosophy and are mainly interested in basic research. Their studies are often reported in professional journals such as the *Journal of Marketing Research* and the *Journal of Consumer Research*. A substantial amount of this research involves theoretical articles and studies concerned with advancing the methodology of the field. Numerous examples can be cited where basic research methodology has been successfully used in applied research. Therefore, advances in basic research typically result in advances in applied research.

Applied and basic research can be differentiated in regard to the thoroughness of the research. A desirable characteristic for basic research is that it be thorough and complete. For applied research, the thoroughness of the research is dictated by the information needs of the decision maker. Consequently, the time and money required to do a thorough study may be inappropriate given the information required for an effective and efficient decision.

This textbook is primarily concerned with applied research. This is reflected in the definition of marketing research discussed earlier. While many of the concepts, approaches, and techniques discussed in this book are applicable to those interested in basic research, our primary focus is on applied marketing research.

TYPES OF RESEARCH

Marketing research can be classified as (1) exploratory research, (2) conclusive research, and (3) performance-monitoring (routine feedback) research. The stage in the decision-making process for which the research information is needed determines the type of research required. Figure 2-1 illustrates this interdependence.

Exploratory Research

Exploratory research is appropriate for the early stages of the decision-making process. This research is usually designed to obtain a preliminary investigation of the situation with a minimum expenditure of cost and time. The research design is characterized by flexibility in order to be sensitive to the unexpected and to discover insights not previously recognized. Wide-ranging and versatile approaches are employed. These include secondary data sources, observation, interviews with experts, group interviews with knowledgeable persons, and case histories.

Exploratory research is appropriate in situations where management is searching for potential problems or opportunities; seeks new insights, ideas, or hypotheses regarding the situation; or desires a more precise formulation of the problem and the identification of the relevant variables in the decision situation. Once these issues have been adequately investigated and the decision situation is thoroughly defined, exploratory research can be useful in identifying alternative courses of action. Here the manager seeks clues to innovative marketing approaches. The objective is to broaden the domain of alternatives identified, with the hope of including the "best" alternative in the set of alternatives to be evaluated.

Conclusive Research

Conclusive research provides information which helps the manager evaluate and select a course of action. The research design is characterized by formal research procedures. This involves clearly defined research objectives and information needs. Often a detailed questionnaire is drawn up, along with a formal sampling plan. It should be clear how the information to be collected relates to the alternatives under evaluation. Possible research approaches include surveys, experiments, observations, and simulation.

Performance-monitoring Research

Once a course of action is selected and the marketing program is implemented, performance-monitoring research is needed to answer the question "What is happening?" Performance monitoring is the essential element to the control of marketing programs in accordance to plans. Deviation from the plan can result from improper execution of the marketing program and/or unanticipated changes in the situational factors. Consequently, effective performance monitoring involves monitoring both the marketing mix variables and the situational variables

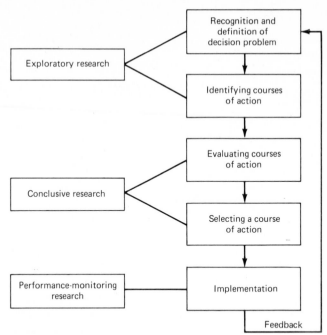

Figure 2-1 Types of research.

in addition to traditional performance measures such as sales, share of market, profit, and return on investment.

THE RESEARCH PROCESS

The formal marketing research project can be viewed as a series of steps called the *research process*. Figure 2-2 illustrates the nine steps in this process. To effectively conduct a research project it is essential to anticipate all the steps and recognize their interdependence. These nine steps represent the framework for the chapters in the book. We will overview these steps now in order to emphasize their sequencing and interdependence. A detailed discussion of each step will be found in the remaining chapters.

Need for Information

Establishing the need for marketing research information is, of course, the first step in the research process. Rarely does the manager's initial request for help adequately establish the need for research information. The researcher must thoroughly understand why the information is needed. The manager is responsible for explaining the situation surrounding the request for help and establishing that research information will facilitate the decision-making process. If the research project is to provide pertinent information for decision making, the need for research information must be precisely defined. Chapter 5 will discuss this area in more detail.

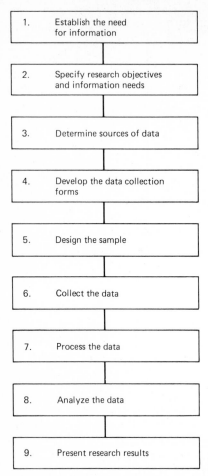

Figure 2-2 Steps in the research process.

Exploratory research may be undertaken to clarify the decision situation in such a way that the need for a formal research project can be determined. It could be that the manager has not properly analyzed whether a significant problem or opportunity exists. Managers often react to hunches and symptoms rather than clearly identified decision situations. Consequently, establishing the need for research information is a critical and difficult phase of the research process. Too often the importance of this initial step is overlooked in the excitement of undertaking a research project. This results in research findings that are not decision oriented.

Research Objectives and Information Needs

Once the need for research information has been clearly established, the researcher must specify the objectives of the proposed research and develop a specific list of information needs. Research objectives answer the question "Why is this project being conducted?" Typically, research objectives are put in writing before the project is undertaken. Information needs answer the question "What specific information is needed to attain the objectives?'' In practice, information needs may be thought of as a detailed listing of research objectives.

The manager should be thoroughly involved at this stage of the research project. Only the manager has a clear perspective as to the character and specificity of the information needed to reduce the uncertainty surrounding the decision situation. It is critical that the potential findings of the study be visualized and the question asked, ''What use are these data for the decision situation?'' This is a useful way to separate data from information before the research project is undertaken. This focus on information rather than data will increase the likelihood that the research findings will facilitate the decision-making process.

In stating research objectives, listing information needs, and visualizing the nature of the research findings, the researcher must anticipate the remaining steps in the research process. The availability of data sources and the limitations of the data-gathering process must be considered. Information needs must be consistent with the ability to gather the data. The format of the research results is dependent on the mode of data analysis. Consequently, each stage of the research process is highly dependent on the other stages.

Data Sources

Once the study objectives have been determined and the information needs listed, the next step is to determine whether the data are currently available from sources internal or external to the organization. Internal sources include previous research studies and company records. External sources include commercial research reports, trade magazine or industry reports, government reports, and so on. If data are found which fit the information needs, the researcher must examine the research design to determine their accuracy. The reputation of the organization which collected and analyzed the data is often a guide to reliability.

If the data are not available from internal or external sources, the next step is to collect new data. The sources include mail, telephone, and personal interviews, observation, experimentation, and simulation. The remaining steps in the research process relate to data collected through these sources.

Data Collection Forms

In preparing the data collection forms, the researcher must establish an effective link between the information needs and the questions to be asked or the observations to be recorded. The success of the study is dependent upon the researcher's skill and creativity in establishing this link. The responsibility for this task rests mainly with the researcher.

The contents of the data collection form depend on whether the data are to be collected by interview or observation. If observation is used, the forms must be designed to facilitate the accurate recording of behavior. The process of developing data collection forms for interviews is more complex; the wording of questions, sequencing of questions, use of direct versus indirect questions, and the general format of the questionnaire are very important. In addition, the willingness and ability of the respondent to answer the question must be considered.

Sample Design

The first issue in designing the sample concerns who or what is to be included in the sample. This means that a clear definition is needed of the population from which the sample is to be drawn. For example, if the research objectives are to determine the attitudes and preferences of current users of a frozen orange juice brand concerning competitive brands, the population would include all adults, teenagers, and children who currently use the brand. In contrast, if the study objectives are to determine the decision criteria used in selecting a brand of orange juice, the population would include all individuals who currently purchase frozen orange juice.

The next issue concerns the method used to select the sample. These methods can be classified as to whether they involve a probability or nonprobability procedure. With probability methods, each element in the population has a known chance of being selected for the sample. Probability methods include simple random sampling, cluster sampling, and stratified sampling. Nonprobability methods include convenience sampling, judgment sampling, and quota sampling.

The third issue involves the size of the sample. In practice, sample sizes vary from just a few individuals to several thousand. The appropriate sample size is influenced by many considerations. These range from precise statistical formulas for determining sample size to managerial considerations regarding cost, value, and accuracy of the information needed for decision-making purposes.

Data Collection

The process of collecting data is critical since it typically involves a large proportion of the research budget and a large proportion of the total error in the research results. In questionnaire studies, a major source of error can be attributed to the interviewing process. Specifically, this error includes improper respondent selection, nonresponse bias, phrasing questions incorrectly, cheating, misinterpreting the respondents' comments, and not accurately recording the comments. Consequently, the selection, training, and control of interviewers is essential to effective marketing research studies.

Data Processing

Once they have been recorded, the processing of the data begins. This includes the functions of editing and coding. Editing involves reviewing the data forms as to legibility, consistency, and completeness. Coding involves establishing categories for responses or groups of responses so that numerals can be used to represent the categories. The data are then ready for hand tabulation or electronic data analysis.

Data Analysis

It is important that the data analysis be consistent with the requirements of the information needs identified in step 2. Three modes of analysis are available:

univariate, bivariate, and multivariate. *Univariate analysis* refers to the examination of one variable at a time. The purpose of univariate analysis is largely description of the data set. A frequency distribution is characteristic of this mode of analysis. *Bivariate analysis* is concerned with the relationship between two variables, while *multivariate analysis* involves the simultaneous analysis of three or more variables. The purpose of bivariate and multivariate analysis is primarily explanatory. With the introduction of the computer, multivariate data analysis has expanded rapidly.[2]

Presentation of Results

The research results are typically communicated to the manager through a written report and oral presentation. It is imperative that the research finding be presented in a simple format and addressed to the information needs of the decision situation. "No matter what the proficiency with which all previous steps have been dispatched, the project will be no more successful than the research report."[3]

A management summary is typically required in the research report. This summary is a one- or two-page review of the key research results. Many managers read the management summary thoroughly and then just skim the body of the report or selectively read those sections dealing with research findings of special interest. Consequently, for many managers, the management summary is the central focus of the research report.

THE MANAGEMENT-RESEARCH RELATIONSHIP

The effectiveness of the research system is dependent upon its relationship with marketing management. Many factors influence the success of this interpersonal contact, such as differences between some managers and researchers in job responsibilities, career objectives, and educational backgrounds.

The research system requires the skills and knowledge of specialized people. A research department may have individuals specializing in various steps of the research process—for example, questionnaire design, field supervision, data processing, data analysis, and report preparation. Specialization involving the marketing mix decision areas is common; individuals or groups may specialize in advertising research, distribution research, product development research, and so on. People trained in statistics, mathematics, psychology, computer science, and economics often qualify for many of these specialized positions. Frequently, these individuals have limited training and perspective regarding the role of applied research in the management decision-making process.

The research specialist who is not management oriented will often accept the request for research help without clearly establishing the need for research.

---

[2] Thomas C. Kinnear and James R. Taylor, "Multivariate Methods in Marketing Research: A Further Attempt at Classification," *Journal of Marketing,* October 1971, p. 56.

[3] Harper Boyd and Ralph Westfall, *Marketing Research: Text and Cases* (Homewood, Ill.: Richard D. Irwin, 1956), p. 195.

This person may fail to ask perceptive questions regarding the decision situation and be uncritical of whether research will facilitate the decision-making process. In addition, many specialists are more concerned with the technical sophistication of the research design and methodology than the information needs of management. This focus leads many researchers to look for decision situations where they can apply the latest research techniques. Many managers view researchers as more concerned with finding an application for their techniques than with supplying information for decision making. This emphasis on technique results in technical jargon and standardized ways of presenting research findings, which tends to inhibit the management-research communication process, especially in the reporting of research results.

In reporting research findings some researchers fail to recognize that their role is advisory; they are not being asked to make the decision for management. The researcher can play a very active and supportive role in the decision-making process, but the responsibility for making the decision rests with management. The researcher may become frustrated by the constraints of this advisory role. The feeling can develop that "I can make better decisions than management."[4]

Why shouldn't the researcher participate in making the decision? First, the objectivity of the research process could be influenced. The researcher's personal biases and vested interests associated with various decision outcomes could decrease the objectivity of the research design and the analysis of the findings. Second, the researcher would weigh the research findings heavily in selecting a course of action. In contrast, the manager can evaluate and weigh the significance of the research findings in the context of experience and knowledge plus the broader policy considerations associated with the decision.

While many researchers are not sufficiently management oriented, many managers are not sufficiently research-oriented. Far too many managers have no training in marketing research and limited perspective as to the nature and role of research in the decision-making process. This inhibits their active involvement in the stages of the research project. This lack of participation can diminish the usefulness of the research findings. If the manager does not view research as a natural aspect of the decision-making process, the researcher is forced to solicit research studies from the manager. This results in myopic and fragmented studies which rarely make a significant contribution to the decision-making process. The effectiveness of marketing research is dependent on the skills and perspective of the manager in using the research function in decision making.

Some managers operate as if the researcher is clairvoyant regarding the nature of the decision situation, the courses of action that appear reasonable, the objective to be accomplished, and the information needed to reduce the decision uncertainty. Few managers are prone to explain these areas lucidly to the researcher. In some cases the manager may be unwilling or unable to

---

[4] Murray Cayley, "The Role of Research in Marketing," *The Business Quarterly,* Autumn 1968, p. 33.

communicate this type of information. Consequently, many research projects are not decision oriented because of the manager's poor communication skills.

The manager may view research as a way to satisfy needs other than those related to decision making. This has been called "pseudo-research."[5]

1 The manager can use marketing research as a way to gain visibility and power in the organization.

2 Marketing research can be used to justify decisions already made. If the research results contradict the decision, the manager can declare the research invalid or simply ignore it altogether.

3 Marketing research can be conducted to establish a scapegoat for marketing decisions that do not accomplish objectives. If the decision is successful, the manager can take full credit; if it is not successful, marketing research is to blame.

4 Marketing research can be used as a promotion tool for service organizations like advertising agencies and media to attract new business and impress current clients.

5 Marketing research can serve to soothe an anxious manager that "something is being done."

6 Managers may support marketing research studies and new research methodology because they believe it is the "faddish thing to do" or the current trend in management practice.

Several barriers to the effective management utilization of marketing research have been identified.[6]

1 Some managers view research as a threat to their personal status as decision makers. They fear that marketing research information may conflict with or invalidate the "knowledge" gained from experience and judgment. The managers may believe that this "knowledge" is what justifies their status and position.

2 The absence of systematic planning procedures in many organizations contributes to the lack of common organizational objectives for managers. In the absence of clear organizational objectives, the managers will substitute their own objectives, which can result in conflict among managers. Research may be seen as a way to support one's view in this internal struggle for power. Managers who believe that marketing research will enhance their position will favor it, while others will oppose it.

3 Some managers are unable to effectively work with, understand, and use the knowledge and skills of research specialists. The interdisciplinary training of specialists makes communication difficult.

4 The isolation of marketing research personnel from the managers can be a problem. The effective use of marketing research assumes that research personnel will have a close and continuous relationship with the managers. Often

[5] Stewart A. Smith, "Research and Pseudo-Research in Marketing," *Harvard Business Review,* pp. 73–76, March–April 1974.

[6] Joseph W. Newman, "Put Research into Marketing Decisions," *Harvard Business Review,* vol. 40, no. 2, pp. 105–112, March–April 1962.

marketing research departments are handicapped in this regard by low organizational status. The weakness of this organizational arrangement is that it depends on the initiative of the manager for effective use of marketing research. Too often managers are unfamiliar with the nature and role of research and are unable to identify problems well enough to ask for the help they need. Those research departments that operate on management request tend to be occupied with routine, short-range operating problems.

The previous discussion has emphasized many of the factors that can influence the effectiveness of the management-research relationship. The more basic areas present in causing conflict have been identified as research responsibility, research personnel, budget, assignments, problem definition, research reporting, and the use of research. Table 2-1 presents the typical positions of top management and marketing research staff on these areas of conflict.[7]

What can be done to minimize this organizational conflict? The research system requires the skills and knowledge of specialists. It also must be sensitive to the needs of management and communicate in management language. Those specialists who find it difficult to communicate with management must be restricted to an analytic role within the research system. The specialist's work can be guided by the use of people who have been referred to as "research generalists."[8]

The research generalist is a kind of intermediary who can work effectively between management and the research specialist. This person can function with ease on the management front and can coordinate both sides in such a way that the knowledge and skills of the specialist can effectively be brought to bear on management decision situations. "The research generalist acts as a friend and serves as a problem definer, an educator, a liaison man, a communicator, and a counselor."[9] This is a demanding and challenging job opportunity. Business school training is a logical prerequisite for those individuals aspiring to such a position.

HISTORY OF MARKETING RESEARCH

To put the nature and role of marketing research in perspective, it is useful to review the history of the field. The development of marketing research during the early part of the twentieth century parallels the rise of the marketing concept. Over this period of time, the management philosophy guiding organizations gradually changed to the consumer orientation of today. During the period 1900 to 1930, management concern was focused primarily on the problems and opportunities associated with production; between 1930 and the late 1940's, this orientation shifted to the problems and opportunities associated with distribution; since the late 1940s increased attention has been focused on consumer needs

---

[7] John G. Keane, "Some Observations on Marketing Research in Top Management Decision Making," *Journal of Marketing,* vol. 33, pp. 10–15, October 1969.

[8] Newman, "Put Research into Marketing Decisions," p. 111.

[9] Ibid.

Table 2-1 Probable Areas of Top Management–Marketing Research Conflict

Top management position	Area	Marketing research position
MR lacks sense of accountability. Sole MR function is as an information provider.	Research responsibility	Responsibility should be explicitly defined and consistently followed. Desire decision-making involvement with TM.
Generally poor communicators. Lack enthusiasm, salesmanship, and imagination.	Research personnel	TM is anti-intellectual. Researchers should be hired, judged, and compensated on research capabilities.
Research costs too much. Since MR contribution difficult to measure, budget cuts are relatively defensible.	Budget	"You get what you pay for" defense. Needs to be continuing, long-range TM commitment.
Tend to be over-engineered. Not executed with proper sense of urgency. Exhibit ritualized, staid approach.	Assignments	Too many nonresearchable requests. Too many "fire-fighting" requests. Insufficient time and money allocated.
MR best equipped to do this. General direction sufficient . . . . MR must appreciate and respond. Can't help changing circumstances.	Problem definition	TM generally unsympathetic to this widespread problem. Not given all the relevant facts. Changed after research is under way.
Characterized as dull, with too much "researchese" and too many qualifiers. Not decision-oriented. Too often reported after the fact.	Research reporting	TM treats superficially. Good research demands thorough reporting and documentation. Insufficient lead time given.
Free to use as it pleases . . . . MR shouldn't question. Changes in need and timing of research are sometimes unavoidable. MR deceived by not knowing all the facts.	Use of research	TM uses to support a predetermined position represents misuse. Isn't used after requested and conducted . . . wasteful. Uses to confirm or excuse past actions.

and desires.[10] The nature and role of marketing activity in these organizations reflects this shift in management philosophy.

Pioneers and Institutions

While numerous people and institutions were involved in the occasional use of marketing research prior to 1910, the period 1910 to 1920 is recognized as the formal beginning of marketing research.[11] In 1911, J. George Frederick established a research firm called The Business Bourse. Charles Coolidge Parlin was

---

[10] Robert L. King, "The Marketing Concept," in G. Schwartz (ed.), *Science in Marketing* (New York: Wiley, 1965).

[11] Material in this section draws heavily from the work of Lawrence C. Lockley, "History and Development of Marketing Research," in Robert Ferber (ed.), *Handbook of Marketing Research* (New York: McGraw-Hill, 1974), pp. 1-3 to 1-15.

appointed manager of the Commercial Research Division of the Curtis Publishing Company that same year. The use of the name "commercial research" had special significance, since most business people considered the term research as too eloquent for a business service. Parlin managed one of the leading research organizations of this period.

The success of Parlin's work inspired several industrial firms and advertising media to establish research divisions. In 1915, the United States Rubber Company hired Dr. Paul H. Nystrom to manage a newly established Department of Commercial Research. In 1917, Swift and Company hired Dr. Louis D. H. Weld from Yale University to become manager of their Commercial Research Department.

In 1919, Professor C. S. Duncan of the University of Chicago published *Commercial Research: An Outline of Working Principles*. This was considered to be the first major book on commercial research. In 1921, Percival White's *Market Analysis* was published. This was the first research book to gain a large readership, and it went through several editions. *Market Research and Analysis* by Lyndon O. Brown was published in 1937.[12] This became one of the most popular college textbooks of the period, reflecting the growing interest of marketing research on the college campus. After 1940, numerous research textbooks were published, and the number of business schools offering research courses rapidly expanded.

Following World War II, the growth of marketing research activity dramatically increased, paralleling the growing acceptance of the marketing concept. By 1948, over 200 marketing research organizations had been formed in the United States.[13] Expenditures on marketing research activities were estimated to be $50 million a year in 1947.[14] Over the next three decades this expenditure level increased more than tenfold.[15]

The growing acceptance of the marketing concept brought a change in emphasis from "market research" to "marketing research." Market research implied that the focus of research was on the analysis of markets. The shift to marketing research broadened the nature and role of research, with the emphasis on contact between researchers and the marketing management process. The publication of *Marketing Research* by Harper Boyd and Ralph Westfall in 1956 reflected this change in orientation.[16]

Methodological Development

Advances in marketing research methodology parallel the development of research methodology in the social sciences, of which marketing is a part. The methodological advances made by psychologists, economists, sociologists, po-

---

[12] Lyndon O. Brown, *Market Research and Analysis* (New York: Ronald Press, 1937).

[13] "Market Detectives," *Wall Street Journal*, Sept. 1947, p. 1.

[14] Donald M. Hobart (ed.), *Marketing Research Practice* (New York: Ronald Press, 1950), p. 9.

[15] "Marketing Research Investment to Hit $600,000,000: Dutka," *Advertising Age*, vol. 39, p. 88, Dec. 9, 1968.

[16] Harper Boyd and Ralph Westfall, *Marketing Research: Text and Cases* (Homewood, Ill.: Richard D. Irwin, 1956).

litical scientists, statisticians, and so on had a pronounced influence on marketing research methodology, and consequently its history is interwoven with the historical development of the social sciences.

Marketing research made major methodological advances from 1910 to 1920. Questionnaire studies or surveys became popular modes of data collection. With the growth of survey research came improvements in questionnaire design and question construction, along with the awareness of biases resulting from the questioning and the interviewing process. Several social scientists who entered the field were interested in working on these applied methodological problems. This established a methodological communication link between marketing and the other social sciences that exists to this day.

During the 1930s, sampling became a serious methodological issue. As statistical training developed beyond descriptive statistics (calculation of means, variances, simple correlation, and construction of index numbers) to an emphasis on inferential statistics, nonprobability sampling procedures came under heavy attack. Modern probability sampling approaches slowly gained acceptance during this period.

Methodological innovation occurred at a fairly steady pace from 1950 through the early 1960s. At this time a major development occurred, the commercialization of the large-scale digital computer. The computer rapidly increased the pace of methodological innovation, especially in the area of quantitative marketing research.

In response to this methodological explosion, two new journals appeared in the 1960s: the *Journal of Marketing Research* and the *Journal of Advertising Research*. In 1966, professors Paul Green and Donald Tull authored an innovative textbook which emphasized the methodological advances made in marketing research.[17] In 1974, the *Journal of Consumer Research* appeared, sponsored by an impressive list of organizations representing the social sciences. This latter publication reflects the growing emphasis on consumer behavior research in business, government, and academia. This focus on consumer behavior reflects the shift of management philosophy to the marketing concept.

SUMMARY

1   The concept of a marketing research system implies a broadly defined role for marketing research in the marketing management process. Here, marketing research is viewed by management as an information center for decision making as opposed to an activity that merely gathers and analyzes data.

2   Marketing research is defined as the systematic and objective approach to the development and provision of information for the marketing management decision-making process. This definition emphasizes the applied-research focus of this book. Information based on experience and judgment differs from marketing research information in terms of objectivity and of how systematically the data was collected and processed.

[17] Paul E. Green and Donald S. Tull, *Research for Marketing Decisions* (Englewood Cliffs, N.J.: Prentice-Hall, 1966).

3 Marketing research can be classified according to the way it interacts with the decision making process. Exploratory research is designed to facilitate recognition of a decision situation and aid in identifying alternative courses of action. Conclusive research is concerned with providing information to evaluate and select a course of action. Performance-monitoring research is designed to facilitate control of the system by measuring the performance of the marketing program.

4 The research process is composed of nine steps starting with the establishment of the need for information and ending with the presentation of the research results. To effectively conduct a research project it is essential to anticipate the nine steps and recognize their interdependence. What is done in one step can greatly influence the other steps.

5 Many factors influence the effectiveness of the management-research relationship. An effective research system is one which is respected by management and focuses on the needs of management. Many sources of conflict can be reduced by proper training of both research and management regarding the role of research in the decision-making process. The creation of the position "research generalist" has substantially increased the effectiveness of the management-research relationship.

6 The history of marketing research parallels the rise of the marketing concept. Early practitioners were concerned with gathering information on markets and developing the applied aspects of survey research. The gradual shift to a focus on marketing research broadened the nature and role of research activities. The emphasis was on gathering information for marketing management decision making. Methodological development in marketing research parallels the development of research methodology in the social sciences. Early methodological development focused on data collection and sampling issues. More contemporary methodological advances relate to computer-based technologies for data analysis.

DISCUSSION QUESTIONS

1 What is a marketing research system?
2 Define marketing research. Elaborate on the components of your definition.
3 Contrast basic and applied marketing research.
4 Discuss the types of marketing research appropriate for various stages of the decision-making process.
5 Specify the sequence of steps in the research process.
6 Why is it essential that a researcher anticipate all of the steps of the research process?
7 What are some of the factors which impinge upon the management-research relationship?

SUGGESTED READING

Cayley, Murray, "The Role of Research in Marketing," *The Business Quarterly,* Autumn 1968, p. 33. A practitioner's view of the role of marketing research in the decision-making process.

Fisk, George, "The Functions of Marketing Research," in Robert Ferber (ed.), *Handbook of Marketing Research* (New York: McGraw-Hill, 1974), pp. 1-16 to 1-30. The author presents a thorough treatment of the two major functions of marketing research: providing information for decision making and developing new knowledge regarding the marketing system.

Keane, John G., "Some Observations on Marketing Research in Top Management Decision Making," *Journal of Marketing,* vol. 33, pp. 10–15, October 1969. An excellent discussion of the role research plays in the management decision-making process.

Lockley, Lawrence C., "History and Development of Marketing Research," in Robert Ferber (ed.), *Handbook of Marketing Research* (New York: McGraw-Hill, 1974), pp. 1-3 to 1-15. A comprehensive discussion of the history of marketing research. The author provides both depth and breadth regarding the evolution of the field.

Newman, Joseph W., "Put Research into Marketing Decisions," *Harvard Business Review,* vol. 40, no. 2, pp. 105–112, March-April 1962. This classic article encourages top managers to recognize the strategic importance of marketing research. The causes of organizational conflict are highlighted, along with recommendations for organizational changes to minimize such conflict.

Chapter 3

An Example of Marketing Research

This chapter is designed to put into operation many of the concepts presented in Chapter 2 and serve the frequently expressed desire of students to see what a research project looks like.[1] The project presented here is not intended to be illustrative of good or effective marketing research. The focus is on the stages of the research process and the types of research that can be utilized.

In addition to being an initial overview of a research project, this chapter is intended to serve as a unifying reference when reading subsequent chapters dealing with specialized aspects of the research process. At several points in the chapter, the student may encounter terms and techniques which are new. In such cases, the authors have tried to identify the chapters where these are explained in detail. The intent is not to have the student turn to these chapters for explanation, but rather to develop an understanding of the sequencing and role of future topics as they relate to the marketing research process. When studying subsequent chapters dealing with specialized aspects of the research process, the reader may find that reference to this chapter will help to bring perspective to the area being studied.

[1] The authors wish to acknowledge the valuable assistance of Lawrence A. Crosby, research assistant, The University of Michigan, in preparing this chapter.

THE PROBLEM SETTING

The research project described here was conducted for the Rigid Container Division of the Society of the Plastic Industry (SPI) by a leading marketing research firm. The Rigid Container Division of SPI represents the majority of U.S. manufacturers of rigid plastic containers. Many of these companies are small manufacturing units with limited marketing and marketing research capabilities. A six-member executive board administers the activities of the Rigid Container Division.

Problem Recognition and Definition

In the last ten years, the plastic packaging industry has experienced dynamic growth, making significant penetration into the markets of more conventional packaging materials such as paper, paperboard, glass, and metal. Sales of plastic packaging totaled around $3 billion in 1974, up from approximately $660 million in 1960. Plastic containers represent about 10 percent of the industry volume.

Several SPI research studies indicated that rigid plastic containers offer important advantages over other container materials. The consumer advantages include their light weight, resistance to breakage, toughness, resealability, and potential for reuse. Plastic containers are attractive to producers in that they are often less expensive than other containers. They store easily because they can be "nested," a feature which reduces shipping costs and warehouse space. In addition, they can be printed with an unlimited variety of colors and designs.

Much of the growth in plastic container sales had stemmed from the initiative of food manufacturers in seeking new packaging concepts for new products being developed. An example of this situation was the development of soft margarine. The manufacturer had requested the development of a reusable container specifically designed for this new product. Similar situations could be cited for other plastic containers for dairy products. An example of a plastic container replacing the traditional package is found with cottage cheese. Here, the advantages of the plastic container were reflected in the consumer's preference for brands of cottage cheese packaged in plastic rather than paper containers. Today, plastic is the dominant packaging form for soft margarine and cottage cheese.

The future outlook for further penetration of the packaging business was optimistic, but expectations were for a much slower growth rate than experienced in the last decade. The constraints on future growth were several: (1) Growing uncertainty regarding the cost of raw materials and the competitive influence this would have on container selection. (2) Future competitive moves from glass, metal, and paper manufacturers. Many of these firms were large and had extensive research and development (R&D) and marketing capabilities. (3) Debate over environmental and safety issues regarding packaging containers. The nonbiodegradable property of plastic was a matter of concern, and the SPI commissioned a leading marketing research firm to analyze the issues in this area. A report was prepared titled "Resource and Environmental Profile Analysis of Plastic and

Nonplastic Containers." (4) Growing concern among SPI members that possibly the high potential markets for plastic containers had been saturated (for example, soft margarine and cottage cheese).

The rapid growth of plastic container sales over the last decade resulted in the modernization and expansion of production facilities to meet this demand. As a result, manufacturing capacity was currently in excess of demand for the majority of SPI members. It was the concern of these members that new markets for plastic products should be identified and programs be developed to capture the market potential. Such action would help solve the excess-capacity problem and would continue the trend of plastic penetration of the container industry. Consequently, the executive board of the Rigid Container Division of SPI concluded that a marketing research study was needed to identify and evaluate the market opportunities for rigid plastic containers.

A leading marketing research firm in Chicago was recommended by the SPI New York office as highly qualified to conduct the study. A preliminary meeting was then arranged. The SPI representatives included a staff member from the New York office and three members representing the Rigid Container Division executive board. The three board members were managers of plastic container manufacturing operations. The purpose of the meeting was to explain why marketing research information was needed. This was to be accomplished by a series of presentations which characterized the plastic container industry and the past, current, and future situation that faced the industry. The previous discussion on problem recognition and definition summarizes the focus of this initial meeting with the marketing research firm. At the end of this meeting, the research firm requested one week to review the problem situation and formulate specific questions.

At the second meeting, the research firm requested a formal statement of objectives and potential courses of action available for reaching the objectives. A lengthy discussion was required before the SPI members committed themselves to specific statements in this regard. They indicated that these two areas had been discussed previously but only in general terms. The following statement was agreed to by the SPI members:

I SPI objective:
   To increase the market penetration of plastic containers to 14 percent by 1980.
II Courses of action:
   A Develop and implement a marketing program to maintain or improve the acceptance of plastic containers in markets where plastic now dominates.
   B Develop and implement a marketing program to expand the acceptance of plastic containers in markets where plastic has a low or moderate penetration.
   C Develop and implement a marketing program to enter new markets currently dominated by paper, paperboard, glass, or metal.
   D Develop and implement a marketing program to work actively with manufacturers of new products.

The discussion turned to the type of information needed to select and implement one or more of the alternatives identified. Again, a lengthy discussion followed, reflecting the complexity of the problem situation. (See Chapter 5.)

The Problem Setting in Perspective

The marketing alternatives of concern to the Rigid Container Division involved broad and extensive information requirements. A program of research for developing a marketing plan was required. This implied the use of multiple data sources and specialized research projects.

One research approach involved studying the reactions of individuals and organizations who influenced the market acceptance of plastic containers. The ultimate consumers can be an influential group in this acceptance process. Consumers may have preferences for packaging characteristics that favor plastic over other packaging materials. The retailer and wholesaler may find packaging characteristics important in the selection of products to handle. Characteristics such as stacking ability, display appeal, and potential for breakage may influence their selection. Manufacturers who must decide on a packaging container for their product may consider many areas in making a decision. The preferences and reactions of consumers, retailers, and wholesalers may be important considerations. Container costs and related investment would be important. Manufacturing considerations, degree of product protection, promotional features, and ecological issues could all enter into the decision. Several research projects would be required to study this complex chain of influence for each market under consideration.

Another area of investigation concerns an analysis of current markets. The task here would be to quantify markets on characteristics such as size, trends in size, current mix of packaging forms, and the fit of packaging requirements with existing plastic container manufacturing processes. This research approach involves the use of published data sources such as research reports, trade association data, and trade periodicals.

Additional studies could be required depending on the breadth of the sponsor's information needs. These might include profitability analysis of current lines of plastic containers, customer analysis, competitive analysis, and environmental analysis.

The information needs of this project are extensive and require a variety of research approaches and studies. These could range from small exploratory studies with consumers, retailers, wholesalers, and manufacturers to more formal studies using observation, interrogation, and experimentation. In addition, studies using published data sources internal and external to the sponsoring organizations could be required. Studies of this breadth are entirely within the capabilities of the research system described in Chapter 2.

THE STUDY PROPOSAL

After several weeks of preparation, a research proposal was developed and sent to each of the executive board members for review. At a subsequent meeting with the research firm and after several changes, the proposal was approved. The following is a summary of the finalized proposal which contains two sections, (1) packaging markets and (2) consumer acceptance.

Study of Packaging Markets

Rationale for the Study The purpose of this study is to identify and characterize packaging markets and screen these markets as to their potential for penetration by plastic containers. The high-potential markets identified through this study will be further screened in the study of consumer acceptance.

Research Objectives

1 To compare current and potential packaging markets with regard to dimensions indicative of market potential.

2 To categorize packaging markets as to the degree of plastic container penetration.

3 To evaluate the high-potential markets in terms of the compatibility of packaging requirements with existing production and material capabilities.

Information Needs

1 Rank container markets by number of containers used per year. Illustrate trends over the past five years.

2 Classify markets as to the most likely plastic manufacturing process (thermoforming, injection molding, spin welding, or blow molding).

3 Classify markets by proportion of containers that are paper, paperboard, glass, metal, and plastic. Illustrate trends over the past five years.

4 Rank container markets by retail price of the product. Illustrate trends over the past five years.

5 Rank container markets by proportion of retail price represented by packaging costs. Illustrate trends over the past five years.

6 Rank container markets by magnitude of packaging cost increase or decrease resulting from a change to a plastic container.

7 Classify markets as to the degree of fit with existing production and material capabilities—high, medium, and low fit.

8 Calculate the plastic container manufacturer's break-even volume for each market. Determine the proportion of market penetration required to break even for each market. Rank the markets or proportion of market penetration required to break even.

Data Sources The data used to meet the information needs will include internal and external reports, publications, and records. (See Chapter 6.) Data that are not available in published form will be gathered by interviews with knowledgeable people in the industry.

The following published sources have been identified:

1 "The Plastic Industry in the Year 2000," by SPI

2 "The Packaging Revolution" from *A Note on the Metal Container Industry,* by Harvard Business School

   3 "1974 Financial and Operating Ratios Survey No. 12," by SPI
   4 "Standard and Poor's Industry Surveys—Containers"
   5 "Economic Forecast—Downtrend in First Half, Uptrend in Second,"
from *Modern Packaging,* January 1975
   6 *1972 Census of Manufacturers*
      a Food Sales—Standard Industrial Classification #20
      b Plastic Sales—Standard Industrial Classification #30794
   7 "U.S. Container and Packaging Materials Production 1960 to 1974,"
from *Modern Packaging,* December 1974
   8 "Value of Packaging Materials 1960 to 1974," from *Modern Packaging,*
December 1974
   9 "End Use Distribution of Selected Containers—Percent of Shipments," from *Modern Packaging,* December 1974
   10 *Standard and Poor's Industry Surveys—Retailing Food*
   11 "Resource and Environmental Profile Analysis of Plastic and Non-
Plastic Containers," by Midwest Research Institute
   12 *Modern Plastics*
   13 *Modern Plastics Encyclopedia*
   14 *Plastics Journal*
   15 *Society of Petroleum Engineering Journal*
   16 *Modern Packaging*
   17 *Modern Packaging Encyclopedia*

Study of Consumer Acceptance

Rationale for the Study   It was the opinion of the research firm that demonstrating consumer acceptance or preference would be the critical factor in
influencing a manufacturer to use a plastic container, in the absence of an
unfavorable cost differential or excessive distribution problems. Consumer preference for a plastic container over existing packaging would provide strong
evidence for a potential sales increase resulting from a change to a plastic
container. In addition, understanding the underlying characteristics of the plastic
container which cause this preference would be useful in developing a promotional program directed to manufacturers. The same information would be useful
to manufacturers in developing a promotional program for trade and consumer
acceptance.

Research Objectives
   1 To determine which container markets have the greatest consumer
acceptance of plastic containers.
   2 To determine the characteristics of plastic containers which represent
advantages compared with paper, paperboard, glass, and metal containers.

Information Needs
   1 Identify the characteristics or attributes which differentiate alternative
packaging materials.
   2 Determine the importance of packaging attributes in container markets.
   3 Determine consumer preference for alternative packaging materials in
container markets.

4   Identify the characteristics of packaging containers which influence consumer preference.

5   Determine which attributes of plastic containers represent important selling points.

6   Determine the characteristics of the ideal packaging container.

7   Determine the likes and dislikes of consumers regarding current packaging containers.

8   Determine what suggestions consumers have for packaging improvement in container markets.

9   Determine which markets have the most inadequate packaging and whether plastic containers represent an improvement.

10   Determine consumer attitudes toward ecological aspects of packaging materials, specifically plastic.

11   Determine consumers' perceptions regarding the cost of alternative packaging materials. Do some containers have a "high price/high quality" image?

12   Determine the nature of the trade-offs consumers will make in selecting a brand/package. How large a price increase will be accepted for a superior packaging form? How much will a lower price offset packaging deficiencies?

13   Determine the characteristics (demographic, life cycle, usage rates) of consumers who are most receptive to plastic containers.

Data Sources

Acquiring data to meet the information needs will involve the interrogation of consumers. The first phase will include a series of exploratory group interviews (see Chapter 18). The purpose is to explore consumer attitudes, feelings, and motives concerning the information need areas such as attributes of packaging, pros and cons of packaging, and ecological issues. Based on these findings, specific questions can be developed for more systematic data collection. The second phase will involve a survey of consumers using a questionnaire administered by personal interview (see Chapters 18 and 19). The main conclusions of the study will be based on the results of this survey.

THE RESEARCH PROJECT

Results of the Study of Packaging Markets

The starting point for this phase of the research project was an extensive list of packaging markets which, at least superficially, seemed to hold good potential for rigid plastic containers. The list was furnished by the SPI, where it had been developed through continuous monitoring and contact with the packaging industry. This list was further screened by SPI to include only those markets where rigid plastic containers were judged to be feasible from the standpoint of both technology and cost.

The next step was to trim from the list those markets with obviously undesirable demand characteristics based on research using secondary data sources (see Chapter 7). While length prohibits presenting these detailed findings,

Exhibit 3-1   Potential Markets for Rigid Plastic Containers

Major plastics markets

Cultured dairy (cottage cheese, yogurt, etc.)
Butter and margarine
Portion packs (e.g., meat cold cuts)
Pantyhose

Minor plastics markets

Shortening
Ice cream
Spreads and dips
Frozen juice
Cosmetic creams and gels
Auto oil and grease
Food sauces
Meat trays

Non-plastics market

Jelly and preserves
Salad dressing
Baby food
Coffee
Drink powders (e.g., Kool-Aid)
Pet foods
Auto parts and kits
Cheese
Household cleaners, wax, car care

the markets which survived this process appear in Exhibit 3-1, where they are classified according to the current penetration of plastic containers. A "major plastics market," for example, is one in which there is already high penetration.

By now, it may have occurred to the discerning reader that there are at least two types of markets with high potential for rigid plastic containers. One would be rapidly growing markets where plastic already has significant penetration, while the other would be large or growing markets where the penetration of plastic could be significantly improved. On the other hand, high-penetration markets with stable or declining primary demand afford little opportunity and therefore do not appear on the list.

Thinking in terms of the concepts of Chapter 2, the Study of Packaging Markets can be viewed as exploratory research for the purpose of identifying specific alternative courses of action to reach the SPI objectives previously discussed. In this case, "alternative courses of action" can be construed as different container markets at which the members' efforts might be directed. The Study of Consumer Acceptance, to which we now turn, concerns not only the identification and evaluation of these specific container market alternatives

but the selection of a course of action as well. This study involves both exploratory and conclusive research.

Results of the Study of Consumer Acceptance

Exploratory Group Studies   This stage of the project involved a series of
group discussion sessions to explore consumer attitudes on the advantages and
disadvantages of different types of containers. The sort of information derived
from these sessions was qualitative in nature and served to guide the quantitative
research conducted later. Group sessions are a fairly well-established technique
in the marketing research business for probing a topic that is not yet well defined.
Chapter 18 will discuss the area of qualitative research in detail.

Design and Procedure   Anywhere from eight to twelve paid participants
attended each of the sessions, which were held at a special facility for group
sessions run by the research firm. The sessions took place in a family-living-
room environment made as comfortable as possible to help set the participants
at ease. The sessions were video tape–recorded for later analysis, but an effort
was made to keep the equipment as unobtrusive as possible, again to minimize
anxiety.

In order to ensure that the sessions were of reasonable length (1½ hours is
usually optimal), it was necessary to restrict the number of uses of plastic
containers discussed in depth in any one session. A master plan was devised
whereby each use was discussed in more than one session but usually in the
context of a different set of other possible uses. Of course, when uses such as
baby food and pet food containers were discussed, it was necessary to have
panel members who were all purchasers of these products. To assure this, a
screening process was employed which we will now examine.

Sample Selection   Each session was conducted with a panel of consumers
who were largely homogeneous in terms of their position in the family life cycle.
While pros and cons exist for this sort of design, recruiting along life-cycle lines
helped in the identification of the most probable users of certain sets of products.
To facilitate the selection process, a screening questionnaire was constructed
to determine marital status, the number and ages of any children living at home,
the occupational status of the adult family members, and usage rates of those
products previously defined as markets for plastic containers. Using this questionnaire, interviewers then selected a convenient sample at a nearby shopping
center (see Chapter 8). Those who agreed to participate were given a time and
place at which to appear.

Moderator and Guide Questions   The group discussions were led by trained
moderators whose function was to channel the conversation along particular
lines. They in turn were directed by a "moderator's guide," which specified the
minimum set of topics which the group was to cover and how the topics were
to be broached. A few sample questions from the guide appear in Exhibit 3-2.

The job of moderating a group session tends to be a very sensitive task. To
be most useful, the conversation needs to be lively and uninhibited but should
not be dominated by a few panel members and should not stray too far from the

Exhibit 3-2 Examples from the Moderator's Guide

When was the last time you found yourself extremely dissatisfied with the container used for a product you had purchased?

Certain types of containers are best suited for certain types of products. Describe for me the kind of product you would expect to find in a glass jar. How about a metal can? Paper or cardboard? Plastic?

In general, what do you consider to be the advantages and disadvantages of glass, metal, paper, and plastic containers?

Let's discuss the kinds of experiences you have had with the containers used for ice cream, jelly, coffee, meat.

Do you think it usually costs more to package a product in plastic rather than glass? Metal? Paper?

Assume that the brand of ice cream you buy was available in the standard paper carton, a plastic container, or a sturdy cardboard container (the cylindrical kind with the separate top). If the price were the same for the three versions, which would you buy? What sort of person can you visualize buying the other two versions?

---

assigned topics. The moderators applied various techniques to help achieve this result. One such technique was to identify panel members holding widely divergent points of view and then guide them into a debate. Another was to call on shy or retiring members directly for their opinions.

Analysis After all the sessions were completed, the tapes were replayed and transcribed, and summary reports were written based on what they contained. Given that the data were qualitative, no statistics were formally presented, such as what percentage said this or that. Instead, the format was to categorize and list comments in such a way as to define the domain of the problem without trying to determine the relative importance of its various aspects. As an aid to the analysis, the individual tapes were edited into a summary tape that included only the most meaningful dialog from each session. In the research business, such tapes are often used for management presentations.

Results At the general level, what emerged from these sessions was as follows:

1 A better understanding of how consumers think about containers, the terms they use, and the attributes and characteristics they consider relevant
2 A more thorough list of the advantages and disadvantages associated with different container types, depending on how they are used
3 Some new ideas on the kinds of products that might be contained in rigid plastic

To help make this discussion more concrete, however, we might consider the results obtained for one packaging market in particular, namely, ice cream. Although per capita consumption of ice cream declined 5.4 percent from 1965 to 1974, it represents a market with minor plastic penetration and would therefore seem to offer good potential for the future. Most ice cream is now contained in paper cartons, which, according to the panel members, have these deficiencies:

1   When the ice cream melts, they leak.
2   They are flimsy and tear easily.
3   Children don't know which end is the top, and they open both.
4   They are susceptible to freezer burn.
5   They tend to absorb moisture.

In comparison, the participants tended to view plastic containers mainly in positive terms, such as the following:

1   They are reusuable.
2   They are resealable.
3   They are strong.
4   They are less messy, because they don't leak.
5   They prevent freezer burn.
6   Sherbet comes like this, and experiences with it have been good.
7   Plastic has a higher quality/price image.
8   They are easy to use and have a wide mouth.
9   There is an incentive value in seeing the ice cream.

In spite of these positive findings from the qualitative research there was not sufficient evidence to say that ice cream in rigid plastic containers would definitely have consumer acceptance. For one thing, the sample was small and not representative. There were no statistics projectable to the general population as to the level of acceptance. Also, it was possible that all nine positive aspects on the list could be easily outweighed by a single important disadvantage not uncovered for some reason. Finally, some other use might exist where the acceptance of plastic would be much more certain. For these reasons and others, the conclusive research discussed in the next section was undertaken.

Survey of Consumers   In contrast to the exploratory group sessions discussed above, the methodology of the survey of consumers was more heavily influenced by an existing body of scientific knowledge. That body of knowledge specifies the manner in which surveys should be conducted and analyzed so as to minimize the amount of error in the results. This survey employed some error-reducing techniques that are not always used in marketing research because the benefits of the reduction in uncertainty do not, in every case, justify the increased cost.

As is the case with most well-developed areas of science, survey research has its own terminology, some of which may be confusing to the uninitiated. Various technical terms are introduced in the rest of this chapter without elaboration or apology, because considerable effort will be expended in defining them in detail in the remainder of the book.

The survey of consumers followed what is a fairly standard series of steps for doing this type of research. The processes which will be discussed are, in the order of their occurrence: questionnaire design and pretesting; sample selection and field work; editing, coding, and data processing; and analysis and reporting.

Questionnaire Design and Pretesting   Some say that questionnaire design is as much an art as it is a science. While this may be true, there is much more to designing a questionnaire than its literary aspects (see Chapter 19). Perhaps one scientific principle in the design of a questionnaire is that the questions should proceed from the general to the specific. For example, in this study respondents were asked to recall some products they had seen contained in plastic. It only made sense that this question should occur before one that specifically mentioned product names. A few other refinements incorporated in the questionnaire were alternate question wordings to avoid an acquiescence bias, the rotation of item lists to avoid an order bias (e.g., the list of attributes and the list of container uses), and precoding of the response categories for machine processing. Some of the questions used in this study have been paraphrased in Exhibit 3-3.

The questionnaire was pretested on a convenience sample of about 75 consumers to make sure that the proper flow existed and that the questions were understandable to ordinary individuals. The pretesting also provided the opportunity to analyze the items for redundancy. This was accomplished by taking the data for the total sample and subjecting them to a technique known as factor analysis (see Chapter 25). The procedure revealed that several of the attributes actually measured the same underlying characteristic, so it was possible to eliminate a few of the items.

Exhibit 3-3   Example of Questions on the Questionnaire

1   Of the packages you currently purchase, which do you feel could be improved? Why?

2   What products do you currently purchase which come packaged in a plastic container?

3   What are the advantages of a plastic container?

4   What are the disadvantages of a plastic container?

5   Would you please evaluate (packaging container) in regard to the degree it possesses the characteristic of (attribute)? (rating scale)

6   How important is the packaging characteristic of (attribute) for a (packaging container)? (rating scale)

7   (Interviewer checks "male" or "female.")

8   What is your marital status?

9   How many people are there in your household?

10   How many children do you have at home?

11   What are their ages?

12   What is the highest grade of school or college that you have completed?

Sample Selection and Field Work   It was determined that the interviews could be successfully conducted over the telephone. Telephone numbers were selected using the method of random-digit dialing (see Chapter 20). Under this procedure, three-digit exchange codes supplied by the telephone company are combined with four-digit random numbers to give every operating telephone in the country an equal probability of selection. An advantage of random-digit dialing is that there is no bias against newly listed or unlisted numbers, as occurs when samples are selected from telephone directories. However, households without telephones are excluded from the target population, and there is some inefficiency in connections made to business numbers. In addition, households with two or more phone listings have a higher probability of being included in the sample. The interviews were conducted at various times of the day over WATS lines. A number of call-backs were made when there was no answer or the line was busy. In all about 500 interviews were completed over the course of several weeks.

Editing, Coding, and Data Processing   At this stage, completed interviews were edited to make sure that they were legible, complete, consistent, and accurate, and that all the instructions had been properly followed (see Chapter 21). In some cases where data were missing, estimates were made of what the responses would have been based on other information in the questionnaire. This was only necessary in a few critical places in the questionnaire. Open-ended questions were then coded to make the data machine-readable. As the coding process was getting under way, a "round robin" was used whereby several individuals coded the same questionnaire. This revealed a few ambiguities in the code book.

As soon as the completed interviews were edited and coded, they were keypunched onto computer cards and verified 100 percent. The research firm had available standard computer programs to process the survey data.

Analysis and Reporting   The objectives of this chapter, together with space limitations, restrict the presentation of the results of the study and the course of action selected and implemented by SPI. Consequently, the following discussion is designed to illustrate the data analysis stage and to discuss a few of the research findings.

The first step in the analysis process was to obtain a description of the sample in terms of demographic characteristics. The sample demographics were then compared with U.S. census data to determine whether the sample was representative of the population. Except for minor sampling variations, the sample and population distributions were very similar.

In like fashion, descriptive statistics were obtained on the response to every item in the questionnaire (see Chapter 22). These statistics included measures of central tendency and dispersion. Among the benefits of doing this was the identification of a number of "wild codes" that needed to be corrected. Some of these univariate statistics were used to make interval estimates of the proportion of consumers in the general population who felt a particular way on a certain issue. For example, it was of interest to the SPI to know that, at the 95 percent confidence level, somewhere between 43 and 51 percent of the population would prefer that their ice cream came in a rigid plastic container. These statistics were especially valuable when compared with similar figures for other products.

There were other cases, however, where a simple univariate analysis was not revealing enough and a cross tabulation or bivariate analysis seemed necessary (see Chapter 23). For instance, 25 percent of the respondents said they would switch brands of ice cream to obtain a plastic container. However, a cross tabulation revealed that the result varied depending on the level of educational attainment, as evidenced in Table 3-1. Only 17 percent of those who graduated from high school said they would switch brands to get plastic, compared with 37 percent of those who had not graduated. Was it safe to conclude, then, that educational attainment was a causal factor affecting the intention to switch brands? The fallacy of this conclusion is evident in Table 3-2. Note that regardless of the level of educational attainment, only 20 percent of those who were aware that plastic is nonbiodegradable said they would switch brands, compared with 43 percent of those who were not aware. The influence of education was that more people with a high school education were aware that plastic was nonbiodegradable (50 percent compared with 25 percent).

Many other two-way relationships were studied, and in addition some more complex multivariate analysis was performed (see Chapter 25 and 26). These results are not reported here, but they were useful to management in decision making.

Table 3-1 Intention to Switch Brands By Level of Educational Attainment

	Total, %	Did not graduate, %	Graduated from high school, %
Would switch	25	37	17
Would not	75	63	83
Total	100	100	100

Table 3-2 Intention to Switch Brands By Level of Educational Attainment and Bio-Awareness

	Did not graduate from high school			Graduated from high school		
	Total, %	Aware, %	Not aware, %	Total, %	Aware, %	Not aware, %
Would switch	37	20	43	17	20	43
Would not	63	80	57	83	80	57
Total	100	100	100	100	100	100

SUMMARY

1 The purpose of this chapter was to illustrate the character and flow of a research project.

2 The first phase of the project involved the recognition by the Rigid Container Division's executive board that a problem existed. The problem was defined as the need to identify and evaluate the market opportunities for rigid plastic containers.

3 The next phase involved specifying the objective of the executive board and identifying potential courses of action to accomplish the objective.

4 The project next turned to identifying the type of information needed to select and implement one or more of the alternatives identified.

5 The information requirements suggested that a series of projects were required. Research objectives and specific information needs were specified for a Study of Packaging Markets and a Study of Consumer Acceptance. The Study of Packaging Markets was an exploratory research study using secondary data sources to identify specific alternative courses of action. The Study of Consumer Acceptance was mainly concerned with conclusive research directed at the selection of a course of action. This study involved a national probability sample of households, with interviews conducted over the telephone.

6 The results of the telephone survey were analyzed by means of univariate and bivariate analysis. Illustrative results were presented for the ice cream container market.

7 The presentation of the research project was not intended to be illustrative of how a research report should be organized and written. Chapter 24 discusses this in detail.

DISCUSSION QUESTIONS

1 How did the marketing research firm ascertain the information needs of SPI?
2 What type of research did the Study of Packaging Markets involve? Why?
3 What type of research did the Study of Consumer Acceptance involve? Why?
4 Evaluate the manner in which the group phase of the Study of Consumer Acceptance was carried out.

SUGGESTED READING

Green, Paul E., and Donald S. Tull, *Research for Marketing Decisions,* 3d ed. (Englewood Cliffs, N.J.: Prentice-Hall, 1975), pp. 265–307. The authors of this leading textbook present a student marketing research project designed to study the market for women's shampoos. The various stages of the research process are explained in detail.

Chapter 4

The Marketing Research Business

In the first two chapters in this section of the book, we discussed the nature and role of marketing research as it relates to marketing decision making. In Chapter 3, we illustrated the marketing research process with the description of a real marketing research study. This example was presented to give "life" to the conceptual material in the first two chapters. In the present chapter, our objective is to add even more "life" to the marketing research process by presenting a description of a very exciting business, the marketing research business; unfortunately, no words on paper can do justice to its dynamic nature.

This chapter will first describe the amount of money that is spent on marketing research, and the types of institutions that use and perform such research. In this context, we shall discuss how companies organize the marketing research function, the types of job opportunities that are available, and the procedures by which the users of marketing research select those who will actually perform it. With a good understanding of the practice of marketing research in hand, the chapter will then address the ethical constraints that affect this field, and finally its legal dimensions.

THE PRACTICE OF MARKETING RESEARCH
Dollar Expenditures

It is difficult to obtain exact dollar figures for the amount of money expended for marketing research activity. However, some good estimates are available to help us understand the magnitude of this business.

A 1973 American Marketing Association study[1] reported that 815 companies surveyed in the United States and Canada spent $233 million for marketing research in 1973. If one allows for reasonable growth since 1973, this figure is likely to be well over $300 million in 1978. These figures understate the expenditures for marketing research, as can be seen by examining Table 4-1. This table presents the worldwide and United States revenues for the top 20 marketing research suppliers. These are companies that do research for other organizations on both an ad hoc and a syndicated basis. Most are large suppliers of syndicated data. We note that these 20 companies had worldwide revenues of $494.3 million in 1977 and United States revenues of well over $300 million. If one considers all the money spent on research where outside research suppliers are not used.

Table 4-1   Top 20 Researchers
(Based on 1977 Marketing/Advertising Research Volume Only)

Rank	Organization	1977 research revenue (in millions)	Percent gain (loss) over 1976	Percent of revenue from outside U.S.
1	A. C. Nielsen Co.	$205.3	18	45
2	I. M. S. International	61.9	17	60
3	Selling Areas—Marketing	40.8	20	—
4	Arbitron Co.	29.0	16	—
5	Burke Int'l. Research	23.1	24	33
6	Booz, Allen & Hamilton	17.5	47	—
7	Market Facts	17.1	19	—
8	Audits & Surveys	12.2	20	—
9	ASI Marketing Research	10.2	(5)	29
10	Marketing & Research Counselors	10.0	33	—
11	Westat Inc.	8.4	29	—
12	National Family Opinion	7.9	27	—
13	Ehrhart-Babic Associates	7.9	13	2
14	Data Development Corp.	7.7	10	—
15	NPD Research	7.3	27	—
16	Yankelovich, Skelly & White	6.9	15	—
17	Louis Harris & Associates	5.8	18	28
18	Walker Research	5.2	26	—
19	Chilton Research Services	5.1	19	—
20	U.S. Testing Co.	5.0	14	—
	Total/Average	$494.3	19	

Source: *Advertising Age*, April 24, 1978, p. 3. Reproduced with permission.

[1] Dik Warren Twedt, *1973 Survey of Marketing Research* (Chicago: American Marketing Association, 1973), p. 28.

**Table 4-2 Consumer Ad Hoc
Research Expenditures by Country**

Country	1975 (in millions)
Argentina	$0.7
Brazil	3.5
Canada	19.0
Denmark	2.0
France	27.0
Germany	30.0
Italy	5.0
Japan	30.0
Mexico	3.0
Sweden	4.5
United Kingdom	36.0
Others*	51.3
Total	$212.0

*Excluding the United States.
Source: Advertising Age, Sept. 13, 1976, p. 30.
Reproduced with permission.

and that done by the thousands of other marketing research supply firms not in the top 20, then annual expenditures on marketing research in the United States should easily exceed $600 million.

Table 4-2 presents estimates made by marketing researchers of the consumer ad hoc marketing research expenditures outside the United States. If syndicated services were added to the $212 million in Table 4-2, the total was estimated by the researchers to be over $400 million.

Marketing research is a big and rapidly growing business, and one offering interesting employment opportunities. We now turn our attention to where the employment opportunities are by examining the institutional structure of the industry.

Institutional Structure

The institutional structure of the marketing research business is complex, with many thousands of different types of organizations being part of the industry. To simplify our discussion we will position each of these organizations into one of three categories. These categories are (1) users, (2) users/doers, and (3) doers. Figure 4-1 presents a graphic representation of this structure. Different types of organizations are listed under each of the three categories. The arrows indicate the direction of the flow of marketing research services. As one would expect, services flow from doers to users. In actuality the industry is more complex than this representation. To display it in all its complexity would reduce any graphic display to chaos.

Users In Figure 4-1 certain organizations are placed in two categories, namely, users and users/doers. These organizations are manufacturers, whole-

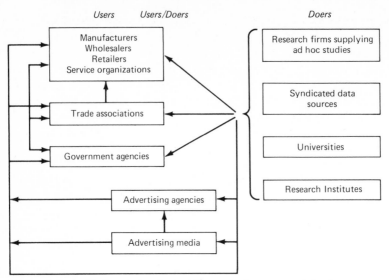

Figure 4-1   Institutional structure of the marketing research business.

salers, retailers, service organizations, trade associations, and government agencies. All of these organizations use marketing research data for the purpose of making marketing decisions of various kinds: product planning and evaluation, distribution planning and evaluation, promotional activity development and assessment, and pricing. However, some do not do any of their own research. These are the organizations designated as users only. Others do some of their own research, while making use of outsiders for the rest. Thus, the graphic representation has these organizations in both categories.

Users/Doers   Certain other institutions are almost always users/doers. Foremost among these are advertising agencies, which undertake research studies for their own planning purposes but also do a great deal of research on behalf of clients. This latter research is usually specially funded by client organizations if large, and often absorbed by the agency for their standard 15 percent of media billings if small. Most agencies have their own research departments, but they also make use of outside suppliers for some studies.

Advertising media are also users/doers. It is important to them to be able to provide accurate information about the size and composition of their audiences, since their advertising revenues per insertion depend on this. This information is communicated to advertising agencies and the clients of agencies. Most media have good reputations for doing competent research in this regard and for providing accurate information. However, the media often make use of outside research suppliers in order to add even more credibility to their audience estimates.

Doers   Doer institutions undertake marketing research solely to provide information for the use of other institutions. Marketing research firms supplying ad hoc studies are one type of doer. We need to distinguish between full-service and limited-service research suppliers. Full-service suppliers will undertake complete research studies for client organizations. That is, they will do problem definition work, questionnaire design, sampling, interviewing, coding, editing, and data analysis and interpretation; and they are prepared to do this for the full range of marketing decision problems. Limited-service suppliers do only some of these activities. These are firms that do only field interviewing or data analysis, for example, or firms that specialize in, say, advertising research or product testing. These limited-service firms often concentrate on one geographic region of the country. This is especially true in interviewing work. These local interviewing firms make themselves available to users/doers and doers. The cost and trouble of maintaining a national interviewing force is too much for most users/doers and doers, and so local firms have set up arrangements with other firms to be able to put together a national interviewing system as needed. (It would not be uncommon for two studies performed through two different doers to end up using the same field interviewers.)

Marketing research supply firms can range from large multinational organizations all the way down to one-person businesses operating out of a basement office. The common denominator is that they all have a client or clients that will pay for the services they provide.

It is important to note the difference between ad hoc studies and syndicated studies. All ad hoc studies are designed to solve *client-specific problems;* syndicated data sources provide information that is *not client-specific*. Syndicated data sources collect certain types of data and then sell these data on a subscription basis to any organization that will buy them. Common types of syndicated data measure retail sales, wholesale product shipments, consumer panels, advertising media audiences, advertising effectiveness, and consumer attitudes. Significant companies in this field include A. C. Nielsen, Selling Areas—Marketing Inc., Audits and Surveys, and Daniel Starch and Staff. A detailed description of the types of syndicated data available and some of the better-known organizations providing them is presented in Chapter 6. We should recognize that many of the firms doing syndicated studies are also in the ad hoc study business. The big users of syndicated data are consumer products companies, advertising agencies, and the advertising media.

Universities through their division of business research are also doers. This research may be undertaken for specific client organizations, but usually it is made public because of university regulations. Government agencies are the biggest users of this group of doers. Commercial firms rarely use universities. Individual professors doing marketing research work on a consulting basis would be included as suppliers of ad hoc studies.

Research institutes can be located within a university structure or independent of the arrangement. They can be providers of both ad hoc or syndicated information. Their ad hoc clients are usually government agencies. An example of a syndicated service here would be the "Index of Consumer Sentiment" published by the Survey Research Center of The University of Michigan.

Career Aspects

A discussion of institutions can hide the fact that it is people pursuing individual careers who actually do the work of marketing research. This section presents an overview of some of the careers available in marketing research. In corporations and suppliers, there are basically four types of jobs: (1) research directors, (2) analysts, (3) technical specialists, and (4) clerical workers.

Research Directors   These individuals are responsible for all activities of the other people in a department. A 1975 study by Krun[2] gives us a good portrait of research directors in large companies. The majority (55 percent) hold a master's degree, with a significant number (33 percent) holding a bachelor's degree and a few (8 percent) a doctoral degree. Most became the research director after holding positions in marketing research or some other marketing staff job. Their role was seen to be largely advisory to top management, but with some policy-making aspects. Another study[3] reported that the average marketing research director in a large company earned between $40,000 and $50,000 in 1977.

Analysts   These individuals do the bulk of the designing and supervision of actual marketing research studies; they are the research generalists referred to in Chapter 2. There are different grades of analysts. Senior analysts in large organizations usually supervise other analysts, who do the majority of project work. In turn, these more junior analysts may have apprentice analysts assisting them. The position of analyst can be an entry-level job for someone pursuing either a B.B.A. or M.B.A. Most large organizations pay competitive salaries to attract new graduates. In the long run, a successful career in marketing research usually pays less than a successful line career in marketing. However, many find the nature of marketing research work worth the sacrifice.

A recent study by Blankenship[4] gives insight into the background and characteristics desired for marketing research generalists. Most managers wanted their new analysts to have a master's degree (51 percent) or a bachelor's degree (40 percent). Most wanted an interdisciplinary degree, with the major to be marketing (68 percent), statistics (60 percent), economics (44 percent), general business (42 percent), or psychology (35 percent). Most (89 percent) indicated that they would hire analysts right out of school. The characteristics they most desired were brightness/intelligence (89 percent), analytic ability (87 percent), imagination/creativity (78 percent), interpersonal skills (66 percent), curiosity (65 percent), writing proficiency (63 percent), and drive/ambition (60 percent). A competent analyst is a person of many analytical and interpersonal skills with

---

[2] James R. Krun, "Marketing Research Chiefs Trend to Progress in Company or Out of It—1975 Study Reveals," *Marketing News,* Jan. 28, 1977, p. 18.

[3] "Where the Money and the Jobs Are," *Media Decisions,* June 1977, p. 66.

[4] Al Blankenship, "What Marketing Research Managers Want in Trainees," *Journal of Advertising Research,* vol. 15, pp. 7–14, February 1975.

a solid understanding of both marketing and marketing research. (A more detailed look at three different analysts will be presented below.)

Technical Specialists   These individuals are available to solve very narrow aspects of marketing research problems. They include, for example, experts in questionnaire design, sampling, data analysis, and computers. Analysts make use of their knowledge when needed.

Clerical Workers   These individuals perform functions as directed by analysts. For example, they type reports, pull sample elements as directed, prepare computer runs, etc.

A Week in the Life of . . .

Following this overview description of the available jobs, we now focus on the analyst's job by outlining the activities undertaken by analysts in three different types of organizations. Excerpts from their daybooks are given here.

Sandra Jenkins, Consumer Products Analyst   The following is a typical week for Ms. Jenkins, who works for a large consumer products company.

Monday a.m.	Made oral presentation to VP of marketing on just-completed product test for new brand.
p.m.	Completed work on a questionnaire for advertising evaluation study; in evening attended group interview done by supplier.
Tuesday	Flew to Denver to supervise the setup of a test market.
Wednesday a.m.	Met with brand manager to discuss problem definition for new study on his brand.
p.m.	Discussed this brand problem with research director and brand manager.
Thursday a.m.	Met with contact analyst from research supplier who is handling field work on pricing study; discussed design issues and timing.
p.m.	Wrote part of report on product test study.
Friday a.m.	Received solicitation from new research supplier seeking our business.
p.m.	Briefed computer people on data analysis runs to be made on image and distribution penetration study involving 2000 respondents.

William Brunner, Industrial Products Analyst   The following is a typical week for Mr. Brunner, who works for a large industrial products company.

Monday a.m.	Returned from Boston after completing a set of interviews with engineers about the potential for a new electrical component we have developed; interviewed a total of twenty engineers in six industries.
p.m.	Began writing report on the project.

Tuesday a.m.	Met with director of sales to design study on sales force turnover.
p.m.	Gave oral report to top management on corporate image advertising results.
Wednesday a.m.	Met with Department of Commerce people to find if they had industry data on the potential for one of our products.
p.m.	Worked with data provided to try to make an estimate.
Thursday	Flew to Chicago to talk to trade association people about their data base and our problems.
Friday a.m.	Began designing a new questionnaire for second round of corporate image advertising.
p.m.	Explained the type of work I do to a new analyst.

Dan Razinski, Supplier Analyst   The following is a typical week for Mr. Razinski, who works for a full-service marketing research supplier.

Monday	Met with client to give findings on branding study; handed in written report, gave oral presentation.
Tuesday a.m.	Prepared bid for field work portion of national study by large petroleum company.
p.m.	Made call on new director of research at large company; explained why we should be one of their suppliers.
Wednesday	Worked on study design for product taste test as directed by client.
Thursday a.m.	Briefed interviewers on media habits questionnaire, made sure their task was clear.
p.m.	Flew to Los Angeles for Friday presentation.
Friday	Made oral presentation to client on study; discussed possible follow-up work.

These three analysts have much in common. They all give oral and written reports, define problems in concert with management, design studies, and execute parts of studies and delegate parts to other people. We note that the industrial products analyst does things similar to what the consumer products analyst does, except that the sample sizes used are smaller and more time is spent searching out secondary data and doing interviewing.

As can be seen, analysts work in an organization context. The next section discusses the organization of the marketing research function in corporations.

Organization[5]

This section considers the question: "Where should the marketing research function be positioned within an organizational structure?" Unfortunately, there is no easy or technically right way to answer this question, for two reasons. First, every organization will differ in the relative importance attached to marketing research and the scale and complexity of research methods employed. Therefore, the marketing research department should be custom tailored to fit

[5] This section is based upon an unpublished paper by J. Craig DeNooyer of the University of Michigan.

the firm's informational requirements. Second, within each firm the organization of the research department is inevitably going to demonstrate dynamism. Very few growing firms find that the exact research structure they instituted 30, 20, or even 10 years ago still adequately meets their expanding corporate needs. Thus, the organizational position of the research function is unavoidably going to be adapted to the enlarged information needs of the marketing-oriented firm.[6]

Despite these limitations, it is possible to give a company and its officers some guidelines as to where the research department should be located within its organization. We will begin with a discussion of the advantages and disadvantages of the most common ways of positioning the research function within a divisionalized firm. Then we will provide some general criteria for managers to use in designing their own organization.

Centralized Organization The first structural option to be considered is that of completely centralizing the research function of a company by locating it at corporate headquarters. In such a case, all research would be under the control of the vice president in charge of marketing. Companies utilizing this approach cite several advantages and a few disadvantages.

Effective coordination and control of the firm's research efforts are two of the major advantages to centralized control. By limiting the number of organizational levels a communiqué must pass through, a firm can speed the decision-making process and increase its ability to adapt to dynamic operating conditions.[7] Also, it induces the research department to work in the company's overall interest rather than a particular division's self-interest. Centralization results in more continuity and coordination between corporate marketing policy and marketing research. In addition, the research undertaken will be more readily transferable to each division of the company with similar needs and problems. A third advantage to centralization is the encouragement of economical, effective, and flexible use of research operations and personnel. This system will help reduce any duplication of efforts. It will permit fuller utilization of research funds, thus saving money. But, perhaps most importantly, it reduces the necessity of finding and hiring scarce, talented research specialists. Where there is a centralized staff, these "top-notch" specialists are able to help all divisions of a firm, even the ones which have only an occasional need for market research.

A fourth major advantage inherent in centralization is an increased usefulness of the research function for corporate executives. By acquiring an overview of the entire firm's marketing objectives, opportunities, and problems, the research department stands more ready to meet the informational needs of company executives.[8] In addition, the department will be free from division-

[6] Richard Crisp, "Organization of the Marketing Research Function," in Robert Ferber (ed.), *Handbook of Marketing Research,* (New York: McGraw-Hill, 1974), pp. 1–66.

[7] Henry Albers, *Principles of Organization and Management,* (New York: John Wiley 1965), p. 1.

[8] Merritt L. Kastens, "Organizing, Planning, and Staffing Market Research Activities in an International Corporation," *Marketing Research in International Operations: Techniques, Tools and Organizational Approaches* (New York: American Management Association, 1963), p. 7.

level biases that might cloud any projects undertaken. This objectivity is essential if marketing research is to be effective. If marketing research can adequately demonstrate its utility to top management, the importance of the department will grow. The final major advantage to centralization is actually a series of benefits—for example, the research department would achieve greater support from top executives; it would achieve greater prestige throughout the company; and there would be one convenient location for the gathering and storing of all pertinent marketing information in a data bank. These benefits greatly facilitate the work of marketing research.

Despite this list of advantages, centralization of the research function also bears three distinct disadvantages. The exclusive structuring of the research function at the corporate level often isolates the research specialists from the day-to-day needs and problems of the various divisions. This separation can result in a lack of effective research on behalf of the divisions and wasted, frustrated effort by the specialist. A less intimate relationship between division managers and researchers hampers the processes of problem definition, the setting of research objectives, and the outlining of informational needs. It is crucial for these steps to be carried out properly in order for any research project to be worthwhile.[9]

A second disadvantage arises when divisional problems are so diverse that any attempt to handle them from a central, corporate department results in a dilution of attention given to each and a lowering of the quality of marketing research information. A single research staff group is limited as to the amount of work it can tackle. If it tries to spread itself too thin, the group is liable to be a "jack of all trades but master of none." A corollary problem appears when corporate-level problems are given top priority and divisional-level problems are virtually forgotten. This causes ill will in each division, and many important marketing decisions have to be made with a lack of pertinent information.

The last major disadvantage is that, under centralization, the researchers are isolated from the point where the action programs based upon their research are put into practice. This separation makes it extremely difficult for the research specialist to discern whether research information is valuable and/or being correctly used. If it is not, the marketing program assumes a higher risk of failure, and the reputation of the marketing research department suffers correspondingly. Years of building up confidence in the validity of marketing research can be wiped out by a few incidents of research findings being misapplied or misunderstood. Unfortunately, the problem does not end here. Given that the company correctly acts upon the research findings, with centralization it runs the risk of not being able to measure the performance of the marketing program, as would be the case if it were organized along divisional lines. These functional shortcomings must be examined and solved by the firm which adopts the centralization of its research department.

    [9] Earl L. Bailey and Lewis Forman, *The Role and Organization of Marketing Research* (New York: National Industrial Conference Board, 1969), p. 12.

Decentralized Organization   The second option open to a divisionalized firm wishing to position its marketing research function is to completely decentralize the department along divisional lines. In this system the market researcher would be responsible to the division manager and not to a top corporate executive. Divisions of companies may be organized by products, by customers, or by geographic regions. The divisional assignment of research personnel would exactly parallel the type of divisional basis used by the company. Thus, research people would be expected to become expert in the research problems of particular products, customer markets, or geographic regions. In many cases decentralization's advantages and disadvantages are inverse arguments of our previous discussion on centralization. Still, there are a few pros and cons that should be highlighted.

Perhaps the most important advantage gained by decentralization is the research group's increased ability to react quickly to and focus its attention on areas where its information is needed most. By working very closely with divisional managers, salespersons, and product managers, the marketing researcher can become quite sensitive to the local or emergency decision situations that arise. One can become totally familiar with a small number of products and understand their market situation. In effect, this form of organization puts the research talent where it is needed most—closer to the consumer of the research.

The second advantage to decentralization is that research findings will receive more attention from divisional personnel and will be used more. Why is this so? One reason is that through decentralization the divisional-level decision-making unit will actually commission the projects to be undertaken. Since they have a personal stake in each product that concerns their division, they will be more likely to pay attention to the research results. A second reason for increased attention to research findings will arise from the fact that decentralization allows researchers to become true specialists in certain areas. If researchers offer opinions or advice in their area of expertise, division managers will be more likely to view this advice as valid and therefore accept it. Since marketing research's function is to provide information that helps managers in their decision-making process, the advantage of increased use of research findings is an important one.

The disadvantages of decentralization can be broken down into two facets: one major objection and a group of minor objections. The major problem is that the research results from a decentralized department may be biased in favor of a particular division's point of view. This bias arises from two sources. First, by interacting closely with its individual division, the research staff may lose sight of overall corporate goals. As a result, the research findings may be biased toward a short-run solution of divisional problems but be in conflict with long-run aims of the entire company. A second source of informational bias may arise because the research function is now responsible only to the division manager whom it serves. All too often the researchers will slant their interpretation of the data to fit what the division manager wishes to hear. "Keeping the boss happy" dominates reporting the undoctored facts. The danger is evident. Overly biased results can never help make good marketing decisions. They can only increase the risk of failure for programs based upon their findings. Consequently, the firm may face a trade-off between a long-run, corporate viewpoint for its research and a more short-run, divisional point of view.[10] The balance ultimately struck between the two will vary within each firm.

A list of less serious objections to decentralization includes the following. There is the possibility of inadequate, corporatewide research controls, standards, and procedures. Decentralization may make no provision for research projects on behalf of the general management. Finding a sufficient number of competent research people can be difficult. Finally, divisionalized research groups may be subject to extreme variation in degree of use. Demands for their services may fluctuate so much between overuse and underuse that the research system becomes grossly inefficient and ineffective.[11] Taken separately, items from this list may not cause a firm irreparable damage. However, if two or more of these conditions are present simultaneously, they may dictate the use of an alternative form of organization for the research function.

Integrated Organization   A viable alternate form to the extremes of centralization and decentralization has proved to be the "integrated" organization structure. This increasingly popular research structure makes use of a central staff (which includes a highly qualified marketing research function) available as needed to counsel with and reinforce individual research departments within each division. This central staff would be responsible to a top-level corporate executive, probably the vice president in charge of marketing. Divisional work would be conducted by division research staffs directly responsible to division managers. Their research projects would deal with divisional marketing problems. The thought behind this matrix organization is that it would help combine the best features of centralization and decentralization into one effective system.[12] Unfortunately, there are also pluses and minuses to this type of research structure.

All the advantages of the hybrid relationship can be summed up as "more coordinated and effective research." Both levels of the research function would contribute to this process. The central research staff would arrange for the exchange of pertinent marketing data to the various divisions, act as a central purchasing agent for all services common to the needs of the research teams, and carry out research projects with companywide implications.[13] In addition, the central corporate staff could set and explain company research standards, undertake projects for departments too small to have their own research staffs, and assist divisional research staffs when they become overloaded with research requests. By having additional research teams located at the divisional level, a

---

[10] Kastens, "Organizing, Planning, and Staffing," p. 6.
[11] Bailey and Forman, *Role and Organization of Marketing Research,* p. 10.
[12] Ibid., p. 16.
[13] Ibid.

company achieves its goal of making the research function part of the firm's marketing team. This allows researchers to become experts in their fields and places their information-gathering techniques closer to the consumer of research.

The main disadvantage to the integrated system is the potential occurrence of control conflicts over the research staffs and their projects. Control conflicts can result when the lines of authority in a company are not clearly delineated.[14] Theoretically the central research staff is organized solely as a helping, advisory branch. But all too often divisional researchers look to corporate staffers as their ultimate bosses instead of their divisional heads. Other control conflicts occur when the corporate staff no longer has any input into what projects are undertaken in each division. Consequently, projects may run counter to the firm's long-run objectives. Clearly an incongruency exists: (1) control conflicts that result from emphasizing the divisional authority and (2) conflicts resulting from emphasis on corporate guidance. The optimum level of power to grant each level will depend upon each firm's preferences.

Any other disadvantages inherent in the integrated system resemble the disadvantages attributed to decentralized research departments—such as high cost, duplication of efforts, and lack of an adequate number of competent specialists. Nonetheless, the control conflict problem is by far the most serious obstacle to implementing the integrated market research system.

Choosing a Structure   Now that the main alternatives to organizing the marketing research function have been outlined, the question becomes: "How is one to choose the structure that is 'best' for one's particular firm?" There are no simple answers, no handy "cookbook" ways to determine the optimum choice. There are, however, a number of criteria which can be followed to help narrow the selection alternatives. In the final analysis, there is no completely right or wrong organizational structure for marketing research in a firm.

The first criterion, and perhaps the most important, is this: The marketing research function should be placed where the marketing decisions are made. The researcher's task is to provide information to marketers to help them in their decision-making process. At whatever level decision making is performed, the research function should be there to help. For example, if a firm makes one or two industrial goods for a few customers, a research staff located at the corporate level might suffice. However, if the firm is like Procter and Gamble, which produces a myriad of products for a host of different customers, it would be better to decentralize or integrate the research function.[15] This would allow all market information to be closer to the person who uses it. In essence, this criterion purports that the research function should reside where the marketing decision-making power resides.

---

[14] Robert J. Small and Larry J. Rosenberg, "The Marketing Researcher as a Decision Maker: Myth or Reality," *Journal of Marketing,* vol. 30, pp. 3–4, January 1975.
[15] Hector Lazio and Arnold Corbin, *Management in Marketing* (New York: McGraw-Hill, 1961), pp. 160–161.

The second criterion to consider when organizing the research department is: Free researchers from undue influence or manipulation by those areas or people for whom they conduct research projects. This rule is suggested to help assure the firm that its research is objectively based. Without an unbiased approach, the best organizational structure in the world will not help the marketer make better decisions. A simple example should suffice to show what is meant by "manipulation" or "influence." If researchers are made to feel that their job hangs in the balance every time they submit some research results that do not correlate with their boss's opinions, it will not be long before all future results say exactly what the manager wants to hear. If this happens, marketing research's reliability and reputation will be ruined.

A third criterion is: The marketing research function should be organized so that the firm can satisfy the demand for research projects quickly and efficiently.[16] If the firm's divisions exhibit a steady volume of requests for research projects, it would be advisable to decentralize the research function. On the other hand, if the demand for research within a firm is sparse or fluctuates widely, it may be more expedient to centralize all research activities in a corporate office. The final criterion is a matter of practicality that many times is overlooked. The research department should report to an executive who has a genuine interest in marketing research, understands how it operates, knows its potentials, and possesses sufficient authority to ensure that the actions called for by the research are undertaken.[17] The firm must take an audit of its present managers in order to determine who supports the use of market research. Then it should examine these managers' job descriptions to determine whether they bear authority in relation to the marketing decision responsibility that will be placed upon them. The importance of the human element in this last criterion cannot be overstressed. The best-laid plans and most detailed blueprints for an optimum research organization will be worthless without the commitment to making them work on the part of those who must staff the structure. Results come from people implementing well-thought-out plans, not from the plans themselves. Marketing research must have support from someone with a great deal of "clout" in the organization.

Utilizing Research Suppliers

One issue that confronts all marketing research directors and a great many analysts is the utilization of research suppliers. These suppliers may be involved with a few aspects of a research study or may be given total responsibility for all aspects of a study. The primary advantages of using research suppliers include: (1) the cost may be less than adding additional personnel and paying the other costs of an internal project; (2) the supplier costs to the user are a variable cost, whereas internal personnel constitute a fixed expense—that is, if the work load varies in the department, outside suppliers can be used at peak times only; (3) suppliers offer special skills not available internally; (4) the users of outside

---

[16] Ibid., p. 158.
[17] Bailey and Forman, *Role and Organization of Marketing Research,* p. 7.

services retain great flexibility, as they pick the best firm available for a specific type of problem; (5) outside suppliers have greater objectivity and are usually not involved in the politics of specific problems; (6) the sponsoring company can remain anonymous.

We must also recognize some disadvantages in the use of research suppliers. These are: (1) the firm may not be completely familiar with the objectives and problems of the company and/or industry; (2) there is a risk, especially in the first purchase from a firm, that the research will not be done well, or done on time; (3) there is a greater risk that results of studies or company activities will become known to competitors; (4) the costs can be higher, as suppliers must earn a profit that allows for slack periods and for studies that lose money.

Selecting a Supplier   Just how does one go about selecting a specific supplier for a project? First of all, a list of possible firms must be drawn up. Learning about and evaluating suppliers are subjects where word-of-mouth influences are high. Buyers seek recommendations from associates within their company, from other researchers outside their company, from advertising agencies, trade associations, and even university professors.[18] Impersonal sources such as trade publications, professional directories,[19] journals, and promotional material of suppliers may also provide prospective supply firms.

The evaluation of prospective suppliers usually involves direct contacts with the firms, discussions with other people for whom they have done work, and the examination of some piece of research they have done. These information sources are used to collect information about the criteria that will be used to make the actual choice. These criteria may include (1) the capabilities of individuals who will be assigned to the project, (2) the degree of specialization needed and provided, (3) technical competence, (4) orientation toward marketing management, (5) education of staff, (6) personal characteristics of key personnel, (7) facilities (field work, data processing, analysis), (8) creativity, (9) ethics, (10) communication skills, (11) ability to perform on time, (12) location close to buyer to allow for better communication, (13) stability, and (14) cost of the project.

The list of firms may be reduced using these criteria, and then the remaining firms may be asked to submit proposals. Proposals are usually provided to prospective clients without charge. The average cost to the supplier of preparing a proposal is $1000 to $2000, with the high end being about $10,000 for a large project.[20] The quality of the proposal constitutes another criterion on which firms would be evaluated.

---

[18] "Using Marketing Consultants and Research Agencies," National Industrial Conference Board Studies in *Business Policy,* no. 120 (New York: NICB, 1966), p. 1.

[19] For example, see *International Directory of Marketing Research Houses and Services* (New York: Marketing Review, New York Chapter of the American Marketing Association); Ernest S. Bradford, *Bradford's Directory of Marketing Research Agencies and Management Consultants* (Middleburg, VA), and *A Geographic Listing of Marketing Consultants and Research Agencies* (Chicago: American Marketing Association).

[20] "Six Consultants Counsel Clients to Improve the Marketing Research They Buy," *Marketing News,* vol. 10, no. 14, p. 13, Jan. 28, 1977.

Sometimes competitive bids for a project are asked for, but this approach is not now a significant way of selecting a supplier. A recent study[21] of 159 research suppliers found that only 14 percent of their business was via competitive bidding. The rest came through negotiations. Furthermore, 72 percent of all suppliers of ad hoc studies refuse to bid competitively, and firms that do bid usually face only one or two other firms in the competition. The 159 suppliers perceived price to be ranked eleventh on a list of important factors for firms choosing a supplier. Quality of work, understanding of the problem, reputation, integrity, experience, referrals, personality of key people, the skills of individuals assigned to projects, specialization, and personal contact all ranked higher in perceived importance.

As in all buying decisions, customers will find some brands they prefer over others. Thus, most experienced buyers of research develop a short list of suppliers with whom they deal on a regular basis. It is often difficult for a new firm to get on the approved list.

Ground Rules for Buyer-Supplier Relationships   In the interaction between the buyers of research and the suppliers, certain ground rules should apply. The supplier should be able to expect certain things from the buyer. These include:

1   A statement of the general background of the management problem at hand
2   A statement of the management problem
3   A statement of the research problem and objectives, and the use to which the research result will be put
4   A chance to discuss these problem statements and background
5   A range of budget available for the project
6   The desired timing
7   An assurance that they will be approached only when there is a reasonable expectation that they will be selected

The supplier also must be able to satisfy certain requirements of the buyer. In general, the supplier must provide information on the list of criteria the buyer is using in making the selection. In summary, this involves presenting details about the company's personnel and operating procedures and providing references. More specific information would be expected about a particular project. This would include:

1   A statement as to the specific personnel responsible for the project
2   A detailed statement of the problem and research objectives to show they understand the problem
3   A detailed description of the research design (pilot studies, sampling plans, field work, coding, editing, data analysis, report format, etc.)

---

[21] Joel B. Haynes and James T. Rothe, "Competitive Bidding for Marketing Research Services: Fact or Fiction," *Journal of Marketing,* vol. 38, pp. 69–71, July 1974.

4 A cost estimate with underlying assumptions spelled out (e.g., length and method of interview; type of report)
5 An accurate timetable

We see that marketing research involves complex relationships among buyers and suppliers. Furthermore, in the process of collecting marketing research information the doers of research are dealing with providers of the required information, who may be respondents to a survey, subjects in an experiment, etc. In all these relationships among buyers, suppliers, and providers, the chance for unethical behavior exists. Thus, a very relevant part of the domain of any practitioner of marketing research is to be aware of the ethics of the field. This is the topic to which we now direct our attention.

ETHICS

Ethics as related to marketing research deal with (1) the judgment that certain types of activities are inappropriate and (2) the judgment that certain types of activities must be undertaken. An example of the former would be the prohibition against using marketing research as a trick to sell products. An example of the latter would be to present the details of how a sample was selected to a client. Ethical issues arise in both the relationship between users and doers of research and the relationship between doers and providers (respondents) of research data.

Codes of Ethics

Because of actual and potential abuses in these areas, a number of codes of ethics have been developed to guide researchers. Exhibit 4-1 presents the American Marketing Association's Marketing Research Code of Ethics as adopted in 1962, with 1972 revisions included. We note that this code deals with user-doer and doer-provider relationships. Some feel that this code does not go far enough, as it deals mostly with prohibition. The Market Research Council developed a code of ethics that deals with things that ought to be done in marketing research. This code is presented in Exhibit 4-2; it gives details on what should be included in a marketing research report.

In a recent article[22] Tybout and Zaltman argued that respondents in marketing research studies are not subject to high enough ethical behavior on the part of doers. Drawing on codes of ethics from nonmarketing consumer researchers (American Psychological Association, American Sociological Association, etc.), they suggest that respondents should have the following basic rights:

1 The right to choose whether or not to participate in a study; included in this are the right to be made aware of this right, to be given sufficient information about the study to decide, and to be explicitly given a chance to choose.

(*Text continues on page 72.*)

---

[22] Alice M. Tybout and Gerald Zaltman, "Ethics in Marketing Research: Their Practical Relevance," *Journal of Marketing Research,* vol. 11, pp. 357–68, November 1974.

Exhibit 4-1   American Marketing Association's Marketing Research Code of Ethics

The American Marketing Association, in furtherance of its central objective of the advancement of science in marketing and in recognition of its obligation to the public, has established these principles of ethical practice of marketing research for the guidance of its members. In an increasingly complex society, marketing management is more and more dependent upon marketing information intelligently and systematically obtained. The consumer is the source of much of this information. Seeking the cooperation of the consumer in the development of information, marketing management must acknowledge its obligation to protect the public from misrepresentation and exploitation under the guise of research.

Similarly the research practitioner has an obligation to the discipline he practices and to those who provide support for his practice—an obligation to adhere to basic and commonly accepted standards of scientific investigation as they apply to the domain of marketing research.

It is the intent of this code to define ethical standards required of marketing research in satisfying these obligations.

Adherence to this code will assure the users of marketing research that the research was done in accordance with acceptable ethical practices. Those engaged in research will find in this code an affirmation of sound and honest basic principles which have developed over the years as the profession has grown. The field interviewers who are the point of contact between the profession and the consumer will also find guidance in fulfilling their vitally important role.

For Research Users, Practitioners and Interviewers

1 No individual or organization will undertake any activity which is directly or indirectly represented to be marketing research, but which has as its real purpose the attempted sale of merchandise or services to some or all of the respondents interviewed in the course of the research.

2 If a respondent has been led to believe, directly or indirectly, that he is participating in a marketing research survey and that his anonymity will be protected, his name shall not be made known to anyone outside the research organization or research department, or used for other than research purposes.

For Research Practitioners

1 There will be no intentional or deliberate misrepresentation of research methods or results. An adequate description of methods employed will be made available upon request to the sponsor of the research. Evidence that field work has been completed according to specifications will, upon request, be made available to buyers of research.

2 The identity of the survey sponsor and/or the ultimate client for whom a survey is being done will be held in confidence at all times, unless this identity is to be revealed as part of the research design. Research information shall be held in confidence by the research organization or department and not used for personal gain or made available to any outside party unless the client specifically authorizes such release.

3 A research organization shall not undertake marketing studies for competitive clients when such studies would jeopardize the confidential nature of client-agency relationships.

For Users of Marketing Research

1 A user of research shall not knowingly disseminate conclusions from a given research project or service that are inconsistent with or not warranted by the data.

2 To the extent that there is involved in a research project a unique design involving techniques, approaches, or concepts not commonly available to research practitioners, the prospective user of research shall not solicit such a design from one practitioner and deliver it to another for execution without the approval of the design originator.

For Field Interviewers

1 Research assignments and materials received, as well as information obtained from respondents, shall be held in confidence by the interviewer and revealed to no one except the research organization conducting the marketing study.

2 No information gained through a marketing research activity shall be used, directly or indirectly, for the personal gain or advantage of the interviewer.

3 Interviews shall be conducted in strict accordance with specifications and instructions received.

4 An interviewer shall not carry out two or more interviewing assignments simultaneously unless authorized by all contractors or employees concerned.

Members of the American Marketing Association will be expected to conduct themselves in accordance with the provisions of this Code in all of their marketing research activities.

Exhibit 4-2 Market Research Council's Code of Ethics

The following "position papers" were developed by the Ethics Committee of the Market Research Council during 1967–1968 and were adopted by an overwhelming vote of the membership as official positions of the Market Research Council in July 1968.

These papers are intended as a first step, not a final step—the thought being that additional papers on other subjects may be added in the future or that these papers may be amended as future developments might warrant.

The Respondent's Right to Privacy

The goodwill and cooperation of the public are necessary to successful public opinion and market research. Actions by researchers which tend to dilute or dissipate these resources do a disservice both to the research profession and to the public.

By its very nature, research must in some measure invade the privacy of respondents. The ringing of a respondent's doorbell or his telephone is an intrusion. If he agrees to participate in a study, his private world of attitudes, knowledge, and behavior is further invaded.

Researchers should recognize that the public has no obligation to cooperate in a study. Overly long interviews and subject matter which causes discomfort or apprehension serve to reduce respondent cooperation. When such interviews cannot be avoided, efforts should be made to explain the reasons to the respondent and to mitigate his anxieties to the extent possible.

One of the greatest invasions of the privacy of respondents is through the use of research techniques such as hidden microphones and cameras. When such a research

Exhibit 4-2 *(Continued)*

technique has been used, a respondent should be told and, if the respondent requests it, any portion of the interview that serves to identify the respondent should be deleted.

Even after the respondent has been interviewed, his privacy is endangered while his interview is being coded, processed, and analyzed. Research agencies have the same responsibility as other professional groups to take all reasonable steps to insure that employees with access to these data observe the canons of good taste and discretion in handling this information.

Since public opinion and market researchers must infringe on the privacy of the public at several stages of the research process, it is unlikely that any set of rules or code of ethics can prevent abuses by unscrupulous or careless researchers, even though such abuses are inexcusable. The best hope of maintaining an attitude of goodwill and cooperation among the public will depend on researchers':

1 Being constantly mindful of the problem
2 Keeping in mind the recommendations above
3 Doing everything in their power to inform the public of the benefits of market and opinion research

Maintaining Respondent Anonymity

Good and accurate research requires obtaining honest and frank expressions of opinions and beliefs. Respondents are more likely (*a*) to participate in a survey and (*b*) to speak honestly and frankly if they believe that they will remain anonymous and will not be called to account for their expressed opinions or stated behavior. For this reason, every researcher should do everything in his power to protect the anonymity of the people he interviews unless he obtains their permission to reveal their names.

This does not preclude follow-up contacts for further research or for verification purposes. However, if there seems to be a reasonable possibility that there will be contacts for any other purposes, it is incumbent on the researcher to warn the respondent of this possibility.

The researcher should be willing to make reasonable efforts to provide evidence on the authenticity of the interviews he has made, providing this does not subject the respondent to harassment.

Disclosure or Release of Survey Results

Implicit in the nature of surveys is the fact that they purport to reflect the opinions or behavior of the population under study. It is the obligation of the researcher to present survey results in such a manner that they do not give a distorted or biased picture of his findings. The client also has this same obligation in reporting survey findings. When others report his findings, the researcher has an additional responsibility to make all reasonable effort to see that they, likewise, present the results impartially.

It is not incumbent on the researcher to insist on an "all-or-nothing" policy in the release of his findings. Only part of the results may be released provided this part does not give a distorted picture of the subject matter it covers.

If the client misuses, misstates, or distorts a survey finding, the researcher should release such other findings and information about how the data were obtained as will put it in proper perspective. Client-researcher agreement prior to release would minimize misunderstandings in this respect.

Any release of findings should include appropriate information about objectives, sample, research techniques, the name of the research organization, etc. that will be helpful in evaluating the results.

Buyer-Seller Relationships

A successful marketing research study is a joint operation involving a research company and its client. It requires mutual respect and confidence between the two parties and imposes certain obligations on each of them.

The buyer of research services has the right to make sure that the work he has contracted for meets all the specifications. He has the right to examine all operations of the research company to see that they are being carried out in the manner agreed upon. However, in doing so he should respect the research company's obligations to the public in matters of anonymity and invasion of respondents' privacy.

The buyer should recognize that the research company is a professional organization engaged in collecting marketing and/or opinion data. The buyer should not, therefore, ask or expect the research company to violate any of the suggested rules of procedure covered elsewhere in this statement. The buyer should not publicly identify the research agency in any release of findings, implying the endorsement of the research agency without prior agreement from the agency.

It is understood that in seeking a research agency the buyer may request proposals from more than one research company. However, generating ideas and planning research designs to solve specific problems are an important part of the services a research agency offers. The buyer, therefore, should not (1) lift ideas from one proposal and give them to another research agency or (2) ask for a proposal from a company which he knows has little or no chance of obtaining his business, unless he so informs them in advance. Soliciting bids for the purpose of obtaining free ideas which will be turned over to another bidder, or for purely technical compliance with a company's policy of obtaining competitive bids, does a disservice to the research firms involved, reflects on the integrity of the client company, and generally lessens the professional level of the research profession.

Kickbacks, rebates, and other "inducements" similarly destroy the professional character of research and should not be solicited, offered, or agreed to.

The research agency has the obligation to express, as they become apparent, any reservations about the usefulness of the proposed research in solving the client's problem. The agency also has the obligation, of course, to do the study contracted for in the manner agreed on. No additional questions designed for another purpose should be included in interviews done for a client without the client's knowledge and consent.

Unless otherwise agreed on by the seller and the buyer, the study report and the compiled tabulated data on which it is based are the property of the buyer. No by-product information should be sold to another buyer unless express permission is obtained from the original buyer.

In the course of conducting research, the researcher may become privy to confidential information relating to the client company. The researcher should not reveal any of this material to any outsider at any time.

Exhibit 4-2   *(Continued)*

Information to Be Included in the Research Firm's Report

Every research project differs from all others. So will every research report. All reports should nonetheless contain specific references to the following items:

1   The objectives of the study (including statement of hypotheses)
2   The name of the organization for which the study is made and the name of the organization that conducted it
3   Dates the survey was in the field and date of submission of final report
4   A copy of the full interview questionnaire, including all cards and visual aids used in the interview; alternatively, exact question wording, sequence of questions, etc.
5   Description of the universe(s) studied
6   Description of the number and types of people studied:
   a   Number of people (or other units)
   b   Means of their selection
   c   If sample, method of sample selection
   d   Adequacy of sample representatives and size
   e   Percentage of original sample contacted (number and type of call-backs)
   f   Range of tolerance
   g   Number of cases for category breakouts
   h   Weighting and estimating procedures used

Where trend data are being reported and the methodology or question wording has been changed, these changes should be so noted.

On request—clients and other parties with legitimate interests may request and should expect to receive from the research firm the following:

   a   Statistical and/or field methods of interview verification (and percentage of interviews verified)
   b   Available data re validation of interview techniques
   c   Interviewing instructions
   d   Explanation of scoring or index number devices

Source: Paper developed by The Market Research Council's Ethics Committee. Reprinted with permission from Leo Bogart.

2   The right to safety; this includes protection of the respondent's anonymity, freedom from a stressful experience, and freedom from deception as to the nature and objectives of the study.

3   The right to be informed; this includes a debriefing of the respondent as to what went on and why, and dissemination of data to respondents if desired.

These views are not generally accepted yet.[23]

[23] For a commentary, see Robert L. Day, "A Comment on Ethics in Marketing Research," *Journal of Marketing Research*, vol. 12, pp. 232–233, May 1975, and Alice M. Tybout and Gerald Zaltman, "A Reply to Comments on 'Ethics in Marketing Research'," *Journal of Marketing Research*, vol. 12, pp. 234–237, May 1975.

Practitioner Attitudes

Some perspectives on practitioners' views of ethical issues were given in a 1968 study by Crawford.[24] In this study he presented a series of situations to research directors and line marketers and asked whether they approved of the activity in the situation. Some of these situations are presented in Exhibit 4-3. You may want to compare their responses with yours (remembering that the study is now 10 years old).

LEGAL ASPECTS

Recently certain activities related to marketing research have come under legal examination. Specific examples include:[25]

    1 The Federal Trade Commission (FTC) successfully moved against encyclopedia firms who were using marketing research as a trick to solicit sales.
    2 The FTC successfully moved against firms using research to identify prospects for a direct-mail scheme.
    3 The FTC successfully moved against supply firms who purported that their data were free from all nonsampling error.
    4 The Internal Revenue Service classified freelance field interviewers as part-time employees of supply firms, thus requiring these firms to pay social security, unemployment insurance, etc.
    5 The Privacy Act of 1974 gives to respondents in federal government–related projects the rights suggested previously by Tybout and Zaltman. It is as yet unclear if and when these rights will be legislated for all marketing research studies.
    6 The Privacy Protection Study Commission of the U.S. Government made 162 recommendations to protect the privacy of individuals. If put into law by Congress and held to apply to government and other research, they could seriously affect the ability of research to obtain respondent information.

    The interest of regulators and legislators in marketing research is likely to increase in the future.

SUMMARY

    1 Marketing research is a big and dynamic business.
    2 Institutions in the marketing research business can be classified as users, users/doers, or doers.
    3 Doers supply both ad hoc studies and syndicated data, on a full- or limited-service basis.

---

    [24] C. Merle Crawford, "Attitudes of Marketing Executives Toward Ethics in Marketing Research," *Journal of Marketing,* vol. 34, pp. 46–52, April 1970.
    [25] This section was developed from work done by Cynthia F. Rice of The University of Michigan.

Exhibit 4-3   Attitudes of Practitioners to Ethically Related Situations

SELECTED RESEARCH TECHNIQUES

1   Ultraviolet Ink

A project director recently came in to request permission to use ultraviolet ink in precoding questionnaires on a mail survey. He pointed out that the letter referred to
an anonymous survey, but he said he needed respondent identification to permit
adequate cross tabulations of the data. The M. R. Director gave his approval.

	Approve	Disapprove
Research directors	29%	70%
Line marketers	22	77

2   Hidden Tape Recorders

In a study intended to probe rather deeply into the buying motivations of a group of
wholesale customers by use of a semistructured personal interview form, the M. R.
Director authorized the use of the department's special attaché cases equipped with
hidden tape recorders.

	Approve	Disapprove
Research directors	33%	67%
Line marketers	26	71

3   One-Way Mirrors

One product of the X Company is brassieres, and the firm has recently been having
difficulty making some decisions on a new line. Information was critically needed
concerning the manner in which women put on their brassieres. So the M. R. Director
designed a study in which two local stores cooperated in putting one-way mirrors in
their foundations dressing rooms.   Observers behind these mirrors successfully
gathered the necessary information.

	Approve	Disapprove
Research directors	20%	78%
Line marketers	18	82

4   Fake Long Distance Calls

Some of X Company's customers are busy executives, hard to reach by normal interviewing methods. Accordingly, the market research department recently conducted a
study in which interviewers called "long distance" from nearby cities. They were successful in getting through to busy executives in almost every instance.

	Approve	Disapprove
Research directors	88%	10%
Line marketers	84	16

5 Fake Research Firm

In another study, this one concerning magazine reading habits, the M. R. Director decided to contact a sample of consumers under the name of Media Research Institute. This fictitious company name successfully camouflaged the identity of the sponsor of the study.

	Approve	Disapprove
Research directors	84%	13%
Line marketers	83	16

6 Exchange of Price Data

X Company belongs to a trade association which includes an active marketing research subgroup. At the meetings of this subgroup, the M. R. Director regularly exchanges confidential price information. In turn, he gives the competitive information to the X Company sales department, but is careful not to let the marketing vice president know about it. Profits are substantially enhanced, and top management is protected from charges of collusion.

	Approve	Disapprove
Research directors	8%	89%
Line marketers	14	82

THE ROLE OF THE MARKETING RESEARCH DIRECTOR

1 Advertising and Product Misuse

Some recent research showed that many customers of X Company are misusing Product B. There's no danger; they are simply wasting their money by using too much of it at a time. But yesterday, the M. R. Director saw final comps on Product B's new ad campaign, and the ads not only ignore the problem of misuse, but actually seem to encourage it. He quietly referred the advertising manager to the research results, well known to all people on B's advertising, and let it go at that.

	Approve	Disapprove
Research directors	41%	58%
Line marketers	33	66

2 Distortions by Marketing Vice President

In the trial run of a major presentation to the board of directors, the marketing vice president deliberately distorted some recent research findings. After some thought, the M. R. Director decided to ignore the matter, since the marketing head obviously knew what he was doing.

	Approve	Disapprove
Research directors	12%	87%
Line marketers	12	86

3 Possible Conflict of Interest

A market testing firm, to which X Company gives most of its business, recently went public. The M. R. Director had been looking for a good investment and proceeded to buy some $20,000 of their stock. The firm continues as X Company's leading supplier for testing.

	Approve	Disapprove
Research directors	40%	57%
Line marketers	58	38

TODAY'S SOCIAL CONCERNS

1 General Trade Data to Ghetto Group

The marketing research department of X Company frequently makes extensive studies of their retail customers. A federally supported black group, working to get a shopping center in their ghetto area, wanted to know if they could have access to this trade information. But since the M. R. Director had always refused to share this information with trade organizations, he declined the request.

	Approve	Disapprove
Research directors	64%	34%
Line marketers	74	25

2 NMAC Request for Recent Price Study

The National Marketing Advisory Council (formed of top marketing executives and marketing educators to advise the Commerce Department) has a task force studying ghetto prices. The head of this study recently called to ask if they could have a copy of a recent X Company study which he understood showed that ghetto appliance prices are significantly higher than in suburban areas. Since X Company sells appliances to these ghetto merchants, the M. R. Director felt compelled to refuse the request.

	Approve	Disapprove
Research directors	56%	39%
Line marketers	46	51

3 Assigning Man to a Ghetto Planning Group

A local Office of Economic Opportunity group recently called to ask that the M. R. Director assign one of his people to the planning group working on the ghetto shopping center mentioned earlier. Since one result of such a center would be to force a good number of ghetto retailers out of business, and since some of these retailers were presently customers of X Company, the M. R. Director refused the request.

	Approve	Disapprove
Research directors	41%	51%
Line marketers	39	57

4 Black Account Executive

The president of an interviewing firm which had been doing most of the field work for X Company wrote to say that a new account executive had been assigned to X. The new man was capable, personable, and black. The M. R. Director wrote back to say that there were no blacks in the department at the moment, and that he felt it would be better all around if a different account man were assigned to X Company.

	Approve	Disapprove
Research directors	5%	94%
Line marketers	7	92

5 Hiring Jewish Marketing Analyst

When interviewing applicants for a newly created analyst position, the M. R. Director was impressed with one man in particular. But he didn't offer him the job, since the applicant referred to himself as Jewish, and it was well known that X Company wanted no Jewish marketing people.

	Approve	Disapprove
Research directors	26%	71%
Line marketers	20	77

4 Careers are available as research directors, analysts, technical special-ists, or clerical workers.

5 A firm may organize the marketing research function so that it is cen-tralized, decentralized, or integrated.

6 Ethical issues arise in user-doer and doer-provider relationships. Various codes of ethics have been developed to direct researchers.

7 Legal constraints are becoming more important in marketing research.

DISCUSSION QUESTIONS

1 What is the institutional structure of the marketing research business?
2 What type of person would make a good research analyst?
3 How can the marketing research function be organized?
4 What are the advantages and disadvantages of each organizational alternative?
5 On what basis should an organizational structure be selected?
6 How should a research supplier be selected?
7 What should buyers and suppliers of research expect from each other?
8 Evaluate Crawford's situations against the American Marketing Association's Mar-keting Research Code of Ethics. Answer each situation yourself.
9 Should legal action be taken to regulate marketing research activity? If so, state specifics.

SUGGESTED READING

Ferber, Robert (ed.), *Handbook of Marketing Research* (New York: McGraw-Hill, 1974), Sec. 1, Chaps. 5, 6, 9, and 10. These chapters present a readable and in-depth look at organizational issues, budgets and controls, ethics, and the use of research suppliers.

Tybout, Alice M., and Gerald Zaltman, "Ethics in Marketing Research: Their Practical Relevance," *Journal of Marketing Research,* vol. 11, pp. 357–368, November 1974. This article explores doer-provider ethical issues in a provocative way. It should stimulate the reader's thinking on the ethics issue.

Cases for Part One

Cosmetic Labeling

Donald Willem, a research director at National Research Associates, was preparing a plan to conduct marketing research to investigate consumer problems associated with the labeling of cosmetic products (lipstick, mascara, make-up, and so on) as well as the impact of the Food and Drug Administration's ingredient-labeling regulation. The completed research proposal was to be presented to the Cosmetic, Toiletry and Fragrance Association (CTFA) in Washington, D.C., within two weeks. Mr. Willem knew that his research proposal would have to offer the potential for clarifying the marketing problems involved in the cosmetic-labeling area before funding would be approved.

The (CTFA) had contacted National Research Associates earlier in the month with regard to preparing a research proposal on the cosmetic-labeling issue. Mr. Willem was left with the impression that several of the leading marketing research shops, such as Market Facts and Opinion Research, would be competing for the research project along with National Research Associates.

Earlier in the week, Mr. Willem had spent an afternoon with Roger Tipps, the representative from CTFA in charge of coordinating the research proposal. Mr. Willem had the impression that Mr. Tipps would be a very influential person in determining who would receive the final research grant.

During the afternoon session, Mr. Willem attempted to ascertain a clear statement of research objectives from Mr. Tipps. While he was not completely successful in this regard, he did learn some useful information about the origin of the project.

For the past decade, CTFA and its member firms had been under constant pressure from consumer groups and government agencies concerning the quantity of factual information available to consumers in the purchase of cosmetics. Increasingly there had been the demand for voluntary action by CTFA to set standards and encourage its members to supply the public with more information on the ingredients of products, for example.

In response to this concern, several CTFA member firms started ingredient-labeling programs. Charles of the Ritz introduced ingredient labels on several of its products; Avon started a labeling program in 1974, and Almay (a hypoallergenic line) began printing ingredient labels in 1973. Despite these efforts, in March 1975 the Food and Drug Adminstration ordered ingredient listing on all cosmetics. The FDA's regulation required the listing of ingredients on cosmetics in order of predominance. Warnings must be on cosmetics that contain ingredients not tested for safety before marketing. Fragrances and flavors are exempted as trade secrets.

Some consumer advocates, such as Betty Furness and Ralph Nader, were unhappy about the fragrance provision. They wanted complete breakdowns on each fragrance. (A given perfume can have as many as 400 ingredients.)

The FDA regulatory action was described as part of an effort to reduce consumer injuries. The FDA said it receives about 650 unsolicited consumer complaints about cosmetics every year but believes that the number of injuries runs much higher.[1]

Proponents of mandatory labeling of ingredients argue that it is important to consumers for two reasons. First, persons with known allergies would be able to identify chemicals in cosmetic preparations to which they are sensitive and thus could avoid them. Second, the ingredient information would be used by consumers in comparing products and evaluating their relative worth. The latter point was highlighted by Mr. Tipps with the following statement to the FDA by the Consumer Federation of America (CFA):

> Simple, inexpensive ingredients are in some cases sold to the unknowing consumer for very high prices. Knowledge on the part of the consumer is the first step toward the prevention of fraud.[2]

To illustrate the effect of the FDA regulation Mr. Willem was shown the Almay label before and after the FDA regulation.

[1]"Cosmetics Must List Ingredients,"*Detroit News,* Feb. 28, 1975.
[2]"Cosmetic Labeling: A Step Forward," *Consumer Reports,* April 1973, p. 216.

[Front of container before regulation]
Almay
Pure Beauty
Liquid
Make-up

Soft Ivory
Hypo-Allergenic • Unscented
1 Fl. OZ. NET

[Back of container before regulation]

Shake before using. Blend evenly over face and throat with smooth, light strokes. Almay Liquid Make-up covers tiny flaws and shadows . . . gives your complexion a beautifully natural finish that stays fresh and pretty for hours.

FOR DELICATE, SENSITIVE, OR ALLERGENIC SKIN
Almay, Schieffelin & Co.
New York, N.Y. 10036
Made in U.S.A.

[Back of container after regulation]

Shake before using. Blend evenly over face and throat with smooth, light strokes. This ingredient disclosure is your proof of our purity: Water, talc, titanium dioxide, mineral oil, propylene glycol, triethanolamine stearate, cholesterol and related sterols, inert inorganic color pigments, magnesium aluminum silicate, cetyl alcohol, glyceryl monostearate, carboxymethyl cellulose, methyl paraben, propyl paraben.

Almay Hypo-allergenic Cosmetics
Almay Inc., New York, N.Y. 10036
Made in U.S.A.

Cosmetic manufacturers were concerned about some of the potential problems that could be created by the FDA ingredient-listing regulation of their products. One difficulty involves production problems caused by shortages of some ingredients. Companies are worried that every time they change a formula, they will have to print new labels. And there is a problem with lead time in silk-screen printing on some of the labels and bottles. Another difficulty centers on particular issues like getting all those little words on the end of (for instance) a lipstick tube. The regulation requires ingredients to be listed in a place where the consumer can see them before actual purchase. This means the ingredients could be on—but not inside—a box. Many lipsticks don't come in boxes at all.

Several cosmetic manufacturers foresaw potential consumer problems arising from the FDA regulation. For example:

1   Now that the names of the ingredients are being seen on the labeling of cosmetics, will consumers be desiring further information on the various ingre-

dients declared? For example, how do you explain sodium lauroyl sarcosinate? Will consumers be left with questions such as: What do they do in the product? What do they do for the skin? Is there enough of it (the particular ingredient) to do the job? Can I get some of it to see if I am sensitive to it?

2   Will the technical terminology associated with ingredient labeling lead to consumer confusion and possible dissatisfaction with cosmetic products?

3   It is not at all certain how consumers will *use* this information, if at all. Some types of product information, for example, are difficult to express in terms the consumer can understand. The resultant confusion can serve to distort, rather than improve, the purchase decision process.

4   Will the ingredient labeling encourage consumers to do more comparison shopping and brand switching in hopes of finding a better price/quality relationship?

5   The romance of cosmetic marketing—or loss of it—was another concern. Will the consumer pay $2.50 for a small shaft of colored, congealed castor oil and wax? They already have in the past by purchasing a tube of lipstick. Of course, it had a romantic name—"Moonbeam Enchantment" or something similar.

In response to the concerns of its member firms, the CTFA established a committee to investigate this area and make recommendations. The committee decided to fund a research project aimed at determining the problems in this area and identifying reasonable courses of action. Consequently, several reputable marketing research firms were contacted and asked to submit a proposal for research.

The Research Proposal

Mr. Willem turned to the task of formulating a research proposal. He knew that the first step was to develop a clear and concise statement of research objectives. While he had several basic ideas in mind, they were not yet formulated adequately for purposes of the research proposal. Experience had taught him that broad and unclear research objectives result in wasted research effort and confusion as to how the research results relate to action alternatives. Consequently, several key questions kept going through his mind. What exactly were the problems he was addressing? Were they problems in which research could be of value? What kinds of information would contribute to the resolution of these problems? What type of action could be taken based on the information?

In addition to defining the research objectives and identifying specific problem areas, Mr. Willem had to develop an outline for the research proposal. What areas were important to cover? What research design should be considered, and what were the specific elements of the design? Mr. Willem knew that the quality of the research proposal was the key to winning the research project.

DISCUSSION QUESTIONS

1   Develop a reasonably clear and concise statement of research objectives. Ask yourself:

   • Why was the request for information made?

- What are the objectives or goals of the decision maker(s)?
- Who is (are) the decision maker(s), and what is the decision-making environment?

2 Prepare a list of five to ten key information needs. (These might be questions on a questionnaire administered to cosmetic users.)
3 A possible research design would be to interview (personal, telephone, or mail) cosmetic users. Can you think of any additional research designs?
4 Develop a reasonably detailed outline of topics to be covered in the research proposal. (Assume you are Mr. Tipps; what areas/questions would you expect to be covered?)
5 Prepare a research proposal.

Case 2

Weston Food Company

The following five episodes deal with the relationship between research and management. In each episode, ask yourself: What is going on? Is the research/management connection effective? Why or why not? How could the situations be improved? What generalizations can be made about how to establish an effective research/management relationship in an organization?

Episode A

Thomas Murphy, director of research for the Weston Food Company, has been striving to establish a cordial relationship with the advertising department for several months. He feels that the research department can supply very useful information regarding the advertising programs of the Weston Food Company.

In response to these efforts, Sam Jones, the advertising manager, calls Mr. Murphy, asking for help in regard to a new advertising program being developed. "We need to know customers' perceptions, attitudes, and preferences toward our new line of diet products."

Mr. Murphy personally directs an extensive research study on the diet product line. Seven weeks later, a thorough report and presentation regarding current users' attitudes, perceptions, and preference patterns is presented to Mr. Jones and his staff. After the presentation, the reaction of Mr. Jones is: "Certainly a lot of interesting data that we weren't aware of; but how does this help us design a new advertising campaign to switch buyers from competitive diet lines to ours and entice potential dieters to try our line?"

Episode B

John Phelps, product manager for Weston's "Magic" scouring pads, calls upon Tom Murphy, director of research, to discuss a problem he has. "Good to see you again, Tom. As you know, sales volume on 'Magic' has not reached the targeted market share. We are seven points off target. I feel it is time to do some research on this problem. It's obvious to me that the culprit is our package design. We just don't catch the eye of the consumer like SOS does. Also, the package does a poor job in conveying the product concept and our point of difference from SOS.''

Mr. Murphy concurs with John Phelps that the packaging is poorly done and that the research department could provide useful information regarding the selection of a new package design.

He goes on to say, ''This type of problem lends itself to controlled experimentation very well. As you know, Barbra Kindle is an expert on experimental design and would be delighted to develop a research proposal that would get right at this problem.''

Mr. Phelps reacts: Sounds excellent to me. Can you have a proposal put together by Thursday?

Mr. Murphy replies: I'll have to check with Barbra first, but let's plan on a Thursday afternoon meeting in Conference Room C.

Mr. Phelps: That's great, I know I can always count on the cooperation of the research department.

Episode C

Tom Murphy, director of research, cautious about vaguely stated research study objectives, has been impressing on a senior staff member, Sid Alsen, the need for clearly written research proposals including management objectives, information requirements, and anticipated uses of expected results. During their conversation, Mr. Murphy receives a call from the marketing department asking for a research staff member to participate in a planning meeting where research needs will be discussed. Mr. Murphy informs Sid Alsen of the call and suggests that he attend the meeting. Before leaving, Alsen is advised: ''Be sure to develop a careful specification of how the information required will be used.''

Later in the afternoon, Sid returns from the meeting thoroughly defeated. ''They told me it wasn't any of my damn business what they were going to do with the information. We are just supposed to get it and they will decide what to do with it.''

Episode D

Ellen Tod, senior research analyst, reviews the marketing plan for the instant potato line and reports to her manager, Thomas Murphy: ''If they had paid any attention to my research report they wouldn't be doing these things. They must be stupid up there; why, I could run that program better!''

Mr. Murphy later receives a call from the planning manager, telling him: ''If that analyst (Ellen Tod) can't just report the facts and stop trying to make us look stupid, we would rather do without!''

Episode E

The following dialog takes place between a product manager, Jim Phiel, and Ellen Tod, senior research analyst.

Ellen Tod: I understand you are interested in a consumer test on product C-11.

Jim Phiel: Yes, we definitely need to get some good market feedback.

Ellen Tod: What will you do if the results are favorable?

Jim Phiel: National introduction, of course. This product has a great future.

Ellen Tod: What if the results are negative?

Jim Phiel: Don't worry about that. I know C-11 will be accepted with enthusiasm.

Ellen Tod: But what happens if your expectations are wrong?

Jim Phiel: Look, if you design a good test, we won't have any problems. There are a lot of hopes riding on the success of this product, and we need some good information behind it.

Part Two

Early Stages of the Research Process

Chapter 5

The Decision to Undertake Research

It has been stated that there are three basic components in any marketing research undertaking: (1) making certain that the right questions are being asked, (2) using appropriate research techniques and controls, and (3) presenting research findings in a clear, comprehensible format that leads to management action.[1]

The purpose of this chapter is to highlight the first component, namely, making certain that the right questions are being asked. Subsequent chapters will deal with the remaining two.

There is probably no activity more critical to the success of the research project than the analysis leading to the decision to undertake research. Frequently, this analysis is poorly executed or superficially passed over in the excitement of doing a research study. The consequences are inadequate information for decision making, wasted research funds, and management dissatisfaction with the marketing research system.

According to some sources, the analysis that was done leading to the decision to build the aircraft carrier *Enterprise* resulted in reports that weighed more than the ship itself. While this is obviously an exaggeration, it does emphasize the

---

[1] William B. Loeander and A. Benton Cocanougher (eds.), *Problem Definition in Marketing,* American Marketing Association, Marketing Research Techniques, ser. 2, Chicago, 1975, p. i.

importance of adequate planning and analysis preceding the decision to undertake an important project such as research. The quality of this preparatory
activity largely determines the success of the research project.

In marketing research, the purpose of this preparatory activity is to establish
an effective link between the early stages of the decision process and the research
process. Figure 5-1 illustrates the nature of this link. The relevance of the
research findings to the information requirements of management is established
at this crucial stage.

PRELIMINARY STEPS IN THE DECISION-MAKING PROCESS

The decision-making process and the management process are often considered
synonymous. An organization's well-being is dependent on the wisdom of the
decisions made by its managers. When confronted with decision situations where
the setting is unique, the manager turns to a more formal approach to decision
making called the decision-making process. A central issue in this process
involves the use of marketing research. As discussed in Chapter 1, the nature
and role of marketing research varies with the needs of management at various
stages of this process.

The purpose of this section is to discuss the issues involved in the first two
stages of the decision-making process: (1) recognition of a decision situation and
(2) definition of the decision problem. Marketing research can play an important
role in the early stages of the decision-making process.

Figure 5-1 Link between the decision process and the research process.

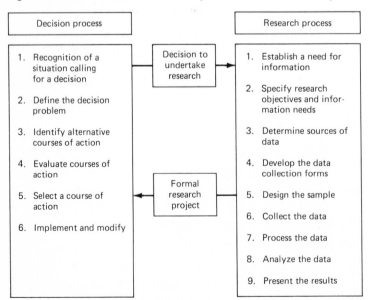

Recognition of a Decision Situation

The first stage of the decision process involves the recognition that a situation exists which calls for a decision. The modern marketing system is highly responsive to changing buyer needs and the variables that influence the availability of resources to serve these needs. The manager is frequently confronted with unique decision situations involving problems and opportunities resulting from the dynamic nature of the situational factors and/or the effectiveness of the marketing program. Typically, these problems and opportunities are first detected in the form of symptoms signaled by the organization's performance-monitoring system. Consequently, the constantly changing marketing system triggers the decision-making process.

Figure 5-2 presents the preliminary steps in the decision-making process and illustrates how the marketing system triggers the recognition of a situation calling for a decision. Here, the behavioral response and performance measures signal symptoms, while the marketing mix and situational factors produce the underlying problems and opportunities. The decision maker's task is to respond to symptoms and analyze the underlying problems and opportunities to determine whether a situation is present that calls for a decision. If the answer is affirmative, the decision maker proceeds to the second stage of the decision process—developing a clear statement of the decision problem. He or she has two courses of action available at this point: (1) define the decision problem based on current information, or (2) turn to exploratory research to aid in defining the decision problem.

Once the decision problem is defined, the decision maker again has two alternatives: (1) proceed through the remaining stages of the decision process, basing the decision on current information, or (2) undertake conclusive research and then proceed through the decision process, basing the decision on a combination of current information and the new information provided by the formal research project.

The remainder of this section will discuss more completely the issues involved in the process of recognizing a situation calling for a decision. Central to this discussion will be an understanding of the distinctions between problems, opportunities, and symptoms. Finally, the role of performance-monitoring research in signaling the presence of symptoms will be discussed.

Problems The word "problem" carries a connotation of trouble; something is wrong and needs attention. The existence of a problem is detected when objectives are established and a measurement of performance indicates that the objectives are not being met. For example, a product's share of market could be below forecasted share. The effectiveness of a new advertising campaign could be below desired awareness levels. The expenses associated with the introduction of a new product could be over budget. Consequently, a problem results when actual performance does not match expected performance.

By "problem" we refer to those independent variables that cause the organization's performance measures to be below objective. Problems can result

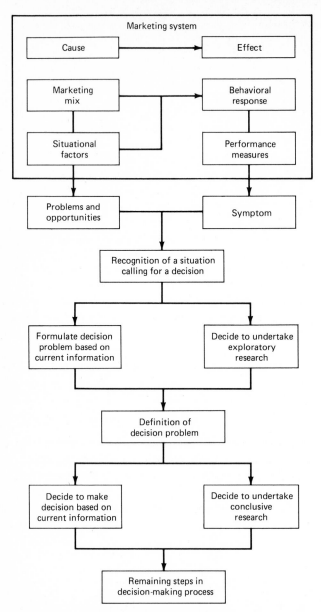

Figure 5-2 Preliminary steps in the decision-making process.

from an ineffective marketing program (product, price, distribution, and promotion) or from changes in the situational factors, or a combination of both.

Opportunities Managers make decisions regarding opportunities as well as problems. By ''opportunity'' we refer to the presence of a situation where performance can be improved by undertaking new activities. An opportunity may result in the establishment of even higher objectives. Opportunities differ from problems in that the manager may not be required to do anything about them. In fact, they may not even be recognized. Most opportunities do not force themselves on managers in the same way that problems do, since most firms have formal methods for detecting the presence of problems via their performance measures but less formal methods for monitoring the opportunities.

The distinction between problems and opportunities is not clear-cut. Problems are usually associated with adversity, but even adversity may be an opportunity in disguise. It has been said that "we are all continually faced with a series of great opportunities brilliantly disguised as insoluable problems".[2]

Symptoms A symptom is a condition that signals the presence of a problem or opportunity.[3] Performance measures act as this signal for marketing management. It is important to recognize that symptoms are not the same as problems and opportunities. For example, a decline in sales volume from forecasted levels is not a problem; it is the symptom of a problem yet to be identified. A symptom can be viewed as the result of a problem or opportunity.

Symptoms occupy a critical position in the process of recognizing that a situation is present calling for a management decision. Once the existence of a problem or opportunity has been recognized, the main issues and causal factors need to be identified. Effective decision making is dependent upon a clear statement regarding the basic problem or opportunity. This statement is often developed only after a thorough investigation of the marketing program and/or the situational factors. Rarely can the problem or opportunity be adequately identified solely on the knowledge that a symptom is present. Decisions are made to solve problems and/or to take advantage of opportunities, not to treat symptoms.

Symptoms often trigger the analysis process designed to identify and define the problems or opportunities. During this process, one may find that the initial variables identified as causing the symptom are the result of even more fundamental variables. An intensive investigation may uncover a complicated sequence of influences which interact to produce the symptom. Once this analysis is completed, the manager can formulate the decision problem and determine the course of action which, it is hoped, will attack the problem and/or exploit the opportunity.

Performance-monitoring Research Management can be alerted to a potential decision situation by performance-monitoring research. It controls the marketing program in accordance with objectives by providing feedback regarding performance. Performance-monitoring research is analogous to the instrument panel in an automobile which monitors fuel level, speed, engine temperature, and oil pressure. When the driver recognizes that a gauge is indicating a performance level which departs from standard, a potential decision problem

---

[2] Quotation by John W. Gardner in Philip Kotler, *Marketing Management,* 3d ed. (Englewood Cliffs, N.J.: Prentice-Hall, 1976), p. 45.
[3] David J. Luck, Hugh G. Wales, and Donald A. Taylor, *Marketing Research,* 4th ed. (Englewood Cliffs, N.J.: Prentice-Hall, 1974), p. 16.

has arisen. In some situations the performance measure is directly associated with the problem, and the nature of the corrective action is obvious. For example, a low fuel-gauge reading is directly associated with the corrective action to refill the gas tank. The driver is typically not confronted with a decision problem in this situation, since the best course of action is clear, and there is a high degree of certainty regarding the outcome.

In most management situations the performance measures are not directly associated with corrective action. Again using our automobile analogy, the engine-temperature gauge may signal a high temperature. There are a number of possible causes, such as low water level, clogged water lines, or a leaking radiator. Depending on the driver's experience with engines, he or she may be able to identify the cause through individual efforts or may be required to call upon a mechanic to diagnose the situation and define the problem. Similar situations can exist in marketing management. A sales decline can signal to management that a potential decision is present. It may be possible to diagnose the cause of the decline using experience and judgment. Alternatively, the manager may decide to bring in a marketing researcher to conduct exploratory research designed to diagnose the situation and define the problem.

Performance-monitoring research provides management with feedback regarding various aspects of the marketing system. Effective management is dependent upon an effective control system which can signal the occurrence of problems and/or opportunities. Performance-monitoring research plays a crucial role in this regard.

Definition of the Decision Problem

Once the manager recognizes that a situation exists calling for a decision, the next step is to clearly define the decision problem. A clearly defined decision problem has two components: (1) a thorough understanding of the objectives surrounding the decision situation and (2) a statement of the problems and opportunities present in the decision situation.

The decision maker has two approaches to defining the decision problem. They can be used in combination, or a single approach can be employed. The first approach is to formulate the decision problem based on the analysis of existing information. This approach relies upon the manager's experience and judgment plus skills in analyzing existing data regarding the decision situation. This approach is typically called a *situational analysis*. The second approach is to use exploratory research to aid in defining the decision problem. If the latter route is selected, there will be a process of interaction between hypotheses previously formulated based on existing information and hypotheses developed from the exploratory research findings. At some point in this interactive process, the decision maker must clearly define the decision problem and proceed to the remaining steps of the decision-making process.

The remainder of this section will discuss the issues involved in the process of defining the decision problem. First, it is important to understand clearly what is meant by a decision problem. Second, the role and responsibility of the decision maker in guiding the definition of the decision problem are emphasized. Next, the two components of the decision problem are reviewed: (1) objectives and (2) statement of problems and opportunities. Finally, the role of exploratory research in the process of defining the decision problem is analyzed in detail.

What Is a Decision Problem? A decision problem exists whenever management has an objective to accomplish and is confronted with a situation involving two or more courses of action to reach the objective. In addition, uncertainty must exist regarding the best course of action. If the manager is certain as to the best course of action, there is no decision problem. If there is only one course of action available, and that is to "do nothing," there is no decision problem.

Decision problems can exist for situations involving both problems and opportunities. Uncertainty can exist regarding the best course of action to solve a problem as well as how to take advantage of an opportunity. Consequently, a decision problem is present in situations regarding problems and opportunities whenever the manager faces a choice among alternative courses of action in which uncertainty exists regarding the outcome of the decision.

Role of the Decision Maker The manager plays a central role in the definition of the decision problem. After recognizing that a potential decision problem exists, it is his or her responsibility to ensure that the following questions are adequately addressed before proceeding further in the decision-making process.

1 What are the decision objectives?
2 What are the problems and/or opportunities associated with accomplishing these objectives?
3 What courses of action are available?
4 What information is needed to properly select among these courses of action?
5 Can the information be obtained?
6 Should the information be obtained?

Objectives of the Decision Maker The decision-making process typically has two sources for objectives. The primary source for objectives is the organization. For example, an organization may have an objective to increase earnings per share by 10 percent next year. The second source involves the personal objectives of the decision maker(s) and those who influence that individual. For example, a marketing manager may have the personal objective of becoming the vice president of marketing or of acquiring more prestige among his or her peers.

In order to understand the motivation for a decision, we must be sensitive to the role played by both organizational and personal objectives. When both sets of objectives coincide, the decision-making process flows more smoothly than when there is conflict between them. The question of how to resolve this conflict in favor of organizational objectives is obviously a complex one, but one approach is to have organizational objectives stated explicitly to others in the organization. In addition, the development of explicit decision criteria for the selection among alternative courses of action often ensures that organizational objectives will predominate in the decision. More will be said on this issue shortly.

In many decision situations the "decision maker" may not be a single individual. Decision making in organizations can involve two or more people who must make decisions as a group. Other situations involve one predominant decision maker who is strongly influenced by other individuals who are part of the decision-making process. In such situations, not only is there potential conflict between organizational and personal objectives but also conflict among the personal objectives of the individuals involved in the decision process.

It is a serious mistake to assume that the decision maker clearly knows what the organizational objectives are and that formulating an explicit statement of these objectives will be viewed with favor. An explicit statement of organizational objectives can force the decision maker to suppress personal objectives. In addition, some individuals may feel that making certain aspects of the decision process explicit can threaten one's status and position as a decision maker.[4]

This situation can present serious problems for the marketing research system. The success of a research study is dependent on a clear understanding of the decision objectives. A major task of the marketing researcher is to skillfully identify the organizational objectives and be sensitive to the personal objectives lurking in the background of the decision process. A successful researcher may be one who can design research to serve the needs of the organization effectively while at the same time enhancing the personal objectives of the decision maker.

Statement of Problems and Opportunities   The process of identifying problems and opportunities is called a situational analysis.[5] Its purpose is to analyze the past and future situation facing an organization to uncover those variables that cause poor performance or represent opportunities for future growth. Specifically, this means that a diagnosis and prognosis must be made of the marketing program and situational variables in the marketing system.

The situational analysis is a creative process in which an attempt is made to isolate and understand the causal variables influencing the marketing system. During this investigation, one must be sensitive to the fact that symptoms are not the same thing as problems and opportunities. Too often, symptoms are defined as the problem or opportunity in the decision situation.

In conducting a situational analysis, a diversity of information sources may be needed to develop insight and hypotheses regarding the causal factors. Flexibility in thinking and the use of multiple information sources is often critical to a successful situational analysis.

---

[4] Joseph W. Newman, "Put Research into Marketing Decisions," *Harvard Business Review,* vol. 40, no. 2, pp. 105–112, March–April 1962.

[5] William B. Loeander and A. Benton Cocanougher (eds.), *Problem Definition in Marketing,* American Marketing Association, Marketing Research Techniques, ser. 2, Chicago, 1975.

It is the manager's responsibility to ensure that a clear and concise statement of problems and opportunities is developed. Depending upon the nature of the decision situation, this statement may be formulated by the manager without the assistance of the marketing research system. Alternatively, the manager may decide that additional information is needed and turn to the marketing research system for assistance. Marketing research personnel and techniques can play an important role in identifying and defining the problems and opportunities.

Role of Exploratory Research   Exploratory research is designed to bring ideas and insight to a decision situation where limited knowledge exists. It can be very helpful in situations where management is searching for potential problems and/or opportunities, or when management desires a more precise formulation of the problem and the identification of the relevant variables in the decision situation.

Exploratory research is often the initial step in a series of studies designed to supply information for decision making. The purpose of this research is to formulate hypotheses regarding potential problems and/or opportunities present in the decision situation. By "hypothesis" we refer to a conjectural statement about the relationship between two or more variables. This statement should carry clear implications for measuring the variables and testing the stated relationships.[6] For example, exploratory research would be appropriate in a situation where management responds to the symptom of declining share of market by asking "What is the problem?" The task of exploratory research would be to identify tentative hypotheses regarding the cause of this decline. Potential hypotheses may be narrowed by further research to the point where a statement of problems and opportunities can be developed. This statement represents the formal hypotheses regarding the causes of the decision situation. These hypotheses can be tested at a later stage of the decision process with conclusive research methods.

Examples of hypotheses developed from exploratory research are as follows:

1   An advertising theme emphasizing the "nutrition value" of food product X will increase brand awareness more than a theme emphasizing "good flavor."

2   A change in the ingredients of product X from artificial chocolate to real chocolate will increase the preference for product X compared with its competition.

3   A 10 percent cut in the retail price of product X will result in a 1 percent market share gain within six months.

Because exploratory research deals with a decision situation where limited knowledge exists, the research design is characterized by flexibility in order to be sensitive to the unexpected and to discover ideas and insights not

[6] See Fred N. Kerlinger, *Foundations of Behavioral Research*, 2d ed (New York: Holt, Rinehart, 1973), pp. 18–26, for a detailed discussion of the characteristics and role of hypotheses in research.

previously recognized. The formulation of hypotheses rarely comes to the mind of the manager or researcher through the application of fixed and rigid procedures. Of all the stages of the decision-making process, identification of problems and opportunities eludes formal description. While the ability to formulate the decision problem must be relegated in part to the realm of inspiration, it is also true that various procedures can assist this creative process. These procedures are (1) search of secondary sources, (2) interviewing knowledgeable persons, and (3) case histories.

Search of Secondary Sources   In many decision situations, a search of the literature can bring useful ideas and insight regarding the nature of the problems and/or opportunities present. A literature search is a logical starting point in that the available data are often inexpensive to acquire and can be gathered quickly.

Secondary data can be defined as data which have been compiled for a purpose other than the present study. Such data often represent the work of others. They may be classified as internal or external to the organization; internal sources include previous research reports, accounting data, sales reports, and so on, while external sources include data such as periodicals, syndicated research studies, government publications, and trade association reports. The novice researcher may not recognize the significance of secondary data sources to exploratory research. This can be a serious mistake both in terms of the cost and time required to do research.

An example may highlight the role of secondary data in problem formulation. A major appliance manufacturer recognized that its share of the market had been slowly declining. This symptom was detected through trade publications which collect data regarding appliance sales for the industry. While the firm's own records indicated a sales increase over past years, the management recognized that their share of total industry sales might be on the decline. Exploratory research was used to identify the cause of the decline in market share.

The first phase of this research involved an analysis of secondary sources such as trade magazine reports and editorials, census publications, trade association reports, and so on. The conclusion drawn from this analysis was that many changes were occurring in the situational factors which represented potential problems—for example, a growing shift of the population to the suburbs and away from the firm's traditional appliance outlets, competitors' moves to build new outlets in the suburbs, competitive action by discounters to open appliance outlets with emphasis on low overhead operations, the growing importance of service, and a declining awareness of brand differences due to quality improvements in all appliance brands. From this analysis, various ideas and insights were gained regarding potential causes of the market share decline. These included a decline in the convenience of store locations and a weakening competitive position with regard to store facilities and operating procedures.

While a literature search can bring valuable insight as to a tentative explanation of the problem or opportunity, it is important to recognize that these explanations are only hypotheses. Further exploratory work may reveal equally attractive hypotheses or lead to a more precise formulation of the current hypothesis.

Interviewing Knowledgeable Persons   After searching secondary sources, additional insight can be gained by talking with individuals who have special knowledge and experience regarding the area under investigation. These may be personnel within the organization, distributors, suppliers, consumers, or anyone directly or indirectly related to the decision situation.

The nature of the interviewing situation can range from informal conversations to more formal yet unstructured research approaches involving groups of individuals who are interrogated by a professional interviewer. These interviews rarely use structured questions, such as those on a questionnaire. Rather, very flexible and free-flowing situations are created designed to search for ideas and uncover the unexpected. At times, various hypotheses may be presented to these individuals to test their reaction and see whether reformulation of the hypotheses is called for. The purpose is to bring additional insight to the identification of problems and/or opportunities. Such approaches have been called focused group interviews, depth interviews, snowball interviews, and the like; they will be discussed in detail in Chapter 18 on data collection methods.

In the case of the appliance manufacturer example, several interviews with knowledgeable persons were conducted. Phone conversations and field interviews were held with editors of trade magazines, distributors, and company personnel. It was found that several competitors were acquiring appliance outlets, new appliance outlets were appearing at convenient suburban locations, and more discounters and large retail chain stores were planning to enter the appliance market. Several focused group interviews with recent appliance buyers brought insight to the buying process and the images buyers had of appliance outlets. Based on this analysis, additional hypotheses were formulated regarding the cause of the market share decline. It was believed that a number of complex factors were operating to cause the problem situation.

Case Histories   The case history approach is an established research method in the behavioral sciences and has been used successfully in marketing research for decades. The design involves the intensive investigation of situations which are relevant to the problem situation. The concept is to select several target cases where an intensive analysis will (1) identify relevant variables, (2) indicate the nature of the relationship among variables, and (3) identify the nature of the problem and/or opportunity present in the original decision situation. For example, the research might investigate selected retail stores, sales territories, markets, salespeople, or industrial buyers. The purpose is to obtain a comprehensive description of the cases and to formulate a better understanding of the variables operating.

The case history method is especially useful in situations where a complicated series of variables interact to produce the problem or opportunity. Cases which can be studied are those reflecting (1) contrasting performance levels, e.g., good and poor markets; (2) rapid changes in performance, e.g., entry of a competitor into a market; and (3) the order in which events occurred, e.g., sales regions which are in various stages of transition from indirect to direct selling efforts.[7]

Data can be obtained through the search of records and reports, observation of key variables, and interrogation of knowledgeable persons. The research style is one of flexibility in the analysis to take advantage of the unexpected and develop insights into the problem situation.

To return once again to the appliance manufacturer example, two cities were selected for intensive case study, one representing a good market and the other a poor market for the firm. The analysis included a plotting of appliance outlets on a map of each city. This map showed the location of outlets by category, with special emphasis on the new types, i.e., discount store outlets, chain store outlets, and so on. Selected stores were visited in each city and observations made regarding sales volume and operating policies. Pictures were taken of the stores which provided an interesting contrast between the firm's traditional appliance outlets and the newer distribution outlets. Finally, buyers in the two contrasting cities were interrogated regarding their buying habits and images of the existing outlets. While the results from this case study were not considered final, sufficient insight into the problem situation was gained to enable a clear problem statement to be developed, and subsequent conclusive research was undertaken to evaluate several courses of action for the firm.

It is important to remember that case histories represent an analysis of past situations which may have limited relevance to future situations. Consequently, conclusions drawn from such studies should be viewed as tentative and suggestive of hypotheses to be tested with conclusive research methodology.

Remaining Steps in the Decision Process

Given a clear statement of the decision problem, the next stage of the decision process is to identify alternative courses of action. (Remember that a decision problem exists only when there are two or more actions to be taken and uncertainty as to which is the best one to take.)

A *course of action* is the specification of how the organization's resources are to be deployed in a given time period. Maintaining the status quo or "doing nothing new" is a course of action just as much as one that specifies a change in the status quo.

The development of alternative courses of action is a crucial stage in the formulation of the decision problem. The management decision can be no better than the best alternative under evaluation. Identifying mediocre courses of action is often an easy task. Implementation of a mediocre action may partially solve a problem or take advantage of an opportunity to some degree. The real management challenge is to identify the best course of action which will result in high performance and give the organization a competitive edge.

Creativity is needed to identify innovative and highly effective courses of action. Various approaches are available that can stimulate the manager's creative

---

[7] Gilbert A. Churchill, Jr., *Marketing Research* (Hinsdale, Ill.: Dryden Press, 1976), p. 67.

process and broaden the domain of alternatives identified.[8] Exploratory research can be especially helpful in identifying innovative courses of action.

Once the alternative courses of action are identified, the next step is one of evaluation. At this point, the manager is faced with the question "What information is needed to properly choose among the courses of action?" This may be answered with the help of information inputs from the manager's experience and judgment plus information currently available through the marketing research system. Alternatively, the manager may decide that new information is needed and request that a formal marketing research study be conducted. The decision to use research implies that the desired information can be obtained and that the cost and time delay associated with collecting it is more than offset by its potential value. The value or benefit of research is typically commensurate with the ability of research information to reduce the management uncertainty regarding the selection of a course of action. Once this information is obtained and presented in a meaningful format, the manager can proceed to the final stage of the decision-making process, namely, the selection of a course of action and the development of a plan for implementation.

A research study designed to evaluate alternative courses of action is called conclusive research. Let us turn now to a discussion of how to get this formal research project under way.

PRELIMINARY CONSIDERATIONS FOR CONDUCTING CONCLUSIVE RESEARCH

Conclusive research provides information which helps the decision maker evaluate and select a course of action. This formal research project contains a series of steps called the research process. (See Figure 5-1.) The nine steps in this process were outlined in Chapter 2. Our discussion here will focus on the initial stages of the research process and the importance of establishing an effective link with the decision-making process.

Establish the Need for Information

Establishing the need for marketing research information is a critical step in the research process. The wisdom of this initial step largely determines the success or failure of the research project.

Role of the Researcher   Rarely does the manager's initial request for help adequately establish the need for research information. Consequently, the researcher has an important role to play in making sure that information is in fact needed and that the research study will provide useful information for decision making. The following questions should be thoroughly addressed by the researcher at this initial stage.

[8] See Sidney J. Parnes and Harold F. Harding (eds.), *Source Book for Creative Thinking* (New York: Scribner, 1962), and Alex F. Osborn, *Applied Imagination,* 3d ed. (New York: Scribner, 1963).

1 Who is the decision maker?

2 What are his or her objectives?

3 Has a clear and concise statement of problems and/or opportunities been developed?

4 What courses of action are to be evaluated?

Decision Maker   The researcher must distinguish between the decision maker and those who represent the decision maker. Often the person who first requests assistance from the marketing research system is not the decision maker. This individual may or may not know how the decision maker views the specifics of the decision situation. Valuable time and effort can be saved if the researcher insists on meeting directly with the individual who has major responsibility for making the decision.

A meeting with the decision maker may be difficult in practice. Many organizations have complicated formal and informal command structures; also, the organizational status of the researcher or the research department may make it difficult to reach the ultimate decision maker in the early stages of the research process. Finally, in many decision situations a number of individuals may influence the decision or act together as the decision maker. Meeting with these individuals as a group or individually may be difficult, and the coordination of a clear statement regarding the decision situation may be even more so. Despite these potential problems, it is essential that the researcher understand the problem situation from the perspective of the decision maker.

Objectives of the Decision Maker   Decisions are made to accomplish objectives. The key to conducting effective research is to thoroughly understand the objectives of the decision maker. As discussed previously, the objectives can be of two types, organizational and personal. The researcher must be sensitive to both types. The identification of objectives can be a difficult assignment in practice.

> Despite a popular misconception to the contrary, objectives are seldom given to the researcher. The decision maker seldom formulates his objectives accurately. He is likely to state his objectives in the form of platitudes which have no operational significance. Consequently, objectives usually have to be extracted by the researcher. In so doing, the researcher may well be performing his most useful service to the decision maker.
>
> Direct questioning of the decision maker seldom reveals all the relevant objectives. One effective technique for uncovering these objectives consists of confronting the decision maker with each of the possible solutions to a problem and asking him whether he would follow that course of action. Where he says "no," further probing will usually reveal objectives which are not served by the course of action.[9]

Statement of Problem and Opportunity   There is probably no activity more critical to the success of the formal research process than a clear and concise

---

[9] Russell L. Ackoff, *Scientific Method* (New York: Wiley, 1962), p. 71.

statement of problems and/or opportunities. Far too often this task is the most neglected phase in initiating the research project. Improper definition of the problem or opportunity can easily lead astray all subsequent efforts to provide useful information for decision making.

The researcher must be sensitive to managers who are reacting to symptoms or vague feelings regarding a possible problem and/or opportunity. The researcher's task is to ask probing questions of the manager to determine the existing degree of knowledge regarding the underlying causes of the decision situation. As discussed previously, exploratory research may be needed to facilitate the development of the statement of problem and opportunity.

Courses of Action   The management decision can be no better than the best alternative being considered. The researcher must be satisfied that the relevant courses of action have been identified and approved by management. Nothing can destroy an otherwise successful research study more than to find that a key alternative was not evaluated.

Given a clear understanding of the courses of action relevant to the decision situation, the researcher can turn to the task of establishing the research objectives and identifying the scientific information needs for evaluating the courses of action.

Research Objectives

Research objectives answer the question ''What is the purpose of the research project?'' For example, the research study discussed in Chapter 3 had the following objectives:

   1   To determine which container markets have the greatest consumer acceptance of plastic containers
   2   To determine the characteristics of plastic containers which represent advantages compared with paper, paperboard, glass, and metal containers

The research objectives should be put in writing and communicated to the decision maker; they explain why the project is being conducted, and it is important that the researcher and decision maker are in agreement.

Research objectives can be stated so broadly that they fail to communicate the specifics of why the study is being conducted. For example, the following lacks the precise detail of the research objective given previously:

   To study consumer reactions to containers

A broad statement like this does not communicate the type of container to be studied, what is to be measured, and how the information might be used. While the degree of detail in the research objectives is dependent upon the nature of the decision situation, generally the more specific the statement of objectives, the lower the risk that management will misperceive the purpose of the study.

Figure 5-3 Pyramid of research objectives and information needs.

In some respects, the more detailed the statement of research objectives the more it coincides with the listing of information needs. Figure 5-3 highlights the pyramiding aspect of research objectives, information needs, and questions on the data collection forms.

Specify Information Needs

After the research objectives have been specified, the next question concerns "What specific information is needed by the decision maker?" A listing of specific information is designed to answer this question.

Research objectives which are specified in great detail often coincide with a more general listing of information needs. In the same manner, a more detailed listing of information needs coincides with the specific questions developed for the questionnaire. Consequently, research objectives serve to guide the research project by giving direction to the specific information to be gathered and the specific questions developed for the questionnaire.

From the other perspective, we can say that each question on the questionnaire should have a direct correspondence to an information need, and each information need should have a direct correspondence to a research objective. If such a correspondence is not established, unneeded data will be collected.

The decision maker should be actively involved in formulating the research objectives and in specifying the information needs, because only the decision maker has a clear perspective as to the character and specificity of the information needed to reduce the uncertainty surrounding the decision situation. Failure to involve the decision maker in this regard can severely hamper the success of the research project.

(An example of specifying research objectives and listing information needs was presented in Chapter 3; a review of this chapter should provide a concrete illustration of the points discussed here.)

In developing the list of information needs, both the manager and researcher should ask, for each item, "Can this information be obtained?" The skills and judgment of the researcher come to the fore at this point.

The data collection process imposes many limitations on the type of information that can be collected. In surveys, buyers or distributors may refuse to disclose certain types of information, or they may not have the knowledge to answer the questions accurately. Consequently, many excellent information needs may be developed, but if it is not possible to collect the information, time and effort will be wasted in the research process. The manager and researcher need to work closely in this regard to assure a correspondence between the information required and the ability of the marketing research system to gather it.

Visualize the Research Findings

Assuming that the information can be gathered, it is important that the potential research findings be visualized and the question asked, "Of what use are these data to the decision situation?" Many managers and researchers find that mocking up the potential research findings is a valuable way to ensure that the data to be collected fit the information needs specified by the decision maker. Often, the decision maker can identify gaps in the original list of needs which can be easily corrected at this preliminary stage of the research project.

The concept of mocking up the potential research findings means that each stage of the research process must be anticipated. For example, in survey research specific questions must first be developed for the questionnaire. Next, the data processing and analysis must be established, then the resulting data can be visualized. At this point, the decision maker would be presented with a mock-up of the data in the form of various tables or graphs containing potential research findings. In essence, the research presentation or report is simulated prior to conducting the project.

The actual data presented may represent a range of optimistic, most likely, and pessimistic. From this mock-up of findings, the manager and researcher may be able to determine whether the data intended to be collected will serve to reduce the uncertainty surrounding the decision situation. If not, the wisdom of collecting the data should be challenged.

Often, the manager can more clearly specify how the data should be analyzed and presented after seeing a mock-up of the potential findings. Additional cross tabulations may be requested, and several multivariate analysis approaches may be required. Often, certain data analysis approaches require that the questionnaire be developed in a certain format, that specific questions be asked, or that the data be tabulated in a certain manner. If these issues are not addressed prior to executing the project, it may be that added costs and delays are incurred at later stages or that the data cannot be obtained. Consequently, the type of directions received from the manager prior to the beginning of the project can be invaluable to its success.

Develop Decision Criteria

Once the research findings have been visualized and the decision maker and researcher are confident that the information needs are complete and the data analysis appropriate, the issue of *decision criteria* should be addressed. Decision criteria are concerned with the rules for selecting among courses of action given various data outcomes.

Developing decision criteria often means setting up a series of "if then" statements. For example:

1 If the research finds a 5 percent potential market share or larger for our new product, then we will proceed to test-market.

	Variable costs	
Market size	$0.10/unit (Contribution = $0.90/unit)	$0.90/unit (Contribution = $0.10/unit)
10,000 (units/$)	Breakeven = 1111 units Market share = 11%	Breakeven = 10,000 units Market share = 100%
100,000 (units/$)	Breakeven = 1111 units Market share = 1%	Breakeven = 10,000 units Market share = 10%

Figure 5-4 Volume and share of market required to break even on cost of research ($1,000 cost of research).

    2 If the research finds a 3 to 5 percent potential market share, then we will reformulate the new product.

    3 If the research finds less than a 3 percent potential market share, then we will abandon the project.[10]

It is important that decision criteria be developed before the decision maker and researcher experience the actual results. Having clear decision rules prior to the research results ensures that organizational objectives take priority over personal objectives and that they assist the data analysis and reporting stages. In addition, decision rules maintain a balance between the weight assigned to information existing prior to the research and the research findings. The absence of decision criteria can result in an inappropriate weight assigned to the research findings depending upon the research outcome and the reaction of management to experiencing the outcome for the first time.

Cost and Value of Research

The evaluation of most activities in an organization is approached on a cost-benefit basis. While it is fairly easy to quantify the costs directly associated with a research project, it is very difficult to quantify the benefits. Consequently, the evaluation of research is inherently subjective.

Given the cost of research, it is possible to determine the number of units of a product that need to be sold to break even on the cost of the research project. Figure 5-4 illustrates this type of calculation for two market sizes and two variable cost structures. The selling price is $1 per unit in all four conditions. The results indicate that the benefit or value resulting from the $1000 research study will have to be greater than a 1 percent share of the market in the best situation and 100 percent in the worst situation. Obviously, the $1000 research cost cannot be justified in the worst situation.

In general, these calculations suggest that it is easier to justify the cost of research as the market size increases and as the ratio of variable cost to selling price decreases. Therefore, the benefits resulting from a $10,000 research project

[10] Eric Marder, "Use One Measure, Do Analysis Before Looking at Data," *Marketing News,* vol. 7, no. 12, p. 1, December 1973.

designed to evaluate alternative advertising campaigns to stimulate demand for long-distance phone calls may be easier to justify than a similar study dealing with a new hobby kit glue. While this type of calculation does not determine the actual benefit derived from such a study, it does indicate the level of benefit needed to cover the cost of research.

There is an additional concept that relates directly to the manager's evaluation of the benefits of marketing research. This concept is the degree of certainty that the manager holds about particular outcomes of the organization's courses of action. For example, a manager might say "I am 95 percent sure that this advertising theme will be a success." This manager should be much less likely to undertake research on the new advertising theme than a manager who says: "I am about 50 percent sure that this advertising theme will be a success." The purpose of marketing research is to reduce the uncertainty about the outcomes of alternative courses of action. Thus, the value of research to a manager increases as the degree of certainty decreases. Again, it is a subjective evaluation by the manager.

In summary, the value of research to a manager increases as (1) the market size increases, (2) the ratio of variable cost to selling price decreases, and (3) the degree of certainty held about outcomes of actions decreases. All three of these factors will be discussed in detail in Chapter 27, and a dollar value for specific marketing research proposals will be calculated.

Controlling the Use of Research

The success of the research project depends heavily upon the ability of the managers and researchers to work effectively together. For most managers, decision making is a highly personalized process which is influenced by the individual's management style and the specifics of the decision situation. The researcher must be sensitive to this situation in developing an effective working relationship with the decision maker. The success of the research project rests upon the quality of this marriage. There are several ways to ensure that research is being used effectively in the decision-making process.

Organizational Design The various organizational designs discussed in Chapter 4 can serve to control the effectiveness of contacts between decision makers and researchers. One design is to assign management responsibility for the initial and final stages of the research process; here the responsibility for the effectiveness of the research rests predominantly in the management camp. The researcher's responsibility is that of adviser regarding the initial and final stages, with primary responsibility for the middle stages of data collection and processing. Typically, the researcher has the right to refuse to conduct a study which he or she views as inappropriate.

An alternative organizational design involves keeping the responsibility for the research process within the research camp while giving the researcher a more powerful organizational role in dealing with the management. For example, the researcher may be required to participate in the majority of management meetings

Exhibit 5-1   Research Request Form

Title: _____   Date prepared: _____

Requested by: _____   Start of project: _____

Approved by: _____   Report due: _____

Date approved: _____   Budget: _____

Project number: _____   Supplier: _____

    1 *Background:* What led to the recognition that research was needed?

    2 *Objectives:* What are the decision objectives?

    3 *Problem/opportunity:* What are the underlying causes of the decision situation?

    4 *Decision Alternatives:* What are the alternative courses of action?

    5 *Research Objectives:* What is the purpose of the research?

    6 *Information Needs:* What type of information is needed?

    7 *Example of Questions:* What kind of questions should be asked?

    8 *Decision Criteria:* What criteria should be used to select the best alternative?

    9 *Value of Research:* Why is the research useful?

regardless of whether the use of research is an issue. Here, the researcher is viewed as part of the management team and is assigned responsibility for identifying decision situations where research is appropriate.

A compromise between these two organizational designs involves the creation of the position of research generalist, someone who serves as an intermediary between the research and management camps. The generalist's main responsibility is to promote effective contacts between decision makers and researchers. The research generalist concept was discussed in Chapter 2.

Research Request Forms   Most organizations require that the decision to undertake research be in writing and approved by upper management and the director of marketing research. This formal request typically involves a standard form which is completed by the decision maker and/or the marketing researcher. Exhibit 5-1 illustrates the type of information requested on such a form.

The purpose of the research request form is to ensure that all of the areas identified on the form have been covered by the decision makers and researchers. There is a degree of commitment associated with things in writing that rarely exists with informal agreements.

Additional forms may be used in some companies for the remaining steps in the research process—for example, project budget estimate forms, project control forms, and project evaluation forms.[11]

Proposal for Research

For projects conducted predominantly within the organization, the research request form usually serves as the research proposal. In practice, most research

[11] For an expanded discussion of this area, see Lawrence D. Gibson, "Use of Marketing Research Contractors," in Robert Ferber (ed.), *Handbook of Marketing Research* (New York: McGraw-Hill, 1975), pp. 1–128 to 1–141.

projects have some phase of the study conducted by outside contractors. Typically, this involves the field interviewing phase. A growing number of organizations are expanding their reliance on outside contractors and using them to conduct more phases of the research process. In some situations, an organization may rely entirely on an outside contractor to conduct the research study. Here, several outside contractors could be asked to submit a proposal for research. The type of information requested from an outside contractor who desires to bid on a research contract might be as follows:

1 Review of decision situation
2 Statement of research objectives
3 Listing of information needs
4 Explanation of research design and procedures
5 Copy of proposed questionnaire and explanation of how questions relate to information needs
6 Justification of sampling plan
7 Explanation of statistical confidence associated with research findings
8 Explanation of data analysis strategy
9 Demonstration of how potential research findings can lead to action-related decisions
10 Proposed budget and documentation of costs
11 Timetable of activities and completion dates
12 Statement of professional qualifications of staff and facilities

When several outside contractors submit their proposals for research, the management group must develop decision criteria to evaluate the proposals. While the criteria selected can be many, the following are often considered important: (1) How well was the decision situation understood? (2) How well does the proposed research fit the information needs of the decision situation? (3) Are the research objectives relevant to the decision situation? (4) How appropriate is the research design to the research objectives? (5) What type of facilities (interviewers, tabulation, computer, etc.) are available? (6) What are the qualifications of the staff? (7) Is the cost of the research appropriate? (8) Are the time requirements reasonable?

In addition to the above criteria, most organizations are looking for outside contractors who are honest and reliable and conduct their business in a professional manner. Contractors who fit these qualifications often enjoy a continuing and cooperative relationship with their clients.

SUMMARY

1 The analysis underlying the decision to undertake research largely determines the success of the research project. Failure to establish an effective link between the decision process and the research process can result in inadequate research findings and management dissatisfaction with the marketing research system.

2   The decision process begins with the recognition that a unique marketing problem exists or that an opportunity is present. Problems are detected when objectives are established and a measure of performance indicates that the objectives are not being met. Opportunities are present in situations where performance can be improved by undertaking new activities. A symptom is a condition that signals the presence of a problem or opportunity. It often triggers the analysis process designed to identify and define problems and opportunities.

3   Performance-monitoring research serves to control the marketing program in accordance with objectives by providing feedback regarding performance. Effective management is dependent upon an effective control system which can signal the existence of problems and/or opportunities.

4   A decision problem is present in situations where the manager faces a choice among alternative courses of action in which uncertainty exists regarding the outcome of the decision. Implicit in any decision problem is a clear statement of objectives plus the identification of problems and/or opportunities.

5   A situational analysis is the process which leads to the identification of problems and opportunities. This involves a diagnosis and prognosis of the marketing program and situational variables in the marketing system.

6   Exploratory research is designed to bring ideas and insight to a decision situation where limited knowledge exists. It facilitates the development of hypotheses regarding potential problems and/or opportunities.

7   Various approaches such as searching secondary sources, interviewing knowledgeable persons, and studying case histories are used in exploratory research.

8   Once the decision problem has been formulated, the next step is to identify alternative courses of action. A course of action is the specification of how the organization's resources are to be developed in a given period. Creativity is needed to identify innovative and highly effective courses of action. Exploratory research can be very useful in this regard.

9   Once the alternatives have been established, the manager may turn to the use of conclusive research. Conclusive research provides information for the evaluation of courses of action.

10   The first step in the conclusive research process is to establish the need for information. The researcher plays a vital role in this process. The decision maker must be clearly identified and the objectives of the decision situation established. A clear statement of problems and/or opportunities must be developed and the alternative courses of action identified. Based on this information, the researcher can formulate the research objectives.

11   Research objectives establish the purpose of the study. They should be in writing and clearly communicated to the decision maker.

12   The specific types of information needed by the decision maker should be identified in writing. The researcher must determine whether it is indeed possible to obtain the type of information requested.

13   The potential research findings should be visualized prior to conducting the study. Preparing a mock-up of the results is a valuable way to ensure that the data to be collected meet the information needs of the decision situation.

14   Decision criteria for selecting among courses of action given various data outcomes should be established prior to conducting the study.

15   The cost of obtaining the information should be weighed against the benefits resulting from a reduction in the decision uncertainty. This type of evaluation is inherently subjective.

16   Various organizational designs can facilitate the establishment of an effective link between the decision process and the research process. Requiring research request forms to be completed prior to undertaking research also strengthens the effectiveness of this link.

17   For research projects conducted within an organization, the research request form serves as the proposal for research. When outside contractors bid on the research project, more elaborate research proposals are required. It is important that clear decision criteria be established for the evaluation of the proposals submitted.

DISCUSSION QUESTIONS

1   Why is the analysis preceding the decision to undertake research so crucial to the success of the project?
2   Distinguish among problems, opportunities, and symptoms.
3   What role does performance-monitoring research play in the management of an organization?
4   What are the essential elements of a decision problem?
5   What are the implications for the marketing researcher of a decision situation characterized by primary (organizational) and secondary (personal) objectives?
6   What is the purpose and nature of a situational analysis?
7   Why is exploratory research often utilized in the initial steps of the decision process?
8   What characteristics of secondary data sources contribute to their significance in exploratory research?
9   Discuss three approaches useful in exploratory research.
10   What is the basic criterion in deciding whether or not to conduct a research project?
11   What are the responsibilities of the researcher in establishing the need for marketing research information?
12   What characteristics should research objectives possess?
13   Should the decision maker be involved in formulating research objectives and listing information needs? Why or why not?
14   Of what use is a mock-up of potential research findings?
15   What are decision criteria? When should they be developed?
16   Why is the evaluation (a priori) of marketing research inherently subjective?
17   How might an organization ensure that marketing research is being used effectively in the decision-making process?

SUGGESTED READING

Gibson, Lawrence D., "Use of Marketing Research Contractors," in Robert Ferber (ed.), *Handbook of Market Research* (New York: McGraw-Hill, 1975), pp. 1-128 to 1-141. The author discusses how to select suppliers, supplier obligations to clients, and the types of relationships between suppliers and clients. Various forms are presented dealing with marketing research problem definition, project proposal and expenditure approval, and supplier evaluation.

Kerlinger, Fred N., *Foundations of Behavioral Research,* 2d ed., (New York: Holt, Rinehart, 1973), pp. 16–26. An advanced text which discusses the subject of problem identification and hypothesis formulation from an academic research perspective.

Loeander, William B., and A. Benton Cocanougher (eds.), *Problem Definition in Marketing,* American Marketing Association, Marketing Research Techniques, ser. 2, Chicago, 1975. An interesting and well-written pamphlet which conceptualizes the problem definition process.

Luck, David J., Hugh G. Wales, and Donald A. Taylor, *Marketing Research,* 4th ed. (Englewood Cliffs, N.J.: Prentice-Hall, 1974), chaps. 2 and 4. A popular marketing research textbook which has an interesting discussion of the marketing research process and the importance of problem discovery and formulation.

O'Dell, William F., "Problem Delineation," in Robert Ferber, (ed.), *Handbook of Marketing Research,* pp. 2-3 to 2-10. The author emphasizes the importance of the marketing researcher's role in the decision-making process and discusses various approaches to facilitate the manager/researcher link.

Osborn, Alex F., *Applied Imagination,* 3d ed. (New York: Scribner, 1963). A well-written book on creativity which has many examples on the application of creative thinking.

Chapter 6

Research Design and Data Sources

The previous chapter discussed the importance of the planning and analysis leading to the decision to undertake a formal research project. It was stressed that the decision problem must be clearly stated and the alternative courses of action specified. The role research can play in both formulating the problem and stimulating the creative process involved in identifying alternative courses of action was emphasized, along with the importance of clearly stated research objectives and detailed information needs. The success of the formal research project is highly dependent upon how skillfully these preliminary issues are addressed.

Once the initial phase of the research process has been adequately performed, the researcher can turn to designing the formal research project and identifying the appropriate sources of data for the study. The primary task of the formal research project is to supply the decision maker with conclusive research information which will increase the level of confidence regarding the best course of action to accomplish objectives.

In this chapter, we first discuss the research designs and the data sources appropriate for exploratory, conclusive, and performance-monitoring research. Next we turn to a more detailed discussion of the basic sources of marketing data. These data sources include (1) interrogation of respondents, (2) observation,

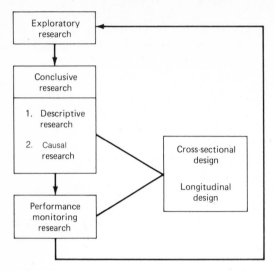

Figure 6-1 Research design.

(3) study of analogous situations, (4) experimentation, and (5) secondary data. We conclude the chapter with a discussion of marketing information systems.

RESEARCH DESIGN

A research design is the basic plan which guides the data collection and analysis phases of the research project. It is the framework which specifies the type of information to be collected, the sources of data, and the data collection procedure. A good design will make sure that the information gathered is consistent with the study objectives and that the data are collected by accurate and economical procedures. There is no standard or idealized research design to guide the researcher, since many different designs may accomplish the same objective.[1]

The objective of the research project logically determines the characteristics desired in the research design. Research objectives are dependent upon the stages of the decision-making process for which information is needed. Three types of research have been identified in this regard: exploratory, conclusive, and performance-monitoring research.

Research designs are typically classified according to the nature of the research objectives or types of research. While this classification is far from perfect, it will organize our discussion of research design. It is important to remember that research designs can serve many research objectives and types of research. The following classification reflects a judgment regarding the research objectives more predominantly associated with a design; it does not imply exclusive association. (See Figure 6-1.)

[1] Julian L. Simon, *Basic Research Methods in Social Sciences: The Art of Empirical Investigation* (New York: Random House, 1969), p. 4.

Exploratory Research

Exploratory research is appropriate when the research objectives include (1) identifying problems or opportunities, (2) developing a more precise formulation of a vaguely identified problem or opportunity, (3) gaining perspective regarding the breadth of variables operating in a situation, (4) establishing priorities regarding the potential significance of various problems or opportunities, (5) gaining management and researcher perspective regarding the character of the problem situation, (6) identifying and formulating alternative courses of action, and (7) gathering information on the problems associated with doing conclusive research.

These objectives all relate to the initial stages of the decision-making process. In decision situations where management has limited knowledge regarding the problem situation and/or alternative courses of action, exploratory research can bring ideas and insight to these areas. These tentative explanations or hypotheses can be further tested with evidence from conclusive research designs.

There is no formal or structured research design for exploratory research. The design is best characterized by its flexibility and lack of structure. The imagination, creativity, and ingenuity of the researcher are essential elements in the design. The data collection strategy is one of diversity and searching in new directions until new ideas or better ideas can no longer be discovered.

The sources of data appropriate for exploratory research include (1) search of secondary data, (2) interrogation of knowledgeable persons, and (3) study of case histories. For a more detailed discussion of how exploratory research can be used in the initial stages of the decision-making process, see Chapter 5.

Conclusive Research

Conclusive research is designed to provide information for the evaluation of alternative courses of action. It can be subclassified into descriptive research and causal research.[2]

Descriptive Research The vast majority of marketing research studies involve descriptive research. Most studies of this nature rely heavily on interrogation of respondents and data available from secondary data sources. Descriptive research is appropriate when the research objectives include (1) portraying the characteristics of marketing phenomena and determining the frequency of occurrence, (2) determining the degree to which marketing variables are associated, and (3) making predictions regarding the occurrence of marketing phenomena.

A significant share of research falls under the first of these objectives, portraying the characteristics of marketing phenomena and determining the

---

[2] This classification follows that of Daniel Katz, "Field Studies," in Leon Festinger and Daniel Katz (eds.), *Research Methods in the Behavioral Sciences* (New York: Holt, Rinehart, 1953), p. 74, and Claire Selltiz et al., *Research Methods in Social Relations,* rev. ed. (New York: Holt, Rinehart, 1959), p. 50.

frequency of occurrence. Consumer profile studies are conducted to describe the characteristics of the users of a product or service. Such profiles can use demographic, socioeconomic, geographic, and psychographic characteristics, as well as consumption rates. Descriptive studies determine buyer perceptions of product characteristics and audience profiles for media such as television and magazines. Market potential studies describe the size of the market, buying power of consumers, availability of distributors, and buyer profiles for a product; product usage studies describe consumption patterns; market share studies determine the proportion of total sales received by both a company and its competitors; sales analysis studies describe sales patterns by geographic region, type, and size on account and product line characteristics; distribution research determines the number and location of distributors; pricing research describes the range and frequency of prices charged for both a company's products and those of its competitors. These examples of descriptive research represent only a sampling of the numerous studies conducted in this area.

Descriptive research often involves determining the degree to which marketing variables are associated. For example, a company may study the degree of association between sales of a product and such buyer characteristics as income and age.

Descriptive information can be used to make predictions regarding the occurrence of marketing phenomena. While data regarding the presence of an association among variables can be used for predictive purposes, these data are not adequate to establish a causal relationship. However, it is not always necessary to understand causal relations in order to make accurate predictive statements. A company may establish an association between the sales of a product and the months of the year, and a sales forecast based on this association may have a high probability of success regarding future sales volume even though the causal relationship has not been established. The concept is to identify variables which are associated with the variable to be predicted and are measurable at the time the prediction is required.

While descriptive research may characterize marketing phenomena and demonstrate an association among variables, statements regarding cause-and-effect relationships are not possible with descriptive research. The decision maker may make predictions that certain actions will result in certain performance outcomes based on the evidence provided from a descriptive study, but this evidence in itself does not demonstrate a cause-and-effect relationship. (Where such evidence is needed, causal research designs are required, which will be discussed shortly.)

The character and purpose of descriptive research is substantially different from that of exploratory research. Effective descriptive research is marked by a clear statement of the decision problem, specific research objectives, and detailed information needs. It is characterized by a carefully planned and structured research design. Since the purpose is to provide information regarding specific questions or hypotheses, the research must be designed to ensure accuracy of the findings. By accuracy we refer to a design that minimizes systematic error and maximizes the reliability of the evidence collected. Systematic error refers to a constant bias in the measurement process, while reliability refers to the extent to which the measurement process is free from random errors. For a detailed discussion of systematic error and reliability in connection with the measurement process, see Chapter 12.

Cross-sectional Design   Descriptive research typically makes use of a cross-sectional research design, i.e. one which involves taking a sample of population elements at one point in time. Frequently this is called the *survey research design*. This is the most popular type of research design and the one with which people are most familiar. The survey design is useful in describing the characteristics of consumers and determining the frequency of marketing phenomena, although it is often expensive and requires skillful and competent research personnel to conduct it effectively.

Decision Maker's Implicit Causal Model   The evidence provided by descriptive research can be very useful when combined with the decision maker's implicit model of how the marketing system functions in regard to the specific area under investigation. This causal model is typically based on the experience and judgment of the decision maker and represents key assumptions regarding the cause-and-effect relationships present in the marketing system. A descriptive study can provide evidence regarding specific questions or hypotheses relating to the current state of the variables present in this causal model. Given this descriptive evidence, the decision maker can draw conclusions regarding the effects of various courses of action and reach a decision as to which course of action will best accomplish objectives. Consequently, descriptive research in itself may not provide evidence directly related to the selection of a course of action. It is when descriptive evidence is incorporated in the decision maker's personal model of the marketing system that it contributes directly to the decision-making process.

The previous discussion can be illustrated with an example. A marketing manager wishes to test the hypothesis that the reason for the decline in share of market for the firm's adult cereal is due to the consumer's misperception that a new natural cereal is more nutritious. This hypothesis was developed from several exploratory group interviews with former users of the firm's cereal product. Descriptive research was conducted to test this hypothesis, and an extensive survey of several hundred adult cereal consumers supported it. The marketing manager combined this descriptive evidence with a personal causal model of how the adult cereal market functions to reach a decision regarding a course of action. The decision was to develop an advertising campaign stressing the adult cereal's superior nutritional standing compared to the natural cereal. The strategy was to correct the market misperception regarding the nutritional value of the firm's adult cereal by clarifying the product positioning of both cereals. The result was a substantial increase in the adult cereal's share of market.

As this example points out, descriptive research presupposes that a sound causal model of the marketing system exists in the mind of the decision maker.

The lower the decision maker's confidence in the wisdom of the causal model, the lower the value of descriptive research in the decision-making process. For example, descriptive research regarding the positioning of a brand is of little value if the decision maker does not know how brand positioning relates to the success of the brand.

Descriptive studies cover an array of research interests, but they require skillful planning if they are to be used effectively in decision making. Far too often, descriptive research is viewed as a fact-gathering expedition.

> Facts do not lead anywhere. Indeed, facts as facts are the commonest, cheapest, and most useless of all commodities. Anyone with a questionnaire can gather thousands of facts a day—and probably not find much real use for them. What makes facts practical and valuable is the glue of explanation and understanding, the framework of theory, the tie-rod of conjecture. Only when facts can be fleshed to a skeletal theory do they become meaningful in the solution of problems.[3]

Descriptive research is easy to conduct when the decision maker gives free rein to collect what are believed to be interesting facts. Typical here is a situation where research objectives are vague, specific research questions or hypotheses have not been formulated, and limited thought has been given to how the evidence can be used in the decision-making process. The result of such fact-gathering expeditions is that the majority of the data turn out to be useless and management has wasted both funds and time. In this situation, possibly an exploratory research study would provide better information, faster and at a lower cost, than a fact-finding descriptive study. Since descriptive studies often cost several thousands of dollars, the collection of interesting but useless facts can be very costly.

Descriptive research designs can utilize one or more of the following sources of data: (1) interrogation of respondents, (2) secondary data, (3) experimentation, and (4) simulation.

Causal Research   The decision-making process calls for assumptions regarding the cause-and-effect relationships present in the marketing system, and causal research is designed to gather evidence regarding these relationships. It requires a planned and structured design that will not only minimize systematic error and maximize reliability but will permit reasonably unambiguous conclusions regarding causality.

Causal research is appropriate given the following research objectives: (1) to understand which variables are the cause of what is being predicted (the effect)—here the focus is on understanding the reasons why things happen; (2) to understand the nature of the functional relationship between the causal factors and the effect to be predicted.

Marketing executives continually think and make decisions based on an implicit causal model of the marketing system. If prices are reduced on a product

---

[3] Robert Ferber, Donald F. Blankertz, and Sidney Hollander, Jr., *Marketing Research*, (New York: Ronald, 1964), p.153.

or the promotion budget is increased, and subsequent unit sales of the product show an upward surge, this effect could be assumed to be caused by the changes in price level and/or the promotion budget. However, can we confidently say that the change in unit sales was caused by the change in price and promotion levels? Certainly not with a high degree of confidence. Many other variables could be the cause. Consequently, causal research must be designed such that the evidence regarding causality is clear. Research designs vary substantially in the degree of ambiguity present in the evidence regarding causality.

The main sources of data for causal research are (1) interrogating respondents through surveys and (2) conducting experiments.

While surveys can determine the degree of association among variables and test hypotheses, they cannot distinguish causality as well as experiments. A skillfully designed experiment can ensure that the evidence regarding causality is reasonably unambiguous in interpretation.

Because of the complexity of the research designs appropriate for experimental research, a separate section of this book has been devoted to their explanation. Chapters 14 through 17 discuss the principles of experimentation and alternative research designs.

Our discussion of conclusive research has emphasized the distinction between descriptive and causal research. In practice, these two approaches may be combined to meet the varied research objectives of a particular study. Even so, it is important to recognize the distinction between them, since they do serve different types of research objectives and differ in the character of the evidence provided for decision making. For example, with causal research, especially in the case of an experiment, the research design may directly evaluate the alternative courses of action under consideration. Here, the independent variables (courses of action) can be manipulated to determine the effect on purchase behavior, attitudes, and so forth. In the case of descriptive research, the evidence is more indirect, and the decision maker's experience and judgment regarding the nature of the causal relationships are required for the effective use of this evidence in the decision-making process.

Performance-monitoring Research

Performance-monitoring research provides information regarding the monitoring of the marketing system. It is an essential element in the control of marketing programs in accordance with plans. The purpose of this research is to signal the presence of potential problems or opportunities.

The objectives of performance-monitoring research are to monitor and report changes (1) in performance measures, such as sales and market share, to determine whether plans are accomplishing desired objectives; (2) in subobjectives, such as awareness and knowledge levels, distribution penetration, and price levels, to determine whether the marketing program is being implemented according to plans; and (3) in the situational variables, such as competitive activity, economic conditions, and demand trends, to determine whether the situational climate is as anticipated when plans were formulated.

The data sources appropriate for performance-monitoring research include (1) interrogation of respondents, (2) secondary data, (3) observation, and (4) experimentation.

Performance-monitoring research can involve a special (ad hoc) study or a continuous research program.

Ad hoc performance monitoring consists of research programs designed to monitor new or special marketing programs of the organization or competitor. Typical here is the monitoring of a test market for a new product. Recent years have shown growing interest in monitoring such situational variables as government regulation, availability of resources, changing life-styles of buyers, concerns of consumer groups, and so forth. The previously discussed cross-sectional research design is appropriate in this situation. This typically involves survey research.

Continuous performance measures are, in general, formal systems designed to monitor the dependent variables in the marketing system. In recent years, increased effort has been directed to monitoring the independent variables as well. The most common performance measures involve product movement data such as units sold, sales volume, and market share. Many organizations have formal systems to monitor the performance of the distribution system, sales force, and promotional programs. Most firms have the sales force submit to management, on a routine basis, formal reports regarding market and competitive conditions.

Longitudinal Design   Continuous performance monitoring typically requires a *longitudinal research design,* that is, one in which a fixed sample of population elements is measured repeatedly. The term "panel" is often used synonymously with longitudinal design. Two types of panels exist: the *traditional panel* and the *omnibus panel.* The traditional panel is a fixed sample where the same variables are repeatedly measured; for example, the Nielsen Retail Store Audit involves a fixed sample of 2500 stores which are measured monthly to estimate the sales of various food and drug items.[4] The omnibus panel is a fixed sample of respondents which is measured repeatedly, but the variables measured are different each time. For example, a food company maintains a panel of households who are asked to evaluate different food products at various points in time.

The longitudinal design has several advantages over the cross-sectional design, the most important being analytical. This is mainly true of the traditional panel, where the respondents and measured variables stay the same. Various data analysis approaches have been developed to analyze this type of data set.[5] These approaches allow the study of changes in attitudes, knowledge, and behavior for the same respondents or households at different points in time. Such

---

[4] Nielsen Retail Index Service (Northbrook, Ill.: A. C. Nielsen Company, 1975).

[5] Francesco M. Nicosia, "Panel Designs and Analysis in Marketing," in Peter D. Bennett (ed.), *Marketing and Economic Development* (Chicago: American Marketing Association, 1965), pp. 222–243.

changes (or lack of change) can be related to changes in marketing program variables (price, promotion, distribution, and product) as well as to changes in situational variables (e.g., competition, economic conditions, and so forth).

Another advantage of the panel design relates to the amount of information which can be collected. Since panel members are often compensated for their participation, they are more cooperative regarding longer and more demanding interviews. Consequently, panels are able to gather extensive background data on the respondents in addition to more detailed data regarding the primary variables of interest.

It is argued that panel data can be more accurate than cross-sectional data. Research evidence suggests that professionally administered panels using the diary reporting procedure (self-administered questionnaire) yield reasonably accurate estimates of retail sales for an array of food and drug items.[6] A comparison of panel and survey estimates of retail sales indicates that more accurate estimates of retail sales exist with panel data.[7] The survey design requires the respondent to recall past purchases, which can be biased because of forgetting and misassociation; bias is reduced in the panel design since there is continuous recording of purchases in the diary as they occur. Additional research suggests that panel members must be paid in order to maintain reporting accuracy. Small payments can produce very accurate reporting. Variations in work loads imposed on the panel members do not significantly influence the reporting accuracy.[8]

The cost of panel data can be lower than the cost of comparable data collected through a survey. The fixed costs associated with developing and maintaining a panel can be spread over the many clients who use it, while a comparable survey requires that the incurred fixed cost be charged directly to a single client.

The main disadvantages of panels stem from the fact that they are not representative. The two major problems are (1) unrepresentative sampling and (2) response bias.

The unrepresentative sampling problem arises from the need to have panel members serve for a long period. As an inducement to service, they are offered gifts and money. It is argued that individuals who are mobile, employed, and uninterested in panel activities, gifts, or money and individuals who are unable to perform the tasks required will not serve on the panel. Despite attempts to match the sample on selected population characteristics such as age, education, occupation, and so on, it is feared that the sample may be unrepresentative in regard to the particular variable being measured.

Another issue relates to the mortality rates of existing panel members and the representativeness of the new members chosen to replace them. Mortality rates (resulting from members moving, losing interest, and dying) can range as high as 20 percent per year for panels operating over a long period of time.

[6] Seymour Sudman, "On the Accuracy of Recording of Consumer Panels: II," *Journal of Marketing Research,* vol. 1, pp. 69–83, August 1964.

[7] J. H. Parfitt, "A Comparison of Purchase Recall with Diary Panel Records," *Journal of Advertising Research,* vol. 7, pp. 16–31, September 1967.

[8] Sudman, "On the Accuracy of Recording of Consumer Panels: II."

Despite these potential biases in representativeness of the sample, the available research evidence suggests that this problem is not a serious issue for professionally administered panels.[9]

The response bias issue is not serious for well-managed panels. The response biases that need to be controlled result from the panel members believing they are "experts," wanting to look good or give the "right" answer, becoming biased from boredom and fatigue, and not routinely completing diary entries.

Research evidence does suggest that new panel members are often biased in their initial responses.[10] New members tend to increase the behavior being measured, e.g., television viewing and food purchasing.[11] Professionally managed panels minimize this type of bias by initially excluding the data of new members from panel results. After the novelty of being on the panel declines, the accuracy of the data increases.

DATA SOURCES

There are four basic sources of marketing data. These are (1) respondents, (2) analogous situations, (3) experimentation, and (4) secondary data.

Respondents

Respondents are a major source of marketing data. There are two principal methods of obtaining data from respondents—communication and observation. Communication requires the respondent to actively provide data through verbal response, while observation requires the recording of the respondent's passive behavior.

Communication with Respondents   The most common source of marketing data is communication with respondents. It is logical to acquire data from people by asking questions. In our daily activities we gather information by asking questions of persons whom we consider knowledgeable. Marketing research is just a more formal and scientific way of gathering such information.

When the information needs of a study require data regarding respondents' attitudes, perceptions, motivations, knowledge, and intended behavior, asking people questions is essential. The respondents can be consumers, industrial buyers, wholesalers, retailers, or any knowledgeable persons who can provide data useful to a decision situation. Effective communication with respondents requires special training and skill if the data are to be useful. Misleading data can result when the questions are biased or require respondents to provide data which they do not possess or choose not to disclose.

The research design can range from questioning a few knowledgeable individuals (qualitative research) to surveys involving hundreds of respondents

[9] W. N. Cordell and H. A. Rahmel, "Are Nielsen Ratings Affected by Non-Cooperation, Conditioning, or Response Error?" *Journal of Advertising Research,* vol. 2, pp. 45–49, September 1962.

[10] D. G. Morrison, R. E. Frank, and W. F. Massy, "A Note on Panel Bias," *Journal of Marketing,* vol. 3, pp. 85–88, February 1966.

[11] A. S. C. Ehrenberg, "A Study of Some Potential Biases in the Operation of a Consumer Panel," *Applied Statistics: A Journal of the Royal Statistical Society,* vol. 9, pp. 20–27, March 1960.

(quantitative research). *Qualitative or exploratory research* usually consists of questioning knowledgeable respondents individually or in small groups (i.e., five to six people). *Group interviews* provide free-flowing, unstructured situations designed to stimulate ideas and insights into a problem situation through group interaction. This typically means asking deeply probing questions over a long time span (i.e., one or two hours). *Depth interviews* use extensive questioning of respondents individually to explore the reasons underlying attitudes and behavior. The focus is on developing hypotheses and insight regarding the "why" of past and future behavior. In contrast, *quantitative research* is designed to explain what is happening and the frequency of occurrence; it is normally conducted by asking a large sample of respondents a few simple questions in a brief time span (i.e., ten to twenty minutes). Formal and structured research procedures designed to control bias in the data are employed.

The data collection methods used in communicating with respondents include personal interviews, telephone interviews, and mail questionnaires. The questions are asked of the respondent and answered verbally with the personal and telephone interview, in writing with the mail questionnaire. The popularity of the telephone interview has increased significantly in recent years.

Observation of Respondents   Observation is the process of recognizing and recording relevant objects and events. It is an important and commonplace activity in our daily activities. Similarly, in marketing, valuable information pertaining to a decision situation can be obtained by observing either present behavior or the results of past behavior.

Observational methods allow the recording of behavior when it occurs, thus eliminating those errors associated with the recall of behavior. This is often less costly and/or more accurate than asking the respondent to recall the same behavior at another point in time. While observation can accurately record what people do and how it is done, it cannot be used to determine the motivations, attitudes, and knowledge that underlie the behavior.

The many issues involved in obtaining data from respondents through communication and observation are discussed in Chapters 18 to 20.

Analogous Situations

A logical way to study a decision situation is to examine analogous or similar situations. Analogous situations include the study of case histories and simulations.

Case Histories   The case history approach is an old and established method of gathering marketing data. It has been used successfully in the behavioral sciences and marketing for decades.[12]

This approach involves the intensive investigation of situations which are

[12] This method of investigation has been widely used in the behavioral sciences and marketing research under the label of "case study." The term "case history" is used here to differentiate the research-oriented case study from the classroom case study most familiar to students. The classroom case study is a pedagogical device designed to put the student in a situation similar to that encountered by a management group. The student's task is to analyze the situation and logically proceed through the decision-making process, ending with a recommendation for action. Research

relevant to a particular problem setting. For example, a researcher might intensively study selected sales territories, selected small markets, or a few consumers. The purpose would be to gain a thorough description and understanding of the variables operating in the situation.

The case history approach is used early in the decision-making process to provide insight into the decision situation. It is used mainly for exploratory research purposes. For a more comprehensive review of this topic, return to our previous discussion in Chapter 5.

Simulation This means the creation of an analogy or likeness of a real-world phenomenon. It is an incomplete representation of reality which tries to duplicate the essence of the phenomenon without actually attaining reality itself. Common examples of simulation are model airplanes, road maps, and planetariums.

What is a *marketing simulation?* It can be defined as an incomplete representation of the marketing system or some aspect of this system. It is a relatively new source of data which is largely computer based. Simulation can be used to gain insight into the dynamics of the marketing system by manipulating the independent variables (marketing mix and situational factors) and observing their influence on the dependent variable(s). A marketing simulation requires data inputs regarding the characteristics of the phenomenon to be represented and the relationships present.

The development of a marketing simulation requires that the builder conceptualize and document the structural components of the system and establish probabilities to represent the behavior of the components.[13] The components or units of the marketing simulation represent objects in the marketing system. Depending on the marketing phenomenon under study, the units can be buyers, households, retailers, etc. The variables in the system establish how the units behave. Variables can be price levels, advertising expenditure, product quality, deals, competitive strategy, and so forth. Probabilities are assigned to the units in correspondence to their response to the variables. The objective is to make the simulation units imitate the behavior of the marketing system units which they represent. The behavior of these units results in the numerical output, or data, from the simulation. For example, the numerical output could be share of market, sales, or profitability. The parameters of the simulation represent the constraints that can be changed only at the direction of the user. These might be level of advertising, price elasticity, proportion of children in the market, competitive advertising levels, and so forth. Parameters allow the user to ex-

---

case histories or case studies are typically more myopic than classroom case studies and are intended to aid the decision-making process by providing ideas and insight into a decision situation. The classroom case study may include one or more case histories as part of the background information in the case.

[13] This discussion follows that of William D. Wells, "Computer Simulation of Consumer Behavior," in Edward C. Bursk and John F. Chapman (eds.), *Modern Marketing Strategy* (Cambridge, Mass.: Harvard Univ. Press, 1964), pp. 104–15.

periment with the simulation, explore alternative marketing strategies, and determine the influence of changes in situational factors.

The development of a marketing simulation requires the skills of a specialist and the cooperation of management. The simulation builder's task is to reduce the complex phenomenon under study to manageable proportions while at the same time replicating the interactions found in the marketing system. The inputs to the simulation represent existing data regarding the system and the organization's experience and judgment as to how the system operates. Once the simulation has been constructed, it can be tested to determine whether the output is consistent with the known performance of the actual system being simulated. "A valid simulation model should behave in a manner similar to the underlying phenomena. This is a necessary validation criterion, but alone may not be sufficient to permit us to rely on its predictive abilities."[14]

Developing a simulation can be a complicated process. A central issue concerns to what extent the simulation should be abstracted from reality. Simulations should neither oversimplify nor overcomplicate. A simulation which is too simple may not be trusted by a decision maker because of its lack of detail or likeness to the real marketing system. However, if it is too complex, the decision maker again may not have confidence in the simulation since it is difficult to understand how it operates. A good simulation model should possess the characteristics of being (1) simple enough for easy comprehension and manipulation by the user, (2) reasonably representative of the domain of implications existing in the marketing system, and (3) complex enough to represent accurately the system being studied.[15]

Simulation models can be classified many different ways. One of the more common classifications is based on the management purpose served by the simulation and includes three types: descriptive, predictive, and prescriptive.

A *descriptive simulation model* is one which illustrates or describes the marketing system under investigation.

> Descriptive models are relatively easy to construct but difficult to manipulate. For this reason, the descriptive model is limited in application to the particular situation which it portrays and does not have general applicability to other situations. For the same reason, descriptive models usually do not lend themselves to portraying dynamic situations or causal relationships between variables, although they may sometimes do so. Descriptive models, however, are valuable for obtaining a "feel" for a situation and for providing a stepping stone for the development of other models with more abstract representation.[16]

A *predictive model* is designed to assist in the prediction of the performance of the marketing system when variables in the system change. For example, a

---

[14] Robert C. Meier, William T. Newell, and Harold L. Pazer, *Simulation in Business and Economics* (Englewood Cliffs, N.J.: Prentice-Hall, 1969), p. 23.

[15] Dimitris N. Chorafas, *Systems and Simulation* (New York: Academic Press, 1965), p. 31.

[16] M. D. Richards and Paul S. Greenlaw, *Management Decision Making* (Homewood, Ill.: Richard D. Irwin, 1966), p. 65.

simulation of the distribution system for a product might predict the loss of sales and shelf space resulting from an interruption in the supply of the product to wholesalers and retailers. A predictive model is useful in studying the effect of different levels of variables in the system but is limited in that it does not allow for the manipulation of the system for purposes of evaluating new courses of action.

A *prescriptive model* is one that allows the user to experiment with changes in the system. This model permits the evaluation of changes in situational factors (e.g., competitive changes) and of the effects of alternative marketing strategies.

How does simulation differ from other data-gathering methods? Simulation requires that a model of the system be conceptualized, developed, and manipulated. The data obtained from simulation consist of numerical outputs resulting from this model. In contrast, the data obtained from respondents, experiments, and secondary sources result directly from the situation being studied.

What are the advantages of simulation compared with other data sources? It can be less expensive than conducting a survey of respondents or test marketing, and the time required to collect and analyze the data may be less. Simulation can be conducted with complete secrecy within an organization; other data sources may not assure this degree of security. Simulation allows the evaluation of alternative marketing strategies and provides "proof" regarding the superiority of one strategy over another. In addition, the consequences of changes in the marketing system can be evaluated without the risk of making changes in the real system. This allows the evaluation of multiple strategies and encourages creativity in that radical strategy changes can be evaluated. Simulation can be useful in determining the sensitivity of a strategy option to departures in the initial assumptions. This is called *sensitivity analysis*. Finally, simulation can be used as a training device for members of the organization. Individuals not directly involved in marketing activities may develop an appreciation of how the marketing system operates and how it affects decisions in their areas, e.g., research and development (R&D) or manufacturing.

The limitations of simulation are the difficulty of developing a valid simulation model and the time and cost of updating the model as conditions change. In situations where the organization has limited background and experience regarding the marketing phenomenon under investigation (e.g., new markets), simulation may not be a feasible data source.

Experimentation

Experimentation is a relatively new source of marketing data. The data from an experiment are organized in such a way that relatively unambiguous statements can be made regarding cause-and-effect relationships.

An experiment is conducted when one or more independent variables are consciously manipulated or controlled and their effect on the dependent variable(s) is measured. The objective of an experiment is to measure the effect of the independent variables on a dependent variable, while controlling for other variables that might confuse one's ability to make valid causal inferences. Various experimental designs have been developed to reduce or eliminate the possible influence of extraneous variables on the dependent variable. Chapters 14 through 17 deal exclusively with the concept of experimentation and the research designs used in this area.

Secondary Data

There are two general types of marketing data—primary and secondary. *Primary data* are collected specifically for purposes of the research needs at hand. *Secondary data* are already published data collected for purposes other than the specific research needs at hand. Consequently, this distinction is defined by the purpose for which the data were collected.

Secondary data can be classified as coming from *internal sources* or *external sources,* the former being available within the organization and the latter originating outside it. External data come from an array of sources such as government publications, trade association data, books, bulletins, reports, and periodicals. Data from these sources are available at minimal cost or free in libraries. The next chapter deals specifically with the data sources available in a library. External data sources not available in a library are usually standardized data which are expensive to acquire. We refer to these data sources as *syndicated sources.* Such sources are predominantly profit-making organizations who provide standardized data to an array of clients. The remainder of this section will discuss internal data sources and syndicated external data sources.

Internal Data   As stated already, these data originate within the organization for which the research is conducted. Internal data collected for purposes other than the research being conducted are *internal secondary data.*

All organizations collect internal data as part of their normal operations. Sales and cost data are recorded, sales reports submitted, advertising and promotion activities recorded, research and development and manufacturing reports made; these are but a few of the data sources available for research purposes within a modern organization. A researcher must be thoroughly familiar with all of these.

Sales and cost data collected for accounting purposes represent a particularly promising source for many research projects. For example, if the research objectives of a project are to evaluate previous marketing activity or to determine the organization's competitive position, sales and cost data can be very helpful.

Many organizations do not collect and maintain sales and cost data in sufficient detail to be used for many research purposes. Sales records should allow for classification by type of customer, payment procedure (cash or credit), product line, sales territory, time period, and so forth. By simple analysis of this type of data the researcher can determine the level and trend in sales, costs, and profitability by customer, territory, and product. More sophisticated analysis could attempt to measure the effect of changes in the marketing program and/or situational variables on sales, costs, and profitability.

The advantages of internal secondary data are their low cost and availability. Unfortunately, many organizations fail to recognize that they have or could have useful internal data available at low cost. These organizations could benefit from specially designed programs to organize and maintain secondary internal data for marketing research purposes.

External Data—Syndicated   The growing demand for marketing data has produced a number of companies which collect and sell standardized data designed to serve information needs shared by a number of organizations; the most common are information needs associated with performance-monitoring research.

Syndicated data sources can be classified as (1) consumer data, (2) retail data, (3) wholesale data, (4) industrial data, (5) advertising evaluation data, and (6) media and audience data. The following section presents an overview of the main types of data available in each of these classifications. A more comprehensive listing and discussion of syndicated data sources is provided in the appendix.

Consumer Data   Several services collect data from consumers regarding purchases and the circumstances surrounding the purchase. The National Purchase Diary Panel, Inc. (NPD) maintains a panel of 13,000 households who keep diaries in which they record all purchases in 50 food and personal care product categories. The Marketing Research Corporation of America (MRCA) maintains a diary panel of 7500 households who record the significant details regarding the purchase of grocery and personal care products. Panel services of this type provide data on sales by brand, type, flavor, or variety purchased; the quantities bought; the price paid; the store patronized; brand switching; demographic and socioeconomic characteristics of the purchase; and so forth.

Various services survey large groups of consumers regarding purchases and the buying situation. Audits and Surveys, Inc., conducts an annual survey of 5000 consumers who participate in leisure sports and recreational activity. The Gallup Organization, Inc., has an annual survey of 15,000 households regarding the purchase of consumer goods and services. Trendex, Inc. conducts a quarterly survey of 15,000 households regarding the ownership and acquisition of consumer durables.

The National Menu Census conducted by Marketing Research Corporation of America provides data regarding the consumption of food products in the home. Data are provided on the menu at each meal, snack items, carry-out foods, and so forth.

Numerous services survey consumers' attitudes and opinions regarding consumption behavior and a variety of contemporary topics relevant to marketing. The Gallup Organization, Inc., Louis Harris & Associates, Inc., The Roper Organization, Inc., and Daniel Yankelovich, Inc., conduct large surveys which monitor consumers' attitudes and opinions on a broad range of social, political, and economic issues as well as trends in life-style and consumption patterns. The Survey Research Center, University of Michigan, monitors consumer consumption patterns, attitudes, and intentions as related to financial issues and the purchase of durable goods. Other services monitor consumers' attitudes and opinions regarding the food-shopping process and their awareness levels for brands and advertisements.

Retail Data   Numerous services rely on retailing establishments for their data. The data collected focus on the products or services sold through the outlets and/or the characteristics of the outlets themselves. Two of the better-known services are A.C. Nielsen's Retail Index and Audits and Surveys' National Total-Market Audit. The Nielsen Retail Index involves a store audit of super-markets, drugstores, and mass merchandisers taken every two weeks. The data reported to a client include total sales by product class, sales by brand, and sales of competing brands. Audits and Surveys' National Total-Market Audit provides bimonthly reports which contain data similar to the Nielsen Retail Index. Many of the product categories included in the audit are different from the Nielsen service.

Wholesale Data   A growing number of services rely on warehouse shipment data to estimate sales at retail. SAMI (Selling Areas—Marketing, Inc.) is a well-known service to manufacturers who sell through retail food stores. Clients who buy SAMI reports can receive monthly data on the movement of each brand in each of 425 product categories. SAMI data estimate sales of a brand and com-petitive brands in each of 36 markets. Such data allow the client to analyze trends in sales or package size and the impact of promotions and competitive actions. The Nielsen Retail Index and SAMI are competitive services in that they provide similar data for similar product categories. SAMI reports become available more quickly than Nielsen data, but the latter represent actual retail purchases, whereas SAMI data represent retail orders from the warehouse.

Industrial Data   There are substantially more syndicated data services available to consumer goods manufacturers than to industrial goods suppliers. The services available for industrial goods are fairly recent and still evolving; an example is Dun & Bradstreet's "Market Identifiers," which provides data on 390,000 Dun & Bradstreet–rated companies. The data can be used to construct sales prospect lists, identify sales territories, establish sales potentials, and so forth. Other industrial services include *Fortune* magazine's *Input/Output* matrix reports and McGraw-Hill's *Dodge Reports*.

Advertising Evaluation Data   Billions of advertising dollars are spent each year on media such as magazines and television with the expectation that these expenditures will result in sales. Consequently, advertisers are interested in data which measure the effectiveness of these expenditures. Our discussion will focus on those services which evaluate advertisements in broadcast and print media.

Several services evaluate advertising in print media. Two of the well-known syndicated readership services are the Starch *Readership Reports* and Gallup and Robinson *Magazine Impact Studies*.

Starch reports measure an advertisement's effectiveness by classifying magazine readership into three groups: (1) those who remember seeing a par-ticular advertisement ("Noted"), (2) those who associated the sponsor's name with the advertisement ("Seen-Associated"), and (3) those who read half or more of its copy ("Read Most"). This evaluation is provided for most consumer magazines and selected business and industrial publications. Starch is the most widely used syndicated readership service.

Gallup and Robinson (G&R) is Starch's major competitor. It uses a more rigorous method in gathering data from magazine readers. G&R first asks the reader to recall and describe advertisements from the closed issue of the magazine, whereas Starch shows the reader the advertisements by turning through the magazine. G&R measures three levels of advertising effectiveness: (1) "Proved Name Registration" (PNR) score, which gives the percentage of readers who remembered the ad and proved its recall by describing the ad; (2) "Idea Playback Profile," a measure of sales message recall; and (3) "Favorable Buying Attitude" score, which measures message persuasiveness. Both Starch and G&R allow the assessment of individual advertisement effectiveness and the tracking of successive campaigns over time.

The services which evaluate television commercials use two basic approaches—the recruited audience method and the normal viewing environment method.

With the recruited audience method, respondents are recruited and brought to a viewing center (theater or mobile viewing laboratory) for purposes of pretesting television commercials. Data are gathered regarding the viewers' attitudes, knowledge, preference, and selection of products. Services which use this approach are McCollum/Spielman Company Audience Studies (ASI), Burgoyne, Inc., PACE (Persuasion and Communication Effectiveness), and Tele-Research, Inc.

With the second approach, the normal viewing environment method, commercials are evaluated in the home. New commercials are pretested by substituting the test commercial for a regular commercial on established programming. This can be done at the network level or in local markets. A sample of viewers is then interviewed to determine the new advertisement's effectiveness. The services which use this approach are AdTel, Ltd.; ARS Division, Research Systems, Inc.; Audience Studies/Com. Lab., Inc.; and Television Testing Company.

Gallup and Robinson, with its Total Prime Time (TPT) Studies, is very prominent in the posttesting of TV commercials. A sample of television viewers is asked to recall their viewing behavior for the previous evening. The recall of sales points and the persuasiveness of the commercial are probed. Two scores—"Commercial Recognition" (CR) and "Proved Commercial Registration" (PCR)—are reported for commercials shown during prime viewing time.

Media and Audience Data   The task of media planner is to identify media that have audience characteristics similar to those of the target market to be reached. The types of data used in matching markets and media typically include demographics, psychographics, and product usage rates. A number of syndicated audience measurement services provide this type of data. The A.C. Nielsen

Company and the American Research Bureau provide audience data for television programs. Other services specialize in providing audience measurement data for a particular medium.

In recent years, two multimedia services have grown in importance—W. R. Simmons & Associates and Target Group Index (TGI). These competitive services allow the media planner to compare audience characteristics over an array of media. For example, Simmons characterizes the audiences for 69 magazines, 2 national newspapers and 5 supplements, and all network television programs. Audience data are provided on demographic characteristics and usage of more than 500 products and services. Similar data are provided by TGI, with over 20 psychographic characteristics in addition.

Media planners need data regarding the advertising effects of competitors. It is important to know how much competitors are spending, where they are spending their advertising dollars, and in what media mix. Several syndicated services provide this type of data.

Perhaps the best-known competitive data service is Leading National Advertisers (LNA). This service monitors over 150,000 ads each year in 86 consumer magazines and 3 national newspaper supplements. Data regarding other media are supplied by services such as BAR (Broadcast Advertisers Report), Media Records, Inc., ACB (Advertising Checking Bureau), and others.

THE MARKETING INFORMATION SYSTEM

Every organization has procedures for acquiring the basic data needed to perform daily activities and assist in the decision-making function. In recent years, many of these procedures have evolved into formal systems for collecting, storing, analyzing, and reporting such data. The introduction of the computer has supported and expanded this trend.

In recent years, interest has grown in the concept of integrating the organization's many data sources into a total system designed to serve the information needs of the organization. From a marketing perspective, we shall refer to this system as a marketing information system (MIS).

The MIS Concept

A *marketing information system* is defined as the systematic and continuous gathering, analysis, and reporting of data for decision-making purposes. Figure 6-2 presents the MIS concept. The marketing information system is shown to stand between the marketing system and the marketing decision maker. There is a flow of data from the marketing system to the marketing information system of the organization. This system is designed to collect and process these data and provide systematic and continuous information flows for decision-making purposes.

We now turn to a discussion of the components of the MIS concept.

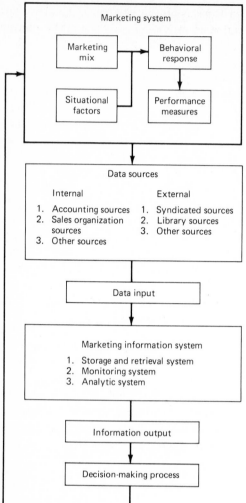

Figure 6-2 Marketing information system concept.

MIS Data Sources

The backbone of a marketing information system is formed by the organization's data sources. Before developing an MIS, an organization must review and overhaul its relevant data sources, identifying and organizing them into systematic structures.

As discussed in a previous section, data sources can be classified as internal and external to the organization. An organization's accounting system and sales organization are important internal data sources for a marketing information system. Syndicated services and library sources represent key external data sources.

The organization's accounting system is a critical data source for marketing decision makers.[17] This system contains data regarding sales, inventory levels, cost allocations, accounts receivable, and so on. Such information is important in monitoring the performance of marketing programs and signaling problems and opportunities.

The organization's sales organization is an excellent source of data.[18] Sales personnel can provide data regarding many aspects of the marketing system. They literally are the organization's eyes and ears in the marketplace. Data can be provided on (1) number of calls made in a time period; (2) circumstances surrounding the sales call; (3) products used by customers; (4) customer expansion plans; (5) competitive activity; and (6) economic and social trends in an area. Many of these data can be standardized and collected through salespeople's periodically completed call reports.

Data purchased from syndicated services can be a valuable input to the MIS. As presented in the appendix to this chapter, these services provide an array of data such as (1) consumer sales; (2) warehouse withdrawals; (3) sales by retail outlet; (4) buyer profiles; (5) pricing and point-of-sale promotional data; (6) media characteristics and evaluation; (7) advertising campaign evaluations; (8) economic, social, and demographic trends; (9) prospect lists; and (10) advertising expenditures in various media. To a substantial degree these data are standardized and can be used for performance-monitoring purposes.

There are a variety of library sources, such as government publications, trade association data, reports, periodicals, and the like. Again, data from these sources are for the most part standardized and can be used for a wide range of information needs.

For a particular organization or industry, other data sources may be as important as those discussed above. For example, valuable data can be provided by an organization's production department and distribution system. Research studies can be conducted periodically to collect standardized data for input to the MIS.

MIS Stages

Marketing information systems can be classified into three stages or levels: (1) the data storage and retrieval system; (2) the monitoring system; and (3) the analytical system.[19]

A data storage and a retrieval system is the most elementary of the three. As a system which automatically accesses stored data, it can be useful in answering factual questions such as: "How many distributors do we have in the central sales zone?" The output of this system is simply the facts which have been stored in it.

A monitoring system is a more sophisticated system designed to provide

---

[17] See *Information for Marketing Management,* National Association of Accountants, New York, 1971.

[18] See *Salesmen's Call Reports,* Conference Board Report No. 570, The Conference Board, New York, 1972.

[19] *Information Systems for Sales and Marketing Management,* Conference Board Report No. 591, The Conference Board, New York, 1973, pp. 3–4.

management with information on what is happening. It reports on areas such as sales levels, share of market, and daily production and inventory levels. This system addresses questions such as: "Where are we?"; "How did we get there?"; and "How do we compare with objectives, competition, and so on?" The output of this system generally requires the data to be manipulated in order to meet the management information needs. This data manipulation may involve the calculation of means, proportions, or indexes. Typically the system allows the data to be presented in various output modes.

An analytical system is the most sophisticated of these. It helps to answer the decision maker's more complex questions, such as: "What caused this to happen?"; "What are the consequences of this course of action?"; and "What will happen if . . .?" The analytical techniques used in this system include an array of statistical and mathematical models designed to perform diagnostic, evaluative, and predictive analyses of the data set.

Analytical systems have been developed to evaluate alternative advertising media schedules and select a schedule which meets specified criteria. They are used to evaluate new-product acceptance, determine sales territory assignments, develop projections of future sales volume trends, and so forth.

While each of these three systems has distinguishing characteristics, in practice the differences are a matter of degree. They basically differ in terms of flexibility, analytical capabilities, and ability to answer more complex management questions.

MIS Attributes

The output of an MIS must have certain attributes if it is to be useful for decision-making purposes.[20] These include (1) timeliness—the information must be available when needed; (2) flexibility—the information must be available in varied formats and detail such that the specific information needs of alternative decision situations can be served; (3) inclusiveness—the information must cover the entire range of information needs; (4) accuracy—the accuracy of the information must fit the needs of the decision situation; and (5) convenience—the information must be easily accessible to the decision maker and presented in a clear and usable manner.

MIS Current Status

With growing acceptance of the computer in the business community, its significant achievements in data processing and analysis created a movement which advocated the MIS concept—a total system which encompasses a significant proportion of the information requirements of the decision maker. This excitement was soon dampened by the practical difficulties of implementing such a concept.[21]

Part of the problem with the MIS concept relates to the failure of its

[20] Ibid., pp. 11–13.

[21] Russell L. Ackoff, "Management Misinformation Systems," *Management Science,* vol. 14, no. 4, December 1967; John Dearden, "MIS Is a Mirage," *Harvard Business Review,* vol. 50, no1, pp. 90–99, January-February 1972.

proponents to recognize that the information needs of decision makers are varied, often complicated, and specific to the skills, knowledge, experience, and personality of the decision maker.[22] No simple combination of data inputs and information outputs is going to meet a significant proportion of the decision maker's requirements for information. This becomes more of a problem the higher the decision maker is in the organization.

Several companies are making progress with systems designed to serve the information needs of middle and lower management. This includes systems designed for product managers, sales managers, and advertising managers.[23] At this organizational level, a segment of routine and reasonably standardized information needs can be identified. Product managers need information regarding sales volume and share of market. They need information on promotion, pricing, and distribution efforts for a specific product. Sales managers have specific information needs regarding the allocation of sales personnel to territories and the control of selling activities. Advertising managers need routine information regarding media characteristics, target populations, and the evaluation of advertising expenditures.

The development of systems to meet routine information needs has emphasized the storage and retrieval level and monitoring level of a marketing information system. Despite some pioneering efforts at the analytical system level, limited progress has been reported in management's acceptance of such systems for more complex decision situations. Consequently, while real progress has been made, the idealized MIS concept—which utilizes all three system levels in an integrated total information system for management decision making—has many hurdles to overcome before reaching its final goal.[24] Presently, we appear to be at a more intermediate stage previously defined as the marketing research system (see Chapter 2). The marketing research system includes many of the diverse data sources found in an MIS but does not have the degree of structure and interactive people-machine concepts found in the total MIS concept. The objective of a marketing research system is to become an information center for marketing decision making by using a combination of research approaches and philosophies which fit the special needs of the organization and individual decision makers.

SUMMARY

1   A research design is the basic plan which guides the data collection and analysis phases of the research project. An effective design assures that the information gathered is consistent with the research objectives and that the data collection and analysis phases involve accurate and economical procedures.

[22] Henry Mintzberg, "The Manager's Job: Folklore and Fact," *Harvard Business Review,* vol. 53, no. 4, pp. 49–61, July-August 1975.

[23] Lawrence D. Gibson et al., "An Evolutionary Approach to Marketing Information Systems," *Journal of Marketing,* vol. 37, pp. 2–6, April 1973.

[24] Charles D. Schewe, "Management Information Systems in Marketing—A Promise Not Yet Realized," *Management Informatics,* vol. 3, no. 5, 1974.

2   The research design for exploratory research is best characterized by its lack of structure and its flexibility. The data collection and analysis strategy is one of diversity and searching in new directions until new ideas or better ideas can no longer be discovered.

3   Conclusive research provides information for the evaluation of alternative courses of action. It can be subclassified into descriptive and causal research.

4   Descriptive research characterizes marketing phenomena, determines the association among variables, and predicts future marketing phenomena. It is characterized by a carefully planned and structured research design. A cross-sectional design or survey research design is typically used in descriptive research projects. This design involves taking a sample of population elements at one point in time. The evidence provided by descriptive research can be very useful in evaluating courses of action when combined with the decision maker's implicit model of how the marketing system functions.

5   Causal research is designed to gather evidence regarding cause-and-effect relationships. The appropriate research designs vary substantially in complexity and in the degree of ambiguity present in the evidence regarding causality. With causal research, the research design may directly evaluate the alternative courses of action under consideration.

6   Performance-monitoring research provides evidence regarding the monitoring of the marketing system. It can involve either an ad hoc study or a continous program of research. Continuous performance monitoring typically requires a longitudinal research design which is often called a panel design. This design consists of taking a fixed sample of population elements which is measured repeatedly. A traditional panel is a fixed sample where the same variables are measured repeatedly. An omnibus panel is a fixed sample of respondents which is measured over a period, but the variables measured are different each time.

7   The basic sources of marketing data are (1) respondents, (2) analogous situations, (3) experiments, and (4) secondary data.

8   There are two main types of data from respondents—those obtained by communication and those obtained by observation. Communication requires the respondent to actively provide data through verbal responses, while observation involves the recording of the respondent's behavior.

9   The study of analogous situations includes the study of case histories and simulations. With the case history approach, there is an intensive investigation of situations which are relevant to a particular problem setting. With simulation, an analogy or likeness of a real world phenomenon is created. Simulation models can be classified as descriptive, predictive, and prescriptive.

10   Experimentation calls for the organization of data in such a way as to permit relatively unambiguous statements regarding cause-and-effect relationships.

11   Secondary data are data collected for purposes other than the specific research needs at hand. Internal secondary data are those available within the organization, whereas external secondary data are provided by sources outside the organization. The latter can be classified into library sources and syndicated sources.

12   External syndicated data sources are predominantly profit-making organizations that provide standardized data. Such data can be classified into (1) consumer data, (2) retail data, (3) wholesale data, (4) industry data, (5) advertising evaluation data, and (6) media and audience data.

13   A marketing information system is defined as the systematic and continuous gathering, analysis, and reporting of data for decision-making purposes. An organization's accounting system and sales organization are important internal data sources, while syndicated services and library sources are key external data sources for an MIS. The three levels of an MIS are (1) the data storage and retrieval system, (2) the monitoring system, and (3) the analytical system. The output of an MIS should have the attributes of timeliness, flexibility, inclusiveness, accuracy, and convenience. The current status of the MIS is marked by growing acceptance of storage and retrieval systems and monitoring systems but very limited acceptance of the total MIS concept.

DISCUSSION QUESTIONS

1   Discuss the nature and role of research design in marketing research.
2   What type of research design is associated with exploratory research?
3   What is descriptive research?
4   How does the research design in descriptive research differ from that in exploratory research?
5   How does the cross-sectional design differ from the longitudinal design?
6   What role does an implicit causal model play in descriptive research?
7   What are the objectives of performance-monitoring research?
8   What advantages does the longitudinal design offer relative to the cross-sectional design?
9   What problems are associated with longitudinal designs?
10   Discuss the four basic sources of marketing data.
11   What is the primary distinction between qualitative and quantitative research?
12   What are the benefits and limitations of simulation?
13   What is meant by a "syndicated source"?
14   What types of data are available from syndicated data sources?
15   What is the role of a marketing information system within an organization?
16   What attributes should MIS output possess?
17   What is the current state of the MIS concept?

SUGGESTED READING

Churchill, Gilbert A., Jr., *Marketing Research: Methodological Foundations* (Hinsdale, Ill.: Dryden Press, 1976). A leading text on marketing research. Chapters 3 and 4 discuss exploratory, descriptive, and causal research designs, while chap. 5 presents secondary data.

Information for Marketing Management, National Association of Accountants, New York, 1971. This is an excellent study of how organizations use internal and external data for decision making. The focus is on accounting data.

Information Systems for Sales and Marketing Management, The Conference Board, Report No. 591, New York, 1973. This report examines the progress of nearly 200 companies in applying marketing information concepts to the requirements of sales and marketing management.

Kerlinger, Fred N., *Foundations of Behavioral Research,* 2d ed. (New York: Holt, Rinehart, 1973). An advanced text on behavioral research. Part 6 deals with research design.

Schewe, Charles D. (ed.), *Marketing Information Systems: Selected Readings,* American Marketing Association, Chicago, 1976. An excellent collection of articles dealing with conceptual issues, design and implementation issues, and an evaluation of the benefits of the MIS and its future.

APPENDIX: Syndicated Sources of Marketing Data

The purpose of this appendix is to catalog the leading syndicated sources of marketing data. For each service, the name of the sponsoring organization, the name of the service, and a brief abstract are presented. Because of the evolving nature of syndicated data services and the rapid entry and withdrawal of services, omissions and inaccuracies are unavoidable. More detailed and contemporary information regarding a particular service can be obtained by contacting the organization directly. For information on how to contact these data services, consult such publications as the American Marketing Association's *International Directory of Marketing Research Houses and Services* (Greenbook), AMA—New York Chapter, 420 Lexington Ave., New York, NY 10017, or *Bradford's Directory of Marketing Research Agencies and Management Consultants in the U.S. and the World,* P.O. Box 276, Dept. A, Fairfax, VA 22030.

The data services have been classified as follows:

A   Consumer Data: Purchase and Consumption Patterns
B   Consumer Data: Attitudes, Opinions, and Behavior Patterns
C   Retail Data
D   Wholesale Data
E   Industrial Data
F   Advertising Evaluation Data: Broadcast Media
G   Advertising Evaluation Data: Print Media
H   Media and Audience Data: Media-Market Fit
I   Media and Audience Data: Competitive Efforts

A   CONSUMER DATA: PURCHASE AND CONSUMPTION PATTERNS

A.1   Organization: Audits and Surveys Company, Inc.
Service: National Sportsman's Consumer Audit

This is an annual survey which provides data regarding consumer participation in leisure sports and recreation activity, plus buying patterns and brand preferences. The data are cross classified by demographic and media characteristics. The sample size is 5000 and the sampling unit consists of males age 15 years and over. The data are gathered by telephone interviews.

A.2 Organization: The Gallup Organization, Inc.
Service: Gallup Macro-Omnibus

This is a survey conducted annually. Data are gathered on the usage rates of consumer goods and services. The data are cross classified by the demographic and socioeconomic characteristics of the users. The sample is 15,000 households, which allows reliable estimates of "low-incidence" usage segments. The data are gathered by personal interview.

A.3 Organization: Market Research Corporation of America
Service: National Consumer Panel

This panel of households has agreed to use a preprinted diary to record the significant details regarding the purchase of grocery and personal care products—the brand, type, flavor, or variety purchased; the quantities bought; the price paid; the store patronized; and so forth. The panel has a weekly reporting period. Repeated use of the same measuring instrument (diary) allows the collection of data on brand switching and brand loyalty. Extensive demographic and socioeconomic data are available for each household. The sample size is 7500 households.

A.4 Organization: National Purchase Diary Panel, Inc.
Service: National Purchase Diary Panels (NPD)

This panel is composed of 13,000 households, who report monthly. Preprinted diaries are used to record household purchasing activities. The data pertain to products purchased frequently in 50 food and personal care product categories; brand name purchased, data, price, store name, special price offer, and so forth. Extensive socioeconomic and demographic characteristics exist for each household.

A.5 Organization: Trendex, Inc.
Service: Trendex

This survey is conducted quarterly. The data concern the ownership and acquisition of consumer durables and allow the tracking of durable purchasing patterns. The sample size is 15,000 households, which allows reliable estimates of low-purchase-frequency durable goods. Telephone interviews are employed.

B CONSUMER DATA: ATTITUDES, OPINIONS, AND BEHAVIOR PATTERNS

B.1 Organization: Burgoyne, Inc.
Service: Food Shopping Habits Study

This is a survey conducted every two years. The data are attitudes, interests, opinions, and behavior patterns regarding the food-shopping process. The sample size is 2800, and the sampling unit is households. The data are gathered by personal interviews.

B.2   Organization: The Gallup Organization, Inc.
Service: Trends

This is a survey conducted at three-week intervals. The data involve attitudes and opinions on a variety of contemporary topics. Trends are analyzed from questions which are repeatedly asked on each survey. The data can be cross classified with demographic and socioeconomic characteristics. The sample size is 1500 households, and the sampling unit is an adult.

B.3   Organization: Louis Harris and Associates, Inc.
Service: Harris Survey

This is a monthly survey which deals mainly with attitudes and opinions relating to public affairs issues. Occasionally, the survey deals with consumer issues and consumer purchase intentions. The sample size is 1600 adults.

B.4   Organization: Marketing Evaluations, Inc.
Service: SCAN

This survey is conducted quarterly. The data collected include brand awareness, attitudes, and usage rates; purchase histories; and advertising awareness. The sample size is 1500 households, which are interviewed personally.

B.5   Organization: The Roper Organization, Inc.
Service: Roper Reports

This survey is conducted ten times a year, monitoring public opinion and consumer behavior on a broad range of existing and emerging social, political, and economic subjects and issues, as well as the public's interests in and attitudes toward various services, products, and life-styles. The sample size is 2000 men and women, age 18 and up. Personal interviews are conducted.

B.6   Organization: Survey Research Center, The University of Michigan
Service: Survey of Consumer Finances

This survey provides data regarding consumer consumption patterns, attitudes, and intentions as related to housing, automobiles, installment debt, household durable goods, and financial assets and transactions. From these data are developed the "consumer sentiment index" and the reasons for consumers turning either optimistic or pessimistic. The survey involves from 1300 to 1500 households that are interviewed by telephone or personally. The reporting frequency is monthly.

B.7   Organization: Daniel Yankelovich, Inc.
Service: The Yankelovich Monitor

This survey is conducted annually. The data include statistics on 35 social trends which measure the country's mood and outlook on life. Annual changes in these trends are analyzed by demographic and socioeconomic segments. The sample consists of 2500 households, where at least one member of the household has attended college. The data are collected by personal interview.

C RETAIL DATA

C.1 Organization: Audits and Surveys, Inc.
Service: Retail Census of Product Distribution

This study of products and brands is based on personal interviews and inspections conducted in some 40,000 retail outlets. The data focus on the number and kinds of outlets in the United States carrying various product categories and the specific brands in stock. The data are analyzed by city size, geographic region, type of outlet, annual store volume, and chain versus independent. The product categories could include automotive, electrical appliances, household products, food, health and beauty aids, photographic supplies, tobacco, and writing instruments. The reporting frequency is annual, and the study results are projectable to all U.S. retail outlets.

C.2 Organization: Audits and Surveys, Inc.
Service: National Total-Market Audit

This service provides bimonthly retail (consumer) sales, retail distribution, and retailer inventory for product categories such as automotive, electrical, food, tobacco, photographic, health and beauty aids, household products, and writing instruments. The service provides data on market size and market shares; sales by outlet type, region, and size of city; inventory levels and percentage of distribution and out-of-stock situations. Retail stores are the sampling units, and the sample size is 5000. The study results are projectable to all U.S. retail outlets.

C.3 Organization: Audits and Surveys, Inc.
Service: National Restaurant Market Index

This service provides data on the commercial restaurant market. Trained enumerators personally call on a national probability sample of 6000 restaurants, projectable to all commercial restaurants in the United States. The clients of this service are institutional food product distributors. The service provides data by product category on brand usage, package sizes, and product types. The data are reported separately for five restaurant types, nine geographic regions, and six city sizes or client sales regions. The reporting frequency is annual.

C.4 Organization: Audits and Surveys, Inc.
Service: Selling-Areas Distribution Index

This service is designed to provide companies using SAMI (warehouse withdrawals to food stores—see next section) with measurements of in-store conditions important in evaluating warehouse movement data. For example, the service reports on number of facings, shelf price, promotional activity, and so forth. The sampling units are 2375 supermarkets in all 28 SAMI areas. The reporting frequency is bimonthly.

C.5 Organization: Burgoyne, Inc.
Service: Retail Distribution Systems: Supermarket and
Grocery Store Panels

This service uses a store audit of food and/or drug retail outlets to provide data on the percentage of stores stocking a brand, average number of facings and percentage of total facings, percentage of stores with displays, and average price. The reporting frequency is monthly, and the sample consists of 1300 food and 600 drug outlets.

C.6 Organization: Burgoyne, Inc.
   **Service: Retail Distribution Systems: Warehouse
   Shipment Panel**

This service uses store audits of supermarkets (see previous discussion of Burgoyne's Supermarket and Grocery Store Panels) to collect data on purchases from warehouse invoices (over $20,000 weekly volume). The sample size is 1300, and the reporting frequency is monthly.

C.7 Organization: Ehrhart-Babie Associates, Inc.
   Service: National Retail Tracking Index

This service provides product movement data from retail food stores in any of 70 market areas. The store audit data collection approach is employed, and the sample size is 1741 retail food stores. An additional service, called "Store Audits—Controlled Sales Tests," samples 25 to 175 stores in a test market area and audits the client's product performance.

C.8 Organization: Market Research Corporation of America
   Service: Metropolitan Drug Audit

This service performs a store audit of 1000 drugstores in any of 55 metropolitan areas. The data provided include share of market, price, shelf space, and promotional efforts. The reporting frequency is quarterly.

C.9 Organization: Market Research Corporation of America
   Service: Metropolitan Supermarket Audit

This service involves a store audit of supermarkets with sales over $1 million. The data provided include brand shares, shelf space, percentage distribution, prices, and promotional efforts. The sample size is 2000, and the reporting frequency is quarterly.

C.10 Organization: A. C. Nielsen Company
   Service: Nielsen Retail Index

This service involves a store audit of 1600 supermarkets, 750 drugstores, and 150 mass merchandisers, taken every two weeks. The types of data provided include share of market, prices, displays, inventory, and promotional efforts. Nielsen retail indexes are available for grocery, drug, pharmaceutical, confectionery, liquor, appliance, perfume, and photographic products.

D WHOLESALE DATA

D.1 Organization: A. C. Nielsen Company
   Service: New Product Service

This service audits the warehouse movement of new products through 150 food chains and independent warehouses. The reporting frequency is bimonthly.

D.2 Organization: Pipeline Research, Inc.
   Service: National Drug Warehouse Audit

This service audits the warehouse movement of drug products through 20 drug chains and independent drug wholesalers. The reporting frequency is monthly.

D.3 Organization: Point-of-Sales Research Company
**   Service: Warehouse Withdrawals—Brand Movement**
**   Data Service**

This service audits the warehouse movement of products sold through supermarket warehouses or drug chains in any of 60 cities. The data include case movement, retail sale estimates, market shares, inventories, and promotional activity for over 6000 products. The reporting frequency is monthly.

D.4 Organization: Selling Areas—Marketing, Inc.
**   (subsidiary of Time, Inc.)**
**   Service: SAMI Reports**

This service audits the warehouse movement of products through food chains and independent food wholesalers. The sample size is from 4 to 25 food wholesalers in each of 28 market areas. This represents about 70 percent of national food sales. The data obtained are of interest to manufacturers who sell products through retail food stores. Data are available on brands in each of 425 product categories. This includes data on share of brand and product category sales, sizes, price, new-item introductions, and so forth. The reporting frequency is monthly.

E INDUSTRIAL DATA

E.1 Organization: Dun & Bradstreet, Inc.
**   Service: Dun's Market Identifiers**

This service involves an annual survey of 390,000 Dun & Bradstreet–rated companies. The data include each company's line of business, size, type, and credit rating. An automated data retrieval system allows the analysis of companies, using up to 20 items of information. Regional Dun & Bradstreet offices can generate "prospect lists" using this system.

E.2 Organization: Fortune Magazine
**   Service: Input/Output Matrix**

This service presents in matrix form (input/output matrix) what each industry in the United States sells to and buys from every other industry. It can be used to describe and forecast buying and selling activity. The service is updated every five years based on data derived from the Census of Manufacturers.

E.3 Organization: McGraw-Hill Information Systems
**   Company**
**   Service: Dodge Reports; Dodge Construction**
**   Potentials**

This service collects data from 165,000 building material manufacturers and distributors and from governmental and educational institutions. The data, useful in the marketing of building products, cover public and private contract totals, by type and number of projects, square feet, and dollar value. Possible geographic classifications include counties, metropolitan areas, states, and individual sales territories. The reporting frequency is monthly.

**E.4 Organization: McGraw-Hill Publications Company,
        Department of Economics
        Service: Annual Survey of U.S. Business' Plans for New
        Plants and Equipment**

This service surveys about 900 industrial or commercial companies regarding planned capital investments. Twenty-six major industries are reported for the coming four-year period. The data are collected by mail questionnaire, and the reporting frequency is annual.

**E.5 Organization: R. L. Polk & Company
        Service: Motor Statistics**

This service surveys distributors and state registries regarding their sales reports and registration counts. The data obtained from these records include market shares for new passenger and commercial vehicle sales and registration by state, county, and town.

F ADVERTISING EVALUATION DATA: BROADCAST MEDIA

**F.1 Organization: AdTel, Ltd. (division of Booz, Allen and
        Hamilton, Inc.)
        Service: AdTel**

This service measures the sales response over a period of time that results from alternative television commercials and consumer promotions. A dual-cable CATV system and two balanced consumer purchase diary panels of 1000 households each are used to control for variables other than those being tested. The panel members keep a diary of the products purchased every week. The impact that a particular television commercial had on sales can be determined by comparing panel sales results.

**F.2 Organization: ARS Division, Research Systems, Inc.
        Service: Television Commercial Pretesting**

This service allows the pretesting of in-home television commercials using test commercials via cable television (CATV). From 400 to 600 persons listed in telephone directories are interviewed. A premeasure of brand preference is made before the showing of the test commercial. A postmeasure is taken several days later to determine recall, changes in brand preference, product usage, television viewing patterns, and demographic and socioeconomic characteristics.

**F.3 Organization: Audience Studies/Com. Lab, Inc.
        Service: ASI Tests**

This service is very similar in data collection and reporting procedure to ARS Division, Research Systems, Inc., discussed previously. The sample is composed of 100 subscribers to one of two cable TV systems. The data include the recall of seeing the commercial and unaided recall of copy details.

**F.4 Organization: Burgoyne, Inc.
        Service: PACE (Persuasion and Communication
        Effectiveness)**

This service has shoppers at shopping centers or supermarkets view competing television commercials in a mobile viewing laboratory. The sample size ranges from 100 to 600, depending on the needs of the client's study. The data are gathered on questionnaires and determine the extent to which competing advertisements stimulate buying interest and communicate the copy points.

F.5   Organization: Gallup and Robinson, Inc.
Service: Total Prime Time (TPT)

This service evaluates TV commercials. A sample of 700 men and 700 women, aged 18 or older and living within the Philadelphia area, are interviewed by telephone regarding their viewing patterns for the previous evening. Recall of commercials is probed as to sales points and persuasiveness.

F.6   Organization: Television Testing Company
Service: Commercial Pre-Testing

This service uses about 400 cable TV households to determine a commercial's impact on brand awareness and intention to purchase. The data are collected by telephone interviews.

G   ADVERTISING EVALUATION DATA: PRINT MEDIA

G.1   Organization: Chilton Research Services
Service: Chilton Ad-Chart Services

This service evaluates the effectiveness of advertisements in magazines. The sample includes about 100 subscribers to the publication. A personal interview is used to determine the degree to which they noticed and/or were informed by the advertising or editorial content of the publication. The data are grouped by product category and purchase influence groups. Over 60 publications are evaluated, and the reporting frequency is the same as that of the publication.

G.2   Organization: Gallup and Robinson, Inc.
Service: Magazine Impact

This service evaluates the effectiveness of advertisements in magazines. The sample includes 150 qualified readers. The study method used is personal placement of the publication with the sample and a telephone interview the following day. Three levels of effectiveness are measured: (1) percentage of readers who remembered the ad, (2) sales message recall, and (3) message persuasiveness.

G.3   Organization: Harvey Communication Measurement
Service
Service: The Harvey Communication Measurement
Service

This service evaluates the effectiveness of advertisements in magazines. A sample of 100 readers is interviewed to determine the effectiveness of the advertising and editorial content of the publication. Open-ended questions are used to probe for ideas and impressions about the advertising.

G.4   Organization: Readex, Inc.
Service: Reader Interest Reports

This service determines the extent to which a magazine's subscribers saw and were influenced by the advertising and editorial content. A magazine is mailed to about 100 subscribers and they are asked to draw a line down the middle of those ads or pages of editorial content which interest them.

G.5   Organization: Daniel Starch and Staff, Inc.
Service: Starch Message Report

This service evaluates the effectiveness of advertisements in general magazines, business publications, and newspapers. Sample sizes per issue range from 100 to 150 adult males (aged 18 and over) plus the same number of adult females. A personal interview is used to determine those who remember seeing a particular ad, those who associated the sponsor's name with the ad, and those who read half or more of the copy. The data are reported on a weekly or monthly frequency, depending on the publication.

H   MEDIA AND AUDIENCE DATA: MEDIA-MARKET FIT

H.1   Organization: American Research Bureau, Inc.
Service: ARB Television/Radio Market Reports

This service measures audience viewing patterns and demographic characteristics. Data are provided on each station's share of viewing households and persons listening. The sample ranges from 800 to 2000 per market surveyed. Mailed diaries and questionnaires are employed to collect the data. The reporting frequency is monthly in large markets and quarterly in others.

H.2   Organization: Audit Bureau of Circulation
Service: ABC Audit

This service reports the paid circulation of newspapers and magazines. Audits of the number of home subscriptions and newsstand sales are used to estimate circulation. All U.S. publishers and magazine distributors are included in the sample. The reporting frequency is weekly.

H.3   Organization: Axiom Market Research Bureau, Inc.
(subsidiary of J. W. Thompson)
Service: Target Group Index (TGI)

This service offers multimedia audience measurement. The data include readership measures for about 120 magazines and newspapers, exposure patterns to TV and radio, brand switching/loyalty, usage or ownership of more than 400 products and services, and psychographic, socioeconomic, and demographic characteristics. The sample includes about 20,000 adults, who are interviewed with self-administered questionnaires. The frequency of reporting is annual.

H.4   Organization: A. C. Nielsen Company
Service: Nielsen Television Index

This service provides estimates of the size and nature of the audience for individual television programs. The data are collected by an audimeter device attached to the television receiver. Data are available on the program's audience size and characteristics, viewing habits, switching, and so on. The sample size is over 1000 TV households. The frequency of reporting is both weekly and semiannual.

H.5 Organization: Opinion Research Corporation
Service: Executive Readership Profile

This service provides readership measures for over 35 general and business publications. Data are available on demographic and background characteristics of the respondents. The sample includes 2500 personal interviews with company executives in 500 of the largest manufacturing firms and 50 of the largest service companies. The reporting frequency is quarterly.

H.6 Organization: Opinion Research Corporation
Service: Teen Readership Profile

This service measures the readership patterns of 500 male and female teenagers for about 40 magazines. The data include leisure-time activities and demographic and socioeconomic characteristics. Personal interviews are employed to collect the data, which are reported bimonthly.

H.7 Organization: Rorabaugh, Inc.
Service: Rorabaugh Reports

This service reports the number of television spots by brand or company, within time periods and by copy type. Advertising expenditures are estimated from standard advertising rates. The sample includes 300 U.S. television stations, which are surveyed using a mail questionnaire. The frequency of reporting is quarterly.

H.8 Organization: W. R. Simmons and Associates Research,
Inc.
Service: Simmons Media/Marketing Service

This service reports on media exposure and product-usage behavior. The data include readership and exposure to magazines, newspapers, television, and radio. These data are cross referenced with product usage, demographic, and socioeconomic characteristics. The sample includes 15,000 male and female heads of households. The data are collected through a series of interactions with the respondent, using personal interviews, a self-administered questionnaire, and a personal viewing diary. The reporting frequency is annual.

H.9 Organization: Lee Slurzberg Research, Inc.
Service: National Black Omnibus

This service reports on magazine readership of the U.S. black adult population. The service covers 16 major black magazines and selected general magazines and includes data on demographic and socioeconomic characteristics. The sample size is 1000 black adults in urban areas, who are interviewed personally. The reporting frequency is quarterly.

I MEDIA AND AUDIENCE DATA: COMPETITIVE EFFECTS

I.1 Organization: Advertising Checking Bureau
Service: ACB Newspaper Research Services

This service counts newspaper advertising linage in all U.S. daily and weekly newspapers. Information is provided on publications carrying the ad, name of sponsor, brand name and price, size, and cost of the ad. Advertising agencies, advertisers, and newspaper publishers use this service to determine competitive promotional activity and new-product entry in local print media. The reporting frequency is weekly.

I.2   Organization: Broadcast Advertiser's Reports, Inc.
Service: BAR Network Television and Radio Service, National Spot Television Service

This service monitors national and local television and radio networks by collecting data on television commercials by product category and brand. These data allow advertisers and agencies to monitor whether their commercials were actually aired. The frequency of reporting is weekly or monthly, depending on the type of data required.

I.3   Organization: Leading National Advertisers, Inc.
Service: National Advertising Investments

This service estimates the expenditures on six media types—television networks, local television, magazines, newspaper supplements, network radio, and outdoor advertising. The reporting frequency is semiannual.

I.4   Organization: Media Records, Inc.
Service: Media Records

This service measures newspaper advertising linage and expenditures by advertisers. The data are available by product category, city, and major newspaper. The sample includes nearly all U.S. newspapers and Sunday supplements. The reporting frequency is quarterly and annual.

I.5   Organization: Publishers Information Bureau, Inc.
Service: PIB Reports

This service determines the advertising space size, copy characteristics, and editorial content of over 80 magazines. The data are classified by industry, company, and product. The reporting frequency is monthly.

I.6   Organization: Rome Research, Inc.
Service: The Rome Report of Business Publications Advertising

This service audits over 650 industrial, business, and professional magazines to determine the advertising space and investment of over 40,000 advertisers. The reporting frequency is semiannual.

Chapter 7

Secondary Data

Once the research objectives and information needs have been specified, the researcher turns to the task of formulating the research design and determining the appropriate sources of marketing data. The previous chapter discussed the research design options available to the researcher and presented an overview of the basic sources of marketing data. This chapter continues the discussion by focusing on secondary data and their role in the research process.[1]

ROLE OF SECONDARY DATA

Figure 7-1 presents the initial steps in the research process with an emphasis on the types of data sources available at the data collection stage. All too frequently the beginning researcher assumes that a survey of respondents is the only way to collect the data for a research project. Actually, survey research should be used only if the data cannot be collected using more efficient data sources. The authors of one book emphasize this point by stating that "a good operating rule is to consider a survey akin to surgery—to be used only after other possibilities

[1] The authors wish to acknowledge the valuable assistance of Nancy S. Karp, Librarian, Graduate School of Business Administration, The University of Michigan, in preparing this chapter.

149

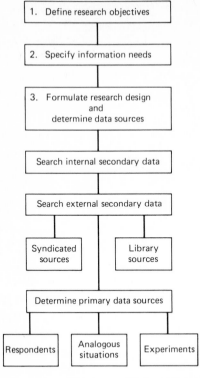

Figure 7-1 Initial steps in the research process.

have been exhausted.''[2] Consequently, the first issue in the data collection stage is to determine whether the data have already been collected.

The data sources available to the marketing researcher can be classified as primary or secondary. *Secondary data* are already published data collected for purposes other than the specific research needs at hand. Such data can be classified as internal or external. *Internal secondary data* are available within the organization (e.g., accounting records and sales reports), whereas *external secondary data* are provided by sources outside the organization (e.g., reports, periodicals, books). *Primary data* are collected specifically for purposes of the research needs at hand. For example, if a retailer collects data from shoppers regarding store image, the resulting data would be primary.

As Figure 7-1 shows, internal secondary data sources should be searched thoroughly before turning to external sources. External secondary data are available from two main sources: (1) syndicated sources and (2) library sources. Syndicated sources, discussed in Chapter 6, are services which collect standardized data to serve the needs of an array of clients. These data are often expensive, and their availability may be restricted to certain clients. Library sources, the focus of this chapter, include an array of publicly circulated publications.

---

[2] Robert Ferber and P. J. Verdoorn, *Research Methods in Economics and Business* (New York: Macmillan, 1962), p. 208.

Once the search of secondary data is completed, the researcher typically will find that primary data must be collected to supplement the secondary data. Rarely will secondary data fulfill the data requirements of a research project. The remaining chapters in this book concentrate on the data collection, analysis, and reporting phases of the research process involving primary data.

It is important that the marketing researcher be familiar with the advantages and disadvantages of secondary data as well as the sources of such data, and these topics will occupy the remainder of this chapter.

Advantages of Secondary Data

The central advantage of secondary data is the saving in cost and time in comparison with primary data sources. Consider the research objective of estimating the market potential for a product. If secondary data are available, the researcher may be able to visit a library, identify the appropriate source, and collect the desired data relating to market potential. This may take a day of the researcher's time and involve minimal cost. Contrast this situation with collecting similar data via a survey. Several weeks or months may be required to design and pretest a questionnaire, train the interviewers, devise a sampling plan, and collect and process the data. In addition, the cost of such a project could involve thousands of dollars. Consequently, it is important to search secondary data sources first before proceeding to primary sources. While it is rare that secondary data completely fulfill the data requirements of a research project, typically they can (1) aid in the formulation of the decision problem, (2) suggest methods and types of data for meeting the information needs, and (3) serve as a source of comparative data by which primary data can be interpreted and evaluated.[3]

Another advantage of secondary data is that it may be beyond the means of the typical organization to collect such data on its own. For example, this would be true of the data collected by the Bureau of the Census.

Disadvantages of Secondary Data

The major disadvantages of secondary data relate to (1) the extent that the data fit the information needs of the project, and (2) the accuracy of the data.

Data Fit Problem   As discussed previously, since secondary data are collected for purposes other than those of the research project at hand, they will rarely completely serve the information needs of the project. The degree of fit can range from completely inadequate to very close. This degree of fit is influenced by three factors: (1) units of measurement, (2) definition of classes, and (3) publication currency.[4]

It is common for the researcher to discover that the secondary data are expressed in units different from those required by the project. For example, a

[3] Jerry E. Drake and Frank J. Millar, *Marketing Research: Intelligence and Management* (Scranton, Pa.: International Textbook Company, 1969), p. 277

[4] Harper W. Boyd, Ralph Westfall, and Stanley F. Stasch, *Marketing Research: Text and Cases,* 4th ed. (Homewood, Ill.: Irwin, 1977), p. 147.

project may require data regarding household income. The researcher may find that income is measured by individual, family, spending unit, or tax return rather than by household. Extreme caution should be exercised in estimating the desired data from measurements in other units.

Another problem relates to the class boundaries used to summarize the data. Assuming the unit of measurement is correct, a researcher could find that household income is composed of $7000 boundaries (0–6999, 7000–13,999, and so on) when the information needs require $5000 boundaries.

The final problem relates to the recency of the data. Marketing decision making typically requires up-to-date information. Many sources of secondary data have long time periods between the collection and publication of the data. For example, government sources, such as census data, can be as much as three years old before they are published. The value of these data for marketing purposes can diminish rapidly with time.

Accuracy Problem   The researcher must determine whether the secondary data are accurate enough for purposes of the research project at hand. A serious limitation of secondary data is the difficulty of evaluating their accuracy. There are a number of sources of error in the sampling, data collection, analysis, and reporting stages of the research process that influence the accuracy of the data. These sources of error can be more easily evaluated when the researcher directly participates in the research process, as is the situation with primary research. The lack of participation in the research process in no way reduces the responsibility of the researcher to evaluate the accuracy of the data used. The following criteria can be used in the difficult task of assessing the accuracy of secondary data: (1) source, (2) purpose of the publication, and (3) evidence regarding quality.[5]

The source of the data is very important in evaluating its accuracy. Secondary data may be secured from an original source or an acquired source. An *original source* is the source that originated the data, while an *acquired source* is a source which procured the data from an original source. The *Statistical Abstract of the United States* is an example of an acquired source. All the data in the *Statistical Abstract* are taken from other government and trade sources. A fundamental rule in using secondary data is to secure data directly from the original source rather than using acquired sources. The reasons for this rule are two. First, the original source is in most cases the only place where the details of the data collection and analysis process are described. Knowledge of the research process is essential in evaluating the accuracy of the data. Second, the original source is generally more detailed and accurate than the acquired source. Errors in transcription and failure to reproduce footnotes and other textual comments can seriously influence the accuracy of the data.

Evaluation of the purpose of a publication is the second criterion for determining the accuracy of secondary data.

---

[5] This discussion follows that of Gilbert A. Churchill, Jr., *Marketing Research: Methodological Foundations* (New York: Dryden Press, 1976), pp. 129–31.

Sources published to promote sales, to advance the interests of an industrial or commercial or other group, to present the cause of a political party, or to carry on any sort of propaganda, are suspect. Data published anonymously, or by an organization which is on the defensive, or under conditions which suggest a controversy, or in a form which reveals a strained attempt at "frankness," or to controvert inferences from other data, are generally suspect.[6]

The above statement should not be interpreted to mean that data from such sources are useless. On the contrary, valuable information can be identified. However, the researcher needs to be sensitive to the purpose of the publication and more cautious in evaluating the data to detect those who would misrepresent and distort statistics to support a position or belief.

The third criterion for evaluating the accuracy of secondary data is to assess the general evidence regarding the quality of the data. If the primary source does not disclose details of the research design, be very cautious. This frequently suggests that the supplying organization has something to conceal. When the details of the research design are disclosed, the researcher should evaluate areas such as (1) sampling plan, (2) data collection procedure, (3) quality of field training, (4) questionnaire technique, and (5) data analysis procedures. A section discussing the limitations of the research design and data should be included. When limited information is available regarding the research design, the researcher can still evaluate the quality of the reporting of the data. Important here are items such as the labeling of tables and figures, the internal consistency of the data, and whether the data support the conclusions drawn in the report.

LIBRARY SOURCES OF SECONDARY DATA

Library sources of marketing data include an array of publicly circulated material, e.g., government documents, periodicals, books, research reports, and trade association publications. What types of research objectives and information needs might call for secondary data? Some examples would be: (1) to estimate the total market potential for corrugated and solid fiber boxes in a given area; (2) to develop a method for establishing sales quotas for television sets by states; (3) to establish national, state, and county sales quotas and a method for estimating the potential market for battery replacements for automobiles; (4) to determine the market potential for industrial lubricants in Cook County, Illinois; (5) to predict the potential market for paper and allied products to merchant wholesalers and the retail trades to 1980; (6) to estimate the market for clothes-washing machines and dryers, dishwashers, and television sets in the Fort Wayne, Indiana, Standard Metropolitan Statistical Area, which consists of Allen County; (7) to select a county in the Syracuse, New York, Standard Metropolitan Statistical Area to locate new supermarkets (the area is composed of Madison, Onondaga, and Oswego counties); and (8) to disperse an advertising budget in proportion to the potential markets, by states, in the South Atlantic region.

[6] Erwin Esser Nemmers and John H. Myers, *Business Research: Text and Cases* (New York: McGraw-Hill, 1966), p. 43.

Secondary data can be used to meet the information needs represented by the above research objectives. The following types of secondary data would be appropriate: (1) employment data, (2) population data, (3) radio and television sales, (4) number of households with television, (5) family median income, (6) aggregate income of the population, (7) occupied housing units, (8) automobile registration, (9) housing units without automobiles, (10) grocery store sales, (11) value of box shipments by end use, and (12) employment by industry group. These types of data are available from library sources.

Government Data Sources

The largest single source of statistical data is the United States government. For years, marketing researchers have relied on this source of data for developing market potentials and sales forecasts, determining sales territories and sales quotas, and locating retail, wholesale, and manufacturing establishments. As the breadth and depth of government data have increased over the years, the relevance of this source of data to marketing information needs has increased dramatically. Consequently, effective marketing research requires a thorough knowledge of government data.

Census Data   Within the federal government, the Bureau of the Census is the leading source of data relevant to marketing. Its vast resources and years of experience combine to give census data a high reputation for quality. The data are generally detailed enough for most marketing information needs. They are reasonably priced and accessible in printed form or on computer tape. The Census Bureau will do individualized computer runs for those willing to pay a small fee.

The available census data are summarized in Table 7-1. Note that some census items are collected through the use of samples. Many census data can

Table 7-1 Subject Items Included in the 1970 Census

	Population items	Housing items
	Complete-count data items (shown for all census areas including city blocks)	
100 percent	Relationship to head of household	Number of units at this address
	Color or race	Telephone
	Age	Private entrance to living quarters
	Sex	Complete kitchen facilities
	Marital status	Rooms
		Water supply
		Flush toilet
		Bathtub or shower
		Basement
		Tenure (owner/renter)
		Commercial establishment on property
		Value
		Contract rent
		Vacancy status
		Months vacant

Table 7-1   Subjects Items Included in the 1970 Census (*Continued*)

	Population items	Housing items
	Sample data items (Not shown in some reports, e.g., *Block Statistics;* summaries are subject to sampling variability)	

20 percent	State or country of birth
	Years of school completed
	Number of children ever born
	Employment status
	Hours worked last week
	Weeks worked in 1969
	Last year in which worked
	Occupation, industry, and
	  class of worker
	Activity 5 years ago
	Income in 1969 by type
		Components of gross rent
		Heating equipment
		Year structure built
		Number of units in structure and
		  whether a trailer
		Farm residence

15 percent	Country of birth of parents Mother tongue Year moved into this house Place of residence 5 years ago School or college enrollment (public or private) Veteran status Place of work Means of transportation to work	Source of water Sewage disposal Bathrooms Air conditioning Automobiles
5 percent (These variables not in *Census Tracts* reports)	Mexican or Spanish origin or descent Citizenship Year of immigration When married Vocational training completed Presence and duration of disability Occupation—industry 5 years ago	Stories, elevator in structure Fuel—heating, cooking, water heating Bedrooms Clothes washing machine Clothes dryer Dishwasher Home food freezer Television Radio Second home
	Derived variables (illustrative examples)	
	Families Family type and size Poverty status Spanish surname Spanish heritage Population density Size of place Foreign stock	Persons per room ("crowding") Household size Plumbing facilities Institutions and other group quarters Gross rent

Source: A Student's Workbook on the 1970 Census, U.S. Department of Commerce, Bureau of the Census, 1975, p. 6.

be very useful to marketers; examples are demographic profiles, housing patterns, and appliance ownership.

The census data are available at many different levels, ranging all the way

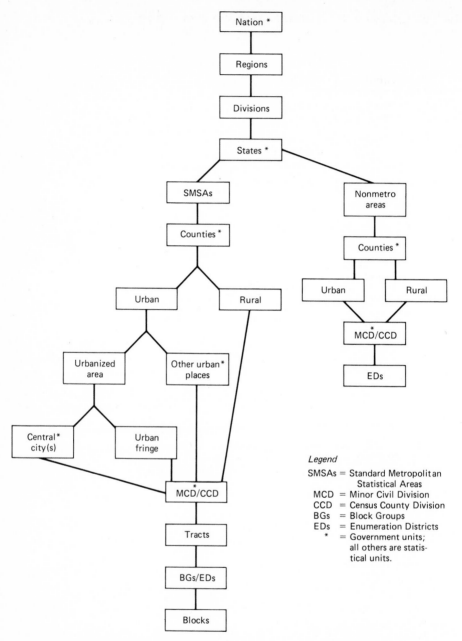

Figure 7-2 Census bureau geographic units and their hierarchical relationships. (*Source:* Teacher's Guide: Approaches to Census Data, *U.S. Bureau of the Census, 1977, p. 16.*)

from the nation as a whole down to city blocks. Figure 7-2 shows the hierarchical relationships among the geographic units used by the Census Bureau. Most census data are published only down to the "tract" level. Some of the levels are governmental units—states, counties, etc.—while others are just statistical units used by the Census Bureau—divisions, standard metropolitan statistical areas (SMSAs), etc. Table 7-2 presents definitions of the geographic units presented in Figure 7-2.

Table 7-2   Definitions of Geographic Units Used by the Census Bureau

Nation:	The U.S. as a whole.
Region:	The U.S. is divided in four regions as follows:
	West: Wash., Oreg., Calif., Mont., Idaho, Nev., Utah, Ariz., N.Mex., Colo., Wyo., Alaska, Hawaii
	South: Tex., Okla., Ark., La., Miss., Ala., Ga., Fla., S.C., N.C., Tenn., Ky., W. Va., Va., Md., Del., D.C.
	Northeast: Pa., N.J., N.Y., Conn., R.I., Mass., Vt., N.H., Maine
	North Central: Ill., Ind., Ohio, Mich., Wisc., Minn., Iowa, Mo., Kan., Nebr., S.D., N.D.
Divisions:	The regions are divided into a total of nine geographic divisions, each of which is composed of a specific group of contiguous states as follows:
	Pacific: Wash., Oreg., Calif., Alaska, Hawaii
	Mountain: Mont., Idaho, Utah, Nev., Ariz., N.Mex., Colo., Wyo.
	West South Central: Tex., Okla., Ark., La.
	East South Central: Miss., Ala., Tenn., Ky.
	South Atlantic: Fla., Ga., S.C., N.C., W. Va., Va., Md., Del., D.C.
	Middle Atlantic: Pa., N.J., N.Y.
	New England: Conn., R.I., Mass., Vt., N.H., Maine
	East North Central: Ill., Ind., Ohio, Mich., Wisc.
	West North Central: Minn., Iowa, Mo., Kans., Nebr., S.D., N.D.
States:	The states of the union.
SMSAs:	A county or group of contiguous counties which contain at least one city of 50,000 inhabitants or more, or twin cities with a combined population of 50,000 or more, the smaller of which must have a population of at least 15,000. At least 75 percent of the labor force of the county must be in the nonagricultural labor force. (There are some other technical distinctions that are omitted here.) There are 243 SMSAs in the U.S.
Counties:	The primary divisions of a state as defined by state law (called parishes in Louisiana; there are none in Alaska).
Urban:	The part of a county containing cities and towns of 2500 population or more.
Rural:	The complement of the urban population, containing farm and nonfarm components.
Urbanized Areas:	A central city of 50,000 or more, or twin cities of 50,000 or more, with the smallest having 15,000 people or more, plus the surrounding urban buildup or fringe (suburbs).
Other Urban Places:	Urban areas not qualifying as urbanized areas; i.e., places of over 2500 but less than 50,000.
Central City:	The area designated by the title of the urbanized area; e.g., Boston does not include Cambridge, etc.
Urban Fringes:	Suburbs of central cities.
MCDs:	Minor civil divisions are component parts of counties representing political or administrative subdivisions called townships, districts, precincts, etc.
CCDs:	Census county divisions were formed by the Census Bureau in 21 states for the purpose of dividing counties into statistical areas; they are used instead of townships, etc.

Table 7-2   Definitions of Geographic Units by the Census Bureau (*Continued*)

Tracts:	Small areas into which large cities and their adjacent areas have been divided for statistical purposes.
BGs:	A subdivision of a tract made up of a number of city blocks.
EDs:	A subdivision of a tract or county MCD/CCD for the purpose of assignment to enumerators for collecting questionnaires; no standard printed reports are available at this level.
Blocks:	The smallest area for which data is available; it is usually a well-defined rectangular piece of land bounded by streets or roads.
Nonmetro Areas:	The parts of a state not included in an SMSA.
Unincorpo-rated Places:	A concentration of population of at least 1,000 which is not legally a city.

Figure 7-3 further illustrates the type of geographic units used. This figure presents the geographic subdivision of an SMSA all the way down to a city block. Clearly, many detailed data of relevance to marketers are available in the census reports.

Census data are not without defects. As with all secondary data, they have the limitation of not being collected for the specific information needs of a marketing research project. At times, definitions have been changed from census to census. Even within a census, definitions can have different meanings. For the researcher who is not familiar with the details of census data, it can be very useful to seek the advice of a professional in this area regarding the specifics of how the data are to be used. Numerous publications, workshops, and conferences sponsored by the U.S. Department of Commerce and the Bureau of the Census are designed to aid the user of census data.

Standard Industrial Classification   Many sources of marketing data are classified according to the Standard Industrial Classification Code, or *SIC Code*. This system of classification was developed by the federal government in connection with taking its Census of Manufacturers. The classification system is based on the products produced or operations performed. The SIC Code classifies all manufacturing into 20 major industry groups, each having a two-digit code (e.g., 25 is Furniture and Fixtures). Each major industry group is further classified into approximately 150 industry groups identified with a three-digit code (e.g., 252 is Office Furniture). Each industry group is further classified into approximately 450 product categories designated by a four-digit code (e.g., 2522 is Metal Office Furniture). This kind of hierarchical system is also used to classify other areas of the economy. For detailed information on how to use the SIC Code, see the *Standard Industrial Classification Manual*.

In addition to government publications, there are a large number of others which contain data applicable to a wide number of research objectives. The task of identifying relevant sources of data can be a difficult one for researchers who are not familiar with the area under investigation. Fortunately, there are many

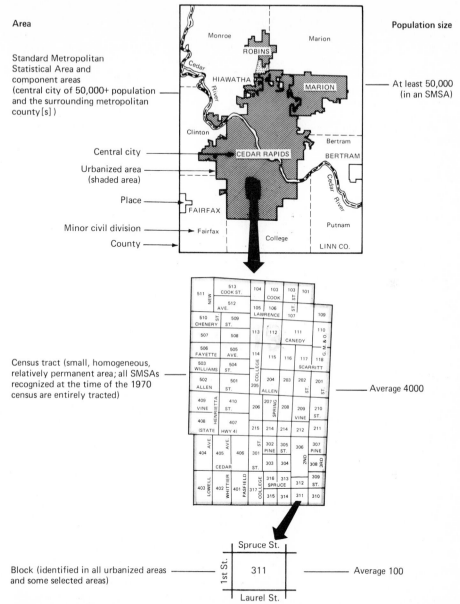

Figure 7-3 Geographic subdivisions of an SMSA. (*Source:* A Student's Workbook on the 1970 Census, *U.S. Bureau of the Census, 1975, p. 8.*)

published guides and indexes to assist them in this pursuit. In addition to published guides and indexes, researchers will find that a competent reference librarian is a valuable source of assistance in identifying relevant sources of data.

In evaluating the quality of the data identified, the researcher must be sensitive to the origin of the data and the research design. At times, this may be difficult to determine. Library data originate from an array of sources such as federal, state, and local governments, colleges and universities, trade associations, chambers of commerce, commercial organizations, foundations, and publishing companies. Some publications mainly present the results of original research, some summarize the research findings of others, and some mainly present interpretations and conclusions regarding the research findings of others.

The appendix to this chapter presents a listing of the main guides and indexes to marketing data, as well as the more predominant sources of marketing data.

SUMMARY

1   Sources of marketing data can be classified as primary or secondary. Secondary data are defined as data collected for purposes other than the specific research needs at hand. Primary data are defined as data collected specifically for purposes of the research needs at hand.

2   Secondary data can be subclassified as internal or external. Internal secondary data are those available within the organization, while external secondary data are those provided by sources outside the organization.

3   External secondary data are available from syndicated and library sources. Syndicated sources refer to data services that collect standardized data to serve the needs of many clients. Library sources include an array of publicly circulated publications.

4   The first phase of the data collection stage of the research process involves a search of internal and external secondary data sources. Primary data sources should be employed after it is determined that the data are not available from secondary data sources. Rarely will secondary data completely meet the data requirements of a research project.

5   The advantages of secondary data are their lower cost and fast retrieval compared with primary data. Additionally, the data may be beyond the means of the organization to collect using primary data research methods.

6   The disadvantages of secondary data are related to the accuracy of the data and the degree of fit between the data and the information needs of the project. The accuracy of secondary data can be evaluated in terms of the (1) source, (2) purpose of the publication, and (3) evidence regarding quality.

DISCUSSION QUESTIONS

1   What is the role of secondary data in the research process?
2   What are the advantages of secondary data relative to primary data?
3   Discuss the shortcomings of secondary data.
4   Suggest some examples of census data useful to marketers.
5   Indicate the main components of the hierarchy of geographic units in descending order of level of aggregation.

SUGGESTED READING

Britt, Stewart H., and Irwin Shapiro, "Where to Find Marketing Facts," *Harvard Business Review,* September-October 1962, pp. 44–52. An extended discussion of how to locate data.

Eckler, Ross A., *The Bureau of the Census* (New York: Praeger, 1972), pp. 93, 122–125, 208, and elsewhere. Discusses the many ways to use census data in marketing research.

Johnson, Barbara, "Census Data: How to Use a Basic, But Often Overlooked, Market Planning Tool," *Industrial Marketing,* April 1972, pp. 24–26. Explains how to use census data in industrial market planning.

Wasson, Chester R., "Use and Appraisal of Existing Information," in Robert Ferber (ed.), *Handbook of Marketing Research* (New York: McGraw-Hill, 1974), pp. 2-11 to 2-25. Interesting discussion on how to use secondary data.

APPENDIX: Library Sources of Marketing Data

The purpose of this appendix is to catalog the predominant library sources of marketing data and to identify the main guides and indexes to marketing data. For each listing, the name of the publication, the publisher, and a brief abstract is presented. Because of the ever-changing nature of library data sources, omissions and inaccuracies are unavoidable. More contemporary information regarding a particular data source can be obtained from a reference librarian.

GUIDES TO BUSINESS LITERATURE SOURCES

Bibliography of Publications of University Bureaus of Business and Economic Research (Denver: Business Research Division, University of Colorado, for the Association for University Business and Economic Research). Annual. Books, working papers, periodical articles, monographs, and other publications are indexed by author, subject, and institution.

Business Information Sources, Lorna M. Daniells, comp. (Berkeley: University of California Press and Paris: Center for Business Information, 1976). Excellent bibliography of reference tools in business and economics. Valuable to the marketer for its coverage of statistics sources and its section on market research sources.

Dissertation Abstracts International (Ann Arbor, Mich.: Xerox University Microfilms, since 1952). Monthly. Includes title key-word and author indexes. The Humanities and Social Science section includes sections on marketing, business administration, banking, and other topics. This source abstracts doctoral dissertations of over 350 institutions.

GUIDES TO MARKETING SOURCES

American Marketing Association Bibliography Series (Chicago). Issued periodically. Contains a series of annotated bibliographies with emphasis on books and periodicals. Each covers a particular topic in some depth.

Data Sources for Business and Market Analysis, Nathalie D. Frank, comp., 2d ed. (Metuchen, N.J.: Scarecrow Press, 1969). Annotated bibliography, arranged by type of source (e.g., research services for marketing, advertising media, government sources) rather than by subject. Emphasis is on original source of data.

Encyclopedia of Business Information Sources (Detroit: Gale Research Company, 1976). Arranged by subject, this work lists periodicals, statistics sources, directories, bibliographies, general works, and other sources.

How to Use the Business Library, With Sources of Business Information, H. Webster Johnson, 4th ed. (Cincinnati, Ohio: South-Western Publishing Company, 1972). A compact guide to materials usually available in a typical business library. Each of 15 chapters deals with a different type of source, such as business directories, business economic services, and financial services.

Journal of Marketing (Chicago). "Marketing Abstracts" section, each issue. Published quarterly by the American Marketing Association. Contains an annotated bibliography of articles published within the last year in major business, economic, and social science periodicals.

Marketing Information Guide (Garden City, N.Y.: The Trade Marketing Information Guide). Monthly. Contains an annotated bibliography of recently published books, periodical articles, government documents, and pamphlets covering a variety of topics.

INDEXES: GENERAL BUT USEFUL

New York Times Index. Since 1913. Semimonthly, with annual cumulation. Detailed subject index includes very brief summaries of articles.

Public Affairs Information Service Bulletin (New York). Since 1915. Weekly, plus periodic cumulations. A subject index to books, pamphlets, government documents, periodical articles, and other publications dealing with economic and social conditions and public affairs. Includes publications from all English-speaking countries.

Reader's Guide to Periodical Literature (New York: H. W. Wilson). Since 1900. Semimonthly and annually. Contains a subject and author index of over 150 U.S. general periodicals.

Social Sciences Citation Index (Philadelphia: Institute for Scientific Information). Since 1969. Quarterly, with annual cumulations. Indexes all articles in about 1400 social science periodicals and selected articles in about 1200 periodicals of other disciplines. Subjects covered include marketing, economics, management, and other areas. Provides a citation index, author (source) index, and permuterm subject index.

INDEXES: BUSINESS

Business Periodicals Index (New York: H. W. Wilson). Published since 1959. Important subject index to selected periodicals in all major fields of business. Covers over 150 English-language periodicals, primarily U.S. Monthly (except for August), with cumulations quarterly and annual.

Funk and Scott Index of Corporations and Industries (Cleveland, Ohio: Predicasts, Inc.). Weekly, plus quarterly and annual cumulations. Indexes U.S. industry, product, and company information from over 750 business and financial publications. There are two sections: industry/product and company. A similar publication, *F & S International,* deals with international business articles.

Wall Street Journal Index (Princeton, N.J.: Dow Jones Books). Since 1957. Monthly, with annual cumulations. Subject index to the Eastern edition. There are two sections: general news and corporate news.

GUIDES TO STATISTICAL SOURCES

American Statistics Index: A Comprehensive Guide and Index to the Statistical Publications of the U.S. Government (Washington, D.C.: Congressional Information Service). Since 1973. Monthly, plus annual cumulations. Excellent guide to the statistical publications of federal government agencies, Congress, and other programs. A typical abstract includes a complete description of the data given. Material is indexed according to subject, author, title, report number, and demographic or other category.

Bureau of the Census Catalog (Government Printing Office). Quarterly, plus monthly supplements and annual cumulations. A comprehensive annotated guide to Census Bureau publications, including data files and special tabulations. Publications cover agriculture, foreign trade, governments, population, and the economic censuses; retail trade, wholesale trade, selected service industries, construction industries, manufacturers, mineral industries, transportation. The catalog also lists available data files and special tabulations, which contain data not found in printed reports. *Guide to Programs and Publications: Subjects and Areas,* Bureau of the Census (Government Printing Office, 1973). This publication provides an extensive listing of the statistical programs and publications of the Census Bureau by showing the geographic areas and major subjects covered in each. Use the *Bureau of the Census Catalog* to update the information in this source.

Directory of Federal Statistics for Local Areas: A Guide To Sources, Bureau of the Census (Government Printing Office, 1966). A still useful guide to federal statistical sources regarding local areas. Covers such topics as population, finance, income, education, and so forth. Most sources listed are published on a recurrent basis. *Directory of Federal Statistics for States: A Guide to Sources,* Bureau of the Census (Government Printing Office, 1967). A guide to federal statistical sources regarding states; similar to the guide for local sources.

Directory of Nonfederal Statistics for State and Local Areas: A Guide to Sources, Bureau of the Census (Government Printing Office, 1969). A guide to statistical data collected by state government agencies, universities, and private organizations. Covers such topics as economic, social, and political data regarding state and local areas. Lists primarily recurrent publications.

Guide to Foreign Trade Statistics, Bureau of the Census (Government Printing Office). Issued periodically. A guide to foreign trade statistics. Description of Census Bureau publications dealing with foreign trade.

Measuring Markets: A Guide to the Use of Federal and State Statistical Data, Department of Commerce (Government Printing Office, 1974). This publication lists and describes federal and state publications, providing statistics useful in consumer market research. Areas covered include population, income, employment, taxes, and sales. Case studies illustrate the use of these data in marketing situations.

Statistical Services of the U.S. Government, Office of Management and Budget (Government Printing Office, rev. ed., 1975). Part I presents the federal statistical system; Part II presents an overview of the economic and social statistical series; and Part III presents the main statistical publications of the government agencies.

Statistics Sources, Paul Wasserman et al., 5th ed. (Detroit: Gale Research Company, 1977). A subject guide to business, industrial, financial, social, and other topics. Detailed subheadings are used under each subject.

GENERAL SOURCES OF STATISTICS

Business Conditions Digest, Bureau of Economic Analysis, Department of Commerce (Government Printing Office). Monthly. This publication contains numerous indicators of current business activity in chart and table form. Researchers find this data useful for developing and updating industry and company forecasts.

Economic Indicators, Council of Economic Advisers (Government Printing Office). Monthly. Presents current statistical series considered to be key indicators of general business conditions. These include gross national product, personal consumption expenditures, and so forth. Researchers find this document useful in developing and updating industry and company forecasts.

Economic Report of the President (Government Printing Office). Annual. This publication documents the President's annual address to Congress regarding the economic condition of the United States. The annual report of the Council of Economic Advisers is included; it reviews economic policy and outlook. Included are statistical series from other documents published by the government dealing with numerous economic indicators.

Federal Reserve Bulletin (Washington, D.C.: Federal Reserve System Board of Governors). This monthly publication contains current financial data on banking activity, savings, interest rates, credit, and domestic nonfinancial statistics; an index of industrial production; and some statistics on international trade and finance.

Handbook of Basic Economic Statistics (Economic Statistics Bureau of Washington, D.C.) Annual, plus monthly supplements. This publication is a compilation of statistics collected by federal government agencies dealing with all areas of the national economy. Complete historical data given for each statistical series.

Historical Statistics of the United States, Colonial Times to 1970, Bureau of the Census (Government Printing Office). This publication is a historical supplement to the *Statistical Abstract.* The comparison of historical data from the *Statistical Abstract* is difficult because of the changes in data classifications and definitions at various points in time. *Historical Statistics* presents these data comparisons using consistent classifications and definitions for all data in the statistical series. Over 12,500 different time series are presented in this document.

Monthly Labor Review, Bureau of Labor Statistics (Government Printing Office). Monthly. This publication presents current data and related articles on employment, earnings, wholesale and retail prices, and so forth.

Predicasts (Cleveland, Ohio: Predicasts, Inc.). An abstract service giving quarterly reviews of 1000 trade journals, business and financial publications, major newspapers, and others. The available information includes abstracts of forecasts and market data condensed to one line. Coverage includes products, industries, and the economy. A related service is Predi-Briefs, a monthly series of abstract listings organized into 34 different fields cataloged by product, country of origin, and type of information.

Statistical Abstract of the United States, Bureau of the Census (Government Printing Office). Annual. The purpose of this valuable publication is to serve as a basic reference for those individuals searching for secondary data. Over 1400 tables presenting social, economic, political, and demographic data appear in this document. These tables serve as an abstract and reference as to data available in other published sources. For many researchers, this publication is the initial reference in their search for external secondary data.

Survey of Current Business, Bureau of Economic Analysis, Department of Commerce (Government Printing Office). Monthly. This important publication provides some 2600 current statistical series covering areas such as indicators of general business, domestic trade, industry statistics, personal consumption expeditures, earnings and employment by industry, and so forth. A historical record of the *Survey of Current Business* is provided twice yearly by *Business Statistics,* Bureau of Economic Analysis, Department of Commerce.

Trade and Securities Statistics (New York: Standard and Poor's Corporation). Monthly, plus cumulations. The publication presents current and historical statistical data covering banking and finance, production and labor, price indexes, income and trade, transportation and communication, and some major industries.

World Almanac and Book of Facts (New York: Newspaper Enterprise Association). Annual. This publication is a handbook of statistics and factual information on a wide variety of subjects, e.g., industry, finance, religion.

Worldcasts (Cleveland, Ohio: Predicasts, Inc.). An abstract service. Two series: World Regional Casts and World Product Casts. Gives quarterly reviews of 800 foreign and domestic journals, bank letters, special studies, and other publications. The available information includes one-line abstracts with subject description (product, country, environmental variables such as population), base period data, short- and long-range forecasts, and a key to indicate source of article. Country summary coverage includes 50 countries, ranging from detailed products to industries and general economics. Product summary volumes contain data for all major countries.

MARKET GUIDES AND DATA

County and City Data Book, Bureau of the Census (Government Printing Office, 1972). This publication contains census data pertaining to counties, SMSAs, and cities. Statistics are provided on population, income, education, employment, housing, retail and wholesale sales, and so forth. The data are compiled from numerous Census Bureau publications.

Market Guide (New York: *Editor and Publisher* magazine). Annual. This publication contains data for 1500 U.S. and Canadian newspaper markets. Data include principal industries, population, transportation facilities, households, banks, retail outlets.

Rand McNally Commercial Atlas and Marketing Guide (Chicago: Rand McNally Company). Annual. This publication contains detailed statistics for counties, cities, standard metropolitan statistical areas (SMSAs), and principal business centers, covering trade, manufacturing, transportation, population, and related data. Each state section includes maps and some business data for counties and cities.

Registration Data. A wide variety of registration data are collected by government. Typically this information is difficult to locate and acquire in a convenient form. Examples of registration data are automobile and boat registrations; licenses for business activities, births, deaths, and marriages; income tax returns; and school enrollments.

Sales and Marketing Management, "Survey of Buying Power" issues (New York: *Sales and Marketing Management* magazine). Annual, Part I: July and Part II: October. This publication contains data on population, effective buying income, and retail sales data for U.S. markets, also comparable data for Canada. Includes tables ranking metropolitan areas and other markets according to population, income, and sales. Gives population, income, and retail sales data for TV markets. Projects data for U.S. and Canadian markets. A separate *Data Service* volume provides additional data. *Sales and Marketing Management* also publishes a "Survey of Industrial Purchasing Power" issue (annual, April).

CONSUMER DATA

Census of Housing, Bureau of the Census (Goverment Printing Office). This census, taken in conjunction with the *Census of Population,* enumerates types of structures, size, year built, occupancy, equipment (such as clothes washers, stoves, and air conditioners), average value, monthly rent, number of persons per room, ethnic category of occupants, and so forth. The 1970 *Census of Housing* provided information by city block for metropolitan areas with populations of 50,000 or more. These data have been found very useful for marketing research purposes. Interim information regarding the percentage distribution of rental and home owner vacancies, general housing characteristics, urban and rural housing data, and other characteristics is furnished by the bureau's *Current Housing Report* series and *Annual Housing Survey.*

Census of Population, Bureau of the Census (Government Printing Office). This census presents population counts by states, counties, standard metropolitan statistical areas (SMSAs), urbanized areas, and census tracts. Census tracts are small, homogeneous, and relatively permanent areas of approximately 4000 in population. The 1970 *Census of Population* identified the population by age, sex, race, national origin, marital status, citizenship, family composition, employment status, income, and other demographic characteristics. The census is taken every 10 years, in the years ending with a zero. Various interim reports are prepared by the Census Bureau. The *Current Population Report* series is a continual updating of population figures. Data are presented on family characteristics, mobility, income, education, population estimates and projections, and other subjects.

Guide to Consumer Markets (New York: Conference Board). Since 1960, annual. Numerous tables and charts provide data on the behavior of consumers in the marketplace. Data appear under the following headings: population, employment, income, expenditures, production and distribution, and prices.

BUSINESS AND INDUSTRY DATA

Agricultural Statistics, Department of Agriculture (Government Printing Office). Annual. This publication presents statistics on prices, production, costs, consumption, and so forth for various agricultural products.

Census of Construction Industries, Bureau of the Census (Government Printing Office). This census is taken every five years, in the years ending with 2 and 7; covers 26 industries. Data include number of establishments, receipts, employment, payments for materials, and other figures. Area statistics reports cover states. Data are arranged according to SIC code numbers. Interim data on housing starts, housing completions, new housing authorized, and other topics are published in the *Current Construction Reports* series.

Census of Manufactures, Bureau of the Census (Government Printing Office). This census is an enumeration of establishments engaged in manufacturing activities. It is taken every five years in the years ending with 2 and 7. Manufacturing establishments are categorized under 450 classes. Statistics are provided on number and size of establishments, capital expenditures, quantity of output, inventories, employment, payroll, and consumption of fuel, materials, and energy. Additional reports cover special subjects, such as concentration ratios and plant and equipment expenditures. Separate state reports provide a geographical approach to the data. Interim reports include the *Annual Survey of Manufactures,* which updates in part the *Census of Manufactures,* and the *Current Industrial Reports,* which contain monthly, quarterly, and annual reports on production, inventories, and orders for commodities. In all three publications, data are arranged by SIC Code number.

Census of Mineral Industries, Bureau of the Census (Government Printing Office). This census is an enumeration of establishments primarily engaged in the extraction of minerals. It is taken every five years, in the years ending with 2 and 7. Statistics are available on some 42 mineral industries regarding such things as number of companies, production, number of employees, capital expenditures, water use, power equipment, and value of shipments. There are also area statistics, covering states. Data are arranged by SIC Code number. *Minerals Yearbook* provides annual data which supplement the *Census of Mineral Industries.*

Census of Retail Trade, Bureau of the Census (Government Printing Office). This publication contains information on 100 kind-of-business classifications. Statistics are available on number of establishments, total sales, sales by merchandise lines, size of firm, employment and payroll for States, SMSAs, counties and cities of 2500 or more. The census is taken every five years in the years ending with 2 and 7, and the data are arranged by SIC code number. An interim publication is the *Monthly Retail Trade.*

Census of Selected Service Industries, Bureau of the Census (Government Printing Office). This publication provides data on more than 150 kind-of-business classifications. Statistics are available on number of establishments, receipts, and payrolls for states, SMSAs, counties, and cities for service organizations such as hotels, barber shops, laundries, and so forth. Data are not available on the professions (with the exception of legal services), nor does the census include the insurance and real estate industries. The census is taken every five years in the years ending with 2 and 7, and the data are arranged by SIC Code number. An interim publication is the *Monthly Selected Service Receipts.*

Census of Transportation, Bureau of the Census (Government Printing Office). This census involves three separate studies—Truck Inventory and Use Survey, National Travel Survey, and Commodity Transportation Survey. The census is authorized every five years, in years ending with 2 and 7.

Census of Wholesale Trade, Bureau of the Census (Government Printing Office). This publication presents data on 118 kind-of-business classifications. Statistics are available on number of establishments, sales, personnel, and payroll for States, SMSAs, and counties. This census is taken every five years in the years ending with 2 and 7, and the data are arranged by SIC Code number. An interim publication is the *Monthly Wholesale Trade: Sales and Inventories.*

Commodity Yearbook (New York: Commodity Research Bureau). Annual. This publication contains data on production, prices, consumption, and import and export flow for approximately 100 individual commodities.

County Business Patterns, Bureau of the Census (Government Printing Office). Annual. This publication presents a county breakdown of business by type, employment, and payroll. The data can be used to develop industrial market potential studies. There is a separate report for each state. Data are arranged by SIC Code number.

Merchandising, "Statistical and Marketing Report" (New York: Billboard Publications). Annual, March issue. Presents tables (some with 10-year figures) and charts covering shipments, sales, product saturation, replacement and trade-in, and import/export figures for home electronics, major appliances, and housewares. "Survey of Consumer Attitudes" semiannual. Presents results from personal interviews regarding such areas as information seeking, discretionary spending, warranties, and so forth. "Statistical and Marketing Forecast" appears annually in the May issue. Presents manufacturer-supplied projections for the coming year regarding unit sales.

Standard and Poor's Industry Surveys (New York: Standard and Poor's Corporation). Updated regularly. Covers 69 major domestic industries, arranged into 36 major industry groups. Text and summary statistics in a basic (annual) and current (quarterly) analysis for each group. Discussion of current situation, recent trends, outlook.

Standard Industrial Classification Manual (1972), Office of Management and Budget (Government Printing Office). This document presents a numerical classification of business establishments according to the product or service involved. Covers all areas of the economy. Widely used by both governmental and private organizations to collect and tabulate data. Commonly known as the *SIC Code.*

Statistics of Income, Internal Revenue Service (Government Printing Office). Annual. This series presents data collected from corporate, proprietorship, and partnership income tax returns and those of individuals. The corporate report presents balance sheet and income statement data broken by industry type, asset size, and so forth. These publications are preceded by a series of preliminary summary reports.

U.S. Industrial Outlook, Domestic and International Business Administration (Government Printing Office). Annual. This publication presents a detailed analysis of about 200 manufacturing and nonmanufacturing industries. For each, information is given on recent developments and outlook. Researchers find this publication useful for forecasting and market planning.

COMPANY DATA AND FACTS: CONSULTANTS AND ASSOCIATIONS

Bradford's Directory of Marketing Research Agencies and Management Consultants in the U.S. and the World (Fairfax, Va.). Biennial. Listings arranged geographically— by state and city, and by foreign country. Each entry describes type of research done. A separate list classifies agencies according to the specific service offered.

Consultants and Consulting Organizations Directory, Paul Wasserman (Detroit: Gale Research Company). 3d ed., 1976. Lists about 5300 firms and individuals, both U.S. and foreign. Each entry briefly describes services and field interest. Includes an index of firms arranged by subject area and state. Updated by semiannual supplements.

Encyclopedia of Associations (Detroit: Gale Research Company). Issued periodically; annually since 1975. 11th ed., 1977. Volume 1, *National Organizations of the United States,* lists active, inactive, and "missing" organizations; each entry briefly describes the organization's activities and lists available publications. Volume 2,

Geographic and Executive Index, and Volume 3, *New Associations and Projects* (issued quarterly). A related publication is the *National Trade and Professional Associations of the United States and Canada and Labor Unions* (Washington, D.C.: Columbia Books, Inc.), annual. Lists associations and publications of associations and has a key-word index.

International Directory of Marketing Research Houses and Services (American Marketing Association, New York Chapter). Alphabetical listing of marketing research houses in the United States and some foreign countries. Each entry describes available services. Firms are also listed by geographic location.

Who's Who in Consulting (Detroit: Gale Research Company, 1973). Biographical information on consultants in a variety of fields. Also an index of consultants arranged by subject area and geographic location.

COMPANY DATA AND FACTS: DIRECTORIES

Directory of Intercorporate Ownership (New York: Simon and Schuster, 1974). Volume 1 lists parent companies; each entry includes divisions, subsidiaries, overseas subsidiaries. Volume 2 is a straight alphabetical listing of all entries in Vol. 1, to aid in identifying parent companies of subsidiaries. This source also lists American companies owned by foreign firms.

Middle Market Directory (New York: Dun & Bradstreet). Annual. Lists over 30,000 companies with a net worth of $500,000 to $999,999. The same data are given as in the directory that follows, except that an officer/directors list is omitted.

Million Dollar Directory (New York: Dun & Bradstreet). Annual. This publication lists over 30,000 companies with a net worth of $1 million or more. This source identifies officers, products, applicable SIC numbers, sales, and number of employees. The companies are also listed geographically and by SIC Code. Includes an alphabetical list of officers and directors, with company affiliation.

Sheldon's Retail Directory of the United States and Canada (New York: Phelon, Sheldon & Marsar, Inc.) Annual. Directory of the largest chain and independent department and specialty stores, arranged by state and city, also by Canadian province and city. Lists merchandise managers and buyers.

Standard and Poor's Register of Corporations, Directors and Executives. Three volumes, annual. Covers U.S., Canadian, and major international corporations, with same information as in the Dun's Directories. A biographical volume provides brief information on 75,000 executives and directors. Companies also arranged in an index volume by state and major city, and by SIC Code number.

State Manufacturing Directories. Directories are published for every state. A typical listing is arranged by geographic location and includes company addresses, officers, products, and related data. A good source of available directories is *Sources of State Information and State Industrial Directories* (Washington, D.C.: Chamber of Commerce of the United States, 1976).

Thomas Register of American Manufacturers and Thomas Register Catalog File (New York: Thomas Publishing Company). Annual. Multivolume source lists companies by specific product or service. A separate alphabetical listing of manufacturers aids in locating small companies. There is also a brand name/trademark index. If the city is known, *telephone directories* provide addresses for companies not listed elsewhere.

COMPANY DATA AND FACTS: FINANCIAL

Company Reports. Company annual reports are useful sources of information. Business
libraries and large public libraries with sizable business collections generally collect
some of these reports, or they can be requested directly from the company. Among
reports filed with the Securities and Exchange Commission, the annual 10-K report
is the most detailed.

Corporation Records. Updated quarterly. Published by Standard and Poor's Corporation,
this is a source of the latest financial statistics on companies. Contains brief background information and news items relating to a company's operation. Updates
material in *Moody's Industrials* and corporation annual reports.

Fortune Double 500 Directory (New York: Time, Inc.). Annual. Published in May–August
issues of *Fortune* magazine. Provides information on sales, assets, profits, and so
forth, for the 1000 largest U.S. corporations, 50 largest banks, and the 50 largest life
insurance, retailing, transportation, utility, and diversified-financial companies. Also
ranks foreign firms and banks.

Moody's Manuals (New York: Moody's Investors Service). Annual, plus weekly or twice
weekly news issues. The six manuals published by Moody's include *Industrial,
OTC Industrial, Municipal and Government, Public Utility, Transportation,* and
Bank and Finance. A typical listing includes location of agency or company, brief
history, description of operation, officers, subsidiaries, detailed current and historical
financial data, securities information. The *Banks and Finance* volume also covers
insurance companies and real estate and investment companies.

ADVERTISING AND PROMOTION DATA

Advertising Age (Chicago: Crain Communications, Inc.). Selected special issues: "U.S.
Agency Billings," annual, February. Covers larger agencies. Each agency profile
lists billings figure, accounts won and lost, billings breakdown by media, gross
income. "International Agency Billings," annual, March. Same data as above are
given, when available. Agencies arranged by country. "100 Leading National Advertisers," annual, August. For each, data on advertising expenditures, sales and
profits, rank of leading product lines and brands, market share, sales, advertising
personnel. "Top 100 Markets," annual, December issue. For each market, discussion
of significant business developments for the last year, the current business climate,
future prospects.

Broadcasting (Washington, D.C.: Broadcasting Publications, Inc.). "Yearbook" issue,
published Spring. Directory of U.S. and Canadian television and radio stations. Also
includes television market data and additional industry-related information.

Journal of Advertising Research (New York: Advertising Research Foundation). Quarterly. This publication presents research studies, literature reviews, and listings.

Standard Directory of Advertisers (Skokie, Ill.: National Register Publishing Co., Inc.).
Annual, plus supplements. Lists U.S. companies doing national or regional advertising. Data include company personnel, name of advertising agency, advertising
budget figures, types of media used. Also a trademark index.

Standard Directory of Advertising Agencies. Issued three times yearly, plus supplements.
Lists agency officers, accounts, and approximate annual billings of about 4400 U.S.
and foreign agencies.

Standard Rate and Data Service, Inc. (Skokie, Ill.). Various titles, many issued monthly. Provides current advertising rates and related data for U.S. radio and TV stations, consumer magazines, business publications, newspapers, other media. Some market data included in the radio, TV, and newspaper volumes. The SRDS is considered the standard source of cost estimation for media planning.

World Advertising Expenditures (New York: Starch INRA Hooper). Biennial. Provides estimates of expenditures in various media categories, arranged by country.

Cases for Part Two

Case 1

Sound Systems Enterprises

Sound Systems Enterprises was a company formed by a group of recent business school graduates. Its objective was to open a retail outlet to sell stereo components in Austin, Texas.

DISCUSSION QUESTIONS

1 What decisions must be made in order to open this retail outlet?
2 What information is needed to make each of these decisions?
3 What marketing research can be used to provide the required information?

Case 2
Twin Pines Golf and Country Club (A)

In mid-May, the Capital Planning Committee of the Twin Pines Golf and Country Club met to discuss a research report that they had just received. This report gave the results of a survey of the club membership on the issue of which capital projects the club should begin this fiscal year. Members of the committee intended to use the report as a basis for selecting among alternative capital projects. A biographical description of the committee members is given in Appendix 1.

Background to the Study

Twin Pines Golf and Country Club was a private club situated in the southwestern corner of Hinsdale, Illinois, a suburb of Chicago. The club was founded in 1936 as an 18-hole golf course and dining room. In 1956, an additional nine holes were built, and in 1969 three outdoor tennis courts were added to the club.

The Capital Planning Committee was a permanent committee of the Twin Pines Club. Its task in recent years involved the overseeing of the maintenance of current facilities. However, in this particular year the Board of Directors of the Club had given an additional task to the committee. They had been asked to make recommendations on new capital facilities. In his letter to the committee, the president of the club stated: "We must be prepared to add new facilities to serve the current and future interests of our members and to attract new members. It is your task to make recommendations in this matter."

In response to this request, the Capital Planning Committee had held a series of meetings where they had discussed possible projects requiring capital expenditures during the next few years. From these meetings they identified five potential projects and the associated capital costs and operating costs per year. These projects were:

	Capital cost	Operating cost per year
An additional nine golf holes complete with automatic watering system on existing lands	$400,000	$45,000
Swimming pool and clubhouse with lockers	80,000	30,000
Tennis clubhouse, court lighting, and bubble cover for winter	120,000	20,000
Three new tennis courts	30,000	10,000
Purchase of 150 acres of land adjacent to club as a buffer against city expansion or for club expansion	300,000	27,000

The committee decided to obtain the opinion of the membership on the five projects before reaching a decision. In December, a research subcommittee was formed which would obtain the views of the membership. It was the expressed intention of the whole committee to recommend the capital project or projects that the membership desired.

The Study

The research subcommittee developed a questionnaire (see Appendix 2) designed to measure the preference of the membership for the five projects. In March, this questionnaire was mailed to all senior and intermediate members of the club. Table 1 shows the number of questionnaires mailed to each class of membership and the associated return rate. The report prepared by the research subcommittee consisted of a set of tables giving what the committee members thought were the main findings of the survey. These are as follows.

Table 1   Questionnaire Returns by Class of Membership

	Number mailed	Number returned	Percent returned
Senior male (club shareholders)	710	540	76
Senior female	650	402	62
Intermediate male (age 21–26)	250	110	44
Intermediate female (age 21–26)	75	32	43
Total	1685	1084	66

Table 2   Project Preference Given Knowledge of the Effect on Annual Fees (Question 4 in the Questionnaire)

Response	Projects					Total responses
	Golf	Swimming pool	Tennis clubhouse	Tennis courts	Land	
Yes	32.5% (352)	37.1% (402)	32.9% (357)	27.4% (297)	23.7% (257)	1665
No	50.6% (549)	59.6% (646)	51.1% (554)	53.6% (581)	60.4% (655)	2985
No opinion	16.9% (183)	3.3% (36)	16.0% (173)	19.0% (206)	15.9% (172)	770
Total respondents	1084	1084	1084	1084	1084	5420

Table 3   Project Preference by Type of Membership (Yes to Question 4 and Categories of Question 1)

Membership type*	Projects					Total responses
	Golf	Swimming pool	Tennis clubhouse	Tennis courts	Land	
Senior male	30.2%[†] (163)	25.9% (140)	27.6% (149)	23.5% (127)	27.2% (147)	726
Senior female	36.4% (146)	38.8% (156)	28.1% (113)	28.7% (115)	19.7% (79)	609
Intermediate male	31.2% (34)	73.6% (81)	67.3% (74)	38.2% (42)	21.4% (24)	255
Intermediate female	29.7% (9)	78.1% (25)	65.6% (21)	40.1% (13)	20.7% (7)	75
Total responses	352	402	357	297	257	1665

*Total response per membership type adds up to more than 100% of the respondents because of multiple responses. Total number of respondents = 1084.
[†]That is, 30.2% of senior male members are in favor of the golf project.

Table 4   Priority Club Should Attach to Projects (Responses to Question 3b)

	High	Medium	Low	No opinion
Additional nine holes	24.7	21.0	45.1	9.2
Swimming pool	28.5	18.7	45.9	6.9
Tennis clubhouse and lights	16.4	16.9	51.2	15.5
Three tennis courts	17.6	15.9	52.0	14.5
Land	19.7	21.4	46.0	12.9

Note: All numbers are percentages by rows. Total number of respondents = 1084.

May 15 Meeting

All members of the Capital Planning Committee were present for the meeting held in the Twin Pines board room on May 15. Mr. John Watts, the committee chairman, opened the meeting by thanking the research subcommittee for their efforts. He also noted that the Board of Directors of the club had asked him to be prepared to make a recommendation concerning capital expenditures at the next board meeting. This meeting was to be held on May 21. Because of this time pressure, it would be necessary for the Capital Planning Committee to reach a decision at the May 15 meeting.

DISCUSSION QUESTIONS

1   What action should the committee take?

2   Why?

Appendix 1   Biographical Description of Capital Planning Committee Members

	Age	Family	Occupation	Club activities
Mr. John B. Watts (Chairman)	62	Married, 2 sons, ages 29 and 27	President, Exeter Tool Company	Golf
Dr. L. Gary Johnston	45	Married, 1 daughter, age 20; 2 sons, ages 17 and 12	Dentist	Golf, tennis
Mr. Joseph R. Taylor	35	Married, 1 son, age 7	Lawyer	Golf
Mr. Robert H. Robertson*	59	Married, 3 daughters, ages 32, 30, and 27	President, Robertson Advertising	Golf
Dr. Malcolm R. Richardson	42	Unmarried	Internal medicine specialist	Golf, tennis
Mr. Kenneth L. Wecker*	69	Widower, 2 daughters, ages 42 and 38	Retired, president of Alpha Associates, Management Consultants	Golf
Dr. W. Lloyd Hains	53	Married, no children	General practitioner	Golf
Mr. Bruce A. Frederick*	46	Married, 1 son, age 16	Sales manager, Beta Electronics	Golf

*Member research subcommittee.

Appendix 2   Questionnaire

1   *Class of Membership*

Please indicate your membership class:

Senior male   ( )
Senior female   ( )
Intermediate male   ( )
Intermediate female   ( )

Appendix 2   Questionnaire (Continued)

2 *Junior members living at home*

Ages of sons	( )	( )	( )	( )	( )
Ages of daughters	( )	( )	( )	( )	( )

3 *Proposed Capital Projects*

Your Capital Planning Committee is presently evaluating a number of possible projects. As part of this evaluation we would like your opinion on the projects listed below:

	Capital cost	Operating cost per year
Nine-hole golf course with automatic watering system	$400,000	$45,000
Swimming pool and clubhouse with lockers	80,000	30,000
Tennis clubhouse, court lighting, and bubble cover for winter	120,000	20,000
Three new tennis courts	30,000	10,000
Purchase of land adjacent (150 acres) to the 16th and 17th holes	300,000	27,000

a What is *your* interest in these projects?

	High	Medium	Low
Additional 9 holes	( )	( )	( )
Swimming pool	( )	( )	( )
Tennis clubhouse and lights	( )	( )	( )
Three tennis courts	( )	( )	( )
Land	( )	( )	( )

b What priority should the club attach to each of these projects?

	High	Medium	Low
Additional 9 holes	( )	( )	( )
Swimming pool	( )	( )	( )
Tennis clubhouse and lights	( )	( )	( )
Three tennis courts	( )	( )	( )
Land	( )	( )	( )

Appendix 2   Questionnaire (*Continued*)

4 *Financing*

Your committee has expressed above the capital and operating costs for each project. Below we have stated these costs in terms of the effect these projects will have on the fees of senior members. Would you be in favor of proceeding with the following projects:

	To finance construction over 10 years	Operating costs	Total	In favor	
				Yes	No
Additional 9 holes	$29	$33	$62	( )	( )
Swimming pool	6	22	28	( )	( )
Tennis clubhouse and lights	9	15	24	( )	( )
Three tennis courts	2	7	9	( )	( )
Land	22	20	42	( )	( )

Part Three

Sampling

Chapter 8

The Basics of Sampling

Without sampling, marketing research as we know it today would not exist. Virtually every marketing research study requires the selection of some kind of sample. When a new product is placed in households for trial, we must select the households to use; when we want to monitor the sales we are experiencing in a geographical area, we must select the stores in the area in which we will record the sales; when we want to conduct a group interview about meat prices, we must select eight to ten people to take part in the group.

The alternative to sampling is to take a census. In a census, we execute our study using *all available elements of a defined population*. Thus, in the examples above, we would use all households for the product placement test, all stores in the area for the sales monitoring, etc.

In this chapter, we shall outline the basic terminology and concepts of sampling and then discuss three types of nonprobability sampling procedures. This chapter lays the basic groundwork necessary for an understanding of the probability sampling procedures that will be discussed in Chapters 9 and 10.

SAMPLING: AN INTRODUCTION

The Benefits of Sampling

Sampling is used very frequently in marketing research because it offers some major benefits over taking a census.

1 *A sample saves money:* The cost of an hour-long in-person interview may be about $20 to $40 per interview. Clearly, we would save money by interviewing 1000 people rather than the 1 million who make up the relevant population.

2 *A sample saves time:* In the above example, we would have 1000 hours of interviewing with a sample versus 1 million hours with a census. To this we must add the time for, say, printing questionnaires, training field interviewers, and preparing the completed questionnaires for data analysis. The problem that led to this study being undertaken is likely to be long forgotten before the census is complete.

3 *A sample may be more accurate:* Surprising as it may seem, this is indeed true. This results from several sources of inaccuracy, called *nonsampling errors,* that occur in the marketing research process. In a census study, we will need more interviewers, more supervisors of interviewers, more people to convert the raw questionnaires to computer input, etc. The smaller the study, the more likely we are to obtain more highly skilled people for each stage of the research process. As the staff gets bigger, the quality of people will fall, and the control and supervision of their activities will become more difficult. Also, a census may take so long that the marketing phenomenon of interest may have changed. For example, questions about the awareness of a new product have meaning only at one point in time. A census awareness level would be biased upward by the passage of time. All of this leads to more errors and less accurate results.

Like a census, a sample includes nonsampling errors too, but to a lesser degree. Unlike a census, a sample also gives us sampling error. This is a statistical concept that will be discussed in detail in Chapter 9. For now, we should just remember that a sample statistic provides an estimate of a population value. To the extent that the two values differ, sampling error has occurred.

Thus, a sample will be more accurate than a census if the total of sampling and nonsampling errors for the sample is less than the nonsampling types of errors for the census.

4 *A sample is better if the study results in the destruction or contamination of the element sampled:* Product usage tests result in the consumption of the product. Clearly, taking a census of Budweiser beer is not the way to run a profitable business. Similarly, interviewing people may sensitize them to the topic of the interview. We can say that they have been "contaminated" with respect to this topic. We may want to interview them again about the same topic to see whether, for example, our advertising campaign has had an impact. We would like to interview people who have not been contaminated by a previous interview. If a census were taken previously, all subjects of interest would have been contaminated.

Some Necessary Sampling Concepts

With the reasons for sampling established, we now turn to the question of how a sample is selected. First we must learn the definition of some basic sampling concepts, that is, the language of sampling. The taxonomy of sampling terms which follows is based on that used by Leslie Kish,[1] as adapted by Earl Babbie.[2]

[1] Leslie Kish, *Survey Sampling* (New York: Wiley, 1965), pp. 6–7.
[2] Earl Babbie, *Survey Research Methods* (Belmont, Calif.: Wadsworth, 1973), pp. 79–82.

Element *An element is the unit about which information is sought.* It provides the basis of the analysis that we will undertake. The most common elements in marketing research sampling are individuals. In other instances, the elements could be products, stores, companies, families, etc. The elements in any specific sample would depend on the objectives of the study.

Population A population is the aggregate of all the elements defined prior to selection of the sample. A properly designated population must be defined in terms of (1) *elements,* (2) *sampling units,* (3) *extent,* and (4) *time.* For example, a survey of consumers might specify the relevant population as:

1 Element: females 18–50
2 Sampling units: females 18–50
3 Extent: Texas
4 Time: from May 1 to June 15, 1979

Alternatively, the population for a study designed to measure buyer reaction to a new industrial chemical might be:

1 Element: chemical engineers
2 Sampling units: companies purchasing over $300,000 of chemicals per year; then chemical engineers
3 Extent: the continental U.S.
4 Time: 1979

Or, if we wished to monitor the sales of a new consumer product, the population might be:

1 Element: our product
2 Sampling units: supermarkets, drugstores, discount stores; then our product
3 Extent: Boston
4 Time: May 5–12, 1979

We cannot overstress how critical it is to define the population to this level of detail; nothing else constitutes proper sampling.

You will note that we have not used the term "universe." A universe is a hypothetical infinite aggregation of elements generated by a theoretical model.[3] The endless tossing of a perfect coin would form such a universe. However, such theory has no place in the world of marketing research sampling. Some authors use the terms "population" and "universe" interchangeably; we will use only "population" in this book.

[3] Ibid., p. 79.

Sampling Unit   Previously, we used the term "sampling unit" in defining a relevant population. It is now time to define it more explicitly. A sampling unit is the element or elements available for selection at some stage of the sampling process. In the most simple type of sampling, single-stage sampling, the sampling units and the elements are the same. For example, in our first population illustration above, both the elements and the sampling units were "females 18–50." This indicates a direct, one-stage sampling process. We would select our sample of females 18–50 directly.

With more complex sampling procedures, different levels of sampling units may be utilized, and then the sampling units and elements differ in all but the last stage. Consider our second illustration above. Our elements of interest are chemical engineers. However, we are reaching these engineers indirectly, through a two-stage process. First, we will select a sample of "companies purchasing over $300,000 of chemicals per year." Then, within these selected companies we will select a sample of chemical engineers. This is a two-stage sampling process. Note that only at the final stage are elements and sampling units identical. Similarly, the third illustration above is also a two-stage process, with the stores constituting the first stage and "our product" the second.

A sampling process may have as many stages as the researcher desires. All he or she must do is specify the sampling unit at each stage. For example, a four-stage sample might be:

Stage 1   Cities over 500,000 population
Stage 2   City blocks
Stage 3   Households
Stage 4   Males 50 and over

The elements of interest in this study would, of course, be "males 50 and over." The terms "primary sampling units," "secondary sampling units," "tertiary sampling units," and "final sampling units" are often used to designate the successive stages of the process.

Sampling Frame   A sampling frame is a list of all the sampling units in the population. The actual sample is drawn from this list. Some of the most creative thinking in a marketing research project may be related to the specification of a sampling frame. A frame may be a class list, a list of registered voters, a telephone book, an employee list, or even a map. In the case of a map we would be sampling pieces of geography. A city block would be an example. The frame list may be printed or stored in a computer file, on tape or disk. Once a population is specified, one then searches for a good sampling frame. Often the availability of a sampling frame defines the population, as no perfect fit is available between population and frame.

Study Population   A study population is the aggregate of elements from which the sample is drawn. Previously, we defined a population as the "aggregate of the elements defined prior to the selection of the sample.'' Unfortunately, practical difficulties arise that cause the actual sample to be drawn from a somewhat different population from the one we defined a priori. What happens is that elements of the population are omitted from the sampling frame. For example, a club membership list may be incomplete, some people have unlisted phone numbers, a map may not include a new street.

The study population, then, is the aggregation of elements from which the sample is actually selected. It is with regard to this study population that we can make proper inferences, even though our real interest is the original population.

The Sampling Process: An Overview

Armed with the sampling concepts we just defined, we can describe in overview the steps in selecting a sample. Figure 8-1 presents this overview.

Step 1   Define the population. This would, of course, include (1) the elements, (2) the sampling units, (3) the extent, and (4) the time.

Step 2   Identify the sampling frame from which the sample will be selected.

Step 3   Decide on a sample size. Here we determine how many elements to include in the sample. Deciding when a sample is too big or too small is a difficult problem. We will discuss this in Chapter 11.

Step 4   Select a specific procedure by which the sample will be determined. Exactly how will the decision be made on which population elements to include in the sample? Much of the rest of this and the next two chapters deals with this issue. (In actuality, Steps 3 and 4 are often done at the same time.)

Step 5   Physically select the sample based upon the procedure previously described in Step 4.

SAMPLING PROCEDURES

There are many different procedures by which researchers may select their samples, but one fundamental concept must be established at the outset—the distinction between (1) a probability sample and (2) a nonprobability sample.

In *probability sampling,* each element of the population has a known chance of being selected for the sample. The sampling is done by mathematical decision rules that leave no discretion to the researcher or field interviewer. Note that we said a ''known chance'' and not an ''equal chance'' of being selected. Equal-chance probability sampling is only a very special case of probability sampling, called *simple random sampling.* What probability sampling allows us to do is calculate the likely extent to which the sample value differs from the population value of interest. This difference is called *sampling error.* We will discuss sampling error in more detail in Chapter 9.

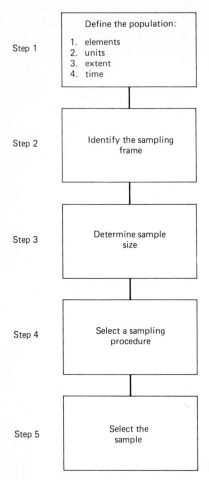

Figure 8-1 Steps in selecting a sample.

In *nonprobability sampling,* the selection of a population element to be part of the sample is based in some part on the judgment of the researcher or field interviewer. There is no known chance of any particular element in the population being selected. We are therefore unable to calculate the sampling error that has occurred. We have absolutely no idea whether or not the sample estimates calculated from a nonprobability sample are accurate or not. We are in the realm of a wish and a prayer.

There are a number of different sampling procedures that fall into the category of nonprobability methods and a number that are probability methods. Figure 8-2 lists them. In the rest of this chapter we will discuss the three kinds of nonprobability samples: convenience, judgment, and quota. Chapter 9 presents a discussion of the most elementary type of probability sampling, simple random sampling. Chapter 10 discusses the more complex probability sampling procedures, stratified and cluster sampling.

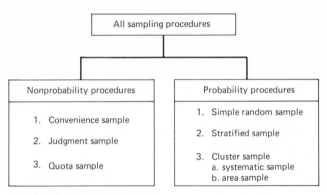

Figure 8-2 Sampling procedures.

Nonprobability Sampling Procedures

Convenience Sampling Convenience samples are selected, as the name implies, on the basis of the convenience of the researcher. Examples here include (1) asking for people to volunteer to test products and then using these people, (2) stopping people in a shopping mall to get their opinion, (3) using student or church groups for conducting an experiment, (4) having "people in the street interviews" by a television station, and so on. In each instance, the sampling unit or element either is self-selected or has been selected because it was easily available. In all cases it is unclear as to what population the actual sample is drawn from. The television interviewer may state that her sample represents the community. Clearly, she is wrong. Most members of the community had no chance of being selected. It is only those who happened to be where the interviewer was at the time of the show who had a chance of being selected. Even the exact chance of these people being selected is unknown.

In such cases, the difference between the population value of interest and the sample value is unknown, in terms of both size and direction. We cannot measure sampling error, and clearly we cannot make any definitive or conclusive statements about the results from such a sample. However, convenience samples can be most easily justified at the exploratory stage of research, as a basis for generating hypotheses, and for conclusive studies where the manager is willing to accept the risk that the study results might have great inaccuracies. Convenience sampling is extensively used in practice.

Judgment Sampling Judgment samples (or purposive samples, as they are also called) are selected on the basis of what *some expert thinks* those particular sampling units or elements will contribute to answering the particular research question at hand. For example, in test marketing, a judgment is made as to which cities would constitute the best ones for testing the marketability of a new product. In industrial marketing research, the decision to interview a purchasing agent about a given product constitutes a judgment sample. He or she must be regarded as a representative of the company by the person who draws the sample.

Other examples could include an instructor's choice of someone to start a class discussion; expert witnesses presenting their views in court; and the selection of stores in an area to try out a new display.

Again, the degree and direction of error are unknown, and definitive statements are not meaningful. However, if the expert's judgment is valid, the sample will be a better one than if a convenience sample were used. Judgment sampling is moderately used in practice.

Quota Sampling   Quota samples are a special type of purposive sample. Here the researcher takes explicit steps to obtain a sample that is similar to the population on some prespecified, "control" characteristics. For example, an interviewer may be instructed to conduct half of the interviews with people 30 years old and over, and half with people under 30. Here, the control characteristic is the age of respondents. Specifying this particular control statement implies, of course, that the researcher knows the population of interest is equally divided among persons 30 years old and over and persons under 30. Obviously this is a simple example, as only one control characteristic was used.

More realistically, in order to be more representative of a population, we would have to "control" on a number of characteristics. Therefore, to properly select a quota sample we must (1) specify a list of relevant control characteristics and (2) know the distribution of these characteristics across our population. Let's look at an example. Suppose we have two control characteristics of interest, age and race, as follows:

1 Age: 2 categories—under 30 and 30 and over
2 Race: 2 categories—white and nonwhite

There are then four sampling cells of interest. They are (1) under 30 and white, (2) 30 and over and white, (3) under 30 and nonwhite, and (4) 30 and over and nonwhite. What we must know is the proportion of the population in each of these cells. This is a much more complex question than just knowing the proportion of the population in a single control characteristic. Note what happens to the number of sampling cells as the number of control characteristics and associated categories increases. Suppose we had four characteristics for control, as follows:

1 Age: 4 categories—(1) under 18, (2) 18–30, (3) 31–50, (4) over 50
2 Race: 3 categories—(1) white, (2) black, (3) other
3 Education: 4 categories—(1) elementary school, (2) high school, (3) college,
                           (4) graduate school
4 Income: 5 categories—(1) under $5000 (2) $5000–$7499, (3) $7500–$9999,
                           (4) $10,000–$14,999, (5) $15,000 and over

This would result in $4 \times 3 \times 4 \times 5 = 240$ sampling cells. We would have to have information on the proportion of the population in each of these 240 cells. Such a description of the particular population that interests us may be extremely difficult or impossible to find. As a matter of fact, often our intent is in measuring the population on these types of characteristics.

However, if up-to-date knowledge of the distribution of the control characteristics is available, we may determine the size of sample to select in each cell. Cell sample size is simply:

Total sample size × proportion desired in the cell

For example, if our total sample is 1200 and the proportion in Cell 1 is .05 (5 percent), the number of people with those characteristics in our sample for Cell 1 would be:

$$1200 \times .05 = 60$$

We would then direct our interviewer to interview 60 people with these characteristics. The same procedure is repeated for all cells. The actual selection of specific sample elements is left to the judgment of the interviewer.

There are some problems with quota samples.

1   The proportion of respondents assigned to each cell must be accurate and up to date. This is often difficult or impossible.

2   The ''proper'' control characteristics must be selected; that is, all characteristics that are related to the measures of interest must be included. For example, if we want to learn people's attitudes toward males having long hair, it would be a mistake not to use age as a control factor, since age is probably related to the attitude toward long hair for males. In any particular study, we may omit a relevant control characteristic and not be aware of it. Consequently, our results can be misleading.

3   The third problem concerns the practical difficulties associated with including more and more control characteristics. As noted before, we end up with too many cells for the interviewers to work with; finding the desired respondents will not be easy.

4   A fourth difficulty concerns the interviewer's selection of the actual respondents to interview. In finding people who fit the desired description, he or she may avoid people who look unfriendly, live in poorly painted houses, live in apartment buildings, etc. An unknown bias is thus introduced into the study. Therefore, a quota sample and population may be exactly the same on measures for which we know the characteristics of both, but differ substantially on measures for which we have only the sample value. Indeed, it is these ''sample only'' measures that are the ones that really interest us to begin with. They are the reason for taking the sample. The sample provides estimates of the unknown population value. If we knew the population value, there would be no reason for sampling. The validity of a quota sample is often presented in terms of the match between known population and sample characteristics. Beware of this. The error in other sample measures is again of unknown size and direction.

Quota samples are useful in preliminary stages of research, and if done with great care they can provide more definitive answers. However, they are likely to be less valid than a probability sample. Quota sampling is very extensively used in practice.

Probability Sampling Procedures

Probability sampling is relatively new in terms of its actual application in marketing research. Before 1950, the nonprobability sample was almost the only kind used in real field studies. Advances in sampling theory and field sampling techniques since then have allowed probability sampling to become a real alternative for marketing researchers.

In probability sampling the chance that a population element will be included in the sample is known, and the sample elements are selected by means of mechanical decision rules. No discretion is left to the researcher or field interviewer in selecting sample elements. There is no guarantee that the results obtained with a probability sample will be more accurate than those obtained with a nonprobability sample; what the former allows the researcher to do is to measure the amount of sampling error likely to occur in his or her sample. This provides a measure of the accuracy of the sample result. With nonprobability sampling no such error measure exists.

We will develop probability sampling concepts in more detail in the next two chapters.

SUMMARY

1 Sampling is an activity carried on in almost all marketing research.

2 The benefits of sampling over a census include saving money, saving time, obtaining more accurate information, and avoiding the destruction or contamination of all the elements in the population.

3 An element is the unit about which information is sought. A population is the aggregate of the elements defined prior to selection of the sample. It is defined in terms of (1) elements, (2) sampling units, (3) extent, and (4) time. A sampling unit is the element or elements available for selection at some stage of the sampling process. A sampling frame is a list of all the sampling units in the population.

4 The steps in the sampling process are: (1) define the population, (2) identify the sampling frame, (3) decide on the sample size, (4) select a specific procedure by which the sample will be determined, and (5) physically draw the sample.

5 In probability sampling each element of the population has a known chance of being selected. In simple random sampling each element has an equal chance of being selected. In nonprobability sampling, the selection of elements is based in some part on the judgment of the researcher.

6 Nonprobability sampling procedures include the use of convenience, judgment, and quota samples. Convenience samples are selected at the convenience of the researcher, judgment samples on the basis of the expert opinion of the researcher, and quota samples on the basis of the distribution of the defined population across control characteristics.

DISCUSSION QUESTIONS

1 Why is sampling so often used in marketing research?
2 Distinguish among the following sampling concepts: element, population, sampling unit, sampling frame, and study population.
3 Distinguish between probability and nonprobability sampling.
4 What is the nature of the error generated by a nonprobability sampling procedure?
5 Distinguish among three types of nonprobability sampling procedures.
6 Why are nonprobability sampling procedures so often used in practice?

SUGGESTED READING

Babbie, Earl, *Survey Research Methods* (Belmont, Calif.: Wadsworth, 1973), chap. 5, pp. 73–81 and 106–110. An advanced but very readable overview of sampling. The emphasis is on verbal description.

Kish, Leslie, *Survey Sampling* (New York: Wiley, Inc., 1965), chap. 1. An advanced discussion of sampling theory.

Slonim, Morris James, *Sampling* (New York: Simon and Schuster, 1960), chaps. 1, 2, and 4. A well-written verbal introduction to sampling. It presents sampling in an intuitive and interesting manner.

Chapter 9

Simple Random Sampling

The previous chapter presented the reader with essential concepts for the understanding of sampling in marketing research and also drew the fundamental distinction between probability and nonprobability sampling procedures. This chapter presents a detailed description of the most elementary type of probability sampling, simple random sampling. Care is taken to present a step-by-step approach, because the principles developed here have direct application to the more frequently used and more complex sampling procedures discussed in Chapter 10. This chapter will also address the issue of the accuracy of sample results. For example, in 1936 a sample of over 2 million persons taken by the *Literary Digest* predicted a victory for Landon over Roosevelt by about 15 percent. "President" Landon must have wondered how the sample could have been so wrong. In contrast, in 1968 George Gallup used a sample of 2000 persons to predict that Richard Nixon would get 43 percent of the vote. In truth, Nixon got 42.9 percent. How can a sample of 2000 persons be more accurate than a sample of 2 million? At the end of this chapter you will understand how.

SIMPLE RANDOM SAMPLING

It is our assumption in writing this chapter that you have had one course in statistics. However, experience tells us that most students have found statistics difficult and welcome a review of basic concepts. Its usefulness to real problems may also have been obscure until now. Our discussion will therefore start with basics, stay at an elementary level, and sacrifice technical elegance for communication purposes. We hope to demonstrate that basic sampling concepts are fundamental to the practice of marketing research.

The discussion that follows is based on classical statistics. There is an alternative type of statistics, called bayesian statistics or decision theory statistics, that can be used in sampling. This approach is more complex and remains for the most part an academic exercise, as most organizations do not use it in practice. The reader is referred to Chapter 27 for the presentation of this material.

Some Terms and Symbols Defined

To begin our discussion of simple random sampling, we must again define some terms.

Parameter   A parameter is a summary description of a measure in the defined population. This is the true value we would obtain if we undertook a census that did not contain any nonsampling errors. The average age of a class in marketing research and the average income of new business school graduates are parameters.

Statistic   A statistic is a summary description of a measure in the selected sample. The sample statistic is used to estimate the population parameter. Thus, the average age of a class in marketing research and the average income of new business school graduates would also be statistics if measured by means of a sample.

Some Symbols to Get Straight   There are certain conventions that are used in sampling and statistics. The following symbols and associated meanings will be used in this book. Basically, Greek letters are used for population parameters and English letters for sample statistics. (See Appendix Table A-7 for a complete listing of the Greek alphabet.) We also distinguish between the symbols for population size, N, and sample size, n.

	Concept	Population symbol	Sample symbol
A. Continuous measures	Mean or average of continuous variable	μ	$\overline{X}$
	Variance of continuous variable	σ^2	s^2
B. Dichotomous or two-answer measures or binomial measures (e.g.: Are you female—yes or no)	Proportion answering "yes"	π	p
	Proportion answering "no"	$(1 - \pi)$	$(1 - p)$ or q
	Variance of proportion	σ^2	s^2

A Population to Examine

Table 9-1 presents a population that we will use to illustrate sampling concepts. This population consists of students who are taking an Introduction to Marketing course from a particular professor. The professor has collected three pieces of information from them:

1 The student number of each student (column 1)
2 The age of each student (column 2)
3 A statement as to whether the student intends to take the course in marketing research before graduation, with answers coded as follows: 1 = yes, the student intends to take marketing research, and 0 = no, the student does not intend to take marketing research (column 3)

The other columns in Table 9-1 will be used in later calculations. The student number will be used only to identify each population element. It is the other two items that interest us from a measurement point of view. We note that age is a continuous variable, and election of marketing research is a dichotomous variable. Let's identify them as follows:

$$\text{Age} = X_1$$
$$\text{Election of marketing research} = X_2$$

Calculation of Population Parameters for Continuous Variables

As a way of clarifying the nature of sample statistics, we will first look at the calculation of parameters taken from a census. Table 9-1 presents a census of the age and the election of a marketing research course as an option of students in an Introduction to Marketing course.

The measure in column 2, age, is a continuous variable. Let's calculate a measure of central tendency and a measure of dispersion for age as follows:

Central tendency: the mean or average $= \mu$
Dispersion: the variance and standard deviation $= \sigma^2$ and σ respectively

Table 9-1 Census of Age and Election of Marketing Research Course as Option of Students

(1) Student number	(2) Age (X_1)	(3) Election of marketing research course 1 = yes, 0 = no (X_2)	(4) $x = X_1 - \mu$	(5) $x^2 = (X_1 - \mu)^2$
1	25	1	1.3	1.69
2	27	0	3.3	10.89
3	29	1	5.3	28.09
4	31	1	7.3	53.29
5	25	0	1.3	1.69
6	29	0	5.3	28.09

Table 9-1 Census of Age and Election of Marketing Research Course as Option of Students (Continued)

(1) Student number	(2) Age (X_1)	(3) Election of marketing research course 1 = yes, 0 = no (X_2)	(4) $x = X_1 - \mu$	(5) $x^2 = (X_1 - \mu)^2$
7	27	0	3.3	10.89
8	24	0	.3	.09
9	27	1	3.3	10.89
10	28	1	4.3	18.49
11	33	0	9.3	86.49
12	29	1	5.3	28.09
13	26	0	2.3	5.29
14	28	0	4.3	18.49
15	28	1	4.3	18.49
16	26	0	2.3	5.29
17	26	1	2.3	5.29
18	36	1	12.3	151.29
19	29	0	4.3	18.49
20	26	0	2.3	5.29
21	21	0	-2.7	7.29
22	19	0	-4.7	22.09
23	24	0	.3	.09
24	22	0	-1.7	2.89
25	20	1	-3.7	13.69
26	22	0	-1.7	2.89
27	19	1	-4.7	22.09
28	20	0	-3.7	13.69
29	19	0	-4.7	22.09
30	24	0	.3	.09
31	25	0	1.3	1.69
32	22	1	-1.7	2.89
33	20	0	-3.7	13.69
34	21	1	-2.7	7.29
35	21	0	-2.7	7.29
36	23	1	-.7	.49
37	21	0	-2.7	7.29
38	23	0	-.7	.49
39	18	0	-5.7	32.49
40	21	1	-2.7	7.29
41	19	0	-4.7	22.09
42	23	0	-.7	.49
43	22	1	-1.7	2.89
44	19	0	-4.7	22.09
45	20	0	-3.7	13.69
46	20	0	-3.7	13.69
47	21	0	-2.7	7.29
48	20	1	-3.7	13.69
49	19	0	-4.7	22.09
50	18	0	-5.7	32.49
	$\Sigma X_1 = 1184$	$\Sigma X_2 = 17$	$\Sigma(X_1 - \mu) = 0$	$\Sigma(X_1 - \mu)^2 = 844.90$

For a population the mean is simply *the sum of the values divided by the number in the population*. Thus

$$\mu = \frac{\sum\limits_{i=1}^{N} X_i}{N}$$

$$= \frac{25 + 27 + \ldots + 18}{50} = \frac{1184}{50}$$

$$= 23.7$$

So the average age in the class is 23.7.

The variance of a population measure is the *sum of the squared deviations about the mean divided by the number in the population*. Thus

$$\sigma^2 = \frac{\sum\limits_{i=1}^{N} (X_i - \mu)^2}{N}$$

Column 4 of Table 9-1 lists the deviations from the mean, and column 5 lists the squares of these deviations. Here

$$\sigma^2 = \frac{(25 - 23.7)^2 + (27 - 23.7)^2 + \ldots + (18 - 23.7)^2}{50}$$

$$= \frac{(1.3)^2 + (3.3)^2 + \ldots + (-5.7)^2}{50}$$

$$= \frac{1.69 + 10.89 + \ldots + 32.49}{50}$$

$$= \frac{844.90}{50}$$

$$= 16.9$$

The standard deviation is *the square root of the variance*:

$$\sigma = \sqrt{16.9}$$
$$= 4.1$$

Calculation of Population Parameters for Dichotomous Variables

Column 3 of Table 9-1 presents the values associated with the dichotomous variable, the election of marketing research as an option. It is dichotomous because only the answers yes or no are allowed. "Yes" is coded 1, and "no" is coded 0 (zero).

In the same way that we calculated the mean, variance, and standard deviation of age, let us now turn to the election of marketing research.

$$\pi = \frac{\sum\limits_{i=1}^{N} X_i}{N}$$

$$= \frac{(1 + 0 + \ldots + 0)}{50}$$

$$= \frac{17}{50}$$

$$= .34, \text{ and } (1 - \pi) = .66$$

The proportion of the population electing marketing research is .34. The variance as before is

$$\sigma^2 = \frac{\sum\limits_{i=1}^{N} (X_i - \pi)^2}{N}$$

$$= \frac{(1 - .34)^2 + (0 - .34)^2 + \ldots + (0 - .34)^2}{50}$$

We note that $(1 - .34)^2$ occurs every time $X_2 = 1$. Thus it occurs .34 of the time. Also we note that $(0 - .34)^2$ occurs every time $X_2 = 0$, or .66 of the time. Thus

$$\sigma^2 = (1 - .34)^2(.34) + (0 - .34)^2(.66)$$
$$= (.66)^2(.34) + (-.34)^2(.66)$$
$$= .2244$$

Then

$$\sigma = \sqrt{.2244}$$
$$= .473$$

The general formula for σ^2 is

$$\sigma^2 = \pi(1 - \pi)$$
$$= (.34)(.66)$$
$$= .2244$$

and

$$\sigma = \sqrt{\pi(1 - \pi)} \qquad\qquad = \sqrt{.2244} = .473$$

What we have done is calculate parameters that describe a known population. Let us now proceed to sample from this population. Our interest in the samples we draw will be to calculate statistics that describe the sample, and to make inferences about how well these statistics estimate the parameters of the population. In the terms of a statistics course, we are interested in both descriptive and inferential statistics respectively.

Calculation of Sample Statistics for Continuous Variables

Earlier we calculated population parameters for the age of students in Table 9-1. Let us now draw a sample from that population and calculate the mean, variance, and standard deviation of the sample. Our method of sampling will be simple random sampling.

There are two conditions that define the existence of simple random sampling. They are: (1) each element has an equal chance of being selected, and (2) each combination of the n sample elements has an equal chance of being selected. Previously we noted only the first condition as defining simple random sampling; this was done to keep the discussion simple. Now we must note that there are other probability sampling procedures in which the elements have an equal chance of selection. However, in all other sampling procedures, constraints are put on the possible combinations of sampling elements such that all combinations of elements are not equally likely. Mechanically, we use a set of random numbers to make the selection. The list of random numbers in Appendix Table A-1, as the name implies, is composed of numbers that have no pattern of occurrence. Any number is as likely to appear in any spot on the table as any other. Each student is identified by a two-digit student number ranging from 01 to 50. Thus, we could use the table to give us a two-digit number between 01 and 50 to select an element for the sample. We would use as many of these two-digit numbers as we wanted elements in the sample.

An example will help make this clear. Suppose we wish to select a sample with $n = 5$. If we start on Appendix Table A-1 (page 634) at an arbitrary point in the 36th row, first column, and move horizontally, we would select a sample consisting of elements numbered 32, 17, 05, 37, and 41. These are the first five two-digit numbers between 01 and 50 that we meet. Our sample values for age and election of marketing research would be:

Student number	Age	Election of marketing research
32	22	1
17	26	1
05	25	0
37	21	0
41	19	0

We have selected a sample of size 5 from a population of size 50. Thus we have selected n/N or 5/50 or 1/10 or .1 of the population elements. We say that the *sampling fraction* is .1.

The sampling fraction can be used to estimate total population usage of a product or service from the total sample usage. Suppose that our sample of five students uses a total of 35 gallons of gasoline a week. Then the estimated total population usage of gasoline would be:

$$\frac{\text{Total sample usage}}{\text{Sampling fraction}} = \frac{35}{.1}$$
$$= 350 \text{ gallons}$$

The mean or average of the sample is simply *the sum of the values divided by the sample size*. Thus

$$\overline{X} = \frac{\sum_{i=1}^{n} X_i}{n}$$
$$= \frac{22 + 26 + 25 + 21 + 19}{5}$$
$$= \frac{113}{5}$$
$$= 22.6$$

Our mean sample statistics value for age is 22.6. We note that this is slightly lower than our true population mean age of 23.7. In most real problems we would not know the true mean age and so would use the sample mean as our best estimate of the true value.

The sample variance is *the sum of squared deviations about the mean divided by the degrees of freedom we have available*.

$$s^2 = \frac{\sum_{i=1}^{n} (X_i - \overline{X})^2}{\text{degrees of freedom (df)}}$$

A sample is capable of allowing us to calculate a number of statistics. The first statistic limits the values that other statistics may take.[1] We say that one degree of freedom was used in calculating the first statistic. More generally, degrees of freedom equals *the number of independent observations on the variables of interest minus the number of statistics calculated*. Or

df = sample size − number of statistics calculated

---

[1] An example might help. If we have two numbers, 2 and 3, we can calculate the mean as 2.5. If someone is told that we have two numbers, that one number is 2, and that the mean of the numbers is 2.5, he or she knows the other number must be 3; it has no freedom to take any value except 3. Thus this sample of $n = 2$ has one degree of freedom ($n − 1$).

In calculating the mean for our sample we used up one degree of freedom, and we must take this into consideration in calculating the variance. Thus, the degrees of freedom for our sample variance are $n - 1$. So

$$
\begin{aligned}
s^2 &= \frac{\sum\limits_{i=1}^{n} (X_i - \overline{X})^2}{n - 1} \\
&= \frac{(22 - 22.6)^2 + (26 - 22.6)^2 + (25 - 22.6)^2 + (21 - 22.6)^2 + (19 - 22.6)^2}{5 - 1} \\
&= \frac{(-.6)^2 + (3.4)^2 + (2.4)^2 + (-1.6)^2 + (3.6)^2}{4} \\
s^2 &= \frac{.36 + 11.56 + 5.76 + 2.56 + 12.96}{4} \\
&= \frac{33.20}{4} \\
&= 8.3
\end{aligned}
$$

Our population variance was 16.9, so our sample has understated it somewhat. Note that if we had divided by n instead of $n - 1$, the variance would have been even smaller. This is generally what happens. Division by n leads to an understatement of the variance.

The standard deviation would be

$$
\begin{aligned}
s &= \sqrt{8.3} \\
&= 2.88
\end{aligned}
$$

We have now calculated descriptive statistics for our continuous variance. Let's look at the numerator of our variance equation. It is

$$
\sum_{i=1}^{n} (X_i - \overline{X})^2
$$

In words, it is the sum of squared deviations about the mean. Or, more simply, we will refer to it as *the sum of squares*, or "SS." We will use this terminology throughout the book. We note, then, that variance is simply

$$
\frac{SS}{df}
$$

Remember this!

We now introduce a simplification of our formula for calculating variance and standard deviation for a continuous variable. This new formula is called the *computational formula* for calculating variance. It is

$$s^2 = \frac{\Sigma X^2 - [(\Sigma\ X)^2/n]}{n-1}$$

and

$$s = \sqrt{\frac{\Sigma X^2 - [(\Sigma X)^2/n]}{n-1}}$$

In our sample of 5,

$$\Sigma X^2 = (22)^2 + (26)^2 + (25)^2 + (21)^2 + (19)^2 = 2{,}587$$
$$(\Sigma X)^2 = (22 + 26 + 25 + 21 + 19)^2 = (113)^2 = 12{,}769$$

Thus

$$s^2 = \frac{2587 - (12{,}769/5)}{4}$$
$$= \frac{2587 - 2553.8}{4}$$
$$= \frac{33.2}{4}$$
$$= 8.3$$

and

$$s = \sqrt{8.3} = 2.88$$

We note that these values for s^2 and s are exactly the same as previously calculated. In all future calculations of s^2 and s we will use the computational formula, as it saves a great deal of work.

Calculation of Sample Statistics for Dichotomous Variables

Now let's calculate the mean, variance, and standard deviation of our dichotomous variable, election of marketing research.

$$p = \frac{\sum\limits_{i=1}^{n} X_i}{n}$$
$$= \frac{1 + 1 + 0 + 0 + 0}{5}$$
$$= \frac{2}{5}$$
$$= .4$$

We note that $q = (1 - p) = (1 - .4) = .6$.
The variance:

$$s^2 = \frac{\sum\limits_{i=1}^{n} (X_i - p)^2}{df}$$
$$= \frac{(1 - .4)^2 + (1 - .4)^2 + (0 - .4)^2 + (0 - .4)^2 + (0 - .4)^2}{5 - 1}$$
$$= \frac{(.6)^2 + (.6)^2 + (-.4)^2 + (-.4)^2 + (-.4)^2}{4}$$
$$= \frac{1.2}{4}$$
$$= .3$$

The standard deviation:

$$s = \sqrt{.3}$$
$$= .548$$

We note that the general formula for the variance is

$$s^2 = pq\left(\frac{n}{n-1}\right)$$
$$= (.4)(.6)\left(\frac{5}{4}\right) = .3$$

We have now calculated statistics for our dichotomous variable. These would be the estimates of the population parameters.

Drawing Inferences about Population Parameters from Sample Statistics for Continuous Variables

The Basic Theory   Earlier we calculated the mean age of a sample we randomly selected from our student population. In order to tell how good an estimate of the population parameter this sample statistic really is, we must understand the theory of statistical inference.

First we assume a second student population that consists of five elements. In this case, the students are identified by the letters A, B, C, D, and E. Suppose we wish to select a single random sample of size $n = 2$ from this population. There are a number of combinations of elements that could form the sample— that is, there are a number of possible samples. Here they are:

Sample number	Elements in sample
1	AB
2	AC
3	AD
4	AE
5	BC
6	BD
7	BE
8	CD
9	CE
10	DE

There are 10 possible combinations of two elements from a population of five. Mathematically, this is simply the calculation of the number of all possible combinations without replacement. The general formula for this is

$$C_n^N = \binom{N}{n} = C(N, n)$$
$$= \frac{N!}{n!\,(N - n)!}$$

In our example, $N = 5$ and $n = 2$, therefore

$$C(5, 2) = \frac{5!}{2!\,3!} = \frac{5 \cdot 4 \cdot 3 \cdot 2 \cdot 1}{2 \cdot 1 \cdot 3 \cdot 2 \cdot 1}$$
$$= \frac{20}{2}$$
$$= 10$$

Each of the 10 possible samples would yield an estimate of the mean of the population.

We now turn our attention back to the population of 50 students in Table 9-1. Previously we selected one sample of five from this population. The number of possible samples of size five from this population is

$$C(50, 5) = \frac{50!}{5!\,45!} = \frac{50 \cdot 49 \cdot 48 \cdot 47 \cdot 46}{5 \cdot 4 \cdot 3 \cdot 2 \cdot 1}$$
$$= \frac{254{,}251{,}200}{120}$$
$$= 2{,}118{,}760 \text{ possible samples}$$

So we selected one of the 2,118,760 possible samples of size $n = 5$. Just consider the number of possible samples from a realistic population of interest.

For example, if there are 70 million voters in a presidential election and we select a sample of 1000, this sample is only one of $C(70$ million, 1000) possible samples.

$$C(70 \text{ million, } 1000) = \frac{70 \text{ million!}}{1000! \, (70 \text{ million} - 1000)!}$$

The important point is that in any population there are many possible samples. We must also understand that classical statistical inference is based on what happens when we repeatedly select different samples from a population. Previously we did select one sample of $n = 5$ from our population, and this sample yielded a mean age of 22.6. Now suppose we select another sample of $n = 5$ and calculate the mean. In this sample the mean might be 23.4 years. If we again repeat the process, we might get a third sample mean of 24.2 years. Seemingly, we have confused ourselves in that we now have three estimates of the population parameter. However, in statistical theory we would not stop at three samples; we would sample again and again, and in repeating this process we would note that certain mean values repeat themselves. Specifically, we would note that sample means closer in value to the population mean tend to repeat themselves more often than those farther removed from the population mean. This should make intuitive sense. We could plot these mean values, and they would seem to be forming the familiar bell (or normal-shaped) curve. This distribution of sample means is called the *sampling distribution of the mean,* or simply the *sampling distribution.* The sampling distribution is important for two reasons: (1) the sample means in this distribution are distributed around the population mean in a known way; (2) using this distribution, we can determine how closely the sample statistics are distributed around the population parameter.

In order to derive these benefits from the sampling distribution, we must formalize the nature of the sampling distribution of the mean. To do this we turn to the *central-limit theorem* of statistics, which states that:

1 If a population distribution for a measure is normal, the sampling distribution of the mean will be normal for all sample sizes.

2 If a population is non-normal for a measure, the sampling distribution of the mean approaches the normal as the sample size increases.

3 The mean of the sampling distribution of the mean is the population mean. In the type of situation where the expected value of an estimator (the mean of the sampling distribution for the statistic) is the parameter or population value, the statistic is said to be *unbiased.*

4 The standard deviation of the sampling distribution of the mean is the population standard deviation divided by the square root of the sample size. Thus,

$$\sigma_{\bar{x}} = \frac{\sigma}{\sqrt{n}}$$

This value is often called the *standard error of the mean.*

In practice we do not know μ or σ, so we estimate them with $\overline{X}$ and s respectively calculated from the one sample we do select; so,

$$s_{\overline{X}} = \frac{s}{\sqrt{n}}$$

Figure 9-1 demonstrates the central-limit theorem. Four different population

Figure 9-1 Distribution of sample means for samples of various sizes and different population distributions. [*Reproduced with permission from Ernest Kurnow, Gerald J. Glasser, and Frederick R. Ottman,* Statistics for Business Decisions (*Homewood, Ill.: Irwin,* © *1959*), *pp. 182–183.*]

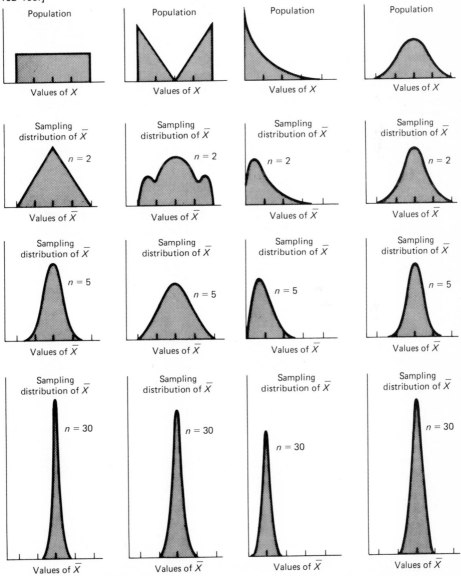

distributions for a variable are presented. Only in the right-hand situation is this distribution normal. However, we note for each population that the sampling distribution of the mean is virtually normal when $n = 5$ (it is truly normal for the normal population) and truly normal when $n = 30$ or greater. So when we calculate the mean from any one sample of $n = 30$, we can be sure that this mean comes from a distribution that is normal with a mean of μ and standard error of $\sigma/\sqrt{n}$.

There is one other aspect about a normal curve that must be understood before we can put all this theory to work. This aspect relates to the area contained under a normal curve. Figure 9-2 shows a normal curve with an amount of area contained within different standard deviations from the mean. Specifically, we note that approximately

   1   68 percent of cases will be within ± 1 standard deviation from the mean.
   2   95 percent of cases will be within ± 2 standard deviations from the mean.
   3   99.7 percent (almost all) cases will be within ± 3 standard deviations from the mean.

We now have all the pieces of theory in place that are needed to determine how good an estimate our sample mean is.

Using the Theory   Our sample of the ages of five students was selected from a population distribution that was close to normal, so we know that the mean we calculated is from a normal distribution of means. We estimate

   1   The mean of the sampling distribution as $\overline{X}$
   2   The standard deviation of the sampling distribution[2] (standard error) as

$$s_{\overline{X}} = \frac{s}{\sqrt{n}} = \frac{\sqrt{\sum_{i=1}^{n} (X_i - \overline{X})^2 \big/ (n-1)}}{\sqrt{n}}$$

In our example, $\overline{X} = 22.6$ and $s = 2.88$, thus

$$s_{\overline{X}} = \frac{2.88}{\sqrt{5}} = \frac{2.88}{2.24} = 1.3$$

Now let's calculate the size of the intervals at ± 1 standard deviation from the mean, then ± 2, then ± 3 standard deviations from the mean. At ± 1 standard deviation, the interval is

   $22.6 \pm 1.3 = 21.3\text{--}23.9$

[2] Technical purists will note that with a population as small as this one, we should apply a correction factor to the formula. However, in practice most populations are quite large, and the correction factor is not needed. So, to aid in student understanding, we are ignoring the point for now. We will address it later in the chapter.

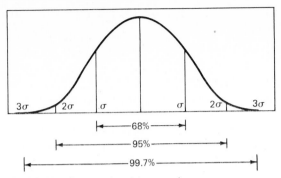

Figure 9-2 Area under the normal curve.

We know that 68 percent of the means from our sampling distribution are contained in this interval, if our calculated sample mean $\overline{X}$ is truly the mean of the sampling distribution. (Remember μ = 23.7.) At ±2 standard deviations, the interval is

$$22.6 \pm 2(1.3) = 22.6 \pm 2.6 = 20.0\text{–}25.2$$

We know that 95 percent of the means from our sampling distribution are contained in this interval, if our calculated sample mean $\overline{X}$ is truly the mean of the sampling distribution. At ±3 standard deviations, the interval is

$$22.6 \pm 3(1.3) = 22.6 \pm 3.9 = 18.7\text{–}26.5$$

We know that 99.7 percent (virtually all) of the means from our sampling distribution are contained in this interval if our calculated mean $\overline{X}$ is truly the mean of the sampling distribution.

We refer to these intervals that we have calculated as *confidence intervals*. The first interval was a 68 percent confidence interval, the second a 95 percent, and the last one a 99.7 percent confidence interval. Note that we must designate the level of confidence before we can calculate an interval; it is our knowledge that the mean comes from a normal distribution of means that allows us to calculate an interval.

Exactly what does a confidence interval mean? Let's use the 95 percent confidence level as an illustration. We noted previously that the mean of the sampling distribution is the population mean, and that we use one sample mean, $\overline{X}$, as an estimator of the mean of the sampling distribution. But we have selected only one sample, and thus we do not know what the true mean of the sampling distribution is. It is therefore possible to select a sample such that the true population mean is not contained within the 95 percent (or other level) confidence interval calculated from the sample. The population mean either is or is not contained within the 95 percent confidence interval calculated from a sample. A 95 percent confidence interval does not mean that there are 95 chances in 100 that the population mean is contained within the interval; it means that if we selected 100 different random samples and calculated 100 different 95 percent confidence intervals, we could expect the true mean to be contained within the 95 percent confidence interval in 95 out of the 100 samples. So again we note that concepts of classical statistics have meaning in terms of repeated sampling.

The 95 percent confidence interval we calculated was 22.6 ± 2.6, or 20.0 to 25.2. Under repeated sampling, we would expect the true population mean to fall within such intervals in 95 samples out of 100. In our example we note that the population mean of 23.7 does fall within the 95 percent confidence interval we calculated from our sample of 5. Also, we can say that our estimate has a *precision* of ± 2.6 years at a 95 percent level of confidence. We note that the size of the precision has meaning only at a designated level of confidence. At 99.7 percent the precision of our estimate is ± 3.9 years.

The calculation of a confidence interval provides us with the measure of *sampling error* and sample accuracy we were in search of earlier. Again we note that it is only the use of probability-based selection procedures that allows us to properly calculate the confidence interval. We know nothing about the sampling distribution of means for nonprobability sampling and thus cannot calculate a meaningful confidence interval. We should note that it is common practice for confidence intervals to be calculated from nonprobability samples; the manager who uses these intervals, however, is implicitly assuming that his or her nonprobability sampling procedure has yielded a simple random sample.

The Effect of Sample Size on Precision   The formula for the standard deviation of the sampling distribution of the mean is

$$s_{\bar{X}} = \frac{\sqrt{\sum_{i=1}^{n} (X_i - \bar{X})^2 \Big/ (n - 1)}}{\sqrt{n}}$$

or more simply it is

$$s_{\bar{X}} = \frac{s}{\sqrt{n}}$$

where s is the standard deviation of the distribution of the variable of interest. We note that $s_{\bar{X}}$ will vary inversely with the square root of the sample size we select. That is, $s_{\bar{X}}$ will get smaller by the square root of the sample size as the sample size increases. Notice that the confidence interval around $\bar{X}$ will get smaller as $s_{\bar{X}}$ gets smaller, and we will be more certain of the accuracy of our estimate.

We can illustrate this by again using our student population, but this time we will assume that the population really has 500,000 elements and not 50, but that the population mean and variance are as before. Now let's assume we selected a number of simple random samples from this population, and that in each case the mean and variance we calculated from these samples were identical, as follows:

$$\overline{X} = 22.6\,;\, s^2 = 8.3\,;\, s = 2.88$$

You will recognize these as the statistics calculated from our sample of 5 taken previously. The different sample sizes are

(1) $n=5$ (4) $n=1000$
(2) $n=30$ (5) $n=2000$
(3) $n=100$

For each sample size we calculate $s_{\overline{X}}$.

(1) $s_{\overline{X}} = \dfrac{2.88}{\sqrt{5}} = 1.3$

(2) $s_{\overline{X}} = \dfrac{2.88}{\sqrt{30}} = \dfrac{2.88}{5.48} = .53$

(3) $s_{\overline{X}} = \dfrac{2.88}{\sqrt{100}} = \dfrac{2.88}{10} = .29$

(4) $s_{\overline{X}} = \dfrac{2.88}{\sqrt{1000}} = \dfrac{2.88}{31.7} = .09$

(5) $s_{\overline{X}} = \dfrac{2.88}{\sqrt{2000}} = \dfrac{2.88}{44.8} = .06$

The associated 95 percent confidence intervals are

(1) $22.6 \pm 2(1.3) = 22.6 \pm 2.6 = 20.0\text{--}25.2$
(2) $22.6 \pm 2(.53) = 22.6 \pm 1.06 = 21.5\text{--}23.7$
(3) $22.6 \pm 2(.29) = 22.6 \pm .58 = 22.0\text{--}23.2$
(4) $22.6 \pm 2(.09) = 22.6 \pm .18 = 22.4\text{--}22.8$
(5) $22.6 \pm 2(.06) = 22.6 \pm .12 = 22.5\text{--}22.7$

As n has increased from 5 to 2000, the confidence interval has decreased from 5.2 to .2, which shows how much more confident in our estimate we can be as the sample size increases. That is, for $n = 2000$ we would expect that the true mean would fall in an interval only .2 wide in 95 samples out of 100.

In this example, the true mean, 23.7, does not fall in the interval from 22.5 to 22.7. This has happened because we forced all the sample means to be the same, no matter what the sample size. We did this just to illustrate the effect of sample size on the size of a calculated confidence interval. In truth, as we increase the sample size, the sample mean would approach the population mean in value. A statistic that approaches the population parameter in value as the sample size increases is called a *consistent estimator.* Obviously we want consistent estimators, so our sample mean for $n = 2000$ would be much closer to 23.7 than the $n = 5$ mean we used above. This should make intuitive sense. The more elements we include, the more representative our sample should be.

The other component of the calculation that affects the size of $s_{\overline{x}}$ and thus our confidence interval is the standard deviation of the distribution of the variable, s. It is the numerator of $s_{\overline{x}}$. Thus, we would like our estimate of $\overline{X}$ to have as small a variance and therefore as small a standard deviation as possible. An estimator that provides this minimum variance and thus the minimum standard error for any given sample size is called the *most efficient estimator.* We want efficient estimators.

Drawing Inferences about Population Parameters from Sample Statistics for Dichotomous Variables

All the theory and procedures we applied to continuous variables also apply to dichotomous variables. The sample mean of the proportion of students electing marketing research in our sample of 5 was .4. This is but one sample mean from a distribution of means of the proportion that would result from repeated samplings of size 5. Again, the central-limit theorem applies. In this case the mean of the sampling distribution of means is π, and the standard deviation of the sampling distribution is $\sqrt{\pi(1 - \pi)/n}$. We do not know these population values, so we estimate them as follows:

$$\text{Mean} = p$$

$$\text{Standard deviation} = s_p = \sqrt{\frac{p(1 - p)}{n}} \text{ or } \sqrt{\frac{pq}{n}}$$

We now calculate the 95 percent confidence interval for our sample of 5. The formula would be

$$p \pm 2\sqrt{\frac{pq}{n}}$$

In our example, $p = .4$ and $n = 5$. The 95 percent interval is

$$.4 \pm 2\sqrt{\frac{(.4)(.6)}{5}} = .4 \pm 2\sqrt{.048}$$
$$= .4 \pm 2(.22) = .4 \pm .44$$
$$= 0 - .84$$

This is a very wide interval because the sample size is small and the value pq of the variable is large. What we can say is that in 95 samples out of 100, we would expect the true proportion mean to be contained in this type of interval. The true mean, .27, is contained in this interval.

Again let us note the effect on the confidence interval of an increase in the sample size to 2000. If $p = .4$ again, the 95 percent confidence interval would be

$$.4 \pm 2 \sqrt{\frac{(.4)(.6)}{2000}} = .4 \pm 2 \sqrt{.00012}$$
$$= .4 \pm 2(.011) = .4 \pm .022$$
$$= .38 - .42$$

Again because we constrained p to equal .4, a result obtained from a sample of 5, the true mean falls outside this tight interval. If the sample size were 2000, the sample mean would move closer to the population value. That is, p is a consistent estimator of π. We would then expect the true mean to fall in this type of small interval in 95 samples out of 100.

Note that for any given sample size the value of s_p is maximum when $p = .5$. This is because $pq = .25$. For no other value of p is pq this large. If $p = .6$, $pq = .24$; if $p = .7$, $pq = .21$; if $p = .8$, $pq = .16$; if $p = 9$, $pq = .09$; if $p = .99, pq = .0099$. What this indicates is that the more undefinitive the results (the closer p is to .5), the larger is the amount of error.

We have now calculated a measure of sampling error for both a continuous and a dichotomous variable.

The Question of Population Size

The discussion to date has made no mention of the size of the population as being important in our calculations. Technically this is not correct, but most marketing-related populations are large enough so that the concern about population size is not important, and this extra level of complexity would have made the previous discussion harder to follow.

The problem of population size is simply that for finite populations we must change the formula we use in calculating the standard error of the sampling distribution of the mean. What we do is apply the *finite population correction* or "finite correction factor" to our previous formula, so that

$$(1) \quad \sigma_{\bar{x}} = \frac{\sigma_X}{\sqrt{n}} \sqrt{\frac{N-n}{N-1}} \quad \text{and} \quad s_{\bar{x}} = \frac{s_X}{\sqrt{n}} \sqrt{\frac{N-n}{N-1}}$$

$$(2) \quad \sigma_p = \sqrt{\frac{\pi(1-\pi)}{N}} \sqrt{\frac{N-n}{N-1}} \quad \text{and} \quad s_p = \sqrt{\frac{pq}{n}} \sqrt{\frac{N-n}{N-1}}$$

The value $\sqrt{(N-n)/(N-1)}$ is the finite correction factor. We note that for large values of N relative to n, the value of $\sqrt{(N-n)/(N-1)}$ is approximately equal to 1. Thus we can just use the basic formula for $\sigma_{\bar{x}}$ and $s_{\bar{x}}$ and σ_p and s_p.

The value of the correction factor is always between 0 and 1. It is zero when $N = n$. That is, when we take a complete census we cannot calculate a standard error. This is as we should expect. Standard error has meaning only for samples, not for a census. The value of the correction factor approaches 1 as N gets bigger relative to n. So we see that multiplying by the correction factor will always lower the size of the standard error (except when it equals 1). Thus, if we choose to ignore the correction factor, we overstate the standard error and increase the size of our confidence interval. We err on the side of conservatism.

In most marketing applications it is safe to ignore the correction factor. As a rule of thumb, some suggest applying the correction factor when the sample includes more than 5 percent of the population (when the sampling fraction exceeds .05). Like all rules of thumb, 5 percent is not a definite guide; others have suggested 10 percent as the magic number. The reader should simply be sensitive to this issue when dealing with small populations.

In our example we selected 10 percent (5/50) of the population. We should have applied the correction factor.

A Warning about Nonsampling Errors

The calculation of confidence intervals about an estimator gives us the feeling that we know just how much error we are dealing with. For most marketing research studies this can be very misleading. Our measurement of error was that of sampling error only. A confidence interval does not take nonsampling errors into account at all. If nonsampling errors occur, a bias is introduced into our estimate of unknown degree and magnitude. Control of nonsampling errors is therefore critical. These are discussed in more detail in Chapter 11.

The Accuracy of Probability Samples

Probability samples can be extremely accurate. In fact, the Gallup and Harris polls have successfully predicted the outcome of every presidential election in which they have applied probability sampling procedures. What about 1948, you say. Did not the polls predict that Dewey would defeat Truman? Indeed they did, but the samples were quota samples, as probability sampling was new at that time.

Let's compare two presidential elections. In 1936 the *Literary Digest* conducted a poll by mail. Their sample size was over 2 million. They predicted a victory for Landon over Roosevelt by about 15 percent, yet in fact Roosevelt won easily. In 1968, using a probability sample of less than 2000 out of over 70 million voters, Gallup predicted that Richard Nixon would get 43 percent of the vote. He got 42.9 percent. The sampling frame used by the *Literary Digest* was more well-to-do than the true population of voters. The poor people who supported Roosevelt did not get a chance to respond to the poll.

The sampling procedures outlined in this chapter provide the tools for the researcher to give accurate estimates of the parameters of interest. The major problem area lies in the nonsampling errors that arise.

In Chapter 10, we shall continue our discussion of probability sampling. Specifically, we shall discuss two types of sampling procedures—stratified sampling and cluster sampling. These procedures are more complex than simple random sampling but are used more often in practice. In Chapter 11, we shall discuss nonsampling errors and the determination of sample size.

SUMMARY

1   A parameter is a summary description of a measure in the defined population. A statistic is a summary description of a measure in the selected sample.

2   The ratio of sample size (n) to population size (N) is called the sampling fraction.

3   We are able to calculate the mean and standard deviation for a population and for a simple random sample. We can do this for both continuous and dichotomous variables. Variance is simply SS/df.

4   Any simple random sample that we draw is just one of the $C(N,n)$ samples that could have been drawn.

5   In simple random sampling, each element has an equal chance of being selected, and each combination of n sample elements has an equal chance of being selected.

6   The central-limit theorem tells us that the mean of the sample that we did select comes from a distribution of sample means that form a normal curve if $n \geq 30$, no matter what the shape of the underlying variable distribution. Also, if the variable distribution is normal, then the sampling distribution of the mean is always normal, no matter what the sample size is.

7   Using our knowledge of the area under a normal curve, we can calculate confidence intervals about our sample mean. Specifically, the 95 percent interval will be $\bar{X} \pm 2s_{\bar{X}}$, and the 99.7 percent interval will be $\bar{X} \pm 3s_{\bar{X}}$, where $s_{\bar{X}} = s/\sqrt{n}$.

8   Precision is the absolute size of the confidence interval about the mean. For example, at the 95 percent level of confidence, absolute precision $= \pm 2s/\sqrt{n}$.

9   A sample statistic whose expected value equals the population parameter is called an unbiased statistic. A sample statistic that has the minimum variance is the most efficient estimator.

10   The confidence interval provides a measure of accuracy of an estimator.

11   Beware of nonsampling errors.

12   Probability samples can provide very accurate estimates if properly executed.

DISCUSSION QUESTIONS

1   What is the difference (if any) between a parameter and a statistic?

2   Identify the symbols which denote common parameters and statistics of both continuous and dichotomous variables.

3   Define the mean and variance in words and in mathematical notation for both a population and a sample, first treating the variable as continuous and then dichotomous.

4   Why is the central-limit theorem critical to measuring sampling error?

5   What is a confidence interval?

6   What affects the size of a confidence interval?

7   What are the desirable properties of estimators?
8   To what extent do confidence intervals increase our certainty with regard to making inferences?
9   Most political pollsters judged the 1976 presidential election to be too close to call. Explain how this could happen.
10 What problems are likely to occur in implementing a field study using simple random sampling?
11 Why do some researchers calculate confidence intervals from data generated from nonprobability samples?
12 Since nonprobability samples do not yield a measure of sampling error, why are these procedures so extensively used in commercial and academic practice?

SUGGESTED READING

Babbie, Earl, *Survey Research Methods* (Belmont, Calif.: Wadsworth, 1973), chap. 5, pp. 82–92. An intuitive overview of simple random sampling.

Kish, Leslie, *Survey Sampling* (New York: Wiley, 1965), chap. 2. An advanced, mathematically oriented discussion of simple random sampling.

Slonim, Morris James, *Sampling* (New York: Simon and Schuster, 1960), chap. 7. An elementary overview of simple random sampling.

Chapter 10

More Complex Sampling Procedures

We now continue our discussion of probability sampling procedures. The first part of this chapter deals with stratified sampling, and the remainder describes two types of cluster sampling, systematic sampling and area sampling. These three sampling procedures are more complex than simple random sampling, but they are also much more frequently used in practice.

STRATIFIED SAMPLING

Purpose

One property that we wanted in our estimators was efficiency—that is, we wanted them to have as small a standard error as possible. Stratified sampling may result in a *decrease in the standard error of the estimator*. Thus the confidence interval we calculate would be smaller.

Method of Selection

A stratified sample is selected as follows:

    1 Divide the defined population into mutually exclusive and collectively exhaustive subgroups or strata. Strata are mutually exclusive if membership in one stratum precludes membership in any other stratum. For example, a pop-

215

ulation may be divided into two strata on the basis of sex; that is, there would be a male stratum and a female stratum. An individual person cannot belong to both strata, and thus they are mutually exclusive. Strata are collectively exhaustive if all possible categories of a variable are used to define the strata. That is, the categories "male and female" define the complete domain of the variable "sex." No other category is possible, and thus the defined strata are collectively exhaustive of the variable, sex.

2   Select an independent simple random sample in each stratum.

An Illustration

How does such a two-stage procedure decrease the standard error of an estimator? It only does so if the designated strata are *more homogeneous* on the variable on which we are calculating our statistics. If the strata are as heterogeneous on this variable as the unstratified whole population, no decrease in the standard error will occur.

Let us illustrate the standard error–reducing property of stratified sampling. Again we use part of the data presented in Table 9-1. The student number and age of students are presented in Table 10-1. We will use the age data to illustrate the standard error–reducing property.

Perhaps you noted in reading Table 9-1 that the ages of students numbered 1–20 seemed higher than the ages of students numbered 21–50. This is indeed true. A piece of information that was missing in Table 9-1 was that students 1–20 are graduate students and students 21–50 are undergraduate students. We would expect graduate students to be older than undergraduates, and they are. Note

Table 10-1   Census of Age of Students

	(1) Student number	(2) Age (X_1)
	1	25
	2	27
	3	29
	4	31
	5	25
	6	29
	7	27
	8	24
	9	27
Graduate	10	28
students	11	33
	12	29
	13	26
	14	28
	15	28
	16	26
	17	26
	18	36
	19	28
	20	26

Table 10-1 (Continued)

	(1) Student number	(2) Age (X_1)
	21	21
	22	19
	23	24
	24	22
	25	20
	26	22
	27	19
	28	20
	29	19
	30	24
	31	25
	32	22
	33	20
Under-	34	21
graduate	35	21
students	36	23
	37	21
	38	23
	39	18
	40	21
	41	19
	42	23
	43	22
	44	19
	45	20
	46	20
	47	21
	48	20
	49	19
	50	18

that the group of students numbered 1–20 has a more homogeneous age profile than the population as a whole, and so does the group of students numbered 21–50. By using a *stratification variable,* "graduate versus undergraduate," we have identified two strata that are more homogeneous than the population on the variable of interest, age. We have present the necessary condition to take advantage of stratification.

The Sample

Now let us draw a simple random sample of $n = 2$ from the graduate stratum and a simple random sample of $n = 3$ from the undergraduate stratum. Note that the ratio of our sample sizes by strata is in proportion to the ratio of the number of population elements by strata. Here the sample ratio 2/3 is proportionate to the population ratio 20/30. This is called *proportionate stratified sampling,* and it occurs when the total sample elements are allocated to strata in proportion to the number of population elements in the strata. The researcher also has the option of allocating the total sample to strata on a basis disproportionate with the population distribution among strata. We shall discuss disproportionate stratified sampling later in this chapter.

As a basis for facilitating the discussion that follows, we identify the following notation:

$N_{st.1}$ = population size in stratum 1
$N_{st.2}$ = population size in stratum 2
$n_{st.1}$ = sample size in stratum 1
$n_{st.2}$ = sample size in stratum 2
$\overline{X}_{st.1}$ = sample mean of stratum 1
$\overline{X}_{st.2}$ = sample mean of stratum 2
$s^2_{st.1}$ = sample variance of stratum 1
$s^2_{st.2}$ = sample variance of stratum 2

Now let's draw a simple random sample of $n=2$ from stratum 1 and $n = 3$ from stratum 2. Conveniently, the sample of $n = 5$ we drew in Chapter 9 was just this kind of sample, so we do not have to select a new sample. Specifically, the sample by strata is:

Student number	Age
Stratum 1	
05	25
17	26
Stratum 2	
32	22
37	21
41	19

Calculation of Statistics within Strata

In Chapter 9 we calculated the mean, variance, and standard deviation of the total sample without stratification. There,

$$\overline{X} = 22.6, \quad s^2 = 8.3, \quad \text{and} \quad s = 2.88$$

Now we calculate the mean, variance, and standard deviation within each stratum. For stratum 1,

$$\overline{X}_{st.1} = \frac{\sum_{i=1}^{n_{st.1}} X_i}{n_{st.1}}$$

$$= \frac{25 + 26}{2}$$

$$= \frac{51}{2}$$

$$= 25.5$$

To find $s_{st.1}^2$ using our computational formula, we calculate

$$\Sigma X_{st.1}^2 = (25)^2 + (26)^2 = 625 + 676 = 1301$$

and

$$\frac{(\Sigma X_{st.1})^2}{n} = \frac{(51)^2}{2} = \frac{2601}{2} = 1300.5$$

$$s_{st.1}^2 = \frac{1301 - 1300.5}{1}$$

$$= .5$$

$$s_{st.1} = .71$$

For stratum 2,

$$\bar{X}_{st.2} = \frac{22 + 21 + 19}{3}$$

$$= \frac{62}{3}$$

$$= 20.7$$

$$\Sigma X_{st.2}^2 = (22)^2 + (21)^2 + (19)^2$$

$$= 484 + 441 + 361$$

$$= 1286$$

$$\frac{(\Sigma X_{st.2})^2}{n} = \frac{(62)^2}{3}$$

$$= \frac{3844}{3}$$

$$= 1281.3$$

$$s_{st.2}^2 = \frac{1286 - 1281.3}{2}$$

$$= \frac{4.7}{2}$$

$$= 2.35$$

$$s_{st.2} = 1.53$$

Table 10-2 summarizes these results. We note that the variance and standard deviation within each stratum are much lower than the variance and standard

Table 10-2 Total Sample and Within-strata Mean, and Variance of Sample

	Mean	Variance	Standard deviation
Without stratification	22.6	8.3	2.88
Within stratum 1	25.5	.5	.71
Within stratum 2	20.7	2.35	1.53

deviation of the total sample. This points out one advantage of stratified sampling—that is, we can do analysis within strata with a smaller standard error than that available for the whole sample. Our within-strata confidence interval would thus be smaller than that generated by the use of the standard error of the whole sample.

Calculation of the Mean and Standard Error for the Whole Sample

We next consider how to calculate the mean and the standard error for the whole sample on the basis of within-strata results. The overall sample mean, $\overline{X}_{st.}$, is simply a *weighted average of the within-strata means*. The weight for a stratum is the ratio of the population size of that stratum to the total population size,

$$\frac{N_{st.j}}{N}$$

where $N_{st.j}$ is the population size within stratum j. Therefore,

$$\overline{X}_{st.} = \sum_{j=1}^{A} \left(\frac{N_{st.j}}{N} \right) \overline{X}_{st.j}$$

where A = the number of strata. In our example we have two strata; thus $A = 2$, and so

$$
\begin{aligned}
\overline{X}_{st.} &= \sum_{j=1}^{2} \left(\frac{N_{st.j}}{N} \right) \overline{X}_{st.j} = \left(\frac{N_{st.1}}{N} \right) \overline{X}_{st.1} + \left(\frac{N_{st.2}}{N} \right) \overline{X}_{st.2} \\
&= (20/50)25.5 + (30/50)20.7 \\
&= .4(25.5) + .6(20.7) \\
&= 10.2 + 12.4 \\
&= 22.6
\end{aligned}
$$

This is exactly the same mean we calculated without stratification.

The ratio $N_{st.j}/N$ is the relative weight attached to each stratum. For future reference, let's call this ratio W_j.

In our example,

$$W_1 = .4 \text{ and } W_2 = .6$$

The calculation of the *standard error* of the mean from within-strata information is more complex. It is *the square root of the weighted combination of the square of the standard error within each stratum*. The weighting factor in this case is the square of the relative weight of each stratum.

The formula[1] is

$$s_{\bar{X}} = \sqrt{s_{\bar{X}}^2}$$

where $s_{\bar{X}}^2 = \sum_{j=1}^{A} \left(\dfrac{N_{st.j}}{N} \right)^2 s_{\bar{X}_{st.j}}^2$

$$= \sum_{j=1}^{A} W_j^2 s_{\bar{X}_{st.j}}^2$$

In our example (using the values in Table 10-2), we have for stratum 1:

$$s_{\bar{X}_{st.1}} = \frac{.71}{\sqrt{2}} = \frac{.71}{1.41}$$
$$= .50$$
$$s_{\bar{X}_{st.1}}^2 = .25$$

and for stratum 2:

$$s_{\bar{X}_{st.2}} = \frac{1.53}{\sqrt{3}} = \frac{1.53}{1.73}$$
$$= .88$$
$$s_{\bar{X}_{st.2}}^2 = .78$$

Therefore

$$s_{\bar{X}}^2 = (.4)^2(.25) + (.6)^2(.78)$$
$$= (.16)(.25) + (.36)(.78)$$
$$= .04 + .28$$
$$= .32$$
$$s_{\bar{X}} = \sqrt{.32}$$
$$= .57$$

[1] Again we will ignore the finite-population correction factor.

Note that we took the square of the weighting factor for each stratum and the square of the standard error. We cannot take a simple weighting of the strata weight and the associated standard errors.

Alternatively, we may calculate $s_{\bar{X}}^2$ directly without first calculating the standard errors within each stratum. The formula to do this is

$$
s_{\bar{X}}^2 = \sum_{j=1}^{A} \frac{\left(\dfrac{N_{st.j}}{N}\right)^2 s_{st.j}^2}{n_{st.j}}
$$

$$
= \sum_{j=1}^{A} \frac{(W_j)^2 s_{st.j}^2}{n_{st.j}}
$$

In our example, with $A=2$,

$$
s_{\bar{X}}^2 = \frac{(W_1)^2 s_{st.1}^2}{n_{st.1}} + \frac{(W_2)^2 s_{st.2}^2}{n_{st.2}}
$$

$$
= \frac{(.4)^2(.5)}{2} + \frac{(.6)^2(2.35)}{3}
$$

$$
= (.16)(.25) + (.36)(.78)
$$

$$
= .04 + .28
$$

$$
= .32
$$

$$
s_{\bar{X}} = \sqrt{.32} = .57
$$

The value of $s_{\bar{X}}$ is identical to that previously calculated.

In Chapter 9 we calculated the standard error of the mean, using the unstratified sample, to be 1.3. We note that by stratifying the sample the standard error has been reduced to .57.

Calculation of Associated Confidence Interval

The 95 percent confidence interval for the stratified sample is $22.6 \pm 2(.57) = 22.6 \pm 1.1 = 21.5$–$23.7$. The unstratified 95 percent interval was 20.0–25.2. Thus the size of the interval has been reduced from 5.2 to 2.2 and the absolute precision from ± 2.6 to ± 1.1. We note that the population mean, 23.7, does fall in this new interval. Note also that the stratified 99.7 percent confidence interval would be smaller than the unstratified 95 percent interval. The 99.7 percent interval is $22.6 \pm 3(.57) = 22.6 \pm 1.7 = 20.9$–$24.3$. Clearly a stratified sampling procedure is more efficient than an unstratified one. This fact helps account for the moderately high use of stratified sampling in practice.

Why do we get such a reduction in standard error and associated precision using a stratified sampling procedure? It is because we use only within-stratum variability in calculating the overall standard error. Across-strata variability becomes irrelevant.

The effect with stratified sampling is that we can increase the precision of our estimates with the same sample size we used in an unstratified fashion.

Alternatively, we could obtain the same precision as with an unstratified sample with a smaller sample and thus a lower cost.

The Number of Possible Samples

The sampling fraction in stratum 1 was $2/20 = .1$, and in stratum 2 it was $3/30 = .1$. Both of these sampling fractions are identical with the sample we selected in Chapter 9, $5/50 = .1$. Under both stratified and unstratified procedures each population element had an equal chance, .1, of being selected. However, with stratified sampling *all possible combinations of elements are not equally likely.* To illustrate, we shall use a population of elements identified as A, B, C, D, and E. This of course is the population that yielded 10 possible simple random samples of size 2. Now assume that elements A and B are from one stratum, while C, D, and E are from another. Again we wish to draw a sample of $n=2$, but this time we restrict the sample to one element from each stratum. The possible sample element from stratum 1 is either A or B, and within stratum 2 it is either C, D, or E. Combining possible elements from each stratum, we get the possible samples as

Sample number	Elements in sample
1	AC
2	AD
3	AE
4	BC
5	BD
6	BE

There are 6 possible samples with stratification, as against 10 without. The possible samples that have been eliminated are those that could occur within a stratum before; for example, AB and CD are no longer possible as samples. Note that it is these within-strata means that are the outliers of our distribution of means in simple random sampling. To illustrate this result, we may assign scores to these population elements as follows:

Element	Score
Stratum 1	
A	1
B	2
Stratum 2	
C	3
D	4
E	5

The mean of this distribution of scores is $15/5 = 3.0$. The possible stratified samples of $n=2$ are:

Sample elements	Sample mean
AC	$(1 + 3)/2 = 2.0$
AD	$(1 + 4)/2 = 2.5$
AE	$(1 + 5)/2 = 3.0$
BC	$(2 + 3)/2 = 2.5$
BD	$(2 + 4)/2 = 3.0$
BE	$(2 + 5)/2 = 3.5$

These sample means cluster reasonably tightly about the true mean of 3.0.

Now we examine the mean values generated by samples that are not allowed to occur in this example of stratified sampling, that is, the within-stratum sample means. These means are:

Sample elements	Sample mean
Stratum 1	
AB	$(1 + 2)/2 = 1.5$
Stratum 2	
CD	$(3 + 4)/2 = 3.5$
CE	$(3 + 5)/2 = 4.0$
DE	$(4 + 5)/2 = 4.5$

These means are less well clustered about the mean of 3.0, i.e., they are the outliers on the distribution of means. In our age example, we get means like 26, 27, etc., in stratum 1 or like 20 or 21 in stratum 2. These types of means are not as likely when we combine elements from different strata, as we do when we estimate the mean with a stratified procedure. Removal of some outliers in stratified sampling would thus decrease the variability of the distribution of sample means. That is, the standard error becomes smaller. All combinations of elements are not equally likely. This is one aspect that distinguishes stratified sampling from simple random sampling. Note that the number of possible samples with stratification is the product of the number of all possible samples within each stratum. In our example the formula with two strata is:

$$\text{Number of possible samples} = C(N,n)_{st.1} \cdot C(N,n)_{st.2}$$
$$= C(2,1) \cdot C(3,1)$$
$$= \frac{2!}{1!\,1!} \cdot \frac{3!}{1!\,2!}$$
$$= 2 \cdot 3 = 6$$

In our student age example, the number of possible samples with stratification is

$$C(20,2) \cdot C(30,3) = \frac{20!}{2!\,18!} \cdot \frac{30!}{3!\,27!}$$
$$= \frac{20 \cdot 19}{2 \cdot 1} \cdot \frac{30 \cdot 29 \cdot 28}{3 \cdot 2 \cdot 1}$$
$$= 190 \cdot 4{,}060$$
$$= 771{,}400 \text{ possible samples}$$

In Chapter 9 we noted that there were over 2 million possible simple random samples of size 5 in a population of 50. The number of possible samples has decreased substantially, although we should note that it is still very large. Further, once again the sampling distribution of the means of these samples will form a normal curve. The standard error will be smaller than with simple random sampling, as we previously noted in our calculations. Thus, we can again calculate a legitimate confidence interval.

Usefulness in Marketing Research

Stratified sampling is moderately used in marketing research. The types of variables often measured in marketing research show high variability that can be reduced by stratification. As an example, suppose that we are asked to monitor the retail sales of Folger's coffee. To do this we want to measure the unit sales level of Folger's in a sample of stores. What stratification variables should we use? First the researcher must answer another question: "What factors contribute to the variability in the variable we intend to measure?" In the Folger's example, variability contributing factors would include:

1 Size of store; big stores would have higher sales than small stores.
2 Day of the week; stores sell more coffee on weekends than early in the week.
3 Region of the country; Folger's is a more established brand in the Western states, so we would find higher sales there than in other regions.

Other factors may also contribute to the variability in sales. If we thought they were important contributors, we would also include them as stratification variables. If we distinguished three sizes of stores, two types of days of the week, and four regions of the country, we would have $3 \times 2 \times 4 = 24$ different cells or strata. The similarity to quota sampling in the way the number of cells expands is obvious. However, in quota sampling we have no error measure.

In the stratum composed of "large stores—weekends—Western regions," we might find case sale numbers like 150, 170, or 205. In the stratum labeled "small stores—weekdays—Eastern region," however, we might find case sale numbers like 10, 6, 7. The across-strata variability is much greater than that within each stratum. We would thus obtain more efficient estimates using stratification.

The stratification variables worked because they are all *correlated* with the sales of Folger's. In general, we add stratification variables as long as they contribute meaningfully to the variability of the variable we are measuring. Of course, we also consider the *cost* of stratification in deciding on the number of stratification variables.

Most studies are designed to measure many variables. What is a good stratification variable for some of these may not be as good for others. In selecting stratification variables, we want those that will contribute most meaningfully across all variables of interest.

Disproportionate Stratified Sampling

The overall sample size, n, can also be allocated to strata on a basis *disproportionate* with the population sizes of the strata. Proportionate allocation is straightforward, so why should we complicate things by allocating on some other basis? The answer lies in the differences in variability within strata. Generally, for a fixed sample size we can reduce the overall standard error of the estimate by sampling more heavily in strata with higher variability. Suppose that we had added another stratification variable to our age example and that by doing so we obtained a population stratum with the elements 21, 21, 21 in it. There is no variability in this stratum, and a sample of one is all that is needed to measure perfectly the mean of this stratum. Alternatively, a stratum with much variability will require a large sample size to produce an efficient estimate of the mean. This is true because in order to calculate the standard error within a stratum we divide the standard deviation within the stratum by the square root of the stratum sample size, $n_{st.j}$.

An optimal allocation of a fixed sample size among strata is one that generates the minimum standard error of the overall estimate. To find this optimal allocation we must know something about the variability within strata before sampling. Experience and past studies may provide such knowledge. Companies doing retail store audits often sample the larger stores at a disproportionately high level because these larger stores exhibit more variability in sales than smaller stores. The result is a smaller standard error and a more reliable estimate. There are mathematical formulas to determine the optimal allocation of a sample to strata, but they are complex and beyond the scope of this book. In general, these formulas indicate that (1) the larger the stratum, the larger the sample, and (2) the greater the variability within a stratum, the larger the sample.

How are the overall mean and standard error calculated with a disproportionate stratified sample? Exactly the same formulas are used as before, in proportionate stratified sampling. This is the case because

$$W_j = \frac{N_{st.j}}{N}$$

That is, it is the size of the population within strata and the total population that determine the weighting factors. The sample sizes within strata are used only to calculate within-strata means and standard errors.

CLUSTER SAMPLING

Overview

In all the probability sampling methods we have discussed so far, the elements that form the sample are selected individually. In cluster sampling, *a cluster or group of elements are randomly selected at one time*. Thus, before we can select a cluster sample, the population must be divided in mutually exclusive and collectively exhaustive groups. We then select a random sample of these groups.

Suppose we had a population of 20 elements divided into 4 equal-sized groups as follows:

Group	Population element number
Group 1	1, 2, 3, 4, 5
Group 2	6, 7, 8, 9, 10
Group 3	11, 12, 13, 14, 15
Group 4	16, 17, 18, 19, 20

If we wanted to select a probability sample of 10 elements, we could select elements individually using simple random sampling, or we could randomly select two of the four groups and use all the elements in those two groups. The situation where we directly select groups and then use *all* the elements in these groups is called *one-stage cluster* sampling. If we had selected a random sample of elements from within the selected groups, we would call this a *two-stage cluster* sample. In both cluster and simple random sampling the sampling fraction would be the same, .5. However, all possible combinations of elements are not equally likely in cluster sampling. Most combinations are impossible.

What if the clusters we select have elements that are not representative of the population? Would not our estimates be biased? The answer is yes. This points out the criterion we should use in forming groups. We want them to be as close in heterogeneity on the variables of interest as the population as a whole. If the groups are exactly as heterogeneous as the population, any one group we select will accurately represent the population; in practice, however, this ideal is never reached. Note that in cluster sampling the criterion used in forming groups is exactly the opposite of that used in stratified sampling. In stratified sampling we want homogeneous groups, whereas in cluster sampling we want heterogeneous groups.

How does the size of the standard error generated from a cluster sample compare with the size of the standard error generated from a simple random sample? The answer depends on the similarity of the heterogeneity in the formed groups compared with the population, as follows:

1 If the groups are exactly as heterogeneous as the population, both methods will yield the same standard error.

2 If the groups are less heterogeneous than the population, the standard error will be greater with cluster sampling than with simple random sampling.

We refer to this comparison of the standard errors generated by various sampling procedures as an assessment of the *statistical efficiency* of the procedures.

In practice, sample clusters are often much less heterogeneous than the population, which means that in most cases they are less statistically efficient than simple random samples. For reasons of cost, however, cluster samples are very extensively used in practice. They are often much cheaper than other procedures for a given sample size. Alternatively, for a given dollar budget we can generate a larger sample using cluster sampling. When we combine the statistical efficiency of a procedure with its cost, we refer to this as the *overall efficiency* or *total efficiency* of the procedure. Cluster sampling is often the most overall efficient procedure. That is, we get a smaller standard error per dollar spent. The next section discusses the most straightforward type of cluster sampling, systematic sampling.

SYSTEMATIC SAMPLING

The Method

In systematic sampling, the researcher selects *every kth element in the frame, after a random start somewhere within the first k elements.* Suppose we wanted to select a systematic sample of $n=5$ from our student population in Tables 9-1 and 10-1. Here

$$k = \frac{50}{5} = 10$$

In general,

$$k = \frac{N}{n}$$

which is the reciprocal of the sampling fraction we desire and is called the *sampling interval.* Thus, to select our systematic sample of $n=5$, we do the following:

1 Obtain a random number between 1 and 10. This element will be our starting point and the first element of the sample.

2 Add 10 to this random number. This element will be the second element of the sample. Add another 10 to get the third element, and so on.

If the random number were 2, our sample would include the elements

2, 12, 22, 32, 42

Once the sampling interval and random starting point have been specified, the elements that are included in the sample become automatic. They form a cluster of elements. In our population of 50, there are only 10 possible systematic samples of size $n=5$ that can be drawn, because each cluster includes $\frac{1}{10}$ of the population. In general, the number of possible samples is equal to k, the sampling interval. With populations that are large relative to the sample size, the value of k, and therefore the number of possible samples, increases substantially.

Because we use all the elements in the cluster generated by systematic sampling, it is called a *one-stage cluster sampling procedure*. Also, it is clear that all possible combinations of elements are not equally likely. We have reduced the number of possible samples from over 2 million with simple random sampling to 10 with systematic sampling.

Fortunately, it can be shown that the mean of the sampling distribution of means generated by repeated systematic sampling is equal to the population mean. That is, the mean from any one systematic sample is an unbiased estimator of the population mean. We may then calculate meaningful confidence intervals as we did with simple random sampling.[2] In fact, if the frame from which we are sampling is truly random, a systematic sample may be thought of as being identical to simple random sampling. In most applications the results are almost identical.

The mean age for the systematic sample we drew is (reading the ages associated with the selected elements from Table 10.1):

$$\overline{X} = \frac{27 + 29 + 19 + 22 + 23}{5}$$

$$= \frac{120}{5}$$

$$= 24.0$$

and $\Sigma X^2 = (27)^2 + (29)^2 + (19)^2 + (22)^2 + (23)^2$

$$= 729 + 841 + 361 + 484 + 529$$

$$= 2944$$

$$\frac{(\Sigma X)^2}{n} = \frac{(120)^2}{5}$$

$$= \frac{14400}{5}$$

$$= 2880$$

---

[2] There are some very technical aspects related to the calculation of standard error that apply here. They are well beyond the scope of this book and have been ignored. In most situations these refinements add little to real managerial understanding of sampling results. We proceed here as if the formulas related to simple random sampling apply. For technical detail see Leslie Kish, *Survey Sampling* (New York: Wiley, 1965), pp. 117–18.

Therefore,

$$s^2 = \frac{2944 - 2880}{4}$$

$$= \frac{64}{4}$$

$$= 16$$

Then

$$s = 4$$

The standard error is

$$\frac{4}{\sqrt{5}} = \frac{4}{2.24}$$

$$= 1.79$$

The 95 percent confidence interval is then

$$24.0 \pm 2(1.79) = 24.0 \pm 3.58$$
$$= 20.4 - 27.6$$

The true mean is again contained within the 95 percent interval. Because of the particular elements that formed the cluster we selected, the standard error is larger than in the simple random sample we selected earlier; thus, so is the confidence interval.

Systematic sampling is more used in practice than simple random sampling, because it is much easier and cheaper to select a systematic sample. With systematic sampling we do not jump back and forth all over our sampling frame wherever our random number leads us, nor do we have to worry about checking for duplication of elements. In simple random sampling both of these problems occur. Because systematic sampling is a close substitute for simple random sampling, we may use it to select elements within strata in stratified sampling.

There is one other benefit of systematic sampling over simple random sampling, which is that we do not need a complete sampling frame to draw a systematic sample. An interviewer instructed to interview every 20th customer can do so without a full list of all customers. Similarly, he or she could select a sample of every third house without a full list of the houses available.

The Problem of Periodicity

There is one major problem with systematic sampling, namely, that we will obtain biased estimates if the list of elements forming the frame forms a cyclical pattern that coincides with a multiple of the size of the sampling interval. This type of frame is said to have *periodicity*. We may illustrate this problem with two examples. Suppose we wanted to interview residents of a student housing complex[3] and selected housing units from a list of all units arranged in numerical order: 1, 2, . . . , 599, 600. Suppose our sampling interval were 10 and our random starting number 5. Our sample would contain the 60 housing units numbered 5, 15, 25, . . . , 585, 595. Now suppose that the complex was built such that the units ending in 5, 25, 45, 65, and 85 were corner units. These corner units had one more bedroom than the other units and had higher rent. They also were allocated to students on the basis of seniority (number of years in the complex) and on the basis of having at least three children. So half of our sample would consist of people with at least three children who had been in the complex a number of years and were willing to pay the higher rent. Our sample would not be representative of the complex. Note here that the cyclical pattern is twice the size of the sampling interval. The pattern could be any multiple of the sampling interval and cause bias in our estimates.

As a second example,[4] consider the problem of a movie theater manager who wants to estimate total popcorn sales by using a sample of certain days' sales. Suppose it is decided to select one day from each week of the year—that is, $n = 52$. The sampling interval is then $365/52 = 7$. The sample would then only allow recording popcorn sales on the same day of the week for all 52 weeks. A sample of Saturdays would obviously overstate sales, whereas a sample of Tuesdays would understate sales.

The researcher must be sensitive to periodicity in a sampling frame if the intention is to use systematic sampling. If periodicity exists, it must be removed from the frame by rearranging the elements, or some other sampling procedure must be adopted.

Implicit Stratification with Systematic Sampling

Ordered frames are not always bad for systematic sampling. If the frame is ordered on what might be used as a stratification variable, selection of a systematic sample will automatically provide a stratified sample. In this situation, a systematic sample will produce a more statistically efficient result than simple random sampling.

Consider the systematic sample of students we selected. We know that the list of students is ordered by whether they are graduate or undergraduate students, in the ratio 20/30. With a sampling interval of 10, we know that the first two sample elements must come from the graduate stratum and the last three from the undergraduate stratum. Thus we automatically selected a proportionate stratified sample of students with our systematic sample.

If the researcher is aware of the implicit stratification that has occurred, it is possible to use stratified formulas to calculate the sample mean and standard

---

[3] This example is adapted from Earl Babbie, *Survey Research Methods* (Belmont, Calif.: Wadsworth, 1973), p. 93.

[4] This example is adapted from Gilbert A. Churchill, Jr., *Marketing Research: Methodological Foundations* (Hinsdale, Ill.: Dryden Press, 1976), p. 293.

error. The result is a smaller confidence interval. In our student age sample, the ages of the students within strata would be:

Stratum 1:   27, 29
Stratum 2:   19, 22, 23

The reader is encouraged to do the necessary calculations to show the reduction in standard error. It should now be intuitively obvious by just looking at the numbers arranged in strata.

In summary, systematic sampling offers potential advantages in (1) ease of sample selection, (2) cost, (3) removal of the need for a complete frame, and (4) implicit stratification of properly ordered frames. Difficulties are related to (1) the problem of possible periodicity and (2) possible technical problems in calculating standard error. Systematic sampling is moderately used in practice.

AREA SAMPLING

The Basics

With simple random sampling, stratified sampling, and most applications of systematic sampling discussed so far, a complete and accurate listing of the elements of the population is required. Unfortunately, for a great many marketing research applications such lists are impossible to generate at a reasonable cost. Lists are not available for such populations as all the adults in the United States, all the inhabitants of a state or city, all users of a particular product, or all university students or church members. It may be possible to obtain such lists, but the cost would be extremely high, and they would probably contain many inaccuracies. Sampling practitioners have developed an ingenious solution to this problem. They reasoned that people reside on a specific piece of land, so why not sample pieces of land and interview the persons who reside there? So the word "area" in area sample originally referred to a piece of land. *An area sample is actually a sampling of areas.* It is extensively used in practice.

We shall illustrate this concept by outlining what a one-stage area sample might look like. Suppose we want to run an in-home usage test of a new formulation of a shampoo. We have decided to run this test in Atlanta. An accurate listing of all households in Atlanta is unavailable, since the city directory and telephone book are both very out of date even right after they are published. So we select an area sample using the following method:

1   List all city blocks in Atlanta, N_B.
2   Choose a simple random or systematic sample of n_B city blocks from the population of N_B city blocks.
3   Attempt to place the product in all households in the chosen blocks, n_B.

This is a probability sampling procedure because the probability of any household being selected is equal to the sampling fraction, n_B/N_B. If Atlanta had 10,000 blocks and we selected a sample of 20 blocks, the probability of any household being selected would be $20/10,000 = .002$. The reason why this probability equals the sampling fraction for the blocks is that we are using all households in the selected blocks as part of the sample.

Multistage Area Samples

An area sample can have as many stages as the researcher desires. Most area samples have more than one stage. What would a two-stage area sample designed for our product usage test look like? The steps would be:

1   List all city blocks in Atlanta, N_B.
2   Choose a simple random sample or systematic sample of n_B city blocks.
3   List the households located in the selected city blocks, N_H.
4   Select a simple random or systematic sample of n_H households from the selected n_B city blocks.

Note that the first two steps of two-stage area sampling are the same as in one-stage area sampling. With the latter, however, we were required to make one list (of blocks), and we used probability sampling procedures only once (to select the blocks). In two-stage area sampling we were required to make two lists (blocks and then households), and we used probability sampling procedures twice (to select blocks and then households). In a two-stage area sample we twice repeated the sequence "list population sampling units, and then sample." Thus, in a k-stage area sample we would go through this sequence k times.

A multistage area sample may be illustrated by describing the five-stage area sampling process used by the Survey Research Center of the Institute for Social Research of the University of Michigan for its many national studies.[5] Figure 10-1 gives a graphic view of the five stages of this process. The five stages are:

Stage 1   The continental United States is divided into 74 "primary areas." These areas are usually counties, groups of counties, or metropolitan areas. A probability sample of primary areas is then made. That is, the researchers list the areas and then sample from this list. The top row of Figure 10-1 depicts the primary areas on the map of the continental United States and shows the selection of one primary area. It is common for the researchers to stratify the primary-area population to assure themselves that their sample will include the proper proportion of primary areas of different types. For example, a geographic stratification would ensure that each region of the country is represented. Multiple stratification variables are often used.

---

[5] This section is based on the *Interviewer's Manual*, rev. ed., Survey Research Center, Institute for Social Research, The University of Michigan, Ann Arbor, 1976, pp. 35–37.

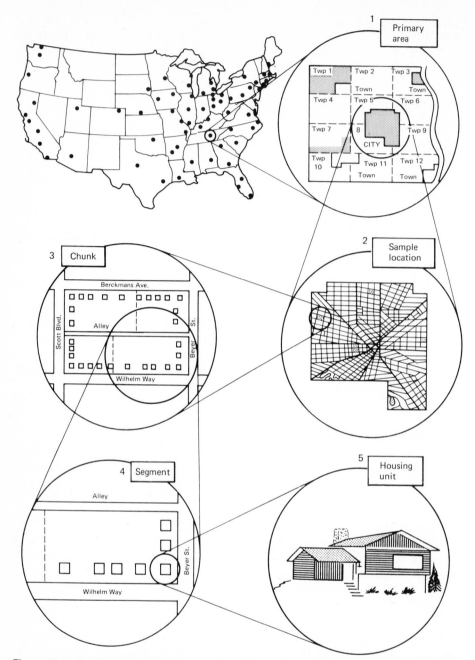

Figure 10-1 An illustration of area sampling. (*Adapted from* Interviewer's Manual, *rev. ed., Survey Research Center, Institute for Social Research, The University of Michigan, Ann Arbor, 1976, p. 36.*)

Stage 2 A listing is made of the large cities, medium-sized towns, and remaining areas in the selected primary areas. In the example on Figure 10-1, the selected area consists of one large city, four medium-sized towns, and open space. This area would probably be stratified into three groups: (1) large cities, (2) smaller cities and towns, and (3) open space. Then one or more of what are called "sample locations" would be selected by probability methods from each stratum. Again the researchers list the population sampling units and select a probability sample.

We should also note that they have again been stratified to ensure a representative sample. The connected circles running from "primary area" to "sample location" on Figure 10-1 illustrate stage 2 for the selection of one sample location from one primary area previously selected.

Stage 3 A listing is made of the geographic areas within the sample location. These geographic areas must have identifiable boundaries—for example, city blocks, rural roads, rivers, or county lines. These geographic areas are referred to as "chunks." On the average, chunks are designed to contain from 16 to 40 dwellings, but they may contain more in large cities. A probability sample of chunks is then selected from each selected sample location obtained in stage 2. The theme of "list sampling units and select a probability sample" should be very obvious. The connected circles running from "sample location" to "chunk" on Figure 10-1 illustrate stage 3 for the selection of one chunk from one sample location previously selected.

Stage 4 A listing is made of all the housing units in the selected chunk, which is then divided into smaller units called "segments," containing from 4 to 16 housing units. A probability sample of segments is then selected. The connected circles running from "chunk" to "segment" on Figure 10-1 illustrate the selection of one segment from a chunk that was previously selected.

Stage 5 From the listing of housing units in segments, a probability sample of housing units is selected. The connected circles running from "segment" to "housing unit" on Figure 10-1 illustrate the selection of one housing unit from one segment that was previously selected. If this process continued to include the listing of persons within housing units and then selected a probability sample of persons, it would be a six-stage area sample. Note that a housing unit does not have to be a single-family dwelling. A full 70-unit apartment building would count as 70 housing units.

The Properties of Multistage Area Samples

Multistage area sampling is much less statistically efficient than simple random sampling. In a simple random sample a single sampling error is calculated. A two-stage area sample is subject to two sampling errors. The selection of the clusters at the first stage is only an estimate of the population of clusters; that is, sampling error occurs. In this way, the selection of elements from within a cluster is only an estimate of the population of elements within that cluster. Thus, a five-stage area sample would contain five sampling errors. The formulas to calculate the standard error from a multistage area sample are too complex to be discussed here. Researchers should be sensitive to this issue and should be prepared to consult a technical expert for the proper calculation. In practice, the results obtained from the final stage are often treated as if they came from a direct probability sampling of a list of final elements. That is, the formulas used are those for simple random sampling and stratified sampling. The net effect of doing this is to understate the sampling error that has occurred. However, for decisions where the risk of such an understatement is explicitly tolerated, we cannot be too critical of such a shortcut procedure.

The technical aspects may seem complex enough at this point, but there are still some basics about the sampling error generated in multistage area sampling that should be understood.[6] Sampling error is decreased by an increase in (1) sample size and (2) the homogeneity of the elements being sampled. Sample size and homogeneity affect sampling error at each stage of a multistage sample design. Thus, to have a small sampling error at the time of selecting clusters, we would like to select a large number from a group of very similar clusters. Similarly, to have a small sampling error at the time of selecting elements from a given cluster, we would like to select a large number from a group of very similar elements. For any given sample size, we cannot increase the number of clusters without decreasing the number of elements within each cluster. Therefore, cluster-level error would seem to be decreased at the expense of element-level error. This is true, but the effect is limited by the fact that elements within area sample clusters tend to be more homogeneous than the population as a whole. For example, the residents of a city block are more similar than those in the county or even city as a whole. Therefore, the sample size within clusters of this type can be quite small and still yield a reasonable sampling error. Clusters, on the other hand, tend to be more heterogeneous. Thus, a large number of clusters may be necessary to reduce the sampling error to a reasonable size at the cluster selection level. This discussion leads to the conclusion that we should select a large number of clusters and a small number of elements within each cluster in order to have the best statistical efficiency.

But what about total efficiency? It does have a role to play. The more clusters we select, the more lists of elements we have to prepare, the more geographical areas we have to send interviewers to, and the more administrative complications we will have to deal with. All these factors increase the cost of the study, so the final sample design involves a tradeoff between statistical efficiency and cost. There is no optimal choice available. The researcher must make this tradeoff based on the objectives of the study, the amount of money available, and the amount of error that is acceptable.

Equal-Probability Area Sampling

Earlier we defined probability sampling as a technique where each element has a known chance of being selected. In all the types of sampling discussed so far, except disproportionate statistical sampling, each element has had an equal

---

[6] This discussion follows an excellent one in Babbie, op. cit., pp. 98–99.

chance of being selected. This is the easiest way to ensure that the sample selected represents the population. In this section we shall discuss how we obtain equal probabilities for each element. Later in the chapter we shall discuss sampling with unequal probabilities for the elements.

There are two ways to assure equal-chance selection of elements in an area sample.

1   Equal-Chance Selection of Clusters—Equal-Proportion Selection of Elements within Clusters   In this method each cluster is given an equal chance of selection regardless of size, then the same proportion of the elements is selected from within each cluster. Thus, each element has an equal chance of being selected. Let us illustrate this result. Suppose we have 1000 elements divided into 50 clusters of different sizes. If we select a sample of 5 clusters, each cluster has a 5/50 chance of being selected. If we then select one-fifth of the elements within each cluster, the total probability of an element being selected is

$$^5/_{50} \times {}^1/_5 = .1 \times .2 = .02$$

In this way bigger clusters have more elements selected. This balances the fact that these clusters had only as high a chance of being selected as smaller clusters. This process would require a sample size of $.02 \times 1000 = 20$ elements. Note that for equal-probability sampling, the probability of an element being selected is equal to the sampling fraction. In this case $20/1000 = .02$.

More typically we would have a specified sample size and would be asked to select the number of clusters and proportion of elements within each cluster. A number of combinations of numbers of clusters and within-cluster proportions could accomplish this task. For example, the following combinations yield a probability of selection of .02:

(1)   10 clusters and $^1/_{10}$ of the elements
$$= {}^{10}/_{50} \times {}^1/_{10}$$
$$= .2 \times .1 = .02$$

(2)   20 clusters and $^5/_{100}$ of the elements
$$= {}^{20}/_{50} \times {}^5/_{100}$$
$$= .4 \times .05 = .02$$

We can apply this procedure to multistage designs, as long as we continue to select the elements at each stage with equal proportion. Let's use the Institute for Social Research design to illustrate this. Suppose that at stage 1 we selected 10 of the 74 "primary areas." These primary areas vary in size, so at stage 2 we select $^2/_5$ of the "sample location sections" in each primary area; each sample location section therefore has an equal probability of being selected equal to:

$$^{10}/_{74} \times {}^2/_5 = .14 \times .4 = .056$$

Now for stage 3, if we select a sample of "chunks" from each sample location section at the rate of 7/400, each chunk will have an equal chance of being selected even if the sample location sections are of different sizes. If the stage 4 proportion to select "segments" is $\frac{1}{4}$ and the stage 5 proportion to select "housing units" is $\frac{1}{5}$, the probability of selecting any housing unit is:

$$\begin{matrix} \text{House-} \\ \text{hold unit} \\ \text{proba-} \\ \text{bility} \end{matrix} = \begin{matrix} \text{stage 1} \\ \text{pro-} \\ \text{portion} \end{matrix} \times \begin{matrix} \text{stage 2} \\ \text{pro-} \\ \text{portion} \end{matrix} \times \begin{matrix} \text{stage 3} \\ \text{pro-} \\ \text{portion} \end{matrix} \times \begin{matrix} \text{stage 4} \\ \text{pro-} \\ \text{portion} \end{matrix} \times \begin{matrix} \text{stage 5} \\ \text{pro-} \\ \text{portion} \end{matrix}$$

$$= \tfrac{10}{74} \times \tfrac{2}{5} \times \tfrac{7}{400} \times \tfrac{1}{4} \times \tfrac{1}{5}$$
$$= .14 \times .4 \times .018 \times .25 \times .2$$
$$= .00005$$

In a household population of 70 million this design would require a sample size of $.00005 \times 70$ million $= 3500$. Of course, given a sample size of 3500 and a sampling fraction objective of .00005, we can adjust the proportions of sampling units selected at various stages as long as their product continues to equal .00005.

What makes this yield equal probability for each household is that we select an equal proportion within each cluster at each stage. Thus different-sized clusters are automatically taken care of. Clearly, if we had selected the same number of sampling units at each stage, the household unit elements would have different probabilities—those from big clusters would have much less chance of being selected than those from small clusters. This process would yield equal probabilities for elements only if all clusters were the same size.

2 Probability Proportionate to Size (PPS)   There is another method of obtaining equal element probabilities that is more statistically efficient than the equal-proportion method discussed above. In the latter method a relatively small number of large clusters are selected, and thus the elements selected to represent all large clusters are selected from a few clusters. In response to this problem, the more recommended method of selecting first-stage clusters is the "probability proportionate to size" (PPS) method.

In a two-stage PPS the procedure would be as follows. In the first stage of the method, each cluster is assigned a chance of selection proportionate to the number of second-stage elements it contains, with the result that larger clusters have a better chance of selection than small ones. Then in the second stage the same number of sampling units are selected from each selected cluster. Thus a smaller proportion of elements will be selected from larger clusters than from small ones, with the result that the probability of all elements being selected at the second stage is the same. As an illustration, suppose we have 10 city blocks as follows:

Block number	Number of households
1	10
2	20
3	30
4	10
5	100
6	30
7	70
8	30
9	50
10	50
Total households	400

The relevant probability proportionate to size for block B is

$$PPS_B = \frac{\text{number of households in block B}}{\text{total number of households}}$$

for block 1,

$$PPS_1 = 10/400 = .025$$

For block 9,

$$PPS_9 = 50/400 = .125$$

We mechanically select a PPS block sample by calculating the cumulative number of households and assigning random numbers in proportion to this cumulative distribution.

Block number	Number of households	Cumulative number of households	Associated random numbers
1	10	10	001–010
2	20	30	011–030
3	30	60	031–060
4	10	70	061–070
5	100	170	071–170
6	30	200	171–200
7	70	270	201–270
8	30	300	271–300
9	50	350	301–350
10	50	400	351–400
Total	400		

If we wanted a sample of three blocks, we would obtain three 3-digit random numbers between 001 and 400. Suppose we obtained the numbers 124, 302, and 027; our sample would be blocks 5, 9, and 2 We then select five households from blocks 2, 5, and 9. The probabilities of selecting elements are:

Probability of element in block B
$$= \text{block probability} \times \text{within-block element probability}$$
For elements in block $2 = {}^{20}/_{400} \times {}^{5}/_{20}$
$$= .05 \times .25$$
$$= .0125$$
For elements in block $5 = {}^{100}/_{400} \times {}^{5}/_{100}$
$$= .25 \times .05$$
$$= .0125$$
For elements in block $9 = {}^{50}/_{400} \times {}^{5}/_{50}$
$$= .125 \times .1$$
$$= .0125$$

The stage 1 and stage 2 probabilities balance each other to give equal probability of selection for all elements. The same result also holds for the unselected blocks.

In a multistage area sample we can use the PPS method for the first two stages to ensure equal probabilities to that point. Then we can select equal proportions from that point on to yield equal probabilities of all elements at the final stage. For example, if we really had a five-stage area sample and used PPS as in the example above, the element probability at the final stage might be:

Element probability $=$ probability after 2 stages $\times$
probability at other stages
$$= .0125 \times .018 \times .50 \times .3$$
$$= .00003$$

PPS is used to help ensure that large clusters are represented in the sample. Alternatively, this may be done by stratifying the first-stage cluster by size and sampling within clusters. PPS and stratification on size would not be used together.

Unequal-Probability Area Sampling

In all the probability sampling methods discussed so far, except disproportionate stratified sampling, each population element had an equal chance of selection. Recall that in our original definition of probability sampling each element only needed a known chance of being selected to be a probability procedure. Often in area sampling, elements are selected disproportionately; that is, elements have different probabilities of being selected. The research may yield unequal probabilities for a number of reasons, including:

1   The researcher wants to do detailed subgroup analysis, and so he or she purposely oversamples a small subgroup to have a large enough sample to do meaningful analysis for that group. Such a subgroup might be working women.

2   The researcher is doing disproportionate stratified sampling to reduce within-stratum and overall sampling error.

3   A sample yields a smaller proportion of a particular subgroup than the population proportion.

4   A PPS design requires knowledge of cluster sizes. If these sizes turn out to be incorrect, the result is that the cluster will be given a disproportionately high or low probability of being selected.

Thus, we may obtain unequal probabilities for element selection from a number of purposeful or accidental happenings. They present no problems as long as the researcher is interested in doing only within-subgroup analysis. Suppose, for example, we were estimating the weekly gasoline consumption among undergraduate and graduate students in our population of 50 students. If we took a sample of 10 from each subgroup, the graduate students would have a probability of selection of $^{10}/_{20} = .5$, and the undergraduates $^{10}/_{30} = .33$. Note that the overall sampling fraction $^{20}/_{50} = .4$ does not equal the probability of each element being selected. This relationship does now hold only within the subgroups. Suppose we estimated the average gasoline consumption of graduate students as $100/10 = 10$ gallons per week, and of undergraduates as $50/10 = 5$ gallons per week. Those estimates are valid, and we can compare them with each other. However, if we combine the subgroups to make an overall estimate, the higher consumption of graduate students would be overrepresented, thus biasing the estimate upwards. This average is

$$\overline{X}_{gasoline} = .5(10) + .5(5)$$
$$= 5 + 2.5$$
$$= 7.5$$

What we want is to have the weights reflect the subpopulation sizes. So the unbiased estimate is

$$\overline{X}_{gasoline} = .4(10) + .6(5)$$
$$= 4 + 3$$
$$= 7$$

You will recognize these weights as the population proportions from the stratified sampling section. This example was easy because we knew all about the subpopulation sizes. More realistically, we are likely to know the probability of selecting an element from subgroups. Can we directly use element probabilities to obtain proper weights? The answer is yes.

The rule is that an element should be assigned a weighting factor *in proportion to the inverse of its probability of being selected.*

In our gasoline example,

1 For graduate students:
   Probability of selection $= .5$

   Inverse $= \dfrac{1}{.5} = 2.0$

2 For undergraduate students:
   Probability of selection $= .33$

   Inverse $= \dfrac{1}{.33} = 3.0$

With this information there are two ways to obtain our overall average of 7 gallons. The first is to multiply the total gallons in each subgroup and the number in the sample in each subgroup by their respective inverse, and then take the average. Here we get

$$
\begin{array}{ll}
\text{Graduates:} & 100 \text{ gallons} \times 2 = 200 \\
& 10 \text{ students} \times 2 = 20 \\
\text{Undergraduates:} & 50 \text{ gallons} \times 3 = 150 \\
& 10 \text{ students} \times 3 = 30
\end{array}
$$

$$
\begin{array}{ll}
\text{Total gallons} & = 200 + 150 = 350 \\
\text{Total students} & = 20 + 30 = 50 \\
\text{Average gallons} & = \dfrac{350}{50} = 7
\end{array}
$$

The 50 is called the *weighted sample size.*

The alternative is to convert the inverses to proportions with respect to each other, then take a weighted average.

$$
\begin{array}{ll}
\text{Graduate inverse} & = 2 \\
\text{Undergraduate inverse} & = 3 \\
\text{Total of inverses} & = 5
\end{array}
$$

$$
\begin{array}{ll}
\text{Proportion graduate} & = {}^2/_5 = .4 \\
\text{Proportion undergraduate} & = {}^3/_5 = .6
\end{array}
$$

You will recognize these as our population weighting factors.

The latter method is much preferred for large studies with small subgroup sampling fractions. For example, if three subgroups had probabilities of element selection of .00005, .000047, and .000052, the respective inverses are 20,000, 21,277, and 19,231. Multiplying by these weights is certainly more complicated than taking their proportions, which are .33, .35, and .31. Note that in equal-probability sampling each element would be assigned the same weight, as the inverses would be equal. This, of course, is as it should be.

Weighting can be handled in a number of ways. If we have our data on computer cards, we can simply duplicate cards for various subgroups to bring them up to the proper proportions. In our gasoline example, we would reproduce the graduate cards twice and the undergraduate ones three times. This method will do for small jobs but is impossible for large ones. Fortunately, most good computer data analysis packages have procedures where the researcher can specify weighting factors. The analysis program then automatically includes them as part of the analysis.

Statistical Inference and Complex Sampling Procedures

Statistical inference was developed on the basis of simple random sampling. Can it be meaningfully applied to samples of the complexity we have seen in this chapter? The evidence leads us to believe that it can. Frankel's significant study in this area concluded that (1) the sample estimates were approximately unbiased, (2) the sample variances of these estimates were approximately unbiased, and (3) the calculated standard error allowed for the calculation of valid confidence intervals.[7]

The reader should now be able to outline the design of a sampling plan to meet his or her objectives. For the complexities of statistical inference in these complex designs, one should consult a technical specialist.

In Chapter 11, we shall look at some of the harsh realities that interfere with the accuracy of our study—realities that go beyond sampling errors. We shall overview nonsampling errors and then discuss the one aspect of sample design that we have not yet addressed. This aspect is the determination of sample size.

SUMMARY

1 Stratified sampling allows for the reduction of the standard error over simple random sampling.

2 To select a stratified sample, one divides the population into mutually exclusive and collectively exhaustive strata and then selects a probability sample from each stratum. The strata are designed to be more homogeneous than the total population.

3 A proportionate stratified sample is one where the sample size is allocated to strata in proportion to the number of population elements in the strata.

4 Sample elements may also be allocated on a basis disproportionate with the population size of strata. The objective here is to oversample the strata with the higher variability in order to reduce the standard error within the strata.

5 The overall mean in stratified sampling is the weighted average of the within-strata means. The weighting factor is the ratio of the stratum population size to total population size, $N_{\text{st.}j}/N$ or W_j.

6 The overall standard error is the square root of the weighted combination of the square of the standard error within each stratum. The weighting factor is the square of the W_j. The standard error is smaller than with simple random

[7] Martin R. Frankel, *Inference from Survey Samples: An Empirical Investigation* (Ann Arbor, Mich.: Survey Research Center, Institute for Social Research, The University of Michigan, 1971), pp. 104–116.

sampling because we use only within-stratum variation to calculate the overall standard error.

7   The number of possible stratified samples is the product of the number of all possible samples within each stratum.

8   For a stratification variable to be useful, it must be correlated with the variable we are measuring.

9   In cluster sampling we randomly select a cluster or group of sampling units at one time. To do this the population is divided into mutually exclusive and collectively exhaustive groups.

10   These groups are designed to be as heterogeneous as the population.

11   Statistical efficiency involves the comparison of the standard errors of different sampling procedures.

12   Overall efficiency involves the comparison of the standard error per dollar spent.

13   In systematic sampling, we select every kth element in the frame, after a random start somewhere within the first k elements.

14   The sampling interval equals N/n and is equal to the number of possible samples in a systematic procedure.

15   A frame with a cyclical pattern that coincides with a multiple of the size of the sampling interval will yield biased results in systematic sampling.

16   A systematic sample of a frame ordered on a stratification variable yields a stratified sample.

17   Area sampling involves selecting pieces of geography.

18   A multistage area sample involves the repeated process of listing sampling units and selecting a probability sample from this list.

19   A multistage sample will have equal probability of the selection of each element if the selection at each stage involves a given proportion of sampling units. The probability of element selection equals the product of the individual proportions.

20   Alternatively, equal element probability can be obtained by selecting the first-stage sampling units with probabilities proportionate to size, and then selecting the same number of second-stage sampling units in each selected first-stage unit.

21   Elements may be selected with unequal probabilities.

22   With disproportionate sampling, the elements must be weighted before meaningful total-sample analysis can be done.

23   An element should be assigned a weighting factor in proportion to the inverse of its probability of being selected.

DISCUSSION QUESTIONS

1   How is a stratified sample selected?
2   What is the objective of stratified sampling?
3   What is proportionate stratified sampling?
4   What is disproportionate stratified sampling?

5 How are the whole-sample mean and standard error calculated from a stratified sample?

6 Under what circumstances does stratified sampling reduce the standard error?

7 Why does stratified sampling reduce the standard error?

8 What is cluster sampling?

9 What are statistical efficiency and overall efficiency?

10 How is a systematic sample selected?

11 What is periodicity? How is it caused and cured?

12 How does implicit stratification occur?

13 What is area sampling?

14 What is multistage area sampling?

15 How does one get equal probability of element selection using a multistage area sampling procedure?

16 Why does one sometimes get unequal probabilities of element selection?

17 How are whole-sample estimates made when elements have unequal selection probabilities?

SUGGESTED READING

Babbie, Earl, *Survey Research Methods* (Belmont, Calif.: Wadsworth, 1973), chap. 5, pp. 92–106, and chap. 6. A verbal overview of the details of stratified and cluster sampling, with details of actual sampling plans.

Kish, Leslie, *Survey Sampling* (New York: Wiley, 1965), chaps. 3–7. An advanced discussion of the mathematics of stratified and cluster sampling.

Slonim, Morris James, *Sampling* (New York: Simon and Schuster, 1960), chaps. 8–10. An intuitive verbal overview of stratified and cluster sampling.

Chapter 11

Practical Aspects of Sampling: Nonsampling Error and Sample Size

In this chapter we will discuss two very pragmatic aspects of sampling in marketing research. The first is nonsampling error, a category encompassing all the problems that can arise to make the very precise-looking statistical calculations of the previous two chapters not really very precise at all. This section will put some practical perspective on the sampling procedures we discussed earlier. We shall then introduce the concept of total error, as a way of assessing the overall accuracy of sample results. The final part of this chapter will discuss the determination of sample size. This issue is one that does have a statistical component to it. However, other aspects of the marketing research process, including study objectives, time requirements, cost, nonsampling errors, and data analysis, all have a bearing on determining sample size. The tradeoffs required among these aspects make the sample size decision a more pragmatic than theoretical one. Hence, we have included it in this chapter.

NONSAMPLING ERRORS

Introduction

Nonsampling errors include all the errors that may occur in the marketing research process except the sampling error that we discussed in Chapters 9 and

10. The concept of nonsampling error simply includes all the aspects of the research process where mistakes and deliberate deceptions can occur. Unfortunately, these mistakes and deceptions occur with great frequency in the marketing research process. We must therefore be aware of (1) what nonsampling errors may occur, (2) what effect these errors may have on our results, and (3) what steps we can take to reduce these errors. This chapter deals with the first two issues, identification of nonsampling errors and possible effects of these errors. The details of how to reduce nonsampling errors will be left to the remaining chapters of the book, since most of them focus on that topic. The chapters that deal with the reduction of nonsampling errors will be identified with the specific error in the list of errors that follows later in this chapter.

The Effect of Nonsampling Errors

Sampling error has two properties that make it useful to the researcher: (1) it is measurable, and (2) it decreases as the sample size increases. Unfortunately, nonsampling errors are not easily measurable, and they do not decrease with sample size. In fact, in all likelihood, nonsampling errors increase as sample size increases. What nonsampling errors do is put a bias in our results of unknown direction and magnitude. One practicing researcher put forth the following view of the effect of nonsampling errors:

> Over the years I have used a simple rule of thumb that the true mean square error of field studies is at least twice the size of reported theoretical sampling error, though there is evidence to suggest that it is larger in many commercial surveys.[1]

Indeed, nonsampling error can render the results of a study useless, even though the researchers calculated a very precise confidence interval. The danger is that a researcher will think the confidence interval tells the whole story. The next section catalogs the nonsampling errors that may occur.

Types of Nonsampling Errors

The first three types of nonsampling errors we will discuss are very directly related to the sampling procedures presented in Chapters 8 to 10.

Defective Population Definition   The study population must be defined to fit the study objectives. Consider the case of the manager of one of the restaurants in a major metropolitan airport. She would like to know what sort of image the restaurant has among those who have some likelihood of eating in the airport. The population is defined as people over 18 years old, getting off planes in the week of September 12 to 19. If the sample is selected from this population, one might get misleading results. It does not include significant numbers of potential customers, i.e., people who are visiting the airport but who are not landing on planes, and people who are just taking off. Also, the sample includes people who

---

[1] Benjamin Lipstein, "In Defense of Small Samples," *Journal of Advertising Research*, vol. 15, p. 39, February 1975.

have no chance of eating at the restaurant, i.e., people who change planes without going into the main terminal where the restaurants are. Meaningful conclusions from the study are questionable.

Frame Is Nonrepresentative of the Population The sampling frame must match the defined population. Consider the case of an investment company that uses the telephone book to select a sample of "potential stock buyers." This frame would not cover the defined population well, as a significant number of high-income people have unlisted phone numbers. These high-income people are the prime potential stock buyers. Again, meaningful conclusions are suspect.

Nonresponse Errors Errors occur because people in the selected sample either refuse to be a part of the sample or are not at home during the sampling period. A sample is a probability sample as selected. If some of the selected elements do not form part of the realized sample, it is not a true probability sample. The resulting error is called nonresponse error.

As an example of this problem, consider the case of a resort developer who attempts to interview people during the day. The study yields some refusals and a lot of "not at homes." We must wonder if the refusals as a group hold different attitudes about the development from those who responded. Also, by interviewing only in the day, the developer missed all families where both the spouses work. This group may be a prime prospect.

Frame problems and nonresponse errors are discussed in Chapter 20. The remaining nonsampling errors, which follow, are related to areas of the research process other than sampling.

Faulty Problem Definition A product manager requests a study to test a media mix. If the true problem is pricing strategy, there is no advantage in having a small confidence interval about the media mix estimates. This issue was discussed in detail in Chapter 5, but its importance must again be emphasized.

Poor Questionnaire Design In a survey of his constituents, a congressman asked: "Should the Congress challenge the do-nothing administration and take action on unemployment?" This is hardly the way to find their true feeling on a complex issue. What good is a confidence interval here? Most questionnaire design problems are more complex than this, relating to question sequence, length, word usage, etc., and the topic is discussed fully in Chapter 19.

Measurement Error Measurement is the process of assigning numbers to observed phenomena. A researcher may try to develop a scale of interest in a new product, but the scaling may be done improperly. This is a complex area which will be discussed in detail in Chapters 12 and 13.

Interviewer-related Errors Interviewers can lead respondents to answer in a particular way either by accident or on purpose. They also have been known to record responses improperly and even to fill out questionnaires without interviewing anyone. In other words, they cheat. This issue is discussed in Chapter 20.

Improper Causal Inferences   A producer of heavy equipment changes the compensation scheme of its sales force, and the following year sales double. Management infers that the new compensation plan caused the sales increase. It is also possible that other factors could have caused it—for example, the economy could have improved, the product was improved, or even the sales-persons have become more experienced. Management has observed an association between sales and compensation and has inferred the cause. The search for causes is discussed in Chapters 14 to 16.

Data Processing Errors   Questionnaires must be prepared for analysis. This involves coding the responses, recording the codes, punching the codes onto computer cards, and so on. Mistakes can occur in all these activities, or a bias could be exhibited in coding responses. These issues are discussed in Chapter 21.

Data Analysis Errors   Simple mistakes can occur in data analysis, such as adding numbers incorrectly. Most errors here are more complex than this. They usually involve the misapplication of data analysis procedures. This topic is discussed in Chapters 22, 23, 25, and 26.

Interpretation Errors   We have all observed that people can interpret a set of data to suit their own purposes. This bias may be explicitly deliberate or subconscious. It can also be related to misunderstandings of study results. This issue was discussed in Chapter 5 and will be treated further in Chapter 24.

Auspices Bias   Error can occur because of the respondents' perception of who is conducting the study. Consider the following question: "We represent the Procter and Gamble Company, and we would like to know your opinion of our product, Pampers." People's true feelings may not come out when they know the source of the study.

Total Error

What should be clear now is that a small sampling error does not necessarily indicate an accurate result. What the user of research must be concerned about is *total error,* where:

Total error = sampling error + nonsampling error

The formal measurement and treatment of nonsampling error is rarely done in practice and is often impossible for most types of nonsampling error. All the researcher can do is try to use the best procedures available to keep nonsampling error low.

THE DETERMINATION OF SAMPLE SIZE

Armed with an understanding of both sampling error and nonsampling error, we now turn our attention to the question of sample size determination. Both types of error bear on this question. First, let us examine sample size in statistical theory.

The Question of Sample Size in Statistical Theory

Previously, in simple random sampling for a known sample size, we calculated the confidence interval of our estimate at a given level of confidence. To do this for a continuous measure we had the following information:

1   An estimate of the mean, $\overline{X}$.
2   An estimate of the standard deviation, s.
3   A sample size.
4   A level of confidence.
5   Using (2) and (3), we calculated the standard error, $s_{\overline{x}}$. We then calculated the relevant confidence interval. The equation to do this at the 95 percent confidence level was:

$$\text{Confidence interval} = \overline{X} \pm 2\,\frac{s}{\sqrt{n}}$$

We have calculated $\overline{X}$ and s, and know n, so we can solve this equation for the confidence interval. Or, we could calculate the precision we obtained using part of the above equation as follows:

$$\text{Precision} = \pm 2\,\frac{s}{\sqrt{n}}$$

Now suppose we want to reach a given level of precision. If we have a value for s, we can solve this equation for the required sample size.[2]

Let's illustrate this conclusion. Suppose that at the 95 percent level of confidence we wish to obtain an estimate of the mean age of students that is within ± 3 years of the true mean age. Additionally, we will assume that we have an estimate of $s = 3.0$. Then the required sample size is obtained by solving the following equation for n:

---

[2] If we know the true standard deviation, σ, we can also calculate the required sample size. Here,

$$\text{Precision} = \pm 2\,\frac{\sigma}{\sqrt{n}}$$

Our presumption is that it is unrealistic to think that we would know σ. In all likelihood this is one parameter we are trying to estimate. We will use statistical values in this section ($\overline{X}$, s, p), although parameters (μ, σ, π) are technically more correct.

$$\text{Precision} = \pm 2 \frac{s}{\sqrt{n}}$$

$$\pm 3 \text{ years} = \pm 2 \frac{3.0}{\sqrt{n}}$$

$$3 = \frac{6}{\sqrt{n}}$$

$$3\sqrt{n} = 6$$

$$\sqrt{n} = \frac{6}{3}$$

$$\sqrt{n} = 2$$

$$n = 4$$

A sample size of 4 will assure us a precision of ± 3 years, if $s = 3.0$.

In this example we expressed the precision in units (years). When we use units to do this, it is called *absolute precision*. We might also have expressed precision as a percentage of the mean value we calculate. Here the precision in units varies depending on the size of the mean. Precision expressed in percentages is called *relative precision*. Let's do an example to calculate sample size to assure a specified relative precision. Assume that $\overline{X} = 25, s = 3.0$, the required precision is ± 10 percent $(.1)$, and the 99.7 percent level of confidence is desired. The required equation is:

$$\pm .b\overline{X} = \pm 3 \frac{s}{\sqrt{n}}$$

where $.b$ is the precision percentage expressed as a decimal. In our example the equation becomes:

$$\pm .1(25) = \pm 3 \frac{(3.0)}{\sqrt{n}}$$

$$2.5 = \frac{9}{\sqrt{n}}$$

$$2.5\sqrt{n} = 9$$

$$\sqrt{n} = \frac{9}{2.5}$$

$$\sqrt{n} = 3.6$$

$$n = 13$$

The required sample size is 13 if $\overline{X} = 25$ and $s = 3.0$.

We could rearrange our relative precision equation as follows (we can ignore the $\pm$ signs as they drop out in the calculation):

$$.b\bar{X} = 3\frac{s}{\sqrt{n}}$$

$$.b\bar{X}\sqrt{n} = 3\,s$$

$$.b\sqrt{n} = 3\frac{s}{\bar{X}}$$

Rearranging the equation in this fashion demonstrates that we really do not need to know both $\bar{X}$ and s but only the ratio of the standard deviation to the mean, $s/\bar{X}$. This ratio is called the *coefficient of variation*.

The troublesome thing about our calculations of required sample size is that we need a value of s for absolute precision and a value for $s/\bar{X}$ for relative precision. If we do have these values, in all likelihood we already know what we want to know about a particular variable. Also, for absolute precision the required sample size varies (1) inversely with the size of the precision desired, (2) directly with s, and (3) directly with the size of the confidence level desired. In most studies we want to measure many variables. To the extent that they differ in terms of precision desired, s, or confidence level, the required sample sizes will differ. There is no one sample size that is statistically optimal for any study. The only way to assure the required precision would be to select the largest sample. In this way the variable requiring the largest sample size would reach its specified precision, and all the others would have tighter precision than specified.

To be sure that we understand how to calculate the required sample size and the limitations of such a calculation, we now calculate n for a dichotomous variable. The confidence interval for a dichotomous variable at the 95 percent level of confidence is

$$p \pm 2\sqrt{\frac{pq}{n}}$$

Thus,

$$\text{Absolute precision} = \pm 2\sqrt{\frac{pq}{n}}$$

Assume we have an estimate of $p = .3$ and that we want $\pm.04$ as the absolute precision at the 95 percent level of confidence. Then

$$.04 = 2\sqrt{\frac{(.3)(.7)}{n}}$$

is the required equation. Solving for n, we get

$$.04 = 2\sqrt{\frac{.21}{n}}$$

Dividing through by 2, we get

$$.02 = \sqrt{\frac{.21}{n}}$$

$$.02 \sqrt{n} = \sqrt{.21}$$

$$\sqrt{n} = \frac{\sqrt{.21}}{.02}$$

$$\sqrt{n} = \frac{.46}{.02}$$

$$\sqrt{n} = 23$$

$$n = 529$$

The required sample size is 529.

To calculate relative precision at the 99.7 percent level of confidence, the equation is:

$$.bp = 3 \sqrt{\frac{pq}{n}}$$

where $.b$ is the precision percentage expressed as a decimal. If the required precision is $\pm$ 5 percent (.05), the equation becomes

$$.05(.3) = 3 \sqrt{\frac{(.3)(.7)}{n}}$$

$$.015 = 3 \sqrt{\frac{.21}{n}}$$

Dividing through by 3, we get

$$.005 = \sqrt{\frac{.21}{n}}$$

$$.005 \sqrt{n} = \sqrt{.21}$$

$$\sqrt{n} = \frac{.46}{.005}$$

$$\sqrt{n} = 92$$

$$n = 8464$$

The required sample size is 8464, reflecting our use of the 99.7 percent level of confidence and a very tight precision specification.

We note that in order to determine required sample size for a dichotomous variable we need to know the mean value p. Regrettably, p is probably the value we are trying to determine in the first place. So beware of people who claim that they have determined the statistically optimal sample size for a study, for such a statement is nonsense. This does not mean that the calculation of required sample size is of no value. It can provide a general guide to the researcher as to the required sample size under differing types of findings. That is, assume different values for $\overline{X}$, s, p, etc., and see what sample sizes are required.

This would be one factor affecting the determination of sample size for the study. Other factors in the decision would be the study objectives, the cost involved, the time requirements, the type of data analysis planned, and the existence of nonsampling errors.

We must note that the sample size calculations we made here were for simple random samples only. In the more complex sampling procedures discussed in Chapter 10 the formulas become more complex. However, the principle is exactly the same; that is, we must specify the level of confidence and precision, and then we use the relevant formula for standard error to find the sample size.

Sample Size and Nonsampling Error

No one should blindly accept the sample size generated by a statistical formula. One reason for not doing so is the existence of nonsampling errors. Some nonsampling errors will get larger as the sample size increases—for example, nonresponse errors, interviewer errors, data processing errors, and data analysis errors. Thus, a decrease in sampling error occurs at the expense of an increase in nonsampling error. A carefully done study with $n = 200$ may have a smaller total error than a study of $n = 2000$. The problem is that many researchers, managers, and media people like to refer to the statistical precision of estimates. Rarely do they mention other possible errors. We should look beyond the statistical formulas to the details of how the study was done. The general public also seems to believe that larger samples are necessarily better than smaller ones, which is incorrect, but the company doing research that will be exposed in the public domain must be aware of this perception. It just seems more credible to say: "Based on a study of 3000 people" than to say: "Based on a study of 250." Researchers must respond to this perception for outside use, but they should never be fooled with the same reasoning for internal use reports. Larger is not necessarily better. Also, a very small sample may yield a statistical precision at a level suitable to the needs of marketing decision makers.

Sample Size and Other Factors

A marketing research study is always a compromise between technical elegance and practical constraints faced by researchers and managers. These constraints affect sample size decisions, and several are discussed below.

Study Objectives   The use that management intends to make of the information provided by a study affects the sample size. A decision that does not need precise informational inputs can make do with a very small sample size. A company may be happy to measure interest in its new product within 15 to 20 percent. In contrast, a political pollster can be off by less than 1 percent and fail in his study objective, to predict the election outcome. The latter obviously needs a larger sample than the former.

Time Constraints   Often research results are needed "yesterday." Of course, some time for presenting results is agreed upon. This time period may be too short to use anything except a small sample. The larger the study, the more time is needed.

Cost Constraints   A limit on the amount of money available for a study obviously could limit the sample size. Alternatively, the existence of a lot of money for a study should not be the sole motivation for a large sample size. Available dollars can be a downward constraint on sample size. It should never be the reason for increasing the sample size beyond that needed to meet the study objectives.

Data Analysis Procedures   Data analysis procedures have an effect on the sample size for a study. The most basic type of analysis that can be performed deals with only one variable at a time. This is called univariate analysis (see Chapter 22). The relationship between sample size and precision of estimates on one variable is exactly what we have been discussing in Chapters 9, 10 and 11. When we examine the relationship of two variables at a time, the sample size issue becomes more complex. This is called bivariate analysis (see Chapter 23). Suppose we wanted to examine the relationship between usage of a product and income. Suppose also that each variable is composed of five categories. Therefore, the cross tabulation of usage by income results in a table of 25 cells. Suppose we had a sample of 250 people. If these people were spread evenly across the crosstab table, there would be only 10 respondents per cell. An even distribution across cells is not likely. However, the point is that some cell sizes will be quite small, and the precision of estimates within cells will obviously be less than those obtained in a univariate analysis. Thus, the types of bivariate analysis planned and the precision required within cells will affect the choice of sample size. A study doing only univariate analysis may only require 200 respondents, whereas a similar study doing bivariate analysis may require over 1000 respondents.

We might want to examine the relationships among more than two variables at a time. This is called multivariate analysis (see Chapters 25 and 26). Different multivariate techniques require different sample sizes to allow the researcher to make valid estimates of population parameters. In general, the more parameters we are estimating the larger the sample size must be. Beyond this statement it is difficult to make simple generalizations. Some multivariate techniques can be used legitimately with small sample sizes. These include factor analysis, cluster analysis, multidimensional scaling, and small regression and analysis of variance models. At the other extreme, some techniques were designed for very large samples. The AID (Automatic Interaction Detector) model is one example of this situation. The details of these analysis models and their sample size requirements are left to Chapters 25 and 26. In summary, the researcher must think ahead to the plan of data analysis in determining sample size.

It should now be clear that the choice of a sample size is situation-specific. It depends on statistical precision requirements, concern for nonsampling error, study objectives, time available, cost, and the data analysis plan. There is no one correct answer for the choice of sample size for a study.

MANAGERIAL SUMMARY OF SAMPLING

To end this section of the book on sampling, we shall present a brief summary of some of the dimensions of various sampling procedures. Table 11-1 is the heart of this summary. It presents comparisons among a census and various sampling procedures on a number of dimensions. The first is the ability of the procedure to generate a measure of sampling error, and the second is the related concept of statistical efficiency. The third dimension is the need for a list of population elements in order to draw the sample, the fourth is the cost of the procedure, and the fifth is the frequency of use in practice. A manager should consider all these aspects when choosing a sampling procedure.

SUMMARY

1   Nonsampling errors include all the errors that may occur in the marketing research process, except the sampling error.

2   The effect of nonsampling error is usually not measurable.

3   Nonsampling error increases with sample size.

4   The researcher should be concerned with total error, which is the sum of sampling and nonsampling errors.

5   Sample size should not be determined by the use of statistical formulas alone.

6   The choice of sample size is made involving a trade-off among sampling error, nonsampling error, study objectives, time constraints, cost constraints, and data analysis plans.

DISCUSSION QUESTIONS

1   What is a nonsampling error?

2   What are the properties of nonsampling errors?

3   Define and then give an example of each type of nonsampling error listed in this chapter.

4   A major marketing research firm once declared one of its survey-based services to be "free from all error, except sampling error." Do you think this could be a true statement?

5   What is absolute precision? What is relative precision?

6   What information is necessary in order to calculate a statistically optimal sample size for (1) a continuous variable, (2) a dichotomous variable?

7   What factors should one consider in determining the sample size for a study?

Table 11-1 Managerial Summary on Sampling

Dimensions	Nonprobability samples				Probability samples			
	Census	Convenience	Judgment	Quota	Simple random	Stratified	Systematic	Area
1. Generation of sampling error	No	No	No	No	Yes	Yes	Yes	Yes
2. Statistical efficiency		—No measurement—			The level compared to	High when stratification variables work	Somewhat low	Low
3. Need for population list	Yes	No	No	No	Yes	Yes	Not necessary in all applications	Only for selected clusters
4. Cost	Very high	Very low	Low	Moderate	High	High	Moderate	Moderate to high
5. Frequency of use in practice	Low	Extensive	Moderate	Very extensive	Low	Moderate	Moderate	Very extensive

Source: Adapted from Keith K. Cox and Ben M. Enis, *The Marketing Research Process* (Pacific Palisades, Calif.: Goodyear Publishing Co.), and the current authors' experience.

SUGGESTED READING

Lipstein, Benjamin, "In Defense of Small Samples," *Journal of Advertising Research,* vol. 15, February 1975. The article presents an excellent overview of nonsampling errors.

Cases for Part Three

Case 1

Milan Food Cooperative

Ms. Joyce Lauchner was the general manager of the Milan Food Cooperative (MFC). She had become concerned of late that she had lost touch with the buying patterns of the cooperative members. MFC just seemed so big now relative to the early days. She wondered whether she could make use of some data that were already available to her to increase her understanding of the members' purchase habits. She hoped that she could use this knowledge to better plan the mix and quantity of goods that MFC carried.

Background of MFC

The MFC was founded in 1974 by Ms. Lauchner and a small group of volunteers. It had grown from 10 original members in January 1974 to 500 members in September 1978. It was located in an old warehouse on the northwest side of Milan, Michigan. Milan was a community of 7500 people located in southeast Michigan, about 40 miles southwest of Detroit. MFC drew membership from a number of communities around Milan, including Ann Arbor and Monroe.

The objective of the MFC was to provide high-quality food products at a price below that available at local supermarkets. To accomplish this end the MFC used shipping cartons as shelves, required shoppers to mark their own prices on goods, carried only the best-selling brands, and generally did not offer the "luxuries" associated with traditional supermarkets. To shop at MFC one had to be a member. The membership fee was $25 per year. Any profits earned by the MFC in a year were returned to the members as a credit against purchases. Ms. Lauchner thought that the members bought most of their food at MFC.

Ms. Lauchner's Concerns

In the early days of the MFC Ms. Lauchner had prided herself on knowing all its members. She had spent a great deal of time in the store and felt she knew what people were buying and how much they were spending. As the membership grew, her administrative duties kept her in her office much more. She no longer knew all the members, nor did she have a good feel for their expenditure patterns. She wanted to develop a better understanding of these aspects of her business and thought that perhaps some of the data that had already been collected on the membership might provide answers.

The Available Data

In June 1978 a questionnaire was used to collect data on the membership. During the month all members came into the cooperative at least once. Thus, data were available on all members. The data consisted of demographic characteristics of the members plus their weekly food expenditures.

The data were available on the cards that were filled out by the members at the time of the interview. Ms. Lauchner had these cards in a filing cabinet in her office. A description of the contents of the cards, along with the actual card values for each member, is presented below.

As a first step in understanding the membership, Ms. Lauchner wanted to know their average weekly expenditure on food. Since time was short, she wanted to do this without having to look at all 500 cards. However, she also wanted the average she calculated to be an accurate one. She wondered how she could do this.

MFC DATA

Explanation of Items A–K on the Table (the Variables)

A = Household identification number; 1–500
B = Weekly food expenditure, actual, e.g., $37.50
C = Number of persons in household; 1–9
D = Annual income of household, actual, e.g., $17,500
E = Education of head of household; 1–5
F = Age of head of household, actual, e.g., 38
G = Weekly food expenditure, coded into seven categories; 1–7
H = Any children under 6 years in household; 1–2

I = Any children 6–18 years in household; 1–2
J = Annual income of household, coded in six categories; 1–6
K = Age of head of household, coded into seven categories; 1–7

Category Definitions for Variables

Variable C (Total Number of Persons in Household)

1 = one person
2 = two persons
3 = three persons
4 = four persons
5 = five persons
6 = six persons
7 = seven persons
8 = eight persons
9 = nine or more persons

Variable E (Education of Head of Household)

1 = less than grade 8
2 = grades 9–11
3 = high school graduate
4 = some college
5 = college graduate

Variable G (Weekly Expenditures on Food)

1 = less than $15
2 = $15–29.99
3 = $30–44.99
4 = $45–59.99
5 = $60–74.99
6 = $75–89.99
7 = $90 or over

Variable H (Any Children Under 6 Years Old in Household)

1 = no
2 = yes

Variable I (Any Persons 6–18 Years Old in Household)

1 = no
2 = yes

Variable J (Annual Income of Household)

1 = less than $3,000
2 = $3,000–5,999
3 = $6,000–9,999
4 = $10,000–14,999
5 = $15,000–24,999
6 = $25,000 or over

Variable K (Age of Head of Household)

1 = less than 25
2 = 25–34
3 = 35–44
4 = 45–54
5 = 55–64
6 = 65–74
7 = 75 or older

A	B	C	D	E	F	G	H	I	J	K
1	12.00	1	2500	1	56	1	1	1	1	5
2	16.50	1	2800	1	70	2	1	1	1	6
3	18.00	1	2000	1	20	2	1	1	1	1
4	17.00	1	4500	1	60	2	1	1	2	5
5	46.50	1	8000	1	40	4	1	1	3	3
6	45.00	1	7000	1	51	4	1	1	3	4
7	15.00	1	3500	1	76	2	1	1	2	7
8	60.00	2	2800	1	20	5	1	1	1	1
9	15.00	2	2500	1	51	2	1	1	1	4
10	18.00	2	4000	1	32	2	1	1	2	2
11	22.50	2	5000	1	47	2	1	1	2	4
12	20.00	2	8000	1	35	2	1	1	3	3
13	97.00	2	5500	1	58	7	1	1	2	5
14	57.00	2	6000	1	27	4	1	1	3	2
15	39.00	2	3000	1	38	3	1	1	2	3
16	30.00	2	4000	1	40	3	1	1	2	3
17	42.00	2	3000	1	19	3	1	1	2	1
18	30.00	2	3000	1	50	3	1	1	2	4
19	30.00	2	6000	1	41	3	1	1	3	3
20	32.00	2	6500	1	34	3	1	1	3	2
21	33.00	2	13000	1	23	3	1	1	4	1
22	30.00	2	15000	1	34	3	1	1	5	2
23	37.50	2	22000	1	42	3	1	1	5	3
24	110.00	3	11000	1	43	7	1	2	4	3
25	53.00	3	6500	1	51	4	1	2	3	4
26	34.00	3	28000	1	50	3	1	2	6	4
27	27.00	4	4000	1	46	2	1	2	2	4
28	39.00	5	12000	1	56	3	1	2	4	5
29	67.50	7	11000	1	48	5	1	2	4	4

A	B	C	D	E	F	G	H	I	J	K
30	22.50	2	1900	1	40	2	2	1	1	3
31	7.50	3	2800	1	20	1	2	1	1	1
32	19.00	3	3200	1	24	2	2	1	2	1
33	22.50	4	5000	1	30	2	2	2	2	2
34	28.50	5	7000	1	33	2	2	2	3	2
35	34.50	5	10000	1	38	3	2	2	4	3
36	52.50	6	2500	1	37	4	2	2	1	3
37	58.00	8	10000	1	42	4	2	2	4	3
38	7.00	1	2500	1	19	1	1	1	1	1
39	26.00	1	500	1	68	2	1	1	1	6
40	15.00	1	2500	1	20	2	1	1	1	1
41	30.00	1	6000	1	34	3	1	1	3	2
42	25.50	1	6000	1	66	2	1	1	3	6
43	7.50	1	1500	1	67	1	1	1	1	6
44	12.00	1	1500	1	72	1	1	1	1	6
45	13.50	2	4000	1	28	1	1	1	2	2
46	18.00	2	2500	1	20	2	1	1	1	1
47	30.00	2	2500	1	21	3	1	1	1	1
48	12.00	2	500	1	26	1	1	1	1	2
49	15.00	2	1500	1	19	2	1	1	1	1
50	7.50	2	500	1	19	1	1	1	1	1
51	10.50	2	1500	1	33	1	1	1	1	2
52	12.00	2	1500	1	36	1	1	1	1	3
53	15.00	2	500	1	30	2	1	1	1	2
54	20.00	2	2500	1	45	2	1	1	1	4
55	16.00	2	500	1	54	2	1	1	1	4
56	15.00	2	500	1	56	2	1	1	1	5
57	26.00	2	6200	1	26	2	1	1	3	2
58	15.00	2	1500	1	39	2	1	1	1	3
59	30.00	2	2500	1	21	3	1	1	1	1
60	22.00	2	2500	1	40	2	1	1	1	3
61	22.50	2	2500	1	48	2	1	1	1	4
62	24.00	2	2500	1	60	2	1	1	1	5
63	20.00	2	3500	1	23	2	1	1	2	1
64	11.00	2	500	1	26	1	1	1	1	2
65	16.50	2	2500	1	64	2	1	1	1	5
66	15.00	2	500	1	70	2	1	1	1	6
67	15.00	2	2500	1	31	2	1	1	1	2
68	30.00	2	6300	1	32	3	1	1	3	2
69	28.00	2	4500	1	44	2	1	1	2	3
70	30.00	2	6000	1	49	3	1	1	3	4
71	37.50	2	3500	1	35	3	1	1	2	3
72	60.00	2	3500	1	22	5	1	1	2	1
73	24.00	2	2500	1	28	2	1	1	1	2
74	7.50	2	2500	1	51	1	1	1	1	4
75	87.00	3	11000	1	69	6	1	1	4	6
76	30.00	3	6300	1	43	3	1	1	3	3
77	21.00	3	2500	1	33	2	1	1	1	2
78	120.00	3	8000	1	39	7	1	1	3	3
79	20.00	3	8500	1	58	2	1	1	3	5
80	22.50	3	2500	1	19	2	1	1	1	1

264 SAMPLING

A	B	C	D	E	F	G	H	I	J	K
81	30.00	3	10000	1	33	3	1	1	4	2
82	40.00	3	6000	1	41	3	1	1	3	3
83	37.50	3	6000	1	47	3	1	1	3	4
84	30.00	4	4500	1	48	3	1	2	2	4
85	38.00	4	2500	1	55	3	1	2	1	5
86	60.00	4	6400	1	36	5	1	2	3	3
87	37.50	5	6000	1	57	3	1	2	3	5
88	75.00	6	4500	1	49	6	1	2	2	4
89	37.50	6	3500	1	32	3	1	2	2	2
90	75.00	4	5000	1	32	6	2	1	2	2
91	51.00	4	6000	1	44	4	2	2	3	3
92	75.00	4	4500	1	40	6	2	2	2	3
93	50.00	5	2500	1	29	4	2	2	1	2
94	39.00	5	6000	1	47	3	2	2	3	4
95	60.00	5	9200	1	58	5	2	2	3	5
96	37.50	5	8000	1	51	3	2	2	3	4
97	80.00	6	12000	1	43	6	2	2	4	3
98	30.00	6	3500	1	39	3	2	2	2	3
99	40.00	6	14000	1	39	3	2	2	4	3
100	75.00	6	4500	1	33	6	2	2	2	2
101	15.00	7	1500	1	49	2	2	2	1	4
102	100.00	7	6000	1	53	7	2	2	3	4
103	30.00	9	2500	1	43	3	2	2	1	3
104	34.50	9	3500	1	60	3	2	2	2	5
105	60.00	1	8500	2	45	5	1	1	3	4
106	45.00	1	11000	2	45	4	1	1	4	4
107	51.00	1	15000	2	53	4	1	1	5	4
108	36.00	1	4000	2	42	3	1	1	2	3
109	37.50	1	4500	2	33	3	1	1	2	2
110	30.00	1	4200	2	59	3	1	1	2	5
111	15.00	1	2500	2	21	2	1	1	1	1
112	20.00	1	6000	2	64	2	1	1	3	5
113	7.50	1	500	2	69	1	1	1	1	6
114	10.00	1	1500	2	39	1	1	1	1	3
115	6.00	1	6000	2	26	1	1	1	3	2
116	15.00	2	2000	2	39	2	1	1	1	3
117	66.00	2	18000	2	62	5	1	1	5	5
118	20.00	2	10000	2	58	2	1	1	4	5
119	50.00	2	11000	2	38	4	1	1	4	3
120	57.00	2	13000	2	29	4	1	1	4	2
121	47.00	2	13000	2	60	4	1	1	4	5
122	48.00	2	12000	2	50	4	1	1	4	4
123	45.00	2	27000	2	40	4	1	1	6	3
124	15.00	2	4500	2	26	2	1	1	2	2
125	22.50	2	1500	2	24	2	1	1	1	1
126	52.50	2	2500	2	29	4	1	1	1	2
127	15.00	2	2500	2	31	2	1	1	1	2
128	20.00	2	8600	2	46	2	1	1	3	4
129	22.50	2	3500	2	30	2	1	1	2	2
130	30.00	2	6000	2	48	3	1	1	3	4
131	30.00	2	4500	2	36	3	1	1	2	3

A	B	C	D	E	F	G	H	I	J	K
132	37.50	2	6000	2	30	3	1	1	3	2
133	30.00	2	6000	2	70	3	1	1	3	6
134	30.00	2	3500	2	39	3	1	1	2	3
135	60.00	2	6200	2	44	5	1	1	3	3
136	50.00	2	6000	2	56	4	1	1	3	5
137	52.00	3	25000	2	59	4	1	1	6	5
138	15.00	3	4500	2	29	2	1	1	2	2
139	40.00	3	3500	2	46	3	1	1	2	4
140	50.00	3	17000	2	32	4	1	1	5	2
141	36.00	4	9000	2	73	3	1	1	3	6
142	30.00	4	6000	2	40	3	1	1	3	3
143	16.50	2	2800	2	59	2	1	2	1	5
144	40.00	2	3500	2	49	3	1	2	2	4
145	33.00	3	2500	2	47	3	1	2	1	4
146	40.00	3	3500	2	52	3	1	2	2	4
147	43.00	3	5000	2	48	3	1	2	2	4
148	44.00	3	6000	2	56	3	1	2	3	5
149	30.00	3	10000	2	24	3	1	2	4	1
150	68.00	4	9000	2	51	5	1	2	3	4
151	36.00	4	8000	2	38	3	1	2	3	3
152	45.00	4	6000	2	47	4	1	2	3	4
153	52.50	4	9900	2	58	4	1	2	3	5
154	75.00	5	12000	2	50	6	1	2	4	4
155	28.00	5	6500	2	49	2	1	2	3	4
156	39.00	5	6000	2	61	3	1	2	3	5
157	37.50	5	6000	2	53	3	1	2	3	4
158	50.00	5	6000	2	42	4	1	2	3	3
159	54.00	5	8500	2	39	4	1	2	3	3
160	21.00	6	12500	2	48	2	1	2	4	4
161	37.50	6	11500	2	47	3	1	2	4	4
162	39.00	6	16000	2	50	3	1	2	5	4
163	90.00	6	6000	2	46	7	1	2	3	4
164	11.00	3	5000	2	46	1	2	1	2	4
165	36.00	3	2800	2	31	3	2	1	1	2
166	35.00	3	3900	2	20	3	2	1	2	1
167	37.50	3	8000	2	29	3	2	1	3	2
168	24.00	3	2500	2	23	2	2	1	1	1
169	30.00	3	17000	2	41	3	2	1	5	3
170	30.00	3	4500	2	37	3	2	1	2	3
171	55.00	4	13000	2	30	4	2	1	4	2
172	23.00	4	2500	2	53	2	2	1	1	4
173	27.00	4	2500	2	31	2	2	1	1	2
174	45.00	6	2500	2	33	4	2	1	1	2
175	45.00	7	2500	2	35	4	2	1	1	3
176	52.00	3	9000	2	38	4	2	2	3	3
177	30.00	3	3500	2	37	3	2	2	2	3
178	45.00	4	12000	2	30	4	2	2	4	2
179	45.00	4	8000	2	41	4	2	2	3	3
180	37.50	4	6000	2	45	3	2	2	3	4
181	45.00	4	4500	2	30	4	2	2	2	2
182	55.00	4	17000	2	34	4	2	2	5	2

A	B	C	D	E	F	G	H	I	J	K
183	25.00	4	4500	2	29	2	2	2	2	2
184	80.00	5	13000	2	36	6	2	2	4	3
185	100.00	5	12500	2	30	7	2	2	4	2
186	60.00	5	8700	2	37	5	2	2	3	3
187	37.50	5	3500	2	36	3	2	2	2	3
188	65.00	5	21000	2	40	5	2	2	5	3
189	35.00	5	4500	2	39	3	2	2	2	3
190	37.50	5	7500	2	28	3	2	2	3	2
191	27.00	6	13000	2	38	2	2	2	4	3
192	58.00	6	11000	2	39	4	2	2	4	3
193	42.00	6	7000	2	33	3	2	2	3	2
194	37.50	6	4500	2	40	3	2	2	2	3
195	40.00	6	6000	2	48	3	2	2	3	4
196	45.00	6	6000	2	32	4	2	2	3	2
197	73.00	7	12000	2	30	5	2	2	4	2
198	39.00	7	12500	2	42	3	2	2	4	3
199	53.50	7	8500	2	36	4	2	2	3	3
200	57.00	8	20000	2	39	4	2	2	5	3
201	42.00	8	22000	2	39	3	2	2	5	3
202	38.00	8	9000	2	38	3	2	2	3	3
203	45.00	8	6000	2	41	4	2	2	3	3
204	52.50	9	6500	2	40	4	2	2	3	3
205	67.50	9	9500	2	45	5	2	2	3	4
206	75.00	9	500	2	35	6	2	2	1	3
207	63.00	1	4000	3	56	5	1	1	2	5
208	65.00	1	10000	3	59	5	1	1	4	5
209	45.00	1	2800	3	22	4	1	1	1	1
210	48.00	1	4500	3	24	4	1	1	2	1
211	57.00	1	5000	3	58	4	1	1	2	5
212	45.00	1	9000	3	36	4	1	1	3	3
213	45.00	1	25000	3	61	4	1	1	6	5
214	30.00	1	10000	3	36	3	1	1	4	3
215	37.50	1	14000	3	58	3	1	1	4	5
216	30.00	1	12000	3	29	3	1	1	4	2
217	30.00	1	12000	3	47	3	1	1	4	4
218	30.00	1	24000	3	32	3	1	1	5	2
219	60.00	1	3500	3	22	5	1	1	2	1
220	18.00	1	3500	3	29	2	1	1	2	2
221	20.00	1	4500	3	74	2	1	1	2	6
222	22.50	1	2500	3	20	2	1	1	1	1
223	30.00	1	6800	3	53	3	1	1	3	4
224	72.00	2	7000	3	30	5	1	1	3	2
225	67.50	2	10000	3	24	5	1	1	4	1
226	65.00	2	12000	3	54	5	1	1	4	4
227	60.00	2	17000	3	37	5	1	1	5	3
228	60.00	2	26000	3	66	5	1	1	6	6
229	45.00	2	18000	3	44	4	1	1	5	3
230	54.00	2	22000	3	42	4	1	1	5	3
231	48.00	2	18000	3	63	4	1	1	5	5
232	46.50	2	26000	3	50	4	1	1	6	4
233	42.00	2	13000	3	38	3	1	1	4	3

A	B	C	D	E	F	G	H	I	J	K
234	35.00	2	14000	3	59	3	1	1	4	5
235	37.50	2	10000	3	61	3	1	1	4	5
236	30.00	2	11500	3	44	3	1	1	4	3
237	45.00	2	30000	3	40	4	1	1	6	3
238	30.00	2	9000	3	29	3	1	1	3	2
239	38.00	2	4500	3	23	3	1	1	2	1
240	40.00	2	18000	3	57	3	1	1	5	5
241	20.00	2	6000	3	21	2	1	1	3	1
242	22.50	2	7000	3	27	2	1	1	3	2
243	25.00	2	18000	3	41	2	1	1	5	3
244	20.00	2	9000	3	34	2	1	1	3	2
245	30.00	2	24000	3	60	3	1	1	5	5
246	37.50	2	11000	3	23	3	1	1	4	1
247	60.00	2	9000	3	59	5	1	1	3	5
248	22.50	2	27000	3	46	2	1	1	6	4
249	15.00	2	3500	3	22	2	1	1	2	1
250	30.00	2	4500	3	63	3	1	1	2	5
251	37.50	2	7000	3	25	3	1	1	3	2
252	40.00	2	3500	3	68	3	1	1	2	6
253	45.00	2	15000	3	54	4	1	1	5	4
254	37.50	2	26000	3	34	3	1	1	6	2
255	45.00	2	17000	3	26	4	1	1	5	2
256	30.00	3	10000	3	50	3	1	1	4	4
257	45.00	3	14000	3	49	4	1	1	4	4
258	37.50	3	4500	3	62	3	1	1	2	5
259	18.00	3	7000	3	58	2	1	1	3	5
260	60.00	3	8000	3	31	5	1	1	3	2
261	45.00	3	8000	3	43	4	1	1	3	3
262	37.50	3	4500	3	27	3	1	1	2	2
263	37.00	3	6000	3	27	3	1	1	3	2
264	40.00	4	28000	3	39	3	1	1	6	3
265	45.00	4	19000	3	67	4	1	1	5	6
266	60.00	4	11000	3	59	5	1	1	4	5
267	30.00	4	6500	3	33	3	1	1	3	2
268	45.00	4	10000	3	68	4	1	1	4	6
269	50.00	4	6000	3	76	4	1	1	3	7
270	60.00	3	16000	3	40	5	1	2	5	3
271	20.00	3	2600	3	38	2	1	2	1	3
272	55.00	3	10000	3	45	4	1	2	4	4
273	50.00	3	10000	3	50	4	1	2	4	4
274	33.00	3	9000	3	40	3	1	2	3	3
275	33.00	3	11000	3	48	3	1	2	4	4
276	45.00	3	19000	3	49	4	1	2	5	4
277	18.00	3	6000	3	32	2	1	2	3	2
278	37.50	3	15000	3	50	3	1	2	5	4
279	45.00	3	8000	3	43	4	1	2	3	3
280	70.00	3	8800	3	58	5	1	2	3	5
281	67.50	4	10000	3	47	5	1	2	4	4
282	69.00	4	15000	3	34	5	1	2	5	2
283	120.00	4	13500	3	48	7	1	2	4	4
284	45.00	4	12000	3	33	4	1	2	4	2

A	B	C	D	E	F	G	H	I	J	K
285	42.00	4	10000	3	40	3	1	2	4	3
286	30.00	4	14000	3	49	3	1	2	4	4
287	39.00	4	10000	3	46	3	1	2	4	4
288	36.00	4	12000	3	57	3	1	2	4	5
289	39.00	4	12000	3	43	3	1	2	4	3
290	37.50	4	6000	3	28	3	1	2	3	2
291	45.00	4	18000	3	49	4	1	2	5	4
292	37.50	4	6000	3	31	3	1	2	3	2
293	45.00	4	6000	3	54	4	1	2	3	4
294	25.00	4	6000	3	29	2	1	2	3	2
295	50.00	4	8000	3	34	4	1	2	3	2
296	40.00	4	17000	3	38	3	1	2	5	3
297	54.00	4	20000	3	45	4	1	2	5	4
298	45.00	4	6000	3	39	4	1	2	3	3
299	60.00	4	8000	3	56	5	1	2	3	5
300	45.00	4	8000	3	49	4	1	2	3	4
301	45.00	4	15000	3	41	4	1	2	5	3
302	35.00	4	8000	3	33	3	1	2	3	2
303	80.00	5	11000	3	49	6	1	2	4	4
304	55.00	5	13000	3	48	4	1	2	4	4
305	37.50	5	10000	3	48	3	1	2	4	4
306	55.00	5	20000	3	42	4	1	2	5	3
307	35.00	5	2500	3	49	3	1	2	1	4
308	52.50	5	15500	3	34	4	1	2	5	2
309	80.00	6	14000	3	49	6	1	2	4	4
310	86.00	6	10000	3	56	6	1	2	4	5
311	110.00	6	13000	3	52	7	1	2	4	4
312	95.00	7	19000	3	39	7	1	2	5	3
313	45.00	7	6000	3	49	4	1	2	3	4
314	60.00	8	21000	3	44	5	1	2	5	3
315	67.50	9	15000	3	47	5	1	2	5	4
316	18.00	3	2500	3	27	2	2	1	1	2
317	47.00	3	11000	3	32	4	2	1	4	2
318	50.00	3	14000	3	29	4	2	1	4	2
319	45.00	3	16000	3	28	4	2	1	5	2
320	36.00	3	12000	3	28	3	2	1	4	2
321	30.00	3	6000	3	22	3	2	1	3	1
322	67.50	3	12000	3	24	5	2	1	4	1
323	22.50	3	6000	3	23	2	2	1	3	1
324	26.00	3	2500	3	32	2	2	1	1	2
325	27.00	3	3500	3	25	2	2	1	2	2
326	45.00	3	6000	3	35	4	2	1	3	3
327	30.00	3	10000	3	19	3	2	1	4	1
328	35.00	3	8000	3	30	3	2	1	3	2
329	52.50	3	8000	3	27	4	2	1	3	2
330	55.00	3	6000	3	20	4	2	1	3	1
331	35.00	3	20000	3	32	3	2	1	5	2
332	51.00	4	4000	3	24	4	2	1	2	1
333	37.50	4	12000	3	32	3	2	1	4	2
334	30.00	4	13000	3	30	3	2	1	4	2
335	75.00	4	8000	3	26	6	2	1	3	2

A	B	C	D	E	F	G	H	I	J	K
336	40.00	4	6000	3	22	3	2	1	3	1
337	37.50	4	4500	3	27	3	2	1	2	2
338	21.00	4	7000	3	30	2	2	1	3	2
339	30.00	4	6000	3	29	3	2	1	3	2
340	22.50	4	9500	3	28	2	2	1	3	2
341	67.50	4	14000	3	25	5	2	1	4	2
342	60.00	4	8000	3	33	5	2	1	3	2
343	87.00	5	14000	3	33	6	2	1	4	2
344	45.00	5	14000	3	29	4	2	1	4	2
345	50.00	5	9000	3	31	4	2	1	3	2
346	48.00	6	6000	3	38	4	2	1	3	3
347	60.00	7	4500	3	29	5	2	1	2	2
348	90.00	4	14000	3	34	7	2	2	4	2
349	45.00	4	14000	3	35	4	2	2	4	3
350	54.00	4	12500	3	30	4	2	2	4	2
351	37.50	4	17500	3	30	3	2	2	5	2
352	33.00	4	4500	3	29	3	2	2	2	2
353	72.00	5	14000	3	36	5	2	2	4	3
354	51.00	5	11000	3	35	4	2	2	4	3
355	36.00	5	14500	3	36	3	2	2	4	3
356	65.00	5	8000	3	32	5	2	2	3	2
357	60.00	5	16000	3	34	5	2	2	5	2
358	45.00	5	21000	3	40	4	2	2	5	3
359	45.00	5	7500	3	29	4	2	2	3	2
360	37.50	5	6000	3	31	3	2	2	3	2
361	67.50	5	6000	3	36	5	2	2	3	3
362	39.00	5	8000	3	40	3	2	2	3	3
363	45.00	5	3500	3	37	4	2	2	2	3
364	37.50	5	4500	3	46	3	2	2	2	4
365	24.00	6	8500	3	38	2	2	2	3	3
366	42.00	6	13000	3	39	3	2	2	4	3
367	60.00	6	6000	3	35	5	2	2	3	3
368	40.00	6	6000	3	41	3	2	2	3	3
369	37.50	6	6000	3	33	3	2	2	3	2
370	60.00	6	6000	3	38	5	2	2	3	3
371	73.50	7	12000	3	38	5	2	2	4	3
372	105.00	7	20000	3	38	7	2	2	5	3
373	52.50	7	6000	3	36	4	2	2	3	3
374	35.00	7	3500	3	37	3	2	2	2	3
375	37.50	7	6000	3	31	3	2	2	3	2
376	50.00	7	7000	3	47	4	2	2	3	4
377	49.00	7	8000	3	44	4	2	2	3	3
378	60.00	8	6000	3	41	5	2	2	3	3
379	67.50	8	6000	3	47	5	2	2	3	4
380	45.00	8	4500	3	51	4	2	2	2	4
381	75.00	8	18000	3	36	6	2	2	5	3
382	52.50	8	9000	3	46	4	2	2	3	4
383	54.00	9	20000	3	45	4	2	2	5	4
384	50.00	9	2500	3	50	4	2	2	1	4
385	75.00	9	18000	3	49	6	2	2	5	4
386	52.50	9	8000	3	44	4	2	2	3	3

A	B	C	D	E	F	G	H	I	J	K
387	35.00	1	4000	4	71	3	1	1	2	6
388	30.00	1	5000	4	28	3	1	1	2	2
389	36.00	1	5000	4	36	3	1	1	2	3
390	18.00	2	13000	4	56	2	1	1	4	5
391	52.00	2	5000	4	35	4	1	1	2	3
392	53.00	2	11000	4	40	4	1	1	4	3
393	45.00	2	10000	4	45	4	1	1	4	4
394	25.00	2	15000	4	24	2	1	1	5	1
395	27.00	2	18000	4	34	2	1	1	5	2
396	15.00	2	4500	4	26	2	1	1	2	2
397	75.00	2	22000	4	41	6	1	1	5	3
398	25.00	2	2500	4	69	2	1	1	1	6
399	22.00	2	17500	4	58	2	1	1	5	5
400	58.00	3	14000	4	40	4	1	1	4	3
401	40.00	3	30000	4	47	3	1	1	6	4
402	37.00	3	8000	4	45	3	1	1	3	4
403	27.00	3	20000	4	60	2	1	1	5	5
404	30.00	3	3500	4	59	3	1	1	2	5
405	50.00	3	4500	4	39	4	1	1	2	3
406	30.00	3	24000	4	62	3	1	1	5	5
407	75.00	3	6000	4	77	6	1	1	3	7
408	45.00	4	30000	4	52	4	1	1	6	4
409	55.00	3	28000	4	48	4	1	2	6	4
410	40.00	3	8000	4	23	3	1	2	3	1
411	60.00	3	22000	4	42	5	1	2	5	3
412	45.00	3	35000	4	44	4	1	2	6	3
413	60.00	4	14500	4	56	5	1	2	4	5
414	26.70	4	18000	4	54	2	1	2	5	4
415	51.00	4	11000	4	51	4	1	2	4	4
416	45.00	4	14500	4	56	4	1	2	4	5
417	57.00	4	10000	4	34	4	1	2	4	2
418	65.00	4	19000	4	47	5	1	2	5	4
419	115.00	4	3500	4	31	7	1	2	2	2
420	45.00	4	4500	4	55	4	1	2	2	5
421	60.00	4	9000	4	49	5	1	2	3	4
422	55.00	4	20000	4	41	4	1	2	5	3
423	75.00	4	22000	4	51	6	1	2	5	4
424	75.00	4	18000	4	33	6	1	2	5	2
425	48.00	4	17000	4	29	4	1	2	5	2
426	45.00	5	6000	4	31	4	1	2	3	2
427	52.50	5	8000	4	43	4	1	2	3	3
428	35.00	5	500	4	28	3	1	2	1	2
429	45.00	5	28000	4	36	4	1	2	6	3
430	52.50	5	4500	4	55	4	1	2	2	5
431	45.00	5	8000	4	48	4	1	2	3	4
432	135.00	6	22000	4	44	7	1	2	5	3
433	70.00	6	24000	4	44	5	1	2	5	3
434	60.00	6	24000	4	39	5	1	2	5	3
435	60.00	3	13000	4	33	5	2	1	4	2
436	51.00	3	10000	4	28	4	2	1	4	2
437	30.00	3	4000	4	32	3	2	1	2	2

A	B	C	D	E	F	G	H	I	J	K
438	53.00	3	8000	4	27	4	2	1	3	2
439	30.00	3	6000	4	23	3	2	1	3	1
440	70.00	4	14000	4	29	5	2	1	4	2
441	30.00	4	8000	4	28	3	2	1	3	2
442	37.50	4	4500	4	30	3	2	1	2	2
443	30.00	5	6000	4	32	3	2	1	3	2
444	48.00	4	13500	4	40	4	2	2	4	3
445	35.00	4	5500	4	29	3	2	2	2	2
446	55.00	4	20000	4	36	4	2	2	5	3
447	40.00	4	25000	4	41	3	2	2	6	3
448	27.00	5	12000	4	43	2	2	2	4	3
449	100.00	5	14000	4	36	7	2	2	4	3
450	57.00	5	9500	4	36	4	2	2	3	3
451	75.00	6	13000	4	40	6	2	2	4	3
452	45.00	6	8000	4	39	4	2	2	3	3
453	85.00	7	18000	4	38	6	2	2	5	3
454	100.00	7	20000	4	48	7	2	2	5	4
455	45.00	7	36000	4	43	4	2	2	6	3
456	50.00	7	4500	4	32	4	2	2	2	2
457	48.00	1	14000	5	24	4	1	1	4	1
458	52.50	1	12500	5	60	4	1	1	4	5
459	34.50	1	14000	5	28	3	1	1	4	2
460	9.00	1	2500	5	25	1	1	1	1	2
461	15.00	1	6000	5	28	2	1	1	3	2
462	13.00	2	13000	5	25	1	1	1	4	2
463	54.00	2	14500	5	47	4	1	1	4	4
464	25.00	2	8000	5	78	2	1	1	3	7
465	30.00	2	28000	5	64	3	1	1	6	5
466	35.00	2	3500	5	76	3	1	1	2	7
467	12.00	2	2500	5	23	1	1	1	1	1
468	39.00	3	13000	5	39	3	1	1	4	3
469	45.00	3	42000	5	54	4	1	1	6	4
470	37.50	3	17000	5	52	3	1	2	5	4
471	40.00	3	24000	5	40	3	1	2	5	3
472	52.50	3	17000	5	40	4	1	2	5	3
473	60.00	3	32000	5	48	5	1	2	6	4
474	37.50	4	17000	5	56	3	1	2	5	5
475	55.00	4	24000	5	44	4	1	2	5	3
476	56.00	4	16000	5	36	4	1	2	5	3
477	75.00	5	23000	5	48	6	1	2	5	4
478	45.00	5	6000	5	37	4	1	2	3	3
479	100.00	5	39000	5	44	7	1	2	6	3
480	72.00	2	14000	5	30	5	2	1	4	2
481	33.00	3	20000	5	36	3	2	1	5	3
482	30.00	3	22000	5	33	3	2	1	5	2
483	37.50	3	8000	5	28	3	2	1	3	2
484	30.00	3	9000	5	32	3	2	1	3	2
485	22.00	3	7000	5	30	2	2	1	3	2
486	60.00	4	5000	5	28	5	2	1	2	2
487	20.00	4	9000	5	30	2	2	1	3	2
488	25.50	4	4500	5	26	2	2	1	2	2

A	B	C	D	E	F	G	H	I	J	K
489	33.00	4	6000	5	32	3	2	1	3	2
490	51.00	4	9000	5	34	4	2	1	3	2
491	45.00	7	26000	5	39	4	2	1	6	3
492	75.00	4	14500	5	34	6	2	2	4	2
493	18.00	4	14000	5	36	2	2	2	4	3
494	40.00	4	15500	5	40	3	2	2	5	3
495	75.00	5	28000	5	42	6	2	2	6	3
496	24.00	5	24000	5	33	2	2	2	5	2
497	115.00	6	24000	5	36	7	2	2	5	3
498	75.00	7	28000	5	37	6	2	2	6	3
499	105.00	7	20000	5	39	7	2	2	5	3
500	75.00	8	33000	5	42	6	2	2	6	3

Case 2

Claude Scott, Political Candidate

Claude Scott is a candidate for mayor of Lincoln, Nebraska. You have been retained by Mr. Scott to determine his chances of winning the coming November election.

Case 3

Amtrak

The marketing manager for Amtrak was trying to develop a marketing plan designed to increase the use of Amtrak by college students. As part of this process, he wanted to obtain information on college students' current attitudes toward and usage of Amtrak. You have been retained by the marketing manager to design the sample for this study.

Case 4

Big Bob's Pizza Place

The manager of Big Bob's Pizza Place wants to run an advertisement in this coming Sunday's paper featuring the "Tuesday Night Price Special" that he plans to start in the restaurant the following Tuesday. The manager has retained you to develop a sampling plan of the customers coming into his restaurant on Tuesday night. He plans to administer a questionnaire to this sample to determine the degree to which the Sunday advertisement influenced them to come to the restaurant.

DISCUSSION QUESTION

For each of the above three cases, prepare a sampling design.

Part Four

Measurement

The Measurement Process

The process of measurement is a commonplace occurrence for college students. Entrance examinations are measuring devices designed to assess the student's potential for college-level work. Once in college, the student is confronted with an array of examinations to measure achievement in courses such as marketing research. Measurement is involved when we count the number of students in a class, classify them as male or female, or judge which students are most attractive in appearance or personality. These are only a few examples of the use of measurement in our daily activities. Typically, the measurement process is taken for granted. Rarely do we stop to think about the differences in the type of measurements taken and the accuracy of the conclusions drawn. This chapter is designed to stimulate the reader's thinking in this regard.

MEASUREMENT IN MARKETING

The process of measurement is a fundamental aspect of marketing research. It is often stated that the best way to really understand a thing is to try to measure it. For this reason, if no other, the topic of measurement is of growing concern to those in the field of marketing.

Decision makers are interested in measuring many aspects of the marketing system; for example, they may want to measure the market potential for a new product, group buyers by demographic or psychographic characteristics, measure buyers' attitudes, perceptions, or preferences toward a new brand, or determine the effectiveness of a new advertising campaign. Consequently, the measurement of marketing phenomena is essential to the process of providing meaningful information for decision making.

Developing effective measures of marketing phenomena is not an easy task. In Chapter 11, measurement error was cited as being a substantial share of the total error in marketing research information. For many research projects, measurement error can be substantially greater than sampling error. Having a clear understanding of the measurement problem and how to control this error is an important aspect of designing an effective marketing research project.

The marketing manager rarely becomes directly involved in the actual measurement process. The task of selecting and designing measurement techniques is the responsibility of the research specialist. However, the decision maker must often approve the measurement techniques that are recommended and needs to be confident that these techniques are effective in controlling measurement error.

In order to control measurement error effectively, the marketing manager should be concerned with three issues. First, the specification of information needs should recognize the degree of difficulty in obtaining accurate measures. Secondly, the alternative measurement procedures for obtaining the information should be recognized. Thirdly, the cost of measurement versus the accuracy of measurement should be evaluated. This chapter and many of the remaining chapters deal with these three issues.

The Measurement Process

In marketing research, the measurement process involves using numbers to represent the marketing phenomena under investigation. Stated formally, the *empirical system* includes marketing phenomena, such as buyer reactions to products or advertisements, while the *abstract system* includes the numbers used to represent the marketing phenomena. Figure 12-1 depicts the measurement process as one of developing a correspondence between the empirical system and the abstract system. The former is composed of the physical sciences (the study of physical things) and the social sciences (the study of people). Marketing is a member of the social sciences in that it involves "human activity directed at satisfying needs and wants through exchange processes."[1]

Definition of Measurement

The previous discussion suggests that measurement is concerned with developing a correspondence between the empirical system (e.g. preference) and the abstract system (e.g., numbers). Therefore, measurement may be defined as *the assignment of numbers to characteristics of objects or events according to rules.*

[1] Philip Kotler, *Marketing Management,* 3d ed. (Englewood Cliffs, N.J.: Prentice-Hall, 1977), p. 5.

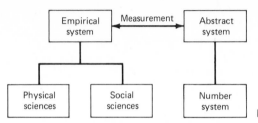

Figure 12-1 The measurement process

Effective measurement is possible when the relationships existing among the objects or events in the empirical system directly correspond to the rules of the number system. If this correspondence is misrepresented, measurement error has occurred. More will be said in this regard shortly.

It is important to note that the definition of measurement suggests that it is the characteristics of objects or events that are measured and not the objects or events themselves. We do not measure a buyer or a product, but rather we measure some characteristic of a buyer or a product. For example, we can measure a buyer's preference, usage rate, income, or attitude. We can measure a product's speed, sweetness, size, or color.

The term "number" in the definition of measurement imposes certain restrictions on the type of numerical manipulations admissible. Numbers are being used as symbols to model the characteristics of interest in the empirical system. The nature of the relationships existing in the empirical system determines the type of numerical manipulations which are valid in the abstract system. There is a great temptation to use all the characteristics of the number system in our data analysis and to disregard the restrictions imposed by the empirical phenomena under study. We now turn to a discussion of the characteristics of the number system, which should provide a better understanding of this issue.

Number System Characteristics

Very early in our educational career we learned four characteristics of the number system 0, 1, 2, 3, 4, 5, 6, 7, 8, and 9. First, each number in the series is unique, and there are ten numbers. Second, the ordering of the numbers is given by convention, e.g., $2 > 1$, $1 > 0$. Third, we can define equal differences, e.g., $3 - 2 = 7 - 6$, $7 - 5 = 3 - 1$. Fourth, we can define equal ratios, e.g., $10 \div 5 = 6 \div 3$.

The manipulation of numbers using mathematics or statistics involves one or more of these four characteristics of the number system. There is a great temptation to use more of these characteristics in our data analysis than may actually exist in the empirical system being modeled. The problem is one of focusing clearly on determining how many of these four characteristics are present in the marketing phenomena under investigation and then restricting our data analysis to using only the appropriate characteristics in our manipulation of the numbers. Often, this restriction hampers the sophistication of data analysis that can properly be performed.

Types of Scales

Scales have been classified in terms of the four characteristics of the number system. These scales of measurement are *nominal, ordinal, interval, and ratio.* The characteristics of these scales are summarized in Table 12-1, and the following paragraphs discuss each of these scales and their characteristics in detail.

Nominal Scale A nominal scale is one where numbers serve only as labels to identify or categorize objects or events. A familiar example is the use of numbers to identify football players. Assume that the quarterback for the blue team is 12, and the quarterback for the green team is 9. Numbers used in this manner serve only as a label to identify the players. The numbers assume equality with respect to the characteristics of the players. For example, we cannot infer that the quarterback of the blue team is superior in ability to the quarterback of the green team due to the higher number of 12. Therefore, the number 12 does not imply a superior characteristic to the number 9—it only serves as a unique label for identification of the player.

Nominal scales are used for the lowest form of measurement, namely, classification and identification. Few restrictive rules are imposed in the assignment of numerals to the objects or events. The rule is simply: Do not assign the same number to different objects or events, or different numbers to the same object or event. For example, we could change the number of our blue-team quarterback from 12 to 56, or any other number desired. The only restriction is

 Table 12-1 Characteristics of Measurement Scales

Scale	Number system	Marketing phenomena	Permissible statistics*
Nominal	Unique definition of numerals	Brands Male-female Store types Sale territories	Percentages Mode Binomial test Chi-square test
Ordinal	Order of numerals	Attitudes Preference Occupation Social class	Percentiles Median Rank-order correlation
Interval	Equality of differences	Attitudes Opinions Index numbers	Range Mean Standard deviation Product-moment correlation
Ratio	Equality of ratios	Age Costs Number of customers Sales (units/dollars)	Geometric mean Harmonic mean Coefficient of variation

*All statistics appropriate for nominal measurement are appropriate for higher scale measurement. The same is true for ordinal- and interval-scale measurement.

Source: Adapted from S. S. Stevens, "On the Theory of Scales of Measurement," *Science*, vol. 103, pp. 677–680, June 7, 1946.

Table 12-2 Reasons for Purchase by Sex

Reason for purchase	Male		Female		Total	
	N	Percent	N	Percent	N	Percent
Weight	10	20	28	56	38	38
Speed	31	62	10	20	41	41
Miscellaneous	9	18	12	24	21	21
	50	100	50	100	100	100

that within the blue team each player must have a unique number for purposes of identification. Consequently, many possible numbers can be used to identify the players, and we cannot argue that one number is better for our quarterback than another number. They all serve the purpose of identification equally.

A substantial proportion of marketing phenomena require nominal-scale measurement. Such nominal-level identification and classification is needed to measure brands, store types, sales territories, geographic locations, heavy versus light users, working versus nonworking women, and brand awareness versus nonawareness. It is a rare marketing research study that does not involve marketing data of this nature.

An illustration of the use of nominal measurement involves a bicycle manufacturer who wants to determine whether there are differences in the reasons why males and females purchase 10-speed bicycles. Former purchasers of the bicycle (50 males and 50 females) were randomly selected and interviewed over the telephone. Table 12-2 presents the results of the survey. It would appear that females are more concerned with the weight of the bicycle, while males are more concerned with speed.

The types of statistical analysis appropriate for nominally scaled data include the mode, percentages, the binomial test, and the chi-square test (see Table 12-1). The mode is the only measure of central tendency which can be used. A mean or median cannot be calculated since they involve higher-level properties of the number system than are present in nominally scaled data.

Ordinal Scale An ordinal scale defines the ordered relationship among objects or events. It involves the number system characteristic of the order of numerals. Ordinal scales measure whether an object or event has more or less of a characteristic than some other object or event. However, this scale does not provide information on how much more or less of the characteristic various objects or events possess.

Let's illustrate ordinal measurement by assuming that our previous bicycle manufacturer is interested in determining the preference ordering of males among the firm's 10-speed bicycle (A) and the two leading competitors (B and C) with regard to the characteristic of speed. A survey was conducted of 200 male potential buyers. The results are reported in Table 12-3.

An ordinal scale can be developed by assigning numerals to the first-, second-, and third-order preference judgments. This involves the assignment of

**Table 12-3   Male Preference Ordering of Bicycles A, B, and C
with Regard to Speed (N = 200)**

| Preference | Proportion of preferences | | | |
ordering	A	B	C	Total
First	.15	.35	.50	1.00
Second	.50	.25	.25	1.00
Third	.35	.40	.25	1.00
Total	1.00	1.00	1.00	

numerals such that the resulting numerical series properly maintains the ordered relationship of the preference judgments. But which set of numbers should be assigned? Obviously, a large number of sets of numbers might be assigned, the only restriction being that the numbers be assigned in such a manner that their order corresponds directly with the ordinal relationships present in the preference judgments. For example, the number 1 can be used to represent the first-order preferences, number 2 for the second-order preferences, and number 3 for the third-order preferences. Alternatively, another set of permissible numerals would be to assign the number 1 to the first-order preferences, the number 3 to the second order-preferences, and the number 30 to the third-order preferences. Other numerical sets include 5, 6, and 7; 1, 20, and 100; and so forth. All of these numerical sets form acceptable ordinal scales, and we cannot argue that one set is better than the others.

A more restrictive rule for the assignment of numerals exists with ordinal measurement than with nominal measurement. An important characteristic of measurement is its power to enable us to establish rules which define the domain of numerical sets that can properly be assigned to the empirical system under investigation.

Ordinal measurement involves the rule that any series of numbers can be assigned that preserves the ordered relationships present in the empirical system. This restriction that the numbers be arranged in serial order substantially eliminates many numerical series from consideration. It is equally true, however, that a great deal of freedom remains regarding which numerical set can be used. This domain of freedom can be formally defined as any order-preserving (i.e., monotonic) transformation of the numerical series chosen. Consequently, with an ordinal scale, the only restriction in the assignment of a new series of numbers is that an increasing monotone transformation be used. Such transformations are illustrated in Figure 12-2(a).

The overall ranking of the three bicycles based on the mode is presented in Table 12-4. The results are presented for both numerical sets 1 and 2. It is important to note that the preference ordering of the three bicycles is identical for both numerical sets 1 and 2. Here, the overall preference ordering is bicycle C first, A second, and B third. We can generalize these findings to all statistics appropriate for the analysis of ordinal data. Consequently, regardless of which order-preserving numerical set is selected for data analysis, the research find-

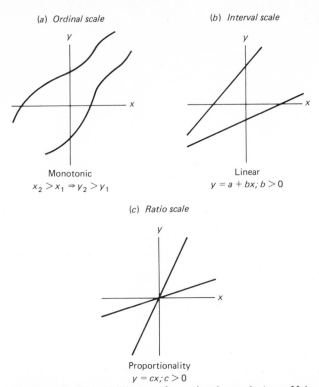

(a) Ordinal scale

y

x

Monotonic
$x_2 > x_1 \Rightarrow y_2 > y_1$

(b) Interval scale

y

x

Linear
$y = a + bx; b > 0$

(c) Ratio scale

y

x

Proportionality
$y = cx; c > 0$

Figure 12-2 Permissible transformation by scale type. [*Adapted from Paul E. Green and Donald S. Tull,* Research for Marketing Decisions, *3d ed.* (*Englewood Cliffs, N.J.: Prentice-Hall 1975*), *p. 60.*]

ings will not change or be dependent upon the numerical set selected. More formally, we can state that for any increasing monotone scale transformation, the conclusions drawn from the data analysis using statistics appropriate for ordinal data *will not change as a result of the assignment of alternative numerical sets.* Some of the statistics appropriate for ordinal data are presented in Table 12-1.

Note that the mean is not an appropriate statistic for ordinal data. What happens if we do calculate the mean? The means for numerical sets 1 and 2 have been calculated to answer this question (see Table 12-4). The result is that the preference ordering of the three bicycles is different for the two numerical assignments. For numerical set 1, bicycle C is first, B is second, and A is last. However, for numerical set 2, bicycle C is first, A is second, and B is third. Bicycles A and B have reversed positions because of the scale transformation. This result is not surprising when we realize that the calculation of a mean involves the equal-interval characteristic of the number system. Since the scale transformation maintained only a monotonic or ranked relationship rather than an equal-interval relationship, the results of our statistical analysis are dependent upon the number series selected. This is a clear example of measurement error occurring in our results.

Table 12-4 Overall Ranking of Bicycles A, B, and C

Descriptive statistic	Ranking		
	1st	2d	3d
Mode (numerical set 1)*	C (1)	A (2)	B (3)
Mode (numerical set 2)†	C (1)	A (3)	B (30)
Mean (numerical set 1)	C (1.75)‡	B (2.05)	A (2.20)
Mean (numerical set 2)	C (8.75)	A (12.15)	B (13.10)

*1st = 1, 2d = 2, 3d = 3.
†1st = 1, 2d = 3, 3d = 30.
‡Mean = (1)(.50) + (2)(.25) + (3)(.25) ÷ 1 = 1.75.

An important segment of marketing data involves ordinal measurement. Most data collected by the process of interrogating people have ordinal properties. For example, the measurement of attitudes, opinions, preference, and perception frequently involves a "greater than" or "less than" judgment. In addition, many characteristics of buyers or purchasing units can involve a ranked characteristic (e.g., occupation, social class, or image). Consequently, a significant share of marketing research data involves ordinal judgments, and the analysis of these data should be subject to the restrictions discussed previously.

Interval Scale   An interval scale involves the use of numbers to rank objects or events such that the distances between the numerals correspond to the distances between the objects or events on the characteristic being measured. Interval scales possess all the requirements of an ordinal scale plus the "equality of difference" characteristic of the number system. The remaining freedom in assigning numbers is reduced to the arbitrary selection of a unit of measurement (distance) and an origin (zero point). Suppose that we have measured four ordered objects A, B, C, and D and determined that the distance between adjacent objects is equal on some characteristic. In the assignment of numbers to the objects, we must arbitrarily decide how to represent the size of the distance between adjacent objects and where to assign the zero points. For example, the numbers 0, 1, 2, and 3 represent an arbitrary assignment of zero to one object and of a one-unit difference between adjacent objects. An alternative number assignment could be 7, 9, 11, and 13. Both numerical assignments are acceptable, and we cannot say that one is better than the other.

The most common examples of interval scales are the Fahrenheit and Celsius scales used to measure temperature. The freezing point of water is assigned a different numerical value on each scale, 32 on Fahrenheit and 0 on Celsius. The unit of measurement and the origin or zero point have been arbitrarily determined for these scales. Equal differences in the temperature are measured by equal-volume expansion in the mercury used in the thermometer.

The arbitrary assignment of the zero point on an interval scale places restrictions on the statements that can be made regarding comparisons of intervals. For example, one cannot say that 100° Celsius is twice as hot as 50° Celsius.

A scale transformation to Fahrenheit demonstrates why. The formula is $C = (F - 32)(5/9)$. Using the formula, the previous Celsius temperatures of 100° and 50° correspond to 212° and 122° on the Fahrenheit scale. Our previous statement that 100° Celsius is twice as warm as 50° does not hold with our new numbers for the Fahrenheit scale. We cannot say that 212° is twice as warm as 122°, because the zero point on each scale is arbitrary. Consequently, comparison of absolute magnitude or ratios is not possible.

The above example with a temperature scale applies to all interval scales. Assume that we have scaled brands A, B, and C on an interval scale regarding buyers' degree of liking of the brands. Brand A receives a 6, the highest liking score, B receives a 3, and C receives a 2. We cannot say that brand A is liked twice as much as brand B. Such a statement assumes that the absolute zero point or the absence of liking has been identified and assigned the value zero on the interval scale. What can we say regarding these intervally scaled data? First, the liking for brand A is more favorable than that for brand B (order of numerals). Second, the degree of liking between A and B is three times greater than the liking between B and C (equality of differences).

The area of freedom in assigning new numerical sets to an interval scale is more restricted than for an ordinal scale. This new numerical assignment involves a positive linear transformation of the form $y = a + bx,$ where b is positive. Here, x is the original scale number and y is the new scale number. Figure 12-2(b) gives examples of two such transformations. Statements comparing intervals are valid with an interval scale because, by taking differences, the nature of the functional relationships is the same regardless of the constants chosen for a and b in the scale transformation formula.

A positive linear scale transformation of an interval scale will not change the research findings when appropriate statistical techniques are used. The majority of such techniques can be used to analyze interval data (see Table 12-1); they include the range, arithmetic mean, standard deviation, product-moment correlation, and so forth. Only a few statistical techniques (such as geometric mean, harmonic mean, and coefficient of variation) could lead to misleading results if applied to interval data.

In marketing, it is very common for attitudinal, opinion, and predisposition judgments to be treated as interval data. To be technically correct, these judgments are ordinal. Researchers disagree as to the amount of measurement error present in the results given by ordinal data treated as interval data. The magnitude of this error must be weighed against the data analysis advantages associated with the more sophisticated statistical techniques applicable to analysis of interval data. It is often argued that while the equality-of-interval characteristic may be violated, the degree of violation is typically small, and the results of most statistical techniques are not affected to the point that significant measurement error exists. In the final analysis, it is the responsibility of the researcher to determine (1) how closely the relationships existing in the marketing phenomena under study approximate an interval scale and (2) the appropriateness of treating the data as intervally scaled. Various data collection instruments for developing interval scales will be discussed in Chapter 13.

Ratio Scale   A ratio scale has all of the properties of an interval scale plus an absolute zero point. With ratio measurement only one number may be assigned arbitrarily, namely, the unit of measurement or distance. Once this is determined, the remaining numerical assignments are completely determined.

Absolute or natural zero point refers to the assignment of the number zero to the absence of the characteristic being measured. For example, in our discussion of the Fahrenheit and Celsius temperature scales, it was stated that the zero points were arbitrarily assigned on both scales. Consequently, the zero points on these scales do not correspond to the absence of heat and are not absolute zero points. The ratio measurement of temperature is known as the Kelvin scale. Here, the zero point is absolute and represents the absence of heat ($-273.15°C$).

A ratio scale implies that equal ratios among the scale values correspond to equal ratios among the marketing phenomena being measured. The statement that the sales of product A are twice as large as the sales of product B is perfectly legitimate with ratio scale data. The scale transformations for a ratio scale involve a positive proportionate transformation of the form $y = cx$; $c > 0$. Figure 12-2(c) presents two such transformations.

A great many very important marketing phenomena possess the properties of a ratio scale. These include sales, market share, costs, ages, and number of customers. In each case a natural or absolute zero exists.

The entire range of statistical techniques can be applied to the analysis of ratio-scaled data. However, the significance of the data analysis techniques gained by having a ratio scale is not great compared with those available for the analysis of interval-scaled data.

DIFFICULTY OF MEASUREMENT

When we discuss the measurement process, most people think in terms of their own experiences with weight, height, and distance. "Since I've been jogging two miles each day, my weight has dropped by five pounds." The measurement of weight, length, and height is typically an easy task involving the use of a ratio scale. The natural zero point and equality of differences are obvious. This type of measurement situation is more characteristic of the physical sciences than of the social sciences, of which marketing is a part. Consequently, the measurement task in marketing is typically more difficult and involves lower scales of measurement than those found in the physical sciences. Figure 12-3 illustrates this type of comparison.

Why is measurement so difficult in marketing? A key problem area relates to the domain of the phenomena studied, namely, the behavior of people. The typical measurement device is that of interrogating people regarding their behavior. The use of a questionnaire is a relatively crude technique which is subject to substantial measurement error.

The measurement task in marketing is complicated by the many concepts or constructs which pervade marketing thought. These concepts or constructs must be precisely defined and measured in a marketing research project if useful information is to be provided for management decision making.

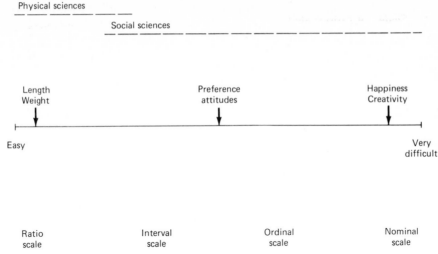

Figure 12-3 Difficulty of the measurement process.

The terms "concept" and "construct" have similar meanings and will be used interchangeably in this book.[2] A construct is defined as *the mental abstraction formed by the perception of a phenomenon.* In marketing, we refer to constructs such as sales, product positioning, demand, attitudes, and brand loyalty. Constructs serve to simplify and synthesize the complex phenomena present in the marketing system.

Some constructs are directly related to aspects of physical realty. For example, the constructs of length and weight are closely related to observations regarding heavy or light and tall or short. The measurement of these constructs is commonplace and fairly easy.

In marketing there are many constructs which do not have observable physical references. Examples include constructs such as predisposition, attitude, preference, and image. These constructs exist in the minds of individuals and are not directly observable. Effective marketing research requires that constructs be defined precisely. This can be done in two general ways—by means of (1) a constitutive definition and (2) an operational definition.[3]

A *constitutive definition* defines a construct with other constructs. This approach is similar to that used in a dictionary where words are used to define other words. A constitutive definition should identify the main features of the construct such that it is clearly differentiated from other constructs. For example, how would you define brand loyalty? Engel et al. define it as "the preferential attitudinal and behavioral response toward one or more brands in a product category expressed over a period of time by a consumer."[4] In this definition, constructs such as preferential attitudes, behavior response, and consumer are used to define the construct "brand loyalty."

[2] For a discussion of their distinction see Fred N. Kerlinger, *Foundations of Behavior Research,* 2d ed. (New York: Holt, 1973), p. 28.

[3] Ibid., p. 30.

[4] James Engel et al., *Consumer Behavior,* 2d ed. (New York: Holt, 1973), p. 552.

An *operational definition* specifies how a construct is to be measured. "An operational definition is a sort of manual of instructions to the investigator. It says, in effect, 'Do such-and-such in so-and-so manner.' In short, it defines or gives meaning to a variable by spelling out what the investigator must do to measure it."[5]

A constitutive definition directs the development of an operational definition. Consider our previous constitutive definition of brand loyalty by Engel et al., which clearly rules out the measurement of brand loyalty solely in terms of consecutive purchases of the brand. For example, the pattern of consecutive purchase of brand B (BBBB) could result from convenience, lack of availability of substitutes, indifference, or lower price rather than from an intrinsic preferential attitude toward the brand. Consequently, an operational definition that is consistent with this constitutive definition of brand loyalty must specify how the preferential attitude is to be measured, what type of behavioral response is consistent with this loyalty state, and how the consumer is to be defined.[6]

Marketing has few examples of standardized constitutive and operational definitions of constructs. This has been a serious hindrance to the effectiveness of marketing research projects, largely reflecting the difficulty of the measurement process in this young field of study.

CONCEPTS OF VALIDITY AND RELIABILITY

Measurement error is minimized when a direct correspondence exists between the number system and the marketing phenomena being measured; in this case the numbers accurately represent the characteristics being measured and nothing else. Obviously, this is an idealized situation which rarely exists in practice. More typically our measurements possess some degree of error in that the numerical scale does not exactly represent the marketing phenomenon under investigation.

There are many ways to describe and classify potential sources of error. The following discussion outlines several of the more common sources.[7]

1   Short-term characteristics of the respondent—personal factors such as mood, fatigue, health, etc. may influence the measurements.
2   Situational factors—variations in the environment in which the measurements are reached.
3   Data collection factors—variations in how the questions are administered and the influence of the interviewing method, e.g., phone, personal, or mail.
4   Measuring instrument factors—the degree of ambiguity and difficulty of the questions and the ability of the respondent to answer them.
5   Data analysis factors—errors made in the coding and tabulation process.

[5] Kerlinger, op. cit., p. 31.
[6] For an interesting discussion of this issue, see J. Jacoby and D. Kyner, "Brand Loyalty vs. Repeat Purchase Behavior," *Journal of Marketing Research,* vol. 10, pp. 1–9, February 1973.
[7] For a more complete discussion see Claire Selltiz et al., *Research Methods in Social Relations,* rev. ed. (New York: Holt, 1959), pp. 150–154.

The total error of measurement consists of two components. The first is *systematic error*, which is error that causes a constant bias in the measurements. For example, assume we are measuring the speed of events at a swimming meet using a stopwatch which systematically runs fast. To the disappointment of the swimmers, this will cause an upward bias in the measured swimming speeds for all events.

The second component of the total error of measurement is *random error*, which involves influences that bias the measurements but are not systematic. For example, in our swimming meet several stopwatches could be used to time the race. Assuming the absence of systematic error, one would find that the recorded times fall within a range around the true time. This random error has been discussed previously in the chapters dealing with sampling.

Returning to our swimming meet example, we can think of the stopwatch time or observed measurement O_m as composed of three elements, (1) the true speed or score T_s, (2) systematic error S_e, and (3) random error R_e. Formally we can state the relationship as

$$O_m = T_s + S_e + R_e$$

where O_m = observed measurement
$\quad\quad T_s$ = true score of the characteristic measured
$\quad\quad S_e$ = systematic error
$\quad\quad R_e$ = random error

Validity and Reliability Defined

The *validity of a measure* refers to the extent to which the measurement process is free from both systematic and random error. The *reliability of a measure* refers to the extent to which the measurement process is free from random errors. Reliability is concerned with the consistency, accuracy, and predictability of the research findings. Validity is concerned with the question: Are we measuring what we think we are measuring? Validity is a broader and more difficult issue than reliability.

Assume we are conducting a survey of buyers to estimate the market share for brand X. For purposes of illustration, assume the market share is actually 10 percent. Let us also assume that four potential conditions exist regarding the influence of systematic and random error on our observed measure of market share. Condition A is no systematic error and low random error; condition B is high systematic error and low random error; condition C is no systematic error and high random error; and condition D is high systematic error and high random error. These four conditions represent extremes, and the more typical situation would lie somewhere in the middle. Figure 12-4 illustrates these four conditions.

The figure also presents the influence of systematic and random error on the distribution of sample means for each of these four conditions. In condition A, the expected value of the distribution of sample means is identical to the true market share of 10 percent. The low random error is reflected in a tight distribu-

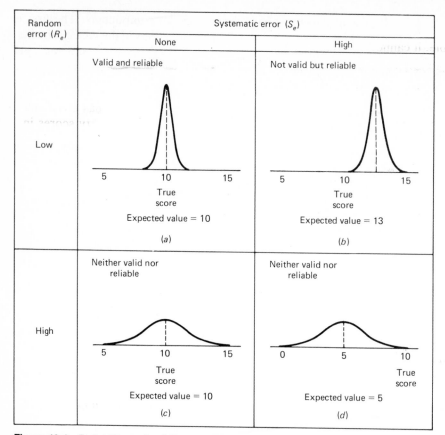

Random error (R_e)	Systematic error (S_e)	
	None	High
Low	Valid and reliable True score Expected value = 10 (a)	Not valid but reliable True score Expected value = 13 (b)
High	Neither valid nor reliable True score Expected value = 10 (c)	Neither valid nor reliable True score Expected value = 5 (d)

Figure 12-4 Reliability and validity.

tion of sample means. Here, repeated samples consistently produce means which are close to the true market share. In this condition, our survey results would be described as both valid and reliable. Condition B has the same tight distribution of sample means, but the influence of the high systematic error has biased the expected value 3 points above the true share of market. Repeated sampling would produce means which are close to the 13 percent result. In this situation, our survey results would be reliable but not valid.

In condition C, the expected value of the distribution of sample means is identical to the true market share of 10 percent, but the high random error causes the distribution of sample means to be highly dispersed. Here, repeated sampling would find many sample means dramatically different from the true market share. In this condition, our survey results would be described as neither valid nor reliable. Finally, condition D has the same high random error as condition C, but here the systematic error is also high, causing the expected value of the sampling distribution to be 5 points below the true market share. In this situation, our survey results would again be described as neither valid nor reliable.

To summarize, for a measure to be valid it must be reliable. Here, systematic error S_e and random error R_e are small or zero. However, if a measure is not reliable, it cannot be valid, and if it is reliable, then it may or may not be valid. Reliability is a necessary but not a sufficient condition for validity. Consequently, the validity of a measure is of main concern since it deals with both systematic and random error. Reliability is a weaker concept since it involves only random error. The ease of measuring reliability compared with validity has given emphasis to the reporting of reliability scores in preference to validity scores in research studies.

Estimation of Validity and Reliability

It is rare to find a decision maker spending the money and taking the time to determine the validity and reliability of research results. The pressures and practical considerations of the typical decision-making situation leave the issue of validity and reliability to those concerned with basic research or academic research projects. Consequently, we will not go into depth regarding the theoretical and complex issues involved with this topic. Rather, we will overview the main methods for estimating validity and reliability. An in-depth discussion of this area can be found in Selltiz.[8]

An easy measure of validity would be to compare the observed measurement with the true measure. However, rarely do we know the true measure, and if we did there would be no reason to measure it in the first place. Consequently, what we do is to infer the validity of the observed measurement using one or more estimation methods. The major ways to estimate the validity of measurement are (1) construct validity, (2) content validity, (3) concurrent validity, and (4) predictive validity.

Construct Validity   Construct validity involves understanding the theoretical rationale underlying the obtained measurements. The approach is to relate the construct of interest to other constructs such that a theoretical framework is developed regarding the marketing phenomenon being measured. Construct validity increases as the correlation between the construct of interest and the related constructs increases in the predicted manner.

To illustrate construct validity, assume that a sales manager believes there is a relationship among job satisfaction, degree of extrovert personality, and job performance of a sales force. Construct validity could be assessed by developing measures of these three constructs and ascertaining the relationship among the measures for a group of sales personnel. Those who have high job satisfaction and extrovert personalities should exhibit high job performance scores; if they do not, one could question the construct validity of the measures and/or question the validity of the hypothesized relationship. If that relationship is sufficiently confirmed from previous research, the conclusion could be drawn that the measures do not measure what we think they measure.

[8] Ibid.

Construct validity can be evaluated with other approaches. If a construct exists, it should be successfully measured by methods that are different or independent. *Convergent validity* involves the measurement of a construct with independent measurement techniques and the demonstration of a high correlation among the measures. Alternatively, if a construct exists, it should be distinguished from constructs which differ from it. *Discriminant validity* involves demonstrating a lack of correlation among differing constructs.

Content Validity   Content validity involves a subjective judgment by an expert as to the appropriateness of the measurement. This is a common method used in marketing research to determine the validity of measurements.

To illustrate content validity, assume we are going to measure the image of retail stores in a grocery chain. Rather than asking a simple question, a multi-item measuring technique is to be developed. Assume that 20 items or questions are proposed which, when combined in an index, represent the measure of store image. The content validity of these 20 items would be determined by having an expert or experts assess the representativeness of the items used to measure store image. The content validity could be challenged if items such as store cleanliness, friendly atmosphere, or price competitiveness were excluded from the list of items. Content validity is frequently called "face validity" because of the emphasis on the expert's critical eye in determining the relevance of the measurements to the underlying construct.

Concurrent Validity   Concurrent validity involves correlating two different measurements of the same marketing phenomenon which have been administered at the same point in time. It is primarily used to determine the validity of new measuring techniques by correlating them with established techniques.

To illustrate concurrent validity, assume that our previous 20-item measurement technique of store image is valid. Also, assume that an alternative and shorter technique is proposed. Concurrent validation would involve administering both techniques under similar or identical conditions and correlating the two measures of store image. A high correlation would establish the concurrent validity of the new technique.

Predictive Validity   Predictive validity involves the ability of a measured marketing phenomenon at one point in time to predict another marketing phenomenon at a future point in time. If the correlation among the two measures is high, the initial measure is said to have predictive validity, sometimes also called *pragmatic validity* or *criterion-related validity*. It is to be distinguished from concurrent validity, where the two correlated measures occur at the same point in time.

To illustrate predictive validity, consider the use of the Scholastic Aptitude Test to predict college performance. Here, the test measures the student's aptitude for college-level work, and this is used as a predictor of future performance at college. The wide use of this test by colleges attests to its predictive validity.

The major methods of estimating the reliability of measurement are the test-retest, the alternative-forms, and the split-half methods.

Test-Retest Reliability   Test-retest reliability involves repeated measurement using the same scaling device under conditions which are judged to be very similar. The results of these measurements are compared to determine their similarity. This approach assumes that the greater the discrepancy in scores the greater the random error present in the measurement process and the lower the reliability.

To illustrate test-retest reliability, let's return to our multi-item technique for measuring retail store image, discussed previously in reference to content validity. Test-retest reliability would involve administering our 20-item measuring technique to a group of store shoppers at two points in time. The results of the two measurements would then be correlated to determine the degree of correspondence. The lower the correlation the lower the reliability.

There are a number of problems with this approach to measuring reliability. First, it may not be logical or possible to administer the measurement twice to the same subject. Second, the first measurement may change the subject's response to the second measurement. Third, situational factors may change, causing the second measurement to change. These types of problems can bias our measurement of reliability.

Alternative-Forms Reliability   Alternative-forms reliability involves giving the subject two forms which are judged equivalent but are not identical. The results of the two measurements are compared to determine the degree of discrepancy in scores, as in the test-retest approach.

Using this approach to determining reliability would require a second set of 20 items to be developed for our retail image–measuring instrument. The two equivalent forms would be administered to the same subjects and the degree of correspondence determined. The problems associated with the alternative-forms approach are the expense and delay associated with developing a second measuring instrument and the difficulty of making them equivalent.

Split-Half Reliability   Split-half reliability involves dividing a multi-item measurement device into equivalent groups and correlating the item responses to estimate reliability. This approach is really a version of the alternative-forms technique.

For example, if we believed that the retail image was composed of a single characteristic or dimension (e.g., favorable-unfavorable image dimension), we could use split-half reliability to measure the internal consistency or internal homogeneity of the 20 items forming the retail image–measuring instrument. Here, each item is assumed to measure this single characteristic independently. The approach would be to randomly divide the 20 items into two groups and determine the degree of correspondence. A high correlation coefficient means that the items are measuring the same characteristic.

SUMMARY

1 The process of measurement is a fundamental aspect of marketing research. It involves the use of numbers to represent the marketing phenomena under investigation.

2 Measurement is defined as the assignment of numbers to characteristics of objects or events according to rules. It is the characteristics of objects or events that are measured, not the items themselves. Measurement error is present when the characteristics of the number system do not represent the relationships present in the marketing phenomena being measured.

3 The four characteristics of the number system—equality of numerals, order of numerals, equality of differences, and equality of ratios—correspond to the four scales of measurement, i.e., nominal, ordinal, interval, and ratio. A nominal scale consists of identifying and categorizing, with no implications of "more or less." An ordinal scale involves the determination of more or less but with no indication as to the distance or interval. An interval scale involves the determination of distance, while a ratio scale involves the additional characteristic of an absolute zero point.

4 Each of these four types of measurement is important in marketing research. Significant marketing phenomena exist at each level of measurement. As we move from nominal to ratio measurement, the rules for assigning numerals to the marketing phenomena become increasingly more restrictive. However, as these rules become more restrictive, the range and sophistication of statistical techniques for data analysis increase.

5 The measurement task in marketing is typically more difficult and involves lower scales of measurement than found in the physical sciences. The problem lies in the measurement of the behavior of people. This often involves measuring concepts or constructs believed to exist in people's minds. The measurement process requires that the construct be operationally defined. Marketing has few examples of standardized operational definitions of constructs.

6 The total error of measurement consists of two components, systematic and random error. The validity of a measurement refers to the extent to which the measurement process is free from both systematic and random error. The reliability of a measure refers to the extent to which the measurement process is free from random error. Measurement can be valid and reliable; not valid, but reliable; or neither valid nor reliable. Reliability is a necessary but not a sufficient condition for validity.

7 The main methods for estimating validity and reliability are (a) construct validity, (b) content validity, (c) concurrent validity, (d) predictive validity, (e) test-retest reliability, (f) alternative-forms reliability, and (g) split-half reliability. Reliability is a weaker concept than validity since it involves only random error. Consequently, reliability is easier to measure than validity and is reported more frequently in research studies.

DISCUSSION QUESTIONS

1 What is measurement?
2 What is the objective of the measurement process?
3 What role does measurement play in marketing?
4 Why is measurement so difficult in marketing?
5 What are the four characteristics of the number system?
6 Distinguish among the four scales of measurement. Give examples of the types of marketing phenomena which each scale might be used to measure.
7 What is measurement error?
8 Distinguish between the validity and reliability of a measure.
9 Discuss the major ways in which the validity of measurement is assessed.
10 How may the reliability of a measure be evaluated?

SUGGESTED READING

Kerlinger, Fred N., *Foundations of Behavior Research* (New York: Holt, 1973), chaps. 3, 25, 26, and 27. A well-written introductory book on behavioral research. It covers the areas of measurement theory, constructs, operational definitions, and reliability and validity.

Selltiz, Claire, et al., *Research Methods in Social Relations,* rev. ed. (New York: Holt, 1959). An excellent discussion of measurement theory and reliability and validity. Somewhat more advanced than Kerlinger.

Stevens, S. S., "On the Theory of Scales of Measurement," *Science,* vol. 103, pp. 677–680, June 7, 1946. An early paper on the theory of measurement scales.

Torgensen, Warren S., *Theory and Methods of Scaling* (New York: Wiley, 1958), chaps. 1 and 2. A more advanced discussion of measurement theory and scaling.

Chapter 13

Attitude Measurement

The marketing manager for a leading hair shampoo aimed at the female market is listening to an exploratory research group discussion on women's reactions to the product. The following statements are typical of this discussion:

"I like the plastic bottle."

"It has lots of suds."

"I don't like the rose smell."

"This is a high-priced product."

"I don't buy it anymore."

"I always purchase that product."

After listening to this discussion for more than an hour, the marketing research manager is asked to comment on what this discussion means and why it is important. How would you respond? It would be important to characterize clearly the meaning of the attitudes expressed by the discussion group, establish why these attitudes are important to the successful marketing of the product, and point out how the significance of these attitudes can be established by formally measuring the attitudes in the context of a conclusive research study.

The objective of this chapter is to address the above issues by building on our discussion of the measurement process in the previous chapter. In the first section the importance of attitudes in marketing will be discussed. The second section provides a detailed discussion of the nature of attitudes, and the final section discusses the many approaches used to measure attitudes and the development of attitude scales.

IMPORTANCE OF ATTITUDES IN MARKETING

The measurement of attitudes is central to many marketing situations. The strategy of market segmentation is often based on attitudinal data. Determining the attitudes of different market segments toward a product can be essential to developing a "positioning" strategy. Attitude measurement is often the basis for evaluating the effectiveness of an advertising campaign. In addition, the assumed relationship between attitudes and behavior helps in the prediction of product acceptance and in the development of marketing programs.

NATURE OF ATTITUDES

An attitude is an individual's enduring perceptual, knowledge-based, evaluative, and action-oriented processes with respect to an object or phenomenon.[1]

Components of Attitude

Attitudes are generally considered to have three main components: (1) a *cognitive* component—a person's beliefs about the object of concern, such as its speed or durability; (2) an *affective* component—a person's feelings about the object, such as "good" or "bad"; and (3) a *behavioral* component—a person's readiness to respond behaviorally to the object.

Link between Attitude and Behavior

Attitudes are important in marketing decision making because of the assumed relationship between attitudes and behavior. Models which conceptualize the construct of attitude typically represent an attitude as a series of sequential components which lead to behavior.[2] Research evidence indicates that the link between attitudes and behavior is not simplistic, and the decision maker and researcher should be cautious in assuming that such a relationship exists in a decision situation. The prediction of future behavior for an aggregate of buyers does appear to be higher than the prediction of behavior regarding an individual buyer.[3] Since most decision situations are concerned with aggregate behavior rather than individual behavior, the attitude-behavior link does have some empirical support for many marketing decision situations. However, attitudes

---

[1] For alternative definitions see D. Krech and R. S. Crutchfield, *Theory and Problems in Social Psychology* (New York: McGraw-Hill, 1948), p. 152; and J. F. Engel, D. T. Kollat, and R. D. Blackwell, *Consumer Behavior* (New York: Holt, 1968), p. 165.

[2] See E. K. Strong, *The Psychology of Selling* (New York: McGraw-Hill, 1925), p. 9; Robert J. Lavidge and Gary A. Steiner, "A Model for Predictive Measurements of Advertising Effectiveness," *Journal of Marketing,* October 1961, p. 61; and Everett M. Rogers, *Diffusion of Innovations* (New York: Free Press, 1962), pp. 79–86.

[3] For a discussion of the research on this issue, see G. S. Day, *Buyer Attitudes and Brand Choice Behavior* (New York: Free Press, 1970).

are only one influence on behavior, and in a particular decision situation other factors could be more influential than attitudes. An obvious example would be an individual who has a highly favorable attitude toward purchasing a new sports car but because of economic constraints has to purchase a less desirable used compact.

The marketing implications of this attitude-behavior link relate to measuring the cognitive and affective components of the buyer's attitude and being able to predict future purchase behavior. Alternatively, by influencing the cognitive and affective components, purchase behavior could be influenced.

Model of Behavioral Response

The purpose of marketing activity is to bring about some response from the targeted market segment. The response may be at the cognitive, affective, or behavioral level. Figure 13-1 shows these three basic levels of response plus a more detailed classification called the *hierarchy-of-effects model*. This model hypothesizes that the buyer passes through the stages of awareness, knowledge, liking, preference, intention-to-buy, and purchase in succession. Recent research by Ray suggests that these stages can occur in different sequences depending on the degree of buyer involvement with the purchase and the degree of differentiation among the alternatives.[4]

Cognitive Component   The cognitive component refers to the respondent's awareness of and knowledge about some object or phenomenon. This is sometimes called the *belief component*. It is expressed by statements such as: "I believe product A does . . ." or "I know that product B will . . . ."

The cognitive component is of considerable importance for many types of information needs. Many decision situations require information regarding the market's awareness/knowledge about product features, advertising campaigns, pricing, product availability, and so forth.

Affective Component   The affective component refers to the respondent's liking and preference regarding an object or phenomenon. Sometimes called the *feeling component*, it is expressed by statements such as: "I dislike product A," "Advertisement X is poor," and "I prefer product A to product B."

The affective component, like the cognitive component, is an important aspect of the information needs for many decision situations. Examples include determining buyers' positive and negative feelings and preferences regarding the organization's marketing program as well as those of competitors.

Behavior Component   The behavioral component refers to the respondent's intention-to-buy and actual purchase behavior. The intention-to-buy stage refers to the respondent's predisposition to action prior to the actual purchase decision. Marketers are interested in respondents' buying intentions as indicators of

---

[4] Michael L. Ray, "Marketing Communication and the Hierarchy-of-Effects" (unpublished research paper No. 180, Stanford University, August 1973).

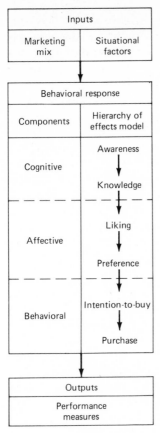

Inputs	
Marketing mix	Situational factors

Behavioral response	
Components	Hierarchy of effects model
Cognitive	Awareness ↓ Knowledge
Affective	Liking ↓ Preference
Behavioral	Intention-to-buy ↓ Purchase

Outputs
Performance measures

Figure 13-1 Model of behavioral response.

future purchase behavior. A well-known survey regarding purchase intentions is conducted by the Survey Research Center at the University of Michigan. The Center asks consumers about their buying intentions for durable goods such as automobiles and appliances during the next few months. The assumption is that the decision process for durable goods involves extensive planning and that purchase intentions should correlate with actual purchase behavior. Despite this logic, the predictive ability of data regarding intentions appears to be lower than many would anticipate.[5]

Behavior refers to what the respondents *have done or are doing*. In marketing, behavior refers to the buyer's purchase and use patterns for a good or service. Information needs typically focus on what is purchased, how much, where, and when the purchase took place, the circumstances surrounding the purchase, and the characteristics of the buyer. The measurement of behavior involves the development of a comprehensive description of the purchase situation.

[5] F. Thomas Juster, "Durable Goods Purchase Intentions, Purchases, and the Consumer Planning Horizon," in Nelson Foote (ed.), *Household Decision Making, Consumer Behavior*, vol. 4 (New York: New York University Press, 1961), pp. 311–342.

Difficulty of Measuring Attitude

As discussed in Chapter 12, the measurement task in marketing is typically more difficult and involves lower scales of measurement than found in the physical sciences. A prime example of this difficulty is the measurement of the construct of attitude, which exists in the minds of individuals and is not directly observable. Attitude scaling refers to the various operational definitions developed for the measurement of this construct.

In measuring attitudes, one must be sensitive to the scale-level assumptions and the restrictions these assumptions impose on data analysis. Typically, attitudes are measured at the nominal or ordinal level, although several more complex scaling procedures allow measurement at the interval level. There is always the temptation to assume that the attitude measurements have the more powerful properties of an interval scale. The researcher must always be sensitive to these questions: (1) What are the characteristics of the construct being measured? (2) What properties of the number system properly relate to this construct?

ATTITUDE-SCALING PROCEDURES

Attitude scaling is the term commonly used to refer to the process of measuring attitudes. Attitude scaling in marketing tends to focus on the measurement of the respondent's beliefs about a product's attributes (cognitive component) and the respondent's feelings regarding the desirability of these attributes (affective component). Some combination of beliefs and feelings typically is assumed to determine intention to buy (behavioral component).

General Methods of Attitude Measurement

Attitude measurement procedures rely on data from respondents. The measuring techniques can be grouped into those based on communicating with respondents and those based on observing respondents.[6]

Communication Techniques

1   Self-reports: Respondents are directly asked to report their beliefs or feelings by responding to one or more questions on a questionnaire. A number of scaling techniques have been developed to measure these beliefs and feelings.

2   Responses to unstructured or partially structured stimuli: The respondents are shown a picture of a product being purchased or used, or some other situation, and are asked to express their reaction. Other approaches include story telling, word-association tests, and sentence completion.

3   Performance of objective tasks: Respondents are asked to memorize and/or report factual information about products. These responses are analyzed and inferences drawn regarding the nature of the respondents' beliefs and

    [6] Stuart W. Cook and Claire Selltiz, "A Multiple-Indicator Approach to Attitude Measurement," *Psychological Bulletin* 62 (1964), pp. 36–55.

feelings. The assumption is that respondents are more likely to remember those things which are consistent with their beliefs and feelings.

Observation Techniques

1 Overt behavior: Individuals are put in a situation which allows behavior patterns to be exhibited and inferences to be drawn regarding the individuals' beliefs and feelings. This technique is based on the assumption that a person's behavior is dependent on beliefs and feelings.

2 Physiological reactions: Respondents are exposed to products or advertisements and their physiological reactions are measured. The measurement device typically is the galvanic skin response technique, which measures sweating of the hand, or the eye dilation technique, which measures changes in the diameter of the pupil of the eye. A limitation of the physiological response approach is that it measures only the intensity of feelings and not direction (positive or negative).

Of these general methods for measuring attitudes, the self-reporting technique is by far the most widely used, and the remainder of this chapter will focus on the various scaling procedures which use it. These procedures are most appropriate for conclusive research studies which require that attitudes be formally measured and quantified using a large sample of respondents. The remaining general methods for measuring attitudes are most appropriate for exploratory research designed to develop the nature of beliefs and feelings present in a decision situation. These remaining methods will be discussed in more detail in Chapter 18, which deals with data collection methods.

Self-Report Techniques

The most common tool of attitude measurement is the self-report method. Several such techniques will be discussed here, with emphasis on the development of unidimensional scales.

Nominal Scale The simplest self-reporting scale is a nominal scale, where the respondent's beliefs are classified in two or more categories. For example, a nominal scale can be developed from responses to the question: "Does your automobile have radial tires—yes or no?" A third category of "don't know" might be included for those respondents who are not informed regarding this feature of their automobile. The result of this scaling is a three-category classification of respondents with respect to their responses—yes, no, and don't know. Here a nominal scale has been developed, and numbers can be assigned to the categories for data analysis purposes. Keep in mind that these numbers can be used only to identify the categories.

Rating Scales Rating scales refer to measurement situations which involve ordinal, interval, and ratio scales. Typically, the focus of the measurement situation is on developing ordinal or interval scales of the affective component.

A rating scale requires the respondent to indicate the position on a continuum or among ordered categories which corresponds to his or her attitude. Numerical values may be part of the scale or be assigned after the respondent completes the self-rating task.

An ordinal scale is formed when respondents order themselves by responding to a question such as: "Do you like, dislike, or are you indifferent to radial tires?" The result of this scaling is a three-category ordinal scale which ranks the respondents according to their feeling about radial tires, i.e., like—indifferent—dislike. Numbers can be assigned to these ordered categories for purposes of data analysis.

Graphic Rating Scales   A graphic rating scale requires the respondents to indicate their position on a continuum which ranges from one extreme of the attitude in question to the other extreme. The format of this graphic continuum is as varied as the imaginations of the researchers who devise such scales.

Figure 13-2 presents two examples of alternative graphic scales (scales A and C).[7] Let's assume that several respondents have sampled a new formulation of cake mix, and we are interested in measuring their feelings regarding the sweetness of the cake mix. Scale A relies on a series of facial expressions to represent the varying degrees of like and dislike. The respondents are asked to indicate which of the facial expressions best represents their reaction to the sweetness level. A most favorable response means the sweetness level is "just right" (extreme smile) while a least favorable response (extreme frown) means the cake is either "too sweet" or "not sweet enough." Such an unfavorable response would require additional questioning of the respondent to determine what was wrong with the sweetness level. Graphic scales of this nature are especially useful when the respondents speak different languages, or when the respondents are children.

Scale C presents a positive-negative continuum. The respondents are asked to indicate their position by checking a location on this continuum. Once the judgments are recorded, the researcher can subdivide the continuum into an appropriate set of categories and assign numerals to the judgments. It is argued that the advantage of this continuous scale is that the respondent is not confronted with a predetermined set of response categories. Rather, the categorization of the scale is left to the respondent, who implicitly determines the number of categories during the judgment process. A disadvantage of this graphic scale is that it requires the respondent to deal with an abstract judgment situation. In addition, since the researcher does not know how the respondents subdivided the continuum, the comparison and grouping of responses across respondents is difficult to justify.

Verbal Rating Scales   Verbal rating scales are probably the most frequently used scales in marketing research. These require the respondents to indicate their position by selecting among verbally identified categories. Scale B in Figure

[7] Jean Morton-Williams, "Questionnaire Design," in Robert M. Worchester (ed.), *Consumer Market Research Handbook* (London: McGraw-Hill, 1972), pp. 85–87.

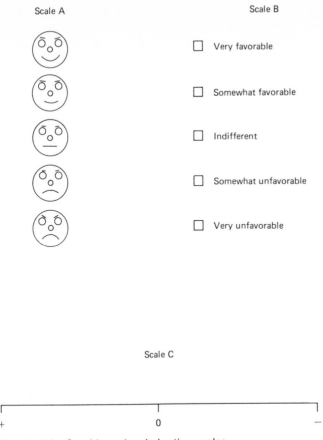

Figure 13-2 Graphic and verbal rating scales.

13-2 is an example; here, the respondents are asked to check the box adjacent to the phrase which best corresponds to their reaction given the question at hand.

It is important to understand the issues surrounding the construction of verbal rating scales.[8] The major issues are: (1) number of categories, (2) odd or even number of categories, (3) balanced versus unbalanced scale, (4) extent of verbal description, (5) category numbering, (6) forced versus nonforced scales, and (7) comparative versus noncomparative scales.

While there is no established *number of categories* which is deemed optimal for a scale, in practice scales of five or six categories are typical.[9] Some researchers argue that more than five or six are needed in situations where small

---

[8] This discussion follows that in Donald S. Tull and Del I. Hawkins, *Marketing Research* (New York: Macmillan, 1976), pp. 336–339.

[9] D. R. Lehmann and J. Hulbert, "Are Three-Point Scales Always Good Enough?" *Journal of Marketing Research,* vol. 9, pp. 444–446, November 1972; see also M. S. Matell and J. Jacoby, "Is There an Optimal Number of Alternatives for Likert-Scale Items?" *Journal of Applied Psychology,* vol. 56, pp. 506–509, December 1972.

changes in attitude are to be measured.[10] Others argue that it is doubtful that the majority of respondents can distinguish between more than six to eight categories. Beyond this point, additional categories do not increase the precision with which the attitude is being measured.[11] Most researchers find that it is as easy to administer and analyze a scale with five or seven categories as it is to use one with, say, three categories. Consequently, researchers typically utilize at least a five-category scale unless special circumstances dictate fewer or more categories.

Should the scale have an *odd or even number of scale categories*? The answer to this issue is unclear. If an odd number of categories is selected, the middle category is typically identified as a neutral position. If an even number is selected, the scale does not have a neutral category, and the respondent is forced to take a position expressing some degree of feeling. The results of a research study comparing an odd (seven-category) scale with an even (six-category) scale concluded that there was no significant difference in the results between scales.[12]

Should the number of favorable and unfavorable categories be *balanced or unbalanced*? A balanced scale has the same number of favorable categories as unfavorable categories. The argument for an unbalanced scale relates to the nature of the attitude distribution to be measured. If the distribution is predominantly favorable, an unbalanced scale with more favorable categories than unfavorable categories would be appropriate. The argument for balanced scales emphasizes the potential biasing of responses which can result from limiting the response categories on the favorable or unfavorable side of the scale.

How extensive should be the *verbal description* of a category? Some researchers believe that clearly defined response categories increase the reliability of the measurements.[13] It is argued that each category should have a verbal description and that these verbal descriptions should have a clear and precise wording such that each response category is differentiated.

In many situations the researcher believes that the respondent's judgments can be treated as interval data. Implicit in this decision is the assumption that the respondent views the differences between verbal descriptions to be equally spaced. When using the phrases "very good," "fairly good," and "neutral" as verbal descriptions for an interval scale, the researcher assumes that the distance between "very good" and "neutral" is twice the distance of that between "fairly good" and "neutral." A research study which measured the relative size of "very" and "fairly" found a respective weight of $+3.74$ and $+1.22$ rather

[10] G. D. Hughes, "Selecting Scales to Measure Attitude Change," *Journal of Marketing Research*, vol. 4, pp. 85–87, February 1967.

[11] P. E. Green and V. R. Rao, "Rating Scales and Information Recovery—How Many Scales and Response Categories to Use?" *Journal of Marketing*, vol. 34, pp. 33–39, July 1970.

[12] G. S. Albaum and G. Munsinger, "Methodological Questions Concerning the Use of the Semantic Differential," paper presented at the Spring 1973 meeting of the Southwestern Marketing Association.

[13] C. Selltiz, M. Jahoda, M. Deutsch, and S. W. Cook, *Research Methods in Social Relations* (New York: Holt, 1959), p. 349.

than the assumed weight of $+2$ and $+1$, respectively.[14] In this situation, the assignment of the weights $+2$ and $+1$ for purposes of data analysis would obviously introduce measurement error in the research results. It is common practice to treat rating scales as interval scales and to compute means and standard deviations on such measurements. The researcher should be sensitive to this practice and remember the potential for measurement error in the research findings.[15]

Should *numbers* be assigned to the response categories? The argument is that they should be used when the researcher believes the respondent's judgments can be treated as interval data. The numbers 5, 4, 3, 2, and 1 could be used on a five-category scale to communicate to the respondent that the intervals between response categories are intended to be of equal distance.

Another issue in constructing a rating scale concerns the use of a *forced versus a nonforced scale*. A forced scale requires all respondents to indicate a position on the attitude scale. The argument for a forced scale is that those who are reluctant to reveal their attitude are encouraged to do so with the forced scale. Those respondents who have no opinion or no knowledge typically mark the "neutral" category on the scale. If a significant proportion of the respondents have no opinion, rather than a reluctance to reveal their feelings, it is best to have a category of "no opinion" or "no knowledge" rather than forcing their response in the "neutral category."[16]

A final issue concerns the use of *comparative and noncomparative scales*. A comparative scale requires the respondents to express their attitude by making a direct comparison with a standard or reference point. This reference point could be the current brand used, an ideal product, or a competitive product. A comparative scale allows the researcher to report the respondents' attitudes relative to a standard that may be of importance in a decision situation. The argument for noncomparative scales is that they allow each respondent to choose his or her own reference point, and that consequently a more accurate measurement of the respondent's attitude is achieved. In practice, the selection of comparative and noncomparative scales is dependent on the specific information needs of the decision situation.

Rank-Order Scale   The rank-order technique involves having the respondent rank various objects with regard to the attitude in question. Thus, the respondent may be required to rank five print advertisements with regard to either awareness of, liking for, preference for, or intention to buy the product advertised.

The rank-order technique is widely used in marketing research. It is comparative in nature and forms an ordinal scale of the objects evaluated.

[14] Cliff Holmes, "A Statistical Evaluation of Rating Scales," *Journal of the Market Research Society*, 1974, vol. 16, p. 91.

[15] J. A. Martilla and D. W. Carvey, "Four Subtle Sins in Marketing Research," *Journal of Marketing*, vol. 39, pp. 8–10, January 1975.

[16] G. D. Hughes, "Some Confounding Effects of Forced-Choice Scales," *Journal of Marketing Research*, vol. 6, pp. 223–226, May 1969.

This technique has important advantages. It is simple in concept, easy to administer, and less time-consuming to administer than other comparative techniques, such as paired comparison. The instructions for ranking objects are easy to comprehend; consequently, the technique can be used on self-administered questionnaires. In addition, it is argued that the technique is similar to the purchase decision process and forces respondents to discriminate among products in a realistic manner.

The limitations of rank-order techniques are important also. The forced-choice and comparative nature of the technique results in a ranking of objects regardless of the attitudinal position of the respondent to the objects as a group. It could be that the respondent "dislikes" all of the objects in the set. In this case, the object ranked first is the least "disliked" of the objects in the set. Obviously the researcher must be sensitive to the attitudinal position of the respondent and be confident that a realistic set of objects is being evaluated.

Another limitation of the rank-order technique is the fact that it produces only ordinal data. While there are scaling techniques which form higher-order scales based on ranked input data, these techniques bring a degree of complexity to the data collection and analysis phase which may be undesirable. Finally, several research studies have found that the ranking and rating-scale techniques yield similar results.[17] Other things being equal, in selecting between these two techniques researchers must weigh the pros and cons of each technique against the specific needs of the research project.

Paired-Comparison Scale   With the paired-comparison technique, respondents are presented with two objects from a set and required to pick one with regard to the attitude in question. Thus, the respondent is required to make a series of paired judgments between objects regarding preference, amount of some attribute present, and so forth.

The data collection procedure typically requires the respondent to compare all possible pairs of the objects. If there are 5 objects ($n = 5$) to be evaluated, there will be 10 paired comparisons $[n(n - 1)/2]$ required in the judgment task. The evaluation of 10 objects requires 45 paired comparisons. The geometric expansion in the number of paired comparisons limits the usefulness of this technique for the evaluation of large object sets.

In Table 13-1, matrix A presents paired-comparison data for five brands of cake mix, A, B, C, D, and E. The judgment task was to pick the cake mix sample which had the most light and fluffy texture. Each cell entry in matrix A represents the proportion of respondents who believed that the "column" brand has more of the attributes in question than the "row" brand. For example, in the brand A versus brand B comparison 90 percent of the respondents believed that brand B was lighter and fluffier than A. An inspection of the column proportions reveals that brand B dominates the other brands on this attribute.

[17] See Jack Abrams, "An Evaluation of Alternative Rating Devices for Consumer Research," *Journal of Marketing Research,* vol. 3, pp. 189–193, May 1966; and H. H. Kassarjian and M. Nakanishi, "Study of Selected Opinion Measurement Techniques," *Journal of Marketing Research,* vol. 4, pp. 148–153, May 1967.

Table 13-1 Paired-Comparison Data

			Matrix A		
	A	B	C	D	E
A	—	.90	.64	.14	.27
B	.10	—	.32	.02	.21
C	.36	.68	—	.15	.36
D	.86	.98	.85	—	.52
E	.73	.79	.64	.48	—

			Matrix B		
	A	B	C	D	E
A	—	1	1	0	0
B	0	—	0	0	0
C	0	1	—	0	0
D	1	1	1	—	1
E	1	1	1	0	—
Total	2	4	3	0	1

How can an ordinal scale be developed given these paired-comparison data? The first step is to convert matrix A to 0–1 scores, which indicate whether the column brand dominates the row brand and vice versa (see matrix B in Table 13-1). Here, "1" is assigned to a cell if the column brand dominates the row brand (if the proportion > .5), and "0" is assigned to a cell if the column brand does not dominate the row brand (if the proportion ≤ .5). The ordinal relationship among brands is determined by totaling the columns. Here, the ordinal scaling of the brands is B > C > A > E > D. Thus, brand B has the lightest and fluffiest texture, followed by C, A, E, and D.

If the researcher requires an interval scaling of the cake mix brands, the paired-comparison data in matrix A of Table 13-1 can be analyzed using a technique called *Thurstone's law of comparative judgment,* which converts ordinal judgments into interval data. While the details are too extensive for the purposes of this book, several excellent explanations of the technique are available for those interested.[18]

The arguments in favor of the paired-comparison technique relate to the simplicity of the judgment task, the comparative nature of the task, and the availability of scaling methods which produce interval data. This interval-scaling feature can be important in assessing differences among competitive products and advertisements.

The paired-comparison technique has important limitations. As the number of objects to be evaluated increases arithmetically, the number of paired com-

---

[18] See Allen L. Edwards, *Techniques of Attitude Scale Construction* (New York: Appleton-Century-Crofts, 1957), pp. 20–29; P. E. Green and D. S. Tull, *Research for Marketing Decisions* (Englewood Cliffs, N.J.: Prentice-Hall, 1974), pp. 184–191; H. A. David, *The Method of Paired Comparisons* (London: Charles Griffin & Co., 1963).

parisons increases geometrically. Consequently, the technique is limited to a small number of objects in order to control respondent fatigue during the judgment process. In addition, research indicates that the order in which the objects are presented can bias the results,[19] that the paired-comparison task is not typical of the actual choice process present in the marketplace, and that simpler noncomparative rating scales provide results similar to those obtained from paired comparisons.[20]

Semantic Differential Scale   This is one of the most popular attitude measurement techniques in marketing research.[21] The main application of the semantic differential has been in connection with company and brand image studies.

An image can be defined as an average of many separate attitudes toward a company, brand, or concept. As discussed previously, each separate attitude has three components—cognitive, affective, and behavioral. Consequently, image measurement requires the respondents to express their position on many attitudes using a multiscale questionnaire.

The semantic differential typically requires the respondents to evaluate an object on a seven-point rating scale bounded at each end by bipolar adjectives. For example:

Retail Store X							
Reliable	__:	__:	X :	__:	__:	__:	__:	Unreliable
Friendly	X :	__:	__:	__:	__:	__:	__:	Unfriendly
Modern	__:	__:	__:	__:	X :	__:	__:	Old-fashioned
Inexpensive	__:	__:	__:	__:	__:	X :	__:	Expensive
Progressive	__:	__:	__:	X :	__:	__:	__:	Not progressive

Respondents are instructed to check the blank location which most accurately reflects their position regarding the object in connection with each of the bipolar adjectives.

The semantic differential was originally developed by Osgood.[22] He developed 50 bipolar adjectives which measured three basic dimensions of an object: (1) evaluative—good versus bad; (2) activity—active versus passive; and (3) potency—strong versus weak. Marketing researchers rarely use the semantic differential in the manner proposed by Osgood. Rather, the technique is typically

[19] P. Daniels and J. Lawford, "The Effect of Order in the Presentation of Samples in Paired Comparison Tests," *Journal of the Market Research Society,* vol. 16, pp. 127–133, April 1974.

[20] R. Seaton, "Why Ratings Are Better Than Comparisons," *Journal of Advertising Research,* vol. 14, pp. 45–48, February 1974.

[21] B. A. Greenberg, J. L. Goldstucker, and D. N. Bellenger, "What Techniques Are Used by Marketing Researchers in Business?" *Journal of Marketing,* vol. 41, pp. 62–68, April 1977.

[22] C. Osgood, G. Suci, and P. Tannenbaum, *The Measurement of Meaning* (Urbana: University of Illinois Press, 1957).

adapted to fit the specific needs of the research project at hand, as the following examples demonstrate.[23]

1 The single-word adjectives are sometimes replaced with descriptive phrases tailored to a particular company, product, or concept. The following could be used, for example, to measure the brand image of a cola soft drink:
Very special drink—just another drink
Fun type of drink—kind of serious drink
Regular people drink it—snobs drink it
2 The polar opposites have been replaced with phrases that may not include extremes and may eliminate the negative portion of the scale. The reason is that some respondents are unwilling to check the extremes of a scale, and some either are unwilling to express a negative view or do not have negative views toward the objects under investigation. The following phrases represent this adaptation:
High-quality product—so-so product
Modern company—somewhat old-fashioned company
3 Many researchers have the respondent evaluate an "ideal product" or "ideal company" in addition to the objects under investigation. This approach allows the objects under investigation to be compared to a norm or standard.
4 Each position on the scale can be assigned a numerical value, such as 7, 6, 5, 4, 3, 2, 1 or +3, +2, +1, 0, −1, −2, −3. The assumption is that the respondents' judgments can be treated as interval data, which makes possible the calculation of the arithmetic mean for an object on each scale. This approach is widely accepted by researchers who use the semantic differential.[24] However, there is a controversy as to whether these measurements can be treated as interval data. Critics argue that the median is the appropriate summary measure.

Semantic differential data are typically analyzed using the profile analysis approach. This involves calculating the arithmetic mean or median for each set of verbal phrases or polar opposites for each object evaluated. These summary measures are usually plotted on the scales such that the profiles of the objects can be compared. Figure 13-3 provides an illustration of the profiles for three brands of beer.[25] Brand X has the most favorable brand image, while brand Z has the least favorable image. All three brand images are on the positive side of the scales.

The popularity of the semantic differential is attributed to its versatility and simplicity. The technique is easy to develop and administer, and the results can be readily communicated to management. In addition, it has been found to be a discriminating and reliable research tool.[26]

The limitation of the semantic differential relates to the requirement that

[23] William A. Mindak, "Fitting the Semantic Differential to the Marketing Problem," *Journal of Marketing,* vol. 25, pp. 28–33, April 1961.

[24] For a more detailed discussion see F. N. Kerlinger, *Foundations of Behavioral Research* (New York: Holt, 1973), pp. 566–581, or C. Holmes, "A Statistical Evaluation of Rating Scales," *Journal of the Market Research Society,* vol. 16, pp. 87–107, April 1974.

[25] Mindak, op. cit.

[26] R. F. Carter, W. L. Ruggels, and S. H. Chaffee, "The Semantic Differential in Opinion Measurement," *Public Opinion Quarterly,* vol. 32, pp. 666–674, Winter 1968–69.

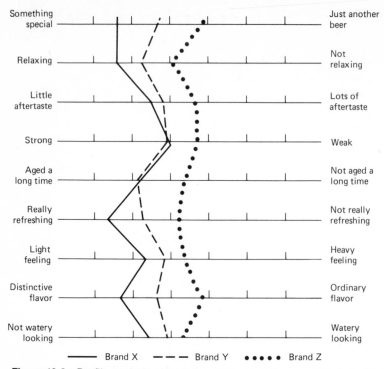

Something   Just another
special   beer

Relaxing   Not
                                                   relaxing

Little   Lots of
aftertaste   aftertaste

Strong   Weak

Aged a   Not aged a
long time   long time

Really   Not really
refreshing   refreshing

Light   Heavy
feeling   feeling

Distinctive   Ordinary
flavor   flavor

Not watery   Watery
looking   looking

——— Brand X   – – – Brand Y   ● ● ● ● Brand Z

Figure 13-3 Profile analysis of beer brand images. (*Source: William A. Mindak, "Fitting the Semantic Differential to the Marketing Problem,"* Journal of Marketing, *April 1961, pp. 28–33.*)

the scales be composed of true bipolar adjectives or phrases. It is argued that the pilot testing necessary to meet this requirement can be expensive and time-consuming. In practice, formal pilot testing is rarely done, and the bipolar adjectives or phrases are developed using the researcher's judgment.

Stapel Scale The Stapel scale is a modification of the semantic differential scale. It is a unipolar 10-point nonverbal rating scale with values ranging from +5 to −5. The scaling technique is designed to measure the direction and intensity of attitudes simultaneously.[27] It differs from the semantic differential in that the scale values indicate how close the descriptor or adjective fits the object evaluated.

Table 13-2 presents the format of a Stapel scale. Respondents are instructed to evaluate how accurately the adjective or phrase describes the object to be evaluated. The following instructions are given to the respondent:

You would select a *plus* number for words that you think describe (Bank A) accurately. The more accurately you think the word describes it, the larger the *plus* number you

[27] I. Crespi, "Use of a Scaling Technique in Surveys," *Journal of Marketing,* vol. 25, pp. 69–72, July 1961.

Table 13-2   Stapel Scale Format

	Bank	
	+5	+5
	+4	+4
	+3	+3
	+2	+2
	+1	+1
Fast service	Friendly	
	−1	−1
	−2	−2
	−3	−3
	−4	−4
	−5	−5

would choose. You would select a *minus* number for words you think do not describe it accurately. The less accurately you think a word describes it, the larger the *minus* number you would choose. Therefore, you can select any number from +5, for words that you think are very accurate, all the way to −5, for words that you think are very inaccurate.[28]

Unipolar judgments can be analyzed the same way that semantic-differential data are treated. Figure 13-4 presents hypothetical results of a profile analysis of two banks based on Stapel-scale data.

The arguments in favor of the Stapel scale relate to its convenience of administration and the absence of the requirement that the scales be composed of truly bipolar adjectives or phrases.[29] Research indicates that the Stapel scale can produce results similar to those of the semantic differential.[30] In addition, the technique has produced satisfactory results when administered over the telephone.[31] Despite these advantages, the Stapel scale has experienced limited use in marketing research in comparison with the semantic differential. It does appear to be a useful technique which should grow in popularity with researchers.

Indirect Scales   The self-report scaling techniques previously discussed require the respondents to report directly what their position is regarding the attitude in question. While this is a very efficient way to measure attitudes, it is argued that under certain circumstances (e.g., reluctance to express an attitude in regard to a controversial issue), respondents may not accurately report their position using direct measurement techniques. A respondent might not be directly aware of his or her position on an issue. Concern with the limitations of

---

[28] Ibid., p. 71.

[29] E. J. Lusk, "A Bipolar Adjective Screening Methodology," *Journal of Marketing Research*, vol. 10, pp. 202–203, May 1973.

[30] D. I. Hawkins, G. Albaum, and R. Best, "Stapel Scale or Semantic Differential in Marketing Research?" *Journal of Marketing Research*, vol. 11, pp. 318–322, August 1974; and J. J. Vidali, "Single-Anchor Stapel Scales Versus Double-Anchor Semantic Differential Scales," *Psychological Reports*, vol. 33, pp. 373–374, October 1973.

[31] Hawkins et al., op. cit.

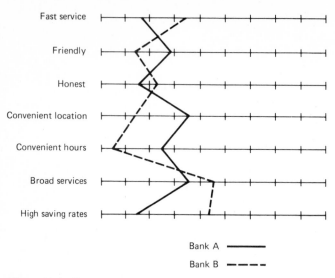

Figure 13-4 Stapel scale comparative profiles.

direct measurement techniques has resulted in the development of indirect self-reporting scaling techniques.[32] While these techniques have been developed to deal with attitude measurement problems present in the field of psychology, marketing researchers have applied them to similar problems in marketing.

Indirect scales combine the respondents' judgments on several questions in order to develop a measure of their position on the attitude in question. Indirect scales are commonly called *attitude scales* and *attitude batteries*.

To ensure that the questions included in the scaling technique contribute efficiently to the measurement of the attitude in question, it is usually necessary to try out a large number of items in a pilot study using 50 to 100 respondents and then apply various criteria for selecting those questions which are most appropriate for the actual scale. It is typical to phrase questions so that the respondent can indicate agreement or disagreement with them. Based on these responses, a score is developed for each respondent which represents his or her position with regard to the attitude in question.

There are four main types of indirect scaling techniques: (1) Likert's method of summated ratings; (2) Thurstone's method of "equal-appearing intervals"; (3) Guttman's cumulative scales; and (4) the Q-sort technique.

Indirect techniques in marketing have not been widely used because of the time and expense involved in developing them and the difficulty of administering the scales. In addition, most attitudes in marketing can be measured effectively using direct attitude measurement techniques. We will briefly discuss the Likert scale, since it is used more frequently than the other three. There are several excellent sources which thoroughly explain the mechanics of how to construct, analyze, and interpret these indirect scaling techniques.[33]

---

[32] Edwards, op. cit.

[33] Edwards, op. cit., and Selltiz et al., op. cit.

The Likert Scale   This involves a series of statements related to the attitude in question. The respondent is required to indicate degree of agreement or disagreement with each of these statements, and responses are given a numerical score that will consistently reflect the direction of the person's attitude on each statement. The respondent's total score is computed by summing scores for all statements. The following example illustrates the use of the Likert scale.

A homemaker is given a card with the following verbal scale.[34]

___ Strongly agree
___ Agree
___ Neither agree nor disagree
___ Disagree
___ Strongly disagree

Next, the homemaker is read or shown a list of statements about the object under investigation. For each statement the homemaker is required to indicate the phrase which best represents his or her position concerning the statement. Assume that the following statements are used to determine the homemaker's attitude toward brand X chocolate cake mix:

1   Brand X is expensive.
2   Brand X is rich in taste.
3   Brand X is light and fluffy.
4   Brand X has real chocolate flavor.
5   Brand X has a moist texture.

The responses to these statements are scored from five to one (strongly agree through strongly disagree) for statements favorable to brand X (statements 2 through 5) and scored from one to five (strongly agree through strongly disagree) for statements unfavorable to brand X (statement 1). The sum of these scores represents the homemaker's total score on the attitude in question. In this example, the total score could range from a high of 25 (very favorable) to a low score of 5 (very unfavorable).

There are five steps in the construction of a Likert scale:[35]

1   The researcher collects a large number of statements considered relevant to the attitude being measured which can be clearly identified as either favorable or unfavorable.
2   These statements are given to a group of respondents representative of the respondent population of interest. The respondents indicate their position on each statement by checking a category on an agreement-disagreement scale.
3   The responses to the various statements are scored by summing the respondent's numerical score on each statement. The responses must be scored

---

[34] Several versions of this scale are used in practice. Some researchers prefer a 7-point scale, while others include a "don't know" category.
[35] Selltiz et al., op. cit., pp. 367–368.

in such a manner that favorable responses toward the object consistently receive the same numerical scores. This will require the reversing of the numerical assignment depending on whether the statement is favorable or unfavorable.

4 The statements are analyzed to determine which of them discriminate most clearly between the high scorers and low scorers. Statements which do not indicate a substantial correlation with the total score or do not elicit different responses from those who score high and those who score low on the overall test are eliminated. This process increases the.internal consistency or reliability of the measurement technique.

5 The remaining statements form the Likert scale, which can be used to measure the attitude in question.

The Likert scale has several advantages over other indirect scaling techniques. It is reasonably easy to construct and administer, and the simplicity of the instructions and the judgment task allow its use on mail surveys. The evidence to date indicates that the Likert scale is more reliable than the Thurstone method.[36]

The arguments against the Likert scale are that it produces only an ordinal scale.[37] Many researchers believe that the Likert data closely resemble those of an interval scale, and so they prefer to use statistical techniques requiring interval data. On balance, most researchers find that the advantages of the Likert scale outweigh the disadvantages of other indirect scaling techniques.

SUMMARY

1 Attitude measurement is important in marketing because of the central role it plays in developing a segmentation/positioning strategy, evaluating the effectiveness of advertising, predicting product acceptance, and facilitating the development of marketing programs.

2 An attitude represents an individual's enduring perceptual, knowledge-based, evaluative, and action-oriented processes with respect to an object or phenomena. The three components of an attitude are (a) cognitive—relating to beliefs, (b) affective—relating to feelings, and (c) behavioral—relating to action tendency.

3 Marketing activities are designed to bring about some response from the targeted market segment. This response can be at the cognitive, affective, or behavioral level. The hierarchy-of-effect model hypothesizes a cognitive-affective-behavioral sequence resulting from the marketing effort. While the order of this sequence may vary depending on the specifics of the marketing situation, the measurement of an attitude component early in the sequence may allow predictions regarding the character of subsequent components.

[36] L. H. Seiler and R. L. Hough, "Empirical Comparisons of the Thurstone and Likert Techniques," in G. F. Summers (ed.), *Attitude Measurement* (Chicago: Rand McNally, 1970), pp. 159–173.

[37] An improved Likert scale is presented in G. Kundu, "A Comparison of the Likert and a New Technique of Attitude Measurement," *Indian Journal of Psychology,* vol. 47, pp. 245–258, September 1972.

4 An attitude is a construct which exists in the minds of individuals. Attitude scaling refers to operational definitions for the measurement of this construct. This is a difficult measurement task, and typically it results in a nominal or ordinal scale.

5 The general methods for measuring attitudes rely on communicating with respondents and on observing respondents. Communication techniques include (a) self-reports, (b) responses to unstructured or partially structured stimuli, and (c) performance of objective tasks. Observation techniques include (a) overt behavior, and (b) physiological reactions.

6 The self-reporting technique, the most widely used method of attitude measurement in marketing, is composed of many specific scaling approaches. Of these approaches, graphic and verbal rating scales are among the most frequently used. The major issues surrounding the construction of rating scales are (a) number of categories, (b) odd or even number of categories, (c) balanced versus unbalanced scale, (d) extent of verbal description, (e) category numbering, (f) forced versus nonforced scales, and (g) comparative versus noncomparative scales.

7 The rank-order scaling approach involves a ranking of objects with regard to the attitude in question. This popular approach results in an ordinal scaling of the objects.

8 The paired-comparison scaling approach involves a series of pairwise judgments among objects in a set. This more complex scaling approach results in an ordinal scale.

9 The semantic-differential scaling approach is a popular way to measure "image," which can be defined as an average of many separate attitudes toward a company, brand, or concept. With this method, an object is evaluated on several rating scales bounded at each end by bipolar adjectives or phrases. The data are analyzed using the profile analysis approach.

10 The Stapel scale is a modification of the semantic-differential scale. It uses a unipolar 10-point nonverbal rating scale to measure how closely the descriptor fits the object evaluated.

11 Indirect scales attempt to measure attitudes in situations where the respondent may not accurately report beliefs and feelings using direct scaling approaches. These more complex approaches include (a) Likert's method of summated ratings; (b) Thurstone's method of "equal-appearing intervals"; (c) Guttman's cumulative scales; and (d) the Q-sort technique. Of these scaling approaches, only the Likert scale has received much attention in the measurement of attitudes in marketing.

DISCUSSION QUESTIONS

1 What is an attitude?
2 What are the three main components of attitudes?
3 Describe the stages of the hierarchy-of-effects model.
4 What questions must the researcher always be concerned with when measuring attitudes?

5   What general methods of attitude measurement exist?
6   What self-report techniques are used in marketing research?
7   Discuss some of the issues involved in constructing a verbal rating scale.
8   What are the advantages and disadvantages of rank-order scales?
9   Describe the methods by which ordinal and interval scales can be derived from paired-comparison data.
10 What advantages and limitations exist for the paired-comparison technique?
11 Explain the profile analysis method of evaluating data from semantic-differential scales.
12 How does the Staple scale differ from the semantic-differential scale?
13 When may an indirect scale offer advantages to the marketing researcher over other self-reporting methods?
14 What are the steps involved in constructing a Likert scale?

SUGGESTED READING

Abrams, Jack, "An Evaluation of Alternative Rating Devices for Consumer Research," *Journal of Marketing Research,* vol. 3, pp. 189–193, May 1966. This article presents research findings comparing various scaling techniques.

Edwards, Allen L., *Techniques of Attitude Scale Construction* (New York: Appleton-Century-Crofts, 1957). An excellent book which thoroughly explains the mechanics and issues involved in constructing, analyzing, and interpreting indirect scaling techniques.

Hughes, G. David, *Attitude Measurement for Marketing Strategies* (Glenview, Ill.: Scott, Foresman, 1971). This interesting book discusses attitude measurement as it relates to marketing.

Selltiz, Claire, Marie Jahoda, Morton Deutsch, and Stuart Cook, *Research Methods in Social Relations* (New York: Holt, 1959). Chapters 5 and 10 of this book deal specifically with measurement issues and attitude scaling techniques.

Summers, Gene F., *Attitude Measurement* (Chicago: Rand McNally, 1970). An excellent book which deals in depth with many aspects of attitude measurement.

Cases for Part Four

New England Soup Company

On May 11, 1975, William Kolander, president of the New England Soup Company of Boston, Massachusetts, was reviewing a research report he had recently received from a Boston-based research house. The report presented the findings of a study on the firm's new formulation of Kolander's Chowder brand of canned soup. The study had also been sent to the firm's sales manager, Kirk George, and the production manager, Edward Corey. A meeting was scheduled for May 12 with the research firm and the New England Soup Company management. The purpose of the meeting was to discuss the research findings and to make decisions concerning Kolander's product offerings.

The Company

The New England Soup Company was a small firm which produced and distributed a line of specialty canned soup products to both the institutional and retail markets. Approximately 62 percent of their 1974 sales volume went to the institutional market ($68,526), and 38 percent went to the retail market ($42,102).

The company was founded by William Kolander in 1957. Kolander's father was a successful owner of several restaurants in the Boston area which were famous for their chowder soup. The young Kolander convinced his father in 1956 that there was a market to sell the chowder to local institutions (restaurants, hospitals, etc.) in the New England area, and he developed a canned chowder under his father's supervision. Production facilities were acquired in the same year.

After losses in the first few years, the business turned profitable in 1960. At this time, Kolander decided to enter the retail market with Kolander's Chowder brand. Both the institutional and retail business grew rapidly during the 1960s, as did the firm's profitability. Expanded production facilities were built in 1968, and two additional specialty soup lines were introduced in 1970. These lines experienced limited success at retail but were reasonably profitable in the institutional market.

Current Situation

The last five years had been a period of level and then declining sales for Kolander's Chowder (1972—6942 cases, 1973—5676 cases, 1974—5105 cases, and 1975[1]—4900 cases). Mr. Kolander attributed this decline in sales to the market entry of two new canned chowders in 1971 and 1972 (see Appendix A). The new competitors were Fisherman's Delight Chowder and Cape Cod Chowder. Both brands were produced locally and appeared very similar in formulation to Kolander's Chowder.

Both of the new competitors had entered the market with a somewhat lower selling price than the Kolander's brand. Consequently, distributors were attracted by the slightly higher margins plus the desire to carry a competitive alternative to Kolander's chowder. Several large retailers had advertised the Fisherman's Delight brand as a "weekly special" at 43 cents per can.

Management Objective

Mr. Kolander recognized that the firm faced a serious competitive threat from the two new brand entries. While there were several long-term issues he was considering, his immediate concern was one of developing a competitive strategy to counter the sales decline of Kolander's Chowder. Specifically, he wanted to recover the lost distribution of the brand and switch customers from competitive brands back to the Kolander's brand. This was to be accomplished within the next 12 months. While increased distribution outside the current market area was a possibility, Mr. Kolander's immediate objective was to improve the market position of Kolander's Chowder within the New England area.

The Research Project

In January 1975, Mr. Kolander contacted a local research firm. After a series of meetings, the research firm recommended that a series of group interviews be conducted with current users of the two competitive chowder brands in order to explore reasons for product usage, reactions to the brands, and perceived

---

[1] Estimated from 1975 company records.

product differences. Through group sessions of this nature, the research firm believed that the cause of declining sales of Kolander's Chowder could be established and potential solutions identified.

The results of the group sessions suggested that an important proportion of the competitive canned chowder users preferred a chowder that was thicker and creamier than the current Kolander's Chowder brand formulation. Of the former Kolander's Chowder users, the desire for a creamier formulation was the predominant reason for switching. Many of these chowder users had switched to either Fisherman's Delight or Cape Cod Chowder.

Based on these findings, the research firm recommended that further research be conducted to evaluate changing Kolander's Chowder to a creamier formulation. For purposes of the test, it was recommended that two creamier formulations be developed, a "creamy" version and an "extra creamy" version. These two new formulations would be evaluated in a taste test along with Kolander's current chowder plus the two competitive brands.

After several meetings regarding specific aspects of the proposed research design, Mr. Kolander decided to approve the project. Appendix B presents the results of this study.

DISCUSSION QUESTION

What action should Mr. Kolander take based on the research findings?

APPENDIX A

New England Soup Company, Audit of Retail Food Outlets (selected tables from the report)

Fifty retail food outlets in the New England market area have been audited annually since 1972. These are deemed representative of the potential distribution outlets for the New England Soup Company of canned soups.

Percentage of Stores Stocking Canned Chowder Brands

Brand	1972	1973	1974
Kolander	94	86	82
Cape Cod	20	36	42
Fisherman's Delight	4	18	24

Number of Brands of Canned Chowder Stocked

Brand	1972	1973	1974
None	3	1	0
One	34	25	23
Two	10	20	24
Three	2	3	2
Four or more	1	1	1
Total stores	50	50	50

Range of Retail Prices of Canned Chowder Soup (in cents)

Brand	1972	1973	1974
Kolander	49–53	48–55	47–54
Cape Cod	48–51	49–53	48–51
Fisherman's Delight	46–50	47–51	47–49

APPENDIX B

Research Report: Evaluation of Two New Formulations of Kolander's Canned Chowder

Research Objectives

To evaluate the preference for two new chowder formulations among users of Kolander's Chowder, Cape Cod Chowder, and Fisherman's Delight Chowder.

Research Design and Procedure

Two hundred male ($n = 100$) and female ($n = 100$) canned chowder users were selected from four geographic locations representative of the New England market area. The subjects were selected using a probability sampling procedure involving a telephone-administered qualifying questionnaire. Each subject was paid $5 for participating in the test.

The subjects came to one of four test locations (local churches). They were tested individually in 30-minute sessions. Subjects were brought into the testing room and seated at stalls. An instruction sheet explained that the subject was to evaluate several samples of chowder, that the test would consist of three parts, and that they would be required to taste a total of 15 cups of chowder. Normal taste-testing procedures were followed.

The first part involved tasting five samples of chowder and ranking them from "most preferred" to "least preferred." The five chowders were Kolander's regular chowder, Fisherman's Delight, Kolander's creamy (version 1), Cape Cod, and Kolander's extra creamy (version 2).

The second and third parts of the test involved tasting five samples again. The samples had different code letters and the subjects were not told the samples were identical to the previous five. After tasting the five samples, the subjects were again asked to rank-order the five samples.

For each subject, the test procedure resulted in three preference orderings of the five chowder samples. The preference orderings were combined to form a composite ordering for each subject, a procedure that resulted in a more reliable measure of each subject's true preference ordering.

Results

The data set consisted of 200 preference orderings of the five chowders. Table 1 presents 20 preference orderings which are representative of the entire data set. The difference between male and female preference orderings was not statistically significant.

The data set was analyzed by calculating the average rank order of each chowder and scaling the chowders on a five-point scale ranging from most preferred (1) to least preferred (5). Table 2 presents the results of this analysis.

Recommendation and Discussion

Recommendation: Change the current Kolander's Chowder formulation to the version 1—"creamy"—formulation and develop a new label which makes this change conspicuous at point of purchase.

The Table 2 results clearly indicate that the current Kolander's Chowder formulation and the "extra creamy" formulation ranked significantly (.05 level of significance) lower than the two competitors' brands and the "creamy" formulation. These findings suggest that the market position of Kolander's Chowder can be improved by a formulation change to the "creamy" version, which ranks higher than the two competitors and should recapture a significant share of sales lost to the Cape Cod and Fisherman's Delight brands.

Table 1 Preference Orderings of Five Canned Chowders

Subject	Kolander's Regular	Fisherman's Delight	Kolander's Creamy	Cape Cod	Kolander's Extra Creamy
1	1	2	3	4	5
2	2	1	3	4	5
3	1	2	3	4	5
4	5	4	3	2	1
5	5	4	3	2	1
6	5	4	1	2	3
7	1	2	3	4	5
8	5	4	3	2	1
9	1	2	3	4	5
10	5	4	3	2	1
11	3	1	2	4	5
12	5	2	1	3	4
13	5	4	3	1	2
14	5	3	1	2	4
15	1	2	3	4	5
16	1	2	3	4	5
17	5	4	2	1	3
18	3	2	1	4	5
19	5	4	3	2	1
20*	4	2	1	3	5
.	.	.	.	.	.
.	.	.	.	.	.
.	.	.	.	.	.
200	.	.	.	.	.
Total =	685	550	482	588	712
n =	200	200	200	200	200
Mean =	3.4	2.8	2.4	2.9	3.6

*The first 20 preference orderings are representatives of the total sample of 200 subjects.

Table 2 Preference Scale (*n* = 200)

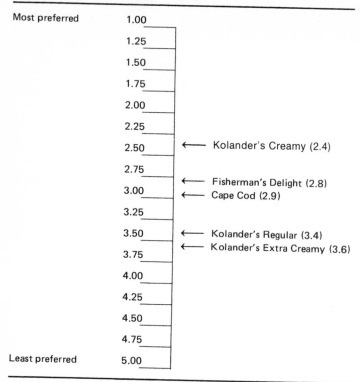

Most preferred	1.00
	1.25
	1.50
	1.75
	2.00
	2.25
	2.50	← Kolander's Creamy (2.4)
	2.75
	3.00	← Fisherman's Delight (2.8) ← Cape Cod (2.9)
	3.25
	3.50	← Kolander's Regular (3.4)
	3.75	← Kolander's Extra Creamy (3.6)
	4.00
	4.25
	4.50
	4.75
Least preferred	5.00

Case 2

Federal Trade Commission—Corrective Advertising[1]

Dr. William Kranz had recently joined the Federal Trade Commission (FTC) staff as a consumer behavior consultant. He was on leave from a leading Midwestern Graduate School of Business Administration and was especially interested in the application of consumer behavior concepts and research to legal issues involving advertising.

In his first few months at the FTC, Dr. Kranz became interested in the area of corrective advertising, specifically in the way information from consumers could be utilized in the legal process involving corrective advertising.

[1] This case was prepared by James R. Taylor and William L. Wilkie. Sections of the case are based on the research report by William Wilkie, "Consumer Research and Corrective Advertising: A New Approach," Marketing Science Institute, Cambridge, Mass., Oct. 1973.

Corrective Advertising

Corrective advertising may be defined as advertising run by a commercial sponsor for the purpose of correcting consumer misimpressions resulting from the sponsor's earlier ads. Corrective advertisements are clearly "remedial" in nature, are run by a private concern in response to earlier commercials of that same firm, and are the outcome of a specific regulatory procedure of the Federal Trade Commission.

Corrective advertising was developed by the FTC as a mechanism for more efficient regulation of false or deceptive advertising. The concept was originally advanced by a group of law students (Students Opposed to Unfair Practices, or SOUP) who sought to intervene in an FTC complaint against Campbell's Soup advertising in 1970. SOUP contended that traditional use of cease and desist orders (under which the company simply withdraws the particular advertisement and does not run it again) would not adequately protect the public interest. Their reasoning was that consumers who may have relied upon the hypothesized deceptions should be informed of such deception in future advertisements run by the company.

From Dr. Kranz's viewpoint, the general framework for FTC's corrective advertising program was reasonably well developed. However, there was no decision system to help determine when corrective advertising was needed and how it should be implemented. For this reason, he believed consumer research could offer significant benefits for both FTC and businesses responding to the program.

Decision Making in Corrective Advertising

The primary objective of a corrective advertisement is to dispel "residual effects" of a deceptive advertisement. Robert Pitofsky, the chief architect of the FTC's program, described three benefits expected from successful corrective advertising:

1 Misleading effects on consumer are dissipated.
2 Adverse competitive effects are dissipated.
3 The wrongdoer is denied the fruits of his violation.[2]

An additional administrative benefit—increased deterrence of deceptive advertising through threat of this stronger remedy—should not be overlooked.

Note, however, that a corrective-advertising order cannot be punitive in intent. While "wrongdoers" may legitimately be denied ill-gotten gains, they cannot be punished beyond this point. This suggests a need for precision in the development of specific remedial orders.

After studying the corrective-advertising cases, Dr. Kranz identified three rather distinct stages, shown in Figure 1, which characterize the FTC's decision process for corrective advertising. Stage 1 determines whether an advertisement

[2] Stanley Cohen, "Enforcer Pitofsky Explains FTC's New Get Tough Policy," *Advertising Age*, Jan. 18, 1971, p. 1.

has the "tendency or capacity to mislead." This often involves lengthy hearings in which various forms of evidence and expert witnesses are introduced. The five FTC Commissioners are then endowed with sufficient expertise to determine whether there has been deception or not. A judgment that deception has or could have occurred provides a necessary but not sufficient condition for corrective advertising.

Stage 2 reflects a decision as to the appropriateness of a corrective remedy as opposed to the more typical "cease and desist" order. The hearing record is examined for evidence on the existence of residual effects from the deceptive advertisement. Corrective advertising may be ordered when it appears that significant residual effects have been felt at either the consumer or competitive level.

Stage 3 requires a specification of all aspects of the corrective remedy. Note that there is not a "yes-no" decision for this stage; a detailed corrective campaign must be developed whether or not the lawyers know how to precisely dispel residual effects.

It appeared to Dr. Kranz that stages 2 and 3 were additions to FTC's traditional regulatory decision process. These new decisions represent a shift from legal reaction to marketing action; FTC is in effect adopting the role of a public advertising agency which designs communications mixes for offending advertisers.

This shift of focus meant that the FTC had to deal with a number of complex issues involved in developing a corrective-communications mix. For example, should companies be required to run corrective ads whether or not future promotional advertising is continued? How long should the corrections be run? Which media should be selected and scheduled? What budget is correct? Should the company be permitted to promote the brand actively during this period? If so, can the promotion be in the same insertion as the corrective message? What characteristics should be built into the copy of the corrective advertisement?

Dr. Kranz believed that the FTC lacked the necessary skills to deal adequately with these complex questions and that it should seriously consider an alternative option. This option was outlined in a report prepared by Dr. Kranz and sent to various members of the FTC.

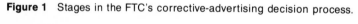

Figure 1   Stages in the FTC's corrective-advertising decision process.

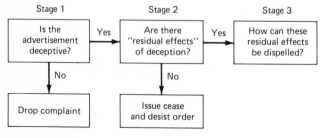

A New Approach to Corrective Advertising

Dr. Kranz identified three areas of concern in corrective advertising: (1) message, (2) audience, and (3) response. The message (M) represents an advertisement which is transmitted to and received by members of an audience (A), who then respond (R) in some fashion.

FTC has traditionally stressed M and A factors in advertising. "Capacity to mislead or deceive" has often been judged from overt characteristics of the message, especially when statements were literally untrue. Special attention has been given to advertisements aimed at certain susceptible audiences such as children and elderly or low-income consumers.

Dr. Kranz believed that corrective-advertising cases should focus on the R factor, namely, behavioral response. The primary objective of corrective advertising is to remove certain residual effects of deception. Residual effects are simply responses (R) which have continued over time. Specification of the particular R variables to be remedied is needed in order to clarify the objectives of corrective advertising. Measurement of this response level can then be used for stages 2 and 3 of the decision process (Figure 1).

A major issue presented by Dr. Kranz's proposal was the appropriate specification and measurement of behavioral response. Should the behavioral response be specified at the cognitive level (awareness and knowledge), at the affective level (liking and preference), or at the behavioral level (intention-to-buy and purchase)?

Dr. Kranz's suggested criteria for selection of an appropriate level of behavioral response include:

1   That it follow as directly as possible from exposure to an advertisement
2   That it reflect claims (deceptive or corrective) made in the advertisement
3   That it reflect the meaning or salience of impact of exposure to such claims in terms of consumer injury or benefit
4   That it offer an opportunity for precision in remedy

Hawaiian Punch Complaint and Order

In the fall of 1972, Dr. Kranz was asked to consult with the FTC staff investigating RJR Foods' advertising for Hawaiian Punch beverages. Since many of the staff members were familiar with Dr. Kranz's evaluation of the FTC's approach to corrective advertising, it was believed that this case offered an opportunity for him to put his recommendations into operation.

The proposed complaint contended that RJR Foods' advertising misrepresented the proportion of natural fruit juice as greater than the actual proportion of 11 percent. Consequently, the complaint implied that there were "residual effects" of the deception. This raised the issue of how these "residual effects" could be corrected (see Figure 1).

The issue before Dr. Kranz was how to measure the "residual effects" such that the FTC could determine when corrective action had dispelled the effects of the deception. Once it was demonstrated that the "residual effects" were dispelled, the corrective advertising could be terminated by RJR Foods.

In a subsequent meeting with the investigating staff, Dr. Kranz proposed that a follow-up consumer survey be used to measure the effect of any corrective action taken by RJR Foods. The details of the survey would have to be negotiated with RJR Foods as a part of the final decision and order. The reaction of the staff was favorable to this approach, and he was asked to participate in future meetings with RJR Foods regarding the proposed complaint.

In the meeting with RJR Foods and its advertising agency, William Esty Company, the proposed complaint was debated along with the staff recommendations as to corrective action and the proposed consumer survey. After several lengthy sessions, RJR Foods tentatively agreed to the FTC consent order requiring "affirmative disclosure"[3] of product content. This order meant that any Hawaiian Punch label or ad which depicted, visually or verbally, fruits or juice, would have to clearly and conspicuously disclose the total percentage of fruit juice concentrate in a single serving. RJR Foods complied with the consent order by inserting the statement that Hawaiian Punch "has not less than 10 percent natural fruit juices" in all of its future advertising of Hawaiian Punch. The details of the consumer survey were to be worked out at future meetings once each side had an opportunity to formulate specific proposals as to the nature of the consumer survey and how it would be implemented.

Dr. Kranz was very pleased with the tentative agreement regarding the consumer survey. While the rationale for the survey was clearly understood by both parties, the specific issues involved in implementing the survey were still subject to difficult negotiation.

The investigating staff had requested that Dr. Kranz develop a consumer research proposal for in-house discussion before the next meeting with RJR Foods. Dr. Kranz did feel that the data should be collected by a telephone survey. The remaining issues in developing the research proposal were less clear. Of immediate concern was the development of a question or series of questions to measure whether residual effects of the Hawaiian Punch advertising had been dispelled by the corrective advertising. In addition, what criterion should be set for determining whether the effects of the deception had been dispelled? How should the population be defined? Should the same criteria be applied to all segments of the population? If not, how should they be varied? Should statistical concepts such as tests of significance be used in deciding whether the residual effects had been dispelled? How big should the sample be? Dr. Kranz immediately began to tackle these questions in preparation for the meeting with staff members.

DISCUSSION QUESTION

Design a telephone survey which addresses the specific measurement and sampling issues of concern to Dr. Kranz.

---

[3] This "affirmative disclosure" consent order represents a partial application of the corrective-advertising approach. It did not require reference to prior advertising.

Part Five

Experimentation and Test Marketing

Principles of Experimentation and Quasi Experimentation: The Search for Causality

In Chapter 11, improper causal inferences were identified as one type of non-sampling error. In this chapter, we shall discuss this problem in the context of different types of research designs. The ability of different designs to distinguish causality will be discussed. The chapter first describes the necessary conditions for causality to be inferred, then the principles of experimental and quasi-experimental design, and finally the managerial aspects of these designs.

THE SEARCH FOR CAUSALITY

Introduction

Marketing managers want to be able to make *causal statements* about the effects of their actions. For example, a brand manager might say: "The new advertising campaign we developed has resulted in a 10 percent increase in sales." In similar fashion, a sales manager might boast: "The new sales training program has resulted in lower sales force turnover." In both of these examples the managers are making a causal statement. Are these statements valid, however? We cannot answer, because we do not have enough information about each situation. The brand manager has observed that sales increased after the change in the advertising campaign. Similarly, the sales manager has observed lower sales force turnover after the change in the sales training program. However, the fundamental question that should be asked in the presence of all causal statements has been neither asked nor answered: *"Are there some other possible factors that could have caused the changes you observed?"*

Our brand manager's increase in sales could have been caused by the increased product penetration in the distribution channel, a strike at a competitor's plant, a new package design, a decrease in price, etc. The decrease in sales force turnover that the sales manager boasted about could have been caused by a new quota payment system, a change in the type of people hired by the company, the fact that poor economic conditions have made job opportunities at other companies scarce, etc. Clearly, marketing managers and researchers must be able to know the conditions where proper causal statements may be applied. Also, it is the nature of marketing decision making that all the conditions allowing the most accurate causal statements are usually not present. In these circumstances, causal inference will still be made by marketing managers. In doing so, they should clearly understand the risk of error they are taking. This error possibility should be explicitly considered and not just ignored. The materials in this chapter provide the framework for understanding the conditions necessary to make proper causal inferences.

The Necessary Conditions for Causality

Before outlining the conditions that allow causal statements to be made, we must first develop a more formal understanding of the concept of causality. The scientific concept of causality is complex and differs substantially from the one held by the average person-on-the-street. Selltiz et al.[1] identify some differences between the scientific and so-called "common-sense" concept of causality. The common-sense view holds that a single event (the "cause") always results in another event (the "effect") occurring. In science, we recognize that an event has a number of determining conditions or causes which act together to make the effect probable. Note that in the common-sense notion of causality, the effect always follows the cause. We refer to this as *deterministic causation*. In contrast, the scientific notion specifies the effect only as being probable. This is called *probabilistic causation*. The common-sense notion talks of proving that X causes Y; the scientific notion holds that we can only infer causality and never really prove it. This inference comes from analyzing data that we have generated. The chance of an incorrect inference is always thought to exist.

The world of marketing fits the scientific view of causality. Marketing effects are probabilistically caused by multiple factors, and we can only *infer* a causal relationship—we can never really prove it definitively. We must always live with the possibility that we have not identified the true causal relationship.

We now examine the conditions under which we can make causal inferences. These are (1) concomitant variation, (2) time order of occurrence of variables, and (3) elimination of other possible causal factors.

[1] This section follows an excellent discussion in Claire Selltiz, Marie Jahoda, Morton Deutsch, and Stuart W. Cook, *Research Methods in Social Relations,* rev. ed. (New York: Holt, 1959), pp. 80–88.

Concomitant Variation   Concomitant variation is the extent to which a cause, X, and an effect, Y, occur together or vary together in the way predicted by the hypothesis under consideration. Consider the example of a marketer of small foreign cars. This company has undertaken a new advertising campaign "to improve the attitudes people hold of our cars and therefore to increase sales." Suppose that in testing the results of this campaign they find that both aims have been achieved—attitudes have become more positive, and sales have increased. We can then say that there is concomitant variation between attitudes and sales. Note that the implied hypothesis here is that "improved attitudes cause sales to increase."

We can now conclude that the hypothesis of a causal relationship between attitudes and sales is tenable. However, it is not yet proved. There are other possible explanations of the observed relationship that are equally tenable. Two examples follow: (1) The increase in sales has resulted in more people becoming more experienced with these cars, which may have resulted in the observed improvement in attitudes. That is, the increase in sales has caused the attitude change. (2) Some other variables may have caused the observed relationship. For example, the company may have improved the quality of their cars during the period in question. Clearly, we must go beyond concomitant variation before making valid causal inferences.

Time Occurrence of Variables   The hypothesis that improved attitudes cause increases in sales can be examined further by collecting data about attitudes from people at various times in their purchase process, specifically (1) before exposure to the advertising campaign, (2) after exposure but before car purchase, and (3) after both exposure and car purchase. If attitudes improved only after exposure to the campaign but prior to car purchase, we would have more evidence that the hypothesis is tenable. If however, attitudes improved only after car purchase, the hypothesis would be untenable. That sales increases caused improved attitudes would be a more tenable hypothesis in this situation.

The general statement of this very intuitive concept is that one event cannot cause another if it occurs after the other event. *The causing event must occur either before or simultaneously with the effect.*

There is one complication in this seemingly straightforward concept, namely, that it is possible for two events to be both a cause and an effect of each other. In our example, improved attitudes may cause increases in sales, *and* increased sales may cause improved attitudes. Thus, the relationship between attitudes and sales could be that of alternately "feeding" on each other. This type of relationship would be demonstrated in a purchase decision study if attitudes improved both before and after the increase in sales occurred.

If we now had demonstrated concomitant variation and proper time occurrence of variables, we would still be left with the fundamental question of causality noted earlier: "Are there some other factors that could have caused the observed relationship between X and Y?"

Elimination of Other Possible Causal Factors   Consider the case of a slightly mixed-up scientist who formulated the hypothesis that soda water caused intoxication. To test this hypothesis a randomly selected group of animals were given soda water mixed with scotch, rye, bourbon, and vodka. Intoxication was observed in each case. The scientist then reasoned: "I have observed concomitant variation between soda consumption and intoxication. Also, the proper time order of events to infer causality is present. My hypothesis is, therefore, correct." Well, we all know that another factor, the presence of alcohol, is the true cause of what he observed. The scientist had not searched for other possible causes. Also, the research design used did not allow for the identification of the true causal relationship. This ability of research design to assist in making proper causal inferences is the subject of the next section of this chapter. First, however, we should note that the brand manager and sales manager who made the causal statements we examined early in this chapter were making exactly the same type of causal statement as our mixed-up scientist; they were no less mixed-up than he, or she.

EXPERIMENTATION

The Use of Experiments in Marketing

The fundamental research tool used to help identify causal relationships is the experiment. The objective of an experiment is to measure the effect of explanatory variables or independent variables on a dependent variable, while controlling for other variables that might confuse one's ability to make causal inferences.

As recently as 20 years ago experimental research was little used in marketing research, but this is no longer the case. Experimentation has been used successfully to reach conclusive answers to such questions as:

1 Can we increase profits by servicing small accounts by mail rather than from branch stores?

2 Can we increase supermarket sales of our product by obtaining additional shelf space?

3 Will the addition of stannous fluoride to our toothpaste reduce users' cavities?

4 Does the number of times that a salesperson calls on a particular account in a given time period affect the size of the order obtained from that account?

5 Is a given newspaper advertisement more effective in color than in black and white?

6 Which of several promotional techniques is most effective in selling a particular product?

7 Is it necessary for an advertisement to change the attitude of subjects in order to cause them to use more of the product?[2]

[2] These examples are from Keith K. Cox and Ben M. Enis, *Experimentation for Marketing Decisions* (Scranton, Pa.: International Textbook Company, 1969), p. 4.

This list could be extended indefinitely, for experimental procedures are useful across the whole domain of marketing decision making. As Cox and Enis note:

> The usefulness of experimental design in marketing extends across the functional areas of promotion, distribution, pricing and product policies. Wherever marketing management is interested in measuring the effects of alternative courses of action, experimentation may be a practical means of reducing the risk involved in deciding among the alternatives.[3]

Some Definitions and Concepts

To understand experimentation properly, we must first learn some basic definitions and concepts.

Experiment An experiment is executed when one or more independent variables are consciously manipulated or controlled by the person running the experiment, and their effect on the dependent variable or variables is measured.

In surveys and observational studies there is no manipulation of independent variables by the researchers. This is the fundamental difference between experimental and nonexperimental research. In searching for causal relationships in nonexperimental situations the researcher must proceed ex post facto—that is, one observes the effect and then searches for a cause. In these circumstances we can never completely be sure of the proper time order of occurrence of variables and the effects of other possible independent variables that have been excluded from consideration. The superiority of experiments in this regard is absolute.

Treatments Treatments are the alternatives or independent variables that are manipulated and whose effects are measured. Examples in marketing include product composition, advertising executions, price levels, etc. In a measurement sense, treatments need only form a nominal scale.

Test Units The test units are the entities to whom the treatments are presented and whose response to the treatments is measured. It is common in marketing for both people and physical entities, such as stores or geographic areas, to be used as test units. For example, people may be asked to try a product and then have their attitudes toward it measured. Here people are the test units. Alternatively, different end-aisle displays may be set up in supermarkets and sales levels measured. Here, supermarkets are the test units.

Dependent Variables These are the measures taken on the test units. Typical marketing examples include sales, preference, awareness, etc. In a measurement sense the dependent variables must form an interval scale.

---

[3] Ibid., p. 5.

Extraneous Variables   These are all the variables other than the treatments that affect the response of the test units to the treatments. These variables can distort the dependent variable measures in such a way as to weaken or invalidate one's ability to make causal inferences. For example, a book publisher attempting to measure the response of buyers to two different cover designs would want to keep other aspects of the book the same for each buyer group. If the publisher allowed the extraneous variable, price, to vary between buyer groups, he could not be sure that he was measuring the effect of the cover. The price change would thus "confound" the experiment.

The researcher has three possible courses of action with respect to extraneous variables. First, one may physically control the variable. In our book example, we could hold constant the price of the book. Second, if physical control is not possible, one may randomize the assignment of treatments to test units. Our book publisher could randomly assign different prices to all buyers. In experiments with human test units, this usually takes the form of randomly assigning the test units to the different treatments. In this way it is hoped that an extraneous factor (such as IQ or age) is equally represented in each treatment group. Obviously we would prefer physical control, but unfortunately in marketing applications we must often rely on randomization.

A third way to control the effects of extraneous variables is through the use of specific experimental designs that accomplish this purpose. Much of the rest of this chapter discusses how specific designs can accomplish this task.

If physical control, randomization, and design features do not eliminate the differential effects of extraneous variables among treatment groups, the experiment is confounded, and no causal statements are possible. We call such an extraneous variable a *confounding variable*. For example, suppose we are using two cities as our test units, and it rains in one city and not the other. If rain affects the dependent variable (say, the number of car washes), our experiment is confounded, and rain is the confounding variable.

Actually we still have one line of defense against the confounding variable. We may statistically control the effects of this variable on the dependent variable with a technique called *analysis of covariance* (ANCOVA), which is discussed in Chapters 16 and 26. To make use of ANCOVA we must be aware of the confounding variable and be able to measure it. Therefore, the kind of extraneous variable that we are most worried about in experimentation is the one that operates differentially among treatment groups and is unknown to the experimenter.

Experimental Design   An experimental design involves the specification of (1) treatments that are to be manipulated, (2) test units to be used, (3) dependent variables to be measured, and (4) procedures for dealing with extraneous variables.

Validity in Experimentation[4]

Two concepts of validity are relevant in experimentation, internal validity and external validity.

Internal Validity   Internal validity is the basic minimum that must be present in an experiment before any conclusion about treatment effects can be made. It is concerned with the question of whether the observed effects on the test units could have been caused by variables other than the treatment. Without internal validity the experiment is confounded.

External Validity   External validity is concerned with the ''generalizability'' of experimental results. To what populations, geographic areas, treatment variables, and measurement variables can the measured effects be projected?

The researcher, obviously, would like an experimental design to be strong in both kinds of validity. Unfortunately, it is sometimes necessary to trade-off one type of validity for another. For example, in order to remove the effects of an extraneous variable, one may create a very artificial environment for an experiment. In doing this, we may have decreased the generalizability of the results to more realistic environments. For example, an advertiser may ask respondents to view advertisements in a trailer. Can the effects that are measured in this environment be generalized to a home viewing environment?

Symbols Defined

To facilitate our discussion of specific experimental designs, we will make use of a set of symbols that are now almost universally used in marketing research.[5]

X Represents the exposure of a test group to an experimental treatment, the effects of which are to be determined.

O Refers to processes of observation or measurement of the dependent variable on the test units.

R Indicates that individuals have been assigned at random to separate treatment groups or that groups themselves have been allocated at random to separate treatments.

- Movement from left to right indicates movement through time.
- All symbols in any one row refer to a specific treatment group.

---

[4] This section follows the now classic presentation of this material in Donald T. Campbell and Julian C. Stanley, *Experimental and Quasi-Experimental Design for Research* (Chicago: Rand McNally, 1966), pp. 5–6.

[5] These symbols are from ibid., p. 6. The specific definitions used are adopted from Seymour Banks, *Experimentation in Marketing* (New York: McGraw-Hill, 1965), pp. 25–26.

- Symbols that are vertical to one another refer to
  activities or events that occur simultaneously.

A few examples should make this symbolic scheme clear. The symbols

$$O_1 \ X_1 \ O_2$$

indicate that one group received a measurement of the dependent variable both
prior to (O_1) and after (O_2) the presentation of the treatment (X_1). Further the
symbols

$$R \ X_1 \ O_1$$
$$R \ X_2 \ O_2$$

indicate that two groups of subjects were randomly assigned to two different
treatment groups at the same time. Further, the groups received different experimental treatments at the same time, and the dependent variable was measured in the two groups at the same time.

Types of Extraneous Variables

Previously, we discussed the need for controlling extraneous variables in order
to ensure that the experiment has not been confounded. That is, we want to be
assured that the experiment is internally valid. In this section we shall classify
these extraneous variables using the scheme suggested by Campbell and
Stanley.[6]

History   History refers to the occurrence of specific events that are external
to the experiment but occur at the same time as the experiment. These events
may affect the dependent variable. For example, consider the design

$$O_1 \ X_1 \ O_2$$

where O_1 and O_2 are measures of the dollar sales of sales personnel and X_1
represents a new sales training program. The difference $O_2 - O_1$ is the measurement of the treatment effect. However, the new sales training program is not
the only possible explanation of a positive difference $O_2 - O_1$; an improvement
in general business conditions between O_1 and O_2 is as plausible a hypothesis
for explaining the observed increase in sales as is the new training program.
The greater the length of time between observations, the greater the chance of
history confounding an experiment of this type. What we need is a procedure
to control the effects of history.

Maturation   Maturation is similar to history except that it is concerned
with changes in the experimental units themselves that occur with the passage

---

[6] Campbell and Stanley, op. cit., p. 5.

of time. Examples would include getting older, growing hungrier, and growing more tired. In our sales training design, sales may have increased because the sales force has become somewhat older and more experienced. Clearly, people change over time. However, so do stores, geographic regions, and organizations. The longer the time between O_1 and O_2 the greater the chance of maturation effects.

Testing   Testing is concerned with the possible effects on the experiment of taking a measure on the dependent variable before presentation of the treatment. There are two kinds of testing effects. The first could be called the *direct* or *main testing effect,* and it occurs when the first observation affects the second observation. For example, consider the case of respondents who have completed a pretreatment questionnaire. If they are asked to complete the same questionnaire after exposure to the treatment, they may respond differently just because they are now "experts" with that questionnaire. The internal validity of the experiment is then compromised.

The second testing effect affects external validity but is important enough to mention here. It is called the *reactive* or *interactive testing effect.* This is the situation where the test unit's pretreatment measurement affects the reaction to the treatment. For example, a pretreatment questionnaire that asks questions about shampoo brands may sensitize the respondent to the shampoo market and distort the awareness levels of a new brand introduction (the treatment). The measured effects are then not really generalizable to nonsensitized persons.

Instrumentation   Instrumentation refers to changes in the calibration of the measuring instrument used or changes in the observers or scorers used. In the sales training study mentioned previously, the dependent variable, sales, was measured in dollars. If there had been a price increase in the company's products between O_1 and O_2, the difference $O_2 - O_1$ could be explained by this change in instrumentation.

An interviewer presenting the pre- and posttreatment questionnaires in different fashions could also cause an instrumentation effect. Similarly, a difference in the presentation of the treatment itself to different test units could cause this effect.

Statistical Regression   Statistical-regression effects occur where test units have been selected for exposure to the treatment on the basis of an extreme pretreatment score. The effect is that such "outliers" tend to move toward a more average position with the passage of time. Suppose that in the sales training example above only poorly performing salespersons had been given the new training program. Subsequent sales increases might be attributed to the regression effect. This is because random occurrences such as weather, family problems, or luck helped define good and poor performance of salespersons in the pretreatment measurement. These same random occurrences will make some of the poor performers better performers in the next year, thus confounding the experiment.

Selection Bias   Selection bias refers to the assigning of test units to treatment groups in such a way that the groups differ on the dependent variable prior to the presentation of the treatments. If test units self-select their own groups or are assigned to groups on the basis of researcher judgment, the possibility of selection bias exists. Test units should be randomly assigned to treatment groups.

Test Unit Mortality   Test unit mortality refers to test units withdrawing from the experiment while it is in progress. What can we conclude if a number of salespersons quit the company between X_1 and O_2? It is possible that those who were not improving quit, or that just the opposite happened.

All these types of extraneous variables constitute alternative explanations of what is observed in an experiment. They are the rivals of the hypothesis that the researcher is testing. One objective of our research designs should be to eliminate the possibility of these effects confounding our results.

Three Preexperimental Designs

What follows is an examination of three preexperimental designs. They are considered preexperimental because inherent weaknesses in the designs make internal validity very questionable. This presentation will be used to highlight the sources of invalidity that may arise in non-true experiments.

The One-Shot Case Study   This design is presented symbolically as:

$$X \qquad O$$

In words, a single group of test units is first exposed to a treatment, X, and then a measurement is taken on the dependent variables. Note that the symbol R does not appear in the design, so there was no random assignment of test units to the treatment group. The test units were self-selected or arbitrarily selected by the experimenter.

An example of this design might be as follows. A sales manager requests volunteers to take part in a new sales training program, and a measure of their sales performance is taken some time after the training program is completed. The impossibility of drawing meaningful conclusions from such a design should be apparent. The level of O is the result of many uncontrolled factors, and it cannot be deemed to be good or bad in the absence of a pretreatment observation of sales performance. Thus history, maturation, selection, and mortality problems all serve to render this design internally invalid.

The One-Group Pretest-Posttest Design   This design is presented symbolically as:

$$O_1 \qquad X \qquad O_2$$

Here, for example, we have added a pretest measurement of sales performance to the one-shot case study design. If we then took the difference between $O_2 - O_1$ as our measure of experimental effect, would we have a valid measure of the effect of the sales training program? Clearly a number of extraneous variables could explain the difference $O_2 - O_1$, rendering this design useless for reaching conclusive answers.

Specifically, (1) the economic situation could have changed (history), (2) the salespersons could have matured (maturation), (3) the premeasure could have affected performance (testing), (4) prices of goods sold could have changed (instrumentation), (5) the test units could have been self-selected (selection), (6) some test units could have dropped out, with an unknown result on O_2 (mortality), and (7) test units could have selected themselves on the basis of the bad year they had just experienced, and they could have a better subsequent year just because of luck (regression). Even if this design had been

$$R \quad O_1 \quad X \quad O_2$$

all sources of invalidity except selection would still apply.

This latter design is the one used by the mixed-up scientist doing the experiment with soda water. He had not controlled for the extraneous variable, intake of alcohol (history).

The Static-Group Comparison   The static-group comparison design is one where there are two treatment groups, one that has been exposed to the treatment and one that has not. Both groups are observed only after the treatment has been presented, and test units are not randomly assigned to the groups. Symbolically, this design is:

Group 1: X O_1
Group 2: O_2

Group 2 is called a control group because it has not received the treatment and so may serve as the baseline for comparison. In marketing we often define the control group treatment as the current level of marketing activity. This design would then be presented symbolically as:

Experimental group: X_1 O_1
Control group: X_2 O_2

where X_2 is the baseline marketing program that we wish to compare X_1 with. For example, in trying out the new sales training program on some salespersons, the sales manager would not be likely to drop all sales training for the other salespersons. The manager is interested in comparing one program with another, so the old program is the control group treatment.

The overwhelming source of invalidity in this design is selection. Test units have not been randomly assigned to treatment groups; therefore, the groups may differ on the dependent variable prior to the presentation of the treatment. The experimental result $O_1 - O_2$ could clearly be attributed to this pretest difference caused by selection procedures. Differential test unit mortality is also possible because of the nature of the treatment. More experimental-group test units may have withdrawn because of the offensive nature of the new sales training program, for example.

Three True Experimental Designs

A true experimental design is one where the researcher is able to eliminate all extraneous variables as competitive hypotheses to the treatment. Three true experimental designs follow.

The Pretest-Posttest Control Group Design   This design is presented symbolically as:

Experimental group: R O_1 X_1 O_2
Control group: R O_3 O_4

where X_1 is the treatment of interest. Again the control group could have a baseline treatment applied to it. The random assignment of test units to the treatment groups eliminates selection bias as a potential confounding variable.

The premise here is that all extraneous variables operate equally on both the experimental and control groups. The only difference between the groups is the presentation of the treatment to the experimental group. Therefore, the difference $O_2 - O_1$ is the sum of the treatment effect plus the effects of the extraneous variables, whereas the difference $O_4 - O_3$ is the sum of the extraneous variables only. In symbols:

$$O_2 - O_1 = TE + H + M + T + I + R + TM \qquad (14\text{-}1)$$
$$O_4 - O_3 = \phantom{TE + {}} H + M + T + I + R + TM \qquad (14\text{-}2)$$

where TE = treatment effect, H = history, M = maturation, T = testing, I = instrumentation, R = regression, and TM = test unit mortality.

If we subtract Equation 14-2 from 14-1, we find that

$$(O_2 - O_1) - (O_4 - O_3) = TE$$

the true treatment effect we sought. So we have found a way to identify the effect of an independent variable. All potential destroyers of internal validity are controlled by this design. Note the fundamental principle of experimental design that is operative here: The experimenter does not care what extraneous variables are operative *as long as they operate equally on all treatment and control groups*. Even with a control group design, the experiment is confounded if an extraneous variable operates differentially among treatment and control groups. The assumption must be that they operate equally.

A major difficulty with this design is the effect of the pretest measurement on the test units' reaction to the treatment (the interactive testing effect). Since this is a potential confounder of external validity, in the experimental group we must add another variable to the equation explaining the difference $O_2 - O_1$. This variable is IT, the interactive testing effect. If we also define EXT to be the symbol indicating the sum of all other extraneous variables, then:

$$O_2 - O_1 = TE + EXT + IT$$
$$O_4 - O_3 = \quad\quad EXT$$

therefore

$$(O_2 - O_1) - (O_4 - O_3) = TE + IT$$

That is, we cannot separate the interactive testing effect from the treatment effect. We must always have some doubt about the generalizability of our treatment.

If the scientist doing the experiment with soda water had used this design, he would not have concluded that soda water causes intoxication, because the control group would have consumed the alcohol without the soda water. Clearly, their level of intoxication would have equaled that of the experimental group. The possibility of the interactive testing effect occurring here is quite small. One should be able to measure pretest levels of intoxication in animals without sensitizing them to the coming treatment. Other researchers may not be quite so fortunate, however. A shampoo marketer using this design to measure the effect of a new advertising campaign may generate an interactive testing effect. Specifically, the pretest may sensitize test units in the experimental group to advertisements in the shampoo product category, and the resultant posttest levels of advertising awareness would not be generalizable to a nonsensitized population. In this case, the researcher would look to other designs that control for this effect.

The Solomon Four-Group Design   This design controls for all extraneous variable effects on internal validity, plus the interactive testing effect. Symbolically:

Experimental group 1:	R	O_1	X	O_2
Control group 1:	R	O_3		O_4
Experimental group 2:	R		X	O_5
Control group 2:	R			O_6

What we have done here is add another experimental group and another control group to the previous design. This second experimental group receives no pretest but otherwise is identical to the first experimental group. The second control group receives only a posttest measurement. What effects do the differences between the various pre- and post- measures give us?

Experimental group 1:	$O_2 - O_1 = TE + EXT + IT$	(14-3)
Control group 1:	$O_4 - O_3 = \quad\quad EXT$	(14-4)
Experimental group 2:	$O_5 - O_1 = TE + EXT$	(14-5)
	$O_5 - O_3 = TE + EXT$	(14-6)
Control group 2:	$O_6 - O_1 = \quad\quad EXT$	(14-7)
	$O_6 - O_3 = \quad\quad EXT$	(14-8)

Equations 14-5 and 14-6 are usually averaged to give

$$O_5 - \frac{O_1 + O_3}{2} = TE + EXT \tag{14-9}$$

Also, Equations 14-7 and 14-8 are averaged to give

$$O_6 - \frac{O_1 + O_3}{2} = EXT \tag{14-10}$$

The experimental treatment effect is then obtained by subtracting Equation 14-10 from 14-9. Thus

$$\left(O_5 - \frac{O_1 + O_3}{2}\right) - \left(O_6 - \frac{O_1 + O_3}{2}\right) = TE + EXT - EXT = TE$$

which is the desired result.

This design also gives us a direct measure of the effect of extraneous variables, EXT, and allows us to calculate the interactive testing effect, IT. This effect is obtained by subtracting Equation 14-9 from Equation 14-3:

$$(O_2 - O_1) - \left(O_5 - \frac{O_1 + O_3}{2}\right) = TE + EXT + IT - TE - EXT = IT$$

i.e., the interactive testing effect.

We have now not only controlled all extraneous variables and the interactive testing effect, but we have also succeeded in measuring their effects. Unfortunately, these benefits come at the expense of increases in the time, cost, and effort needed to conduct the experiment, and consequently this design is little used in marketing practice. However, it does serve as a standard against which to compare other designs. What we would like is a smaller design that controls extraneous variables and the interactive testing effect. Such a design is the posttest-only control group design.

Posttest-Only Control Group Design   This design is written as:

Experimental group:	R	X	O_1
Control group:	R		O_2

It is essentially the last two groups of the Soloman four-group design. Here the O_1 and O_2 measurements are composed of the following parts:

$$O_1 = TE + EXT$$
$$O_2 = \phantom{TE + {}} EXT$$

Therefore

$$O_1 - O_2 = TE + EXT - EXT = TE$$

i.e., the treatment effect.

Since there is no pretest in this design, the interactive testing effect cannot occur. Also, the extraneous variables have been controlled, and we have a nonconfounded measure of the treatment effect. But wait: suppose the pretreatment measures on the dependent variable were different between the experimental and control group? Would not this confound the experiment? Indeed, it would. What we must assume is that the random assignment of test units to the groups has resulted in the groups being approximately equal on the dependent variable prior to the presentation of the treatment to the experimental group. We also must assume that test unit mortality affects each group in the same way. With large enough samples and proper randomization these assumptions are not unreasonable, a fact which, when combined with the reactive nature of a great deal of marketing research, helps explain why this design is probably the one used most often in marketing practice. The soda-testing scientist, the sales manager, and the shampoo manufacturer could all use this design to obtain a nonconfounded measure of their treatment effect.

QUASI EXPERIMENTATION

In designing a true experiment, the researcher often creates artificial environments in order to have control over independent and extraneous variables. As a result, serious questions are raised about the external validity of the experimental findings. One response to this problem has been the development and use of quasi-experimental designs.

A quasi-experimental design is one where the researcher has control over data collection procedures (i.e., the "when" and "to whom" of measurement) but lacks complete control over the scheduling of the treatments (i.e., the "when" and "to whom" of exposure) and also lacks the ability to randomize test units' exposure to treatments.[7]

With loss of control of test unit assignments and treatment manipulations, the possibility of obtaining confounded results is great. The researcher must then

---

[7] This definition and section draw heavily on Campbell and Stanley, op cit., pp. 34–64; Banks, op cit., pp. 37–45; and James Caporaso, "Quasi-Experimental-Experimental Approaches to Social Science: Perspectives and Problems," in James A. Caporaso and Leslie L. Roos, Jr. (eds.), *Quasi-Experimental Approaches: Testing Theory and Evaluating Policy* (Evanston, Ill.: Northwestern University Press, 1973), pp. 3–38.

be aware of what specific variables are not controlled. An attempt must be made to incorporate the possible effects of these uncontrolled variables into the interpretation of the findings. We now turn to an examination of selected quasi-experimental designs.[8]

Specific Designs

Time-Series Experiment   A time-series experiment may be presented symbolically as:

$$O_1 \quad O_2 \quad O_3 \quad O_4 \quad X \quad O_5 \quad O_6 \quad O_7 \quad O_8$$

The essence of this design is the undertaking of a periodic measurement on the dependent variables for some test units. The treatment is then introduced, or occurs naturally, and the periodic measurements are continued on the same test units in order to monitor the effects of the treatment.

Note how this design conforms to our definition of a quasi experiment. The researcher does have control over *when* measurements are taken and *on whom* they are taken. However, there is no randomization of test units to treatments, and the timing of treatment presentation, as well as exactly which test units are exposed to the treatment, may not be within the researcher's control. A common example of this type of design in marketing involves the use of consumer purchase panels. These panels provide periodic measures on their purchase activity (the O's). A marketer may undertake a new advertising campaign (the X), and examine the panel data to look for the effect. Here, the marketer has control over the timing of his advertising campaign but cannot be sure when the panel members were exposed to the campaign, or even whether they were exposed at all. Also other consumers outside the panel would be exposed to the campaign. Attempting to make causal inferences from this type of situation is common in marketing.

This design is, of course, very similar to the preexperimental one-group pretest-posttest design, $O_1 \quad X \quad O_2$. Does not the time-series design suffer from all the same problems? The answer is no; the fact that we have taken many pretest and posttest measurements provides more control over extraneous variables. To illustrate this increase in control, let's examine some possible results of this type of design (see Figure 14-1). Assume that X represents a change in advertising campaign, and the O's represent the market share of the product in question. The following conclusions about the advertising campaign seem reasonable:

1   In situation A, the campaign has had both a short-run and a long-run positive effect.

---

[8] Only a few simple possible quasi-experimental designs are discussed here. For other useful designs see Campbell and Stanley, op. cit., pp. 34–64; Banks, op. cit., pp. 37–45; and Caporaso and Roos, op. cit., pp. 11–31.

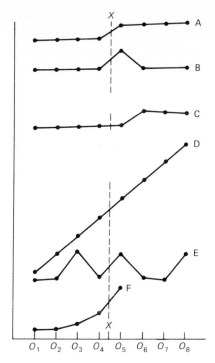

Figure 14-1 Some possible results of a time-series experiment. (*Adapted from Campbell and Stanley, op. cit., p. 38.*)

2 In situation B, the campaign has had a short-run positive effect.

3 In situation C, the campaign may have had a longer-term effect. Since the reaction was delayed for a period, we cannot be as sure as we were in A and B.

4 In situations D, E, and F, the changes that occur after X are consistent with the pattern prior to X. Therefore, we cannot infer that the advertising campaign had an effect.

Note that the one-group pretest-posttest design would have measured only O_4 and O_5. With these measures only, we could easily infer an effect of the campaign, $O_5 - O_4$, in situations D, E, and F; we could also miss the effect in C and the nature of the effects in A and B.

The multiple observations in this design also provide additional control of extraneous variables. For example, the maturation effect on $O_5 - O_4$ can be ruled out as a cause, because this effect would also show up in other observations. It would not affect the O_4 to O_5 period alone. By similar reasoning, main testing, instrumentation, and statistical regression effects can be ruled out. If we then randomly or with good judgment select our test units and take strong measures to prevent test unit mortality (i.e., panel members dropping out), we can at least partially rule out the effects of selection bias and test unit mortality.

The fundamental weakness of this design is the experimenter's inability to control history. But all is not lost; the experimenter could maintain a careful log of all possible relevant external happenings that could have an effect. If this process failed to turn up any unusual competitive activity, economic changes, etc., the experimenter might reasonably conclude that the treatment has had an effect.

The other weakness of this design is the possibility of an interactive testing effect from the repeated measurements being made on test units. For example, panel members may become "expert" shoppers, thus making generalizations to other populations more difficult. This design is used a great deal, and it can provide meaningful information if used carefully.

Multiple Time-Series Design   In some studies utilizing the time-series design, it may be possible to find another group of test units to act as a control group. For example, an advertiser may try out a new campaign in a few cities only. Panel members in these cities would constitute the experimental group, while members from other cities would constitute a control group. In symbols, this design is:

Experimental group:	O	O	O	X	O	O	O
Control group:	O	O	O		O	O	O

If the researcher is very careful in selecting the control group, this design can add more certainty to the interpretation of the treatment effect than is obtainable with the straight time-series experiment. This is so because the treatment effect is tested both in its own group and also against the control group. The main problem with this design lies in the possibility of an interactive effect in the experimental group.

Equivalent Time-Sample Design   An alternative to finding a control group is to use the experimental group itself as its own control. In symbols this design might be:

$$O \quad X_1 \quad O \quad X_0 \quad OOO \quad X_1 \quad OO \quad X_0 \quad O$$

where X_1 is the experimental treatment and X_0 is the absence of the treatment. Here the treatment is repeatedly presented, measurements are repeatedly taken, and periods of treatment absence are spaced between. This design is best utilized when the effect of the treatment is transient or reversible.

An example of its use would be the testing of the effect of in-store conditions, such as music, on total purchases per customer.[9] Here we could use a single store, whose customers make up the test units, and utilize equivalent sets of days with and without music over a period of many months.

The biggest problem with this design is the possibility of the interactive testing effect occurring. It is basically a reactive design because of all the measurements taken, and therefore it is best used where the repeated measurements are nonreactive. In situations like the store example, we are able to measure per-customer sales without sensitizing customers to the treatment. If

[9] Adapted from Banks, op. cit., p. 39.

we did repeated interviewing of customers about in-store music, sensitization would no doubt be a problem.

Nonequivalent Control Group Design   This is the last quasi-experimental design to be examined in this chapter. Here, the experimental group and the control group are both given pretest and posttest measurements, but the two groups do not have preexperimental test unit selection equivalence. Symbolically, this design is:

Experimental group: O_1 X O_2
Control group: O_3 O_4

This is a quasi-experimental design because the groups were not created by the random assignment of test units from a single population. However, the existence of even a nonequivalent control group improves the ability of the researcher to interpret results in comparison with the one-group pretest-posttest design discussed previously. In this design the researcher has control over who is exposed to the treatment. Clearly, the more similar the experimental and control groups in composition, and the closer the pretest measurements, the more useful the control group becomes. If these criteria are met, this design can effectively control the effects of history, maturation, main testing, instrumentation, selection, and test unit mortality. Regression may provide one major source of problems in this design, that is, if either group has been selected on the basis of extreme scores. In such cases some of the differences in pretest and posttest measures may result from regression effects. Care must be taken to avoid this problem. The possibility of an interactive testing effect is also present in this design.

MANAGERIAL ASPECTS OF EXPERIMENTATION AND QUASI EXPERIMENTATION

In this section, we shall discuss the types of issues that are important to managers in the use of experimental and quasi-experimental designs.

Comparison with Other Procedures

There are many procedures for collecting data in marketing research—for example, the use of secondary data, observation, survey, and simulation. They can all provide useful information for marketing decision making. However, since they are basically descriptive techniques, none of these procedures allows for the identification of causal relationships. Only experimental and quasi-experimental designs can identify such relationships; the other procedures can only find correlation. The cause and effect cannot be separated. Yet all too often descriptive studies are used to argue causal relationships. For example, the National Tourism Council does a survey. In this survey, the respondents are measured on what is assumed to be an effect variable, say, the amount of money spent on vacations in Georgia. Then, in the same survey, the respondents are measured on a series of hypothesized causal variables. If one of these "causal" variables, say, awareness of Georgia tourism advertisements, is found to be correlated with the effect, the advertising is assumed to have caused dollars to be spent on tourism in Georgia. Clearly, this is ex post facto reasoning. What is observed is concomitant variation only. The time order of the two variables is not established, nor have other possible variables been eliminated. Only experimentation and quasi experimentation can do this.

This does not mean that a correct causal relationship cannot be established in descriptive studies, for the researcher may be absolutely correct with a causal guess. The point is that one can never be sure. Descriptive studies are the most frequently used type of study in marketing research practice, and they will continue to be used to state causal relationships. Constraints of time, money, and so on may make this the only type of study available to a manager. In using them for causal purposes the manager should be aware of the risk of error that is being taken.

Laboratory versus Field Environments

There are two types of environments in which an experiment may be conducted. The first is a laboratory environment, that is, one where the experimenter conducts the experiment in an artificial environment constructed expressly for the purpose of the experiment. The field environment is the alternative. Here, the experiment is conducted in actual market situations, and no attempts are made to change the real-life nature of the environment. An example of a laboratory experiment would be the showing of test commercials to test units in a theater. This same experiment could be conducted in the field by having test commercials run on actual television programs.

Validity   Laboratory environments provide the researcher with maximum control over possible confounding variables. They have higher internal validity. A consequence of the artificial nature of a laboratory, however, is the loss of generalizability to more realistic situations. Thus, they have lower external validity. Experiments conducted in the field have lower internal validity and higher external validity. Often a field experiment provides so little control over extraneous variables that we must be content to conduct a quasi experiment.

Cost   Laboratory experiments are generally less expensive than field experiments. They tend to be smaller in size (i.e., with a smaller number of test units), shorter in duration, more tightly defined geographically, and therefore much easier to administer.

Time   The simpler nature of laboratory experiments also means that they require less time to execute.

The researcher must trade off these factors in selecting an environment for an experiment. Table 14-1 presents a summary of these factors.

Table 14-1 Laboratory versus Field Experimentation

Factor	Laboratory	Field
Internal validity	High	Low
External validity	Low	High
Cost	Low	High
Time	Low	High

Control of Invalidity

In presenting alternative experimental and quasi-experimental designs, we discussed possible sources of invalidity in detail; this section contains a managerial summary of these points. Table 14-2 presents the sources of invalidity of preexperimental and experimental designs, and Table 14-3 presents the same information for quasi-experimental designs. In these tables, a minus sign indicates a definite weakness in that design controlling the relevant sources of invalidity; a plus sign indicates that the factor is controlled; a question mark indicates a possible source of concern; and a blank indicates that the factor is not relevant. Use these tables only when sure that you understand why each design is classified as it is.

Limitations of Experimentation

The manager should recognize the following limitations of experimentation:[10]

   1   It is not always possible to control the effects of extraneous variables. Differential effects among treatment groups can easily occur in field experiments.
   2   In field experiments, lack of cooperation from wholesalers and retailers can limit experimental activity.
   3   Lack of knowledge about experimental procedures on the part of marketing personnel may limit the usage of experimentation, and in addition it may lead to experimental conclusions being discarded as not meaningful.
   4   Experiments can be costly and time-consuming.
   5   In using people as test units, care must be taken that the experimenter does not say and do things that bias test unit responses.

In the next chapter, we shall discuss certain statistical assumptions of experimental designs. These assumptions are not always met in real experiments.

Stages in Executing an Experiment

Once the researcher has a firm understanding of alternative procedures to experimentation, has considered what environment might be used, has a good understanding of how to control sources of invalidity, and has recognized the

---

[10] Adapted from Cox and Enis, op. cit., pp. 108–109.

Table 14-2 Sources of Invalidity of Preexperimental and Experimental Designs

Design	History	Maturation	Testing	Instrumentation	Regression	Selection	Mortality	Interaction of testing and X
	Source of invalidity							
	Internal							**External**
Preexperimental designs:								
One-shot case study X O	–	–				–	–	
One-group pretest-posttest design O X O	–	–	–	–	?			–

Static-group comparison
  X   O
        O
	+	?	+	+	+	–	–	

True experimental designs:								
Pretest-posttest control group design R O X O R O O	+	+	+	+	+	+	+	–
Soloman four-group design R O X O R O O R X O R O	+	+	+	+	+	+	+	+
Posttest-only control group design R X O R O	+	+	+	+	+	+	+	+

Adapted from Donald T. Campbell and Julian C. Stanley, *Experimental and Quasi-Experimental Design for Research* (Chicago: Rand McNally, 1966), p. 8.

limitations of experimental procedures, he or she is ready to begin the necessary steps for the proper execution of an experiment. These steps are:[11]

1 State the problem.
2 Formulate an hypothesis.
3 Construct an experimental design.

[11] Adapted from Oscar Kempthorne, *The Design and Analysis of Experiments* (New York: Wiley, 1952), p. 10.

Table 14-3 Sources of Invalidity of Quasi-experimental Designs

Design	History	Maturation	Testing	Instrument decay	Regression	Selection	Mortality	Interaction of testing and X
	Source of invalidity							
	Internal							**External**
Times series O O O X O O O	−	+	+	?	+	+	+	−
Multiple time series O O O X O O O O O O O O O	+	+	+	+	+	+	+	−
Equivalent time sample O X_1O X_0O X_1O	+	+	+	+	+	+	+	−
Nonequivalent control group O X O O O	+	+	+	+	−?	+	+	−

Adapted from Seymour Banks, *Experimentation in Marketing* (New York: McGraw-Hill, 1965), p. 44.

4 Formulate made-up results and check to see that these results are the type required by the problem statement. In other words, be sure that the design answers the question at hand.

5 Check that the types of results that are possible can be analyzed by available statistical procedures. (See Chapters 15 and 16.)

6 Perform the experiment.

7 Apply statistical-analysis procedures to the results to see whether effects are real or just error or noise in the experiment.

8 Draw conclusions with concern for both internal and external validity.

Once again the emphasis is on a meaningful statement of a problem and the provision of information relevant to this problem. Then and only then are the technical aspects of design and analysis useful to the marketer.

The Future of Experimentation and Quasi Experimentation

Marketing research textbooks written 20 years ago contained little or no mention of the use of experimental and quasi-experimental procedures in marketing research. This accurately reflected the practice of the day. Since then these procedures have gained substantially in use and are now considered as a viable alternative to other types of studies. Cox and Enis[12] identify four reasons why they expect this trend to continue.

[12] Cox and Enis, op. cit., pp. 109–110.

1 Experimentation works. Meaningful marketing results are generated by the procedures.

2 The costs of making wrong causal inferences in marketing are increasing.

3 Educational levels are rising, with an associated increase in the understanding of these procedures.

4 The capabilities of computerized analysis procedures have eliminated the tedium of hand analysis on results.

The modern marketing manager should understand what can be accomplished by experimental and quasi-experimental designs. This chapter has presented materials designed to aid in this understanding. One question that has been left unanswered is: "When will I know if the effect I have measured is greater than that due to sampling error?" In Chapters 15 and 16 we shall examine this question and also look at some specific statistical design procedures. In Chapter 17 we shall examine in detail the most important quasi-experimental activity undertaken in marketing research, namely, test marketing.

SUMMARY

1 Causality may be inferred when concomitant variation, the proper time order of occurrence of variables, and the elimination of other possible causal factors have all occurred.

2 An experiment is executed when one or more independent variables are consciously manipulated and controlled by the person running the experiment, and their effect on the dependent variable is measured.

3 Treatments are the alternatives which are manipulated and whose effects are measured.

4 Test units are the entities to whom the treatments are presented and whose response to the treatments is measured.

5 Dependent variables are the measures taken on the test units.

6 Extraneous variables are all the variables other than the treatments that affect the response of the test units to the treatments. They may be physically controlled, or randomization may be used to obtain control of them.

7 Internal validity is concerned with the question of whether the observed effects could have been caused by variables other than the treatments.

8 External validity is concerned with the generalizability of experimental results.

9 Categories of extraneous variables are history, maturation, testing, instrumentation, statistical regression, selection bias, and test unit mortality.

10 Specific designs differ in their ability to control extraneous variables. These specifics are summarized in Tables 14-2 and 14-3.

11 Experimental and quasi-experimental procedures are the only ones that allow proper causal inferences to be made. All other study types proceed ex post facto.

DISCUSSION QUESTIONS

1 What is the fundamental question that should be asked when searching for causality?
2 What are the necessary conditions to infer causality?
3 What is an experiment?
4 How does an experiment differ from surveys or observational studies?
5 What scale of measurement must the independent and dependent variables form in an experiment?
6 How may one control the effects of extraneous variables?
7 What are internal and external validity?
8 Describe seven different types of extraneous variables.
9 What is the interactive testing effect?
10 How can a design described as $R \quad O_1 \quad X \quad O_2$ be confounded?
11 What design could control these confounding variables?
12 Under what circumstances is it impossible for even the best design to control an extraneous variable?
13 What is a quasi experiment?
14 How does a time-series experiment allow for the control of extraneous variables?
15 Compare laboratory and field experiments.
16 How does one choose between these two environments?
17 Outline the limitations of experimentation in marketing.
18 What steps should be taken in executing an experiment?

SUGGESTED READING

Campbell, Donald T., and Julian C. Stanley, *Experimental and Quasi-Experimental Design for Research* (Chicago: Rand McNally, 1966). This short monograph provides the classic presentation of specific research designs to control extraneous variables.
Selltiz, Claire, Marie Jahoda, Morton Deutsch, and Stuart W. Cook, *Research Methods in Social Relations*, rev. ed. (New York: Holt, 1959), chaps. 3 and 4. A classic presentation of descriptive and causal analysis.

Chapter 15

The Basics of Designed Experiments

The previous chapter examined the design procedures that allow one to make proper causal inferences. Now we address the issue of statistical significance in experimentation. Specifically, we shall describe procedures that allow us to determine when a measured effect is greater than that due to sampling error. We shall do this in the context of some specific design procedures. The chapter begins with an overview of four experimental design procedures: (1) completely randomized design, (2) randomized block design, (3) Latin square design, and (4) factorial design. Next follows a discussion of hypothesis testing as it relates to experimentation, and then the statistical data analysis procedure is described that allows one to identify when effects are significant. This procedure is called the analysis of variance (ANOVA). In this chapter, we shall apply ANOVA to the simplest experimental design procedure, the completely randomized design. The application of ANOVA to the randomized block, Latin square, and factorial designs is left until Chapter 16.

At first glance, this chapter and the next may appear quite difficult, but this is an incorrect impression; the symbols and the calculations need not be alarming. Read these chapters one section at a time, and they should present no difficulty. The discussion will start with basics, stay at an elementary level, and sacrifice technical elegance for communication purposes. What you will see in these chapters is essentially the application of a principle we established in

Chapter 9 while describing simple random sampling: that variance equals the sum of squares divided by degrees of freedom, SS/df. If you prefer not to develop a complete understanding of the calculation of ANOVA for a completely randomized design (CRD), simply read the overview of the four design procedures that follows.

FOUR DESIGN PROCEDURES: AN OVERVIEW

The procedures discussed here can be applied to any of the designs presented in Chapter 14; what we are adding now is the flesh that goes with the bones given in Chapter 14. Again, all that the statistics allow us to do is to identify when an effect is greater than one would expect by chance.

Completely Randomized Design

A completely randomized design is the simplest type of designed experiment. It is useful when the researcher is investigating *the effect of one independent variable*. This independent variable need only be a nominal scale, so that it may have many categories. Each category of the nominal independent variable is a treatment. As an example, suppose that the independent variable of interest is "type of sales training program," and it has three categories:

1 No sales training
2 Head office lectures for sales training
3 On-the-job sales training

So we have one independent variable, type of sales training program, with three categories. Each category represents a treatment, with category 1 representing the control group treatment.

In a completely randomized design the experimental treatments are assigned to test units on a completely random basis. In our sales training example, salespersons would randomly receive the three treatments without any regard for external factors such as their previous experience, age, size of sales territory to which they will be assigned, etc. If sales were our dependent variable, we would then compare the average sales level of each of the three treatment groups to see which treatment was best.

Randomized Block Design

In the completely randomized design, all extraneous variables were assumed to be constant over all treatment groups. But what if this were not true? What if those receiving on-the-job sales training tended to be assigned to larger territories than those in other treatment groups? Would not the results obtained be misleading? Indeed they would. The size-of-territory effect would be obscuring the measurement of the treatment effect. What we would like to do is "block out" this extraneous effect. One procedure for doing this is the randomized block design.

This design is built upon the principle of combining test units into blocks based on some external criterion variable. For example, size of sales territory could be such a criterion variable. These blocks are formed[1] with the anticipation that the test units' scores on the dependent variable within each block will be more homogeneous, in the absence of treatment, than those of test units selected at random from all test units.

For example, let's divide our sales territories into three blocks based upon sales potential as follows:

Block number	Sales potential per year
Block 1	$200,000–$999,999
Block 2	$1,000,000–$1,999,999
Block 3	$2,000,000–$2,999,999

The sales levels we would expect test units to have within these blocks would be more homogeneous than sales levels we would expect if we ignored the blocking and selected test units at random. Note that the assumption here is that the blocking factor, sales potential per year, is correlated with the dependent variable, salesperson sales level. Note also that the blocking is done prior to the presentation of the treatment.

Once the blocks have been established and test units identified by block, we are ready to assign treatments. In this design each treatment must appear at least once in each block. Thus each block must have, at a minimum, a number of test units equal to the number of treatments. In our example, we would need at least three salespersons in each sales potential block, each receiving a different sales training treatment.

The fundamental reason for doing blocking is to allow the researcher to obtain a measure of sampling error smaller than that which would result from a completely randomized design. This occurs because some of the variation in the dependent variable is assigned to the blocking factor, leaving a smaller sampling error. Exactly how this is done statistically will be discussed later in Chapter 16.

The parallel between blocking in experimentation and stratification in sampling should be apparent. In both situations, we form subgroups so that *the variable of interest is more homogeneous within the groups than it would be across all groups*. The result of this process is a smaller measure of sampling error.

In the randomized block design the researcher can make use of only one blocking factor. However, one may define the blocking factor by using more than one external variable. For example, in our sales training situation we could have defined our blocking factor using both sales potential in territories and age of salespersons. Assume that the sales potential categories were defined as before and age was categorized as:

---

[1] Allen L. Edwards, *Experimental Design in Psychological Research,* 3d ed. (New York: Holt, 1968), p. 155.

Category 1   18–30
Category 2   Over 30

Then with three sales potential categories and two age categories, we would have a blocking factor composed of $3 \times 2 = 6$ blocks as follows:

Block number	Description
Block 1	$200,000–$999,999 potential and age 18–30
Block 2	$1,000,000–$1,999,999 potential and age 18–30
Block 3	$2,000,000–$2,999,999 potential and age 18–30
Block 4	$200,000–$999,999 potential and age over 30
Block 5	$1,000,000–$1,999,999 potential and age over 30
Block 6	$2,000,000–$2,999,999 potential and age over 30

Note that blocks, like independent variables in experimentation, are nominally scaled.

The number of variables used to create a blocking factor can be extended beyond two. The problem is that the number of blocks required in the blocking factor increases as a multiplicative function of the number of categories in the external variables used. The other problem with blocking by using more than one external variable is that the researcher can measure only the overall effect of the blocking factor. One cannot isolate the separate effects of the variables defining the blocking factor. A possible partial solution to this problem is the Latin square design.

Latin Square Design

In situations where the researcher wishes to control and measure the effects of two extraneous variables, the Latin square design may be used. Table 15-1 illustrates the layout of a Latin square design applied to our sales training example. The rows and columns of Table 15-1 designate the extraneous variables that are to be controlled and measured. In our example, we have identified three categories for the row variable, age of salesperson, and three categories for the column variable, sales potential per year. The three treatments are identified by the letters A, B, and C, where A = no sales training, B = head office lectures for sales training, and C = on-the-job sales training. The number of categories of each variable to be controlled exactly equals the number of treatments. This is a necessary condition for using the Latin square design, and it is the reason why we have three age categories in this situation while there were only two in the randomized block design discussed previously. Without this condition we would not have a square design. Our example yields a 3×3 Latin square. If we had four treatments, we would have to designate four categories for the row and column variables. This would be a 4×4 Latin square.

Another necessary condition for the use of the Latin square design relates to the way in which the treatments are assigned to cells of the square; they are assigned to cells randomly, subject to the restriction that each treatment occurs once with each blocking situation. Since each row and column category defines

Table 15-1 Latin Square Design for Sales Training Experiment

Age of salespersons	Sales potential per year (in thousands)		
	$200–$999	$1000–$1999	$2000–$2999
18–25	A	B	C
26–30	B	C	A
Over 30	C	A	B

A = no sales training, B = head office lectures, for sales training, and C = on-the-job sales training.

a blocking situation, each treatment must appear once in each row and once in each column. The treatments in Table 15-1 conform to this restriction.

Factorial Design

In marketing we are often interested in the *simultaneous effects of two or more independent variables*. The three design procedures discussed so far allow for the use of only one independent variable. If we wish to examine two or more independent variables in an experimental situation, we must use a factorial design. Suppose that, in our sales training example, the interest was in measuring the effects of the sales training procedure and the compensation scheme used. Suppose that there were two categories of compensation schemes to be tested, as follows:

Category number	Compensation type
Category 1	Straight salary
Category 2	Straight commission

So we have two independent variables: (1) type of sales training and (2) compensation scheme. Both form a nominal scale. The first has three categories, the second two. In a factorial design the categories of the independent variables are called *levels*. In the design each level of each independent variable appears with each level of all other independent variables. In our example, we would say that we have a 3×2 factorial design. This design would yield $3 \times 2 = 6$ cells in a design matrix. Table 15-2 shows the layout of our 3×2 factorial experiment. If we were running an experiment with four independent variables, with 2, 3, 3, and 4 levels respectively, we would have $2 \times 3 \times 3 \times 4 = 72$ cells in our design matrix. Obviously, one adds independent variables and levels with great care.

Note that we no longer call the individual independent variable categories "treatments." They are called levels. The treatments are now the various combinations of levels that occur. In Table 15-2, we have six treatments defined by the combinations of training and compensation, $A_1B_1, A_1B_2 \ldots A_3B_2$.

A factorial design allows us to measure the separate effects of each vari-

Table 15-2   3 × 2 Factorial Design for Sales Training and Compensation Experiment

			B	
			B_1 Straight salary	B_2 Straight commission
A	A_1	No sales training	A_1B_1	A_1B_2
	A_2	Head office lectures	A_2B_1	A_2B_2
	A_3	On-the-job training	A_3B_1	A_3B_2

able working alone. Thus the sales training effect calculated from a factorial design would be exactly the same as that calculated from a completely randomized design, but the factorial design would also give us the individual effect of the compensation schemes. These individual effects of each independent variable are called the *main effects*.

There is one other type of effect that is important in factorial designs. This effect is used to recognize that a number of independent variables working together often have a total effect greater than the straight sum of their main effects. This extra effect is called an *interaction effect*. More formally, interaction occurs when the relationship between an independent variable and the dependent variable is different for different categories of another independent variable. In our example, the relationship between sales level (the dependent variable) and type of sales training program (the first independent variable) may vary depending upon which compensation scheme was used (the second independent variable). If this were so, we would say that the two independent variables, type of training and compensation scheme, interact.

Tables 15-3 and 15-4 illustrate the meaning of main and interaction effects. Table 15-3 presents a simplified version of our sales experiment. Here we just have two training programs, A_1 and A_2, and two compensation schemes, B_1 and B_2. The entries in the cells represent average salesperson sales in thousands of dollars during the experiment. We note that, regardless of the compensation scheme used, training program A_1 yields \$10,000 more sales on average than A_2. The main effect of A_1 is then \$10,000. Note also that, regardless of the sales training program used, compensation scheme B_1 yields \$50,000 more sales than B_2 on average. The main effect of B_1 is then \$50,000. The total effect of treatment A_1B_1 is \$10,000 + \$50,000 = \$60,000. There is no interaction between sales training and compensation.

Table 15-3   An Illustration of Main Effects

		Compensation scheme	
		B_1	B_2
Training program	A_1	\$200,000	\$150,000
	A_2	\$190,000	\$140,000

Table 15-4 An Illustration of Interaction Effects

		Compensation scheme	
		B_1	B_2
Training program	A_1	$200,000	$180,000
	A_2	$190,000	$140,000

Table 15-4 presents the same design matrix with different results. Here the effect of the training program depends on the compensation scheme used. Specifically, A_1 is $10,000 better than A_2 when B_1 is used and $40,000 better when B_2 is used. Similarly, B_1 is $20,000 better than B_2 when A_1 is used and $50,000 better when A_2 is used. Here the effect of one independent variable on the dependent variable is different for different levels of the other independent variable. We have interaction. Statistical analysis procedures for factorial experiments can separate both the main effects and the interaction effect.

We should note that the number of interactions rises as the number of independent variables increases. For example, a listing of main and interaction effects for two and three independent variables follows:

Number of independent variables and description	Main effects	Interaction effects
2: A and B	A, B	AB
3: A, B, and C	A, B, C	AB
		AC
		BC
		ABC

In marketing, interaction among marketing variables is likely to be the rule rather than the exception. The factorial design is thus a very important one given its ability to identify and measure interaction. It may be used in a completely randomized design, with randomized blocks, or with a Latin square. These latter two refinements are beyond the scope of this book.[2] We will examine the statistical analysis of a completely randomized factorial design later in the next chapter.

A final noteworthy aspect about interaction: The randomized block design assumes that there is no interaction between the blocking factor and the independent variable, and the Latin square design assumes that there is no interaction between the two blocking factors.

Usage in Practice

Almost all real marketing problems involve the need for the control of extraneous variables or the simultaneous application of more than one marketing variable. Thus randomized block, Latin square, and factorial designs are the most used in practice.

[2] The interested reader should consult a book on experimental design—for example, Edwards, op. cit.

Commonly used blocking factors in marketing include store size, days of the week, time of the year, and geographical regions, all of which often contribute extraneous variation in the dependent variables that interest marketers. For example, one might be interested in measuring the effects of different prices on coffee sales. Suppose that these sales are measured in food stores on each day of the week and in different regions of the country. The actual sales of coffee that we observe might be affected by the different prices plus the different sizes of stores, the day of the week, and the region of the country. What we do is control the effects of these extraneous variables to get a clear measure of the price effect.

HYPOTHESIS TESTING IN EXPERIMENTATION

To determine whether or not a measured effect is greater than that which could occur by chance, we do statistical hypothesis testing. Hypothesis testing is a procedure that is familiar to those who have had a basic statistics course. Again, we assume that the reader has had such a course but would benefit from a review. This section provides such a review as it relates to experimentation.

The Concept of a Null Hypothesis

Hypothesis testing begins with the statement of an hypothesis in a *null form,* i.e., a form which *supposes that a population parameter takes on a particular value or set of values.* For example, we might wish to test to see whether the mean age of a class was 25 years. The null hypothesis (H_0) is:

$$H_0: \mu = 25$$

It is the null hypothesis that one evaluates in hypothesis testing. A null hypothesis may be rejected and some alternative hypothesis accepted. Alternatively, the null hypothesis may not be rejected in the test. In this situation, we do not conclude that the null hypothesis is valid. We do not accept a null hypothesis. All we can say is that we do not have the evidence to reject it. It may later be proved incorrect with the collection of new sample data. Note that we test the value of a population parameter with data generated by a sample; thus, the sample value might differ from the population value simply because of sampling error. By examining the sampling distribution of a statistic we can determine whether the sample value is different enough from the proposed null hypothesis value to have occurred just by sampling error. If this difference were greater than that due to sampling error, we would reject the null hypothesis. Stating the null hypothesis as we did above implies a number of *alternative hypotheses.* One such hypothesis is that the mean age is not 25. We can write the null and alternative hypotheses as:

$$H_0: \mu = 25$$
$$H_1: \mu \neq 25$$

In testing this null hypothesis, we would reject it if the mean age were either greater or less than 25. We are thus interested in the sampling distribution of mean ages on both sides of 25. This type of test is called a "two-tailed" test since we will examine both ends of the sampling distribution to see at what level of chance the mean value our sample generated could have occurred just because of sampling error.

Another alternative hypothesis in this situation is that the mean age is greater than 25. We write:

$$H_0: \mu = 25$$
$$H_1: \mu > 25$$

Here, our interest is only in the upper part of the sampling distribution of means. A hypothesis test applied here is called a "one-tailed" test since we have a specific direction in mind for the alternative hypothesis. The final alternative hypothesis here is that the mean age is less than 25. Again this would be a one-tailed test.

It is possible to phrase the null hypothesis to cover a range of values. For example,

$$H_0: \mu \leq 25$$

implies an alternative hypothesis

$$H_1: \mu > 25$$

With a direction given to the alternative hypothesis, a one-tailed test applies. The researcher should take care to phrase the null hypothesis in such a way as to accept the alternative hypothesis that is really of interest if the null hypothesis is rejected.

In experimentation, the null hypothesis is that *the treatment effects, and any interaction effects that might apply, equal zero*. If τ_j represents the effect of treatment j, we can write the null hypothesis as:

$$\tau_1 = \tau_2 \ldots = \tau_j = 0$$
or $\tau_j = 0 \, (j = 1, 2, \ldots j)$

where j = a specific treatment. The alternative hypothesis is that

$$\tau_j > 0 \quad (j = 1, 2 \ldots j)$$

If the treatments have had no effect, we would expect the scores on the dependent variable to be the same in each group. Thus, the mean values would be the same in each group. So our null hypothesis is equivalent to the statement that

$$\mu_1 = \mu_2 \ldots = \mu_j = \mu$$

Table 15-5 Summary of Hypothesis Testing Errors

Sample conclusions	True condition	
	H_0 is true	H_0 is false
Do not reject H_0	(1) Correct decision (2) Confidence level (3) Probability = $1 - \alpha$	(1) Type II error (2) Probability = β
Reject H_0	(1) Type I error (2) Significance level (3) Probability = α	(1) Correct decision (2) Power of the test (3) Probability = $1 - \beta$

where $1, 2, \ldots, j$ represent treatment groups, and μ represents the whole population mean without regard to groups. ANOVA is the hypothesis-testing procedure used in experimentation. It is essentially a procedure for simultaneously testing for the equality of two or more means.

Possible Errors

In hypothesis testing the decision maker either rejects or does not reject H_0. The decision may or may not be correct. If H_0 is true and is not rejected, the decision is correct. Also, if H_0 is false and is rejected, the decision is correct. Alternatively, the rejection of a true H_0 or the nonrejection of a false H_0 would indicate that an error had been made. These errors are named *type I* and *type II errors* respectively. They are also referred to as α error and β error respectively. Table 15-5 presents a summary of sample conclusions and their possible outcomes.

Also summarized in Table 15-5 are the probabilities of being correct and of making each type of error. The usual beginning point in testing a null hypothesis is to specify the level of type I error the researcher is willing to tolerate. The researcher knows that a null hypothesis is tested with sample data, so he or she expects some sampling error to be in the data. The farther the sample result is from the null hypothesis, the more likely that H_0 is not true. However, one recognizes that the sample estimate one has generated may have come from the tail of the sampling distribution of the statistic about the true value H_0. It may be an outlier. In specifying an α error level, the researcher indicates that an α proportion of the outlying part of the sampling distribution of the statistic will be assumed to be too far from H_0 not to reject H_0. In doing so, one recognizes the probability of making a type I error equal to α. This designation of α is referred to as the *significance level* of the hypothesis test. For example, a researcher may specify $\alpha = .05$, indicating that there is a probability of .05 that a type I error has been made. We say the test is performed at the .05 significance level.

Instead of looking at the probability of making an α error, we could also consider the probability of not rejecting H_0 when it is true. This probability is $1 - \alpha$ and is referred to as the *confidence level* of the test. The more confidence we want in the test, the smaller we make α. A test performed at the .05 significance level is thus performed at the $1 - .05 = .95$ confidence level. The confidence level discussed here is exactly the same concept as the confidence level we discussed in connection with calculating confidence intervals in Chapter 9 (which dealt with simple random sampling). It relates to the proportion of the sampling distribution of a statistic that is within a certain distance from the true population value.

Now we examine the possible outcomes when H_0 is false. If we do not reject H_0 when it is false, we have made a type II or β error. This occurs when we observe what we think is an outlier of the sampling distribution of the statistic about H_0, when we really are looking at a value drawn from a sampling distribution about a value other than H_0. The farther an observed value of a statistic is from H_0 the more likely it is that it comes from another sampling distribution. Thus, the smaller we set α, the larger the probability of a type II error. We call this probability of a type II error β.

If H_0 is false and we reject it, we have made a correct decision. We describe the probability of rejecting a false null hypothesis as the *power of the test*. The measure of this probability is $1 - \beta$. β and therefore $1 - \beta$ take on a specific value only when a specific alternative hypothesis value for a statistic is given. More detail on the nature of β will be provided in Chapter 22. For now, it is enough to recognize that β increases as α decreases for a given sample size. In practice β is often determined only after the sample has been selected, or it is just ignored. The problem with this approach in marketing is that the cost of a type II error to an organization may be much greater than the cost of a type I error. Consider this example presented by Cox and Enis.

In the case of making a type I error in the choice of the best promotional strategy for a new product introduction, suppose that we reject the true hypothesis (conclude that one promotional strategy was better than the others) even though all were, in fact, equally effective. Since we have to select one of the equally effective alternatives, there is actually little risk associated with our choice of strategies.

On the other hand, we might accept the hypothesis (conclude that there is no difference in the effectiveness of the three promotional strategies) when one promotional strategy is, in fact, more effective than the others. This type II error could be very expensive, in terms of opportunity costs, if we select one of the less effective strategies.[3]

Obviously, then, there are compelling managerial reasons for choosing a level of significance (α) in the .10 to .25 range instead of the traditional .01 or .05 levels used in social science research.

Steps in Hypothesis Testing

The steps we will use in hypothesis testing are:

[3] Keith K. Cox and Ben M. Enis, *Experimentation for Marketing Decisions* (Scranton, Pa.: International Textbook Company, 1969), p. 11.

1   Formulate a null and alternative hypothesis.

2   Select the appropriate statistical test given the type of data the researcher has.

3   Specify the significance level, α.

4   Look up the value of the test statistic in a set of tables (see Appendix A) for the given α; these tables give points on the sampling distribution of the statistic in question that occur with different α probabilities.

5   Perform the statistical test chosen in (2) on the data available; this yields a value of the relevant statistic.

6   Compare the value of the statistic calculated in (5) with the value looked up in (4). If (5) is greater than (4), we reject the null hypothesis, because the value of (5) has come too far out on the sampling distribution to be considered by us as part of the sampling distribution about H_0.

In the next sections of this chapter, we will apply these steps to test for the significance of experimental effects in a completely randomized design.

STATISTICAL ANALYSIS OF EXPERIMENTS

We are now ready to develop an understanding of the ANOVA procedure. ANOVA is a method of analysis that applies when the researcher is dealing with *one intervally scaled dependent variable and one or more nominally scaled independent variables*.[4] ANOVA is related to a number of other data analysis procedures that will be discussed in Chapter 26. An understanding of the basics of ANOVA will add greatly to our understanding of these other techniques.

There are actually three different ANOVA procedures.[5] They are:

Model I: Fixed Effects   In this model the researcher makes inferences only about differences among the *j* treatments actually administered, and about no other treatment that might have been included. In other words, no interpolation between treatments is made. For example, if the treatments were high, medium, and low advertising expenditures, no inferences are drawn about advertising expenditures between these points.

Model II: Random Effects   In the second model, the researcher assumes that only a random sample of the treatments about which one wants to make inferences have been used. Here, one would be prepared to interpolate results between treatments.

Model III: Mixed Effects   In the third model, the researcher has independent variables that are both fixed and random types.

---

[4] There are statistical techniques that can be applied to ordinal dependent variables in experimentation. These techniques are more advanced than the approach taken in this book, and so they are not addressed here.

[5] This section draws on William L. Hayes, *Statistics* (New York: Holt, 1963), pp. 356–358 and 439.

The major differences among these models relate to the formulas used to calculate sampling error and to some data assumptions. In this book, we shall show the calculations for the fixed effects model only, since the basic approach and the principles to be established are the same for the other models.[6] Also, in marketing research most experiments fit the fixed effects model, as the experiments usually include all treatments which are important in relation to the decision to be made.

In applying the fixed effects model the researcher makes assumptions about the data. Specifically:[7]

1 For each treatment population j, the experimental errors are independent and normally distributed about a mean of zero with an identical variance.

2 The sum of all treatment effects is zero.

3 In the calculations presented here, each treatment group has the same number of observations. This assumption is not generally necessary, but it makes the calculations easier.

Completely Randomized Design (CRD)

ANOVA applied to a CRD is called "one-way" ANOVA because it is being applied to categories of one independent variable. Table 15-6 presents results generated by a CRD. The measures on the dependent variable, Y, are taken on the test units. Here there are four test units in each of three treatments. We have $4 \times 3 = 12$ test units. The units are stores in the relevant geographic region where each of three coupon plans was applied. The dependent variable is the number of cases of cola sold the day after the different coupons were run in the local papers. The treatments are the three categories of the independent variable, T.

T_1 Coupon plan 1
T_2 Coupon plan 2
T_3 Coupon plan 3

So we have 3 treatments, 12 test units, and an interval-dependent variable measure on each test unit.

In Table 15-6 we define the mean of each treatment group as:

$$\overline{Y}_{.j} = M_{.j} = \frac{\Sigma Y_{.j}}{n}$$

The use of the period (.) in front of the j implies that we are calculating the mean by adding all i's in the jth treatment group. Note also that $\Sigma Y_{i.}$ would indicate the sum of all j's for a given i, and $\Sigma Y_{..}$ would indicate the sum of all i's and all j's. In our example,

[6] The interested reader should consult a more advanced book; for example, see ibid., pp. 356–457.
[7] Ibid., pp. 364–365.

Table 15-6 Completely Randomized Design with Three Treatments (Coupon Plans)

	Treatments (j)		
	Coupon plan 1	Coupon plan 2	Coupon plan 3
Test units (i)	20	17	14
	18	14	10
	15	13	7
	11	8	5
Treatment totals	$\Sigma Y_{.1} = 64$	$\Sigma Y_{.2} = 52$	$\Sigma Y_{.3} = 36$
Treatment means	$\bar{Y}_{.1} = M_{.1}$ $= \Sigma Y_{.1}/n_1$ $= 64/4 = 16$	$\bar{Y}_{.2} = M_{.2}$ $= \Sigma Y_{.2}/n_2$ $= 52/4 = 13$	$\bar{Y}_{.3} = M_{.3}$ $= \Sigma Y_{.3}/n_3$ $= 36/4 = 9$
		Grand total	$\Sigma Y_{..} = 64 + 52 + 36 = 152$
		Grand mean	$\bar{Y}_{..} = M = \Sigma Y_{..}/(n_1 + n_2 + n_3)$ $= 152/12 = 12.7$

Note: $n_1 = n_2 = n_3 = n_j = 4.$

$$\bar{Y}_{.1} = M_{.1} = \frac{64}{4} = 16$$

$$\bar{Y}_{.2} = M_{.2} = \frac{52}{4} = 13$$

$$\bar{Y}_{.3} = M_{.3} = \frac{36}{4} = 9$$

We also define the *grand mean* of all observations across all treatment groups as $\bar{Y}_{..}$ or M. Here

$$M = \frac{64 + 52 + 36}{12} = 12.7$$

These various means will be used in order to understand the meaning of ANOVA. In an experimental context, we want to determine whether the treatments have had an effect on the dependent variable. By "effect" is meant a functional relationship between the treatment T_j and the dependent variable Y. That is, do different treatments give systematically different scores on the dependent variable? For example, in our coupon plan situation, if the plans have had differing effects on sales, we would expect the amount of sales in the stores in treatment T_1 to differ systematically from T_2 and T_3. If in fact they do, the mean of each treatment group would also differ. In ANOVA an effect is defined as *a difference in treatment means from the grand mean*. What we are doing in ANOVA is determining whether differences in treatment means are large enough to have occurred other than just by chance.

Some Notation and Definitions   Let Y_{ij} be the score of the ith test unit on the jth treatment. For example, in Table 15-6,

$$Y_{11} = 20, \quad Y_{42} = 8, \text{ etc.}$$

We define any individual test unit's scores as equal to

$$Y_{ij} = \text{grand mean} + \text{treatment effect} + \text{error}$$
or $Y_{ij} = \mu + \tau_j + \epsilon_{ij}$

We note that this model is a simple linear, additive model with values specified in terms of population parameters. Since we are going to be using sample results to make our inferences, we can rewrite this model as

$$Y_{ij} = M + T_j + E_{ij} \tag{15-1}$$

where M = the grand mean
T_j = the effect of the jth treatment
E_{ij} = the statistical error of the ith test unit in the jth treatment

In this model the treatment effect is defined as the difference between the treatment mean and the grand mean.

$$T_j = M_{.j} - M$$

The reason we use M as the base from which to compare the various $M_{.j}$'s is that even if we did not know from which treatment a test unit came, we could still guess the grand mean as their score on the dependent variable. Knowledge of treatment group memberships improves our ability to predict scores as an improvement over M.

The error for an individual unit, E_{ij}, is estimated by the difference between an individual score and the treatment group mean to which the score belongs.

$$E_{ij} = Y_{ij} - M_{.j}$$

It is a measure of the difference in scores that occur which are not explained by treatments. This is the measure of sampling error in the experiment. It is also called experimental error. For example, if all scores within a treatment are close together, the individual scores will be close to the treatment mean and the error will be small, and vice versa. This deviation is a measure of the random variation within each treatment in an experiment.

We can rewrite Equation 15-1 as

$$Y_{ij} = M + (M_{.j} - M) + (Y_{ij} - M_{.j}) \qquad (15\text{-}2)$$

$$\begin{array}{ccccc} \downarrow & & \downarrow & \downarrow & \downarrow \\ \text{Individual} & = & \text{grand} & + & \text{treatment} & + & \text{error} \\ \text{score} & & \text{mean} & & \text{effect} \end{array}$$

Alternatively, we can write any observation as a deviation from the grand mean. We do this by moving M to the left side of Equation 15-2. We write

$$(Y_{ij} - M) = (M_{.j} - M) + (Y_{ij} - M_{.j}) \qquad (15\text{-}3)$$

$$\begin{array}{ccc} \downarrow & \downarrow & \downarrow \\ \text{Individual score} & \text{deviation of group} & \text{individual score} \\ \text{deviation from} & = \text{mean from grand} & + \text{deviation from} \\ \text{grand mean} & \text{mean, i.e., treat-} & \text{group mean,} \\ & \text{ment effect} & \text{i.e., error} \end{array}$$

Partitioning the Sum of Squares   The idea of ANOVA is built around the concept of the sum of squared deviations from the grand mean and from group means. We partition the total sum of squares into components. We begin by squaring the deviation from the grand mean, M, for each score in the sample and then sum these squared deviations across all test units, i, in all groups, j. We do this by squaring Equation 15-3 for all individuals in all groups. It becomes

$$\sum_{i=1}^{n}\sum_{j=1}^{t}(Y_{ij} - M)^2 = \sum_{i=1}^{n}\sum_{j=1}^{t}[(M_{.j} - M) + (Y_{ij} - M_{.j})]^2 \qquad (15\text{-}4)$$

All the $\sum_{i=1}^{n}$ means is that we are adding across all individuals in a treatment, and

all $\sum_{j=1}^{t}$ means is that we are doing this for all treatments. Equation 15-4 expanded becomes

$$\sum_{i=1}^{n}\sum_{j=1}^{t}(Y_{ij} - M)^2 = \sum_{i=1}^{n}\sum_{j=1}^{t}(M_{.j} - M)^2$$

$$+ \sum_{i=1}^{n}\sum_{j=1}^{t}(Y_{ij} - M_{.j})^2 + 2\sum_{i=1}^{n}\sum_{j=1}^{t}(M_{.j} - M)(Y_{ij} - M_{.j}) \qquad (15\text{-}5)$$

This is simply squaring an equation of the form

$$A = B + C$$

to get

$$A^2 = B^2 + C^2 + 2BC$$

We note that the sum of deviations about any mean equals zero.[8] Therefore the

$$2 \sum_{i=1}^{n} \sum_{j=1}^{t} (M_{.j} - M)(Y_{ij} - M_{.j})$$

part of Equation 15-5 is zero, as

$$\sum_{i=1}^{n} (Y_{ij} - M_{.j}) = 0$$

and

$$\sum_{j=1}^{t} (M_{.j} - M) = 0$$

We also note that

$$\sum_{i=1}^{n} \sum_{j=1}^{t} (M_{.j} - M)^2 = \sum_{j=1}^{t} n_j (M_{.j} - M)^2$$

where n_j is the number of subjects in group j. This is so because $M_{.j} - M$ is a constant (as we are dealing with means only) for each individual i in a particular group j. We can then multiply this constant by the number in the group to yield an equivalent number. Equation 15-5 then becomes

$$\sum_{i=1}^{n} \sum_{j=1}^{t} (Y_{ij} - M)^2 \quad = \quad \sum_{j=1}^{t} n_j (M_{.j} - M)^2 \quad + \quad \sum_{i=1}^{n} \sum_{j=1}^{t} (Y_{ij} - M_{.j})^2 \qquad (15\text{-}6)$$

↓	↓	↓
Total sum of squared deviations from the grand mean	= weighted sum of squared deviations of group means from grand mean	+ sum of squared deviations within groups
↓	↓	↓
Total sum of squares (SS_T)	= sum of squares between groups	+ sum of squares within groups
	↓	↓
	treatment effect sum of squares (SS_{TR})	+ error sum of squares (SS_E)

What we have done is divide the total sum of squares into two components.

---

[8] This basic finding of statistics is easily illustrated. $10 + 5 + 15 = 30$ and the mean is $30/3 = 10$. The sum of deviations $= (10 - 10) + (5 - 10) + (15 - 10) = 0 + (-5) + 5 = 0$.

These components are the sum of squares *within* groups and the sum of squares *between* groups. These are measures of variation. If the treatments have had no effect, the scores in all treatment groups should be similar. If this were so, the variance of the sample calculated using all test unit scores, without regard to treatment groups, would equal the variance calculated within treatment groups. That is, the *between*-group variance would equal the *within*-group variance. If the treatments *have* had an effect, however, the scores within groups would be more similar than scores selected from the whole sample at random. Thus, the variance taken within groups would be smaller than the variance between groups. Therefore, we could compare the variance between groups with the variance within groups as a way of measuring for the presence of an effect. This is exactly what is done.

But how do we get variance from the sum-of-squares terms we have in Equation 15-6? Since variance equals SS/df, all we need to do is divide each component of Equation 15-6 by its appropriate df, and we will have the necessary variance terms. To obtain the required degrees of freedom we apply the rule we learned in Chapter 9. For the sample as a whole we used up one degree of freedom to calculate the grand mean; therefore, the relevant number of degrees of freedom for the SS_T is the total number of test units minus one. For the SS_{TR} the number of degrees of freedom is always one less than the number of treatments, because once we have determined $t - 1$ group means and the grand mean, the last group mean can only take on one value. The degrees of freedom for the error term equals the number of test units minus the number of treatment groups, because we only use the t within-group means to calculate the error sum of squares. In summary:

	General formula	Our example
Df for SS_T =	$tn - 1$	$(3 \times 4) - 1 = 11$
Df for SS_{TR} =	$t - 1$	$3 - 1 = 2$
Df for SS_E =	$tn - t$	$(3 \times 4) - 3 = 9$

Note: df for $SS_{TR} + SS_E = df$ for SS_T.

Knowledge of the SS_{TR} and SS_E, plus their relevant degrees of freedom, allows us to calculate an estimate of the associated treatment and error variances. These estimates of population variances are called *mean squares* (*MS*) in experimental situations. This term recognizes the fact that they are estimates of population variances.

One more piece of information is needed before we can determine the significance of an effect. Since our test of effect involves taking the ratio of MS_{TR} to MS_E, we need to know the sampling distribution of this ratio under the null hypothesis (that there is no effect). It can be shown that this ratio is distributed as the F statistic with $t - 1$ df for the numerator and $tn - t$ df for the denominator. The critical values of the F distribution are given in Table A-5 of Appendix A. If the treatments have had no effect, the scores in all treatments should be

Table 15-7   ANOVA Table for Completely Randomized Design

Source of variation	Sum of squares, SS	Degrees of freedom, df	Mean square, MS	F ratio
Treatments (between groups)	SS_{TR}	$t - 1$	$MS_{TR} = \dfrac{SS_{TR}}{t - 1}$	$\dfrac{MS_{TR}}{MS_E}$
Error (within groups)	SS_E	$tn - t$	$MS_E = \dfrac{SS_E}{tn - t}$	
Total	SS_T	$tn - 1$		

similar, and so the treatment and error mean squares should be almost identical. The calculated F would then equal 1, or nearly so. The larger the treatment effect, the larger the ratio MS_{TR} to MS_E will be. The calculated F value will then get larger. The F distribution in Table A-5 of Appendix A gives the F values that can occur at various type I error levels given the null hypothesis of no effect. What we do is compare the calculated F against the table value for F at a designated α. If the calculated F exceeds the table F, we reject the null hypothesis. Table 15-7 presents the various components of the calculation of the experimental F value in formula form.

A Calculated Example   We now apply what has been developed to see whether there is a significant treatment effect in the data presented in Table 15-6.

Total Sum of Squares[9]

$$SS_T = \sum_{i=1}^{n} \sum_{j=1}^{t} (Y_{ij} - M)^2$$
$$= (20 - 12.7)^2 + (17 - 12.7)^2 + \cdots + (5 - 12.7)^2$$
$$= 232.7$$

Treatment Sum of Squares

$$SS_{TR} = n_j \sum_{j=1}^{t} (M_{.j} - M)^2$$
$$= 4[(16 - 12.7)^2 + (13 - 12.7)^2 + (9 - 12.7)^2]$$
$$= 98.7$$

Error Sum of Squares

$$SS_E = \sum_{i=1}^{n} \sum_{j=1}^{t} (Y_{ij} - M_{.j})^2$$
$$= (20 - 16)^2 + (17 - 13)^2 + \cdots + (5 - 9)^2$$
$$= 134$$

[9] We could, of course, use the computational formula for SS that was presented in Chapter 9.

Table 15-8   ANOVA for Coupon Experiment with Completely Randomized Design

Source of variation	Sum of squares, SS	Degrees of freedom, df	Mean squares, MS	F ratio
Treatments	98.7	2	49.4	3.3
Error	134.0	9	14.9	
Total	232.7	11		

Note that once we have obtained SS_T and SS_{TR} we can calculate SS_E by subtracting SS_{TR} from SS_T. However, we can double-check our calculations by using the formula for SS_E.

By applying the appropriate df to these SS, we can obtain the mean squares necessary to calculate F. Table 15-8 presents the calculations of F for these data.

The calculated F value is

$$F = \frac{49.4}{14.9} = 3.3$$

at 2 and 9 df. We must now look up the critical value of F in Table A-5. In this table, degrees of freedom for the numerator are the column headings, and degrees of freedom for the denominator are the row headings. The table gives critical values at different levels of confidence $(1 - \alpha)$. The intersection of a given row and column at a given $1 - \alpha$ gives the critical values at the α level of significance. In our example, the critical F value at $\alpha = .1$ for 2 and 9 df is 3.01. Our calculated F was 3.3, so our F value could have occurred by chance less than 10 percent of the time, and we reject the null hypothesis of no treatment effect.

Note that our result would not be significant if we had set $\alpha = .05$, as the critical value is 4.26. Given our choice of $\alpha = .1$, we conclude that the choice of coupon plan does make a difference in sales. We would then examine the data to see which plan was best. In this case, it is obviously plan 1.[10] Note that all an F test does is tell us that there has been a significant effect. We must dig back into the data to see which treatment is causing the effect.

We have now established the procedure for determining the significance of an effect in a completely randomized design. The procedures for other designs apply exactly the same principles; the only difference relates to some extra computations. These procedures are presented in detail in the next chapter.

SUMMARY

1 ANOVA is simply the calculation of different variances, SS/df.

---

[10] It is not always as easy as this to see which treatment is the best; there may be a large number of treatments, or results may be less clear-cut. More advanced procedures are available to determine which treatment is best—for example, in Hayes, *Statistics*, pp. 459–489.

2 In a completely randomized design, treatments are assigned to test units on a completely random basis.

3 In a randomized block design (RBD), test units are combined into blocks based on some external criterion variable. Treatments are then randomly assigned within blocks of test units.

4 RBD allows the measurement and control of one blocking factor.

5 In a Latin square design (LS), test units are combined into blocks based on two external criterion variables. Treatments are then randomly assigned to blocks subject to the restriction that each treatment occurs once within each blocking situation.

6 LS design allows the measurement and control of two blocking factors.

7 A factorial design allows for the analysis of the main effects of more than one independent variable, plus the effect of the interaction among independent variables.

8 Interaction occurs when the relationship between an independent variable and the dependent variable is different for different categories of another independent variable.

9 A null hypothesis is a statement that a population parameter takes on a particular value or set of values.

10 A null hypothesis may be rejected or not rejected. If it is rejected, the alternative hypothesis is accepted. A null hypothesis is never accepted.

11 In experimentation the null hypothesis is that the treatment effects and interaction effects equal zero.

12 Type I error occurs when one rejects a true null hypothesis. It occurs with a probability of α and occurs where α is called the significance level of the hypothesis test.

13 $1 - \alpha$ is the probability of not rejecting a true null hypothesis. It is called the level of confidence.

14 Type II error occurs when one does not reject a false null hypothesis. It occurs with a probability of β.

15 $1 - \beta$ is the probability of rejecting a false null hypothesis. It is called the power of the test.

16 From a management point of view, the cost of a type II error may be greater than that of a type I error.

17 The steps in hypothesis testing are: (1) Formulate a null and alternative hypothesis, (2) select the appropriate statistical test, (3) specify the significance level, (4) find the critical value of the test statistic in tables, (5) calculate the statistic using the sample data, and (6) compare the statistic values. If (5) is greater than (4), reject the null hypothesis.

18 The fixed effects model allows inferences only about the different treatments actually used. It is most relevant in marketing.

19 In ANOVA an effect is defined as a difference in treatment means from the grand mean.

20 Experimental error is the difference between an individual score and the treatment group mean to which the score belongs.

21 ANOVA is calculated by partitioning the SS_T into SS_{TR} and SS_E and dividing each of these by their relevant degrees of freedom to yield an estimate of treatment and error variances called the mean squares (MS_{TR} and MS_E). That is, the one-way ANOVA model is partitioned as follows: $SS_T = SS_{TR} + SS_E$.

22 The relevant statistics for a significance test is the F statistic, where $F = MS_{TR}/MS_E$.

DISCUSSION QUESTIONS

1 What is a CRD?
2 How does an RBD (randomized block design) aid the experimenter?
3 Why are LS (Latin square) designs so utilized in marketing field experiments?
4 What is a factorial design?
5 Describe the steps in hypothesis testing in general.
6 What is the null hypothesis in an experiment?
7 Distinguish between significance level and confidence level.
8 What are type I and type II errors?
9 What is the power of the test?
10 What is the fixed effects model?
11 How is an effect measured?
12 How is experimental error measured?
13 Explain in words how the MS_{TR} and MS_E are calculated in one-way ANOVA.
14 How is the F test done?

SUGGESTED READING

Cox, Keith K., and Ben M. Enis, *Experimentation for Marketing Decisions* (Scranton, Pa.: International Textbook Company, 1969), chaps. 1–3. A well-written, easy-to-read description of ANOVA and the uses of experimentation in marketing.

Hayes, William L., *Statistics* (New York: Holt, 1963), chap. 12. A detailed mathematical treatment of ANOVA in CRDs.

Meddis, Ray, *Elementary Analysis of Variance for the Behavioral Sciences* (New York: McGraw-Hill, 1973), chaps. 1–6. Presents an elementary, step-by-step approach to the ANOVA calculations.

Chapter 16

More Complex Designed Experiments

Chapter 15 described in detail the ANOVA model as it applies to a completely randomized design (CRD). This chapter presents the same type of detail for ANOVA as it applies to the randomized block design (RBD), Latin square (LS) design, and factorial design. Again, at first glance, this chapter may appear difficult, and again this impression is incorrect. What you will see in this chapter is a straightforward extension of the approach to ANOVA for the CRD. The same principle applies. Here we will develop a measure of the estimated variance, or mean square, for various components of the total sum of squares for the RBD, LS design, and factorial design. In doing so, we again use the principle that variance equals SS/df. The only real difference from a CRD is that we divide the total sum of squares into more components with the other three designs.

Again, remember that the dependent variable is assumed to be intervally scaled and that the independent variables and blocking variables are assumed to be nominally scaled.

RANDOMIZED BLOCK DESIGN

ANOVA for a randomized block design (RBD) involves only one more step than that for a CRD. Table 16-1 presents the data for our CRD coupon experiment as if the experiment had been blocked. Note that the table is the same as Table 15-6, except that the i's now represent blocks instead of test units, and we have calculated row totals and means in addition to column totals and means. Let's assume that the blocks represent different store sizes. In essence, we are saying that we expect some variation in cola sales just due to the differences in the size of the test unit stores. Block 1 represents the largest stores, block 2 the next largest, and so on. We must also assume that treatments were randomly assigned to test units within blocks to apply the RBD.

Partitioning the Sum of Squares In the RBD we define an individual observation as

$$Y_{ij} = \text{grand mean} + \text{treatment effect} + \text{block effect} + \text{error}$$

or, in population parameter terms,

$$Y_{ij} = \mu + \tau_j + \beta_i + \epsilon_{ij}$$

Again, we will be estimating this model with sample results, so we state the model as

$$Y_{ij} = M + T_j + B_i + E_{ij} \tag{16-1}$$

where B_i is the effect of the ith block and the other terms are defined as in the CRD. We have previously defined the M and T_j items in this model. We must define the blocking effect and also redefine the error term. We define blocking effect in a parallel manner to the treatment effect, the only difference being that the blocking effect is stated in terms of row means instead of column means.

$$B_i = (M_{i.} - M)$$

Here knowledge of blocking group membership *improves our ability to predict scores as an improvement over the grand mean.* We assume that $\sum_{i=1}^{n} B_i = 0$. That is, the net block effect is zero. We can rewrite Equation 16-1 as

$$
\begin{array}{ccccccccc}
Y_{ij} & = & M & + & (M_{.j} - M) & + & (M_{i.} - M) & + & E_{ij} \\
\downarrow & & \downarrow & & \downarrow & & \downarrow & & \downarrow \\
\text{Individual} & = & \text{grand} & + & \text{treatment} & + & \text{blocking} & + & \text{error} \\
\text{score} & & \text{mean} & & \text{effect} & & \text{effect} & &
\end{array}
\tag{16-2}
$$

We can then solve this equation for E_{ij} to get the measurement of error effect.

$$
\begin{aligned}
E_{ij} &= Y_{ij} - M - (M_{.j} - M) - (M_{i.} - M) \\
&= Y_{ij} - M - M_{.j} + M - M_{i.} + M \\
&= Y_{ij} - M_{.j} - M_{i.} + M \text{ or } [Y_{ij} + (M - M_{.j} - M_{i.})]
\end{aligned}
$$

Table 16-1   Randomized Block Design with Three Treatments and Four Blocks

Blocks (i) store sizes	Treatments (j)			Block totals	Block means
	Coupon plan 1	Coupon plan 2	Coupon plan 3		
1	20	17	14	$\Sigma Y_{1.} = 51$	$\bar{Y}_{1.} = M_{1.} = 51/3 = 17$
2	18	14	10	$\Sigma Y_{2.} = 42$	$\bar{Y}_{2.} = M_{2.} = 42/3 = 14$
3	15	13	7	$\Sigma Y_{3.} = 35$	$\bar{Y}_{3.} = M_{3.} = 35/3 = 11.7$
4	11	8	5	$\Sigma Y_{4.} = 24$	$\bar{Y}_{4.} = M_{4.} = 24/3 = 8$
Treatment totals	$\Sigma Y_{.1} = 64$	$\Sigma Y_{.2} = 52$	$\Sigma Y_{.3} = 36$		
Treatment means	$\bar{Y}_{.1} = M_{.1}$ $= \Sigma Y_{.1}/n_1$ $= 64/4$ $= 16$	$\bar{Y}_{.2} = M_{.2}$ $= \Sigma Y_{.2}/n_2$ $= 52/4$ $= 13$	$\bar{Y}_{.3} = M_{.3}$ $= \Sigma Y_{.3}/n_3$ $= 36/4$ $= 9$		
	Grand total			$\Sigma\Sigma Y_{..} = 64 + 52 + 36 = 152$	
	Grand mean			$\bar{Y}_{..} = M = \Sigma\Sigma Y_{..}/(n_1 + n_2 + n_3)$ $= 152/12 = 12.7$	

The error terms thus represent the difference between an individual score, Y_{ij}, and the net difference between the grand mean and the sum of the treatment and block means. If the blocking effect is significant, this error term will be smaller than an error defined without blocking. As an illustration, look at score Y_{21} in Table 16-1. This score is 18. The error without blocking is

$$Y_{ij} - M_{.j} = 18 - 16 = 2$$

With blocking, the error is

$$Y_{ij} + M - M_{.j} - M_{i.} = 18 + 12.7 - 16 - 14 = .7$$

A similar pattern would be found with the other scores. Thus blocking reduces the size of experimental error. We may rewrite Equation 16-2 as

$$Y_{ij} = M + (M_{.j} - M) + (M_{i.} - M) + (Y_{ij} - M_{.j} - M_{i.} + M) \tag{16-3}$$

If we move M to the left side of Equation 16-3, sum the resultant deviations across all blocks and all treatments, and square both sides, we get

$$\sum_{i=1}^{n} \sum_{j=1}^{t} (Y_{ij} - M)^2 = n_j \sum_{j=1}^{t} (M_{.j} - M)^2$$

$$+ t_i \sum_{i=1}^{n} (M_{i.} - M)^2 + \sum_{i=1}^{n} \sum_{j=1}^{t} (Y_{ij} + M - M_{.j} - M_{i.})^2$$

You should recognize this result as

$$SS_T = SS_{TR} + SS_B + SS_E$$

It follows from the fact that all the cross products again become zero because each involves a sum of individual deviations about a mean. Also, we may write

$$t_i \sum_{i=1}^{n} (M_{i.} - M)^2 \quad \text{instead of} \quad \sum_{i=1}^{n} \sum_{j=1}^{t} (M_{i.} - M)^2$$

because we are again adding constant means over the t treatments. It is just simpler to multiply by t than to add the same thing t times. Note that this result was obtained by exactly the same principle as that used in a CRD.

The relevant df for the block is $n - 1$, because once this number of block means are determined, the other is automatically fixed given the grand mean value. If we subtract the treatment and block degrees of freedom from the total degrees of freedom, we get the error degrees of freedom as

Error df = total df − treatment df − block df

$$= (tn - 1) - (t - 1) - (n - 1)$$
$$= tn + 1 - t - n$$

In our example, the error $df = (3 \times 4) + 1 - 3 - 4 = 6$. More generally, the same result may be obtained by applying the formula

Error $df = (t - 1)(n - 1)$

Table 16-2 presents the ANOVA table for an RBD.

A Calculated Example   We shall now apply the RBD ANOVA procedure to the data in Table 16-1.

Total Sum of Squares

$$SS_T = \sum_{i=1}^{n} \sum_{j=1}^{t} (Y_{ij} - M)^2$$
$$= (20 - 12.7)^2 + (17 - 12.7)^2 + \cdots + (5 - 12.7)^2$$
$$= 232.7$$

Thus SS_T is exactly the same here as with the CRD, as we would expect.

Treatment Sum of Squares

$$SS_{TR} = n_j \sum_{j=1}^{t} (M_{.j} - M)^2$$
$$= 4[(16 - 12.7)^2 + (13 - 12.7)^2 + (9 - 12.7)^2]$$
$$= 98.7$$

Table 16-2   ANOVA Table for Randomized Block Design

Source of variation	Sum of squares, SS	Degrees of freedom, df	Mean square, MS	F ratio
Treatments (between columns)	SS_{TR}	$t - 1$	$MS_{TR} = \dfrac{SS_{TR}}{t - 1}$	$\dfrac{MS_{TR}}{MS_E}$
Blocks (between rows)	SS_B	$n - 1$	$MS_B = \dfrac{SS_B}{n - 1}$	$\dfrac{MS_B}{MS_E}$
Error	SS_E	$(t - 1)(n - 1)$	$MS_E = \dfrac{SS_E}{(t - 1)(n - 1)}$	
Total	SS_T	$tn - 1$		

Table 16-3 ANOVA Table for Coupon Experiment with Blocking for Store Size

Source of variation	Sum of squares, SS	Degrees of freedom, df	Mean square, MS	F ratio
Treatment	98.7	2	49.4	70.6
Block	129.8	3	43.3	61.9
Error	4.2	6	0.7	
Total	232.7	11		

Note that the SS_{TR} is exactly the same as with the CRD.

Block Sum of Squares

$$SS_B = t_i \sum_{i=1}^{n} (M_{i.} - M)^2$$
$$= 3[(17 - 12.7)^2 + (14 - 12.7)^2 + (11.7 - 12.7)^2 + (8 - 12.7)^2]$$
$$= 129.8$$

Error Sum of Squares

$$SS_E = SS_T - SS_{TR} - SS_B$$
$$= 232.7 - 98.7 - 129.8$$
$$= 4.2$$

Table 16-3 presents the calculated F values for the treatment and block effect.

For the treatment effect, the critical value of F for $\alpha = .1$ at 2 and 6 df is 3.46. For the blocking factor, the critical value of F for $\alpha = .1$ at 3 and 6 df is 3.29. Both the treatment and the block effects are statistically significant, but note in this case that even at $\alpha = .01$ the treatment effect is now significant (critical $F = 10.9$). By blocking we have obtained a smaller measure of error and thus a more reliable measure of the treatment effect. All the SS_B comes out of the SS_E for the CRD; that is,

$$SS_E \text{ (with blocking)} = SS_E \text{ (without blocking)} - SS_B$$

In our example,

$$SS_E \text{ (with blocking)} = 134.0 - 129.8 = 4.2$$

LATIN SQUARE DESIGN

If we wanted to block out and measure the effects of two extraneous variables, we could use the Latin square (LS) design. In an LS design the number of categories of each blocking variable must equal the number of treatment categories, and each treatment must appear once and only once in each row and column of the design. Table 16-4 shows selected LS designs of different sizes. The letters *A, B*, etc. represent treatments. To generate the treatment assignment pattern for a particular study, one would pick the appropriate-sized layout from Table 16-4 and randomize the column order. For example, a 3 × 3 LS might yield the following treatment pattern when the columns are randomized with the random numbers 3, 1, 2:

    C   A   B
    A   B   C
    B   C   A

One would then randomize the row assignments within columns, subject to the constraint that each treatment may appear only once in each row. One such result of this process could be the following LS:

    B   C   A
    C   A   B
    A   B   C

We can now illustrate the LS design with a numeric example. Suppose that we ran our coupon experiment again to see whether the results could be replicated in other areas. The only difference is that this time we want to block out and measure the effect on sales of both store size and day of the week. In doing so, we must expect significant variation in cola sales simply because of these factors. For one reason or another, we have been unable to measure sales on the same day of the week for each test unit. Since there are three treatments (coupon plans), we must have three categories of store size and three categories of days of the week to use the LS design. Table 16-5 presents the data generated from

Table 16-4   Illustrative Latin Square Layout

3 × 3				4 × 4			
A	*B*	*C*		*A*	*B*	*C*	*D*
B	*C*	*A*		*B*	*C*	*D*	*A*
C	*A*	*B*		*C*	*D*	*A*	*B*
				D	*A*	*B*	*C*

5 × 5						6 × 6					
A	*B*	*C*	*D*	*E*		*A*	*B*	*C*	*D*	*E*	*F*
B	*C*	*D*	*E*	*A*		*B*	*C*	*D*	*E*	*F*	*A*
C	*D*	*E*	*A*	*B*		*C*	*D*	*E*	*F*	*A*	*B*
D	*E*	*A*	*B*	*C*		*D*	*E*	*F*	*A*	*B*	*C*
E	*A*	*B*	*C*	*D*		*E*	*F*	*A*	*B*	*C*	*D*
						F	*A*	*B*	*C*	*D*	*E*

Table 16-5 Latin Square Design with Three Treatments

Rows (*i*)	Columns (*j*)			Row totals	Row means
	1 Mon.–Tues.	**2** Wed.–Thurs.	**3** Fri.–Sun.		
1 Large stores	25 (*B*)	15 (*C*)	50 (*A*)	$\Sigma Y_{1..} = 90$	$M_{1..} = 90/3 = 30.0$
2 Medium stores	5 (*C*)	25 (*A*)	25 (*B*)	$\Sigma Y_{2..} = 55$	$M_{2..} = 55/3 = 18.3$
3 Small stores	15 (*A*)	15 (*B*)	14 (*C*)	$\Sigma Y_{3..} = 44$	$M_{3..} = 44/3 = 14.7$
Column totals	$\Sigma Y_{.1.} = 45$	$\Sigma Y_{.2.} = 55$	$\Sigma Y_{.3.} = 89$	$\Sigma Y_{...} = 189$	
Column means	$M_{.1.} = 45/3$ $= 15.0$	$M_{.2.} = 55/3$ $= 18.3$	$M_{.3.} = 89/3$ $= 29.7$		$M = 189/9$ $= 21.0$

Treatments (*k*)	*A**	*B*	*C*
Treatment totals	$\Sigma Y_{..1} = 90$	$\Sigma Y_{..2} = 65$	$\Sigma Y_{..3} = 34$
Treatment means	$M_{..1} = 90/3$ $= 30.0$	$M_{..2} = 65/3$ $= 21.7$	$M_{..3} = 34/3$ $= 11.3$

*For example, $\Sigma Y_{..1} = 15 + 25 + 50 = 90$; i.e., we add the scores at all the places where *A* appears.

this LS design experiment. The pattern of treatment assignments is the one generated previously by randomization with these three plans:

A Coupon plan 1
B Coupon plan 2
C Coupon plan 3

The treatment designation is noted next to the cola sales on Table 16-5.

Partitioning the Sum of Squares   In the LS design we define an individual observation as

$$Y_{ijk} = \text{grand mean} + \text{row effect} + \text{column effect} + \text{treatment effect} + \text{error}$$

where Y_{ijk} = the measured result when the kth treatment is applied to the ith row and the jth column. In population parameter terms, the model is

$$Y_{ijk} = \mu + \alpha_i + \beta_j + \tau_k + \epsilon_{ijk}$$

Again we will be estimating this model with sample results, so we state the model as

$$Y_{ijk} = M + R_i + C_j + T_k + E_{ijk} \tag{16-4}$$

where R_i = the effect of the ith row block (i.e., store size)
         C_j = the effect of the jth column block (i.e., day of the week)
         T_k = the effect of the kth treatment (i.e., coupon plan)
         E_{ijk} = the experimental error of the ijk observation
         $i, j, k = 1, 2, \ldots, t$ where t = the number of treatments

The three effects of interest are:

1 Row effect (i.e., effect of store size) = $(M_{i..} - M)$, the difference between the row mean and the grand mean, adding across all j's and k's.
2 Column effect (i.e., effect of day of the week) = $(M_{.j.} - M)$, the difference between the column mean and the grand mean, adding across all i's and k's.
3 Treatment effect (i.e., effect of coupon plan) = $(M_{..k} - M)$, the difference between the treatment mean and the grand mean, adding across all i's and j's.

We assume that the net effect of each effect is zero. That is,

$$\sum_{i=1}^{t} R_i = 0 \qquad \sum_{j=1}^{t} C_j = 0 \qquad \text{and} \qquad \sum_{k=1}^{t} T_k = 0$$

Table 16-6 ANOVA Table for Latin Square Design

Source of variation	Sum of squares, SS	Degrees of freedom, df	Mean square, MS	F ratio
Between rows	SS_R	$t-1$	$MS_R = \dfrac{SS_R}{t-1}$	$\dfrac{MS_R}{MS_E}$
Between columns	SS_C	$t-1$	$MS_C = \dfrac{SS_C}{t-1}$	$\dfrac{MS_C}{MS_E}$
Between treatments	SS_{TR}	$t-1$	$MS_{TR} = \dfrac{SS_{TR}}{t-1}$	$\dfrac{MS_{TR}}{MS_E}$
Error	SS_E	$(t-1)(t-2)$	$MS_E = \dfrac{SS_E}{(t-1)(t-2)}$	
Total	SS_T	t^2-1		

We can then rewrite Equation 16.4 as

$$Y_{ijk} = M + (M_{i..} - M) + (M_{.j.} - M) + (M_{..k} - M) + E_{ijk}$$

$$\begin{array}{ccccccccc}
\text{Individual} \\ \text{score}
& = & \text{grand} \\ \text{mean}
& + & \text{row} \\ \text{effect}
& + & \text{column} \\ \text{effect}
& + & \text{treatment} \\ \text{effect}
& + & \text{error}
\end{array}$$

We can solve this equation for E_{ijk} to get the measurement of error.

$$E_{ijk} = Y_{ijk} - M - (M_{i..} - M) - (M_{.j.} - M) - (M_{..k} - M)$$
$$= Y_{ijk} + 2M - M_{i..} - M_{.j.} - M_{..k}$$

If both blocking factors are correlated with the dependent variable, this error measure will be smaller than that obtained with a CRD or RBD that uses only one blocking factor.

If we moved M to the left side, added all these deviations across all rows and columns, and squared the equation, we would obtain the required SS. The model would then be

$$SS_T = SS_R + SS_C + SS_{TR} + SS_E$$

as again all the cross products fall out to zero. Table 16-6 shows the ANOVA layout for an LS design. SS_R, SS_C, and SS_{TR} each have $t - 1$ df. With $(t)(t) - 1$ or $t^2 - 1$ df in the whole sample, this leaves $(t - 1)(t - 2)$ df for the error term.

A Calculated Example   We shall now apply the LS design ANOVA to the data in Table 16-5.

Total Sum of Squares

$$SS_T = \sum_{i=1}^{t} \sum_{j=1}^{t} (Y_{ijk} - M)^2$$
$$= (25 - 21)^2 + (15 - 21)^2 + \cdots + (14 - 21)^2$$
$$= 1302$$

Row Sum of Squares

$$SS_R = t \sum_{i=1}^{t} (M_{i..} - M)^2$$
$$= 3[(30 - 21)^2 + (18.3 - 21)^2 + (14.7 - 21)^2]$$
$$= 383.9$$

Column Sum of Squares

$$SS_C = t \sum_{j=1}^{t} (M_{.j.} - M)^2$$
$$= 3[(15 - 21)^2 + (18.3 - 21)^2 + (29.7 - 21)^2]$$
$$= 356.9$$

Treatment Sum of Squares

$$SS_{TR} = t \sum_{k=1}^{t} (M_{..k} - M)^2$$
$$= 3[(30 - 21)^2 + (21.7 - 21)^2 + (11.3 - 21)^2]$$
$$= 526.7$$

Error Sum of Squares

$$SS_E = SS_T - SS_R - SS_C - SS_{TR}$$
$$= 1302 - 383.9 - 356.9 - 526.7$$
$$= 34.5$$

Table 16-7 presents the calculated F values for the treatment and the two blocks. For the treatment and blocking factors, the critical value of F for $\alpha = .1$ at 2 and 2 df is 9.0. Therefore, both blocking factors and the treatment are significant. Note that none of these effects would have been significant at $\alpha = .05$, as the critical F is 19.0. If we had used a CRD or blocked with just one of our two blocking factors in an RBD, the treatment effect would not have been significant at $\alpha = .1$. This is so because the SS_R and SS_C would be added back into the LS design SS_E to give the SS_E for the CRD. As for the RBD, either SS_R or SS_C would be added back to the LS design SS_E to give the SS_E for the RBD. In either instance, the SS_R or SS_C is large enough to render the calculated F ratio nonsignificant, at $\alpha = .1$. Here we needed two blocking factors to find a significant treatment effect. The value of blocking in marketing experiments should be clear.

Table 16-7 ANOVA Table for Coupon Experiment with 3 × 3 Latin Square Design

Source of variation	Sum of squares, SS	Degrees of freedom, df	Mean square, MS	F ratio
Row effect (store size)	383.9	2	192.0	11.1
Column effect (days of week)	356.9	2	178.5	10.3
Treatment	526.7	2	263.4	15.2
Error	34.5	2	17.3	
Total	1302.0	8		

Again note that we must look into the data to see that treatment A is the best coupon plan.

FACTORIAL DESIGN

In a factorial design (FD) we measure the effects of two or more independent variables and their interactions. Suppose that in our coupon experiment we are interested not only in the effect of coupon plans, but also in the effect of the media plans that support the coupon plans. Table 16-8 presents data generated from such an experiment. You should recognize these as the data we used in Table 15-6 for our CRD. All we have done here is regroup the data and presented them as if they came from an FD.

Partitioning the Sum of Squares In the FD with two independent variables, we define an individual observation as

$$Y_{ijk} = \text{grand mean} + \text{effect of treatment } A$$
$$+ \text{effect of treatment } B + \text{interaction effect } AB + \text{error}$$

where Y_{ijk} = the kth observation on the ith level of A and the jth level of B. For example, here

$$Y_{111} = 20, \qquad Y_{231} = 7$$

In population parameter terms, the model is

$$Y_{ijk} = \mu + \alpha_i + \beta_j + (\alpha\beta)_{ij} + \epsilon_{ijk}$$

Again, we will be estimating this model with sample results, as we write

$$Y_{ijk} = M + A_i + B_j + (AB)_{ij} + E_{ijk} \tag{16-5}$$

Table 16-8 A 2 × 3 Factorial Design with Media Plans and Coupon Plans As Independent Variables

		Coupon plans (j)				
		B_1	B_2	B_3	Media totals	Media means
Media plans (i)	A_1	20 18	17 14	14 10	$\Sigma Y_{1..} = 93$	$M_{1..} = 93/6 = 15.5$
	A_2	15 11	13 8	7 5	$\Sigma Y_{2..} = 59$	$M_{2..} = 59/6 = 9.8$
Coupon totals		$\Sigma Y_{.1.} = 64$	$\Sigma Y_{.2.} = 52$	$\Sigma Y_{.3.} = 36$	$\Sigma Y_{...} = 152$	
Coupon means		$M_{.1.} = 64/4 = 16$	$M_{.2.} = 52/4 = 13$	$M_{.3.} = 36/4 = 9$		$M = 12.7$

Treatment cell (ij)	A_1B_1	A_1B_2	A_1B_3	A_2B_1	A_2B_2	A_2B_3
Cell total Cell mean	$\Sigma Y_{11.} = 38$ $M_{11.} = 38/2$ $= 19$	$\Sigma Y_{12.} = 31$ $M_{12.} = 31/2$ $= 15.5$	$\Sigma Y_{13.} = 24$ $M_{13.} = 24/2$ $= 12$	$\Sigma Y_{21.} = 26$ $M_{21.} = 26/2$ $= 13$	$\Sigma Y_{22.} = 21$ $M_{22.} = 21/2$ $= 10.5$	$\Sigma Y_{23.} = 12$ $M_{23.} = 12/2$ $= 6$

Note: $n_{ij} = 2$ for all i's and j's.

where A_i = the effect of the ith level of A (media plan), $i = 1, \ldots, a$, where a is the number of levels in A

B_j = the effect of the jth level of B (coupon plan), $j = 1, \ldots, b$, where b is the number of levels in B

$(AB)_{ij}$ = the effect of the interaction of the ith level of A and the jth level of B

E_{ijk} = the error of the kth observation in the ith level of A and the jth level of B, i.e., the ij cell

In our example $n_{ij} = 2$ for all ij cells.

The four effects of interest are:

1 A_i effect (i.e., media plan) = $(M_{i..} - M)$, the difference between the row mean and the grand mean.

2 B_j effect (i.e., coupon plan) = $(M_{.j.} - M)$, the difference between the column mean and the grand mean.

3 Error = $(Y_{ijk} - M_{ij.})$, the difference between an individual observation and the cell mean to which it belongs. That is, the only difference within a cell should be random chance.

4 Interaction effect $(AB)_{ij}$ = any remaining variation in the data after main effects and error have been removed.

We can rewrite Equation 16-5 as

$$Y_{ijk} = M + (M_{i..} - M) + (M_{.j.} - M) + (AB)_{ij} + (Y_{ijk} - M_{ij.})$$

and solve for the interaction term, $(AB)_{ij}$:

$$\begin{aligned}(AB)_{ij} &= Y_{ijk} - M - (M_{i..} - M) - (M_{.j.} - M) - (Y_{ijk} - M_{ij.})\\ &= Y_{ijk} - M - M_{i..} + M - M_{.j.} + M - Y_{ijk} + M_{ij.}\\ &= M + M_{ij.} - M_{i..} - M_{.j.}\end{aligned}$$

In our example,

$$(AB)_{11} = 12.7 + 19 - 15.5 - 16 = 0.2$$

and

$$(AB)_{23} = 12.7 + 6 - 9.8 - 9 = -0.1$$

Results like this suggest that there is little interaction in the data. We may now rewrite Equation 16-5 as

$$Y_{ijk} = M + (M_{i..} - M) + (M_{.j.} - M) + (M + M_{ij.} - M_{i..} - M_{.j.}) + (Y_{ijk} - M_{ij.})$$
$$(16\text{-}6)$$

If we moved M to the left side, added all the deviations across all scores k in all

Table 16-9   ANOVA Table for a Two-factor Factorial Design

Source of variation	Sum of squares, SS	Degrees of freedom, df	Mean square, MS	F ratio
Treatment A	SS_{TRA}	$a - 1$	$MS_{TRA} = \dfrac{SS_{TRA}}{a - 1}$	$\dfrac{MS_{TRA}}{MS_E}$
Treatment B	SS_{TRB}	$b - 1$	$MS_{TRB} = \dfrac{SS_{TRB}}{b - 1}$	$\dfrac{MS_{TRB}}{MS_E}$
Interaction AB	$SS_{INT(AB)}$	$(a - 1)(b - 1)$	$MS_{INT(AB)} = \dfrac{SS_{INT(AB)}}{(a - 1)(b - 1)}$	$\dfrac{MS_{INT(AB)}}{MS_E}$
Error	SS_E	$ab(n - 1)$		
Total	SS_T	$abn - 1$		

ij cells, and squared the equation, we would obtain the required SS. The model would then be

$$SS_T = SS_{TRA} + SS_{TRB} + SS_{INT(AB)} + SS_E$$

where SS_{TRA} = sum of squares of treatment A
SS_{TRB} = sum of squares of treatment B
$SS_{INT(AB)}$ = sum of squares for interaction of A and B

This result occurs because all the cross products fall out to zero, as we would now expect. Table 16-9 shows the ANOVA layout for a two-factor FD. Each factor has one degree of freedom less than its number of categories, and the interaction term has $(a - 1)(b - 1)$ df. With $abn - 1$ df in the whole sample, this leaves $ab(n - 1)$ for the error term.

A Calculated Example   Now let us apply the FD to the data in Table 16-8.
Total Sum of Squares

$$SS_T = \sum_{i=1}^{a} \sum_{j=1}^{b} \sum_{k=1}^{n} (Y_{ijk} - M)^2$$
$$= (20 - 12.7)^2 + (17 - 12.7)^2 + \cdots + (5 - 12.7)^2$$
$$= 232.7$$

Again note that the SS_T is the same as in the CRD and RBD, as it must be.
Treatment A Sum of Squares

$$SS_{TRA} = bn \sum_{i=1}^{a} (M_{i..} - M)^2$$
$$= (3)(2)[(15.5 - 12.7)^2 + (9.8 - 12.7)^2]$$
$$= 97.5$$

Treatment B Sum of Squares

$$SS_{TRB} = an \sum_{j=1}^{b} (M_{.j.} - M)^2$$
$$= (2)(2)[(16 - 12.7)^2 + (13 - 12.7)^2 + (9 - 12.7)^2]$$
$$= 98.7$$

Note that this is the SS_{TR} we found for the CRD. In other words, the main effect of the coupon plan is identical under both analysis procedures, as we would expect.

Interaction Sum of Squares

$$SS_{INT(AB)} = n \sum_{i=1}^{a} \sum_{j=1}^{b} (M + M_{ij.} - M_{i..} - M_{.j.})^2$$

$$= 2[(12.7 + 19 - 15.5 - 16)^2$$
$$+ (12.7 + 15.5 - 15.5 - 13)^2 + (12.7 + 12 - 15.5 - 9)^2$$
$$+ (12.7 + 13 - 9.8 - 16)^2 + (12.7 + 10.5 - 9.8 - 13)^2$$
$$+ (12.7 + 6 - 9.8 - 9)^2$$
$$= 0.7$$

Error Sum of Squares

$$SS_E = \sum_{i=1}^{a} \sum_{j=1}^{b} \sum_{k=1}^{n} (Y_{ijk} - M_{ij.})^2$$
$$= SS_T - SS_{TRA} - SS_{TRB} - SS_{INT(AB)}$$
$$= 232.7 - 97.5 - 98.7 - 0.7$$
$$= 35.8$$

Table 16-10 presents the calculated F values for the two treatments and the interaction. For treatment A, the critical F for $\alpha = .05$ at 1 and 6 df is 5.99. Therefore, the media effect is significant. For treatment B, for $\alpha = .05$ at 2 and 6 df the critical F is 5.14. Thus, the coupon effect is also significant. Since the calculated interaction F is less than 1, we know it is not significant without even using the F table. We can now go back to the data to see that it is media plan A_1 and coupon plan B_1 that yield the best results.

This two-factor ANOVA is called "two-way" ANOVA. The factorial procedure can be extended to N independent variables. This is called "N-way" ANOVA. The calculations for an ANOVA greater than two-way are too complex to present here. The analysis of such an experiment is, however, easily handled by modern computer programs. In any event, the principle of these more advanced calculations is exactly the same as you have just learned.

Table 16-10 ANOVA Table for Media and Coupon Experiment Using a Two-factor 2 × 3 Factorial Design

Source of variation	Sum of squares, SS	Degrees of freedom, df	Mean square, MS	F ratio
Treatment A (media)	97.5	1	97.5	16.3
Treatment B (coupon)	98.7	2	49.4	8.2
Interaction (AB)	0.7	2	.4	.1
Error	35.8	6	6.0	
Total	232.7	11		

Analysis of Covariance

In Chapter 14 we noted that the RBD and LS designs could be used to control extraneous sources of variation in the dependent variable. To make use of these procedures, we need to design our experiment with relevant blocking factors in mind; in other words, we must be aware of the possible extraneous variables before undertaking the experiment. But what happens if we discover an extraneous source of variation *after* we run the experiment? Fortunately, there is a technique that does allow us to do an ex post facto analysis of the data to control for this extraneous variation. It is called the *analysis of covariance* (ANCOVA). We shall leave the details of ANCOVA for Chapter 26. For now, you should simply be aware that ANCOVA can control extraneous variation ex post facto. What this demonstrates again is a basic principle of the analysis of experiments, namely that, if you can measure extraneous factors, you can control their influence on the dependent variable. This control may be done either with a blocking procedure or ex post facto with ANCOVA.

SUMMARY

1 The CRD measures the effect of one independent variable without statistical control of extraneous variation. Its basic composition is $SS_T = SS_{TR} + SS_E$.

2 The RBD design measures the effect of one independent variable with statistical control of one extraneous factor. Its basic composition is $SS_T = SS_{TR} + SS_B + SS_E$.

3 The LS design measures the effect of one independent variable with statistical control of two extraneous factors. Its basic composition is $SS_T = SS_R + SS_C + SS_{TR} + SS_E$.

4 The FD measures the main and interaction effects of two or more independent variables. Its basic composition for a two-way ANOVA is $SS_T = SS_{TRA} + SS_{TRB} + SS_{INT(AB)} + SS_E$.

5 ANCOVA may be used to control extraneous variation ex post facto.

DISCUSSION QUESTIONS

1 Into what components is the SS_T partitioned in an RBD, LS design, and two-factor factorial design?
2 How is the estimate of the variance of each component obtained from the partitioned SS?
3 How does an RBD or LS design decrease the experimental error that would be calculated in a CRD?
4 What happens to the size of SS_{TR} calculated in a CRD when an RBD is used instead?
5 Explain how the F test for treatment effect is performed in an RBD, LS design, and FD.
6 How can extraneous variation in a dependent variable be controlled ex post facto?

SUGGESTED READING

Cox, Keith K., and Ben M. Enis, *Experimentation for Marketing Decisions* (Scranton, Pa.: International Textbook Company, 1969), chaps. 4–6. A readable presentation of the calculations of ANOVA for the RBD, LS design, and FD.

Edwards, Allen L., *Experimental Design in Psychological Research* (New York: Holt, 1968), chaps. 9–13. An advanced discussion of the RBD, LS design, and FD.

Chapter 17

Test Marketing

In the previous three chapters we have developed the conceptual tools to understand and identify causality. This was not an academic exercise, for a significant proportion of marketing research in practice is causally oriented. A recent survey[1] by Bellenger et al. estimated that 36 percent of consumer product companies use formal experimental designs, and 67 percent of them use informal (quasi) experimental designs. For industrial products companies and those marketing both consumer and industrial products, these usage rates are considerably lower. However, the fundamental point remains, namely that experimental and quasi-experimental procedures are extensively used in practice. They are used because they work.

The topic of this chapter is test marketing (or market testing, as some authors call it), a field-oriented testing activity that may be either an experiment or a quasi experiment depending on how it is structured. In most cases it attains only quasi-experimental status. Our reason for dedicating a chapter to test marketing relates to our underlying philosophy for this book, which is that we

[1] Danny N. Bellenger, Jac L. Goldstucker, and Barnett A. Greenberg, "What Techniques Are Used by Marketing Researchers in Business?", *Journal of Marketing,* vol. 41, pp. 64–65, April 1977. Although this study suffers from serious nonresponse error, it still provides a feel for the use of various procedures in marketing research practice.

want the reader to get beyond technical concepts and into the flavor of the real world of marketing research. Test marketing represents a very real activity that allows the reader to observe the use of experimental and quasi-experimental procedures, and it allows the tying in of some of the syndicated data services discussed in Chapter 6. Also, since test marketing is a heavily used activity in marketing research, it merits presentation here. The Bellenger study estimated that test marketing is used by 62 percent of consumer goods companies, 34 percent of industrial goods companies, and 40 percent of those companies marketing both types of products.

This chapter first describes the possible uses of test marketing, then discusses when test marketing should be undertaken as well as noting its limitations. A number of implementation decisions in test marketing will be covered, specifically the choice of the number of cities to use, the criteria for selecting test cities, the distinction between standard test cities and control test cities, and the length of time a test should run.

INTRODUCTION TO TEST MARKETING

As stated above, test marketing is a much used and important activity in marketing research; yet it is a very controversial subject in the marketing research community. The marketing research director of a major consumer goods company recently described test marketing as "an archaic device." Still, others have put forward the proposition that new forecasting techniques may make test marketing obsolete.[2] We shall discuss the reasons for some of the negative attitudes toward test marketing later in the chapter. Yet, despite all the negatives, the use of test marketing remains high, and it is in fact growing. A recent article noted:

> A few years ago, some marketers were forecasting the imminent demise of test marketing. Growing sophistication of pre-market testing and computer modeling would make costly tryouts of new products unnecessary, they predicted. Somehow it just hasn't worked out that way. Contrary to the experts' opinion, test marketing has become more important in today's slow-growth, high-cost business environment.[3]

Test Marketing Defined

Before proceeding further, we need a formal definition of test marketing. Achenbaum defines test marketing from the research-oriented person's point of view as follows:

[2] "New Product Forecasting Techniques May Make Test Markets Obsolete," *Marketing News,* vol. 10, no. 10, Nov. 19, 1976, pp. 1 and 4.
[3] Sally Scanlon, "Calling the Shots More Closely," *Sales and Marketing Management,* May 10, 1976, p. 43.

It is a controlled experiment, done in a limited but carefully selected part of the marketplace, whose aim is to predict the sales or profit consequences, either in absolute or relative terms, of one or more proposed marketing actions.[4]

Achenbaum goes on to explain that, at the other extreme, some people define test marketing loosely as "trying something out in the marketplace."[5] He recognizes that most test marketing activity falls between these two extremes. Cost and time pressures are the main reasons why the research-oriented extreme is not often used. But Achenbaum notes that: "No matter what choice is made, one thing is common to all such tests: the results are used as if they were predictive"[6] of the whole marketplace. It should not be surprising that, with so much test marketing activity positioned toward the loose end of the definitional spectrum, it is easy to find examples of test market failures.

In our definition of test marketing, we shall take account of the practice of this activity. Specifically we define test marketing as *the implementation and monitoring of a marketing program in a small subset of the target market areas for the product in question.* This definition takes in designs that are not even good quasi experiments, let alone experiments, but this is the nature of this activity.

The Selection of Alternatives to Test

A product manager was overheard to say to a researcher in discussing the introduction of a new product: "I want to test at least two price levels, three different advertising executions, two coupon alternatives, two package designs, three point-of-purchase presentations, and two product formulas." This test could be designed as a controlled experiment, using a factorial design; but look how many test cities we would need to conduct this experiment! At a minimum it would require:

$$2 \text{ (prices)} \times 3 \text{ (advertising executions)} \times 2 \text{ (coupons)} \times 2 \text{ (packages)}$$
$$\times 3 \text{ (point-of-purchase presentations)} \times 2 \text{ (product formulas)} = 144 \text{ cities}$$

Obviously, the cost of such a test would be unreasonably high. This points out that true field experiments can test only a few levels of a few variables.

What the product manager must do in this situation is eliminate some combinations of variables prior to undertaking the test market. Basically, all the possible combinations of marketing variables must be reduced to a few alternative strategies. For example, two strategies might be:

1   Price $1.15, advertising using hidden-camera interviews, 10-cents-off coupon, plastic package, end-aisle display, and the strong product formula.
2   Price $0.98, advertising using "slice of life" execution, 15-cents-off

---

[4] Alvin R. Achenbaum, "Market Testing: Using the Marketplace as a Laboratory," in Robert Ferber (ed.), *Handbook of Marketing Research* (New York: McGraw-Hill, 1974), p. 4-32.
[5] Ibid.
[6] Ibid.

coupon, cardboard packages, middle-aisle display, and medium-strength product formula.

This test could be conducted in two cities (at a minimum). However, it does not allow the measurement of separate main effects or interaction effects. We can only grossly measure the effect of the two strategies. Hence, most test marketing would be best described as a quasi experiment.

How do researchers reduce to a few strategies the number of possible combinations they are interested in? They use personal judgment, based on the experience of both the manager and the company, and also they undertake research on each aspect of the strategy prior to the test market. For example, a researcher could (1) test the product formula within a home placement test, (2) do copy testing on the advertising executions, and (3) consult previous company experience with similar products to compare end-aisle displays with middle-aisle displays and to study the results of various coupon plans. A great many judgments must be made, and a great deal of research undertaken, prior to the test market.

THE USES OF TEST MARKETING

No matter how formal or informal the design of a test market, there are two fundamental uses for it.[7]

1 Test marketing can serve a *managerial control function*. That is, it can allow an organization to gain needed information or experience before undertaking a project on a grand scale.

2 Test marketing can serve a *predictive research function*. That is, it can predict the outcome of alternative courses of action. This input can be used to decide whether or not to undertake a course of action.

Test Marketing as a Managerial Control Tool

In undertaking any new marketing activity there is risk that something will go wrong. This is especially true in the marketing of new products or brands, but it is also true in established product categories where some innovation is being introduced. A test market here would be designed as a pilot operation for later larger-scale national introduction. It would give us needed experience in many areas, including the following:

1 We could gain experience in physically handling the product—i.e., shelf life, breakage, storage, shipping, etc. We could identify costly mistakes and thereby avoid them on a national basis. Consider the case of Nabisco's "Legendary Pastries."[8] A few months after the product was introduced in a test market, the cans of cherry topping began exploding. It seems that an apparently

---

[7] This section follows an excellent discussion in ibid., pp. 4-33 to 4-38.

[8] Sally Scanlon, "Is the Chemistry Changing?", *Sales Management, The Marketing Magazine,* Apr. 16, 1973, p. 33.

innocuous ingredient in the mix was fermenting the cherries. Consider the problem if Nabisco had put this product into national distribution.

2   It could give us experience in simply learning how things get done in marketing this product. We could learn the difficulties of gaining distribution, of producing a new commercial, of making our price hold at retail, etc. This experience would be used later in our national roll-out.

In designing test marketing programs for managerial control purposes we need not worry about having a correct experimental design. We are simply gaining experience, not making sales or profit projections, and therefore not making "go/no-go" decisions.

Test Marketing as a Predictive Research Tool

Of more interest to marketing researchers is test marketing as a predictive device. In fact, most test markets are used in this manner, no matter how badly designed. There are two situations in which test marketing is used as a predictive device, (1) in new-product or new-brand introductions, and (2) in the evaluation of alternative marketing programs for existing brands—i.e., to evaluate either individual marketing variables or programs. These two uses require reasonably tight experimental or quasi-experimental executions in order to generate reasonable predictions. Their only real difference from each other, from a methodological point of view, is that the testing of alternative marketing programs requires a control group (i.e., the present program).

In new-product or new-brand tests management wants to know how its new product or brand will do in terms of sales and profits in a national introduction. The reader may well wonder how one projects from test market results to a national performance, and indeed this is a very difficult problem. Projections are often made with what turns out to be a very large error when the national results are compared with the projection. Gold has suggested an approach to this problem,[9] offering three different methods for making this projection.

1   **Buying Income Method**   Here sales of the test brands are expanded by the ratio of the test area's buying income to the buying income of the country. In formula:

$$\text{National sales estimate} = \frac{\text{total U.S. income}}{\text{test area income}} \times \text{test area sales}$$

2   **Sales Ratio Method**   Here sales of the test brand are compared with the sales of another brand where a logical sales relationship may be expected. That is:

[9] Jack A. Gold, "Testing Test Marketing Predictions," *Journal of Marketing Research,* vol. 1, p. 10, August 1964.

National sales estimate =

$$\frac{\text{national sales of other product}}{\text{test area sales of this other product}} \times \text{test area sales of test product}$$

The firm may have related experience with other brands that they assume to be similar to the new brand.

3   The Share-of-Market Method   Here sales of a test brand are related to sales of the product category as a whole in the area where the new brand is being tested. In formula:

$$\text{National sales estimate} = \frac{\text{test area sales of new brand}}{\text{test area sales of this whole product category}}$$
$$\times \text{ national sales of this whole product category}$$

In Gold's study the share-of-market method was found to be the most accurate,[10] but it also is the most expensive, as it requires the auditing of all the competitive brands in the product category. It also assumes that the test product will not expand sales of the product category.[11]

More recently, a number of new procedures for projecting test market results have been proposed which are more sophisticated mathematically than Gold's approach. Our intention here is not to present the details of the mathematics of these approaches, but rather to give a brief overview of the similarities among them. Basically, these approaches have the following steps:

1   In undertaking a test market, collect purchase data from a panel in the test market area.

2   Obtain measures from the panel on the cumulative growth in the number of new buyers of the brand under study and the rate of repurchase activity for this brand over a number of purchase cycles.

3   Formulate a mathematical model to describe the demand for this brand. The model is expressed in terms of the measures taken in (2) above, that is, cumulative growth rate and repurchase rate, plus the size of the panel relative to the national population.

4   Use this model, and the growth and repurchase rates obtained from the consumer panel in the test market, to project national sales levels.

Proponents of this type of method have reported very accurate projections

---

[10] Ibid., p. 16.

[11] For a more detailed discussion of Gold's approach, see Edwin M. Berdy, "Testing Test Market Predictions: Comments," *Journal of Marketing Research,* May 1965, pp. 196—198. Also see Gold's reply, *Journal of Marketing Research,* May 1965, pp. 198–200.

from panel results to national outcomes.[12] Note that the Gold approach takes only gross measures of test market results, whereas the latter approaches measure purchase activity on an individual household basis by using a panel. An individual firm should develop projection formulas of its own to fit its own circumstances.

We shall now close this section on the uses of test marketing by listing some of the specific types of information a test market might provide for a company:[13]

1 Sales in units and dollars
2 Market share
3 Profitability and return on investment
4 Consumer behavior and attitudes with respect to the product, i.e., who does and doesn't buy; who makes the buying decision; how the product is used; repurchase patterns; perceptions of the product, etc.
5 Effectiveness of alternative marketing strategies, and possibly of the various components such as coupon plans, advertising executions, etc.
6 Reaction of the trade to the product and its marketing program, i.e., willingness to stock it, location on shelf, use of point-of-purchase materials, assessment of the sales force's presentation, etc.

In obtaining this information the company can make use of any of a number of syndicated test marketing services, some of which are discussed later in this chapter. Also, the firm is likely to need customized studies to measure some of the variables of interest.

THE DECISION TO UNDERTAKE TEST MARKETING

The decision to undertake test marketing involves the examination of the costs of the test market against the expected benefit. This section examines some of the specific areas of costs that are related to test marketing, the potential benefits having been discussed in the previous section. The problems associated with test marketing will also be discussed here.

Costs of Test Marketing

There are both direct and indirect costs of test marketing. The direct costs include:[14]

---

[12] The reader who is interested in the details of these newer approaches should consult a number of excellent references, including J. H. Parfitt and B. J. K. Collins, "Use of Consumer Panels for Brand-Share Prediction," *Journal of Marketing Research,* vol. 5, pp. 131–145, May 1968; David H. Ahl, "New Product Forecasting Using Consumer Panels," *Journal of Marketing Research,* vol. 7, pp. 160–167, May 1970; Gerald J. Eskin, "Dynamic Forecasts of New Product Demand Using a Depth of Repeat Model," *Journal of Marketing Research,* vol. 10, pp. 115–129, May 1973; Benjamin Lipstein, "Modelling and New Product Birth," *Journal of Advertising Research,* vol. 10, pp. 3–11, October 1970.

[13] This list is adapted from F. Ladik, L. Kent, and P. C. Nahl, "Test Marketing of New Consumer Products," *Journal of Marketing,* vol. 24, pp. 29–34, April 1960.

[14] Adapted from Jay E. Klompmaker, G. David Hughes, and Russell I. Haley, "Test Marketing in New Product Development," *Harvard Business Review,* May-June 1976, p. 129.

1 A pilot plant to make the product (if the test is for a new product)
2 Commercials
3 Payments to advertising agency for services
4 Media time at a higher rate because of low volume
5 Syndicated research information
6 Customized research information and associated data analysis costs
7 Point-of-purchase materials
8 Couponing and sampling
9 Higher trade allowances to obtain distribution

Klompmaker et al. note that the typical two-city test market in 1975 had direct costs of $250,000, and a four-city test $500,000. Long-running, complex tests can have direct costs of over $1 million.

To these costs we must also add the indirect costs of the test to the company, which include:

1 Opportunity cost of lost sales that would have occurred in a successful national introduction
2 Cost of management time spent on the test market
3 Diversion of sales force activity from money-making products
4 Possible negative impact on other products carrying the same family brand
5 Possible negative trade reactions to your products if you develop a reputation of "bombing"
6 Cost of letting your competitors know what you are doing, allowing them to develop a better strategy or beat you to the national market with a new product like yours

These costs are indeed high. In deciding whether or not to undertake a test market we must also consider some of the problems associated with test marketing.

Problems of Test Marketing

A number of problems occur with test marketing, and they will be listed later in this section. All of them, however, give rise to one overriding negative consequence—the lack of projectivity of the test market results to the national roll-out of the product. In 1965 *Printer's Ink—Consumer Advertising* undertook a review of test marketing and noted:

> Says the marketing chief of a large company: "Why? We never got clear answers (from test marketing). We never got accurate predictions on sales and profits."
>   Leaders of the marketing research community themselves are among the first to admit this. Says Bart Panitierre, GF Corporate Marketing Research Director, "Life would be wonderfully simple if the so-called national sales picture were one smooth canvas. It's not. It's really a mosaic—a rather uneven one—made up of hundreds of local markets each having a different shape and color. Test markets are only sample chips. Their results are difficult to project now to a national pattern,

though the better the choice of sample chips, the better the odds on an accurate prediction—providing, of course, you are fair in handling the chip and running the market tests."

One research director—Arthur Koponen, then at Colgate-Palmolive—said, "Projectivity is a myth."[15]

There are a number of reasons for this poor projectivity in test marketing:[16]

1 The salespersons in the selected area are stimulated beyond normal activity levels by just the mere awareness that a test is being conducted in their market.

2 The trade is made aware of the test and gives artificially high distribution and retailer support.

3 Special introductory offers and promotions are often made to the trade and to consumers because it is so important to get and maintain distribution during the test to measure repurchase activity. Their offers are then not available at the scale of the test for a national roll-out.

4 Competitive efforts, both deliberate and coincidental, have profound effects on the test market results. These efforts are then different on a national basis. At an extreme, competitors can attempt to destroy your ability to make judgments from a test by increasing their efforts in your test cities out of proportion with their national effort. In 1957, Purex began a test of a liquid bleach in Erie, Pennsylvania. In response Procter & Gamble increased its advertising efforts in Erie and also went into a heavy cents-off campaign for its Clorox brand. Purex had to cancel the test, as no meaningful results were possible.[17]

5 Measurement accuracy can yield ambiguous data. Auditing store sales can often give inaccurate data because of poor store records or incomplete knowledge of the store's billing and handling systems. Also, only a sample of stores is used, with a resultant sampling error occurring. These sample results must also be weighted properly to take account of large versus small stores in the population of stores. This is especially a problem when the measurements are made on a temporary basis for this one test.

6 Competitors may use your test market to learn of your activities and monitor your results. They may then beat you to the national market with this type of product. Having this competitor in the national market would obviously make the test results less projectable. This happened to Lever Brothers in testing their "Mrs. Butterworth" syrup, and also to Procter & Gamble in testing "Bounce" fabric softener. Calgon used P&G's test to beat P&G to the national market with its "Cling Free" brand.

[15] K. Ford, "Management Guide: Test Marketing," *Printer's Ink,* Aug. 27, 1965, as quoted in Achenbaum, op. cit., p. 4-33.

[16] Adapted from David H. Hardin, "A New Approach to Test Marketing," *Journal of Marketing,* vol. 30, pp. 28–31, October 1966.

[17] U.S. Federal Trade Commission 1963, *United States of America before Federal Trade Commission in the Matter of Procter & Gamble Company,* Corporation Docket No. 6901.

When to Test Market

With a firm understanding of the costs and limitations of test marketing in hand, we are ready to turn to a checklist of points to consider in deciding when to test market:

1 Consider the cost and risk of failure against the profit and probability of success. A product with low costs and low risk of failure may not need testing.

2 Consider the plant investment to go national versus that required for the test. Lean toward a direct national roll-out if little extra plant investment is necessary, and vice versa.

3 Consider the likelihood and speed with which the competition will copy and/or preempt your product or campaign. The faster they will respond, and the more likely they are to do so, the more reason there is for skipping the test.

4 Consider the effects of a national failure on the trade and on consumers. Will the company's reputation and other products suffer?

Thus, if the costs and risk are low, little incremental plant investment is needed for a national roll-out, competitors are likely to be able to copy your program quickly, and a failure is not likely to have major long-term consequences on the company's reputation, you would probably not do test marketing before a national launch. A company may consider one of these factors important and decisive enough on its own. For example,[18] Pillsbury developed a powdered soft drink to compete with Kool-Aid (General Foods), Wyler's (Borden), and Hawaiian Punch (R.J.R. Foods), all well-established competitors. Pillsbury's product, called "Squoze," had half the sugar and half the calories of the other mixes. Pillsbury reasoned that they would lose out if they gave their product a test market, because the competitors would easily match them and preempt the national market; so they skipped the test market.

DESIGNING TEST MARKETS

Three design issues will be covered in this section: (1) the choice of how many cities to use in the test, (2) the criteria to be used for selecting cities, and (3) the length of time the test should run.

The Number of Cities

Ladik et al.[19] offer the following guidelines:

1 Select at least two cities for each program variation to be tested.

2 Where projectivity is important, at least four geographic areas should be used.

We would of course consider the cost of adding more cities against the expected benefits. In general, the greater the risk of loss on a national basis, the more

---

[18] Scanlon, "Calling the Shots More Closely," p. 48.
[19] Ladik et al., "Test Marketing of New Consumer Products."

alternative programs should be considered; and the greater the regional differences in relation to your product, the more cities should be used.

Criteria for City Selection

No one city or group of cities can represent the whole United States. However, we should try to select cities that have the following characteristics:[20]

1 The markets should not be overtested.

2 The markets should have normal historical development in the product class.

3 The markets should represent a typical competitive advertising situation.

4 The markets should not be dominated by one industry.

5 Special resident profile markets should be avoided (for example, college towns and retirement areas).

6 If sales are different by region, each region should be tested.

7 The markets should have little media spillover into other markets and should receive little outside media impact.

8 The markets should have a media usage pattern similar to the national pattern.

9 The markets should not be too small to provide meaningful results or so large that testing becomes too expensive.

To this list we might add:

10 The markets should have representative distribution channels.

11 The competitive situation should be similar to the national situation.

12 Sales auditing and other research services should be available.

13 The company must be able to ship the product to the test areas at a reasonable cost.

14 The demographic profile of the cities should be "representative."

Obviously, not all these criteria are met by any one city or cities. This list is just the standard to shoot for.

In test marketing we distinguish between the two types of test cities: (1) control markets and (2) standard markets. *Control markets* (or minimarkets, as they are called) are cities where a research supply house has paid retailers to guarantee that they will carry products that it designates. The research company (1) handles the placing of products on shelves in retail stores, (2) services these products regularly to ensure that the required in-stock condition is maintained, (3) audits product class sales, and (4) observes competitive action that would affect the test. In other words, the environment is controlled to allow for tight designs. Control markets offer the advantages of (1) speedier access to distribution and readings on results, (2) reduced cost per market, (3) no distraction of sales force attention from other lines, and (4) greater secrecy, as most control

---

[20] Adapted from ibid.

markets are small and are not automatically audited by A. C. Nielsen or SAMI, etc. Thus, competitors must expend more time and effort to monitor your results.

The major drawback to control markets is the fact that true trade reaction to your product cannot be obtained, and this is often important to the marketer. These markets tend to be smaller, making national projections more difficult. Also, they generally do not have isolated media. This results in spillover of advertising into other areas where the product is not available. This wastes money, and in addition it can cause ill will for consumers and retailers who cannot buy the advertised product. Control markets are a fairly recent development in test marketing. The research companies who run these control markets have reported extensive use of this service. They also report success in having control market tests reasonably accurately predict national sales levels.

The alternative to control markets is the use of what are called *standard markets,* where the company must fight for trade support in the same fashion as in a national roll-out. There is no guarantee of getting retail distribution at all, let alone getting particular shelf facing and special stocking. This type of test provides a more realistic picture of the likely trade reaction to your product. It is, however, more expensive, slower, more distracting to the sales force, and more easily monitored by the competition. This type of test is still the dominant one in practice. Exhibit 17-1 lists both standard and control markets that are frequently used for test markets in practice. The names of some of the larger research supply houses that run a particular control market are also indicated.

The Length of a Test

The average test market runs from 6 to 12 months.[21] How does one decide how long a test should run for a particular situation? The following factors are relevant:

1   The test must run long enough for repurchase activity to be observed. This gives a measure of the "staying power" of a new product or program. The shorter the average repurchase period, the shorter the test can be. Cigarettes, soft drinks, perishable foods are purchased every few days, whereas shaving cream, toothpaste, etc., are purchased only every few months. The latter type of product would require a longer test than the former. The product should be allowed to go through a number of repurchase cycles.

2   How soon will competitors react? The faster this reaction, the shorter the test.

3   The cost of the test must also be considered. At some point the value of additional information is outweighed by its costs.

The Use of Research Suppliers

Marketing research suppliers are very active in the business of test marketing. Their primary activities include (1) providing retail store and warehouse sales or shipment information through audits, (2) selling consumer panel data on

---

[21] Scanlon, "Calling the Shots More Closely," p. 43.

Exhibit 17-1 Frequently Used Test Markets

Standard Markets	Control Markets
Albany-Schenectady-Troy	**Burgoyne, Inc.**
Atlanta	*Mini Markets:*
Boston	Binghamton, N.Y.
Buffalo	Charleston, S.C.
Cincinnati	Omaha
Cleveland	Providence, R.I.
Columbus, Ohio	Tucson
Dallas-Fort Worth	*Micro Markets:*
Dayton	Bangor, Me.
Denver	Eureka, Cal.
Des Moines	Gainesville, Fla.
Fort Wayne, Ind.	Lima, Ohio
Fresno, Calif.	Odessa, Texas
Grand Rapids-Kalamazoo	**Marketest,** division of Market Facts
Houston	*Binghamton, N.Y.
Indianapolis	Columbus, Ohio
Jacksonville	*Dayton
Kansas City	*Erie, Pa.
Madison, Wis.	*Fort Wayne, Ind.
Minneapolis-St. Paul	*Fresno, Cal.
New Orleans	Grand Rapids
Oklahoma City	Nashville
Omaha	*Orlando
Orlando	Springfield, Mass.
Peoria, Ill.	*Wichita
Phoenix	**Nielsen Data Markets**
Portland, Me.	*Boise, Idaho
Portland, Ore.	*Green Bay, Wis.
Providence, R.I.	*Portland, Me.
Quad Cities: Rock Island & Moline,	*Savannah, Ga.
Ill.; Davenport & Bettendorf, Iowa	*Tucson
Rochester, N.Y.	
Rockford, Ill.	
Sacramento, Cal.	
St. Louis	
Salt Lake City	
San Diego	
Seattle	
South Bend, Ind.	
Spokane	
Syracuse	
Tampa-St. Petersburg	
Tucson	

*Indicates cities in which the company maintains permanent distribution, merchandising, and auditing services.
Source: Sally Scanlon, "Calling the Shots More Closely," *Sales and Marketing Management,* May 10, 1976, p. 46.

purchases and attitudes, and (3) providing control market tests. They are also able to design and execute customized research for a company doing test marketing. Exhibit 17-2 presents a listing of some of the major companies providing test market services. A more detailed description of these companies was presented in Chapter 6.

Test marketing can be a very useful activity if executed with great care, and with no illusions about the precision of estimates that it will produce. It provides the most realistic test of alternatives under consideration.

Exhibit 17-2   Guide to Test Market Services

If you're looking for help with test market auditing and evaluation or control market testing, the following are leaders in those fields. They are by no means the only companies that offer such services, nor does their inclusion constitute an SMM recommendation.

For names of other research companies, consult such publications as the American Marketing Association's 1976 *International Directory of Marketing Research Houses and Services* (*Greenbook*), AMA-New York Chapter, 420 Lexington Ave., New York, NY 10017, or *Bradford's Directory of Marketing Research Agencies and Management Consultants in the U.S. and the World.*, P.O. Box 276, Dept. A, Fairfax, VA 22030.

Store/Warehouse Auditing Services

Audits & Surveys, Inc.
Burgoyne, Inc.
Ehrhart-Babic Associates, Inc.
Market Audits, Inc.
Market Facts, Inc.
A. C. Nielsen Co.
Selling Area-Marketing, Inc. (SAMI)
Store Audits, Inc.

Consumer Diary Panels

Consumer Mail Panels, division of Market Facts
Home Testing Institute, Inc.
Market Research Corp. of America (MRCA)
National Family Opinion, Inc.
National Purchase Diary Panel, Inc.

Control Market Tests

Audits & Surveys
Burgoyne, Inc.
Ehrhart-Babic
Market Audits
Marketest, division of Market Facts
Nielsen Data Markets (see A. C. Nielsen above)
Store Audits

Source: Sally Scanlon, "Calling the Shots More Closely," *Sales and Marketing Management,* May 10, 1976, p. 48.

SUMMARY

1   Test marketing is frequently used but is a controversial subject in marketing research.

2   Definitions of test marketing range all the way from "controlled experiments" to "trying something out." We define test marketing as the implementation and monitoring of a marketing program in a small subset of the target market areas for the product in question.

3   Selection of alternatives to test must involve other research and judgment prior to the test market.

4   Most test markets are quasi experiments at best.

5   Test marketing may be used as a managerial control function or as a predictive research function. The latter use may involve either new-product or new-brand introductions, or the evaluation of alternative marketing programs for existing brands.

6   In projecting test market results to a national product, the researcher may use the buying income method, the sales ratio method, the share-of-market method, or panel methods.

7   Direct costs of test marketing run at about $250,000 for a two-city test. Indirect costs are also high.

8   Test marketing often yields estimates of national outcomes that are inaccurate.

9   Reasons for unsatisfactory results include abnormal behavior by salespersons and the trade, special campaigns by the company doing the test, competitive actions, and measurement accuracy problems.

10   Consider test marketing when the costs and risk of failure are high, and/or the plant investment of a national roll-out is high relative to the test, and/or the competition is not likely to respond quickly, and/or the effects of a national failure on your company's reputation would be high.

11   In designing a test market, the researcher must make decisions with respect to what information to collect, the number of cities to use, the specific cities to use, and the length of time the test should run. One must also decide what marketing research supplier services to use.

DISCUSSION QUESTIONS

1   What is test marketing?
2   On what basis does one select alternative courses of action for use in a test market?
3   What are the two fundamental uses of test marketing?
4   How can test market results be projected to national results?
5   What information can a test market provide?
6   What are the costs of test marketing?
7   Why do test marketing results often give poor projections?
8   Under what circumstances should a company undertake test marketing?
9   What type of cities should be used in test marketing?

10 What is a control market?
11 What are the pros and cons of control markets?
12 How long should a test market run?

SUGGESTED READING

Achenbaum, Alvin R., "Market Testing: Using the Marketplace As a Laboratory," in
      Robert Ferber (ed.), *Handbook of Marketing Research* (New York: McGraw-Hill,
      1974), part 4, chap. 3. This article presents a definitive overview of the nature of test
      marketing.
Klompmaker, Jay E., G. David Hughes, and Russell I. Haley, "Test Marketing in New
      Product Development," *Harvard Business Review,* May-June 1976. This article
      presents a readable review of test marketing practice, based on interviews with
      directors of marketing research.

Cases for Part Five

Continental Brands

In early January, Mr. Dan Roper, product manager for Ultra Shine brand of floor wax, began analyzing the results of a market experiment that Decision Facts, a marketing research supply house, had just completed for Continental Brands. This market experiment was designed to measure the effect of alternative media plans (1) on Ultra Shine's sales and (2) on certain consumer attitude measures. Mr. Roper intended to use the results of the experiment to formulate his media plans for the next fiscal year. He had to submit his marketing plan for the coming fiscal year to his superiors by February 15. With this deadline in mind, he had arranged a meeting for two days from now with the advertising agency account executive who handled Ultra Shine. He intended to present guidelines for a media plan to the agency at that time.

Background

Continental Brands was one of America's largest package goods merchandisers. The company marketed a total of 25 brands in the floor wax, general-purpose cleaner, laundry products and over-the-counter drug markets. Each brand was assigned to a product manager. For a brand with large sales a product manager would be assigned to it exclusively, whereas for smaller brands a product manager would handle up to three brands. Product managers were responsible for all marketing decisions related to their brand or brands.

Ultra Shine was considered to be a major brand, with current yearly sales of $50 million and profits of $5,750,000. Media advertising amounted to $4,800,000. Ultra Shine was one of five brands of floor wax that Continental marketed. It was introduced to the market in 1961. The basic appeal used to promote Ultra Shine from its introduction through the present was its toughness based upon its special plastic formulation. Ultra Shine was profitable in its first year on the market, and by 1965 had obtained the position of number one brand in the market. It still held this position. There were over 20 national brands of floor wax on the market, plus many local brands. Ultra Shine's main competition came from three other plastic-formulated brands: Plastic-Shine, Able's Plastic Wax, and Space Age Clear Shine. All of these brands sold for about the same price as Ultra Shine and had equivalent distribution penetration at retail. Mr. Roper considered advertising to be Ultra Shine's main weapon in holding its market position.

From 1960 to 1968 the floor wax market had been growing at the rate of about 8 percent a year. The advent of permanent-shine floor tile in the middle 1960s and products that clean and shine floors with just a damp sponging in the 1970s had decreased this growth rate to 4 percent. This trend combined with increased competition action had resulted in a decline in Ultra Shine's sales growth rate from 10 percent in 1970 to just over 3 percent. Ultra Shine's share of the market had decreased from 12 percent in 1970 to 10 percent.

Since its introduction, Ultra Shine had made almost exclusive use of spot television commercials. In the year prior to the analysis, 95 percent of all Ultra Shine advertising was on spot television. The commercials currently being run featured an in-home demonstration of Ultra Shine's resistance to heel marks and toy scratches.

Mr. Roper had suspected for some time that Ultra Shine's loss in market share was due to an overconcentration of advertising on spot television. In early 1977, in consultation with the advertising agency account executive, he commissioned Decision Facts, a research supply house, to undertake a market experiment to test the effectiveness of alternative media plans. The cost of the study was $22,000, exclusive of media advertising dollars. The following gives excerpts from the report submitted by Decision Facts.

The Research Report

Objectives

1 To test the relative effectiveness of alternative media plans for Ultra Shine

2 To recommend the best media plan

Media Plans Tested

1 Spot television only (control market)
2 Spot radio 50 percent, spot television 50 percent
3 Newspapers 50 percent, spot television 50 percent

The media expenditures were the same for all three markets, and the creative aspects had the same theme.

Test Markets Used

Three cities were selected for the media plan test such that the following characteristics were as evenly matched as possible in all three cities:

1 Economic characteristics
2 Distribution penetration of Ultra Shine and its three major competitors

The cities were also to be isolated from outside media. Those selected were metro Atlanta, metro Denver, and metro Seattle. The economic characteristics of these cities were as shown in the table.

	Atlanta	Denver	Seattle
Population	1,200,000	1,400,000	1,400,000
Households	580,000	470,000	503,000
Income per household	$15,000	$15,000	$15,300
Retail sales index*	123	111	115

*On national base of 100.

Data Collected

The data were collected by means of telephone interviews. The following purchase-related measures were taken:

1 Brand of floor wax usually purchased
2 Brand of floor wax last purchased
3 Brand of floor wax intend to purchase next

Also collected were attitude measures. These were collected on a 7-point scale, with a 1 indicating the lowest level on the attitude measure and 7 the highest level. The following attitude measures were collected: (1) toughness, (2) shine, (3) ease of application, (4) length of wearing, (5) modernity, (6) convenience, and (7) speed of drying.

Sample Plan

In each test city the sample was selected randomly from the telephone directory. To qualify to answer the questionnaire, a respondent had to be a user of floor wax. The size of the realized sample of floor wax users was Atlanta 500, Denver 496, and Seattle 489.

Timing

The changes in media assignments took place in September, and the interviewing was undertaken in December.

Results

(Only selected tables from the report are presented here.)

Brand Usually Purchased

| | (Only the top four national brands are presented) | | |
	Atlanta	Denver	Seattle
	Spot TV	Spot radio and spot TV	Newspaper and spot TV
Ultra Shine	11%	16%*	9%
Plastic-Shine	10	8	8
Able's Plastic Wax	12	9	10
Space Age Clear Shine	8	12*	7

*Significant difference from control levels at .05 level of chance.

Brand Last Purchased

| | (Only the top four national brands are presented) | | |
	Atlanta	Denver	Seattle
	Spot TV	Spot radio and spot TV	Newspaper and spot TV
Ultra Shine	10%	14%*	10%
Plastic-Shine	10	9	8
Able's Plastic Wax	11	10	9
Space Age Clear Shine	6	12*	9*

*Significant difference from control levels at .05 level of chance.

Mr. Roper's Position

The report by Decision Facts contained action recommendations. However, Dan Roper was the type of person who liked to draw his own conclusions from research data. He therefore set aside the recommendation section of the report and began formulating his own conclusions about the action he should take now.

DISCUSSION QUESTIONS

1 Evaluate the experimental design used by Continental Brands.
2 If you think the design can be improved, indicate in detail how you would do so.
3 What marketing conclusions can be drawn from the results of the study? What action would you recommend for Ultra Shine?

Attitude Measures

Attributes	Ultra shine			Plastic-shine			Able's plastic wax			Space age clear shine		
	A Spot TV	D Spot R and TV	S Newspaper and spot TV	A Spot TV	D Spot R and TV	S Newspaper and spot TV	A Spot TV	D Spot R and TV	S Newspaper and spot TV	A Spot TV	D Spot R and TV	S Newspaper and spot TV
Toughness	6.0	6.5*	6.0	5.9	6.0	5.8	5.7	5.8	5.6	5.2	5.0	5.7*
Shine	5.9	6.1	5.8	6.0	5.8	6.1	5.4	5.8	5.1	5.7	5.9	6.0
Ease of application	5.4	5.4	5.5	5.6	5.4	5.5	6.1	5.9	5.7	4.7	4.6	4.9
Length of wearing	6.2	6.1	6.4	6.0	6.0	6.0	5.2	5.0	4.9	5.1	5.2	5.0
Modernity	5.4	5.6	5.5	5.8	5.6	5.8	5.1	5.4	5.5	4.9	4.6	4.4
Convenience	4.5	4.0*	5.1*	4.9	4.9	4.8	4.7	4.9	4.7	4.9	4.5	4.6
Speed of drying	4.2	5.1*	4.6	4.1	4.4	4.2	4.0	3.9	4.1	3.7	3.6	4.1

*Significant difference from control levels at .05 level of chance.

Note: A = Atlanta, D = Denver, S = Seattle.

Case 2

Allied Research, Inc.

In early March, Edward Little, the president of Allied Research, Inc., was approached by Paul Lawrence, the president of the Central Mid-West Region of the Red Cross Society. In lieu of a financial contribution, Mr. Lawrence requested that Mr. Little contribute his research skills to the Red Cross this year.

The Research Question

Mr. Lawrence noted that for some time he and some other members of the Mid-West Red Cross executive board believed that random telephone solicitation, either with or without a second call to those contacted by the first random call, would be an effective way to recruit blood donors. Currently, telephone solicitations were made only from lists of previous blood donors. Mr. Lawrence requested that Mr. Little design a test to determine whether random telephone solicitation was an effective way to recruit blood donors. He was also interested in the possible effect of a second call. He went on to note that the attempt to recruit donors by random calls was to be in addition to the telephone calling from current donor lists.

Presently the Red Cross continuously operated six blood donor clinics in the central mid-west region. Mr. Lawrence gave Mr. Little a copy of Exhibit 1, showing the number of pints of blood each of their clinics obtains in an average week, by the days of the week. The Red Cross also undertook special blood drives about four times a year. Mr. Lawrence noted that the next special drive was due to run during the week of April 15. Average blood intake increased during these special campaigns.

Exhibit 1   Number of Pints of Blood Obtained in Six Locations by the Days of the Week, for an Average Week

	Days of the week					
Location	Monday	Tuesday	Wednesday	Thursday	Friday	Saturday
City Hall, downtown	100	46	56	34	109	90
Northway Shopping Center	94	36	44	29	85	79
Fairview Armed Forces Base	50	20	26	15	49	44
Southway Shopping Center	42	16	24	10	50	40
St. Anthony's Church	36	20	22	15	44	39
Red Cross headquarters	112	55	61	48	121	105

   Mr. Little agreed to assist the Red Cross in this matter and said that he would be able to develop a complete study design by the end of the week. They decided to meet on Friday afternoon to go over Mr. Little's study design. Mr. Lawrence then left, and Mr. Little began considering what design would be most appropriate for the circumstances of the Red Cross.

DISCUSSION QUESTION

Prepare an experimental design.

Part Six

Obtaining Information from Respondents

Chapter 18

Data Collection Methods

Previous chapters have emphasized the role of exploratory research both in formulating problems and in stimulating the creative process involved in identifying alternative courses of action. It was stressed that the decision problem must be clearly stated and the alternative courses of action specified before the conclusive research project can be initiated.

Once the need for conclusive research is established, the researcher must clearly state the objectives of the proposed research and develop a specific list of information needs. The next step in the formal research project is to determine whether the desired data are currently available from secondary data sources. These sources can be internal or external to the organization. Typically, secondary data sources do not completely meet the information needs of the study, and the researcher turns to formulating a research design based on primary data sources. These include (1) respondents, (2) analogous situations, and (3) experiments. Previous chapters have discussed the data sources of analogous situations and experimentation. This chapter focuses on the remaining primary data source, namely, respondents.

Respondents are a major source of marketing data. There are two methods of acquiring data from respondents—communication and observation. Communication requires the respondent to actively provide data through verbal response, while observation involves the recording of the respondent's behavior.

Before turning to a discussion of the data collection issues that arise in connection with respondent data, let us first overview the types of data that can be collected from respondents.

TYPES OF RESPONDENT DATA

In a fundamental sense, all marketing decision making is concerned with taking action today so that future objectives can be accomplished. In this context, marketing research can be viewed as a forecasting technique designed to facilitate the process of predicting market behavior. The types of data that can be obtained from respondents for use in forecasting market behavior are (1) past behavior, (2) attitudes, and (3) respondent characteristics.

Past Behavior

Evidence regarding the respondent's past behavior has wide usage as a predictor of future behavior. In our personal activities we all use evidence of past behavior to predict the future behavior of our friends and relatives. In similar fashion, a marketing research study can gather evidence on a respondent's behavior regarding purchase and use of some product or brand to predict future behavior. The specific evidence gathered regarding this past behavior can be as follows: (1) What was purchased/used? (2) How much was purchased/used? (3) How was it purchased/used? (4) Where was it purchased/used? (5) When was it purchased/used? and (6) Who purchased/used it?[1] Consequently, there are many dimensions to understanding past behavior. The researcher must be sensitive to the key behavioral dimensions relevant to predicting future behavior when specifying the data required to meet the information needs of a study.

Attitudes

Attitudes are important in marketing because of the assumed relationship between attitudes and behavior. Attitudinal data are used to identify market segments, to develop a "positioning" strategy, and to evaluate advertising programs.

An attitude is generally considered to have three main components: (1) a *cognitive* component—a person's beliefs about the object of concern, such as its speed or durability; (2) an *affective* component—a person's feelings about the object, such as "good" or "bad"; and (3) *behavioral* component—a person's readiness to respond behaviorally to the object.

The measurement of attitudes was discussed extensively in Chapter 13. The emphasis was on the quantification of attitudes, using self-report scaling techniques. This chapter will discuss additional techniques for identifying the nature of attitudes and their measurement.

---

[1] Fred T. Schreier, *Modern Marketing Research—A Behavioral Science Approach* (Belmont, Calif.: Wadsworth, 1963), p. 251.

Table 18-1 Life-style Characteristics

Activities	Interests	Opinions
Work	Family	Themselves
Hobbies	Home	Social issues
Social events	Job	Politics
Vacation	Community	Business
Entertainment	Recreation	Economics
Club membership	Fashion	Education
Community	Food	Products
Shopping	Media	Future
Sports	Achievements	Culture

Source: Adapted from J. T. Plummer, "The Concept and Application of Life-Style Segmentation," *Journal of Marketing*, vol. 38, p. 34, January 1974.

Respondent Characteristics

"Respondent characteristics" refers to describing respondents on certain different variables. These include demographic, socioeconomic, and psychological characteristics. For many products, variables of this nature have been found to be correlates of purchase behavior. In addition, variables such as age, sex, marital status, family size, income, occupation, and education level have been found useful in sample stratification and validation.

A popular way of describing respondents is in terms of their life-style, defined as *a distinctive mode of living of a society or segment thereof*.[2] Life-style focuses on respondent activities, interests, opinions, and demographic characteristics as determinants of style of living. The first three of these, listed in more detail in Table 18-1, are called A-I-O items, which stands for activities, interests, and opinions.

The term *psychographics* is closely related to the concept of life-style. It is a broader term which includes the life-style concept. One definition is as follows:

Psychographics is a quantitative research procedure which seeks to explain why people behave as they do and why they hold their current attitudes. It seeks to take quantitative research beyond demographic, socioeconomic and user/non-user analysis, but also employs these variables in the research. Psychographics looks into three classes of variables, of which life-style is one. The others are psychological and product benefits.[3]

[2] W. Lazer, "Life-style Concepts and Marketing," in S. A. Greyser (ed.), *Toward Scientific Marketing* (Chicago: American Marketing Association, 1964), p. 130.

[3] Emanuel Demby, "Psychographics and from Whence It Came," in William D. Wells (ed.), *Life Style and Psychographics* (Chicago: American Marketing Association, 1974), p. 28.

METHODS OF COLLECTING RESPONDENT DATA

As stated earlier, the two basic methods of collecting data from respondents are communication and observation. We shall examine the communication method first. Discussion of the observation method begins on page 442.

Communication Method

The communication method of data collection is based on the questioning of respondents. It is logical to ask respondents questions if you want to know what brand of soup they buy, which television programs are viewed, or why a particular store is shopped. Such questions may be asked verbally or in writing, while the responses may be in either form. The data collection instrument used in this process is called a *questionnaire*. The questionnaire has come to be the predominant data collection instrument in marketing research. It is estimated that over half of the United States public has participated in one or more research studies of this nature.[4]

Advantages of the Communication Method　The main advantage of the communication method is its *versatility*. Versatility refers to the ability of the method to collect data on a wide range of information needs. The vast majority of marketing decision problems involve people. Consequently, the information needs focus on people's past behavior, attitudes, and characteristics. The communication method can gather data in all three of these areas.

Additional advantages relate to the *speed* and *cost* of the communication method as compared with the observation method. The speed and cost advantages are highly dependent. The communication method is a faster means of data collection than observation in that it provides more control over the data collection process. The researcher does not have to predict when and where the behavior will occur or wait for it to occur. For example, it would be much faster and cheaper to ask the respondent about the purchase of a dishwasher than to try to anticipate and observe the purchase.

Disadvantages of the Communication Method　There are several important limitations of the communication method. The first relates to the respondent's *unwillingness to provide the desired data*. The respondent may refuse to take the time to be interviewed or refuse to respond to particular questions. The second limitation concerns the respondent's *inability to provide the data*. The respondent may not recall the facts in question or may never have known them to begin with. The final limitation involves the *influence of the questioning process* on the responses. The respondents may bias their responses in order to give a socially acceptable answer or in order to please the interviewer. While the limitations can seriously reduce the validity of the communication method, they can also be controlled by properly designing the data collection instrument.

[4] Frank D. Walker, "Their Opinion Counts," in W. S. Hale (ed.), *Proceedings: 20th Annual Conference* (New York: Advertising Research Foundation, 1974), p. 14.

More will be said in this regard in the following chapter on designing data collection forms.

Communication Techniques Classified by Structure and Directness

There are various ways to classify the data collection techniques which utilize the method of communication. A useful classification scheme is to categorize techniques by their degree of structure and their degree of directness.[5] Figure 18-1 presents the four classes which emerge from this classification scheme: (1) structured, direct; (2) unstructured, direct; (3) unstructured, indirect; and (4) structured, indirect.

Structure refers to the degree of standardization imposed on the data collection process. A formal questionnaire is typically used to bring structure to the data collection process. With a highly structured approach, the questions asked and the responses permitted are completely predetermined. A multiple-choice examination in a marketing research course would be an example of a questionnaire with a high degree of structure. With a highly unstructured data collection approach, the questions to be asked are loosely predetermined and the respondents are encouraged to express their views freely. An intermediate degree of structure would involve standardized questions but an "open-ended" response format.

A direct data collection approach is one where the objective of the study

Figure 18-1 Communication techniques classified by structure and directness.

	Structured	Unstructured
Direct	Survey questionnaire	Focus-group interview Depth interview
Indirect	Performance of objective task technique	Thematic apperception test Role playing Cartoon completion Word association Sentence completion

[5] This classification scheme was first suggested by Donald T. Campbell, "The Indirect Assessment of Social Attitudes," *Psychological Bulletin,* vol. 47, p. 15, January 1950.

is obvious to the respondent from the nature of the questions asked. In contrast, an indirect approach asks questions in a manner that disguises the objective of the study.

Structured-Direct   The most common data collection technique is the structured-direct questionnaire, which requires that the questions be asked with exactly the same wording and in exactly the same sequence for all respondents. This standardization is designed to control response bias by ensuring that the respondents are responding to exactly the same question. The response to a standardized question may require the selection of an alternative from a predetermined set of responses.

Conclusive research projects typically require a structured-direct questionnaire. The standardized questions and fixed-response alternatives can evolve from previous research which used less structured techniques. In addition, the structured questions-and-responses categories usually require extensive pretesting to ensure that the questions measure what they are designed to measure. The structured-direct questionnaire requires extensive time and skill to develop. More will be said in this regard in the following chapter.

There are several advantages of the structured-direct approach,[6] the greatest being administrative simplicity and ease of data processing, analysis, and interpretation. The structured question format is designed to control response bias and increase the reliability of the data. In addition, it can be administered over the telephone, through the mail, and by personal interview.

The disadvantages of the structured-direct approach are the same as the limitations of the communication method: the respondents may not be able to provide the desired data, they may not be willing to provide the data, and the questioning process may bias their responses. In addition, structured questions and fixed-response alternatives may result in loss of validity for certain types of data. If the data required from the respondent are clear-cut, limited in scope, and well known, the structured-fixed alternative question may be very appropriate. However, when the information needs involve exploring the nature of recently formed or evolving beliefs and feelings, the structured approach could seriously influence the validity of the data.

Unstructured-Direct   With the unstructured-direct approach the purpose of the research study is clear to the respondent. There is a great degree of flexibility in how the questions are asked and in the degree of probing. The response format is open-ended, and respondents are encouraged to freely express their beliefs and feeling on the issues presented by the interviewer.

There are two techniques that use the unstructured-direct approach: (1) the focus group interview and (2) the depth interview.[7]

---

[6] Claire Selltiz et al., *Research Methods in Social Relations,* rev. ed. (New York: Holt, 1959), pp. 257–263.

[7] The discussion of these two techniques follows the presentation in D. N. Bellenger, K. L. Bernhardt, and J. L. Goldstucker, *Qualitative Research in Marketing,* Monograph Series No. 3 (Chicago: American Marketing Association, 1976), pp. 7–33.

Exhibit 18-1 Guide for Focus Group Interviews on Automobile Insurance

1 Do you have insurance on your automobile now?
  a (for those who do have it) Why?
    What are the most important reasons why you have automobile insurance?
    What are some other reasons?
    What reasons have you heard—for instance advertising—that you think are *not* important?
    Have you ever driven without insurance?
    How did that happen?
    Would you do it again?
    What do the others in the group think? Would they do it?
  b (for those not carrying insurance) Why not?
    Have you ever had it?
    Why did you drop it?
    Do you expect to get some? When?
2 Turn the discussion to types of auto insurance coverage.
  a What is collision insurance? (Try to get the group to define it, but make sure they know that it means insurance that pays for damage to the owner's car as a result of an accident, no matter whose fault.)
    Do you have collision insurance?
    Why? (probe)—Have you ever had it? (if yes) Why did you drop it?
    Do you expect to get it again?
    (Encourage discussion between those who do have it and those who don't on the merits of this type of insurance.)
  b (repeat the preceding discussion for):
    Liability Insurance (Bodily Injury and Property Damage)—that which pays for damage done by a driver to other cars or property or to other people. Comprehensive Insurance (Fire, Theft, etc.)—that which pays for loss or damage to a car as a result of fire, theft, natural hazards, vandalism, etc. Medical Payments Insurance—that which pays medical expenses of guests in the car.

Source: J. W. Newman, *Motivation Research and Marketing Management* (Boston: Harvard Business School, Division of Research, 1957), p. 130. Used with permission of the Harvard Business School, Division of Research.

Focus Group Interview The focus group interview, or group depth interview, is one of the most frequently used techniques in marketing research. It can be defined as *a loosely structured interview conducted by a trained moderator among a small number of respondents simultaneously*. This technique has its origins in the group therapy methods used by psychiatrists. While the interview does require a preinterview organization of topics or interviewer guide, the setting emphasizes flexibility, and the value of the technique lies in discovering the unexpected which results from a free-flowing group discussion. Exhibit 18-1 presents an example of a focus group interviewer guide.

Focus group interviews can be used for a number of different purposes. Recent interviews with researchers suggest the following uses:[8]

[8] Ibid., pp. 18–19.

1   To generate hypotheses that can be further tested quantitatively

2   To generate information helpful in structuring consumer questionnaires

3   To provide overall background information on a product category

4   To get impressions on new product concepts for which there is little information available

5   To stimulate new ideas about older products

6   To generate ideas for new creative concepts

7   To interpret previously obtained quantitative results

The respondent group should be composed of people with fairly homogeneous characteristics. One organization, which conducts approximately 600 focus groups per year, avoids combining full-time married homemakers with children at home and unmarried working women, because their life-styles and objectives are substantially different. They also avoid grouping men and women together as well as teenagers and younger children.[9] Thus, it is important to maintain as much homogeneity or commonality among group members as possible. This avoids interactions and conflicts among group members on issues not relevant to the study objectives.

The size of the group can be as many as 10 or 12 people for consumer goods research. Experience suggests that a group with less than 8 people results in the discussion being dominated by a few respondents, and having more than 12 people tends to diminish the opportunity for some respondents to participate. It is argued that for non–consumer goods research (architects, doctors, industrial purchasers, engineers, investors, contractors, etc.) 6 or 7 people may be best for maximum interaction among participants.

With regard to the selection of respondents, most researchers believe that careful screening is essential to the success of the focus group interview. First, the group members must have had adequate experience with the object or issue being discussed. Second, those respondents who have previously participated in a group session should not be included a second time. Some research organizations allow the respondents to participate a second time if they have not participated in a session within the last year. The reason for this rule is that former participants often play the role of expert by dominating the discussion and trying to "show off" for the first-time participants.

Another issue in respondent selection relates to allowing people to participate in a group which contains a relative, neighbor, or friend. Since friends sometimes tend to talk to each other and not to the whole group, many researchers will not select respondents from church groups or other organizations where participants have established relationships.

Most researchers believe the physical setting to be very important to the effectiveness of the group session. The atmosphere should encourage a relaxed feeling and one where informal and spontaneous comments are encouraged. It

[9] Myril D. Axelrod, "10 Essentials for Good Qualitative Research," *Marketing News,* March 14, 1975, p. 10.

is best to establish a "coffee klatsch" or "bull session" atmosphere in this regard.

A living room environment is considered more appropriate than a conference board room setting, which may inhibit many of the respondents or encourage them to play the role of expert. While a living room in a private home is ideal, most research organizations have participants come to a central facility which has a specially designed laboratory furnished like a comfortable, but not elaborate, living room. The advantage of a laboratory lies in the availability of facilities for recording the session and for allowing the client to indirectly observe the group session in process.

How long is a group session? The typical focus group interview lasts 1½ to 2 hours. This period of time is needed to establish rapport with the respondents and explore in depth their beliefs, feelings, ideas, and insights regarding the discussion topic.

The number of group sessions to be conducted depends on the nature of the issue at hand, the number of market segments involved, and the time and cost constraints of the project. Typically the researcher must concentrate the group session on those segments most critical to the topic being considered. It is very desirable to replicate the focus group session for each market segment being studied.

Clients frequently observe the focus group session, and it is better to have this done from behind a two-way mirror rather than to have the client present in the room with the participants. The client can let the moderator know during short breaks in the session if there are areas needing more exploration. This detached location of the client avoids the danger of disruptions of the group session by having the participants observe the client's reactions or note taking.

The moderator's role is of prime importance to the success of the focus group technique. Highly skilled moderators are required to ensure that proper respondent rapport is established, that the discussion is directed along relevant dimensions, and that the degree of probing and depth of insight are sufficient to accomplish the research objectives. In addition, the moderator is central to the analysis and interpretation of the data. Great skill, experience, knowledge of the discussion topic, and intuitive insights regarding the nature of group dynamics are required to accomplish this task. Consequently, the moderator is often a trained psychologist who has developed special moderator skills through intensive study and practice.

The moderator's skill is clearly demonstrated by the ability to maintain a high degree of interaction among group members. Unskilled moderators typically find themselves conducting individual interviews with each of the participants rather than stimulating interaction within the group. Only with interaction can the group interview (1) provide the desired spontaneity of response by participants, (2) produce the degree of emotional involvement essential to produce "depth"-level responses, and (3) produce the kind and degree of rapport which facilitates a "give and take" exchange of attitudinal and behavioral information.[10]

---

[10] Bellenger et al., op. cit., pp. 12–16.

The key qualifications for moderators are:[11]

1 *Kindness with firmness*—In order to elicit necessary interaction, the moderator must combine a disciplined detachment with understanding empathy.

2 *Permissiveness*—While an atmosphere of permissiveness is desirable, the moderator must be at all times alert to indications that the group atmosphere of cordiality is disintegrating.

3 *Involvement*—Since a principal reason for the group interview is to expose feelings and to obtain reactions indicative of deeper feelings, the moderator must encourage and stimulate intensive personal involvement.

4 *Incomplete understanding*—A most useful skill of the group moderator is his or her ability to convey lack of complete understanding of the information being presented.

5 *Encouragement*—Although the dynamics of the group situation facilitate the participation of all members in the interaction, there may be individuals who resist contributing.

6 *Flexibility*—The moderator should be equipped prior to the session with a topic outline of the subject matter to be covered. By committing the topics to memory before the interview, the moderator may use the outline only as a reminder of content areas omitted or covered incompletely.

7 *Sensitivity*—The moderator must be able to identify, as the group interview progresses, the informational level on which it is being conducted, and determine if it is appropriate for the subject under discussion. Sensitive areas will frequently produce superficial rather than depth responses. Depth is achieved when there is a substantial amount of emotional response, as opposed to intellectual information. Indications of depth are provided when participants begin to indicate how they feel about the subject, rather than what they think about it.

Does the sex of the moderator influence the effectiveness of the group session? There are two views in this regard. This first holds that the sex of the moderator should be the same as that of the group members to ensure proper rapport. The second view is that the sex of the moderator should be different from that of the group members. The argument is that the participants will not assume that the moderator knows what they are discussing and will be more explanatory in their responses.

What special techniques can the moderator use in running a group session? When one person tries to dominate the discussion, the moderator can stop the proceedings and poll each participant regarding the issue at hand. This technique is also useful to encourage the shy person to express a viewpoint and participate in the discussion. At the close of the session, each person can be asked to summarize what the group has resolved. Another useful technique is to call each of the participants a day or so after the completed session and have them express their viewpoints again. Many times viewpoints change due to passage of time or more reflective thinking on the issues.

[11] Donald A. Chase, "The Intensive Group Interview in Marketing," *MRA Viewpoints,* 1973.

Should the same moderator be involved in all group sessions on the topic? Most researchers believe so. With each session the moderator becomes more effective and gains additional insights as to the analysis and interpretation of the sessions.

The major advantage of the focus group interview rests on the premise that if you want to understand your consumers, you have to listen to them. There is much to be gained from listening to consumers describe a product in their own vernacular, and from having them portray how they buy products and how they perceive product benefits and limitations, using highly personalized terms. Data such as these can bring insight to potential problems and opportunities and can identify possible marketing program strategies that have not occurred to the manager.

When compared with other data collection techniques, the focus group interview has these specific advantages:[12]

1. *Synergism:* The combined effect of the group will produce a wider range of information, insight, and ideas than will the cumulation of the responses of a number of individuals when these replies are secured privately.

2. *Snowballing:* A bandwagon effect often operates in a group interview situation in that a comment by one individual often triggers a chain of responses from the other participants.

3. *Stimulation:* Usually after a brief introductory period the respondents get "turned on" in that they want to express their ideas and expose their feelings as the general level of excitement over the topic increases in the group.

4. *Security:* The participants can usually find comfort in the group in that their feelings are not greatly different from other participants and they are more willing to express their ideas and feelings.

5. *Spontaneity:* Since individuals aren't required to answer any given question in a group interview, their responses can be more spontaneous and less conventional, and should provide a more accurate picture of their position on some issues.

6. *Serendipity:* It is more often the case in a group rather than individual interview that some idea will "drop out of the blue."

7. *Specialization:* The group interview allows the use of a more highly trained, but more expensive, interviewer since a number of individuals are being "interviewed" simultaneously.

8. *Scientific scrutiny:* The group interview allows closer scrutiny of the data collection process in that several observers can witness the session and it can be recorded for later playback and analysis.

9. *Structure:* The group interview affords more flexibility than the individual interview with regard to the topics covered and the depth with which they are treated.

10. *Speed:* Since a number of individuals are being interviewed at the same time, the group interview speeds up the data collection and analysis process.

[12] John M. Hess, "Group Interviewing," in R. L. King (ed.), *New Science of Planning* (Chicago: American Marketing Association, 1968), p. 194.

The focus group interview is an exploratory research technique which can be extremely valuable in developing hypotheses regarding problems and opportunities, facilitating the development of a clear statement of the decision problem, and stimulating the creative process designed to formulate alternative courses of action. Conclusive research is the next logical step in the testing of these hypotheses and the evaluation of the courses of action. In special circumstances, the decision maker's experience and judgment may be sufficient for a course of action to be selected without gathering conclusive research evidence. Most typically, however, such evidence is required, and the decision maker would be making a serious error to assume that the focus group interview could provide evidence of a conclusive nature.

We have just touched upon a major disadvantage of the focus group interview, namely, that the decision maker cannot use the evidence in a conclusive research manner. The evidence is not projectable to a target segment for two reasons. First, the sample is not representative of the target segment in the sense that quantitative statements can be made regarding the significance of the research findings. Second, the evidence itself is highly dependent upon the experience and perception of the moderator and other observers. The danger is that the decision maker may use the exploratory findings as conclusive evidence to support preconceived notions about the decision situation.

As in any area of human endeavor, there are individuals who will compromise proper research procedures for personal gain. With the focus group interview, these improper procedures involve poor recruitment of participants, poor physical environment, and an unskilled moderator.

Depth Interview The depth interview may be defined as an *unstructured personal interview which uses extensive probing to get a single respondent to talk freely and to express detailed beliefs and feelings on a topic.* The purpose of this technique is to get below the respondent's surface reactions and discover the more fundamental reasons underlying the respondent's attitudes and behavior.

The depth interview can extend over an hour or more with the interviewer typically committing to memory the outline of topics to be covered. The actual wording of questions and their sequencing are left to the discretion of the interviewer, who tries to identify general areas for discussion and then encourages the respondent to discuss freely, in depth, the topic of interest. The interviewer will probe responses that are of interest by asking such questions as "That's interesting, can you tell me more?" and "Why do you say that?"

While not an active participant in the discussion, the interviewer has a critical role in the success of the depth interview technique. It is the interviewer's responsibility to create an environment where the respondent is relaxed and free to present beliefs and feelings without fear of criticism or lack of understanding. As in the focus group interview, the interviewer's role is central to the success of this technique.

The advantage of the depth interview over the focus group interview relates to the greater depth of insight that can be uncovered and the ability to associate the response directly with the respondent. With the focus group interview it is difficult to determine which respondent made a particular response. In addition, the interviewer can develop a high level of rapport with the respondent, which results in a freer exchange of responses than may be possible with the focus group technique.

As with the focus group interview, the primary use of the depth interview is exploratory research. The technique is useful in developing hypotheses, defining decision problems, and formulating courses of action.

The depth interview is seldom used in marketing research. The disadvantages of the technique contribute to its limited use, and its success rests entirely with the skills and experience of the interviewer. Since there are few adequately qualified interviewers and those who are qualified are highly paid, the technique has not experienced wide acceptance as a regular research tool. The length of the interview combined with the high interviewer cost means that the number of persons interviewed in a project is small. The small sample size and the complete reliance on the interviewer for analysis and interpretation are important limitations that restrict this technique's use to special problem situations.

Unstructured, Indirect   Unstructured-indirect data collection techniques are called *projective techniques*. They come from clinical psychology and are designed to obtain data indirectly about respondents' beliefs and feelings. Structured-direct data collection techniques presume that the respondents clearly understand their beliefs and feelings and are willing to communicate these data directly. However, in certain situations, this may not be the case. Projective techniques are designed to explore the "whys" of behavior. A projective technique can be defined as any indirect form of questioning in which an environment is created which encourages the respondent to freely project beliefs and feelings regarding the topic of interest.

Projective techniques require the respondents to interpret the behavior of others, rather than directly asking them to report their beliefs and feelings. In interpreting the behavior of others, the respondents are indirectly projecting their own beliefs and feelings into the situation.

While the majority of projective techniques are easily administered and interpreted, their use in marketing research has been limited to special situations where attitudes cannot be directly measured. The most commonly found in marketing research are (1) the Thematic Apperception Test, (2) role playing, (3) cartoon completion, (4) word association, and (5) sentence completion.

Thematic Apperception Test   The Thematic Apperception Test (TAT)[13] is the most frequently used projective technique in marketing research. TAT involves use of one or more pictures or cartoons which depict a situation relating to the product or topic under investigation. The cartoon format is most frequently used. The pictures or cartoons are neutral, in that few clues as to positive or

---

[13] "Thematic" stands for themes that are elicited, and "apperception" stands for the perceptual-interpretative use of pictures.

negative feelings are present in the situation. The respondent is presented with this ambiguous situation and asked to describe what has happened or what will happen as a result of the situation. This leaves the respondent free to indirectly project personal beliefs and feelings into the interpretation of what is happening.

Role Playing   Role playing, or the third-person technique, presents the respondent with either a verbal or visual situation. Rather than directly expressing personal beliefs and feelings regarding the situation, the respondent is asked to relate the beliefs and feelings of another person to the situation. This third person can be a friend, a neighbor, or a "typical" person. In describing the reaction of others, it is believed, the respondent will reveal personal beliefs and feelings regarding the situation.

A popular version of this technique is to provide the respondent with a description of what a person has purchased and ask the respondent to characterize that person. It is assumed that the respondent's beliefs and feelings toward the products on the list will be reflected in the description of the purchaser.[14]

Cartoon Completion   The cartoon completion technique presents the respondent with a cartoon drawing containing one or more people in a particular situation. The respondent is asked to complete a cartoon in response to the comment of another cartoon character. The cartoon captions are typically depicted with a bubble next to the cartoon character. Examples are: "My friend bought a digital watch," "We are planning to purchase a microwave oven," "Our neighbors purchased a foreign car," and the like.

Word Association   The word association technique consists of presenting a series of words to the respondent, who is required to call out each time the first word that comes to mind in response.

The words read to the respondent are carefully selected and sequenced to reveal his or her beliefs and feelings. A version of this procedure is to ask the respondent to quickly give as many single words as possible in response to each word presented by the interviewer.

Word association tests are analyzed by the frequency with which a response is given, by the amount of hesitation in responding, and by the number of respondents who cannot respond to a test word after a reasonable time period. The common responses are analyzed to reveal patterns of beliefs and feelings. Respondents who hesitate are assumed to be sufficiently emotionally involved that an immediate response is delayed. Nonresponse is assumed to indicate a very high level of emotional involvement.

Sentence Completion   The sentence completion test is similar to the word association test and requires the respondent to finish an incomplete sentence. The beginning phrase is read to the respondent, who is asked to complete the sentence. The meaning of the beginning phrase is disguised such that there is no correct response. The respondent is instructed to reply with the first thoughts that come to mind, and the responses are analyzed for their content. Since this

---

[14] Mason Haire, "Projective Techniques in Marketing Research," *Journal of Marketing*, vol. 14, pp. 649–656, April 1950; see also C. R. Hill, "Haire's Classic Instant Coffee Study—18 Years Later," *Journalism Quarterly*, vol. 45, pp. 466–472, August 1968.

test requires more thought in the responses, it is argued that it provides better results than the word association test.

Projective techniques, like the depth interview, have significant disadvantages which contribute to their limited use in marketing research. Since they typically require personal interviews using highly skilled interviewers and interpreters to analyze the data, they tend to be a very expensive research tool. The high cost per respondent interviewed has resulted in the use of small nonprobability sample sizes, which result in high sampling errors. Projective techniques are complex and can be highly misleading in the hands of an amateur.[15]

Despite these limitations, projective techniques have been found to be useful in many situations.[16] Their proper use still lies in exploratory research designed to discover hypotheses to be tested using more structured and direct research techniques.

Structured-Indirect The structured-indirect approach is often called the *performance of objective task technique*. Respondents are asked to memorize and/or report factual information about the topic of interest. These responses are analyzed and inferences are drawn about the nature of the respondents' underlying beliefs and feelings regarding the topic.

The central assumption of this technique is that respondents are more likely to recall those things which are consistent with their beliefs and feelings. Presumably greater knowledge reflects the strength and direction of the other attitude components. This contention is based on research findings regarding selective information processing, findings which indicate that people tend to (1) selectively expose themselves to information, (2) selectively perceive the information, and (3) selectively retain information which is consistent with their attitudes. Consequently, asking respondents to recall factual information about a topic is a way to indirectly measure the direction and strength of their attitudes. Those respondents who possess the most knowledge regarding product X are assumed to have highly positive attitudes toward the product.

The structured-indirect approach is rarely used in marketing research. It represents an attempt to gain the advantages of indirect attitude measurement with the data collection and processing advantages of structured approaches. Whether the measurement of factual information is a valid indicator of the direction and strength of the underlying attitude structure is a subject of concern to many researchers.

Communication Media

The previous section classified communication techniques on the basis of a combination of structure and directness. Another classification scheme focuses on the types of communication media available for obtaining data from respond-

---

[15] P. Sampson, "Qualitative Research and Motivation Research," in R. M. Worcester (ed.), *Consumer Market Research Handbook* [London: McGraw-Hill (U.K.), 1972], pp. 7–28.
[16] H. L. Steck, "On the Validity of Projective Questions," *Journal of Marketing Research*, vol. 1, pp. 48–49, August 1964.

ents. Three communication media are available: (1) personal interview, (2) telephone interview, and (3) mail interview.

Structured communication techniques can use all three of these. Nonstructured techniques typically require the personal interview. The telephone interview has been used successfully with the focus group technique, using a conference call arrangement with, say, doctors at various geographic locations. Telephone and mail interviews do not usually lend themselves well to unstructured techniques.

Personal Interview   The personal interview consists of an interviewer asking questions of one or more respondents in a face-to-face situation. The interviewer's task is to contact the respondent(s), ask the questions, and record the responses. The questions must be asked in a clear manner and recorded accurately. The recording of responses can take place either during or after the interview.

The face-to-face interviewing process may cause the respondents to bias their responses (for example, because of desire to please or impress the interviewer).[17] This potential for social motives to bias personal interview data will be discussed in more detail in the section on criteria for selecting a communciation medium.

Telephone Interview   The telephone interview consists of an interviewer asking questions of one or more respondents via the telephone instead of by direct personal contact. Telephone interviewing is the most widely used of the three communication media.[18] The reasons for its popularity are its efficient and economical procedures and its application to a wide range of information needs.

With the telephone interview, the lower degree of social interaction between the interviewer and respondent reduces the potential for bias in comparison with the personal interview. The basic limitations of the telephone interview relate to the limited amount of data that can be obtained and the potential bias that can result from an incomplete listing of the target population (i.e., unlisted telephones and non–phone ownership).

Mail Interview   The mail interview consists of a questionnaire mailed to the respondent and the return by mail of the completed questionnaire to the research organization. It is as popular as the personal interview but less so than the telephone interview.[19]

Mail interviews are flexible in their application and relatively low in cost, and they lack the potential for bias resulting from the interview-respondent interaction. The major disadvantage relates to the problem of nonresponse error.

Many approaches can be used to distribute and collect the questionnaire.

---

[17] J. B. Lansing and J. N. Morgan, *Economic Survey Methods* (Ann Arbor: The University of Michigan Press, 1971), p. 160.

[18] Walker, "Their Opinion Counts," p. 15.

[19] Ibid.

It can be left and/or retrieved by an individual rather than using the mail.[20] It can be distributed in magazines and newspapers. Warranty cards can be attached to products and data collected regarding the characteristics of the purchaser and the purchase decision process.

Criteria for Selecting Communication Media

Several criteria are relevant for evaluating which communication media best meet the needs of a research project, namely: (1) versatility, (2) cost, (3) time, (4) sample control, (5) quantity of data, (6) quality of data, and (7) response rate. The importance assigned these criteria will vary with the specific needs of the research project.

Versatility   The personal interview is the most versatile of the three communication media. Telephone interviews are less versatile than personal interviews, while the mail interview is the least versatile. Versatility refers to the ability of the medium to adapt the data collection process to the special needs of the study or the respondent.

The personal interview has high versatility in that the interviewing process involves a face-to-face relationship between the respondent and interviewer. The latter can explain and clarify complex questions, administer complex questionnaires, utilize unstructured techniques, and present visual cues such as advertisements and product concepts to the respondent as part of the questioning process. The telephone interview is not as versatile as the personal interview in that the interviewer is not in a face-to-face relationship with the respondent. Consequently, it is more difficult to use unstructured techniques, to include complex questions, and to require in-depth answers to open-ended questions. When the research design involves structured questions with simple instructions which can be answered easily by the respondent, the interviewer's role can often be eliminated, and the mail interview may be the more appropriate medium for the study.

The researcher must determine the degree of versatility required in a research project and select the communication media which best meet the needs of the study. In practice, most research projects do not require the high versatility that the personal interview provides.

Cost   The number of hours of labor tends to determine the relative cost of the three communication media. Labor costs include the salaries of the interviewers and the supervisory costs associated with controlling the quality of the data collection process.

The personal interview is typically the most expensive medium per completed interview. Telephone interviews are usually more expensive than those conducted by mail. When the questionnaire is short, the cost of the telephone interview usually compares with that of the mail interview.

[20] R. V. Stover and W. J. Stone, "Hand Delivery of Self-Administered Questionnaires," *Public Opinion Quarterly,* vol. 38, pp. 284–287, Summer 1974.

While the cost of a communication medium is highly dependent upon the specific details of the research design, a general estimate of data collection cost per completed interview would be as follows: (1) personal interview—$5 to $25, (2) telephone interview—$3 to $12, and (3) mail interview—$3 to $10.[21]

Time   Among the three communication media, the telephone interview is the fastest way to obtain data. With a short questionnaire, an interviewer can complete perhaps 10 or more interviews per hour. Using the same questionnaire, a personal interviewer would be fortunate to complete two or three interviews per hour. Obviously the travel time between interviews represents a serious time constraint on the personal interviewer's completion rate. Consequently, personal interview studies are typically longer in elapsed time from the beginning of field work to project completion than telephone or mail interview studies.

The total project completion time can be shortened by increasing the number of interviewers working on the study when the personal or telephone interview is used. With the telephone interview it is reasonably easy to train, coordinate, and control the staff of interviewers.[22] Since the interviewing staff can phone from a central location, the project supervisor can easily monitor the interviews and control the quality of the interviewing. Consequently, a large interviewing force can be efficiently used with telephone interviewing to meet the time constraint placed on a research project.

While the number of personal interviewers can also be increased to meet the time constraints placed on a project, the problems associated with training, coordinating, and controlling a large interviewing staff are compounded very fast to a point where it is neither feasible nor economical to increase the number of interviewers on the project. Consequently, personal interview studies are typically longer in elapsed time than mail or telephone studies.

It is very difficult to shorten the elapsed time for completing a mail study. Once the questionnaires are mailed, there is little the researcher can do to speed their completion and return. Typically, it takes two or three weeks to secure the bulk of the replies. A series of follow-up mailings may be required to stimulate the return of the remaining questionnaires. Each follow-up mailing may require two or more weeks to determine whether an acceptable response rate is going to be achieved. While several months could be required to complete a mail study, if the number of interviews to be completed is large, the elapsed time may not be as great as that required to conduct a similar study using personal interviews.

Sample Control   Sample control refers to the ability of the communication media *to reach the designated units in the sampling plan effectively and efficiently.* The three communication media differ significantly in this regard.

The personal interview offers the best degree of sample control. As discussed

[21] The cost per interview, which includes data collection, analysis, and report, would be: (1) personal interview—$20 to $50, (2) telephone interview—$6 to $20, and (3) mail interview—$6 to $18.

[22] J. O. Eastlack, Jr., and H. Assael, "Better Telephone Surveys through Centralized Interviewing," *Journal of Advertising Research,* vol. 6. pp. 2–7, March 1966.

in Chapter 10, area sampling procedures exist which overcome the problems created by the absence of a complete listing of the sampling frame. The sampling frame is the list of population units from which the sample will be drawn. Sampling procedures which do not require a list of the sampling units rely heavily upon the personal interviewer in the process of selecting the sample. Working through the personal interviewer, the researcher can control which sampling units are interviewed, who is interviewed, the degree of participation of other members of the unit in the interview, and many other aspects of the data collection process.

The telephone interview is highly dependent upon a sampling frame. One or more telephone directories usually serve as the sampling frame, with respondents being selected from directories serving the population of interest using probabilistic selection procedures.

Telephone directories are often poor sampling frames in that they are an incomplete listing of persons in an area. This incomplete listing can result from three situations: (1) not everyone has a phone, (2) phone directories are old and do not reflect new phones in service since the directory was published, and (3) some people have unlisted phones.

Telephone ownership in the United States is very high. In 1971 it was estimated that 93 percent of households had telephones.[23] Telephone ownership is near 100 percent in most areas of the country, with the exception of central cities, low-income areas, and rural areas. Consequently, phone ownership is typically not a serious problem for most telephone studies.

In some areas, estimates as to the percentage of phones not listed in new phone directories run as high as 30 percent.[24] This can be a serious source of bias, since recent research indicates that persons with voluntary unlisted numbers differ from persons with listed phone numbers on a number of important demographic characteristics.[25]

As telephone directories grow older, an increasing proportion of persons who have moved to the area do not have an opportunity to list their phone in the current directory. Since persons who move frequently differ from less mobile persons on a number of demographic characteristics, older phone directories become less representative of the population of phone owners.

Due to the problem of unrepresentative phone directories, the telephone interview permits only limited control over the sample. A recent procedure designed to overcome this problem is called *random-digit dialing*.[26] This pro-

---

[23] *Statistical Abstract of the United States,* 1973, 94th ed. (U.S. Bureau of the Census, 1973), p. 496.

[24] G. J. Glasser and G. D. Metzger, "Random-Digit Dialing As a Method of Telephone Sampling," *Journal of Marketing Research,* vol. 9, pp. 59–64, February 1972.

[25] J. A. Brunner and G. A. Brunner, "Are Voluntary Unlisted Telephone Subscribers Really Different?" *Journal of Marketing Research,* vol. 8, pp. 121–124, February 1971; S. Roslow and L. Roslow, "Unlisted Phone Subscribers Are Different," *Journal of Advertising Research,* vol. 12, pp. 35–38, August 1972.

[26] S. Sudman, "The Uses of Telephone Directories for Survey Sampling," *Journal of Marketing Research,* vol. 10, pp. 204–207, May 1973; M. Hauck and M. Cox, "Locating a Sample by Random Digit Dialing," *Public Opinion Quarterly,* vol. 38, pp. 253–260, Summer 1974.

cedure involves the random generation of at least some of the digits used in the sampling plan. A central interviewing facility can be used to place calls, using the Wide Area Telephone Service (WATS).[27] This procedure allows a geographically wide sampling plan. However, even with these improved procedures, telephone surveys still rely on simple random sampling or systematic sampling. As discussed in the sampling chapters, alternate sampling procedures exist which are more efficient than either of these.

The mail interview, like the telephone interview, requires a listing of the population elements. Ideally, this frame is composed of both names and addresses. Typically, telephone street directories are used for a listing of the general population. The problems in the use of this type of list have already been discussed.

Several commercial research firms have panels of respondents who have agreed to answer mail questionnaires sent to them. Such an organization is National Family Opinion (NFO). This firm maintains a panel of over 150,000 United States families who have agreed to cooperate without compensation in completing questionnaires mailed to them on a variety of subjects. A current demographic profile is maintained for each family. Other organizations which maintain mail panels are the Home Testing Institute and Market Facts, Inc.

Mailing lists for specialized groups of respondents can be purchased from firms that specialize in this area. Catalogs are available which contain thousands of lists, many of which can be segmented in various ways.[28] Even with a mailing list that contains the target population, the researcher still has the problem of limited control over the person or persons at the mailing address who complete the questionnaire, as well as whether it will be returned.

Quantity of Data   An established rule is that the largest amount of data can be collected using the personal interview, followed by the mail interview, and then the telephone interview. There is growing evidence that the mail and telephone interview can collect more data than previously assumed. In situations where the respondents are emotionally involved in the topic, all three media can provide substantial amounts of data. At normal involvement levels, however, the personal interview can collect substantially more data than the other two.

The main advantage of the personal interview stems from the social relationship between the interviewer and the respondent. This social setting typically motivates the respondent to spend more time in the interview setting. The University of Michigan Survey Research Center finds that a 75-minute interview is feasible with the personal interview, while the telephone interviews must be limited to 30 or 40 minutes.[29] It is much easier for the respondent to terminate the telephone or mail interview, because of their impersonal nature, than is the case with the personal interview.

An advantage of the personal and telephone interview over the mail interview

[27] Eastlack and Assael, op. cit.

[28] 1973–1974 *Catalog of Mailing Lists* (New York: Fritz S. Hofheimer, Inc., 1972).

[29] Personal communication with Richard T. Curtin, Director, Surveys of Consumer Attitudes, Survey Research Center, University of Michigan.

is that less effort is required of the respondent in the data collection process. Here, the interviewer asks the questions, probes the responses, and records the answers. The personal interview has the added advantage of allowing the visual presentation of rating scale categories and other support material that can facilitate the respondent's comprehension of the questions asked. These advantages all contribute to the respondent's willingness to provide a greater quantity of data.

Quality of Data   Quality of data refers to the degree to which the data are *free from potential bias resulting from the use of a particular communication medium.* When the subject matter is unemotional and the questionnaire is properly designed and administered, quality data will generally result regardless of which medium is used.

Researchers have found substantial differences among the three media when sensitive or embarrassing questions are involved, e.g., bank loans, income, or sexual behavior. For sensitive topics, there is evidence that mail surveys collect better-quality data than personal interviews.[30] Telephone interviews most likely would lie between these two media.

Another source of bias can result from respondent confusion regarding the question asked. Since the respondent cannot seek clarification from the interviewer with the mail interview, it offers the greatest chance for inaccurate results resulting from confusion. The telephone interview would offer more potential for bias from confusion than the personal interview because of the lack of an interviewer's physical presence.

The mail interview has another potential bias which can result from the respondent's reading through the questions before answering them or changing answers earlier in the questionnaire as a result of responses given later in the questionnaire. Both the personal and telephone interview are not subject to this type of bias.

The quality of data obtained in telephone interviews tends to be better than from personal interviews in that the data collection process can be better supervised and controlled. Fewer interviewers are needed for the telephone survey, and they can be trained and supervised at a central location.

Both the telephone and personal interview have an important advantage over the mail interview in that they can be used to collect data near the time the behavior occurs. This reduces the bias associated with failure to recall events accurately.

A final consideration regarding the quality of data obtained concerns cheating by the interviewer. Cheating is easier with the personal interview, since the phone interview can be directly monitored and the former cannot. Since the mail interview does not have an interviewer, it is not subject to bias resulting from

---

[30] B. Dunning and D. Cahalan, "By Mail versus Field Self-Administered Questionnaires: An Armed Forces Survey," *Public Opinion Quarterly,* vol. 34, pp. 618—624, Winter 1973-74; F. Wiseman, "Methodological Bias in Public Opinion Surveys," *Public Opinion Quarterly,* vol. 36, pp. 105–108, Spring 1972.

Table 18-2   Median Income Variation by Number of Callbacks

Number of call at which interviewed	Median Income	Number of interviews
1	$4188	427
2	5880	391
3	6010	232
4	6200	123
5	6010	77
6+	7443	59
All	$5598	1309

Source: J. B. Lansing and J. N. Morgan, *Economic Survey Methods* (Ann Arbor: The University of Michigan Press, 1971), p. 161. Used with permission of the University of Michigan Press.

cheating. Properly designed personal interview studies have procedures for controlling cheating which can be effective in minimizing this source of bias.

Response Rate   Response rate refers to the percentage of the original sample that is actually interviewed. A low response rate can result in a high nonresponse error, which can invalidate the research findings. Nonresponse error refers to the difference between those who respond to a survey and those who do not respond.

Nonresponse error is one of the most serious sources of error confronting the researcher.[31] Table 18-2 illustrates the type of difference that can exist between those who respond and those who do not respond. The median income of respondents for each of a series of callback interviews is shown. A policy of no callbacks (median income of $4,188) would have produced an estimate of income 25 percent below that found after extensive callbacks (median income of $5,598). This finding represents a clear example of nonresponse error.

The probability of nonresponse error increases the lower the survey response rate. However, it is important to recognize that a low response rate in itself does not imply that a high nonresponse error is present in the data. It is only when there is a difference between respondents and nonrespondents on the variables of interest that nonresponse error occurs. If the reason for nonresponse is independent of the key variables of interest, there should be little difference between the respondent and nonrespondent groups.

Nonresponse can result from two sources: (1) not-at-homes and (2) refusals. Nonresponse caused by the respondent not being at home can seriously affect telephone and personal interviews, but it has limited influence on mail surveys. Since respondents are more likely to answer a phone than answer the door when a stranger is present, the telephone interview has less of a not-at-home problem than the personal interview.

[31] P. Ognibene, "Traits Affecting Questionnaire Response," *Journal of Advertising Research,* vol. 10, pp. 18–20, June 1970; R. L. Day and J. B. Wilcox, "A Simulation Analysis of Nonresponse Error in Survey Sampling," in F. C. Allvine (ed.), *Relevance in Marketing: Marketing in Motion* (Chicago: American Marketing Association, 1971), pp. 478–483.

Once a potential respondent has informed the interviewer of an unwillingness to be interviewed, there is little that can be done to reverse the respondent's position. While the offer to call at another time may be favorably received by some respondents, the majority still refuse the interview.

While the mail interview avoids the nonresponse caused by not-at-homes, it is seriously influenced by the refusal to respond. However, the failure to complete and return the questionnaire on time does not imply a strong unwillingness to respond. Many respondents may be influenced to respond if reminded.

The major emphasis on reducing nonresponse in personal and telephone interviews centers on establishing contact with the potential respondent. A series of callbacks is required to reduce the proportion of not-at-homes.[32] Most situations require a minimum of three callbacks. The callback schedule should be varied by time of day and days of the week. An excellent guide for scheduling telephone and personal interviews is provided by the Bureau of the Census.[33] This study provides estimates of the proportion of people at home between 8:00 A.M. and 9:00 P.M. on an hourly basis.

The reduction of nonresponse in mail surveys focuses on motivating the respondent to answer the questionnaire and return it. The response rate of the mail interview is directly related to the respondent's interest in the survey topic.[34] If the target population's interest in the survey topic varies, a serious source of nonresponse error can be introduced to the results.

Some of the more successful ways to increase the response rate of mail surveys are as follows:[35]

1 Use an advance letter or telephone call notifying the respondent of the study and requesting cooperation.
2 Use first-class postage in mailing to the respondent and provide hand-stamped return envelopes.
3 Consider the use of a monetary incentive in those situations where motivation needs to be stimulated.
4 Use a postcard or letter in follow-up contacts requesting completion and return of the questionnaire. Other follow-ups include phone contacts, telegraph, a new questionnaire, and personal contact.

A five-step procedure for securing returns to mail surveys has been proposed by Robin.[36] These steps include (1) a prequestionnaire letter, (2) a questionnaire with cover letter, (3) a follow-up letter, (4) a second questionnaire, and (5) a third

[32] W. C. Dunkelberg and G. S. Day, "Nonresponse Bias and Callbacks in Sample Surveys," *Journal of Marketing Research*, vol. 10, p. 160, May 1973.
[33] Bureau of the Census, *Who's Home When* (Government Printing Office, 1973).
[34] R. F. Mautz and F. L. Neumann, "The Effective Corporate Audit Committee," *Harvard Business Review*, vol. 48, p. 58, November-December 1970.
[35] For an expanded discussion of this topic which includes an extensive series of references, see Donald S. Tull and Del I. Hawkins, *Marketing Research* (New York: Macmillan, 1976), pp. 391–394.
[36] S. S. Robin, "A Procedure for Securing Returns to Mail Questionnaires," *Sociology and Social Research*, vol. 50, pp. 24–35, October 1965.

follow-up letter. A seven-day interval between mailings is recommended.[37] A 77.8 percent response rate has been achieved using this five-step procedure in a mail survey to dentists.[38]

Mail surveys which are conducted by experienced researchers should achieve response rates over 50 percent, and some surveys achieve rates as high as 80 percent. An 80 percent response rate is suggested as the standard for mail surveys by the Advertising Research Foundation.[39] In practice, most fall substantially below this rate. A mail survey which achieves an 80 percent return rate is very comparable to many personal and telephone interview studies in the proportion of completed interviews.

For all three communication media, the decision regarding the number of callbacks involves weighing the benefits of reduced nonresponse error against the additional cost of the callback campaign. The central issue is: "How different is the nonrespondent group from the respondent group?" Several methods for estimating the degree of nonresponse error have been proposed and will be briefly discussed.[40]

1   *Sensitivity analysis.* Determine how different each successive callback group is from the previous respondent group. If the management decision is insensitive to this difference, cease future callbacks.

2   *Trend projection.* Based on the results of successive waves of callbacks, if a trend develops on the variables of interest, it can be used to estimate the characteristics of the nonrespondent group.

3   *Subsample measurement.* A specially designed telephone or personal interview is used to estimate the results of the nonrespondent group. This estimate is then incorporated into the data set of those who responded to the survey.

4   *Subjective estimate.* The researcher, given the nature of the survey topic, uses experience and judgment to estimate the degree of nonresponse error.

Selection of Communication Medium.   Which communication medium should be selected for a study? The answer is the medium which is best capable of meeting the information needs of the study given the time and cost constraints. It should be emphasized that the three communication media are not mutually exclusive. Various combinations of media can be used in the research design; this allows the researcher to design a study which builds on the strengths of all three media.

Observation Method

Observation involves the recording of the respondent's behavior; it is the process of *recognizing and recording the behavior of people, objects, and events.*

---

[37] R. C. Nichols and M. A. Meyer, "Timing Postcard Follow-ups in Mail Questionnaire Surveys," *Public Opinion Quarterly,* vol. 30, pp. 306–307, Summer 1966.

[38] A. F. Williams and H. Wechsler, "The Mail Survey: Methods to Minimize Bias Owing to Incomplete Response," *Sociology and Social Research*, vol. 54, pp. 533–535, July 1970.

[39] Paul L. Erdos, "Data Collection Methods: Mail Surveys," in Robert Ferber (ed.), *Handbook of Marketing Research* (New York: McGraw-Hill, 1974), p. 2-102.

[40] For an expanded discussion of this topic see Tull and Hawkins, op. cit., pp. 394–396.

Informal observation is used extensively by decision makers. All marketers take special note of customer buying patterns, competitive advertising and pricing, product availability, and so forth. The danger in drawing conclusions from informal observation, as in the case of informal communication, is that the potential for both sampling and nonsampling errors is very large. Consequently, techniques for formal observation are designed to control these errors and provide valid data for decision making. This section presents the techniques used in formal observation.

It is rare for a research design to rely entirely on the observational method. Estimates suggest that no more than 1 percent of research projects are of this nature.[41] Consequently, the observational method has major weaknesses when compared with other data collection methods. In practice, observational techniques are used in conjunction with other data collection techniques. It is important to understand the advantages and disadvantages of the observational method to position its role in the array of data collection tools available to the researcher.

Advantages of the Observation Method   The observation method has several advantages when compared with the communication method. First, it does not rely on the respondent's willingness to provide the desired data. Second, the potential bias caused by the interviewer and the interviewing process is reduced or eliminated. Therefore, observational data should be more accurate. Third, certain types of data can be collected only by observation. Obviously, those behavior patterns of which the respondent is not aware can be recorded only by observation.

Disadvantages of the Observation Method   The observation method has two major weaknesses which significantly limit its use. First is the inability to observe such things as awareness, beliefs, feelings, and preferences. In addition, it is difficult to observe a host of personal and intimate activities such as applying makeup and deodorant, eating, family games with the children, and late-evening TV watching. Second, the observed behavior patterns must be of a short duration, occur frequently, or be reasonably predictable if the data collection costs and time requirements are to be competitive with other data collection techniques. This requirement limits the observation method to a unique set of circumstances.

Observational Techniques Classified

Observational techniques can be classified five ways: (1) natural or contrived observation, (2) disguised or undisguised observation, (3) structured or unstructured observation, (4) direct or indirect observation, and (5) human or mechanical observation. Observational techniques will typically possess degrees of these characteristics rather than the dichotomous distinction as presented.

---

[41] Michael L. Ray, *Unobtrusive Marketing Research Techniques* (Cambridge, Mass.: Marketing Science Institute, 1973), p. 13.

Natural versus Contrived Observation   Natural observation involves observing behavior as it takes place normally in the environment, e.g., shopping in a grocery store. Contrived observation involves creating an artificial environment and observing the behavior patterns exhibited by persons put in this environment, e.g., having people shop in a simulated grocery store.

The advantage of a more natural environmental setting is the increased probability that the exhibited behavior will more accurately reflect true behavior patterns. Against this must be weighed the added costs of waiting for the behavior to occur and the difficulty of measuring behavior in a natural setting.

Disguised versus Undisguised Observation   Disguise refers to whether or not the respondents are aware they are being observed. The role of the observer should be disguised in situations where people would behave differently if they knew they were being observed. Various approaches such as two-way mirrors, hidden cameras, and observers dressed as sales clerks can be used to disguise the observations.

Researchers disagree as to how much the presence of the observer will affect people's behavior patterns. One position is that the observer effect is small and short-term,[42] and the other is that the observer can introduce serious bias in the observed behavior patterns.[43]

Structured versus Unstructured Observation   Structured observation is appropriate when the decision problem has been clearly defined and the specification of information needs permits a clear identification of the behavior patterns to be observed and measured. Unstructured observation is appropriate in situations where the decision problem has yet to be formulated and a great deal of flexibility is needed in the observation to develop hypotheses useful in defining the problem and in identifying opportunities. This distinction is similar to that observed in the discussion of communication methods.

Structured observation is more appropriate for conclusive research studies. When using the structured approach, the researcher must specify in detail what is to be observed and how the measurements are to be recorded. The structuring of the observation reduces the potential for observer bias and increases the reliability of the data.

Unstructured observation is more appropriate for exploratory research studies. Here, the observer is free to monitor those behavior patterns which seem relevant to the decision situation. Since there is great opportunity for observer bias, the research findings should be treated as hypotheses to be tested with a conclusive research design.

Direct versus Indirect Observation   Direct observation refers to observing behavior as it actually occurs. Indirect observation refers to observing some

---

[42] F. Kerlinger, *Foundations of Behavioral Reseearch,* 2d ed. (New York: Holt, 1973), p. 538.
[43] E. J. Webb, D. T. Campbell, K. D. Schwartz, and L. Sechrest, *Unobtrusive Measures: Nonreactive Research in the Social Sciences* (Chicago: Rand McNally, 1966), pp. 113–114.

record of past behavior. Here, the effects of behavior are observed rather than the behavior itself. This involves the examination of *physical traces,* a process which includes such things as counting the number of empty liquor containers in trash cans to estimate the liquor consumption of houses.[44] A *pantry audit* is an example of the use of physical traces. Here, the observer asks the respondent if the pantry can be inspected for certain types of products. The successful use of the indirect observation approach rests with the ability of the researcher to identify creatively those physical traces which can provide useful data for the problem at hand.

Human versus Mechanical Observation   In some situations it is appropriate to supplement or replace the human observer with some form of mechanical observer. The reason could be increased accuracy, lower costs, or special measurement requirements. The major mechanical devices used in observation include the (1) motion picture camera, (2) Audimeter, (3) psychogalvanometer, (4) eye-camera, and (5) pupilometer.

The *motion picture camera* can be used to record shopping behavior in supermarkets, drugstores, and the like. Here, the observer evaluates the film and measures the desired behavior. The use of several observers plus repeated viewing allows more accurate measurement of behavior.

The *Audimeter* is a device developed by the A. C. Nielsen Company to record when radio and television sets are turned on and the station to which they are tuned. The observations made from a sample of households are important in determining which programs are aired and which are canceled.

The *psychogalvanometer* measures changes in perspiration rate from which inferences are drawn regarding a person's emotional reaction to stimuli present at the time of the measurement. The stimuli presented might include brand names, copy slogans, or advertisements. It is assumed that the stronger the reaction, the more favorable the person's attitude.

The *eye-camera* measures the movements of the eye. It is used to determine how a person reads a magazine, newspaper, advertisement, package, and the like. Measurements are taken on the sequence of what is observed and the time spent looking at various sections.

The *pupilometer* measures changes in the diameter of the pupil of the eye. An increase in pupil diameter is assumed to reflect the person's favorable reaction to the stimuli being observed.

SUMMARY

1   Respondents are a major primary source of marketing data. Data can be collected from respondents by means of communication and observation. Communication requires the respondent to provide data actively through verbal response, while observation involves the recording of the respondent's behavior.

---

[44] H. G. Sawyer, "The Meaning of Numbers," speech before the American Association of Advertising Agencies, 1961. Reported by Webb et al., op. cit., pp. 41–42.

There are three types of respondent data: (1) past behavior, (2) attitudes, and (3) respondent characteristics.

2 The advantages of the communication method are (1) versatility, (2) speed, and (3) cost, and its possible disadvantages are (1) the respondent's unwillingness to provide data, (2) the respondent's inability to provide data, and (3) the influence of the questioning process.

3 The structured-direct questionnaire is the most common data collection technique. Here, the questions asked and the possible responses are predetermined. In addition, the objective of the study is obvious to the respondent from the questions asked. This technique is used for conclusive research purposes.

4 The unstructured-direct approach involves a high degree of flexibility in how the questions are asked and in the degree of probing. The two techniques which use this approach are (1) the focus group interview and (2) the depth interview. The former is the more popular of the two, and the primary use of both techniques is for exploratory research.

5 The unstructured-indirect approach uses projective techniques designed to attain data indirectly about respondent's beliefs and feelings. The most common techniques used in marketing research are (1) the Thematic Apperception Test, (2) role playing, (3) cartoon completion, (4) word association, and (5) sentence completion. These techniques have experienced limited use in marketing research, their primary use being for exploratory research purposes.

6 The structured-indirect approach assumes that asking respondents to recall factual information about a topic is a way to indirectly measure their attitudes. This approach is rarely used in marketing research.

7 Three communication media are available: (1) personal interviews, (2) telephone interviews, and (3) mail interviews. All three media can be used with structured techniques, while the personal interview is typically required for unstructured techniques. The criteria for selecting among these media are (1) versatility, (2) cost, (3) time, (4) sample control, (5) quantity of data, (6) quality of data, and (7) response rate.

8 The advantages of the observation method are: (1) it does not rely on the respondent's willingness to provide the data, (2) the potential for bias from the interviewer and interviewing process is reduced, and (3) certain types of data can be collected only with this method. The disadvantages are: (1) one cannot observe constructs and certain behavior patterns, and (2) cost and time constraints limit observation to behavior patterns which are short in duration, occur frequently, or are predictable. These disadvantages seriously limit the use of the observation method.

9 Observational techniques can be classified as (1) natural or contrived, (2) disguised or undisguised, (3) structured or unstructured, (4) direct or indirect, and (5) human or mechanical.

DISCUSSION QUESTIONS

1 What major types of respondent data exist?
2 List the advantages and disadvantages of communication methods.

3 Discuss two major unstructured, direct communication techniques.
4 What uses in marketing can focus group interviews serve?
5 Discuss some of the issues involved in carrying out focus group interviews.
6 What are some of the desirable characteristics for focus group moderators?
7 Discuss the advantages and disadvantages of focus groups.
8 How does the depth interview differ from the focus group method?
9 What unstructured, indirect techniques are most often used in marketing?
10 List the communication media commonly used in respondent data collection; what criteria are used to select among them?
11 Identify the techniques used for estimating nonresponse error when communication media are used.
12 What are the advantages and disadvantages of observation methods?
13 Discuss the classification of observational techniques.
14 What major mechanical devices are employed in observation techniques in marketing?

SUGGESTED READING

Bellenger, Danny N., Kenneth L. Bernhardt, and Jac L. Goldstucker, *Qualitative Research in Marketing,* Monograph Series No. 3, (Chicago: American Marketing Association, 1976). An excellent introduction to the contemporary use of the focus group interview, depth interview, and projective techniques.

Erdos, P. L., *Professional Mail Surveys* (New York: McGraw-Hill, 1970). A leading practitioner discusses the procedures used in conducting mail surveys.

Ferber, Robert (ed.), *Handbook of Marketing Research* (New York: McGraw-Hill, 1974). This book presents the work of leading practitioners on various topics in marketing research. Of special interest are chapters on data collection methods (personal, telephone, and mail interviews) and group interviews.

Goodyear, J. R., "Qualitative Research Studies," in J. Aucamp (ed.), *The Effective Use of Market Research* (London: Staple Press, 1971), pp. 47–65. The author provides interesting examples of focus group and depth interviews.

Lansing, J. B., and J. N. Morgan, *Economic Survey Methods* (Ann Arbor: The University of Michigan, 1971). An excellent treatment of survey research procedures and issues.

Newman, J. W., *Motivation Research and Marketing Management* (Cambridge, Mass.: Harvard University Press, 1957). A classic work on qualitative research in marketing.

Webb, E. J., D. T. Campbell, K. D. Schwartz, and L. Sechrest, *Unobtrusive Measures: Nonreactive Research in the Social Sciences* (Chicago: Rand McNally, 1966). A classic work in the area of observational methods.

Chapter 19

Designing Data Collection Forms

Previous chapters have discussed the types of primary and secondary marketing data, and now we consider the issues involved in designing data collection forms for primary data collection. The emphasis is on constructing forms appropriate for conclusive research, where the research design requires a structured data collection method capable of providing valid and relevant data for decision making.

The last chapter emphasized that there are various unstructured data collection techniques which require the use of forms. The nature of these forms can range from fairly structured questionnaires to rough topical outlines. The discussion presented in this chapter will apply only indirectly to the construction of forms for unstructured data collection.

Data collection forms are a central component of most research studies. All three communication media—personal, telephone, and mail interviews—rely on a questionnaire. Since questionnaire studies are far more prevalent than observational studies, the bulk of this chapter will be devoted to issues involved in questionnaire construction. While much of this discussion will be relevant to the issues involved in developing data collection forms for observation the final section of this chapter will be specifically devoted to observational forms.

IMPORTANCE OF QUESTIONNAIRE

A questionnaire is a *formalized schedule for collecting data from respondents*. The function of the questionnaire is that of measurement. Questionnaires can be used to measure (1) past behavior, (2) attitudes, and (3) respondent characteristics.

The measurement of attitudes has grown in importance, and so has the number of attitude measurement techniques, several of which have been discussed in Chapters 13 and 18. These techniques are typically incorporated into a questionnaire. The issues involved in questionnaire design directly relate to developing and administering these attitude measurement techniques.

Measurement error is a serious problem in questionnaire construction. For example, the Survey Research Center at the University of Michigan asked half of the sample in their May 1977 consumer survey this question regarding attitudes toward a gasoline price increase: "Are you in favor of the proposed standby gasoline tax, starting with 5 cents and rising to 50 cents, which will be imposed if we do not meet conservation goals?" The results were that 27 percent favored the additional taxes while 65 percent opposed them. The other half of the sample was asked: "If the United States had to choose between becoming dependent on uncertain foreign oil supplies or curbing gasoline use with rising taxes, which would you favor?" In contrast to the previous finding, 71 percent favored the higher tax alternative, with only 13 percent opting for uncertain oil sources.[1] What could cause such a marked difference in responses? The answer lies in the question wording. The first question does not pose an explicit alternative to the consumer. Rather, the consumer is offered the implicit alternative of higher gasoline prices versus lower gasoline prices. It is not hard to see that consumers would prefer lower prices. The second question poses the alternative of higher prices now versus more dependence on foreign oil supplies. The lesson to be learned from this example is that when a preference question is asked without posing realistic alternatives, the results can be meaningless.

Let's consider another example. Two rather similar ways of asking a question to a sample of nonworking housewives are developed. The first question is: "Would you like to have a job, if this were possible?" The second question is: "Would you prefer to have a job, or do you prefer just to do your housework?" The second question makes explicit the implied choice in the first question. Each question was put to half of a sample of nonworking housewives. The first question resulted in 19 percent stating they would not like to have a job, while the second question resulted in 68 percent who would not like to have a job.[2] This dramatic difference again emphasizes the importance of questionnaire wording. The researcher must ask: "Do the questions measure what they are supposed to measure?" If the answer is no, measurement error is present.

[1] F. Thomas Juster, "A Note on Energy Policy and Automobile Demand," *Economic Outlook USA*, Summer vol. 4, no. 3 (Ann Arbor: Survey Research Center, The University of Michigan, 1977), p. 43.
[2] E. Noelle-Neumann, "Wanted: Rules for Wording Structured Questionnaires," *Public Opinion Quarterly*, vol. 34, p. 200, Summer 1970.

Both of the previous examples illustrate the importance of controlling measurement error in questionnaire construction. Rarely will sampling error result in outcomes of the magnitude observed in these examples. This point is expressed in the following quotation by one of the leading researchers in marketing research.

> . . . that error or bias attributable to sampling and to methods of questionnaire administration were relatively small as compared with other types of variation—especially variation attributable to different ways of wording questions.[3]

Consequently, a skilled researcher is needed to design the questionnaire such that the questions asked measure what they are supposed to measure.

QUESTIONNAIRE COMPONENTS

A questionnaire typically has five sections: (1) identification data, (2) request for cooperation, (3) instructions, (4) information sought, and (5) classification data.

Identification data typically occupy the first section on a questionnaire—data regarding the respondent's name, address, and phone number. Additional data would include items such as the time and date of the interview plus the interviewer's name or code number.

The *request for cooperation* is an opening statement designed to gain the respondent's cooperation regarding the interview. This statement typically first identifies the interviewer and/or the interviewing organization. Next, the purpose of the study is explained, and the time required to complete the interview is given.

The *instructions* refer to comments to the interviewer or respondent regarding how to use the questionnaire. These comments appear directly on the questionnaire when using a mail survey. With the personal and telephone survey, a separate sheet titled "Interviewer Instructions" would explain the purpose of the study, the sampling plan, and other aspects of the data collection process. In addition, the questionnaire may contain special instructions regarding the use of specific questions, e.g., attitude scaling technique.

The *information sought* form the major portion of the questionnaire. The remainder of this chapter deals with designing this aspect of the questionnaire.

The *classification data* are concerned with the characteristics of the respondent. These data are provided directly by the respondent in the case of a mail survey. With the personal and telephone interview surveys the data are collected from the respondent by the interviewer, or in some cases the personal interviewer may estimate more sensitive types of data based on observation, e.g., income. Classification data are typically collected at the end of the interview. However, some sampling procedures require that classification data be collected at the beginning of the interview to determine whether the person qualifies as part of the sampling plan.

---

[3] Samuel A. Stouffer et al., *Measurement and Prediction, Studies in Social Psychology in World War II*, vol. 4 (Princeton, N.J.: Princeton University Press, 1950), p. 709.

QUESTIONNAIRE DESIGN

The design of a questionnaire is more of an art form than a scientific undertaking. There are no series of steps, principles, or guidelines which guarantee an effective and efficient questionnaire. Questionnaire design is a skill which the researcher learns through experience rather than by reading a series of guidelines. The only way to develop this skill is to write a questionnaire, use it in a series of interviews, analyze the weaknesses, and revise the questionnaire.

What we do know about questionnaire design comes from the experience of researchers who have specialized in this area. From this accumulated experience has emerged a series of rules or guidelines which can be useful to the beginning researcher confronted with the task of designing a questionnaire. While these rules are useful in avoiding serious errors, the fine tuning of questionnaire design comes from the creative inspiration of the skilled researcher. Consequently, while the guidelines discussed in this section lay the foundation for questionnaire design, ultimately the quality of the questionnaire depends on the skill and judgment of the researcher, a clear understanding of the information needed, a sensitivity to the role of the respondent, and extensive pretesting.

The discussion of questionnaire design will be organized as a series of seven steps. At each of these steps, various guidelines for questionnaire construction will be presented. While these rules are presented as part of a step-by-step approach to questionnaire development, in practice the steps are highly interrelated. Decisions made early in the sequence will often influence choices later in the sequence, and vice versa. The seven steps, as presented in Figure 19-1, are (1) review preliminary considerations, (2) decide on question content, (3) decide on response format, (4) decide on question wording, (5) decide on question

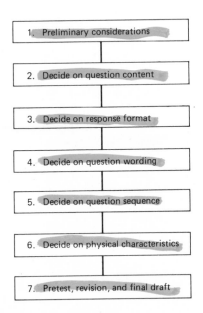

1. Preliminary considerations

2. Decide on question content

3. Decide on response format

4. Decide on question wording

5. Decide on question sequence

6. Decide on physical characteristics

7. Pretest, revision, and final draft

Figure 19-1 Steps in questionnaire design.

sequence, (6) decide on physical characteristics, and (7) carry out pretest, revision, and final draft.

Review Preliminary Considerations

The preliminary considerations for conducting conclusive research were discussed in Chapter 5, which focused on methods of establishing an effective link between the decision-making process and the research process. Central to this process is the development of research objectives and the listing of information needs. The research design must be formulated and the steps in the research process visualized and planned. Consequently, many decisions must be made before the questionnaire can be designed.

Previous Decisions   The questionnaire design stage presumes that the research project is well under way and that many decisions have already been made. Decisions regarding questionnaire design must build upon and be consistent with decisions relating to other aspects of the research project.

Previous decisions regarding the type of research design and the sources of data directly influence the character and the role of the questionnaire in the research project (see Chapters 6 and 7). It is essential to have a clear picture of the target population and to know the details of the sampling plan (see Chapters 8 through 11). Questionnaire design is highly influenced by the characteristics of the respondent group. The more heterogeneous the respondent group, the more difficult it is to design a single questionnaire which is appropriate for everyone. Typically, the questionnaire must be designed to be comprehensible to the least able respondent. The measurement scales and communication media that will be used must be specified (Chapters 13 and 18). The data processing and analysis stages must be visualized, as well as the nature of the research findings. The tactical aspects of questionnaire design are closely related to these final stages of the research process. A review of Chapter 3 would illustrate the nature of these decisions in the context of an actual research project.

Link between Information Needs and Data to Be Collected   Before designing the questionnaire, the researcher must have a detailed listing of the information needs as well as a clear definition of the respondent group. The questionnaire is the link between the information needed and the data to be collected. Figure 19-2 illustrates the nature of this linkage.

The questions on the questionnaire should flow logically from the list of information needs. It would seem obvious that no question should be included on the questionnaire unless it relates to a specific information need.[4] In practice, however, there is a strong tendency to include questions which appear "interesting" but have no specific link to the information needs. Unnecessary questions add expense to the survey and increase the demands placed on the respondent.

---

[4] Unnecessary questions can be justified if they facilitate gaining the respondent's cooperation or add continuity to the questioning process.

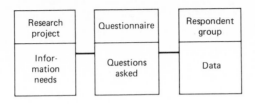

Figure 19-2 Information needs–data linkage.

Decide on Question Content

The content of the questions is influenced by the respondent's ability and/or willingness to respond accurately.

Ability to Answer Accurately   Assuming the desired data are relevant to the decision problem, the researcher must be sensitive to the respondent's ability to provide the data. Many types of data cannot be accurately collected from respondents. Inaccurate data can result from two sources: (1) the respondent is uninformed, and (2) the respondent is forgetful.

Respondent Is Uninformed   We are frequently asked questions on issues we do not have the answers to. As students, we confront this situation far too often. Questions on a questionnaire may confront respondents with the same situation. They could be asked to provide data about their spouse's monthly gross income or credit card purchases when they do not possess accurate data. They could be asked questions about advertisements, products, brands, or retail outlets of which they are unaware.

Researchers have discovered that respondents, like students, will often answer questions even though they have no knowledge of the topic, perhaps because of unwillingness to admit this lack of knowledge. This situation represents a serious source of measurement error.

Often the phrasing of the question will encourage the respondent to answer it by implying that the answer should be known. Consider the question: "What is the current interest rate you receive on your savings account?" It implies that the respondent should know the answer. An alternative would be: "Do you know the current interest rate on your savings account?" This question implies that some people do not know the interest rate, which makes it easier for the respondent to admit a lack of knowledge. If the respondent answers this question affirmatively, the first question could then be asked.

Respondent Is Forgetful   We are frequently asked questions which we were able to answer at one time, but now we have forgotten. As students, we are continually confronted with this situation.

Research studies have shown that we forget most events fairly rapidly after we learn about them.[5] The rate of forgetting is very rapid over the first few days. Consequently, the farther in the past the learning took place, the higher the chance of forgetting.

[5] J. F. Engel, D. T. Kollat, and R. D. Blackwell, *Consumer Behavior,* 2d ed. (New York: Holt, 1973), pp. 340–341.

The probability of forgetting is influenced by the importance of the event and the repetition of the event. It is easier to remember important events such as the first person we kissed, the first person on the moon, the first car we purchased, and the like. In contrast, how many of us can remember the second person kissed, the second person on the moon, and the second car we purchased? It is also easier to remember events that are repeated frequently, e.g., frequently purchased products or frequently viewed advertisements.

When the information needs of a study require questions asking the respondent to recall unimportant or infrequently occurring events, the researcher has a potentially serious problem in designing the questionnaire. He or she must not overestimate the ability of the respondent to recall the event and the surrounding circumstances accurately. This is an easy mistake to make when the topic of the questionnaire is personally important to the researcher or decision maker.

When faced with collecting data about unimportant or infrequent events, there are several options available. First, the researcher can try to interview those respondents most likely to remember, e.g., recent purchasers. Second, the questionnaire can include techniques which stimulate the respondent's recall of the event.

Several studies suggest that questions which rely on unaided recall—questions that do not give cues as to the event—can underestimate the actual occurrence of the event.[6] The aided-recall approach is an attempt to overcome the memory problem; it provides the respondent with cues regarding the event of interest. Students should be familiar with the distinction between aided and unaided recall. An essay question is an example of unaided recall, while a multiple-choice question is an example of aided recall.

An unaided question designed to measure the respondent's awareness of a commercial could be: "What products do you recall were advertised last night on television?" The aided-recall approach would list a number of products for the respondent and then ask: "Which of these products were advertised on television last night?"

The advantage of the aided recall comes from the cue used to stimulate the respondent's memory. The degree of stimulation can vary from limited hints to the presentation of the actual event. This latter approach to aided recall is called the *recognition method*. With increased attempts to stimulate the respondent's memory comes the possibility of suggestion bias resulting from the presentation of the cues. When using the aided-recall approach, researchers often recommend that it is useful to have several levels of successive stimulation. This allows the researcher to analyze the influence of the question sequence and select a level of stimulation most appropriate for the study.

Willingness to Respond Accurately Assuming that the respondent can accurately answer the question, the next issue is to determine his or her will-

---

[6] J. H. Myers and W. H. Reynolds, *Consumer Behavior and Marketing Management* (Boston: Houghton Mifflin, 1967), pp. 65–67.

ingness to do so. Unwillingness to respond accurately could be reflected in (1) refusing to respond to a question or a series of questions, i.e., item nonresponse error, and (2) deliberately providing an incorrect or distorted response to a question, i.e., measurement error.

There are three reasons for unwillingness to respond accurately: (1) the situation is not appropriate for disclosing the data, (2) disclosure of the data would be embarrassing, and (3) disclosure is a potential threat to the respondent's prestige or normative views.

It is important to remember that the respondent has limited motivation to respond accurately to the questions. With the personal and telephone interview, the interviewer's presence can cause the respondent to be more concerned with how the interviewer may react to the responses than with the accuracy of the responses. This is especially the situation if the questions are embarrassing or a threat to prestige and normative viewpoints. The result can be item nonresponse or, worse yet, inaccurate responses.

The respondent's willingness to answer questions is conditioned by the interviewing context. A question regarding personal hygiene habits may be appropriate when asked by a nurse or doctor as part of a physical examination but may be inappropriate when asked by an interviewer conducting a study for a pharmaceutical manufacturer.

The respondent's willingness to answer a question is also a function of his or her understanding of whether the data are needed for a legitimate purpose. The collection of classification data can be a serious problem in this regard. The respondent may be hesitant to provide accurate data when abruptly faced with personal questions regarding age, occupation, and income. The following request for personal data does not explain to the respondent how the data are to be used: "Next, I would like to ask you some questions about yourself. What is your . . .?" Even a brief explanation such as the following can make such a request legitimate for most respondents: "To better understand how the reactions to this new product differ among people with different age, income, and occupational characteristics, we need to know your . . ."

Questions which embarrass the respondent or have an element of prestige or adherence to social norms can result in a biased response. This is especially the situation when the personal or telephone interview is employed. Researchers have found that questions on topics such as sexual behavior and attitudes, number of automobile accidents, or purchase of personal hygiene products and alcoholic beverages can embarrass the respondent and result in a refusal to answer or the distortion of the response.

Questions which have an element of prestige or adherence to social norms include level of education, income earned, and amount of time spent reading or watching educational television. The answers to these types of questions typically result in an upward response bias.

Various approaches have been developed to deal with the bias resulting from the respondent's unwillingness to respond accurately.

1 *Counterbiasing statement:* Begin the question with a statement which

suggests that the behavior in question is rather common and then ask the question to the respondent.[7]

2 *Indirect statement:* Present the respondent with the sensitive question phrased to refer to "other people." It is assumed that the respondent's own behavior or attitude will be reflected in the response.

3 *Labeled response categories:* Present the respondent with a card which lists the sensitive response alternatives and has them identified by letters or numbers. The respondent uses the letter or number to indicate a response to the sensitive question.

4 *Randomized response technique:* Present the respondent with two questions, either of which can be answered "yes" or "no." One question is the sensitive issue (e.g., "Have you shoplifted in the last month?"), while the other question is the insensitive issue (e.g., "Were you born in January?"). A random procedure (e.g., flipping a coin) is used to determine which of the two questions the respondent will answer. Since the response format of the two questions is identical (i.e., yes or no), the interviewer does not know which question the respondent has answered.

The following formula is used to estimate the proportion of respondents who answered "yes" to the sensitive question.[8]

$$P(\text{yes} \mid \text{sens. quest.}) = \frac{P(\text{yes}) - P(\text{insens. quest.}) \quad P(\text{yes} \mid \text{insens. quest.})}{P(\text{sens. quest.})}$$

In the shoplifting study, if the proportion of respondents who answered "yes" is .10, the proportion born in January is .05 (census of population), and the probability of answering each question is .5, the estimate of the proportion of respondents answering "yes" to the shoplifting question is:

$$P(\text{yes} \mid \text{shoplifting}) = \frac{.10 - (.5)(.05)}{.5} = .15$$

Decide on Response Format

Once the problems related to the content of the questions have been analyzed, the next issue concerns the type of questions to use. The concern here involves the degree of structure imposed on the person's responses. The three types of questions range from unstructured to structured response formats: (1) open-ended questions, (2) multiple-choice questions, and (3) dichotomous questions.

Open-ended Questions   An open-ended question requires the respondents to provide their own answer to the question. This is often referred to as a free-response or free-answer question. For example, the respondent could be asked, "What is your reaction to this new cake mix?" With the mail interview, space would be provided for the respondent to write the answer. With the personal

[7] Donald S. Tull and Del I. Hawkins, *Marketing Research* (New York: Macmillan, 1976), p. 261.

[8] C. Campbell and B. L. Joiner, "How to Get the Answer Without Being Sure You've Asked the Question," *The American Statistician,* vol. 27, pp. 229–231, December 1973.

and telephone interview, the respondent would verbally report the answer to the interviewer, who would then record the answer on the questionnaire.

Advantages of Open-ended Questions   Open-ended questions serve as an excellent first question to a topic. They allow general attitudes to be expressed which can aid in interpreting the more structured questions. In addition, they establish rapport and gain the respondent's cooperation in answering more specific and structured questions. Introductory open-ended questions are especially important in mail surveys.

Open-ended questions influence responses less than multiple-choice or dichotomous questions. Respondents are not influenced by a predetermined set of response alternatives and can freely express views divergent from the researcher's expectations. This characteristic makes open-ended questions useful for exploratory research purposes.

Finally, open-ended questions can provide the researcher with insights, side comments, and explanations which are useful in developing a "feel" for the research findings. The final report may include quotations from open-ended questions to bring realism and life to the more structured research findings.

Disadvantages of Open-ended Questions   A major disadvantage of open-ended questions is the high potential for interviewer bias. Interviewers rarely record the respondent's answers verbatim. This results in the interviewer summarizing the respondent's answers or deleting those aspects of the answer deemed unimportant. In addition, those interviewers who write slowly or do not take shorthand typically fail to record parts of the answer due to time constraints. The more the interviewer summarizes and edits the respondent's answers, the more the recorded responses will vary from the actual responses. A tape recorder should be used if verbatim responses are required.

A second major disadvantage of open-ended questions lies in the time and cost associated with coding the responses. For a large survey, extensive coding procedures are required to summarize the divergent responses in a format useful for data analysis and presentation. The time and cost of this coding process can be a significant portion of the total cost of the research project.

Sometimes, in order to gain the advantages of open-ended questions yet avoid some of the time and cost associated with the editing and coding process, precoded questions are used. A precoded question is a multiple-choice question which is presented to the respondent as open-ended. The response alternatives are not read to the respondent. Rather, the interviewer selects the appropriate response alternative based on the respondent's reply to the open-ended question.

This approach works well when the response is easily formulated in the respondent's mind and the possible answers are limited in variety, e.g., number of household members, age of the refrigerator, or monthly grocery expenditures. However, questions which are not well formulated in the respondent's mind and result in a variety of answers have a high probability of interviewer bias.

Other disadvantages include the implicit extra weight given to respondents who are more articulate and tend to raise more points in their answers. Also, open-ended questions are less suited for self-administered questionnaires. The reason is that respondents tend to write more briefly than they speak, and there is also the problem of illegible handwriting. Finally, compared with questions that have structured response formats, open-ended questions are three to five times as costly because of the complexity associated with the data processing.[9]

In general, open-ended questions are most appropriate for exploratory research purposes and research designed to develop more structured questions.[10] While the cost of developing effective structured questions can be high, it must be weighed against the disadvantages of open-ended questions.

Multiple-Choice Questions   A multiple-choice question requires the respondent to choose an answer from among a list provided in the question proper or following the question. The respondent may be asked to choose one or more of the alternatives presented.

Advantages of Multiple-Choice Questions   Multiple-choice questions overcome many of the disadvantages associated with open-ended questions. Most importantly, they reduce interviewer bias and the cost and time associated with data processing. Typically, the interviewer will find this type of question easier and faster to administer. Finally, self-administered questionnaires have a difficult time maintaining respondent cooperation unless the bulk of the questions have a structured-response format.

Disadvantages of Multiple-Choice Questions   Against these advantages must be weighed several disadvantages. First, the design of effective multiple-choice questions requires considerable time and cost. Typically, an exploratory study using open-ended questions is required to formulate the response alternatives. If the latter do not include one or more of the predominant responses, substantial bias can be introduced into the results. Even with an alternative of "other (specify)," there is a tendency for the respondent to choose from among the alternatives specified rather than using the "other" alternative. Second, multiple-choice questions tend to bias the data by the order in which the response alternatives are given the respondent.

Issues in Multiple-Choice Question Design   There are two issues in the design of multiple-choice questions: (1) number of alternatives, and (2) position bias.

The *number of alternatives* to include in a question is typically influenced by the following two guidelines. First, the response alternatives should be *collectively exhaustive,* that is, they should include all the possible response alternatives. The inclusion of the alternative labeled "other (please specify)" accompanied by a space to record the answer is an attempt to comply with this guideline. It is hoped that those major response alternatives which were excluded will be identified in the "other" alternative. Second, the response alternatives should be *mutually exclusive,* that is, the respondents should be able to identify one alternative which clearly represents their response. In some situations the

[9] Jeffrey L. Pope, "12 Ways to Cut Marketing Research Costs," *Marketing News,* June 6, 1975, p. 6.

[10] This conclusion is consistent with S. L. Payne, "Are Open-ended Questions Worth the Effort?" *Journal of Marketing Research,* vol. 2, pp. 417–418, November 1965.

researcher may desire to have the respondent make two or more choices, but multiple responses create special data processing problems.

If the set of response alternatives is reasonably short, they may be included in the question proper. In most cases there are too many alternatives to be included here, and they are listed at the end of the question. With a long list of alternatives, the choices should be listed on a card and given the respondent for inspection.

Another important issue concerns *position bias*. With a list of numbers, such as prices or number of store visits, there is a bias toward the central position of the number array. When ideas are involved, the first alternative on the list has a greater chance of choice. To control position bias, the researcher should alternate the order in which alternatives are listed. This procedure will average out the response bias. Unfortunately it is not easy to rotate most numbers, since they logically should appear as a sequence, for example, 5, 6, 7, 8, and 9. Even if they are presented out of order, the respondent may sort them into sequence before making a choice.

Dichotomous Question   A dichotomous question is an extreme form of the multiple-choice question which allows the respondent only two responses, such as yes–no, did–did not, agree–disagree, and so on. Typically the two alternatives of interest are combined with a neutral alternative, such as "no opinion" or "don't know."

Advantages of Dichotomous Questions   The advantages of the dichotomous question are essentially the same as those mentioned for multiple-choice questions. The interviewers find the questions quick and easy to administer. There is less chance of interviewer bias, and the responses are easy to code, process, and analyze.

Disadvantages of Dichotomous Questions   There is a risk of assuming that the respondent group approaches the topic of interest in dichotomous terms when, in reality, there may be many grades of feeling present or indecision may predominate. Forcing respondents to express their views in a dichotomous manner when they are not thus polarized can produce results which contain substantial measurement error. Dichotomous questions are especially susceptible to error resulting from how the question is worded. For example, early in this chapter, error resulting from implied versus explicit alternatives was illustrated. In addition, the positive or negative posture of the question can have a strong effect on the nature of the response.

Issues in Dichotomous Question Design   The central issue concerns whether to include a neutral response alternative in the question. If it is not included, the respondent is forced to select between the two positions presented. If a neutral alternative is available, and especially if it is shown to the respondent, the latter can avoid taking a position on the topic by selecting the neutral alternative. When the neutral alternative is included, the number of nonresponses should decline and the number of neutral responses increase. If a significant group of respondents are truly neutral, the inclusion of the neutral alternative should increase the accuracy of the results. However, a source of bias can enter when respondents who are not neutral select the neutral alternative for reasons of convenience, embarrassment, or the like. If the proportion of respondents who are truly neutral is large, it is best to include the neutral alternative. If it is believed that the proportion of neutral respondents is small, it is best to force the respondents to select between the two positions of interest.

Decide on Question Wording

The heart of the questionnaire consists of the questions asked. These questions represent the link between the data and the information needs of the study. It is critical that the researcher and the respondent assign the same meaning to the questions asked. If not, serious measurement error will be present in the research results.

The researcher should never be misled into believing that there is a "right" and "wrong" way of asking questions. In a real sense, survey data are created rather than unobtrusively collected. The manner in which data are collected determines to a large degree the character of the data. Consequently, the researcher must be very sensitive to the effect of the question wording on the character of the results to be obtained.

Since no single wording of a question is correct, it is important for the researcher to understand clearly what effect a particular wording can have on the results. The split ballot technique, which splits the questionnaires into groups and assigns alternative questions to each group, can be used for this purpose. The comparison of alternative questions determines how question wording affects the results. This technique allows a better interpretation of the survey results than is possible when a single version of the question is used.

The following are nine general guidelines which the researcher should consider in designing the wording of a question: (1) use simple words, (2) use clear words, (3) avoid leading questions, (4) avoid biasing questions, (5) avoid implicit alternatives, (6) avoid implicit assumptions, (7) avoid estimates, (8) avoid double-barreled questions, and (9) consider the frame of reference.

Use Simple Words   The words used in the questionnaire should be consistent with the vocabulary level of the respondents. If in doubt, it is best to err on the side of simplicity.

Questions designed for children obviously must have a simpler vocabulary than those designed for, say, medical doctors. When designing a questionnaire for the general public, keep in mind the often surprising fact that the vocabulary skills of most seventh graders (12 years of age) are greater than those of many adults. For example, a significant proportion of the general population does not understand the word "Caucasian."[11] Consequently, when designing a questionnaire, researchers must be certain that it is comprehensible to persons with minimal vocabulary skills.

[11] Alan E. Bayer, "Construction of a Race Item for Survey Research," *Public Opinion Quarterly,* Winter 1972–73, p. 596.

Use Clear Words Words which are "clear" have a single meaning which is known to all the respondents. Unfortunately, identifying words which are clear or unambiguous is more difficult than one might expect. Many words which appear to be clear to everyone can have different meanings among population groups and geographic locations.

Consider the words "dinner" and "lunch." Studies indicate that middle- and upper-class families use "dinner" to refer to the evening meal and "lunch" to refer to the noon meal. In contrast, many working-class families refer to the evening meal as "supper" and the noon meal as "dinner." In designing a question which refers to mealtime, it would be better to use "noon meal" and "evening meal" rather than "lunch" and "dinner." Since comparable responses cannot be expected from respondents who assign different meanings to a word, serious measurement error would be present if the words "lunch" and "dinner" were used in the question.

In a study of soup usage in the home, the question "How often do you serve soup at home?" resulted in responses which suggested that soup usage was lower than believed by the management. Additional research indicated that to many respondents the word "served" meant a special occasion, such as when entertaining. Soup eating by the family alone was not considered to be "served." A revised question with better wording was: "How often do you use soup at home?"[12]

Researchers have found that words such as "usually," "regularly," "kind," "normally," and "frequently" are ambiguous. It is difficult to be sensitive to all of the commonly used words which some respondents interpret one way, others another way. In this regard, Payne advises that the researcher consult a leading dictionary and thesaurus and ask the following six questions of each word in the question:

1 Does it mean what we intended?
2 Does it have any other meanings?
3 If so, does the context make the intended meaning clear?
4 Does the word have more than one pronunciation?
5 Is there any word of similar pronunciation that might be confused?
6 Is a simpler word or phrase suggested?[13]

Avoid Leading Questions A leading question is one where the respondent is given a cue as to what the answer should be to the question. Leading questions often reflect the researcher's or decision maker's viewpoint regarding the ques-

---

[12] J. M. Bowen, "Questionnaire Design for the Personal Interview," in *Fieldwork, Sampling and Questionnaire Design* (Amsterdam: European Society for Opinion Surveys and Market Research, 1973), pt. 1, p. 88.

[13] S. L. Payne, *The Art of Asking Questions* (Princeton, N.J.: Princeton University Press, 1951), p. 41.

tion's answer. A leading question causes a constant measurement error in the research findings.

In a question to measure the claim service of automobile insurance companies, the following statement preceded the question on claim service: "It has been alleged that some low-rate companies are much tougher in adjusting claims than standard-rate companies, and that you are more likely to have to go to court to collect the sum due you."[14] This statement would probably influence the response to the questions on the companies' claim service which followed. Consequently, statements designed to clarify a question can have an influence on the responses to the questions they clarify. The researcher should be sensitive to this source of measurement error.

Consider the question: "Do you own a Zenith television set?" This would be a leading question if the reported ownership of Zenith television sets were higher in this case than when the question simply asked: "What brand of television set do you own?" The use of a brand or company name in a question can cause the respondent to believe that this company is the sponsor of the survey. There is a tendency for the respondent to express positive feelings toward the survey sponsor, which can result in measurement error.

Avoid Biasing Questions   A biasing question includes words or phrases which are emotionally colored and suggest a feeling of approval or disapproval.[15] Most researchers would recognize the biasing effect of a question that began, "Don't you agree with Ralph Nader in the belief that . . ." or "Do you believe that the oil monopolies should be . . .?" No reputable researcher would phrase questions in this manner. Unfortunately, the biasing effect of words and phrases is far more subtle than these examples suggest.

The mere suggestion of an attitude or position associated with a prestigious or nonprestigious person or organization can seriously bias the respondent's reply. The question, "Do you agree or disagree with the American Dental Association's position that advertising presweetened cereal to children is . . ." would have such an effect. The nature of the bias would be increased support reported for the position held by the prestigious person or organization over that reported when the person or organization is not included in the question.

It is difficult to avoid leading questions because those words or phrases that bias one respondent group can be neutral with another group. A pretest of the questionnaire is one way to identify which respondent groups find the question biased.

Avoid Implicit Alternatives   In a previous section of this chapter, examples were presented which indicated a marked difference in the answers to questions which pose implicit and explicit alternatives to the respondents.[16] Other research

---

[14] J. Stevens Stock and Barbara K. Auerback, "How Not to Do Consumer Research," *Journal of Marketing,* vol. 27, p. 21, July 1963.

[15] A. N. Oppenheim, *Questionnaire Design and Attitude Measurement* (London: Heinemann Educational Books, Ltd., 1966), p. 59.

[16] See section on importance of the questionnaire.

has demonstrated equally dramatic results.[17] As a rule, it is best to state clearly all relevant alternatives to a question unless there is a special reason for not doing so.

When using explicit alternatives, research indicates that the order in which the alternatives are presented can affect the response. When the number of alternatives is long and complex or close in preference, the alternatives presented at the end of the list have a higher chance of being selected.[18] Consequently, the split-ballot technique should be used to ensure that each alternative appears at each location on the alternative listing.

Avoid Implicit Assumptions It is easy to design a question where the answer is dependent upon a number of implicit assumptions. Consider the question, "Are you in favor of curtailing the amount of sugar allowed in children's cereals?" Implicit in this question is that this action will result in some favorable outcome, e.g., lower rate of tooth decay. An improved wording would be: "Are you in favor of curtailing the amount of sugar allowed in children's cereal if it would result in . . .?" The failure to make explicit the assumptions in a question often results in overestimating the respondent's support for the issue at hand.

Avoid Estimates The questions should be designed in such a way that the respondent does not have to answer by giving an estimate or making a generalization. Consider the question: "How many boxes of powdered soap do you purchase in a year?" This question requires the respondent to determine the number of boxes of powdered soap purchased in a month and multiply by 12. The survey results would be more accurate if the question were: "How many boxes of powdered soap do you purchase in a month?" The yearly figure can be determined by multiplying by 12.

Avoid Double-barreled Questions A double-barreled question occurs when the wording calls for two responses. Consider the question, "What is your evaluation of the snowmobile's ride and acceleration?" Here, two questions have been asked under the guise of a single question. As a rule, when the question includes "and," the researcher should review it to see whether two responses are required.

Consider Frame of Reference By frame of reference we refer to the respondent's viewpoint in responding to the question. Consider these two questions: "Are automobile manufacturers making satisfactory progress in controlling automobile emissions?" and "Are you satisfied with the progress automobile manufacturers are making in controlling automobile emissions?" The viewpoint of the first question is that of an objective evaluation based on how people in general would react to this question. The second question is oriented to the respondent's personal feeling regarding the issue of automobile emissions and

---

[17] E. Noelle-Neumann, op. cit., pp. 200–201, and S. L. Payne, op. cit., pp. 55–74.
[18] M. Parten, *Surveys, Polls, and Samples* (New York: Harper & Row, 1950), p. 211.

is more subjective in this respect. The objectives of the research study will determine which frame of reference is more appropriate. The point is that the researcher must be aware that the respondent's viewpoint can seriously influence the study results.

Decide on Question Sequence

Once the wording of the questions has been determined, the next step is to establish their sequence, i.e., the order or flow of the questions in the questionnaire. The sequencing of the questions can influence the nature of the respondent's answers and be the cause of serious error in the survey findings. While this aspect of questionnaire design draws heavily on the skills of an experienced researcher, several guidelines are presented which the beginning researcher should find useful.

Use a Simple and Interesting Opening Question   The opening question must capture the respondent's interest and curiosity immediately, or the respondent may terminate the interview. Often, the opening question does not relate to the information needs of the study; its sole purpose is to gain the respondent's cooperation and establish rapport. In this regard, a simple question which asks the respondent to express an attitude is a good starter, since most people like to express their feelings and can do so easily. This approach gives respondents confidence that they can answer the remaining questions in the interview.

Ask General Questions First   Within a topic, general questions should precede specific questions. Consider the following two questions: "What considerations are important to you in buying cereal?" and "When buying cereal, is the sugar content important to you?" If these questions were asked in reverse order, sugar content would appear more frequently in the answer to the first question than if the questions were asked in the order given here. Consequently, asking general questions first and specific questions second reduces the chance of sequence bias.

Place Uninteresting and Difficult Questions Late in Sequence   Sequence any questions which are embarrassing, sensitive, complex, or dull well down in the questionnaire. After rapport has been established by the interviewer and the questioning process, the respondent is less apt to object to more demanding and personal questions.

Arrange Questions in Logical Order   The flow of the questioning process must be logical from the respondent's perspective. A question sequence designed to facilitate data processing or established from the perspective of the researcher can cause respondent confusion, frustration, and indecision, and it can seriously influence cooperation and rapport.

When the information needs of a study are extensive and different groups within the sample need to be asked different questions, it is helpful to "flow

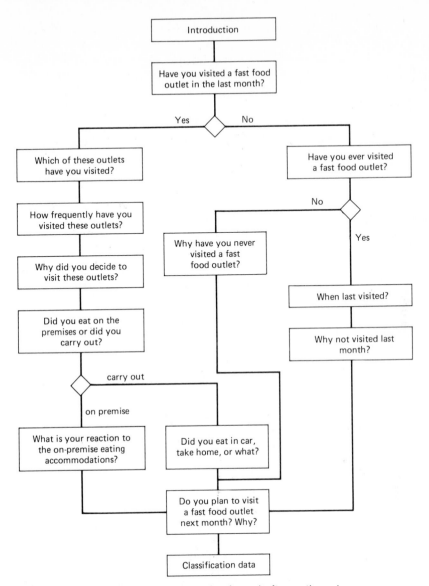

Figure 19-3 Example of a flow chart plan for a draft questionnaire.

chart'' the question sequence. Figure 19-3 presents a flow chart plan for a questionnaire. Flow charting can be very helpful in visualizing the structure of the questionnaire and in ensuring that the questions asked flow logically.

Decide on Physical Characteristics

The physical appearance of the questionnaire can be influential in securing the cooperation of the respondent. This is particularly the case with mail surveys. The quality of the paper and printing often determines the respondent's first reaction to the questionnaire. It is important that the name of the organization sponsoring the survey (often fictitious to avoid bias) and the project name should appear clearly on the first page.

With the personal and telephone interview, the questionnaires should be numbered serially. This facilitates control of the questionnaire in field operations and during data processing. Mail questionnaires may not be identified numerically when respondent anonymity is important.

Finally, the format of a question can influence the response. For both self-administered and interviewer-administered questionnaires, researchers have discovered that the more lines or space left for recording the response to open-ended questions, the more extensive the reply.

Carry Out Pretest, Revision, and Final Draft

Before the questionnaire is ready for field operations, it needs to be pretested and revised. Pretesting refers to the initial testing of one or more aspects of the research design. We are concerned here with pretesting the questionnaire design, for regardless of the researcher's skill a pretest is needed to search out areas for improvement. Most questionnaires require at least one pretest and revision before they are ready for field operations.

Preferably, the questionnaire should be pretested in the manner intended for the final study. However, with an early draft of the questionnaire it is best to pretest using personal interviewers, even though the survey is to be administered by mail or telephone. It is important that only the best interviewers be used for pretest work. A skilled interviewer can respond to requests for explanation, detect areas of confusion, and probe the nature of this confusion. The interviewer should be sensitive to words which are not understood by all respondents, should test question sequence, and should note mechanical difficulties and the like. Ultimately, the revised questionnaire should be pretested in the manner intended for the final survey.

The open-ended response format can be used in the pretest to determine appropriate response categories for what will become a multiple-choice question in the final questionnaire. A new pretest should be conducted to uncover any problems with the standardized response categories created.

The number of people interviewed in a pretest can range from 15 to 30. The sample should be similar to those interviewed in the main study.

Whenever significant changes are made in the questionnaire, another pretest should be conducted. If the pretest results suggest minor changes, the questionnaire is ready for the final draft and distribution to field operators.

OBSERVATIONAL FORMS

Observational forms are easier to design than questionnaires, since the question-asking process is eliminated and design problems related to controlling nonsampling error are reduced. Even so, there are still important issues in the construction of observational forms. The researcher needs to make very explicit the types of observations to be made and how they are to be measured. The measurement process can involve an observer with observational forms, a mechanical recording device, or a combination of both.

The design of observational forms should flow logically from the listing of information needs, which must clearly specify those aspects of the behavior to be observed. It is often useful to characterize the information needs as the "who, what, when, and where" of behavior. Consider the information needs for a study designed to observe shoppers purchasing cereal. They should specify in detail:

1 Who is to be observed?—Purchasers, lookers, males, females, couples, couples with children, children alone.
2 What is to be observed?—Brands purchased, size, brands considered, influence of children and adults, price of product, package inspected.
3 When is observation to be made?—Days of week, hours, day and time of purchase recorded.
4 Where should observations be made?—Type of store, location, how selected.

Observational forms should be simple to use. They should be designed so that they logically follow the behavior observed. They should permit the observer to record the behavior in detail, rather than requiring a summary regarding a number of behavior patterns. The physical characteristics of the form should follow the same rules given for questionnaires. Finally, observational forms need the same degree of pretesting and revision as questionnaires.

SUMMARY

1 A questionnaire is a formalized schedule for collecting data from respondents. It can collect data on past behavior, attitudes, and respondent characteristics. The questionnaire is a critical component of the research project in that a poorly designed questionnaire can be a major source of error in the research results.

2 The five sections to a questionnaire are (1) identification data, (2) request for cooperation, (3) instructions, (4) information sought, and (5) classification data.

3 While a number of guidelines are useful in designing a questionnaire, its quality depends on the skill and judgment of the researcher. The steps in questionnaire design are (1) review preliminary considerations, (2) decide on question content, (3) decide on response format, (4) decide on question wording, (5) decide on question sequence, (6) decide on physical characteristics, and (7) carry out pretest, revision, and final draft.

4 The design of the questionnaire is dependent upon previous decisions regarding the nature of the research design, sources of data, target population, sampling plan, communication media, measurement techniques, and the data processing and analysis plan. The questionnaire is the link between the information needed and the data to be collected.

5 Question content is influenced by the respondent's ability and willingness to respond accurately. The question response format can be open-ended, multiple-choice, or dichotomous.

6 The guidelines for designing the question wording are (1) use simple words, (2) use clear words, (3) avoid leading questions, (4) avoid biased questions, (5) avoid implicit alternatives, (6) avoid implicit assumptions, (7) avoid estimates, (8) avoid double-barreled questions, and (9) consider the frame of reference.

7 The guidelines for determining the question sequences are (1) use simple and interesting opening questions, (2) ask general questions first, (3) place uninteresting and difficult questions late in the sequence, and (4) arrange questions in logical order.

8 The physical characteristics of the questionnaire can influence the degree of respondent cooperation and the character of the responses. The questionnaire needs to be pretested and revised before it is ready for use in the field.

9 Observational forms are easier to design than questionnaire since the design problems associated with the question-asking process have been eliminated. The data collection forms should flow logically from a clear specification of the types of observations to be made and how they are to be measured.

DISCUSSION QUESTIONS

1   What role does the questionnaire play in the research project?
2   What are the typical components of a questionnaire?
3   What decisions precede the questionnaire design stage?
4   What criterion governs the inclusion of questions in the questionnaire?
5   How does the respondent affect the content of the questions?
6   How can a researcher overcome the problems associated with collecting data about unimportant or infrequent events?
7   Why may a respondent be unwilling to respond accurately to a given question?
8   What approaches are available for dealing with the bias resulting from a respondent's unwillingness to respond accurately?
9   What are the advantages and disadvantages of open-ended questions?
10 List the advantages and disadvantages associated with multiple-choice questions.
11 What guidelines govern the design of responses to multiple-choice questions?
12 Under what conditions would dichotomous questions be inappropriate?
13 What general guidelines should one utilize in designing the wording of a question?

SUGGESTED READING

Erdos, P. L., *Professional Mail Surveys* (New York: McGraw-Hill, 1970), chaps. 6 and 7. A leading practitioner presents guidelines for designing self-administered questionnaires.

Kornhauser, A., and P. B. Sheatsley, "Questionnaire Construction and Interview Procedure," in C. Selltiz et al., *Research Methods in Social Relations* (New York: Holt, 1959). A well-written and practical guide to questionnaire construction.

Oppenheim, A. N., *Questionnaire Design and Attitude Measurement* (London: Heinemann Educational Books, Ltd., 1966). An interesting and extensive discussion of the issues involved in questionnaire design.

Payne, S. L., *The Art of Asking Questions* (Princeton, N.J.: Princeton University Press, 1951). A classic work on questionnaire design. Required reading for all researchers interested in this topic.

Chapter 20

Field Operations

The methods of collecting data and the design of data collection forms have been discussed in the previous two chapters. This chapter completes the section on collecting data from respondents by discussing field operations.

The field operation is that phase of the project during which researchers make contact with the respondents, administer the data collection instruments, record the data, and return the data to a central location for processing. The wisdom behind the research design and the skill involved in developing the data collection instrument will be wasted if the field operation is poorly administered. An important source of error in the research process can be identified with the field operation.

The planning of the field operation is highly influenced by the data collection method employed; for example, the field operation for a personal interview study is substantially different from that for a mail interview study. However, given these differences, there are some basic issues which are common to all field operations.

This chapter will first discuss the common issues in planning and controlling field operations. Next, the more specific aspects of field operations associated with alternative data collection methods will be introduced. The last part of the chapter will be devoted to the sources of error in field operations and the presentation of various guidelines for controlling these errors.

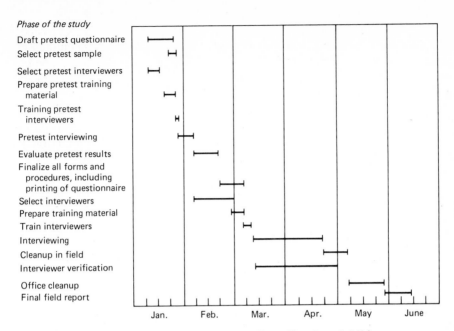

Figure 20-1 Field time schedule flow diagram. (*From Hauck, p. 2-149.*)

PLANNING FIELD OPERATIONS

Four aspects of planning are common to all field operations: (1) time schedules, (2) budgets, (3) personnel, and (4) performance measurement.[1]

Time Schedule

Every project must have a time schedule specifying (1) when the project is to begin and end and (2) the sequencing of activities within this time frame. The number of days needed to complete various activities must be estimated and the degree of overlap among activities determined. It is very important that realistic time periods be established so that the project can be completed in a reasonable amount of time. Often target completion dates are set which do not realistically reflect the time required to carry out field operations properly. Attempts to cut corners to reach unreasonable completion dates can be costly and decrease the accuracy of the results.

   Figure 20-1 presents a detailed time schedule for a personal interview study. Experience suggests that those activities most likely to be underestimated in time requirements are the final approval and printing of the questionnaire, the selection of interviewers, the evaluation of the pretest, and the cleanup in the field. It is best to leave room in the schedule for inaccurate time estimates and unforeseen events.

[1] This section follows closely the discussion presented by Mathew Hauck, "Planning Field Operations," in Robert Ferber (ed.), *Handbook of Marketing Research* (New York: McGraw-Hill, 1975), pp. 2-147 to 2-154.

Budget

The budget involves the assignment of costs to specific activities identified in the field time schedule. The budget and the time schedule are closely interrelated. In most cases they are prepared together, since changes in one can result in changes in the other.

The main cost categories for a personal interview study are (1) office wages and salaries, (2) materials and supplies, (3) telephone, (4) field supervisors or interviewing services, (5) interviewer's compensation, and (6) reproduction of questionnaires and other field forms. These cost categories can be further segmented and assigned to the stages of the data collection process: (1) pretest, (2) selection and hiring of interviewers, (3) interviewer training, (4) final field reports, and (5) data collection.

Effective budgeting and cost control requires a detailed breakdown of the major cost categories into their smallest components.[2] Specific categories need to be reviewed to see whether the costs have been underestimated, and a reserve fund is needed for unforeseen contingencies. Finally, the budget should be reviewed and possibly approved by those individuals responsible for carrying out the activities associated with the cost category.

Personnel

The success of the field operation depends on the quality of the personnel used to execute the plans. Skilled personnel are required, along with the clear assignment of responsibility for all aspects of the plan, if completion dates are to be met and costs controlled. Finally, the personnel must clearly understand what is expected of them and how this performance will be measured.

Performance Measurement

To control activities and accomplish objectives, clear performance measures are required. Too often, the number of interviews to be completed is the only measure clearly specified for a study, yet it is just as important to specify the number of expected refusals, noncontacts, and other noninterviewing situations. Table 20-1 presents these performance measures in a format where expected results can be compared with actual results. The ratios presented at the bottom of the table are used to derive the figures in the body of the table. These ratios can be determined by pretest results and/or the past experience of the researcher.

The totals in Table 20-1 should be broken down by region, interviewing agency, supervisor, and other categories useful for control purposes. The personnel responsible for accomplishing the expected results should participate in determining whether they are reasonable.

Most research projects exceed their initial research budgets. The causes are changes in the research design, poor time scheduling, and inaccurate budget estimates. Upon the completion of a study, the final costs should be compared with the budget so that future budget estimates can be more accurate.

[2] Seymour Sudman, *Reducing the Costs of Surveys* (Chicago: Aldine, 1968).

Table 20-1 Study Performance Measures: Expected and Actual

Performance Measure	Expected	Actual
1 Total eligible respondents	——	——
1.1 Interviews	——	——
1.2 Refusals	——	——
1.3 Noncontacts (assumed eligible)	——	——
1.4 Other (specify)		
_____	——	——
2 Total ineligible respondents	——	——
2.1 Moved	——	——
2.2 Other (specify)		
_____	——	——
3 Total sample	——	——
Response rate $(1.1 \div 1)$	____%	____%
Refusal rate $(1.2) \div (1.1 + 1.2)$	____%	____%
Contact rate $((1 - 1.3) \div 1)$	____%	____%
Eligibility rate $(1 \div 3)$	____%	____%

Source: Adapted from Mathew Hauck, "Planning Field Operations," in Robert Ferber (ed.), *Handbook of Marketing Research* (New York: McGraw-Hill, 1975), p. 2-151.

DATA COLLECTION METHODS

This section presents those aspects of field operations which differ according to whether personal interview, telephone interview, mail interview, or observation is used to collect the data.

Personal Interview

The use of interviewers in a face-to-face setting presents special problems relating to their selection, training, and supervision. Researchers have three options in this regard—they can use their own research organization, contract with an outside field work agency, or do both. No matter which option is chosen, sufficient time and money must be assigned to this very expensive and complicated aspect of the field operation.

Finding qualified interviewers is a difficult task. First, the researcher must specify the job qualifications needed for the project. Next, applicants must be located, screened, and hired in those geographic locations required by the sampling plan. Typically, outside field work organizations are hired to conduct the interviewing. These organizations maintain contact with interviewers and have files on their qualifications.

Once the interviewers are selected, they must be trained. The objective of training is to establish a high degree of commonality in the data collection process among interviewers. Because of time constraints and geographic dispersion in the sampling plan, most training programs consist of written instructions to the interviewer covering areas such as the purpose of the study, how to carry out the sampling plan, and how to approach the respondent, establish rapport, ask the questions, and the like. For complex studies, the training may be conducted by supervisors in person at one or more central locations.

The pretest results should provide valuable insights as to the nature and extent of the training required. It is important to allot enough time in the schedule for adequate training.

Following the training program, the interviewer begins the interviewing process. During this process there should be constant monitoring to determine whether the interviewing is adhering to plans. Completed interviews need to be inspected for completeness, accuracy, neatness, and so forth. If the work of an interviewer is unsatisfactory, retraining or dismissal may be required.

How should the interviewer be compensated—hourly or by the interview? The common answer is to pay by the hour, since an incentive pay scheme may cause the interviewer to rush through the interview and seriously reduce the quality of the data gathered. This could be reflected in cheating or falsification of interviews, failure to ask all the questions, and failure to probe answers adequately.

The argument for an incentive pay scheme, where personnel are paid per interview, is that the interviewers can earn more money by planning their activities more efficiently. It is argued that target completion dates are reached more often and that the quality of data collected can be higher if only those interviews which meet specified standards are acceptable for payment. The important element in the successful use of the incentive pay scheme appears to be the extensive use of controls.

Finally, the success of the field work is dependent on the skill and experience of the field supervisor. The competence of a new supervisor should be checked by contacting previous clients, and only the highest-quality supervisors should be used in field work.

Telephone Interview

Most of the issues involved in the selection, training, and supervision of personal interviewers apply equally well to telephone interviewers. This is particularly the case if the telephone interviews are to be conducted from several geographic locations. However, if they are to be conducted from a central location, the ability to control the field work closely becomes an important distinguishing factor. The entire interviewing process can be directly monitored and the quality of the interview evaluated. Poor-quality interviewing can be detected early and corrected. In addition, problems resulting in a delay in the interviewing time schedule can be detected immediately and, one hopes, corrected.

Delays in the interviewing time schedule usually are attributed to (1) an inadequate population list, (2) a higher rate of callbacks required than planned, and (3) interviews taking longer than expected because of questionnaire length and/or complexity. Problems of this nature typically result from inadequate pretesting of the questionnaire and the data collection process.

A major budget item is the cost of the phone calls, especially if WATS lines are not available.

Mail Interview

The mail interview is distinguished from other data collection methods in that more aspects of the data collection process are under the central control of the researcher. This results from the elimination of the interviewer from the field operation. Consequently, mail surveys are more likely to meet time schedules and stay within budgets than other data collection methods.

The time schedule should classify activities into phases, such as (1) drafting the questionnaire, (2) pretesting, (3) questionnaire finalization and reproduction, (4) first mailing, (5) second or third mailing if used, (6) check of nonrespondents, and (7) data collection from a subsample of nonrespondents. The experience of the researcher is the key to developing realistic time schedules for mail surveys.

Observation

The nature of the plans for observational field operations depends on the complexity of the research design and whether personal or mechanical recording is to be used. When field personnel are to be used, the previous discussion regarding personal interviews applies here. When mechanical recording is to be used, special problems are presented. The budget and time schedule must consider the equipment costs, setup time, maintenance, breakdown, and the like.

ERRORS IN FIELD OPERATIONS

The validity of the research results is directly related to the number and size of sampling and nonsampling errors. This section describes sources of error connected with field operations. Previous sections of the book have discussed sampling and nonsampling errors as they relate to other aspects of the research process.

The main sources of error to be discussed here are (1) sample selection errors, (2) nonresponse errors, and (3) interviewing errors.

Sample Selection Errors

The chapters on sampling have discussed the quota sampling procedure. It was noted that this nonprobability sampling procedure is very common in marketing research and requires the interviewer to select the individuals to be included in the study, subject to various quotas specified in the sampling plan. This interviewer control of the sample selection process is likely to result in respondent selection error.

Despite formal quotas and procedures for sample selection, interviewers will sometimes try to bend or falsify rules and select respondents who are most convenient or offer the least resistance. For quotas on economic levels, interviewers tend to focus on the middle-income levels and to avoid high- and low-income respondents.

Probability sampling procedures which appear to eliminate interviewer sample selection errors still contain the potential for error. The interviewer usually participates in the probability procedure used to identify the list of dwelling units, select the dwelling unit, and select the individual to be interviewed in the unit. In listing dwelling units, interviewers tend to underlist low-income blocks. Random selection procedures for selecting from the list are typically biased by the interviewer in favor of middle-income dwellings. Within the dwelling unit, interviewers tend to select the more accessible persons in the unit.

Nonresponse Errors

Nonresponse error, described in detail in Chapter 18, refers to the difference between those who respond to a survey and those who do not respond. It can be one of the most serious sources of error confronting the researcher. We will briefly build on the earlier discussion of the topic and emphasize its importance to field operations.

Nonresponse can result from two sources: (1) not-at-homes and (2) refusals. The nonresponse problem appears to be increasing. In the 1960s, researchers obtained response rates of 80 to 85 percent using three or four callbacks, but in the 1970s response rates have dropped to 60 to 65 percent. The nonresponse is equally divided between not-at-homes and refusals.[3]

The most common procedure for increasing the response rate is to make callbacks. The cost of a callback program can be reduced by the use of the telephone and/or the self-administered questionnaire. The telephone can be used to contact respondents and make appointments for the personal interview. When appropriate, a self-administered questionnaire with a stamped, self-addressed envelope can be left at the dwelling of all not-at-homes.

Interviewing Errors

With the personal and telephone interview, the interviewer can be a serious source of error. This error is related to (1) interviewer-respondent rapport, (2) asking the questions, (3) recording responses, and (4) cheating.

Interviewer-Respondent Rapport   An interview involves a social interaction between two people. During this interaction, the respondent's perception of the interviewer can directly affect the latter's ability to establish proper rapport. Interviewers who can establish effective relationships with respondents are able to collect more complete and accurate data.

With the personal interview, the interviewer's style of dress should resemble that of the respondent. The interviewer's dress and grooming are important in establishing rapport in that they are regarded by most people as indications of a person's attitudes and orientation. The demeanor of the interviewer should be pleasant, if nothing else.

As a general rule, the more the interviewer and respondent have in common, the greater the opportunity for rapport. Basically, the respondent should see the interviewer as capable of understanding his or her viewpoint.

[3] *Report on the ASA Conference on Surveys of Human Populations* (Washington, D.C.: American Statistical Association, 1973), p. 3.

Asking the Questions   A series of guidelines appropriate for most interviewing situations has been developed and is briefly outlined in this section.[4]

(1) *Be thoroughly familiar with the questionnaire.* The interviewer must study the questionnaire carefully, question by question, and practice reading it aloud. Each question must be read without error or stumbling over words and phrases. The interviewer's role resembles that of an actor reading lines in a play or motion picture. The questions must be read naturally and in a conversational mode.

(2) *Ask the questions exactly as they are worded in the questionnaire.* Researchers have found that even a slight change in wording can distort results. The interviewer must be sensitive to inadvertent changes in a question, such as leaving out part of a question, changing a word, or adding a few words at the end of the question for conversational purposes.

(3) *Ask the questions in the order in which they are presented in the questionnaire.* In the design of the questionnaire, the question sequence was established to ensure that questions early in the sequence will not bias the answers to questions later in the sequence. In addition, the question sequence was designed from the respondent's perspective to create a sense of continuity in the topic covered.

(4) *Ask every question specified in the questionnaire.* The respondent's answer to one question may answer another question later in the questionnaire. In this situation, the interviewer should never skip the question which appears to have been answered earlier. It is the interviewer's responsibility to ask every question, even when it has clearly been answered previously. This can be done by letting the respondent know that the interviewer is aware of the earlier response and is asking the respondent's cooperation in answering again. The interviewer might say, for example: "We have already touched on this, but let me ask you . . ."

(5) *Use probing techniques to get the respondent to answer the question.* The questions have been designed to be understood by all respondents in the sampling plan. However, at times the interviewer may find respondents who misunderstand or misinterpret what is asked, who are reluctant to give a complete answer, or who get sidetracked on another topic in answering the question. The quality of the data collected depends upon the interviewer's skill in overcoming these problems through the use of *neutral* probing techniques.

Probing techniques are intended to perform the following two functions without introducing bias: (1) motivate the respondents to communicate more fully so that they can enlarge on, clarify, or explain the reasons behind what is said, and (2) help the respondent focus on the specific content of the interview so that irrelevant or unnecessary data can be avoided.[5]

There are several kinds of neutral probing techniques which may be used to stimulate a fuller, clearer response.

---

[4] This section follows closely the material in *Interviewer's Manual*, rev. ed., Survey Research Center, Institute for Social Research, University of Michigan, Ann Arbor, 1976, pp. 11–13.

[5] Ibid., p. 15.

Table 20-2 Commonly Used Probes

Interviewer's probe	Standard abbreviation
Repeat question	(RQ)
Anything else?	(AE or Else?)
Any other reason?	(AO?)
Any others?	(Other?)
How do you mean?	(How mean?)
Could you tell me more about your thinking on that?	(Tell more)
Would you tell me what you have in mind?	(What in mind?)
What do you mean?	(What mean?)
Why do you feel that way?	(Why?)
Which would be closer to the way you feel?	(Which closer?)

Source: Interviewer's Manual, rev. ed., Survey Research Center, Institute for Social Research, University of Michigan, Ann Arbor, 1976, p. 16.

1 *Repeating the question.* A very effective approach is to repeat the question just as it is written in the questionnaire. Typically, further probes are unnecessary.

2 *An expectant pause.* The interviewer's silence or pause is an effective cue to the respondent that a more complete response is expected. This is often difficult for new interviewers to do.

3 *Repeating the respondent's reply.* Respondents often are stimulated to further comments on hearing their thoughts repeated. This can be done while the interviewer is recording the comments on the questionnaire.

4 *Reassure the respondent.* If the respondent appears hesitant to respond, it may be helpful to use a comment such as: "We're just trying to get people's ideas on this," or "There are no right or wrong answers, just your ideas on it." If the respondent needs an explanation of a word or phrase, the interviewer should not offer a definition, rather the responsibility for the definition should be returned to the respondent. This might be done as follows: "Just whatever it means to you—anything you would call . . ."

5 *Neutral questions or comments.* Several examples of the most commonly used probes and their "key word" phrases or abbreviations are presented in Table 20-2. The standard abbreviations are to be recorded on the questionnaire in parentheses next to the question asked. The new interviewer will find it useful to have a copy of Table 20-2 available for easy reference during the interview.

6 *Asking for further clarification.* Asking the question: "I'm not quite sure I know what you mean by that—could you tell me a little more?" can arouse the respondent's desire to cooperate with the interviewer who appears to be trying to do a good job. It is often effective to appear somewhat bewildered by the respondent's answer when asking this question.[6]

In summary, effective probing requires that the interviewer recognize immediately just how the respondent's answer has failed to meet the objectives of the specific question. Next, the interviewer must be able to select an appropriate

[6] Ibid., pp. 15–16.

probing technique to elicit the data required by the question. Each question should have instructions indicating how forcefully the interviewer should probe.

(6) *Keep track of changes made in the questionnaire.* If the interviewer makes any changes—even inadvertent ones—in the wording, phrasing, or order of questions, they should be clearly noted on the questionnaire. This allows the researcher to analyze the potential bias and decide how the data should be coded.

(7) *Provide a logical reason for collecting personal data.* If the respondent asks why the interviewer needs to know age, religion, income and the like, the following explanation could be used:

> Well, as I was saying earlier, we are talking with people of different ages and various occupations in all parts of the country. We put all of the interviews together, and then count them up to see whether men feel differently from women, whether young people feel differently from older people, and so on. To do this we need to know a few things about the people we talk to. So, I have just a few questions on that type of thing.[7]

Recording Responses   Even though an error-free job of asking questions has been accomplished, the next concern is recording the data in an unbiased form which can be interpreted accurately by the coders. Each interviewer must use the same format and conventions in recording the interviews and in editing each completed interview.

Rules for Recording Responses   The interviewer should record not only what was said but also how it was said. It should transmit a picture of the respondent's personality and the interview situation. The following six rules are designed to aid in accomplishing this type of recording.

1   Record responses during the interview.

2   Use the respondent's own words.

3   Do not summarize or paraphrase the respondent's answers.

4   Include everything that pertains to the question objectives.

5   Include all probes and comments by entering them next to the question in parentheses.

6   Hold the respondent's interest by repeating the response as it is written down.[8]

Tips on Note Taking   The skill of note taking is developed with practice. Practice recording the comments of friends, or a news broadcast.[9]

1   When starting the interview, try to find a place where you will be able to write comfortably.

2   When the respondent starts to talk, begin to write immediately.

[7] Ibid., p. 13.
[8] Ibid., pp. 20–21.
[9] Ibid., pp. 21–22.

3 Abbreviate words and sentences. During the editing process, put these in along with punctuation.

Mechanics of Recording and Editing Interviews   The following procedures are suggested to facilitate the recording and editing process:[10]

1 Use a pencil to record.

2 Writing must be legible.

3 Use parentheses to indicate the interviewer's words or observations.

4 Do not put anything the respondent says in parentheses.

5 During editing, cross-reference the responses to one question that also apply to other questions.

6 Each question must have an answer or an explanation as to why it was not answered.

7 Check to see that the identification data are complete—name, date, interviewer number, project number, and the like.

Cheating   What is cheating? In practice, it is hard to define. Obviously, the personal interviewer who sits at home and fills out the questionnaire is cheating. More frequently, cheating is defined as the falsification of a question or questions within the questionnaire. This type of cheating is extremely difficult to detect. Phone calls to respondents to determine whether the personal interview took place will not detect the partial falsification of the questionnaire. The monitoring of phone interviews is an effective way to control cheating with the telephone interview.

SUMMARY

1 Four areas are common to planning all field operations: (1) time schedules, (2) budgets, (3) personnel, and (4) performance measurement. The time schedule specifies when the project is to begin and end, and also the sequencing of activities within this time period. The budget involves the assignment of costs to the specific activities identified in the time schedule. Skilled personnel are required, along with the clear assignment of responsibility for activities, if completion dates are to be met and costs controlled. Finally, clear performance measures are required if activities are to be controlled and objectives met.

2 Field operations differ according to whether personal interview, telephone interview, mail interview, or observation is used to collect the data. When interviewers are used to collect the data, they must be selected, trained, and supervised, which involves time-consuming and expensive activities. When telephone interviews are conducted from a central location, the ability to control the interviewing activity closely is an important distinction from personal inter-

[10] Ibid., pp. 22–23.

viewing. With the mail interview, the elimination of the interviewer from the data collection process allows the centralization of the field operation directly under the researcher's control. When observers are used in observational studies, the nature of the field operation is similar to that of the personal interview study. If mechanical recording is to be used, special problems are presented for field operations.

3   The main sources of error in field operations relate to (1) sample selection errors, (2) nonresponse errors, and (3) interviewing errors. The more control the interviewer has over who will be interviewed, the greater the opportunity for sample selection error. Nonresponse error refers to the difference between those who respond and those who do not. Nonresponse can result from (1) not-at-homes and (2) refusals. The callback procedure is most commonly used to increase the response rate.

4   The major sources of interviewing error occur in the areas of (1) interviewer-respondent rapport, (2) asking the questions, (3) recording errors, and (4) cheating.

5   For the new interviewer, a series of guidelines is available regarding the process of asking questions and recording answers. These guidelines, combined with practice sessions, will be useful in improving the new interviewer's skills and reducing interviewing errors.

DISCUSSION QUESTIONS

1   What four areas are important in the planning of field operations?
2   What are the problems peculiar to the use of the personal interview in field operations?
3   Evaluate the use of the telephone interview in field operations.
4   What are the main sources of error in field operations?
5   What is nonresponse error?
6   How can the interviewer contribute to measurement error?
7   What guidelines should an interviewer be given regarding the asking of questions?

SUGGESTED READING

Hauck, Mathew, "Planning Field Operations," in Robert Ferber (ed.), *Handbook of Marketing Research* (New York: McGraw-Hill, 1975), pp. 2-147 to 2-159. The author presents a user-oriented discussion of planning and controlling field operations.

Interviewer's Manual, rev. ed., Survey Research Center, Institute for Social Research, University of Michigan, Ann Arbor, 1976. An excellent document which is designed to instruct personal interviewers on the procedures of conducting survey research.

Mayer, Charles S., "Quality Control," in Ferber, *Handbook of Marketing Research*, pp. 2-160 to 2-177. The author presents an interesting discussion of the issues and procedures appropriate for controlling field operations.

Cases for Part Six

National Watchband

Mr. James Aesop was director of marketing for National Watchband, one of the nation's largest suppliers of replacement watchbands. He was in the process of evaluating a proposed questionnaire for a telephone survey of watch owners concerning their reaction to "fashion" watchbands (see Exhibit 1 for questionnaire). In particular, he wondered whether the questionnaire would provide managerially relevant information, and whether it could be answered by a respondent on the telephone.

Watchbands were sold from display racks in jewelry, department, and discount stores. Traditionally, watchbands had been of two types: either metal or the conventional leather and nylon. The latter were composed of well-established, not very exciting designs. Recently, so-called fashion watchbands had made a significant impact on the market. These bands were predominantly leather, were extra wide, and had bold designs. Mr. Aesop thought that their appeal was to youthful buyers.

National had not entered the fashion segment, as management had judged this type of band to be a short-lived fad. This judgment proved to be incorrect.

Exhibit 1   Questionnaire

Do you wear a watch?

       Yes _____   No _____

(If they answer "no," tell them you are sorry, but "they don't qualify for the study," and then thank them for their trouble.)

1 How many watches do you own?
       Number of watches _____

What are their price ranges?

	1.	2.	3.
Under $15	___	___	___
$15–$30	___	___	___
$30–$50	___	___	___
$50–$100	___	___	___
$100 +	___	___	___

For what purposes are they used?

	1.	2.	3.
Everyday	___	___	___
Evening	___	___	___
Special occasion	___	___	___

How often is each type worn?

	TYPES		
	1.	2.	3.
Frequently	___	___	___
Occasionally	___	___	___
Seldom	___	___	___
Never	___	___	___

2 What type(s) of watchband(s) do you have on your watches? (Please specify by watch.)

	1.	2.	3.
1. Metal expansion	___	___	___
2. Metal nonexpansion	___	___	___
3. Traditional leather	___	___	___
4. Fashion leather (pop, vinyl, wide)	___	___	___
5. Nylon	___	___	___
6. Rubber	___	___	___
7. Other	___	___	___

3 How long ago did you last buy a watchband?
       Months _____   Years _____

Exhibit 1   Questionnaire (*Continued*)

4 What type of watchband was it?
    Type _____
    Don't know _____

5 Where did you buy your last watchband?
    Type of store _____
    Don't know _____

6 How much did you pay for it?
    Price _____
    Don't know _____

7 What made you decide that you needed a new watchband?

8 What factors led you to choose the particular watchband you did? (influencers)

9 Was the purchase of your last watchband a planned or spur-of-the-moment purchase?
    Planned _____   Spur-of-the-moment _____

10 When do you plan to purchase your next watchband?
    (a) Time _____   Only with next watch purchase _____
    (b) Why?
    (c) Where?
    (d) What type?
    (e) What price will you pay?
    (f) Don't know _____

11 Of all the different watchbands currently available, which do you consider the most fashionable?
    Why?

12 Do you buy fashions according to style?
    Yes _____   No _____

13 Now please tell me which of the following statements best applies to you.
    (a) To keep in style I buy new fashions as soon as I see them advertised.
    (b) I try to keep up with the styles worn by my most fashion-conscious friends.
    (c) I try to keep in style with most of the people I know.
    (d) I like to see that a style is going to be around for a while before committing myself to it.

14 Do you see leather "fashion" watchbands as a passing fad?
    Yes _____   No _____

15 Could you please give us the following statistical information:
    1. Your age _____

Exhibit 1   Questionnaire (Continued)

   2. Your occupation _____
   3. Male _____   Female _____
   4. Into which of the following would your income fall?
       Under $2000   _____
       $2000–$6000   _____
       $6000–$10,000   _____
       $10,000–$15,000   _____
       $15,000 and over   _____

Thank you very much for helping us out.

                  Respondent's Name _____
                  Telephone   _____

The fashion segment experienced rapid growth over a two-year period and was still growing. It was at this point that the management of National Watchband asked marketing research to undertake an inexpensive study to determine whether or not National should enter the fashion segment.

Discussion Question

Evaluate and revise the proposed telephone questionnaire. Be prepared to explain the bases for your evaluation and the reason for any changes in the questionnaire.

Case 2

A Day in the Careers of Pamela Palmers and Sandy Sanders—Professional Interviewers

Pamela Palmers and Sandy Sanders, professional interviewers for Tri-State Interviewing, were currently working on a project involving in-store interviews with female supermarket shoppers. The study was concerned with determining homemakers' reactions to two brownie mix formulations. One version (Sample R) was the formula used in the client's current brownie mix, which had achieved a substantial market share. The second version (Sample G) was a new R&D formulation. The client was concerned with homemakers' preferences for the two formulations and their comments/reactions in depth.

    Ms. Palmers and Ms. Sanders had spent the previous afternoon in a briefing session with the client concerning the study procedure and questionnaire execution. Both women were to interview as many female shoppers as possible in the period from 9 A.M. to 9 P.M. The two brownie samples would be prepared locally by a home economist from the client's R&D facilities.

The questionnaire and "contact sheet" are attached.

The following interviews are representative of those conducted by Ms. Palmers and Ms. Sanders during the one-day brownie taste test.

Typical Interviews: Pamela Palmers (PP)
(Kroger Supermarket, Saturday, July 14th)

Contact No. 1 (9:08 A.M.)

A middle-aged woman approaches the test area with a few items in her cart from the entry displays.

PP: Good morning! I am Pamela Palmers, and we are having a brownie taste test this morning. I would like to have you try our two brownie samples and give us your reaction.

Resp.: Why yes, I love brownies.

PP: Please sit down at our test table and try the brownies.

(The respondent sits down and proceeds to taste each of the brownies marked "G" and "R.")

PP: After you have had time to try each brownie, I'd like to ask you a few questions. It will only take a few minutes. Can I get you a cup of coffee?

Resp.: Yes—black, please.

PP: Which of the two brownie samples did you prefer?

Resp.: Sample "G."

PP: What did you particularly like about the brownies?

Resp.: I liked the taste of "G."

PP: What was there about the taste of "G" that you liked?

Resp.: The chocolate taste was good.

PP: In what way was the chocolate taste good?

Resp. It wasn't too bitter and it wasn't too sweet-tasting, it was just the right taste.

PP: Sorry for the delay—I am writing this down, and I want to be sure I am writing it just as you are telling it to me. What else did you like about Sample "G"?

Resp.: Well, I like the color; it's a nice light brown, just a perfect chocolate color for a brownie.

PP: What else did you like?

Resp.: I guess I've told you everything I liked about Sample "G."

PP: What did you like about Sample "R"?

Resp.: There wasn't anything I liked about it.

PP: What did you particularly dislike about the brownies?

Resp.: Well, Sample "R" was sweet, and the texture was terrible.

PP: In what ways was the texture terrible?

Resp.: It's too fluffy; I hate cake brownies.

PP: What else didn't you like about Sample "R"?
Resp.: That's about it.
PP: What did you dislike about Sample "G"?
Resp.: It's a little crumbly.
PP: What else didn't you like?
Resp.: Nothing, it is really an excellent brownie.

Recorded Answer—Question 2

(Sample G), I liked the taste (taste), the chocolate taste was good (good). It wasn't too bitter and it wasn't too sweet-tasting, it was just the right taste (P). Well, I liked the color, it's a nice light brown, just a perfect chocolate color for a brownie. (P) I guess I've told you everything I liked about Sample G. (Sample R) There wasn't anything I liked about it.

Recorded Answer—Question 3

(Sample R) Well, sample R was sweet and the texture was terrible (texture). It's too fluffy, I hate cake brownies (P) That is about it. (Sample G) It is a little crumbly (P) nothing, it is really an excellent brownie.

Contact No. 4 (10:43 A.M.)

A family with two children, aged approximately four and seven, enters the test area. The female is pushing the cart, with the four-year-old riding.

PP: Good morning, sir. I'm Pamela Palmers, and we are having a brownie taste test. Won't you try one? Coffee is available on the table.

(The male picks up a brownie and proceeds to the table for a cup of coffee.)

PP: I would like to have your wife try two samples of our brownies and answer a few brief questions. Do you mind watching the children while she tries the brownies? It will just take a minute.

(The male smiles at Ms. Palmers and suggests to his wife that she try the brownies. The interview is then completed.)

Contact No. 7 (11:32 A.M.)

A middle-aged woman enters the test area pushing the cart at a brisk pace.

PP: Good morning! I'm Pamela Palmers, and we are conducting a brownie taste test this morning. I would like to have you try our brownies and answer a few questions.

Resp.: Sorry, honey, I'm in a hurry.

(She proceeds down the aisle, stopping briefly to grab a loaf of bread. Interview was not completed.)

Contact No. 18 (3:32 P.M.)

A young woman enters the test area and smiles as she sees Pamela.

PP: Mary, how good to see you. I didn't know you shopped at Krogers.

Resp.: Sometimes they have good specials. What are you doing here, running one of those surveys?

PP: How about helping me out and trying our brownies?

Resp.: Love to.

(Mary sits down and tastes the two samples.)

PP: Which of the two brownie samples did you prefer?

Resp.: "G."

PP: What did you particularly like about the brownies?

Resp.: They taste homemade, especially "G."

PP: In what way does Sample "G" taste like homemade?

Resp: It's very chewy and not too sweet.

PP: What else did you like about Sample "G"?

Resp.: Nothing.

PP: What did you particularly like about Sample "R"?

Resp.: It's very light.

PP: What do you mean by light?

Resp.: The weight of the sample, it is more like a cake in its texture.

PP: What else did you like about Sample "R"?

Resp.: That's about it.

PP: What did you particularly dislike about the brownies?

Resp.: Sample "R" had a strong chocolate flavor.

PP: What do you mean by strong chocolate flavor?
Resp.: Rather sweet chocolate taste.
PP: What else didn't you like about sample "R"?
Resp.: Nothing else, I guess.
PP: What did you particularly dislike about sample "G"?
Resp.: Could be somewhat more chewy.
PP: What else didn't you like?
Resp.: That's it; it is really a good brownie, like I make at home.
(The rest of the interview is completed and Pamela and Mary discuss personal matters for a few minutes.)

Contact No. 24 (8:03 P.M.)
A middle-aged couple enters the test area. Pamela approaches their cart, smiles at both and addresses the female:
PP: Good evening. I am Pamela Palmers, and we are conducting a brownie taste test this evening. I would like to have you try our brownies and answer a few brief questions. It will only take a minute or so.
(Turning to the male, and smiling.)
PP: We have coffee available on the table, and you are free to try the brownies yourself while I talk with your wife.
(The female looks at her husband. He nods his head in approval. The female sits down and tries the brownies. The interview is completed.)

Typical Interviews: Sandy Sanders (SS)
(A&P Supermarket, Saturday, July 14th)

Contact 1 (9:22 A.M.)
A young woman and a year-old child approach the test area. The young child is riding quietly in the cart.
SS: Hi, we are testing brownies this morning—please try some.
Resp.: Okay.
SS: "Please sit down at the table and taste the two samples I have labeled "R" and "G." Would you like some coffee?
Resp.: Yes, cream and sugar.
(The woman tries each of the brownies.)
SS: How did you like the brownies?
Resp.: They were good.
SS: Which of the two brownie samples did you prefer?
Resp.: Sample "G."
SS: What did you like about Sample "G"?
Resp.: The nice flavor. The texture of "G" was good; I like a moist brownie.
SS: By moist, do you mean chewy?
Resp.: Yes, I like a chewy brownie.
SS: How about Sample "R"? You had said they were both good.
Resp.: I like "R," but it didn't have the flavor of "G."

SS: Is there anything else?
Resp.: No.
SS: What didn't you like about the brownies?
Resp.: I like my brownies warm.
SS: Anything about Sample "G" you didn't like?
Resp.: It was a little heavy.
SS: Anything else?
Resp.: No.
SS: How about Sample "R"?
Resp.: Rather sweet.
SS: Anything else?
Resp.: No.

Recorded Answer—Question 2

Both good (G) nice flavor, texture good, moist
(moist), chewy (R/ok, flavor not as good
(P) No.

Recorded Answer—Question 3

Not warm enough (G) heavy (P) no (R)
sweet (P) no

Contact No. 3 (10:24 A.M.)
An elderly couple slowly push their cart to the test area.
SS: Hello, would you like to try some brownies this morning?
Resp.: (male) No, can't eat that stuff—dentures.
(The couple passes through the test area. Interview not completed.)

Contact No. 4 (10:27 A.M.)
A middle-aged couple enters the test area. They have with them two girls aged five and eight. The eight-year-old is pushing the cart, while the husband and wife are talking about the grocery list.
SS: How are you this morning? We are testing brownies; would you be interested?
Resp.: (female) No, not today.
(Interview not completed.)

Contact No. 14 (2:13 P.M.)

A middle-aged woman briskly pushes her cart toward the test area.

SS: Hi, we are testing brownies this morning. Would you care to try our two versions and answer some questions?

Resp.: How long will it take?

SS.: Just two or three minutes. We have coffee also.

Resp.: I don't drink coffee—do you have tea?

SS: No.

Resp.: How about milk?

SS: No.

Resp.: Well, I'll try them quickly.

SS: Please sit down at the table. Here are the two samples. I think you will like them.

(The woman quickly tastes each sample.)

SS: Which did you prefer?

Resp.: Sample "R."

SS: What did you like about "R"?

Resp.: It was tasty, more like homemade.

SS: Anything else?

Resp.: It was light; the other one was too chewy.

SS: Anything else?

Resp.: No.

SS: How about "G," what did you like about it?

Resp.: Nothing.

SS: What did you particularly dislike about the brownies?

Resp.: "G" was too chewy, and the flavor was poor.

SS: What do you mean—poor?

Resp.: It was flat.

SS: Anything else?

Resp.: No.

SS: How about "R"?

Resp.: It was great.

(The rest of the interview is completed.)

Contact No. 21 (4:30 P.M.)

A young teenage couple enters the test area. The male is pushing the cart.

SS: Hi, we are having women try brownies this afternoon. Do you have time to try them and answer some questions?

Resp.: (female) No.

Resp.: (male) They look good—you don't mind if I try one?

(He picks up three brownies, and the couple proceeds. Interview not completed.)

Contact No. 27 (7:42 P.M.)

A young couple enters the test area. A boy, about five, is trying to push the cart while his father guides it from the front.

SS: Hello, we are having women taste two versions of brownies this evening. Would you please try them for us? We have coffee if you would like some.

Resp.: (male) Go ahead, honey, I'll grab a cup of coffee and meet you in the cereal section.

SS: Please be seated at our test table and try the two samples marked "R" and "G."

(The woman tastes each sample.)

SS: Which sample did you like best?

Resp.: They were both good.

SS: You must have liked one better than the other.

Resp.: Well, "G" was a little better, but not much.

SS: What did you like about "G"?

Resp.: It was light and mild.

SS: Do you mean its weight?

Resp.: No, its color.

SS: Anything else?

Resp.: Not really.

SS: What did you like about "R"?

Resp.: It had a rich flavor.

SS: What do you mean by rich?

Resp.: The texture was light and delicate.

SS: Anything else?

Resp.: No, that's it.

SS: What did you particularly dislike about the brownies?

Resp.: As I said before, I liked them equally well. They're both excellent.

SS: There must be something you didn't like—was the color too dark on "R"?

Resp.: No, it was fine.

(The interview is complete.)

At 9:32, Sandy meets Pamela at a nearby cocktail lounge. They both order drinks and proceed to check their completed questionnaires for completeness and legibility. By 11:03 they have completed their work and proceed to the local post office to mail the questionnaires to the client's home office.

Discussion Question

How would you evaluate the interviewing skills of Pamela Palmers and Sandy Sanders? What specific suggestions would make to improve their effectiveness?

QUESTIONNAIRE

Store _____   Date _____

Interviewer _____   Time _____

BROWNIE STUDY

1. Which of the two brownie samples did you prefer?
       Sample R ( )   Sample G ( )   No preference ( )

2. What did you particularly like about the brownies? (Probe and clarify fully)

_____

_____

_____

3. What did you particularly dislike about the brownies? (Probe and clarify fully)

_____

_____

_____

4. How frequently do you serve brownies to your family?
   Once a week ( ) Every two weeks ( ) Once a month ( ) Less frequently ( )

5. Do you make your brownies from a mix or from scratch?
   Mix ( )   Scratch ( )   Both ( )

6. If mix, or both, what brand of mix do you usually buy?
   Brand name(s) _____ , _____

(7 through 11: demographic information)

CONTACT SHEET

Interviewer _Pamela Palmer_   Firm _Tri-State_

Place _Kroger_   Address _1436 Maple_

City/State _St. Louis, Mo._   Date _Sat. July 14th_

	Contact Time	Couple	Female	Completed Yes	Completed No
1	9:08 A.M.		✓	✓	
2	9:20 A.M.		✓		✓
3	9:31 A.M.	✓		✓	
4	10:43 A.M.	✓		✓	
5	11:14 A.M.		✓		✓
Total	28	15	13	16	12

CONTACT SHEET

Interviewer _Sandy Sanders_ Firm _Tri-State_

Place _A + P_ Address _1592 Maple_

City/State _St. Louis, Mo._ Date _Sat. July 14th_

	Contact Time	Couple	Female	Completed Yes	Completed No
1	9:22 am		✓	✓	
2	9:50 am	✓		✓	
3	10:24 am	✓			✓
4					
.					
.					
.					
.					
Total	39	18	21	12	27

Part Seven

Final Stages of the Research Process

Chapter 21

Data Processing

Picture yourself as a marketing research analyst. You are sitting in your office when a delivery service drops two large boxes of questionnaires on your desk, the results of six weeks of field interviewing done by a research supply house that you hired to do the interviewing for a study. You decided earlier that you would directly supervise all the work for this study yourself, except for the field work. Your task now is to get this pile of questionnaires into a form that allows you to do analysis on the data they contain. Just what must be done to accomplish this task?

A description of the functions necessary to prepare raw data collection forms, called instruments, for data analysis constitutes the topic of this chapter. We shall begin with a description of some of the basic terms and concepts of data processing as applied to marketing research. Next we discuss the decision whether a particular respondent's instrument should be prepared for data analysis. It may not be filled out properly, and thus we may not want to use it. Other sections will cover the editing of data collection instruments, coding, data cleaning, creation of new variables, and data weighting.

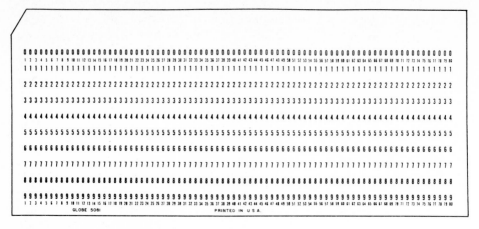

Figure 21-1 The computer card.

SOME BASIC CONCEPTS

Our basic task in data processing is to *convert the raw data in the data collection instrument into a computer-readable form*. We can then make use of computerized data analysis procedures to extract information from the data. Before we see how this is done, there are some concepts and terms that we need to understand.[1]

Case A case refers to *a specific unit of analysis* for the study. Quite often the unit of analysis is the respondent to a questionnaire, so each respondent would be considered a case, and the total number of cases would equal the sample size.

The Computer Card The data provided by a research instrument must be converted into a computer-readable form, and the computer card is the basic device used for this purpose. Figure 21-1 presents a computer card. It is divided into 80 vertical columns. The column numbers appear at the bottom (and under the top row of zeros) of the card. Data are put on the card by punching holes within the columns. Within each vertical column there are 12 spaces available for punches. Ten of these spaces are designated by the numbers 0, 1, 2, 3, 4, 5, 6, 7, 8, 9 running from the top to the bottom of each column. The other two spaces for punches are located above the zero space. They are unnumbered but are sometimes called the 11 and 12 punch, counting from the zero space. By means of a keypunch machine, one can use combinations of punches within a column to form alphabetical letters or special characters. These types of letters and characters will not be used in the data processing discussed in this chapter. Our interest here is in having only one numeric punch (0–9) within each column, as most computer data analysis programs can only handle numeric data.

---

[1] This section follows an excellent discussion in Earl Babbie, *Survey Research Methods* (Belmont, Calif.: Wadsworth, 1973), pp. 187–191.

How is information on a questionnaire converted into punches in a computer card? One or more specific columns of the computer card are assigned to a variable, and then numeric punches are assigned within that column to represent the available responses for that variable. For example, the respondent's year in college might be assigned to column 20 of the computer card. If the respondent is a senior, a 1 could be punched in column 20. If the respondent is a junior, a 2 could be punched in column 20, and so on. If a variable contains more than 10 categories or requires two or more digits to represent the data, the specific variable in question would be assigned as many columns as needed to present the data. For example, the respondent's scores on the Scholastic Aptitude Test (SAT) would require three columns, as the score is out of 800. Columns 71–73 might be assigned for this variable, and the exact score would be punched in the columns. If one's score were 625, the 6 would be punched in column 71, the 2 in column 72, and the 5 in column 73. The data collection instrument for a study may require far more than 80 columns to punch the data properly, but this presents no problem. Each respondent can have as many computer cards as are necessary to represent the data. All that is required is that specific columns within a specific card represent a variable. For example, columns 56–57 of card 3 might represent the respondent's age. The data on the computer cards are read into a computer by a card reader. This device is able to locate the columns on the card and identify the specific punch within each column. The computer can then make use of the data.

Data Deck   The data deck is made up of all the computer cards necessary to represent the data on all the questionnaires. For example, if we had used a questionnaire that needed three cards to represent the data on it, and had a sample size of 400, we would have $3 \times 400 = 1200$ cards in our data deck. It is this data deck that is read into the computer.

Data Storage   Once the data are read into the computer, the researcher may use the computer capabilities to store the data from the data deck in either a computer disk file or on a computer tape. The problems of dropping or losing the data deck are thus removed. Also, data stored in a computer disk file or on tape are much easier for the computer to access for later data analysis. All the physical problems of carrying the data deck to the computer for each data analysis run are eliminated; for a data deck running into thousands of cards, this is a must. Tape storage has the advantage over the disk file of allowing the researcher to transport the data. One can easily carry in one hand a large data set that is stored on tape, whereas a disk file cannot be transported. Also, tape storage is cheaper than disk storage. In practice, data from old studies are usually saved on tape.

Data Matrix   The data storage on disk file or tape may be thought of as forming a data matrix (see Figure 21-2). Each row of the matrix represents a case, and each column represents a variable. We note that the total number of

			Variables (1 to m)				
			Column numbers				
			1	2	. . .		m
		1	2	625			4
		2	3	710			1
		3	1	521			3
		4	1	601			2
		5	4	706			1
Cases	Row	6	3	507			5
(1 to n)	Numbers	7	2	429			1
		.					
		.					
		.					
		n	1	764			2

Variable 1 = Year in college
  (1 = 1st year, 2 = 2d year, 3 = 3d year, 4 = 4th year)
Variable 2 = SAT score (out of 800)
Variable m = Region of the country parents live in
  (1 = Northeast, 2 = Southeast, 3 = Southwest
  4 = Northwest, 5 = Midwest)

Figure 21-2 The concept of a data matrix.

rows equals the number of cases, n, and the total number of columns equals the number of variables, m. We refer to this as an $n \times m$ (n by m) data matrix. The data presented in this sample matrix are the values associated with the specific cases for three variables—year in college, SAT score, and region of the country parents live in. Note that each variable, no matter how many digits it requires, occupies only one column of the data matrix. The number of cases and variables in a data matrix is limited only by the capacity of the computer. It is not uncommon in practice to have a data matrix that is 2500×200 or even larger. It is on this data matrix that computer programs perform data analysis.

With the basic concepts in hand, we now turn to examine the individual steps in the flow of data processing.

DATA PROCESSING FLOW

Figure 21-3 presents an overview of the sequence of functions to be performed in data processing. These include (1) deciding whether to use the data collection instrument for analysis, (2) editing it, (3) coding it, (4) keypunching and verifying the data, (5) preparing the data deck into a computer-readable form, (6) cleaning the dataset, (7) generating new variables as necessary, (8) weighting the data in accordance with sampling plan and results, and (9) storing the dataset on disk or tape. The next section of this chapter presents a discussion of each of these functions.

Identification of Acceptable Instruments

Upon receiving a data collection instrument from the field, the researcher should examine it to determine whether it is acceptable for use in the study. The exact criteria for judging an instrument unacceptable vary from study to study, but those listed on page 502 are typical.

Figure 21-3 Data processing flow.

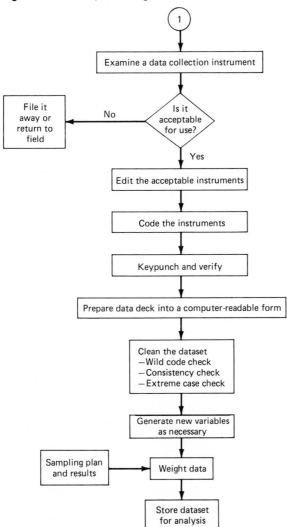

   1   A significant portion of the instrument is left unanswered, or key elements
are left unanswered.
   2   It is clear from answers given that the respondent did not understand the
task required in filling out the instrument.
   3   The answers show too little variance. For example, the answers to a
series of attitude questions are all 3s on a 7-point scale. This is evidence that the
respondent is not taking the task seriously.
   4   The wrong sample element has filled out the instrument. For example,
the study calls for respondents to be working women, and a man has completed
the instrument.
   5   The instrument is physically incomplete. For example, a page may not
have been included or may have been taken off in the field.
   6   The instrument is received after an established cutoff date. If one waited
for all instruments to be returned from the field, the study likely would not be
completed on time.

   If the researcher thinks that the particular defect in question could be
corrected within reasonable time and cost constraints, the data collection instrument may be returned to the field. Otherwise, the instrument is filed away.
   All data collection instruments should be subjected to this type of preliminary
examination before being sent through the rest of the data processing flow. Above
all, the criteria for accepting or rejecting an instrument should be established
before the instruments are received.

Editing

Editing means reviewing the data collection instruments to ensure maximum
accuracy and unambiguity.[2] It is important that editing be done consistently. In
a small study one person may perform the editing function, and consistency is
likely to be high. In a large study that requires many editors, an editing supervisor
is necessary to ensure that consistency is maintained among editors. This person
would have to sample-check different editors on different sections of the instrument. Alternatively, each editor could be made responsible for a different section
of the instrument and edit all instruments for this section.
   In performing the editing function one must be concerned with:

   1   **Legibility**   To be properly coded later, the data must be legible. Sometimes an illegible response can be corrected by contacting the person who
recorded it, and sometimes the correct response can be inferred from other parts
of the instrument. If no definitive answer is available, the response should be
designated as missing data. To sum up, the editor takes the ambiguity out of the
recorded data, so that the coder knows exactly what to do.

   2   **Completeness**   Questions that are not answered may be treated in one
of three ways. First, the editor may contact the interviewer to try to determine

---

[2] Donald S. Tull and Gerald S. Albaum, *Survey Research: A Decisional Approach* (New York:
Intext Educational Publishers, 1973), p. 168.

whether the respondent did not answer the question, or whether the interviewer just failed to record the response. In doing this, there is a risk that the interviewer will not remember this particular interview correctly. Alternatively, the respondent may be contacted again for a response to a specific question. The second approach is to designate this particular piece of data as missing data. Finally, if the editor deems that too many data items are missing, the whole instrument may be sent back to the field or removed from the study.

3   Consistency   At this point, a preliminary check is made on the consistency of the data. (A more detailed check will be performed later by the computer.) For example, the editor might verify that respondents who claim to buy gasoline by credit card do hold credit cards. The editor may ask the interviewer to resolve any inconsistencies, designate the responses to these questions as missing data, or remove the instrument from the study.

4   Accuracy   The editor needs to be attentive for evidence of inaccuracy in the data. The most important area here relates to possible interviewer bias or cheating. Such activities may be spotted by looking for a common pattern of responses in the instruments of a particular interviewer or recorder.

5   Response Clarification   Sometimes the responses to open-ended questions are difficult to interpret clearly. The recorder's words may have abbreviated the answer too much, or some words may be ambiguous. The editor may designate a meaning to the response or ask the interviewer what was meant. The risk of error is high in both instances. Obviously, good field work in the first place can prevent many problems from arising.

Difficulties also occur when questions are not answered in the way the instructions to the instrument required. This is especially a problem in mail surveys. For example, a respondent may be asked to underline a number on a 7-point rating scale. Suppose he or she underlines the numbers 4 and 5. Does this mean that 4.5 is intended as the response? The editor must decide whether to designate the response as a 4 or as a 5, or record it as missing data.

Coding

Coding involves the assignment of a designated numeric symbol into a designated computer card column, to represent a specific response on a data collection instrument. We saw examples of this earlier in the chapter in our discussion of the computer card and how it is used.[3]

Closed and Open-ended Questions   For structured or closed-ended questions, the coding scheme is usually designated prior to the undertaking of field work. This may go as far as having the actual codes printed on the data collection

---

[3] For a detailed discussion of coding, see Philip S. Sidel, "Coding," in Robert Ferber (ed.), *Handbook of Marketing Research* (New York: McGraw-Hill, 1974), pp. 2-178 to 2-199.

instruments. For example, a designation of sex may appear on the instrument as:

2/31	What is your sex?
1	Female
2	Male

The numbers on the left side of the question indicate the coding scheme. Here 2/31 indicates that the response to this question will appear in the 31st column of the 2d card for this respondent. A 1 in this column designates a female and a 2 designates a male. This same approach can be used for coding numeric data that either are not to be coded into categories or have had their relevant categories specified. A respondent's age may be requested and coded as:

1/6–7	What is your age? _____

or as:

1/6	What is your age?
1	0–18
2	19–35
3	36–50
4	over 50

In both cases the codes can be specified prior to the field work. If the codes are written on all questions on the questionnaire, it is said to be wholly precoded.

Open-ended questions present a more complex problem for coding. Here the verbatim responses of respondents are recorded by the interviewer. How does one convert data like these into a punch in a computer card? There are two general approaches to this problem. The first is the preparation of a relatively well-developed coding scheme prior to the completion of the field work. To be able to do this, the researcher must be guided by the results of previous studies or by some overriding theoretical considerations. The major task of the researcher is then to train coders so that they will convert the verbatim response into the correct code category.

The second approach involves waiting until the instruments return from the field before developing the coding scheme. Here the researcher lists, say, 50 to 100 of the responses to the specific question. He or she then examines this list and decides what categories are appropriate to summarize the data. The researcher then trains the coders in this scheme and also alerts them to watch for other responses that occur with some frequency. If this happens, it may be necessary to go back and revise the coding scheme and thus have to recode all instruments on this question.

Rules and Conventions for Code Construction   These are a number of rules or conventions that make the coding function work well. These are:

1 *Establish mutually exclusive and collectively exhaustive code categories.* It is easy to make categories collectively exhaustive—for example, by adding the code category "other," "no information," or "none" to the major categories for the variable in question.[4] By "mutually exclusive" is meant that every response must fit into one and only one code category. Categories must not overlap; this is the one hard and fast rule of all coding. The other items in this section are best described as useful conventions, not rules.

2 If uncertainty exists about possible uses for a particular variable in analysis, the data should be coded so as to *retain a great deal of detail.* It is possible to combine code categories at the time of analysis if such detail is not required. However, it is impossible to "expand" codes for analysis if they have been recorded with too little detail. We may therefore want to code in more detail than we intend to use in analysis. An example of this would be to code the respondent's exact age, and then combine ages into categories at the time of analysis.

3 Follow the following card layout conventions:[5]
   a Use only one punch per column, as most computer programs cannot read multipunched cards.
   b Use only numeric codes, not special characters or blanks.
   c The card position for a variable may consist of as many columns as are necessary, but no more than one variable may be assigned to a single column.
   d Use standard codes for missing data, if at all possible. For example, some researchers always use 9 for a one-column variable and 99 for a two-column variable, etc., for designating missing data. The researcher may have a number of different types of missing data such as "don't know," "does not apply," "refused to answer," etc. If this detail is to be preserved, a standard code should be set for each one. This facilitates coding and later interpretation of data analysis.

4 In choosing breakpoints for continuous variables, consider the following questions:[6]
   a Into how many categories should the variable be cast given the plan of analysis that has been developed?
   b Should the categories be equal-interval (0-9, 10-19, 20-29, etc.), or should they be constructed so that each category has about the same number of cases?
   c Should the extreme categories be open (under $9,000; $60,000 and over) to take in a wide range of extreme scores, or should the intervals be fixed?

In making these decisions the researcher must recognize that the use of equal intervals allows for easier statistical analysis later and that the number of categories selected affects the detail of the information retained from the instru-

---

[4] Ibid., p. 2-181.
[5] Ibid., pp. 2-128 to 2-184.
[6] Ibid., p. 2-183.

ments. The more categories one has, the greater the detail. In the end, the number and definition of categories selected must satisfy the user of the research. The researcher must consult with the manager on this issue.

5   Put a respondent and card identification number on each card in the data deck. Figure 21-4 presents an illustration of part of a data deck in which each respondent has three computer cards. Column 1 of each card presents the card identification number. Since there are three cards for each respondent, we see the number 1, 2, 3 repeating in column 1 for each of the n respondents. Columns 2 to 4 of each card present the case number. Obviously, we expect a sample size of less than 1000. With the cards arranged in this manner, we can instruct the computer to check to see that the required number of cases are in the data deck and that the sequence of cards within each case is the same. If cards are not in the same order within each case, correct data analysis is impossible, because the computer expects to find a given variable in the same card and column location for each case. Case identification numbers also facilitate data cleaning later.

Multiple Responses[7]   The problem of multiple responses arises in two contexts. The first is where the researcher expects to receive a single answer. In this case the decision may be to select one of the answers on some established priority basis—for example, the answer written down first. Alternatively, one may develop code categories to represent combinations of responses. For example, a "7" punch may represent those respondents who said that flavor and baking time were important cake mix attributes. Finally, one may designate this response as missing data.

In situations where the researcher expects more than one answer, two procedures are available. The first is to treat each possible response as a separate variable, with a separate card column. For example, a question may ask what sports a respondent plays. Each sport would be answered "yes" or "no" and assigned to a unique column. The second option is available where the researcher has a specific number of responses expected. The researcher could assign a separate column for "first responses," another for "second responses," and so on. The codes within each column would be the same, representing the available options. For example, a "1" in the first response column could indicate that flavor was the first response for this respondent as an important attribute for cake mix. A "1" in the second response column would indicate that flavor was the second response as an important attribute for cake mix. In analysis, the researcher could examine each response column separately or combine them to get total responses. Care should be taken in combining data of this type; it is possible that an attribute placed second or third, etc., by a great many respondents could have more total mentions than another attribute that had more first mentions. A simple sum of mentions across the columns could confuse managers. They should be consulted as to the importance they place on second- or third-mention levels, etc., before a combining scheme is developed.

It should be recognized that coding is a potentially boring task. After working

[7] See Babbie, op. cit., p. 193.

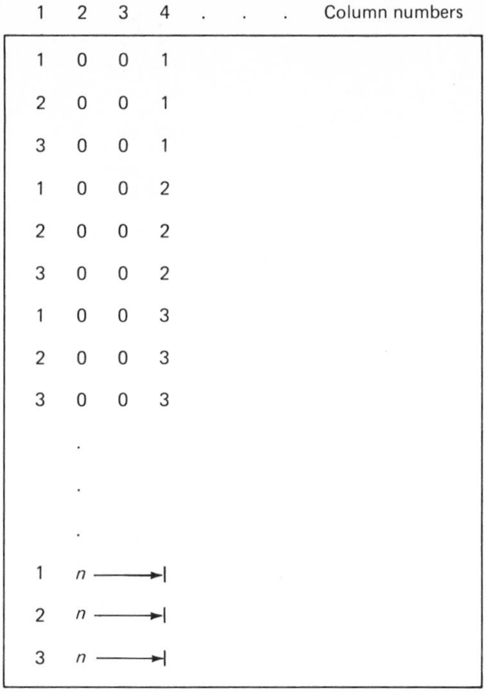

```
  1   2   3   4   .   .   .    Column numbers

  1   0   0   1

  2   0   0   1

  3   0   0   1

  1   0   0   2

  2   0   0   2

  3   0   0   2

  1   0   0   3

  2   0   0   3

  3   0   0   3

             .

             .

             .

  1   n ——►|

  2   n ——►|

  3   n ——►|
```

Figure 21-4 Illustrative data deck with respondent and card identification numbers.

hard and creatively to develop the coding scheme, the actual coding process may seem very tedious. In addition, this function is often not a highly paid job, which results in problems with quality of personnel. Coding errors often occur unless the researcher maintains close supervision over the coding. A manager can keep the coders on their toes by asking to see how a sample of instruments were coded. By doing this one will also get a better feel for the report that is going to emerge later.

The detail of the coding scheme needs to be documented, and this documentation is placed in what is called a *codebook*.

Codebook   A codebook is the place where all the needed information about variables in the data set is documented. It has three functions. First, it serves as a guide to the coders; second, it guides researchers to locate the variables they desire to use in a particular data analysis run; and third, it allows for the proper identification of variable categories as computer output is interpreted. The researcher would literally be lost without a good codebook.

The contents of the codebook vary. For a very simple study, one may just write the relevant column number and punch number on the instrument itself. A completely precoded questionnaire could serve as its own codebook.

In more complex studies, it is useful to have a codebook that contains more information. The researcher often wants the details of open-ended questions documented, or wishes to refer to variables by number for designation in a computer run. So a codebook might contain (1) the question number, (2) the

Table 21-1 An Illustrative Codebook

Question number	Variable number	Card column	Format*	Variable name	Category definitions
35	46	1/52	I1	Sex	1 = Female 2 = Male 9 = Missing data
36 . . .	47 . . .	1/53–54 . . .	I2 . . .	Age . . .	Two-digit number 00–98 99 = Missing data
74	121	3/21–23	F3.2	Grade point average	Three-digit number 000–400 with decimal place two places to left in field given by format

*The use of "I" refers to an integer value in card column(s). The number after the "I" indicates the number of digits in the variable. For example, I1 indicates a one-digit integer variable, I6 a six-digit integer variable, and so on.

The use of "F" indicates that other variables in the card column(s) can take on real values. That is, the variable with an F can have a decimal place. The position of the decimal is given by the number after the decimal place, and the number of digits is given by the number before the decimal. For example, F3.2 indicates a real variable containing three digits with the decimal place position before the second digit. That is, the decimal is two places from the end of the field.

variable number, (3) the relevant card columns, (4) the format (any implied decimal places), (5) the variable name, and (6) the category definitions. Table 21-1 presents a portion of an illustrative codebook. A quick look at the codebook informs us exactly how the variables (sex, age, and grade point average or GPA) appear in the data deck and how we will refer to them in later analysis. For example, GPA will be called variable 121, is in card columns 21–23 of card three, and has an implied decimal place two places to the left of the end of the field, i.e., between columns 21 and 22. We never punch the decimal place; we need only tell the computer with the formal statement. The GPA was obtained in question 74 on the instrument. For a complex open-ended question, the description of the code categories may be quite lengthy.

Actual Coding Once the code categories are established, the actual coding can take place. Here, the coders write the proper codes in the designated location on 80-column paper or on some special "code sheet." These sheets may be thought of as a paper version of a computer card. Once this is done, the coding is completed.

Keypunching and Verifying

The coding sheets completed in the previous step are delivered to keypunchers, who punch the exact number on the sheets into computer cards. We have now converted the data in the data collection instrument into holes in computer cards. However, we must be careful here, as it is very easy for a keypunch operator to make a mistake. It is therefore wise to have the data deck verified after it has been punched. It is put into a verifier (a machine that compares the key that an operator punches with the hole already in a card), and an operator keys from the coding sheets again. If the key pressed by the operator differs from the one found on the previously punched card, the operator is signaled that an error has occurred. He or she may then check to see whether the original punch was incorrect. If the punch was in error, this fact is noted with a notch in that column, and correction is made later. The result of this process should be an accurate data deck.

Prepare Data Deck into a Computer-readable Form

The data deck must now be presented to the computer in such a way that data analysis computer programs can make use of it. Most programs that a researcher is likely to use are contained within a package of programs. One such package of programs is called the Statistical Package for the Social Sciences (SPSS).[8] There are many others, but we shall use SPSS to illustrate the structure of these packages. Figure 21-5 gives an overview of what is done to make an SPSS data file out of the raw data deck. The data deck is read into the computer along with a number of descriptors, including (1) variable numbers and names, (2) variable format, (3) missing-data codes, and (4) variable-category descriptors (if the user desires to have them on computer printouts). The result of this is an SPSS datafile ready for analysis. It has in essence made an SPSS-readable data matrix out of the data deck, and all SPSS analysis programs can make use of this one datafile. We can do an analysis run without worrying about properly locating and defining missing-data codes for the variables of interest in our data deck. All we need to do is refer to the desired variable numbers in the SPSS datafile. This leads to great efficiencies in data analysis.

An item that *must* be included as a variable in the datafile is the case identification number. This will help expedite the data cleaning that is to follow.

Clean the Dataset

We now have a dataset structured as a computer datafile, but we must still attempt to clean the dataset of possible errors. Three types of checks are run on the dataset, namely, (1) a wild code check, (2) a consistency check, and (3) an extreme-case check.

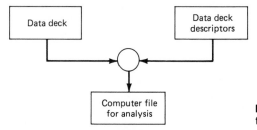

Figure 21-5 Creation of a computer file for analysis.

[8] N. H. Nie, D. H. Bent, and C. H. Hull, *SPSS, the Statistical Package for the Social Sciences* (New York: McGraw-Hill, 1970).

Wild Code Check   The first items we want to get out of our dataset are so-called "wild codes," i.e. codes that are not defined in the codebook for a particular variable. For example, the variable "sex" may have three legitimate codes (the third being for missing data). A number 4 or greater for this variable would be a wild code, probably the result of an error in coding or punching. This check can be done by having the computer list the numbers of responses in each category of each variable, which will tell us whether a wild code exists. But in which case does it occur? This represents no problem if we have made case number a variable. All we do is command the computer to print out the case numbers for those cases that have the wild code, then examine the data collection instruments for these cases and make the appropriate correction in the datafile. Most computer analysis packages allow us to do this easily.

Consistency Check   The next step is to check the consistency of responses within each case. During the editing task we did a preliminary consistency check, but the one performed by the computer can be much more complete. For example, we might check to see that those who have a mortgage also own a house. There are two types of consistency checks: one-way and two-way.[9] In a one-way consistency situation A is true if B is true, but the reverse need not hold. In a two-way consistency situation A is true if and only if B is true, and vice versa. The house and mortgage example above would be an example of a one-way consistency check. That is, those having a mortgage must own a house, but some homeowners may not have a mortgage. A two-way consistency check could be done in a study of university students. A check could be made between credit hours obtained and year of standing in school (senior, junior, etc.). If a junior is someone with between 60 and 90 credit hours, a two-way check could be made between credit hours and year of standing. That is, people with between 60 and 90 credit hours would be checked to see that they were classified as juniors, and junior-classified people would be checked to see that they have the proper number of credit hours. A good data analysis package should have the commands necessary to do this type of checking. Again, once an error is found, the case number is printed out, the data collection instrument is examined, and the correction is made.

Extreme-Case Check   An extreme case is defined as a response on a variable that is well out of the ordinary. For example, an SAT score recorded as 796 in the datafile may be substantially higher than all other scores. We could command the computer to print out the case numbers of all cases with SAT scores above 775. We would then check to see whether these scores were correct. This is another way of identifying possible coding or punching errors.

[9] See John B. Lansing and James N. Morgan, *Economic Survey Methods* (Ann Arbor: Institute for Social Research, The University of Michigan, 1971), p. 237, for a more detailed discussion.

Generating New Variables

Once the originally coded dataset is cleansed, we can proceed to add new variables to this dataset that will be used later in analysis. Again, the computer's capabilities make this task simple. There are a number of circumstances where we might generate new variables:[10]

    1 We may want to add data not collected in the interview. For example, we may want to add census information about the area in which a respondent lives.

    2 We may want to collapse an interval variable, such as income, into categories, or combine the categories of some variables to give a variable with fewer categories.

    3 We may want to form a variable to be defined by combinations of other variables. For example, the variable "stage of family life cycle" is formed using age, marital status, presence of children, etc.

    4 We may want to create an index to represent a number of variables. For example, we may simply add a set of scaled measures about a product to form an index related to interest in the product. More complex indices are also possible.

    These new variables are placed in the dataset for each case and assigned a variable number. They must also be entered in the codebook with a detailed description as to how they were formed.

Weighting

There is one last task that may need to be performed on the datafile, namely, weighting the data in accordance with the sampling plan or because of unexpected sampling results. (Weighting was discussed in detail in Chapter 10.) Basically, we need to weight if the probability of element selection varies across subgroups, and if we wish to do analysis with the whole sample. We command the computer to assign the appropriate weights to cases. If we desire to do subgroup analysis, we simply command the analysis program to ignore the weighting.

Storing

We now have a dataset completely ready for analysis. It is generally stored on disk file or tape, with a copy made on another tape to be put away for safe keeping. We are ready to do data analysis.

ALTERNATIVE PROCESSING FLOWS

Although the data processing flow presented in the previous section represents the traditional approach, there are alternative ways of getting the data from acceptable data collection instruments into the computer. Babbie calls these

[10] Ibid., pp. 238–240.

alternatives *data processing tracks*.[11] We shall use his terminology here in describing these tracks.

Track One Processing   This is the traditional method that we have just presented. In review, its steps are (1) coding of instruments, (2) transferring of codes to coding sheets, and (3) keypunching and verifying of a data deck.

Track Two Processing   It is possible to eliminate the step requiring the transferring of codes to coding sheets by doing what is called *edge coding*. The outside margin of each page of the data collection instrument is marked with spaces representing the columns of a computer card. The coder writes the relevant codes in these spaces instead of on the coding sheets. The edge-coded instruments are then delivered to keypunchers for punching and verifying.

Track Three Processing   It may be possible to eliminate both the coding step and the transferring of codes to coding sheets. That is, we may be able to have the keypunchers directly punch and verify the data from the edited data collection instrument itself. To do this, we need an instrument that is made up of closed-ended questions that are wholly precoded. Also, the instrument must be laid out in such a way that the keypuncher can easily follow the flow of responses.

Track Four Processing   It is possible to eliminate the manual keypunching and verifying of the data by having coders use special mark-sensed coding sheets to record the data codes. These sheets can then be read into the computer by an optical scanner. The computer can then store the data in a disk file or punch out a data deck of computer cards. Here the coder does not write the code number but fills in appropriate spaces on the mark-sensed sheets with a special pencil. Most coders find this a more difficult task than recording the number themselves. The marks must be made with care, as the optical scanner has tight tolerances and errors can easily result. Also, if the mark-sensed sheets are damaged, the scanner may be unable to read them.

Track Five Processing   In order to get around the coding problems inherent in track four processing, the respondents themselves could be asked to indicate their responses by filling out the mark-sensed sheets themselves. Students completing a multiple-choice examination are often asked to do this. Both coding and keypunching are thus eliminated in the flow. For this technique to work properly, the respondents must have the proper pencil and must understand exactly how to record their responses on the sheets. Close supervision by the researcher is a necessity. Thus, mail instruments are not compatible with this approach. Also, closed-ended questions are the only type possible here.

[11] Babbie, op. cit., pp. 197–200.

Track Six Processing[12]   This track is appropriate for telephone interviewing only. Here the questionnaire is programmed into a computer with cathode-ray tubes (CRT) for display.[13] The interviewer sits in front of the CRT and commands the computer to display the questions one at a time. Precoded answers are also displayed on the CRT. The respondent indicates a response, and the interviewer types this response directly into a computer file. Thus editing, coding, keypunching, and verifying of written questionnaires are eliminated. The data are ready for instant cleaning and analysis. The major drawbacks of this system are its costs in equipment, software, and staff. One company puts this figure at $200,000.[14] Very large studies that are well structured and use telephone interviews are the types that can make the most effective use of this system. A number of companies offer this type of service.

Selection of a Track   One's choice of a data processing track depends on the availability of computer hardware, optical scanners, etc. It also depends on the time and cost constraints imposed on the study and the degree of complexity in the data collection instrument. Generally, the more complex the instrument, the more one would tend to do traditional track one processing. Other tracks would tend to be used as the instrument became more structured and as time and cost constraints put pressure on the researcher. If we can get the respondent to fill out a mark-sensed card, we obviously save time and money. The CRT track saves time but costs more money. The researcher must pick a data processing track that fits the type of study being undertaken and the constraints imposed upon its execution.

We now know exactly what the research analyst described earlier in the chapter must do to get data collection instruments ready for analysis. Data processing is not the most exciting area of marketing research, but it is very important. Since a significant proportion of nonsampling errors occur in data processing, the researcher and manager must be attentive to this area.

SUMMARY

1 Data processing is the conversion of raw data in a data collection instrument into a computer-readable form.

2 A traditional approach to data processing includes the functions of (a) deciding whether to use the data collection instrument, (b) editing, (c) coding to coding sheets, (d) keypunching and verifying, (e) preparing the resultant data deck into a computer-readable form, (f) cleaning the data, (g) generating new variables, (h) weighting, and (i) storing the dataset on disk or tape.

3 It is possible to eliminate some of these functions by using edge coding, by keypunching directly from the data collection instruments, by using mark-

---

[12] Babbie does not discuss this option, but we continue to use his terminology.

[13] Jack J. Honomichl, "Computers Speed Up Interviewing Process, Also Can Supply Instant Survey Results," *Advertising Age,* Feb. 14, 1977, pp. 14 and 76.

[14] Ibid.

sensed coding sheets, or by recording respondent answers directly into the computer.

DISCUSSION QUESTIONS

1 How are responses to a questionnaire represented on a computer card?
2 How does one identify data collection instruments that are unacceptable for data processing?
3 What should an editor do in examining an instrument?
4 What are the fundamental rules of code construction?
5 How should multiple responses be handled?
6 What is a codebook? What should it contain?
7 How is a dataset cleaned?
8 Why would one want to create new variables?
9 What are the alternative data processing tracks?
10 How does one select a track?

SUGGESTED READING

Babbie, Earl, *Survey Research Methods* (Belmont, Calif.: Wadsworth, 1973), chap. 10. A most readable discussion of all aspects of data processing.
Sidel, Philip S., "Coding," in Robert Ferber (ed.), *Handbook of Marketing Research* (New York: McGraw-Hill, 1974), sec. 2, part B, chap. 9. An in-depth and very readable discussion of everything connected with coding.

Chapter 22

Univariate Data Analysis

Once the data that one has collected have been properly converted to a computer file, as described in the previous chapter, we are ready to turn our attention to data analysis. Improper data analysis can be a significant source of nonsampling error. The primary objective of the data analysis chapters in this book is to provide an overview of when specific analysis techniques may properly be used. In order to reach this objective we shall identify a number of data analysis techniques, list the circumstances where they may be used, and give examples of their use. We shall not attempt to list all techniques nor to explain their computational aspects in any detail, because we believe that the purpose of data analysis is to provide meaningful information for decision making and that much valuable information can be provided by means of relatively simple data analysis procedures.

Some marketers and others mistakenly think that data analysis is the most important aspect of marketing research. Our premise is that the most sophisticated data analysis available cannot make up for poor problem definition, bad study design, improper sampling, poor measurement, bad field work, or sloppy data processing. Data analysis is just one of many activities that must be done correctly to yield relevant information for decision making. However, it too must be done properly.

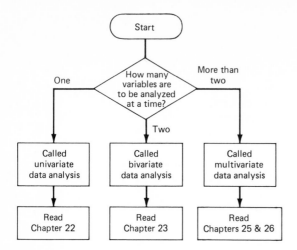

Figure 22-1   Overview of data analysis techniques.

We shall begin this first chapter on data analysis by distinguishing among univariate, bivariate, and multivariate data analysis procedures. Then we shall distinguish between procedures whose objective is description of the sample-based dataset at hand and procedures whose objective is inference about the population from which the dataset was selected. Finally, we shall discuss a number of descriptive and inferential techniques appropriate for univariate analysis.

OVERVIEW OF DATA ANALYSIS PROCEDURES

The fundamental data analysis question facing a marketing manager or researcher is: "What data analysis technique should be used?" The answer is provided by outlining specifics about the situation faced by the marketer. There are three overview questions that help the marketer begin to identify the appropriate technique, namely: (1) How many variables are to be analyzed at the same time? (2) Do we want description or inference questions answered? and (3) What level of measurement (nominal, ordinal, interval) is available in the variable or variables of interest?

Number of Variables to Analyze

The first specific aspect of the situation that must be clarified relates to the objectives of the analysis. This is *the number of variables the marketer wishes to have analyzed at the same time*. Figure 22-1 shows this decision question, the possible outcomes to the question, and where in this book the relevant techniques are discussed.

If one wishes to examine the analysis of one variable at a time, this is called *univariate data analysis*, and it constitutes the topic of the chapter you are currently reading. The relationship of two variables at a time is examined by means of *bivariate data analysis*, the subject of Chapter 23. The relationships of more than two variables at a time call for *multivariate data analysis*, to be covered in Chapters 25 and 26.

Description versus Inference

The second question that must be answered is whether one is interested in the *description of the sample* or in making *inferences about the population* from which the sample was drawn. Descriptive statistics is a branch of statistics that provides researchers with summary measures for the data in their samples. It provides answers to such questions as: (1) What is the average age in the sample? (2) What is the dispersion of ages in the sample? and (3) What is the level of association between age and income in the sample? Inferential statistics is a branch of statistics that allows researchers to make judgments about the whole population based upon the results generated by samples. It is based upon probability theory. It provides answers to such questions as: (1) Is the average age of the population 25? (2) Is the level of association between age and income in the population greater than zero? (3) Are the population treatment means in an experiment equal to each other? Both descriptive and inferential statistics have important applications in marketing research. Marketers must know which type of analysis they are interested in.

Level of Measurement

The third question that must be answered is whether the variable or variables to be analyzed have been measured at a nominal-, ordinal-, or interval-scale level.[1] Both descriptive and inferential techniques vary by the scale level inherent in the variable or variables being analyzed.

If marketers know the number of variables to be analyzed at a time, whether the interest is in description or inference, and the scale level of the variable or variables, they are then in a position to select the appropriate statistical procedure. The rest of this chapter identifies and describes the relevant techniques for the analysis of one variable at a time. In presenting this material we recognize that a computer will be doing the calculations. This does not negate the need for us to know when to use what procedure, because the computer will calculate any statistic we ask it to even if that statistic is not appropriate for the data.

OVERVIEW OF UNIVARIATE DATA ANALYSIS PROCEDURES

Figure 22-2 presents an overview of statistical techniques available for univariate data analysis.[2] It is often important in studies to do a univariate analysis on some

---

[1] There are procedures available for ratio data only. However, they have little relevance to real marketing research problems. Any ratio data in marketing research are usually analyzed by procedures relevant to interval data.

[2] For a complete classification scheme for univariate, bivariate, and multivariate analysis see Frank M. Andrews, Laura Klem, Terrence N. Davidson, Patrick M. O'Malley, and Willard L. Rodgers, *A Guide for Selecting Statistical Techniques for Analyzing Social Science Data* (Ann Arbor: Institute for Social Research, the University of Michigan, 1974).

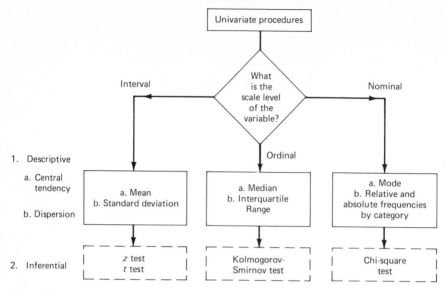

Figure 22-2 Overview of univariate data analysis procedures.

variables. For example, the manager might want a description of the sample's demographic characteristics, of the usage of the company's product, or of respondent attitudes toward a competitive activity. In each situation, one can gain useful information by examining statistics related to one variable at a time. To make sure we are looking for the right procedure, we begin the process described in Figure 22-2 by asking if we want to analyze one variable at a time. Only if this question is answered positively does Figure 22-2 provide us with a guide to the correct procedure. The next question that must be answered concerns the scale level of the variable to be analyzed. It may be nominal, ordinal, or interval. Below each of these possible answers to the scale-level question on Figure 22-2, two sets of boxes are presented. The first set presents the relevant descriptive statistics. The top part of these boxes presents the appropriate measure of central tendency, while the bottom part presents the appropriate measure of dispersion. The boxes defined by dotted lines, positioned below the descriptive statistics boxes, present the appropriate tests of statistical inference for each data type. We note that statistics appropriate for lower scales can be applied to higher scales. For example, a mode and median can properly be calculated for interval data. However, the opposite is not true; the mean is not an appropriate statistic for ordinal or nominal data.

It is not our purpose in the data analysis chapters of this book to give details of every descriptive statistic and every test of inference for every measurement level. This task would take too long. The discussion presented in these chapters will deal with only those techniques that are most relevant to marketing research practice. Thus in this chapter we will not discuss the interquartile range statistic nor the Kolmogorov-Smirnov test, for these are not in the mainstream of marketing research practice.[3] What follows, then, is a discussion of those statistical procedures with which we feel a practicing marketing researcher should be familiar.

DESCRIPTIVE STATISTICS

The objective of descriptive statistics is to provide summary measures of the data contained in all the elements of a sample. In doing so the marketing researcher is usually concerned with measures of central tendency and measures of dispersion. We now turn our attention to identifying these measures by measurement scale level.

Measures of Central Tendency

Three measures of central tendency are often used in marketing research: the mean, the median, and the mode.

Interval Data—The Mean   The mean is the appropriate measure of central tendency for interval data. The reader should be very familiar with the concept of a mean, since we made use of it for both a continuous variable and a proportion in Chapter 9, when discussing simple random sampling. To review, the mean is *the sum of the values divided by the sample size*. In formula,

$$\overline{X} = \frac{\sum\limits_{i=1}^{n} X_i}{n}$$

Thus, if our sample yielded the values 22, 26, 25, 21, and 19, the mean would be $113/5 = 22.6$.

It is also possible to calculate a mean when interval data are grouped into categories or classes. Here the formula for the mean is

$$\overline{X} = \frac{\sum\limits_{i=1}^{k} f_i X_i}{n}$$

where f_i = frequency of the ith class
X_i = midpoint of the ith class
k = number of classes

Table 22-1 illustrates such a calculation.

[3] The reader who needs this test should see Sidney Siegel, *Nonparametric Statistics for the Behavioral Sciences* (New York: McGraw-Hill, 1956), p. 47–52.

**Table 22-1   Calculation of the Mean Using Grouped
Interval Data**

Age classes	Number in class, f_i	Mid point, X_i	$f_i X_i$
15 to under 20	10	17.5	175
20 to under 25	20	22.5	450
25 to under 30	30	27.5	825
30 to under 35	20	32.5	650
$k = 4$	$\Sigma f_i = 80 = n$		$\Sigma f_i X_i = 2100$

$$\overline{X} = 2100/80 = 26.25$$

Ordinal Data—The Median   If our data form an ordinal or interval scale,
we may legitimately make use of the median as a measure of central tendency.
The median for ungrouped data is defined as *the midvalue when the data are
arranged in order of magnitude*. Table 22-2 presents an ordered set of observations and identifies the median. The median may also be calculated for grouped
data. The formula for doing so is complex and would add little to our understanding
of the concept here.[4] What is important is that the median can be applied to
either ordinal or interval data.

Nominal Data—The Mode   The mode is a measure of central tendency
appropriate for nominal or higher-order scales. It is *the category of a nominal
variable that occurs with greatest frequency*. It should not be applied to ordinal
or interval data unless these data have been grouped first. For example, in Table
22-1 the modal class is formed by the ages 25 to under 30.

Sometimes a variable is bimodal. That is, two classes have relatively similar
frequencies. This should be a tip-off to the researcher to look for some other
variable in the situation that may be causing this situation. For example, coffee
sales recorded at both large and small stores could yield a bimodal distribution.
The researcher should have been aware of this. Also, if the distribution is
bimodal, the mean and median do not describe the variable well. They are simply
some "midpoints" between the modes. It is therefore a good idea to look at
measures of dispersion.

**Table 22-2   Identification of the Median
for Ungrouped Data**

Observation, X_i	Score or value of X_i
X_1	10
X_2	20
X_3	70 ← median
X_4	140
X_5	500

[4] The interested reader should consult almost any basic statistics book. For example, see
Morris Hamburg, *Statistical Analysis for Decision Making* (New York: Harcourt Brace Jovanovich,
1977), p. 28.

Measures of Dispersion

Measures of central tendency do not provide enough information for researchers to fully understand the distribution they are examining. For example, the numbers 10, 15, 20 and 5, 10, 30 both have a mean of 15. Clearly, we need a measure of the spread of the distribution of the variable, i.e., a measure of dispersion.

Interval Data—The Standard Deviation   The appropriate measure of dispersion for interval data is the standard deviation, the measure we calculated for a continuous variable and a proportion in Chapter 9. In formula, the standard deviation of a sample is

$$s = \sqrt{\frac{\sum\limits_{i=1}^{n} (X_i - \overline{X})^2}{n - 1}}$$

We calculated this value in detail in Chapter 9 and will therefore not repeat it here.

Whether or not a particular size of standard deviation constitutes a large or small dispersion depends on the size of the mean with which it is associated. For example, to be told that a standard deviation is 100 does not help us much. However, if we are told that in this case the mean is 200, we can conclude that the variable has a large dispersion. If the mean were instead 2000, we could conclude that the variable had a small dispersion. We formalize this type of conclusion by calculating what is called the coefficient of variation. In formula

$$CV = \frac{s}{\overline{X}}$$

where CV is the coefficient of variation. Thus CV is the standard deviation expressed as a percentage of the mean. In our example above,

$$CV_1 = \frac{100}{200} = .5 \text{ and } CV_2 = \frac{100}{2000} = .05$$

Nominal Data—Relative and Absolute Frequencies   For nominal data or better, we may legitimately calculate relative and absolute frequencies as measures of dispersion. Table 22-3 illustrates such a calculation for the nominal variable "region of the country." Absolute frequencies are just the numbers in the sample that appear in each category of the nominal variable. Thus, in our example in Table 22-3, 210 elements were found to have come from the East. Relative frequencies are the percentages of the total elements that appear in each category, thus 20.2 percent (210/1040) of the elements are from the East.

Often, just describing what is in the sample is not enough. We may also

**Table 22-3 Presentation of Relative and Absolute Frequencies
for Nominal Variable**

Region of the country	Absolute frequency (number)	Relative frequencies (percentage)
East	210	20.2
West	405	38.9
North	109	10.5
South	316	30.4
Total	1040	100.0

want to make inferences from the sample to the population from which it was drawn. It is to this issue that we now turn our attention.

INFERENTIAL STATISTICS

The appropriate test of statistical inferences also varies by the scale level of the data available.

Interval Data

Two different tests, the z test and the t test, are appropriate for interval data. The choice between the two depends on the researcher's knowledge of the population standard deviation and the sample size used. These tests are tests about the size of the population mean.

In order to understand properly the following discussion on inference, the reader must understand the basics of hypothesis testing, contained in the section of Chapter 15 headed "Hypothesis Testing in Experimentation." In summary, the reader must be familiar with the concepts of (1) a null and alternative hypothesis, (2) a one- and two-tailed test, (3) type I and II errors, and (4) the steps in hypothesis testing. The reader who feels in need of a review of this material should read the few relevant pages in Chapter 15.

z Test The z test allows researchers to compare the mean generated from a sample with a mean hypothesized to exist in the population, and to decide whether the sample mean allows them to conclude that the hypothesized population mean is true. The z test is appropriate for interval data for situations where (1) the sample size is any size and the population standard deviation σ is known; or (2) the sample size is greater than 30 and the population standard deviation σ is unknown. In situations where $n < 30$ and σ is unknown, the t test should be used. It will be discussed shortly.

Let us illustrate the z test for the continuous variable "age," using the steps in hypothesis testing laid out in Chapter 15. Also, let us assume that a sample of university students taking marketing research has yielded the following information: $\overline{X} = 24$, $s = 5$, and $n = 100$.

Step 1: Formulate null and alternative hypotheses. In this situation the null and alternative hypotheses are:

H_0: $\mu = 23$
H_1: $\mu \neq 23$

So the researcher wants to know whether the sample mean age of 24 will allow the conclusion that the population mean age is 23. The alternative hypothesis, H_1, is phrased so that we know that a sample value too far above or below 23 will allow us to reject H_0. Thus, we will be using a two-tailed test. If $H_1: \mu < 23$ were the alternative hypothesis, we would reject H_0 only if the mean age were too far above H_0. This would be a one-tailed test. It is important to know which test one is doing, because the number of tails affects the position in a statistical table that one consults to find the critical value of the statistic involved.

Step 2: Select the appropriate statistical tests. The appropriate test here is the z test because $n > 30$ and we are testing a hypothesis about means. This test is based on the nature of the sampling distribution of the mean as discussed in Chapter 9. We know by the central-limit theorem that the mean value we generated from our sample comes from a sampling distribution of means that forms a normal curve. Also, we know the area under a normal curve, and thus the number of sampling means located within a certain number of standard errors of the mean of this distribution. Because of this we can determine the probability that any sample mean could have come from a sampling distribution of means that lies about the hypothesized population mean. This was essentially what we were doing in Chapter 9 when we calculated confidence intervals.

The critical values of the z statistic are given in Table A-2 of Appendix A for a two-tailed test, and in Table A-3 for a one-tailed test. The values in these tables are given for a mean of zero and a standard deviation of 1. Thus to use these tables we will have to convert data from a sample to remove the effects of the unit of measurement. The values in the first column and first row of the table are combined to give the z values (i.e., the number of standard deviations about the mean that interest the researcher). The values in the body of the table give the area contained in the tail or tails of the distribution. This provides a measure of the probability of rejecting a true null hypothesis. In other words, these values are α, the probability of making a Type I error.

For example, in Table A-2 for $\alpha = .05$, we find that this is 1.96 (1.9 from column 1 + .06 from row 1) standard deviations from the mean. We note that this represents the 95 percent confidence level. In Chapter 9 it was stated that the 95 percent confidence interval was $\overline{X} \pm 2$ times the standard error; in truth it is $\overline{X} \pm 1.96$ times the standard error, but we simply rounded it off to facilitate the discussion in that chapter. What the 1.96 tells us is that the probability of getting a value of z greater than 1.96 is less than .05. In Table A-3 we note that the probability of getting a value of z greater than 1.96 is less than .025. Thus, here we would be using a test with $\alpha = .025$. For $\alpha = .05$ in a one-tailed test, we note that $z = 1.64$. Thus the probability of getting a z value greater than 1.64 in a one-tailed test is less than .05.

Step 3: Specify the significance level. The researcher must specify a significance level, α. In doing so one must recognize that the smaller one sets α, the bigger β will be for any given sample size. In our example we shall use $\alpha = .1$.

Step 4: Look up the z value for $\alpha = .1$. We note in Table A-2 that $z = 1.64$ for $\alpha = .1$. This is our critical value of z. If the z calculated from the data exceeds 1.64, we will reject the null hypothesis.

Step 5: Perform the statistical test. If the population standard deviation is known,

$$z = \frac{\overline{X} - \mu}{\sigma_{\overline{X}}} = \frac{\overline{X} - \mu}{\sigma/\sqrt{n}}$$

If σ is not known,

$$z = \frac{\overline{X} - \mu}{s_{\overline{X}}} = \frac{\overline{X} - \mu}{s/\sqrt{n}}$$

In our example σ is not known, so we use the latter formula. What the formula does is express the difference between the observed mean $\overline{X}$ and the hypothesized mean μ as a measure expressed as a number of standard errors. The question is: Is the difference $\overline{X} - \mu$ expressed in standard error (the calculated z value) large enough to be likely to occur by sampling error less than .1 of the time?

In our example,

$$z = \frac{24 - 23}{5/\sqrt{100}} = \frac{1}{.5}$$
$$= 2.0$$

Thus the difference $24 - 23$ is equal to 2 standard errors.

Step 6: Compare z values. The calculated z value exceeds the z value for $\alpha = .1 (2.0 > 1.64)$, and thus we reject the null hypothesis. We may not conclude that the average age in the population is 23.

The z test may also be applied to a proportion. Here, for a situation where $n > 30$ and σ_p is known,[5]

$$z = \frac{p - \pi}{s_p} = \frac{p - \pi}{\sqrt{pq/n}}$$

where p = sample proportion
π = hypothesized proportion
s_p = standard error of the proportion

In a situation designed to measure market share, a sample might generate an

---

[5] For small n the binomial distribution must be used. This is so atypical of real marketing research problems that it is not discussed here.

estimate of market share p. We might wish to compare this with a target market share of over π. If $p = .3$, $n = 30$, $H_0\colon \pi \leq .25$, $H_1\colon \pi > .25$,

$$z = \frac{.3 - .25}{\sqrt{(.3)(.7)/30}} = \frac{.05}{.084} = .60$$

The difference between the observed and hypothesized proportion is .60 standard errors. At $\alpha = .01$ in the one-tailed test, $z = 2.32$. Therefore, because the calculated z is less than the critical z from the table, we cannot reject the null hypothesis that $\pi \leq .25$. Therefore, we cannot conclude in a managerial sense that we have reached our target market share of over 25 percent. We note that this is true even though the sample market share was 30 percent.

The Issue of Type II Error   For any given α, n, and related sample results, it is possible to calculate the probability of making a Type II error, β, and the resultant power of the test, $1 - \beta$. However, these are complex statistical topics which are almost never calculated in real marketing research problems. Thus, we have omitted their calculation from the current discussion.[6]

t Test   The t test is appropriately used in hypothesis testing about means for all sample sizes when σ is unknown. The reason we use z when $n > 30$ is that the t distribution and the z distribution are virtually identical when $n > 30$, and the values of the t distribution have not been calculated for large sample sizes. In a t test we estimate σ by using s. The critical values of the t statistics are presented in Table A-4 of Appendix A. The critical value of t varies by the α level selected, the number of degrees of freedom in the sample, and whether a one- or two-tailed test is needed. For example, we note that for $\alpha = .05$ in a one-tailed test with 10 degrees of freedom, $t = 1.812$. There are always $n - 1$ degrees of freedom in a t test of the mean, because we are using s as an estimate of σ, and s has $n - 1$ degrees of freedom. The t table gives values of t that can occur simply as a result of sampling error.

Let us quickly illustrate a t test. Suppose that in attempting to estimate yearly rates of cola consumption per capita,

$H_0\colon$ $\mu = 100$ gallons
$H_1\colon$ $\mu > 100$

and a sample has yielded the following:

$\overline{X} = 120$, $s = 15$, $n = 7$

[6] The interested reader should consult any good basic statistics book. For example, see Hamburg, op. cit., pp. 271–280.

Here

$$t = \frac{\overline{X} - \mu}{s_{\overline{x}}} = \frac{\overline{X} - \mu}{s/\sqrt{n}}$$

$$= \frac{120 - 100}{15/\sqrt{7}} = \frac{20}{5.67}$$

$$= 3.53$$

The critical value of t at $\alpha = .1$ for a one-tailed test at 6 df is 1.44. Since our calculated t exceeds the critical t, we reject the null hypothesis and accept the alternative that per capita cola consumption in the population exceeds 100 gallons.

Nominal Data

Researchers are interested in more than just hypotheses about the mean. Often they wish to make inferences about how respondents are distributed across the possible categories of a nominal variable. For example, in a sample of families who purchase returnable bottles, the researcher might want to know whether these respondents are distributed equally in all occupational categories. The chi-square test is a procedure for comparing a hypothesized population distribution across categories against an observed distribution.

Chi-square Test   In a chi-square test an hypothesized population distribution is compared with a distribution generated by a sample. The formula for chi square is

$$\chi^2 = \sum_{i=1}^{k} \frac{(O_i - E_i)^2}{E_i}$$

where k = number of categories of the variable
O_i = observed number of respondents in category i
E_i = hypothesized number of respondents in category i

Table A-6 of Appendix A gives the critical values of the chi-square distribution. These are the values of chi square that can occur by chance (due to sampling error) for various degrees of freedom and various α levels. The number of degrees of freedom is given on the left side column of Table A-6. It is referred to as n on the table. In a univariate chi-square test, the degrees of freedom equals $k - 1$, since for a given sample size once the number of respondents in $k - 1$ categories is known, the number in the k category is automatically determined. The top row in Table A-6 gives the value of $1 - \alpha$. So if we want $\alpha = .05$, we look in the column for $1 - \alpha = .95$. Let us see how to find a critical value of chi square. Suppose that we have a variable with 7 df and have specified that $\alpha = .05$. Then we look down the $1 - \alpha = .95$ column until it intersects with the row representing 7 df. The critical chi square would be 14.1.

Column 1 of Table 22-4 gives the observed distribution of returnable-bottle users across occupational categories. The null hypothesis here is that there is no difference in the population of returnable-bottle users across occupational categories. Thus we would expect an equal number of respondents in each occupational category. These expected numbers are given in column 2 of Table 22-4. The remaining columns of the table present the steps necessary to calculate chi square in this situation. We see that the calculated chi square equals 10. If we set $\alpha = .1$, the critical chi square from Table A-6 at 3 df is 6.25. Since the calculated chi square exceeds the critical chi square, we reject the null hypothesis and conclude that users of returnable bottles differ in occupational category. Note that the chi-square test merely tells us that there is a significant relationship. We must then go back and look at the distribution itself to see the nature of the relationship. Here we see that students form the modal category.

It is not necessary to have the null hypothesis that all categories have an equal number of respondents; the chi-square test may be used to compare observed results with any hypothesized distribution.

Of course, a good computer data analysis package would provide all the procedures presented in this chapter. The purpose of this chapter has been to allow the reader to know which statistics to ask the computer to generate in a univariate context.

SUMMARY

1 The choice of data analysis procedure depends upon the number of variables to be analyzed at the same time, whether the interest is in description or inference, and the level of measurement of the variable or variables.

2 Descriptive statistics provide summary measures of the data contained in the sample.

3 Inferential statistics allow the researcher to make judgments about the population based upon the sample results.

4 The mean and standard deviation are the relevant descriptive measures of central tendency and dispersion, respectively, for interval data.

5 The median is the relevant descriptive measure of central tendency for ordinal data.

6 The mode and relative and absolute frequencies are the relevant descriptive measures of central tendency and dispersion, respectively, for nominal data.

Table 22-4 Calculation of Chi Square for Occupational Categories

Occupational category	O_i	E_i	$O_i - E_i$	$(O_i - E_i)^2$	$(O_i - E_i)^2/E_i$
Labor	15	25	−10	100	4
Clerical	20	25	−5	25	1
Managerial	30	25	5	25	1
Student	35	25	10	100	4
Total	100	100			10

$df = k - 1 = 3$; calculated $\chi^2 = 10$; critical χ^2 at 3 df and $\alpha = .1 = 6.25$.

7 The z test is the appropriate inferential test about means for interval data when σ is known for any sample size, or for situations where σ is unknown and $n > 30$.

8 The t test is the appropriate inferential test about means for interval data when σ is unknown.

9 The chi-square test is the appropriate inferential test for the distribution of subjects across a nominal variable.

DISCUSSION QUESTIONS

1 What is univariate data analysis?

2 Distinguish between descriptive and inferential statistics.

3 Why are (1) measures of central tendency and (2) measures of dispersion both necessary to describe a variable?

4 From a sample of Tide users, the following frequency count was generated for the categories of the variable, age:

Age	Frequency
55 and over	100
40–54	120
25–39	80
18–24	60
	$n = 360$

Is Tide usage spread evenly across the population in terms of age?

5 The manager of a movie theater hypothesized that twice as many of the theater's patrons were under 30 as were 30 and over. A sample of patrons yielded the following results:

Age	Frequency
under 30	220
30 and over	120
	$n = 340$

Is the theater manager's hypothesis about the population of patrons correct?

6 A sales manager had promised the entire sales force a special trip if average daily sales per salesperson were $1000 or more. A sample of 10 salespersons yielded the following results: Average daily sales per salesperson = $1050; standard deviation = $150. Can the sales manager conclude that the entire sales force has reached the goal?

7 A political research firm undertook a sample of registered voters in a small community to see whether a particular candidate would win the election. The sample size was 50, and the result was that 51 percent of the sample favored this candidate. If people voted as they say they will, do the results indicate that this candidate will win the election?

8 A company had adopted the following decision rule with respect to introducing a new product: If average monthly consumption is 100 ounces or more, we will enter into test market. An in-home placement test of $n = 50$ yielded the following results: Average monthly consumption = 96 ounces; standard deviation = 15. Given their decision rule, what decision should they make?

SUGGESTED READING

Andrews, Frank M., et al., *A Guide for Selecting Statistical Techniques for Analyzing Social Science Data* (Ann Arbor: Institute for Social Research, The University of Michigan, 1974), pp. 1–4 and 19. This guide lists all relevant univariate statistics on the above pages and provides references as to where to find a detailed description of them. It is an extremely useful document for all who have data analysis problems.

Hamburg, Morris, *Statistical Analysis for Decision Making* (New York: Harcourt Brace Jovanovich, 1977), chap. 1. A good discussion of descriptive statistics for univariate analysis. Chapter 7 presents a very readable basic statistical discussion of hypothesis testing.

Chapter 23

Bivariate Data Analysis

In most marketing research studies the interests of the researcher and manager go beyond the univariate data analysis discussed in Chapter 22. They are often interested in the relationship between variables taken two at a time. Typical questions for which bivariate analysis can provide answers include: (1) What is the relationship between using our brand and media viewing habits? (2) What is the relationship between sales force turnover and sales manager age? (3) Is there a difference between attitudes toward our brand and toward other brands?

This chapter presents those data analysis procedures that are appropriate for bivariate relationships. Again, the appropriate technique depends upon the scale level of the variables involved and whether the researcher wants a descriptive statistic or an inferential test. We shall also discuss some issues related to the interpretation of cross-tabulation tables.

OVERVIEW OF BIVARIATE PROCEDURES

Figure 23-1 presents an overview of some bivariate descriptive statistics and inferential tests. Here we must be sure that we want to analyze two variables at a time. If this is the case, the scale level of the variables involved then guides us to the appropriate statistic. Not all possible combinations of bivariate rela-

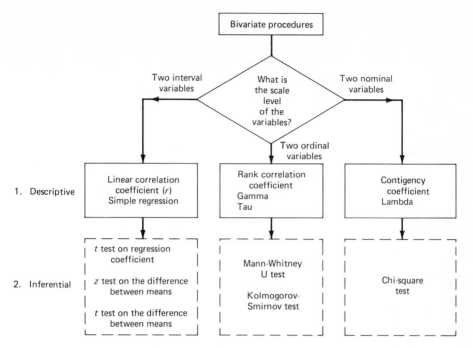

Figure 23-1 Bivariate data analysis procedures.

tionships are presented in Figure 23-1. For example, it is possible to analyze an interval and an ordinal variable together, or a nominal and an ordinal variable, etc. These types of bivariate relationships are not discussed here, as they have little application in marketing research. Further, some of the procedures presented in Figure 23-1 do not as yet have wide application in marketing research and will not be discussed here. Instead, this chapter will be devoted to the bivariate procedures that are most relevant to real marketing research problems. Specifically, from descriptive statistics for interval variables we shall discuss (1) the linear correlation coefficient, r, and (2) simple regression. Also, from inferential statistics for interval variables we shall discuss (1) the t test on the regression coefficient, (2) the z test on the difference between means, and (3) the t test on the difference between means. Finally, from inferential statistics for nominal variables, we shall discuss the chi-square test.[1]

DESCRIPTIVE STATISTICS

Often the interest of the researcher is in describing the nature of bivariate relationships generated from a sample. This section presents a description of

[1] The reader who is interested in the other statistics presented in Figure 23-1, or in bivariate statistics for variables of different scales, should consult Sidney Siegel, *Nonparametric Statistics for The Behavioral Sciences* (New York: McGraw-Hill, 1956), pp. 63–156, and Frank M. Andrews et al., *A Guide for Selecting Statistical Techniques for Analyzing Social Science Data* (Ann Arbor: Institute for Social Research, The University of Michigan, 1974), pp. 5–13.

two relevant descriptive statistical procedures appropriate for use with two interval variables. They are (1) the linear correlation coefficient and (2) simple regression.

Linear Correlation Coefficient

Linear correlation is a measure of the degree to which two interval variables are associated. For example, suppose we have data giving grades on a marketing management course, X, and data on grades in a marketing research course, Y. Our interest is in determining the level and direction of relationship between these two variables—for example, are high grades on X associated with high grades on Y, or vice versa, or is there no relationship between the two? The linear correlation coefficient, r_{XY}, is a measure of the linear relationship between X and Y.

In examining the relationship between two interval variables, a useful beginning is to plot the data on a scatter diagram. Figure 23-2 is an example of a plot for two variables, X and Y. If we draw the means of the two variables, $\overline{X}$ and $\overline{Y}$ on the scatter diagram, a first impression of possible relationships can be obtained. Drawing in the mean values divides the scatter diagram into four quadrants, labeled 1, 2, 3, and 4 in Figure 23-2. For data points in quadrant 1, both the X and Y values are above their respective means; i.e., they have positive deviations from their means. For quadrant 2, X values have negative deviations and Y values positive deviations; for quadrant 3, both have negative deviations; and for quadrant 4, X values have positive deviations and Y values have negative deviations. We note that if the data points tend to be in diagonal quadrants, this would be evidence of a relationship between the two variables. For example, if most points were in quadrants 1 and 3, positive deviations on X would be associated with positive deviations in Y (quadrant 1), and negative deviations in X would be associated with negative deviations in Y (quadrant 3); i.e., as X increases, Y increases. X and Y would be positively related.

On the other hand, if data points tend to be in quadrants 2 and 4, negative deviations in X are associated with positive deviations in Y (quadrant 2), and vice versa (quadrant 4). This situation would indicate a negative relationship between X and Y. The intent of the correlation coefficient, r_{XY}, is to quantify the relationship between the variables.

We begin this process by developing a distance measure between each point's X and Y value and the mean of X and Y. We define:

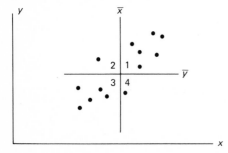

Figure 23-2 An example of a scatter diagram and associated quadrants.

$$x = (X_i - \overline{X}) \tag{23-1}$$

and

$$y = (Y_i - \overline{Y}) \tag{23-2}$$

These measures are deviations from their respective means, as discussed above. Each deviation calculated in the equations above has a sign attached. If the value of X_i or Y_i is greater than the mean, the sign is positive. If the value X_i or Y_i is less than the mean, the sign is negative. By multiplying the two deviations together we get a signed value. The sign of this number tells us something about the quadrant a data point falls into. We define:

$$xy = (X_i - \overline{X})(Y_i - \overline{Y}) \tag{23-3}$$

Thus:

1   If x is positive and y is positive, xy is positive, and the data point falls in quadrant 1.
2   If x is negative and y is positive, xy is negative, and the data point falls in quadrant 2.
3   If x is negative and y is negative, xy is positive, and the data point falls in quadrant 3.
4   If x is positive and y is negative, xy is negative, and the data point falls in quadrant 4.

We see that xy is positive in quadrants 1 and 3 and negative in 2 and 4. Data points in quadrants 1 and 3 indicate a positive relationship between X and Y, as noted previously, and data points in quadrants 2 and 4 indicate a negative relationship between X and Y. Therefore, the sign of xy indicates the direction of relationship.

If we added up all the xys for each data point, to get $\sum_{i=1}^{n} xy$, the sign of this number will indicate the overall direction of relationship. For example, if the data come mostly from quadrants 1 and 3, positive values of xy will outweigh negative values, and $\sum_{i=1}^{n} xy$, will be positive, indicating a positive relationship between X and Y. The opposite is true if the data come mostly from quadrants 2 and 4. If the data are evenly split among all four quadrants, positive and negative values of xy will tend to cancel, and $\sum_{i=1}^{n} xy$ will be zero.

The value of $\sum_{i=1}^{n} xy$ is an improvement over visual examination of the scatter diagram. However, it has two significant weaknesses. First, the value of

$\sum_{i=1}^{n} xy$ is partially dependent on the number of data points, n. As n increases, the value of $\sum_{i=1}^{n} xy$ also increases. Comparison of relationships involving different numbers of observations would then not be meaningful. Second, the value of $\sum_{i=1}^{n} xy$ depends in part on the unit of measurement being used on X and Y. For example, if an exam is marked out of 25 we would get a smaller value for $\sum_{i=1}^{n} xy$ than if the exam was marked out of 50, and a smaller value if it was out of 50 than if out of 100, etc.

We must then eliminate the effects of sample size and units from our measure of association $\sum_{i=1}^{n} xy$. We may eliminate the effects of sample size by dividing through $\sum_{i=1}^{n} xy$ by the degrees of freedom in the sample size, $n - 1$. This gives us a measure of the covariance of X and Y:

$$\text{Cov } (X, Y) = \frac{\Sigma (X_i - \bar{X})(Y_i - \bar{Y})}{n - 1}$$

Note that we will use Σ by itself to indicate addition across all n cases.

Covariance is positive if the values of X_i and Y_i tend to deviate from their respective means in the same direction. It is negative if they tend to deviate in the opposite direction. If X and Y were statistically independent, the Cov $(X, Y) = 0$. We eliminate the effect of units by dividing Cov (X, Y) through by the standard deviations of X and Y. We define this value as the correlation coefficient, r_{XY}. Thus

$$r_{XY} = \frac{\Sigma (X_i - \bar{X})(Y_i - \bar{Y})}{(n - 1)(s_X)(s_Y)}$$

This formula may be simplified to yield

$$r_{XY} = \frac{\Sigma (X_i - \bar{X})(Y_i - \bar{Y})}{\sqrt{\Sigma (X_i - \bar{X})^2 \, \Sigma (Y_i - \bar{Y})^2}} \tag{23-4}$$

or alternatively

$$r_{XY} = \frac{\Sigma \, xy}{\sqrt{\Sigma x^2 \Sigma y^2}} \tag{23-5}$$

We see then that correlation is just a standardized measure of covariation. This standardization allows two correlations to be compared independently of the units in which observations are measured. The correlation coefficient may take on any value between -1.00 and $+1.00$. When $r = 1.00$, this indicates a perfect positive correlation. When $r = -1.00$, this indicates a perfect negative correlation. If $r = 0$, there is no relationship between the variables. Thus correlation provides a measure of the direction and strength of the relationship between two variables.

Correlation is a measure of the extent to which two variables share variation between them. The exact percentage of variation shared by two variables is calculated by squaring r. This r^2 is called the *coefficient of determination.*

In general, if r is bigger than 0.8 (sign of relationship ignored), the relationship between the variables is very strong; if r is between 0.4 and 0.8, the relationship is a moderate to strong one; and if r is less than 0.4, the relationship is a weak one.

A Numeric Example The first two columns of Table 23-1 present the grades of 10 students in a course in marketing management, X, and in marketing research, Y. Figure 23-3 presents a scatter plot of the grades in the two courses. What we want to know is the correlation coefficient between the grades in the two courses. We have calculated the necessary values for Equation 23-5 on Table 23-1. Thus

$$r_{XY} = \frac{1200}{\sqrt{1290 \times 1450}}$$
$$= \frac{1200}{1368}$$
$$= .88$$

Table 23-1 Marketing Management (X) and Marketing Research (Y) Grades for 10 Students

X	Y	$x = (X - \overline{X})$	$y = (Y - \overline{Y})$	xy	x^2	y^2
75	85	1	10	10	1	100
80	85	6	10	60	36	100
60	65	-14	-10	140	196	100
55	60	-19	-15	285	361	225
85	80	11	5	55	121	25
95	95	21	20	420	441	400
70	60	-4	-15	60	16	225
75	80	1	5	5	1	25
80	80	6	5	30	36	25
65	60	-9	-15	135	81	225
$\Sigma X = 740$	$\Sigma Y = 750$	$\Sigma x = 0$	$\Sigma y = 0$	$\Sigma xy = 1200$	$\Sigma x^2 = 1290$	$\Sigma y^2 = 1450$
$\overline{X} = 74.0$	$\overline{Y} = 75.0$					

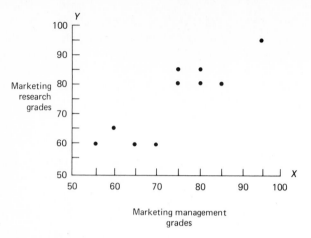

Figure 23-3 Scatter diagram of course grades.

The percentage of variation shared by these two variables is given by the coefficient of determination:

$$r^2 = (.88)^2 = .77$$

This represents the amount of variation in one of the variables we can explain by knowledge of the other variable.

Often the interests of the research go beyond the direction and strength of association between two variables. In this circumstance, simple regression is often useful.

Simple Regression

Regression is a method of analysis that applies when the research is dealing with one intervally scaled dependent variable and a number of intervally scaled independent variables. The purposes of regression are to show *how* the independent variables in the analysis are related to the dependent variable, and to make *predictions* about scores on the dependent variable based upon knowledge of independent variable scores. We begin our study of regression by examining the special case where we have one dependent variable and only one independent variable. Regression used in this context is called *simple regression*. The data on course grades presented in Table 23-1 will again be used. The marketing management grade, X, will be designated as the independent variable, and the marketing research grade, Y, will be designated as the dependent variable. We could fit a linear relationship to these data by drawing an eye-fitted line through the scatter plot in Figure 23-3. However, we want to be more precise than this, so we look for a mathematical procedure to define the required straight line.

Partitioning the Sum of Squares   We begin this process by defining:

Y_i = the ith observation on the dependent variable
$\overline{Y}$ = the mean of all the Y's
$\hat{Y}_i$ = the predicted value of the ith observation of the dependent variable

We can write any observation as a deviation from the mean value, $\overline{Y}$.

Total deviation for ith observation $= (Y_i - \overline{Y})$

This represents the total deviation of Y_i, because if we know nothing about X values, we can still guess $\overline{Y}$ as our estimate of Y. Total deviation must then be expressed as deviation from $\overline{Y}$. In a fashion completely parallel to that for analysis of variance, we can partition this deviation into components:[2]

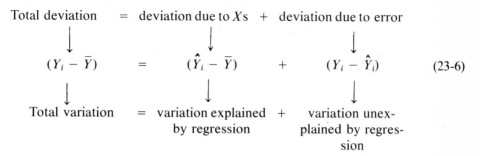

$$\text{Total deviation} = \text{deviation due to } Xs + \text{deviation due to error}$$

$$(Y_i - \overline{Y}) = (\hat{Y}_i - \overline{Y}) + (Y_i - \hat{Y}_i) \qquad (23\text{-}6)$$

$$\text{Total variation} = \underset{\text{by regression}}{\text{variation explained}} + \underset{\substack{\text{plained by regres-}\\ \text{sion}}}{\text{variation unex-}}$$

Figure 23-4 graphically shows this partitioning of total deviation. We note that the explained deviation is the amount the total deviation is reduced by our knowledge of the regression line from the level of deviation present by knowledge of $\overline{Y}$. If we add the deviation in Equation 23-6 across all observations and square this equation, we can partition the sums of squares in a fashion exactly as we did in ANOVA. We then get:

$$\Sigma(Y_i - \overline{Y})^2 = \Sigma(\hat{Y}_i - \overline{Y})^2 + \Sigma(Y_i - \hat{Y}_i)^2$$

$$SS_{\text{total}} = SS_{\substack{\text{explained}\\ \text{by}\\ \text{regression}}} + SS_{\substack{\text{unexplained}\\ \text{by}\\ \text{regression}}}$$

$$\begin{matrix}\text{Total} \\ \text{variation}\end{matrix} = \begin{matrix}\text{explained} \\ \text{variation}\end{matrix} + \begin{matrix}\text{unexplained} \\ \text{variation}\end{matrix}$$

Presenting the deviations in this fashion provides a conceptual understanding of how a regression aids our understanding of the dependent variable. However, we still have not developed a procedure to fit a line to the data.

[2] See Chapters 15 and 16.

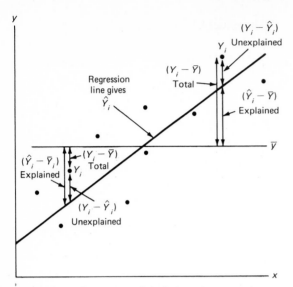

Figure 23-4 Partioning of deviations in regression.

Fitting the Regression Line We want to be able to predict a Y value based on knowledge of an X value and to note the direction of relationship (positive or negative) and rate of change (slope level) between X and Y. These tasks require us to fit a mathematical linear equation to the data. Of course, we want an equation that fits the data well. A good fit could be one that minimizes the error or unexplained deviation. The criterion actually used is to minimize the sum of the squares of the errors. The "least squares" solution has desirable statistical properties that are well dealt with in texts on regression. Intuitively, we can see that large errors are avoided as much as possible, thereby providing a good fit; thus, we want to fit a line of the form

$$Y = a + bX$$

where a = the value of the intercept on the Y axis
         b = the slope of the line

Using our knowledge of the X and Y values, we solve for a and b. One way to do this is to first cast the X values as deviations from their mean: $x = X - \overline{X}$. Now we are solving for an equation of the form $Y = a + bx$. We want to find the values of a and b that minimize the sum of squared errors $\Sigma(Y_i - \hat{Y}_i)^2$.

The mathematical knowledge necessary to develop the formulas for the a and b values is beyond the scope of this book. The resultant formulas are

$$a = \overline{Y}$$

$$b = \frac{\sum\limits_{i=1}^{n} Y_i x_i}{\sum\limits_{i=1}^{n} x_i^2}$$

A Numeric Example   Let us do a regression with the data on grades that we used to calculate the correlation coefficient. The basic data and calculations are presented in Table 23-2. The resultant equation is:

$$\hat{Y}_i = 75.0 + .93x_i \tag{23-7}$$

In making predictions it is sometimes easier to deal with X_i values and not the deviations x_i. Thus Equation 23-7 becomes:

$$\hat{Y}_i = 75.0 + .93(X_i - \bar{X})$$
$$\hat{Y}_i = 75.0 + .93(X_i - 74.0)$$
$$\hat{Y}_i = (75.0 - 68.8) + .93X_i$$
$$\hat{Y}_i = 6.2 + .93X_i \tag{23-8}$$

We note in Equation 23-8 that the b value or slope remains the same. The intercept only has shifted.

The Meaning of the Coefficients   What exactly do the coefficients we calculated mean? The a tells us the predicted value of Y when X is zero. In our example we would predict a score of 6.2 in the marketing research course even if the grade in marketing management were zero. Obviously, such a person should not even be allowed to take marketing research. This points up a general comment, namely, that the a coefficient is generally of less interest to us than the b coefficient.

The b represents *the amount of change we would predict in Y for a one-unit change in X*. Thus, in our example we would predict a .93 increase in the grade in marketing research for each increase of one grade point obtained in marketing management. A negative sign on a b coefficient would indicate that as X increases, Y decreases. Graphically, b is the slope of the regression line.

We may use the regression equation to generate predicted values of Y. These $\hat{Y}_i$'s are presented for the given X_i's in Table 23-2. We can then calculate the difference between the observed and predicted values, $Y_i - \hat{Y}_i$. If we square these values and add them across all observations, we get the sum of squares error, $\Sigma(Y_i - \hat{Y}_i)^2$. These values are calculated in Table 23-2. The sum of squares error here is 334.17. No other values of a and b would give this small an SS_{error}. This is the meaning of a "least squares" solution.

Explained Variation   The question naturally arises as to how much of the variation in Y was explained by our knowledge of X. This question is answered

Table 23-2 Regression Calculations for Data in Table 23-1

X_i	Y_i	$x_i=(X_i-\bar{X})$	$Y_i x_i$	x_i^2	$\hat{Y}_i=75+.93X_i$	$(Y_i-\hat{Y}_i)$	$(Y_i-\hat{Y}_i)^2$
75	85	1	85	1	75.9	9.1	82.81
80	85	6	510	36	80.6	4.4	19.36
60	65	-14	-910	196	62.0	3.0	9.00
55	60	-19	-1140	361	57.3	2.7	7.29
85	80	11	880	121	85.2	-5.2	27.04
95	95	21	1995	441	94.5	0.5	0.25
70	60	-4	-240	16	71.3	-11.3	127.69
75	80	1	80	1	75.9	4.1	16.81
80	80	6	480	36	80.6	-.6	0.36
65	60	-9	-540	81	66.6	-6.6	43.56

$\Sigma X_i = 740$, $\bar{X} = 74.0$

$\Sigma Y_i = 750$, $\bar{Y} = 75.0$

$\Sigma x_i = 0$

$\Sigma Y_i x_i = 1200$

$\Sigma x_i^2 = 1290$

$\Sigma(Y_i-\hat{Y}_i) = 0$

$\Sigma(Y_i-\hat{Y}_i)^2 = 334.17$

$a = \bar{Y} = 75.0$

$$b = \frac{\Sigma Y_i x_i}{\Sigma x_i^2} = \frac{1200}{1290} = .93$$

$$\hat{Y}_i = 75.0 + .93\,x_i$$

by calculating the ratio of explained variation to total variation. Previously we defined the coefficient of determination, r^2, as the amount of variation explained in a correlation context. The same concept applies here, except that in simple regression

$$r_{XY}^2 = \frac{\text{explained variation}}{\text{total variation}}$$
$$= \frac{\Sigma(\hat{Y}_i - \bar{Y})^2}{\Sigma(Y_i - \bar{Y})^2}$$
$$= \frac{SS_{\text{explained}}}{SS_{\text{total}}}$$

r_{XY}^2 is again called the coefficient of determination, and it represents the proportion of the total variation in Y explained by fitting the regression line.

From Table 23-1, we note that for our grades example

$$SS_{\text{total}} = \Sigma(Y_i - \bar{Y})^2 = \Sigma y^2 = 1450$$

Also from Table 23-2, we note that

$$SS_{\text{error}} = \Sigma(\hat{Y}_i - Y_i)^2 = 334.17$$

Thus

$$\begin{aligned} SS_{\text{explained}} &= \Sigma(\hat{Y}_i - \bar{Y})^2 \\ &= SS_{\text{total}} - SS_{\text{error}} \\ &= 1450 - 334.17 \\ &= 1115.83 \end{aligned}$$

Therefore,

$$r_{XY}^2 = \frac{1115.83}{1450} = .77$$

This is exactly the value of r^2 we obtained by squaring the correlation coefficient, as we would expect.

In practice, the size of r^2's obtained from regression vary greatly. In forecasting applications where the environment is quite stable, r^2's may be as high as .8 or .9. In situations where the environment changes a great deal, or where one is trying to predict individual attitudes or behavior, r^2's may be in the .15 to .3 range. These latter, small r^2's indicate that the lack of ability of marketers to fully understand the world in which they are working. However, all is not lost. Individual coefficients may still provide useful information even though the total r^2 is small.

Correlation and simple regression allow the researcher to describe the relationship between two individual variables. For example one could describe the relationship between (1) age and amount of credit card usage, (2) income and wine consumption per year, (3) advertising expenditures and attitudes toward a brand, (4) years of education and expenditures on housing per year, or (5) number of advertising insertions and brand awareness. These are but a few examples of possible situations where correlation and simple regression could be useful.

It should be recognized that correlation and regression provide measures of association, not causation. However, marketing managers may use these procedures to help them better understand the nature of the implicit or explicit causal model they are using.

INFERENTIAL STATISTICS

As with univariate analysis, the interest of the researcher often goes beyond describing sample relationships to making judgments about population parameters. In theory it is possible to test a hypothesis about any descriptive statistic. Thus, for example, we could test hypotheses about the size of the population correlation coefficient. However, in this chapter we will restrict our attention to a few bivariate inferential tests. Specifically, for interval data we shall discuss (1) the t test on the regression coefficient, (2) the z test on the difference between means, and (3) the t test on the difference between means. These tests are somewhat mathematically detailed, and for some readers they will constitute a restatement of material already covered in a basic statistics course. Thus, the discussion of these tests is contained in the appendix at the end of this chapter.

One bivariate inference test will be discussed in the main body of the chapter, namely, the chi-square test, which is appropriate for examining the relationship between two nominal variables. It is discussed here because of its usefulness in analyzing cross-tabulation tables, and because it is often not covered in basic statistics courses. Finally, we shall position the bivariate analysis of variance test that is described in detail in Chapter 15.

The Chi-Square Test

Perhaps the most common type of bivariate analysis in practice is the cross tabulation of two nominal variables. In truth we need not have nominal variables to do this; interval or ordinal variables can be analyzed in this fashion if we first group them into classes or categories. Typical questions addressed by cross tabulation might be: (1) Is there a relationship between age and media habits? (2) Is there a relationship between region of the country and brand preference? (3) Is there a relationship between life-style types and car ownership?

As we see from the examples, the objective of cross tabulation is to identify a relationship between variables. In data from a sample we might observe what appears to be a relationship between two nominal variables. The question naturally arises as to whether this observed relationship is simply the result of

Table 23-3   Cross Tabulation of Income and Brand Purchased Last

		B			
		Brand purchased last			
	Income	B_1 Brand 1	B_2 Brand 2	B_3 Brand 3	Total
A	A_1 Less than $10,000	50	200	125	375
	A_2 $10,000–$20,000	200	100	350	650
	A_3 Over $20,000	100	25	50	175
	Total	350	325	525	1200

sampling error, and the chi-square test is designed to answer this question. The null hypothesis for a chi-square test is that the two variables are *independent* of each other. The alternative hypothesis is that they are not independent, that is, that there is a relationship between the two variables.

We now illustrate the chi-square test. Table 23-3 presents the cross tabulation of an income measure and a measure of brand purchased last. The cell entries indicate the numbers in the sample that form the various combinations of income and brand categories. For example, we note that there were 50 people earning less than $10,000 who purchased brand 1 last. The expected number in each cell is not that they are all equal this time, as with the univariate chi square. This is so because the totals for each category of each variable are not the same. For example, with 650 people earning $10,000–$20,000, we should certainly not expect the cells to be equal. What then should be the expected cell values? To answer this question we turn to one of the elementary rules of probability theory.

We note in Table 23-3 that we have defined income as variable A and the categories of income as A_1, A_2, and A_3. "Brand purchased last" is defined as variable B, and the categories as B_1, B_2, and B_3. The various combinations of A_iB_is are the occurrences of various events. Let us use A_1B_1 to illustrate the required theory.

If A and B are independent, the probability of A_1 and B_1 occurring is the product of the probability, A_1 times B_1. This is the multiplication theorem of statistics. In symbols,

$$P(A_1 \text{ and } B_1) = P(A_1)P(B_1)$$

Also we note that

$$P(A_1) = \text{relative frequency of } A_1 \text{ to all } A\text{'s}$$
$$= \frac{A_1}{A} = \frac{375}{1200}$$

$P(B_1)$ = relative frequency of B_1 to all B's

$$= \frac{B_1}{B} = \frac{350}{1200}$$

$$P(A_1 \text{ and } B_1) = \frac{375}{1200} \times \frac{350}{1200} = .091$$

The expected number in cell A_1B_1 is then

$$n[P(A_1 \text{ and } B_1)] = 1200 \left(\frac{375}{1200} \times \frac{350}{1200} \right)$$

$$= 109.38$$

In general, the formula for expected value is

$$E_{ij} = \frac{n_{A_i} n_{B_j}}{n}$$

where E_{ij} = expected number in cell ij

n_{A_i} = number of elements in category A_i

n_{B_j} = number of elements in category B_j

For A_1B_1 the expected number is

$$E_{11} = \frac{(375)(350)}{1200} = 109.38$$

We can repeat this process for all cells.

Table 23-4 presents the observed and expected numbers for each cell and the calculation of the associated chi square. The relevant formula is

Table 23-4   Calculation of Bivariate Chi Square

Cell number	O_{ij}	E_{ij}	$O_{ij} - E_{ij}$	$(O_{ij} - E_{ij})^2$	$(O_{ij} - E_{ij})^2/E_{ij}$
1,1	50	109.38	−59.38	3526.0	32.2
1,2	200	101.56	98.44	9690.4	95.4
1,3	125	164.06	−39.06	1525.7	9.3
2,1	200	189.58	10.42	108.6	0.6
2,2	100	176.04	−76.04	5782.1	32.8
2,3	350	284.38	65.62	4306.0	15.1
3,1	100	51.04	48.96	2397.1	47.0
3,2	25	47.40	−22.40	501.8	10.6
3,3	50	76.56	−26.56	705.4	9.2
Total	1200	1200.00			252.2

$\chi^2 = 252.2$

$$\chi^2 = \sum_{i=1}^{R} \sum_{j=1}^{C} \frac{(O_{ij} - E_{ij})^2}{E_{ij}}$$

where R = number of categories of the row variable

            C = number of categories of the column variable

            O_{ij} = observed number in cell ij

            E_{ij} = expected number in cell ij

The calculated chi square is 252.2. The number of degrees of freedom is $(R - 1)(C - 1)$, since once the number of elements in $R - 1$ row categories and the total is known, the number in the last category is determined. A similar argument holds for column degrees of freedom. In our example there are $(3 - 1)(3 - 1) = 4$ degrees of freedom. If $\alpha = .01$, the critical value of chi square at 4 df is 13.3 (see Table A-6 of Appendix A). Since the calculated chi square exceeds the critical value, we reject the null hypothesis that income and brand purchased last are independent.

In using the chi square, we should have all the expected cell sizes equal to at least 5. If this is not the case, it is generally recommended that cells be combined to give an expected frequency of at least 5. It is also important to have the two measurements independent of each other. That is, we should not use the chi square to compare repeated measures on the same variable.

The chi-square test may tell us that two variables are not independent. However, it does not tell anything about the nature of the relationship. To determine this, one must look back into the table of interest. In Table 23-3, we see that as income increases, "brand last purchased" shifts from brand 2 to brand 3 and then to brand 1. A researcher often confronts many cross-tabulation tables. A good strategy to use in evaluating these tables is first to examine the chi square for significance, then examine closely those tables with significant chi squares. Fortunately, all good data analysis programs offer the chi-square test as part of a cross-tabulation output. There are a number of other issues related to interpreting cross-tabulation tables that will be addressed later in the chapter; but first there is one other bivariate inferential test that we must note.

Analysis of Variance

One relevant bivariate inferential test is not listed in Figure 23-1—the one-way analysis of variance (ANOVA) test discussed in Chapter 15. This test is appropriate when the researcher has one nominal independent variable and one interval-dependent variable. It tests the null hypothesis that two or more means are equal. We shall not discuss it here, since it was presented in detail in Chapter 15. Our purpose now is simply to position one-way ANOVA relative to other bivariate techniques.

INTERPRETATION OF CROSS-TABULATION TABLES

The position of crosstab tables in marketing research practice is so important that we must go beyond the mere concern about significance discussed previously in our examination of the chi-square test. Certain fundamental issues related to the interpretation of these tables must be clarified: (1) the use of percentages and (2) the elaboration of discovered relationships with the introduction of additional variables.

Use of Percentages

In doing the chi-square test we use the raw frequency counts in each cell. This is fine for this test, but raw frequencies are often difficult to interpret. To aid in the interpretation of significant relationships it usually helps to cast the data in the crosstab table in percentage form. The problem is that the researcher has three alternative ways to calculate percentage: (1) row percentages, such that the percentages in each row add to 100 percent; (2) column percentages, such that the percentages in each column add to 100 percent; or (3) cell percentages, such that the percentages added across all cells equal 100 percent. Table 23-5 presents four tables. The first is a set of raw frequencies in a crosstab between income and consumption of types of wines. The other three tables present the raw frequencies presented in row, column, and cell percentage form.

Which of these percentages is most useful to the researcher? We may try to determine a general rule by examining Table 23-5. Clearly, cell percentages tell us little about the relationship between income and type of wine consumed. They are generally useful only in identifying the size of particular segments, not for assisting one in understanding relationships. If we looked at the column percentages, we could make conclusions such as the following: 65.2 percent of those consuming cheap wine earn less than $15,000, while only 34.8 percent of those consuming cheap wine earn $15,000 and over. This sort of conclusion seems to imply that type of wine consumed is having an effect on income earned. This is obviously not what we mean in this case. Clearly, we expect that income is having the effect on type of wine consumed and not the other way around. Examination of the row percentages shows us the type of relationship we were looking for. Here we could make conclusions such as: 88.2 percent of those earning less than $15,000 consume cheap wine, while only 11.8 percent of these people consume premium wine. This conclusion implies that income is affecting the type of wine consumed.

The rule, then, is to *cast percentages in the direction of the causal factor.* Thus, if the causal factor is the row factor, calculate (by computer) row percentages, and vice versa.

Elaboration of Relationships[3]

Care must be taken in the use of crosstab tables. It is possible that the true relationship is more complex than one that can be properly identified by looking at the cross tabulation of two variables. This is especially true if the user believes that there is a causal relationship between the variables. One might ask: Does

---

[3] For a more detailed treatment of this subject see Herman J. Loether and Donald G. McTavish, *Descriptive Statistics for Sociologists* (Boston: Allyn and Bacon, 1974), pp. 264–305. A good discussion is also given in Gilbert A. Churchill, Jr., *Marketing Research: Methodological Foundations* (Hinsdale, Ill.: Dryden Press, 1976), pp. 367–375.

Table 23-5 Alternative Way of Presenting Cross-tabular Results

A. Raw Frequencies

Income	Type of wine consumed		Total
	Cheap	Premium	
Less than $15,000	75	10	85
$15,000 and over	40	80	120
Total	115	90	205

B. Row Percentages

Income	Type of wine consumed		Total
	Cheap	Premium	
Less than $15,000	88.2%	11.8%	100.0
$15,000 and over	33.3	66.7	100.0

C. Column Percentages

Income	Type of wine consumed	
	Cheap	Premium
Less than $15,000	65.2%	11.1%
$15,000 and over	34.8	88.9
Total	100.0	100.0

D. Cell Percentages

Income	Type of wine consumed	
	Cheap	Premium
Less than $15,000	36.6%	4.9%
$15,000 and over	19.5	39.0
	Total 100.0	

this relationship hold when other variables are considered? For example, how are type of wine consumed and income related for different age groups, or different regions of the country, or different sexes, etc.? What we need to do is elaborate on the relationship that was discovered in two-way tables. We do this by obtaining the cross tabulation of the same variables as before, except that now we get one cross tabulation of these variables for each category of some other variable or variables. Thus, we could see whether there was a different relationship for males and females, etc.

The original association between the two variables is called the *total or zero-order association*. The tables showing the association between the two variables within categories of other variables are called *conditional tables* and reveal *conditional associations*.[4] The variables on which the crosstab is conditional are called *control variables*. Therefore, one might ask for the crosstab of income and type of wine consumed, controlling on age. When conditional tables are developed on the basis of one control variable, they are called *first-order conditional tables*. It is also possible to control on more than one variable. Here conditional tables are developed for elements within the various combinations of control categories. For example, one control combination might be "females from California," in the use of the two control variables, sex and region of the country. We would then obtain a table for each combination of sex and region. When two controls are present, the tables are called *second-order conditional tables;* if three control variables are present, they are called *third-order conditional tables,* and so on. The more control variables one adds, the more tables one will obtain, and the harder will be the interpretation of the results. For example, if one had three control variables with 2, 3, and 4 categories, respectively, one would then get $2 \times 3 \times 4 = 24$ conditional tables. Thus, one adds control variables with care, usually being guided by some theory of the underlying relationship in doing so. Our discussion of this elaboration process will be limited to first-order conditional tables.

The possible outcomes of elaboration depend on the original conclusion. Suppose the original zero-order table leads to the conclusion of a relationship between the variables. Then from the conditional tables one might (1) retain the original conclusion of a relationship existing, (2) specify a different relationship by control categories, or (3) identify the original relationship as spurious. On the other hand, the original table may have led to the conclusion of no relationship. Then from the conditional tables one might (1) retain the original conclusion that there was no relationship or (2) identify a relationship. The next two sections of this chapter illustrate these outcomes.

Zero-Order Relationship Found

This section presents illustrations of the various possible outcomes of conditional table analysis when a zero-order relationship is found.

Retain Original Conclusion of a Relationship Existing   Table 23-6 illustrates a situation where the original conclusion of a relationship existing is retained. The numbers in parentheses in the table indicate the frequency counts for the cells. Part A of the table shows the relationship between income and credit card usage, obtained using the whole sample. Clearly, higher income is associated with greater use of credit cards. Part B of the table shows this same crosstab presented for two age categories. We note that the conclusion about income and credit card usage is retained.

---

[4] Loether and McTavish, op. cit., pp. 266–267.

Table 23-6 Retain Original Conclusion of a Relationship Existing

A. Total Sample (n = 1000)

Use credit cards	Under $15,000		$15,000 and over	
		Income		
Yes	(100)	25.0%	(500)	83.3%
No	(300)	75.0	(100)	16.7
Total	(400)	100.0	(600)	100.0

B. Conditional on Age

B-1 For ages 18–35 (n = 350)

Use credit cards	Under $15,000		$15,000 and over	
		Income		
Yes	(34)	29.6%	(199)	84.7%
No	(81)	70.4	(36)	15.3
Total	(115)	100.0	(235)	100.0

B-2 For ages over 35 (n = 650)

Use credit cards	Under $15,000		$15,000 and over	
		Income		
Yes	(66)	23.2%	(301)	82.5%
No	(219)	76.8	(64)	17.5
Total	(285)	100.0	(365)	100.0

Specification of Original Relationship A good question to ask about a crosstab relationship is: Under what conditions does this relationship hold? For example, it is possible that the relationship between credit card usage and income could have been different for the different age categories. If the relationship between the dependent variable (credit card usage) and the independent variable (income) is different for different categories of the control variable (age), we say that the independent variable and control variables are interacting. The search for this type of statistical interaction is called *specification of the relationship*. Table 23-7 illustrates a situation where interaction is present. Again we present the whole sample and conditional tables. In this instance, the same initial relationship between income and credit usage is present, except that it is not as strong as before. The conditional tables reveal two different relationships between income and credit card usage. Conditional table B-1 (of Table 23-7) gives one picture. Here, lower income is slightly more associated with credit card usage. It appears that younger people earning less than $15,000 are more likely to use credit cards than older people of the same income. B-2 shows a different pattern.

Table 23-7　Specification of Relationship

A.　Total Sample (n = 1000)				
	Income			
Use credit cards	Under $15,000		$15,000 and over	
Yes	(175)	43.8%	(350)	58.3%
No	(225)	56.2	(250)	41.7
Total	(400)	100.0	(600)	100.0

B.　Conditional on Age				
B-1　For ages 18–35 (n = 350)				
	Income			
Use credit cards	Under $15,000		$15,000 and over	
Yes	(100)	76.9%	(150)	68.2%
No	(30)	23.1	(70)	31.8
Total	(130)	100.0	(220)	100.0

B-2　For ages over 35 (n = 650)				
	Income			
Use credit cards	Under $15,000		$15,000 and over	
Yes	(75)	27.8%	(230)	60.5%
No	(195)	72.2	(150)	39.5
Total	(270)	100.0	(380)	100.0

It shows a stronger positive relationship between income and credit card usage than that found in the whole sample table. Age and income are interacting to affect credit card usage.

　　Identification of a Spurious Relationship　Table 23-8 illustrates the situation where the zero-order table reveals a relationship between two variables, while the conditional tables reveal that the relationship was spurious. That is, the original relationship *disappears* when a control variable is present. In this example, the cross tabulation is between attendance at theater movies and ownership of a television set. The whole-sample table reveals that those owning television sets are more likely to attend theater movies. Graphically, this hypothesis can be represented as:

X ⎯⎯⎯⎯⎯⎯⎯⎯⎯⎯⎯⎯⎯⎯⎯⎯→Y

Ownership of a	Attendance at
television set	theater movies
(cause)	(effect)

This result seems somewhat illogical, since it is not clear how television ownership is causing attendance at theater movies. We might hypothesize that a third variable is operative that is causing both television ownership and attendance at movie theaters. This variable might be income. Graphically, this hypothesis can be represented as

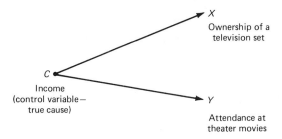

Here income is hypothesized to be causing both X and Y. If the original relationship between X and Y is indeed a causal one, we would expect it to be maintained within categories of the control variable. Part B of Table 23-8 reveals that this is not true. For those earning less than \$15,000, the pattern of attendance at theater movies is the same whether the individual owns a television set or not. Specifically, both television ownership and attendance are low. For those earning \$15,000 and over, the pattern of attendance is the same for both categories of television ownership. Here, both television ownership and attendance are high. Thus the original relationship was spurious.

No Zero-Order Relationship Found

This section presents illustrations of the various possible outcomes of conditional-table analysis when no zero-order relationship is found.

Retain Original Conclusion of No Relationship   Table 23-9 illustrates the situation where the whole-sample table revealed no relationship between two variables and the conditional tables show no relationship. The crosstab is between home ownership and region of the country. The control variable is income.

Identify a Relationship   Table 23-10 illustrates the possibility of a control variable assisting the researcher in identifying a relationship where none seems to exist on the basis of examining zero-order results. In this context the control variable is acting to suppress the observed relationship between two variables, and it is called a *suppressor variable*. This can happen when a relationship in one conditional table is equally sized but in the opposite direction of the other conditional table. The result is that the relationships cancel each other when presented in the zero-order situation.

Table 23-10 presents the cross tabulation of income and credit card usage, controlling for sex. The total-sample table shows no relationship between income and credit card usage. On the other hand, the conditional tables for male and

Table 23-8   Identification of a Spurious Relationship

A.   Total Sample (n = 1430)

Attendance at theater movies	Television ownership			
	No		Yes	
Yes	(240)	36.4%	(610)	79.2%
No	(420)	63.6	(160)	20.8
Total	(660)	100.0	(770)	100.0

B.   Conditional on Income

B-1   For income under $15,000 (n = 550)

Attendance at theater movies	Television ownership			
	No		Yes	
Yes	(40)	9.1%	(10)	9.1%
No	(400)	90.9	(100)	90.9
Total	(440)	100.0	(110)	100.0

B-2   For income $15,000 and over (n = 880)

Attendance at theater movies	Television ownership			
	No		Yes	
Yes	(200)	90.9%	(600)	90.9%
No	(20)	9.1	(60)	9.1
Total	(220)	100.0	(660)	100.0

Source: Adapted from Herman J. Loether and Donald G. McTavish, *Descriptive Statistics for Sociologists* (Boston: Allyn and Bacon, 1974), pp. 276–287.

female show strong but opposite relationships. Males earning $15,000 and over are much more likely to use credit cards than those males earning under $15,000. Exactly the opposite is true for females. Note that this is a special case of interaction. Here sex and income are interacting to hide the effect on credit card usage.

Concluding Comment on Cross Tabulation

In any dataset containing even a small number of variables, there are a great many possible crosstab tables. If one attempts to elaborate on these, the number of possible tables becomes huge. Obviously, researchers cannot just go on a "shopping trip" to find relationships, for they would be overwhelmed with computer output. They must have a model of the problem that focuses on the interrelationships among relevant variables to do proper cross-tabulation analysis. A good definition of the problem at hand combined with the specification of information needs can go a long way in guiding the data analysis process.

SUMMARY

1   Bivariate analysis involves analyzing two variables at a time.

2   The choice of statistical procedure to use depends on the scale level of the variables and on whether the researcher wants a descriptive statistic or an inferential test.

3   Linear correlation (r) is a measure of the degree to which two interval variables are associated.

4   The coefficient of determination (r^2) is the amount of variation in one variable that can be explained by knowledge of the other.

5   Simple regression is appropriate for one intervally scaled dependent variable and one intervally scaled independent variable.

6   Simple regression shows how the independent variable is related to the dependent variable.

7   The simple regression model can be presented as:

$$SS_{total} = SS_{explained} + SS_{unexplained}$$

Table 23-9   Retain Original Conclusion of No Relationship

A.   Total Sample (n = 1000)

Home ownership	Region of the country			
	East		West	
Yes	(205)	41.0%	(201)	40.2%
No	(295)	59.0	(299)	59.8
Total	(500)	100.0	(500)	100.0

B.   Conditional on Income

B-1   For income under $15,000 ($n$ = 300)

Home ownership	Region of the country			
	East		West	
Yes	(60)	40.0%	(63)	42.0%
No	(90)	60.0	(87)	58.0
Total	(150)	100.0	(150)	100.0

B-2   For income $15,000 and over ($n$ = 700)

Home ownership	Region of the country			
	East		West	
Yes	(145)	41.4%	(138)	39.4%
No	(205)	58.6	(212)	60.6
Total	(350)	100.0	(350)	100.0

Table 23-10   Identification of a Relationship

A. Total Sample (n = 1000)

	Income			
Use credit cards	**Under $15,000**		**$15,000 and over**	
Yes	(160)	40.0%	(240)	40.0%
No	(240)	60.0	(360)	60.0
Total	(400)	100.0	(600)	100.0

B. Conditional on Sex

B-1   For Males (n = 500)

	Income			
Use credit cards	**Under $15,000**		**$15,000 and over**	
Yes	(30)	15.0%	(200)	66.7%
No	(170)	85.0	(100)	33.3
Total	(200)	100.0	(300)	100.0

B-2   For females (n = 500)

	Income			
Use credit cards	**Under $15,000**		**$15,000 and over**	
Yes	(130)	65.0%	(40)	13.3%
No	(70)	35.0	(260)	86.7
Total	(200)	100.0	(300)	100.0

8   The simple regression equation is:

$$\hat{Y}_i = a + bX_i$$

where a is the intercept and b is the slope or the amount of increase in $\hat{Y}$ predicted to occur with a 1-unit increase in X.

9   A t test on the b coefficient provides a measure of the null hypothesis that the population regression coefficient is zero. (See appendix.)

10   The coefficient of determination in regression (r^2) equals

$$\frac{\text{Explained variation}}{\text{Total variation}} = \frac{SS_{\text{explained}}}{SS_{\text{total}}}$$

11   The difference between two sample means may be tested to see whether the population means are really different. This may be done with a z or t test, depending on the circumstances. (See appendix.)

12   The chi-square test evaluates the null hypothesis that two nominal variables are independent.

13 One-way ANOVA is appropriate with one intervally scaled dependent variable and one nominally scaled independent variable. It tests the null hypothesis that two or more means are equal.

14 Cast percentages in cross-tabulation tables in the direction of causation.

15 Total-sample cross-tabulation tables may be elaborated by using control variables.

16 If a total-sample relationship is found, this elaboration may find the same relationship, interaction, or spuriousness.

17 If no total-sample relationship is found, this elaboration may find no relationship again or identify a relationship.

DISCUSSION QUESTIONS

1 What questions must one answer in order to select the appropriate bivariate statistical procedure?

2 What is linear correlation?

3 What is the coefficient of determination?

4 When can simple regression be used?

5 How does one test to see whether a simple regression has explained a significant portion of the variation in the dependent variable?

6 When should the z and t tests on the difference between means be used?

7 What is the chi-square test a test for?

8 In what alternative ways may percentages be calculated in a crosstab table? Which way is the best?

9 What is elaboration?

10 What may be found in elaboration?

11 A marketing manager was given the following table of frequency counts to show the nature of the relationship between age and attendance at NFL games. What conclusion should be drawn?

	Age		
Attend NFL games	**Under 40**	**40 and over**	**Total**
Yes	66	31	97
No	24	23	47
Total	90	54	144

12 The same marketing manager also had a table of frequency counts between age and attendance at college football games. What conclusion should be drawn?

	Age		
Attend college football games	**Under 40**	**40 and over**	**Total**
Yes	42	71	113
No	51	65	116
Total	93	136	229

13 The same study used in questions 11 and 12 yielded the following data concerning
the number of NFL home games attended in a year and the number of years the
person has lived in the city:
What is the relationship between the two variables?

Case	Number of home games attended	Years lived in city
1	7	30
2	2	6
3	1	2
4	3	12
5	7	20
6	4	23

SUGGESTED READINGS

Andrews, Frank M. et al., *A Guide for Selecting Statistical Techniques for Analyzing
Social Science Data* (Ann Arbor: Institute for Social Research, the University of
Michigan, 1974), pp. 5–13 and 26–29. This excellent document classifies and gives
references for all the statistics discussed in this chapter, plus many more not discussed
here.

Loether, Herman J., and Donald G. McTavish, *Descriptive Statistics for Sociologists*
(Boston: Allyn and Bacon, 1974), chaps. 6 to 8. A very readable and in-depth
discussion of bivariate descriptive statistics and an elaboration of bivariate relationships.

——— and ———, *Inferential Statistics for Sociologists* (Boston: Allyn and Bacon, 1974),
chaps. 7 and 8. A very readable discussion of hypothesis testing in a bivariate
context.

Siegel, Sidney, *Nonparametric Statistics for the Behavioral Sciences* (New York: McGraw-
Hill, 1956), chaps. 5, 6, and 9. This most readable of all statistics books presents a
discussion and examples of the statistics appropriate for bivariate relationships
involving ordinal and nominal data.

APPENDIX: Bivariate Inference Tests

This appendix contains a description of a number of bivariate inference tests, specifically
(1) the t test on the simple regression coefficient, (2) the F test on the explained sum of
squares in regression, (3) the z test on the difference between means, and (4) the t test
on the difference between means. All tests presented here assume that the variables of
interest are intervally scaled.

The t Test on the Regression Coefficient

The null hypothesis that interests the researcher with respect to simple regression is that the slope is zero. In formula, the null and alternative hypotheses are:

$H_0: \beta = 0$

$H_1: \beta \neq 0$

where β is the population regression coefficient. In essence, we are testing to see whether the X values make a significant contribution to the explanation of the Y values. We begin the t test by first calculating the standard error of the estimate.

Standard error of the estimate.   The measure of the scatter of the actual Y_i values about the regression line, $\hat{Y}_i$, is called the standard error of the estimate. It is the standard deviation of Y_i about $\hat{Y}_i$.

$$\text{Standard error of the estimate } = s_{YX} = \sqrt{\frac{\Sigma(Y_i - \hat{Y}_i)^2}{n-2}}$$

We divide by $n - 2$ to adjust for sample bias effect on this estimator because one degree of freedom is used up in fitting the regression line, and there are $n - 1$ degrees of freedom in the sample. The slope of the regression line requires one degree of freedom. A small standard error of the estimate indicates a tight scatter of observations about the regression line, and vice versa. We could use this value to calculate a confidence interval about the regression line. However, this is not our interest here. For our purposes the standard error of the estimate will be used as an intermediate step in testing the null hypothesis that $\beta = 0$.

From the data in Table 23-2,

$$\Sigma(Y_i - \hat{Y}_i)^2 = 334.17$$

$$\text{thus} \quad s_{YX} = \sqrt{\frac{334.17}{10-2}}$$
$$= \sqrt{41.77125}$$
$$= 6.5$$

Standard error of the regression coefficient.   We may also calculate the standard error or standard deviation of the sampling distribution of the regression coefficient. It is a measure of the amount of sampling error present in the determination of b:

$$s_b = \frac{s_{YX}}{\sqrt{\Sigma x^2}}$$

$$\text{or } s_b = \frac{s_{YX}}{\sqrt{\Sigma(X - \bar{X})^2}}$$

In our example,

$$s_b = \frac{6.5}{\sqrt{1290}}$$

$$= \frac{6.5}{35.9}$$

$$= .18$$

The t *test.*   The standard error of the regression coefficient can be used to test the statistical significance of the b coefficient. We do this by use of the knowledge that:

$$t = \frac{b}{s_b}$$

We then compare this computed t value with the value in t distribution given in Table A-4 of Appendix A, at $n - 2$ degrees of freedom.

In our example,

$$b = .93 \quad \text{and} \quad s_b = .18$$

then

$$t = \frac{.93}{.18}$$

$$= 5.17$$

At 8 degrees of freedom and $\alpha = .05$, for a two-tailed test, the critical value of t is 2.306. Therefore our b coefficient is statistically significant. We conclude that the population regression coefficient is not zero. Thus, knowledge of grades in marketing management is significantly helping us explain grades in marketing research. For $n > 30$, the value of t calculated is compared with z values of the normal distribution, given in Table A-2 of Appendix A.

F Test on the Explained Sum of Squares

Since we have calculated SS associated with the regression and for error, we are in a position to convert these SS to variances (or mean squares) by dividing by the relevant number of degrees of freedom. We could then compare the regression-associated variance with the error variance and determine whether the regression has explained a statistically significant portion of the variation in Y. This is exactly the same type of procedure we followed in the one-way ANOVA presented in Chapter 15. Here too the F statistic is the appropriate test. Specifically,

$$F = \frac{\text{variance explained by regression}}{\text{variance unexplained}}$$

$$= \frac{SS_{\text{explained}}/df}{SS_{\text{unexplained}}/df}$$

Table 23-A1 presents the calculation of the F value for our grades data. As always, there are $n - 1$ degrees of freedom in the sample. The b coefficient requires one degree of freedom, thus leaving $n - 2$ for the error term. The calculated F is 26.71. The critical

Table 23-A1   ANOVA Table for Grades Data

Source of variation	SS	Df	MS	F
$SS_{\text{explained}}$ $\Sigma(Y_j - \overline{Y})^2$	1115.83	1	1115.83	26.71
$SS_{\text{unexplained (error)}}$ $\Sigma(Y_j - \hat{Y}_j)^2$	334.17	$n - 2 = 8$	41.77	
SS_{total} $\Sigma(Y_j - \overline{Y})^2$	1450.00	$n - 1 = 9$		

F (given in Table A-5 of Appendix A) at $\alpha = .05$, and at 1 and 8 degrees of freedom, is 5.32. Thus we conclude that the regression has explained a significant proportion of the variance in Y.

Previously, we calculated $t = 5.17$ for the b coefficient. This value is the square root of the F value we just calculated. We then note the fundamental relationship between the F and t distributions:

$$F = t^2$$

A t test on the b coefficient or an F test on the variance will lead to similar conclusions with regard to statistical significance in simple regression. In regression with more than one independent variable, the difference between the t and F tests will become important. This will be discussed in Chapter 26; for now, we merely note the two procedures.

The z Test on the Difference between Means

A question that often arises in marketing research is whether or not an observed difference between two means generated by a sample is large enough to be a significant difference. That is, are the population means really different from each other? For example, we might want to know whether the mean consumption levels of two brands of cola are the same, or whether the mean attitude scores of male and female salespersons about their jobs are the same, or whether the mean sales levels generated by two coupon plans are equal. To do this we may use either the z or t test on the difference between the mean values. The choice between a z and t test is made on essentially the same basis as in univariate analysis. Specifically, we use z when the population standard deviation, σ, is known for both measures under consideration, or if $n > 30$ for both measures. We use t when the population standard deviation is unknown for either measure when $n \leq 30$.

The null hypothesis is usually that the two population means are equal. However, it is possible to test that the difference between two means is some specific value. The relevant formula if σ is known is

$$z = \frac{(\overline{X}_1 - \overline{X}_2) - (\mu_1 - \mu_2)}{\sigma_{\overline{X}_1 - \overline{X}_2}}$$

where $\overline{X}_1 =$ sample mean for the first variable
$\overline{X}_2 =$ sample mean for the second variable
μ_1 and $\mu_2 =$ hypothesized population means for the two variables

$\sigma_{\bar{X}_1 - \bar{X}_2}$ = standard error of the difference between the means (standard deviation of the sampling distribution of the difference between means)

The central-limit theorem applies to this sampling distribution of the difference between means, except that the formula for the standard error is different. Specifically,

$$\sigma_{\bar{X}_1 - \bar{X}_2} = \sqrt{\sigma_{\bar{X}_1}^2 + \sigma_{\bar{X}_1}^2} = \sqrt{\frac{\sigma_1^2}{n_1} + \frac{\sigma_2^2}{n_2}}$$

where σ_1^2 and σ_2^2 are the population variances for the two variables of interest and n_1 and n_2 are the respective sample sizes.

Suppose that we knew the following related to the average weekly consumption of two cola brands.

Brand A: $\bar{X}_1 = 50$ ounces per week; $\sigma_1 = 12$; $n_1 = 40$
Brand B: $\bar{X}_2 = 60$ ounces per week; $\sigma_2 = 16$; $n_2 = 40$

Here the null and alternative hypotheses are

H_0: $\mu_1 = \mu_2$ or $(\mu_1 - \mu_2) = 0$
H_1: $\mu_1 \neq \mu_2$ or $(\mu_1 - \mu_2) \neq 0$

The standard error is

$$\sigma_{\bar{X}_1 - \bar{X}_2} = \sqrt{\frac{(12)^2}{40} + \frac{(16)^2}{40}} = \sqrt{10} = 3.16$$

and so the calculated z value is

$$z = \frac{(50 - 60) - (\mu_1 - \mu_2)}{3.16} = \frac{-10 - 0}{3.16}$$
$$= -3.16$$

The calculated z value exceeds the critical z value of -1.96 at $\alpha = .05$ for a two-tailed test. Therefore, we reject the null hypothesis and conclude that brand B has significantly more consumption than brand A.

If σ_1 and σ_2 are unknown and not assumed to be equal, we use s_1 and s_2 to estimate $s_{\bar{X}_1 - \bar{X}_2}$ as follows:

$$s_{\bar{X}_1 - \bar{X}_2} = \sqrt{s_{\bar{X}_1}^2 + s_{\bar{X}_2}^2} = \sqrt{\frac{s_1^2}{n_1} + \frac{s_2^2}{n_2}} \tag{23-9}$$

If σ_1 and σ_2 are unknown but assumed to be equal, we can pool our sample results to estimate $s_{\bar{X}_1 - \bar{X}_2}$ using this formula:

$$s_{\bar{X}_1-\bar{X}_2} = \sqrt{\left(\frac{n_1s_1^2 + n_2s_2^2}{n_1 + n_2 - 2}\right)\left(\frac{n_1 + n_2}{n_1n_2}\right)} \qquad (23\text{-}10)$$

It is just a matter of plugging the value of n_1, s_1, etc., into the relevant formula and getting $s_{\bar{X}_1-\bar{X}_2}$. If n_1 and $n_2 > 30$, we can calculate z as follows:

$$z = \frac{(\bar{X}_1 - \bar{X}_2) - (\mu_1 - \mu_2)}{s_{\bar{X}_1-\bar{x}_2}}$$

The t Test on the Difference between Means

The t statistic can be calculated when σ_1 and σ_2 are unknown in a manner parallel to the calculation for z:

$$t = \frac{(\bar{X}_1 - \bar{X}_2) - (\mu_1 - \mu_2)}{s_{\bar{X}_1-\bar{X}_2}}$$

where t has $n_1 + n_2 - 2$ degrees of freedom. The value of $s_{\bar{X}_1-\bar{X}_2}$ can be calculated using either Equation 23-9 or 23-10, depending on whether the researcher assumes that the population variances are equal or not. Suppose a sample yielded the following results:

Coupon plan$A$: $\bar{X}_1 = 20$ sales per day; $s_1 = 3$; $n_1 = 10$
Coupon plan$B$: $\bar{X}_2 = 16$ sales per day; $s_2 = 2$; $n_2 = 5$

and the researcher assumes that $\sigma_1^2 = \sigma_2^2$. Thus, the formula in Equation 23.10 should be used, and

$$s_{\bar{X}1-\bar{X}2} = \sqrt{\left(\frac{(10)(3)^2 + (5)(2)^2}{10 + 5 - 2}\right)\left(\frac{10 + 5}{(10)(5)}\right)}$$
$$= \sqrt{(8.46)(.3)} = \sqrt{2.54} = 1.59$$

then $t = \dfrac{(20 - 16) - (\mu_1 - \mu_2)}{1.59} = \dfrac{4 - 0}{1.59} = 2.52$

At $\alpha = .1$ and 13 df, the critical t value from Table A-4 of Appendix A for a two-tailed test is 1.77. Since the calculated t is greater than the critical t, we reject the null hypothesis that the means are equal.

Difference between Proportions

We may apply the same type of hypothesis-testing procedures to the difference between two proportions when $n > 30$.[1] If σ_1 and σ_2 are known (i.e., if π_1 and π_2 are known), we use the formula

$$z = \frac{(p_1 - p_2) - (\pi_1 - \pi_2)}{\sigma_{p_1-p_2}}$$

---

[1] When $n < 30$, the binomial distribution should be used. This situation will not be discussed in this book.

where p_1 and p_2 are the two observed sample proportions, and

$$\sigma_{p_1-p_2} = \sqrt{\sigma_{p_1}^2 + \sigma_{p_2}^2} = \sqrt{\frac{\pi_1(1-\pi_1)}{n_1} + \frac{\pi_2(1-\pi_2)}{n_2}}$$

When π_1 and π_2 are not known (and therefore σ_1 and σ_2 are not known), we use the formula

$$z = \frac{(p_1 - p_2) - (\pi_1 - \pi_2)}{s_{p_1-p_2}}$$

Since the null hypothesis is that $\pi_1 = \pi_2$, we are assuming that $\sigma_1 = \sigma_2$, and so we can pool our sample results to estimate $s_{p_1-p_2}$ using the formula

$$s_{p_1-p_2} = \sqrt{(p^* \, q^*)\left(\frac{n_1 + n_2}{n_1 n_2}\right)}$$

where

$$p^* = \frac{n_1 p_1 + n_2 p_2}{n_1 + n_2} = \frac{\text{total number of yes answers in the two samples}}{\text{total number of answers in the two samples}}$$

and

$$q^* = 1 - p^*$$

That is, p^* is a pooled estimate of p.

Let us illustrate the latter situation where π_1 and π_2 are not known. Suppose that the two different product concepts are tested with the following results:

Concept A: $p_1 = .20$; $n_1 = 40$
Concept B: $p_2 = .24$; $n_2 = 60$

where p_i = the number of people who indicated they would buy the ith product concept. Here:

H_0: $\pi_1 = \pi_2$
H_1: $\pi_1 \neq \pi_2$
$$p^* = \frac{(40)(.20) + (60)(.24)}{40 + 60} = .224$$

and

$$s_{p_1-p_2} = \sqrt{(.224)(.776)\left(\frac{40 + 60}{(40)(60)}\right)}$$
$$= .085$$

Then

$$z = \frac{(.20 - .24) - (\pi_1 - \pi_2)}{.085} = \frac{-.04 - 0}{.085}$$

$$= -.47$$

That is, the difference between the two proportions is equal to .47 of a standard error. For $\alpha = .05$ and a two-tailed test, the critical $z = 1.96$. Since the calculated z is less than the critical z, we cannot reject the null hypothesis that the two population proportions are equal.

Chapter 24

Reporting Research Findings

The final step in the research process is the preparation and presentation of the research report. A research report can be defined as *the presentation of the research findings directed to a specific audience to accomplish a specific purpose.* This presentation can be written or given orally, or both.

The research report is important for two reasons. First, for many executives, it is the only aspect of the research project which they see, and their evaluation of the entire matter rests with the effectiveness of the written and oral presentation. Second, for marketing research systems, the research findings represent the main service provided to the management group, and their reaction concerning the usefulness of this service is one of the key determinants of how frequently it will be used in the future.

Most decision makers are not interested in the details of the research process. Their focus is on the information (not data) provided and how well it fits their information needs for the decision at hand. However, it is important that the decision maker be provided with enough details of the research project to judge the limitations of the study and the sources of error present in the findings.

Writing the research report and presenting it orally is a skill that one learns through practice. The ability to write clearly and to present a verbal report effectively comes from years of practice throughout one's educational career.

This chapter is not intended to improve the reader's skills in this regard, but rather to serve as a tool to supplement existing communication skills in the task of preparing and presenting the research report.

The chapter is divided into four main sections: (1) guidelines for preparing the written research report, (2) guidelines for preparing the oral presentation, (3) the format of the presentation, and (4) the presentation of data.

WRITTEN REPORT GUIDELINES

Researchers who are effective in report writing agree that there are a series of guidelines which should be followed.

Consider the Audience

The research report is designed to communicate information for use by a decision maker, so obviously it must be tailored to his or her needs. Most decision makers are interested in a clear, concise, accurate, and interesting report which directly focuses on their information needs with a minimum of technological jargon. They are concerned with how the research findings help them reach a decision. Consequently, in preparing the report the researcher must constantly keep the study objectives in mind and clearly demonstrate how the research findings relate to the information needs of the decision situation.

Be Concise Yet Complete

The real skill of the researcher is tested in fulfilling this requirement. Obviously, completeness does not mean that every detail of the research project is found in the report. Rather, it means covering the important points of the project to the exclusion of the unimportant. Since importance is a matter of degree, the researcher's discretion is required in determining what is to be included and how much emphasis is given to each area. The information needs of the decision maker are central to establishing the importance of an area.

Be Objective Yet Effective

The research report must be an objective presentation of the research findings. The researcher violates the standard of objectivity if the findings are presented in a distorted or slanted manner. The professional researcher recognizes that while it is very important to be effective in communicating the research findings, this should never be interpreted as "selling" the results by means of deception.

The findings can be presented in a manner which is objective, yet effective. The writing style of the report should be interesting, with the sentence structure short and to the point. The vocabulary must be appropriate for the audience in that only familiar words are used. Popular clichés and slang terms should be avoided.

At times the researcher will be confronted with a situation where the research findings will not be easily accepted by the decision maker. The findings may conflict with the decision maker's experience and judgment or may unfavorably reflect on the wisdom of previous decisions. In such situations, the above-mentioned commitment to objectivity is tested; the professional researcher has the obligation to present and defend the research findings in an objective manner and convince the decision maker that they are valid. This does not mean that the decision maker must accept the research findings to the exclusion of information based on experience and judgment.

ORAL PRESENTATION GUIDELINES

The oral presentation is often used to support the written report. The nature of the setting can range from a small meeting with the decision maker to a more formal presentation to a larger group of individuals. The guidelines discussed previously apply equally well to the oral presentation.

The oral presentation serves several purposes which the written report cannot. First, it allows the decision maker to ask questions and have points clarified. Second, when a number of persons are involved, it allows them to interact concerning the interpretation of the research findings. In this regard, the researcher must remember that various individuals may view the results negatively and react verbally in this regard during the presentation. The professional researcher must maintain objectivity in presenting the results and be effective in convincing dissenting individuals as to the interpretation of the data.

Tips on Oral Presentation   The beginning researcher may find the following tips useful:

1   Start the presentation with an overview of the presentation plan—tell the audience what you are going to tell them.
2   Use visual aids effectively—charts and tables should be simple and easy to read.
3   Practice the presentation several times, and have someone comment on how to improve your presentation's effectiveness.
4   Have a contingency plan for equipment failure.
5   Check the equipment thoroughly before the presentation.
6   Talk to the audience or decision maker rather than reading from a sheet of paper or the projection screen.
7   Face the audience at all times.
8   Avoid distracting mannerisms with hands and the like—hold the podium, since that's what it is for.

REPORT FORMAT

While there is no single report format which is appropriate for all situations, the following outline is generally accepted as the basic format for most research projects.[1]

---

[1] Gilbert A. Churchill, Jr., *Marketing Research* (Hinsdale, Ill.: Dryden Press, 1976), p. 595.

  1 Title page
  2 Table of contents
  3 Management summary
    a Objectives
    b Results
    c Conclusion
    d Recommendations
  4 Body of report
    a Introduction
    b Methodology
    c Results
    d Limitations
  5 Conclusions and recommendations
  6 Appendix
    a Sampling plan
    b Data collection forms
    c Supporting tables not included in body

Title Page

The title page should contain a title which conveys the essence of the study, the date, the name of the organization submitting the report, and the organization for whom the report is prepared. If the research report is confidential, the name of those individuals to receive the report should be specified on the title page.

Table of Contents

The table of contents lists the sequence of topics covered in the report, along with page references. Its purpose is to aid readers in finding a particular section in the report. When the audience for the report is diverse, the table of contents must be designed to aid people with different interests in finding those sections of the report of most concern to them.

    If the report contains numerous tables and figures, they are typically listed at the end of the table of contents by page number.

Management Summary

Most decision makers require that the research report contain a one- or two-page management summary. This is possibly the most important section of the research report, in that most executives choose to read only the management summary. This is especially the case if the written report is supported with an oral presentation. Other executives will use the management summary as an overview and then read selected parts of the report for more detail.

    The management summary is not a miniature of the main report. Rather, it provides the decision maker with the key research findings which bear on the decision problem. A good management summary is written specifically for the decision maker and is designed to be action-oriented.

    The management summary concisely states the objectives of the research project and the nature of the decision problem. Next the key results are presented, along with the conclusions. Conclusions are opinions and interpretations based on the research. Finally, the management summary ends with specific recommendations for action.

Body of Report

The details of the research project are found in the body of the report. This section includes (1) introduction, (2) methodology, (3) results, and (4) limitations.

Introduction   The purpose of the introduction is to provide the reader with background information needed to understand the remainder of the report. The nature of the introduction is conditioned by the diversity of the audience with regard to their familiarity with the research project. The more diverse the audience, the more extensive the introduction.

The introduction must clearly explain the nature of the decision problem and the research objectives. Background information should be provided as to the product or service involved and the circumstances surrounding the decision problem. The nature of any previous research on the problem should be reviewed.

Methodology   The purpose of the methodology section is to describe the nature of the research design, the sampling plan, and the data collection and analysis procedure. This is a very difficult section to write. Enough detail must be conveyed so that the reader can appreciate the nature of the methodology used, yet the presentation must not be boring or overpower the reader. The use of technical jargon must be avoided.

The methodology section should inform the reader whether the design was exploratory or conclusive. The sources of data—secondary or primary—should be explained. The nature of the data collection method—communication or observation—must be specified. The reader needs to know who was included in the sample, the size of the sample, and the nature of the sampling procedure.

The methodology section is designed (1) to summarize the technical aspects of the research project in a style which is comprehensible to the nontechnician and (2) to develop confidence in the quality of the procedures used. The technical details should be minimized in this section and placed in an appendix for those who desire a more detailed methodological discussion.

Results   The bulk of the report is composed of the research findings, which should be organized around the research objectives and information needs. This presentation should involve a logical unfolding of information in a manner similar to a story. The reporting of findings must have a definite point of view and fit together into a logical whole; it is not just the presentation of an endless series of tables. Rather, it requires the organization of the data into a logical flow of information for decision-making purposes.

Limitations   Every research project has weaknesses which need to be communicated to the reader in a clear and concise manner. In this process, the researcher should avoid belaboring minor study weaknesses. The purpose of this section is not to disparage the quality of the research project, but rather to enable the reader to judge the validity of the study results.

The limitations in a marketing research project generally involve sampling and nonresponse inadequacies and methodological weaknesses. The writing of the conclusions and recommendations section is naturally affected by the recognized and acknowledged study limitations. It is the researcher's professional responsibility to clearly inform the reader of these limitations.

Conclusions and Recommendations

The conclusions and recommendations must flow logically from the presentation of the results. The conclusions should clearly link the research findings with the information needs, and based on this linkage recommendations for action can be formulated.

Many feel that it is not advisable to have the researcher make recommendations. It is argued that the recommendations for action must reflect a blend of the decision maker's experience and judgment with the findings from the research study. Since few researchers possess this degree of experience and judgment, it is felt that the researcher's recommendations may be weighed more heavily in favor of the research findings.

Alternatively, many executives and researchers feel strongly that the research report should include recommendations. It is argued that as long as the decision maker recognizes the context in which recommendations are made, there are clear benefits from having them in the research report. First, it forces the researcher to focus on the decision problem and think in terms of action. Second, it forces the researcher to appreciate the broader management issues and the role of research in the decision-making process. Finally, the researcher may identify recommendations not otherwise considered by the decision maker. In the final analysis, however, the action taken is the responsibility of the decision maker, and the recommendations put forth in the research report may or may not be followed.

Appendix

The purpose of the appendix is to provide a place for material which is not absolutely essential to the body of the report. This material is typically more specialized and complex than material presented in the main report, and it is designed to serve the needs of the technically oriented reader. The appendix will frequently contain copies of the data collection forms, details of the sampling plan, estimates of statistical error, interviewer instructions, and detailed statistical tables associated with the data analysis process.

PRESENTATION OF DATA

The research data can be presented in tabular or graphic form. The tabular form (tables) consists of the numerical presentation of the data (see Table 24-1 for an

Table 24-1   Weekly Traffic Count by Store Location (August 7–13, 1978)

Store	Number of persons entering	Percentage of total
West	4,731	25
North	4,821	26
East	3,514	19
South	3,534	19
Central	2,210	11
Total	18,810	100

illustration), while the graphical form (figures) involves the presentation of data in terms of visually interpreted sizes.

Tables and graphs should contain the following elements:

1   *Table or figure number.* This permits easy location in the report.
2   *Title.* The title should clearly indicate the contents of the table or figure.
3   *Boxhead and stub head.* The boxhead contains the captions or labels to the columns in a table, while the stub head contains the labels for the rows.
4   *Footnotes.* Footnotes explain or qualify a particular section or item in the table or figure.

Three types of graphic presentation will be discussed: (1) the pie chart, (2) the bar chart, and (3) the line chart.

Pie Chart

The pie chart is a circle divided into sections such that the size of each section corresponds to a portion of the total. Figure 24-1 presents the data shown in Table 24-1 in the form of a pie chart. Notice how clearly this figure depicts the relative differences in weekly traffic count by retail store.

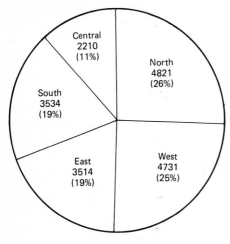

Total traffic count = 18,810

Figure 24-1   Pie chart of weekly traffic count by retail stores (August 7–13, 1978).

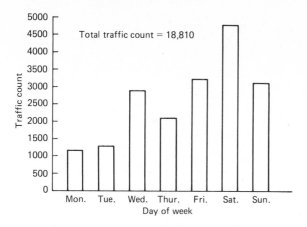

Figure 24-2 Bar chart of traffic count of retail stores by day of week (August 7–13, 1978).

Bar Chart

A bar chart depicts magnitudes of the data by the length of various bars which have been laid out with reference to a horizontal or vertical scale. The bar chart is easy to construct and can be readily interpreted. Figure 24-2 presents a bar chart depicting differences in retail store traffic count by day of the week.

Line Chart

The data presented in Figure 24-2 (bar chart) can be presented in the form of a line chart. Figure 24-3 presents a line chart depicting differences in retail store traffic count by day of the week.

A line chart is preferred over a bar chart in the following situations: (1) when the data involve a long time period, (2) when several series are compared on the same chart, (3) when the emphasis is on the movement rather than the actual amount, (4) when trends of frequency distribution are presented, (5) when a multiple-amount scale is used, or (6) when estimates, forecasts, interpolation, or extrapolation are to be shown.[2]

SUMMARY

1   A research report is the presentation of the research findings to a specific audience for a specific purpose. The presentation can be written or given orally, or both.

2   The guidelines for the written and oral reports are: (1) Consider the audience, (2) be concise yet complete, and (3) be objective yet effective.

3   The main elements of the written report are (1) the title page, (2) the table of contents, (3) the management summary, (4) the body of the report, (5) the conclusions and recommendations, and (6) the appendix.

[2] M. E. Spear, *Practical Charting Techniques* (New York: McGraw-Hill, 1969), p. 74.

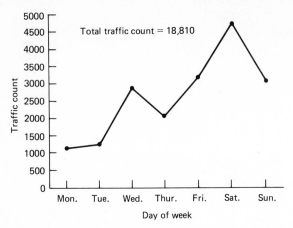

Figure 24-3 Line chart of traffic count of retail stores by day of week (August 7–13, 1978).

4   The research data can be presented in tabular or graphic form. The types of graphic form are (1) the pie chart, (2) the bar chart, and (3) the line chart.

DISCUSSION QUESTIONS

1   Why is the research report important?

2   What general guidelines exist for the preparation of written research reports?

3   How might an oral presentation supplement a written research report?

4   What components are typically included in a research report?

5   What are the alternative means of displaying data graphically?

SUGGESTED READING

Casey, R. S., *Oral Communication of Technical Information* (New York: Reinhold Book Division, 1958). An excellent discussion for those interested in improving their oral presentation skills.

Dawe, J., and W. J. Lord, Jr., *Functional Business Communications* (Englewood Cliffs, N.J.: Prentice-Hall, 1968). An extensive treatment of all aspects of business communications. Those chapters dealing with the research report are chap. 3 and chaps. 7–12.

Gallagher, William J., *Report Writing for Management* (Reading, Mass.: Addison-Wesley, 1969). An excellent book on report writing.

Spear, M. E., *Practical Charting Techniques* (New York: McGraw-Hill, 1969). A very thorough book and a useful reference when writing the report.

Part Eight

Advanced Topics

Chapter 25

Multivariate Data Analysis I: Interdependence Methods

In Chapters 22 and 23 we examined data analysis as it relates to univariate and bivariate situations. These analysis types are the heart of current data analysis in marketing research practice. As a result, we presented the appropriate univariate and bivariate procedures in some detail.

In the next two chapters we present a brief overview of a number of *multivariate data analysis procedures,* which involve the simultaneous analysis of more than two variables. The objectives of our discussion of these techniques are (1) to make the reader aware of the existence of the techniques, (2) to position each technique in terms of the type of input data required, and (3) to discuss the type of output generated by each technique.

Great care should be taken in applying the techniques presented in this and the next chapter. There are a number of problems and statistical assumptions related to each technique that we do not discuss at all. The reader should recognize that these techniques are extremely dangerous *when used by unskilled people*. Unfortunately, a proper step-by-step description of how each procedure works, the assumptions made, and the problems in using them would at least double the size of this book. We leave it to a more advanced course in marketing research to cover this material in the required depth.

Emanuel Demby perhaps explained it best in an article where he described the factors that make a successful marketing researcher. He noted that most successful marketing researchers have certain common traits, including these:

> They rarely go to multivariate analysis until they have tested hypotheses through crosstabulation.
>
> If multivariate findings run counter to what was learned in bivariate analysis, they tend to trust the latter. (Once, an excellent statistician brought me a factor analysis I had challenged, giving me a fascinating explanation for the solution. Just as he finished, the computer house called to say that they had made a mistake in running the program. The researcher walked out of my office, mumbling, "But I had it all worked out. . . .")
>
> The smartest marketing researcher I know asks such naive questions of his statistical consultant that he is later able to communicate complex analyses to his non-statistician management. Apparently, you don't have to be a great statistician to be a success in marketing research, but you do have to know how to use statisticians.[1]

Despite this there is a growing understanding in marketing research of the need for, and usefulness of, multivariate data analysis procedures. There are a number of reasons for this trend. First, marketing problems are usually not completely described by one or two variables. Many variables combine to yield marketing outcomes. Second, the advent of high-speed computers and associated analysis software has made the solution of multivariate statistical procedures relatively easy. Problems that were virtually impossible to solve by human calculation twenty years ago can now be solved in less than a second with a computer. Third, improved understanding of statistical concepts among marketing researchers and managers has increased the likelihood of multivariate procedures being used to make decisions.

This chapter begins by distinguishing multivariate procedures that do not specify a dependent variable from those that do specify a dependent variable. Then three procedures are discussed which do not require that a dependent variable be specified. These procedures are factor analysis, cluster analysis, and multidimensional scaling.

INTERDEPENDENCE VERSUS DEPENDENCE METHODS

The multivariate analysis chapters in this book are organized around a scheme suggested by Kendall.[2] This scheme divides procedures into interdependence and dependence procedures. The fundamental differentiating aspect between the two is whether or not one or more variables have been designated as dependent on other variables. In *dependence methods,* one or more variables are designated as being predicted by (depend on) a set of independent variables.

---

[1] Emanuel H. Demby, "Success in Marketing Research? Here are 15 Key Factors That Will Help You Achieve It," *Marketing News,* Jan. 28, 1977, p. 5.
[2] Maurice G. Kendall, "Factor Analysis As a Statistical Technique," *Journal of the Royal Statistical Society,* vol. 121, 1950, pp. 60–73.

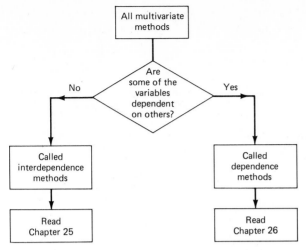

Figure 25-1 Interdependence versus dependence methods.

Regression is an example of this type of analysis. In *interdependence methods,* no variable or variables are designated as being predicted by others. It is the interrelationship among all the variables taken together that interests the researcher. Factor analysis is an example of this type of procedure. Figure 25-1 illustrates this fundamental distinction and notes where in this book the various methods are presented.

This chapter discusses three interdependence methods: factor analysis, cluster analysis, and multidimensional scaling.

FACTOR ANALYSIS

Factor analysis is a procedure that takes a large number of variables or objects and searches to see whether they have a small number of factors in common which account for their intercorrelation.[3] For example, we might attribute the high association between grades in business administration courses to the factor of intelligence, or the association between certain chemical attributes of coffee to the factor of acidity (pH level).

Marketing Applications

Factor analysis has a number of possible applications in marketing research. These include data reduction, structure identification, scaling, and data transformation.

Data Reduction Factor analysis can be used for reducing a mass of data to a manageable level. For example, the researcher may have collected data on 50 attributes of a product. The analysis and understanding of these data may be

[3] Karl Schuessler, *Analyzing Social Data* (Boston: Houghton Mifflin, 1971), p. 4.

aided by reducing the attributes to a minimum number of factors that underlie the 50 attributes. These factors may then be used in further analysis in place of the original attributes.

Structure Identification   Factor analysis may be used to discover the basic structure underlying a set of measures. For example, the above 50 attributes may reduce to two factors identified by the researcher as (1) sweetness/bitterness and (2) degree of freshness. The assumption is that at least some of the measures taken are redundant. The factor analysis then finds the underlying structure of the redundancy by placing the measures on underlying factors or dimensions.

Scaling   A researcher may wish to develop a scale on which subjects can be compared. A problem in developing any scale is in weighting the variables being combined to form the scale. Factor analysis helps the process by dividing the variables into independent factors. Each factor represents a scale measure of some underlying dimension. Further, factor analysis gives the weights to use for each variable when combining them into a scale.

Data Transformation   A number of dependence analysis techniques require independent variables that are themselves uncorrelated (e.g., multiple regression). Factor analysis can be used to identify factors that are uncorrelated. These factors can then be used as input in the relevant dependence method.

Thus, the following have all made use of factor analysis: the development of personality scales, market segments based upon psychographic data, the identification of key product attributes, similarities among magazines, and uncorrelated factors for regression analysis.[4]

Steps in Factor Analysis

There are essentially three steps in a factor analysis solution. The first is to develop a set of correlations between all combinations of the variables of interest. Since we are using correlations, we must then be assuming that the input variables are intervally scaled.[5] The second step is to extract a set of initial factors from the correlation matrix developed in the first step. The third step is to "rotate" the initial factors to find a final solution. The concept of rotation will be discussed later in the chapter. There are a number of decisions that a researcher must make at each of these steps that determine the type of factor analysis that will take place.

Calculation of Correlations   With respect to the calculation of the correlation matrix, two broad classes of factor analysis may be distinguished. These are (1) R-factor analysis and (2) Q-factor analysis. In R-factor analysis, these correlations are calculated *between variables;* in Q-factor analysis, they are

---

[4] For a more detailed review see Gilbert A. Churchill, Jr., *Marketing Research: Methodological Foundations* (Hinsdale, Ill.: Dryden Press, 1976), pp. 561–564.

[5] There are some advanced factor-analysis procedures that do not require interval variables as input. These techniques are beyond the scope of this book.

calculated *between cases.* Cases could be people, products, or whatever else the variables have been measured on, so a Q-factor analysis would group cases on specific factors. Such a procedure could then be used to find similar products or people who belong to different segments.

Figure 25-2 shows how R- and Q-type correlations are developed from the basic data matrix. The solid arrow going down indicates that R-type correlations are calculated between variables by using data from all cases. With m variables in the data matrix, the result of this process is an m by m correlation matrix among variables. The dotted arrow going horizontally to the right indicates that Q-type correlations are calculated between cases by using data from all variables. With n cases in the data matrix, the result of this process is an n by n correlation matrix among cases. The calculation of correlation coefficients has been discussed in detail in Chapter 23, where the example given is of an R-type correlation coefficient, since it shows the relationship between two variables. To calculate a Q-type correlation coefficient we simply treat the cases as if they were variables, and vice versa.

Figure 25-2   Development of R-type and Q-type correlation matrices.

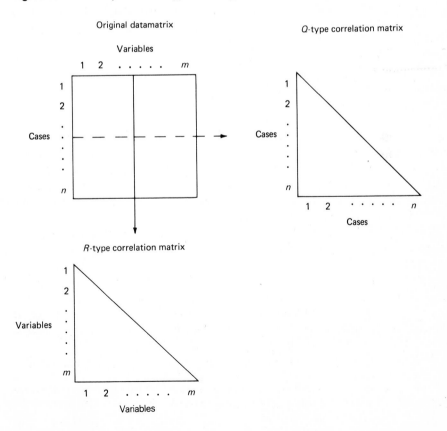

Extraction of Initial Factors   There are many methods for extracting the initial factors from the correlation matrix. In general, these methods are far too numerically complex to even begin to discuss here, but one of them is worthy of our consideration. It is used extensively in practice and will serve to illustrate the nature of factor extraction. It is called the *principal factors method*.

The object of factor extraction is to find a set of factors that are formed as a linear combination of the variables in the correlation matrix. Thus, if the variables X_1, X_2, and X_3 were highly correlated with each other, they would be combined together to form one factor. A linear combination could be defined as follows:

$$z = b_1 X_1 + b_2 X_2 + \cdots + b_m X_m$$

Here z is the linear combination, and it is called a *principal component* or a *principal factor*. The principal-factors methodology involves searching for the values of the b's above which form a linear combination that explains more variance in the correlation matrix than any other set of b's. This is called the first principal factor. This explained variance is then subtracted from the original input matrix to yield a residual matrix. Then a second principal factor is extracted from this residual matrix. This factor explains more of the variance in the residual matrix than any other. The procedure is then repeated until there is very little variance remaining to be explained. The nature of this procedure is such that the factors extracted are uncorrelated with each other. The factors are said to be *orthogonal*.

Rotation   The initial factors are often very difficult to interpret. Thus the initial solution is rotated to yield a solution that is more amenable to interpretation. There are two broad classes of rotation—(1) *orthogonal rotation*, which maintains the factors as uncorrelated with each other, and (2) *oblique rotation*, which allows the factors to be correlated with each other. The basic idea of rotation is to yield factors that each have some variables that correlate highly and some that correlate poorly. This avoids the problem of having factors with all variables having midrange correlations, and thus it allows for easier interpretation.

An Example[6]

Factor analysis is best understood by looking at an example. The one presented here is designed to reduce a set of coffee attributes to a set of underlying factors. Table 25-1 presents the set of 14 coffee attributes on which data were collected on a 10-point semantic differential scale. This table also gives the correlation matrix between the various combinations of attributes. Table 25-2 presents the principal factors extracted from the correlation matrix, plus the orthogonally rotated factors (varimax rotation), and the obliquely rotated factors.

Let us first examine the unrotated principal-factor matrix. We note that

[6] This example is adapted from Bishwa Nath Mukherjee, "A Factor Analysis of Some Qualitative Attributes of Coffee," *Journal of Advertising Research*, vol. 5, pp. 35–38, March 1965.

Table 25-1 Coffee Attributes and Intercorrelations among Attribute Ratings

14 coffee attributes investigated

Pleasant flavor — Unpleasant flavor

Stagnant, muggy taste — Sparkling, refreshing taste

Mellow taste — Bitter taste

Cheap taste — Expensive taste

Comforting, harmonious, smooth, friendly taste — Irritating, discordant, rough, hostile taste

Dead, lifeless, dull taste — Alive, lively, peppy taste

Tastes artificial — Tastes like real coffee

Deep, distinct flavor — Shallow, indistinct flavor

Tastes warmed over — Tastes just brewed

Hearty, full-bodied, full flavor — Watery, thin, empty flavor

Pure, clear taste — Muddy, swampy taste

Raw taste — Roasted taste

Fresh taste — Stale taste

Overall preference

Excellent quality — Very poor quality

Note: Ten blank boxes separated each set of opposing statements. Subjects checked the position which came closest to describing how they felt toward the product.

Intercorrelations among attribute ratings

	1	2	3	4	5	6	7	8	9	10	11	12	13	14
1. Pleasant flavor	1.00	.76	.81	.79	.83	.81	.74	.66	.65	.71	.76	.65	.71	.75
2. Sparkling taste		1.00	.78	.85	.77	.87	.83	.65	.70	.78	.85	.69	.74	.83
3. Mellow taste			1.00	.77	.85	.81	.77	.60	.65	.64	.75	.69	.69	.74
4. Expensive taste				1.00	.78	.87	.83	.76	.69	.81	.81	.64	.71	.87
5. Comforting taste					1.00	.82	.77	.66	.60	.69	.82	.69	.69	.74
6. Alive taste						1.00	.88	.70	.74	.80	.81	.65	.77	.87
7. Tastes like real coffee							1.00	.67	.76	.75	.79	.62	.76	.87
8. Deep distinct flavor								1.00	.51	.84	.70	.54	.59	.70
9. Tastes just brewed									1.00	.67	.65	.67	.80	.75
10. Hearty flavor										1.00	.83	.65	.72	.76
11. Pure clear taste											1.00	.66	.73	.76
12. Roasted taste												1.00	.78	.61
13. Fresh taste													1.00	.73
14. Overall preference														1.00
Mean rating*	4.5	4.3	4.4	4.6	4.4	4.2	4.2	4.3	4.3	4.2	4.3	4.4	4.6	6.9
Standard deviation	1.6	1.3	1.4	1.4	1.3	1.4	1.6	1.5	1.5	1.5	1.4	1.2	1.4	2.7

*The ten scale categories were assigned successive integers beginning with one at the favorable side of the scale. Thus ratings could vary from one (very "good") to ten (very "bad") on an attribute.

Source: Bishwa Nath Mukherjee, "A Factor Analysis of Some Qualitative Attributes of Coffee," *Journal of Advertising Research*, vol. 5, p. 36, March 1965. Used with permission.

Table 25-2 Factor Loadings

	Principal factor matrix					Rotated (varimax) matrix				Oblique factor matrix			
	I	II	III	IV	h^2	A	B	C	D	A	B	C	D
1.	.86	−.01	−.20	.04	.78	.63	.38	.36	.34	.34	.01	.07	−.03
2.	.91	−.01	−.01	−.09	.83	.48	.43	.53	.38	.14	.04	.23	.04
3.	.86	.11	.28	.002	.83	.70	.26	.38	.36	.36	.13	−.003	−.01
4.	.91	.15	−.001	−.10	.87	.46	.53	.54	.29	.16	−.05	.34	−.07
5.	.87	−.002	−.31	.10	.87	.74	.38	.30	.32	.47	.01	−.004	−.08
6.	.93	.03	−.02	−.16	.90	.49	.43	.59	.35	.12	.07	.30	−.01
7.	.90	−.02	.04	−.21	.86	.42	.38	.64	.37	.03	.11	.33	.04
8.	.77	.36	.11	.16	.77	.31	.74	.27	.22	.24	−.40	.32	−.10
9.	.79	−.28	.24	−.09	.76	.23	.24	.52	.62	−.15	.11	.14	.37
10.	.87	.25	.22	.17	.89	.28	.75	.33	.39	.14	.38	.31	.07
11.	.89	.11	.05	.10	.82	.51	.55	.36	.36	.28	−.15	.17	−.01
12.	.76	−.29	.04	.27	.74	.43	.28	.16	.67	.18	−.08	−.18	.38
13.	.84	−.27	.19	.12	.83	.33	.32	.36	.70	.01	−.03	−.001	.41
14.	.90	.04	.08	−.23	.86	.38	.43	.65	.34	.002	.08	.39	.01
Percent common variance	90.0	4.1	3.3	2.6									
Percent total variance	74.4	3.4	2.7	2.6									

Source: Adapted from Bishwa Nath Mukherjee, "A Factor Analysis of Some Qualitative Attributes of Coffee," *Journal of Advertising Research*, 5 (March 1965), p. 37. Used with permission.

there are four factors underlying the 14 attributes. The elements in this matrix listed under the factors are called unrotated factor loadings. The loadings measure which variables are involved in which factor pattern, to what degree and in what direction. They can be interpreted like correlation coefficients. The square of the loading equals the proportion of the variation that a variable has in common with an unrotated factor.

Another way to conceptualize this relationship is to remember that a loading is a correlation coefficient between a variable and a factor. In essence, when we square a loading we are calculating a coefficient of determination, r^2, between a variable and a factor. Thus, the squared loading represents the amount of shared variation between a variable and a factor.

The h^2 measures are called *communalities*. Communality is the proportion of a variable's total variation that is involved in the factors. Mathematically h^2 equals the sum of the squared loading of a variable on all factors. For example, for attribute 1:

$$h^2 = (.86)^2 + (−.01)^2 + (−.20)^2 + (.04)^2 = .78$$

Communality may be interpreted as a measure of uniqueness. By subtracting h^2 from 1.0, the degree to which a variable is unrelated to the others may be calculated. Here we note that 78 percent of the variation in scores on attribute 1 can be predicted from the other variables, leaving 22 percent uniquely related to this attribute.

To get the percentage of total variance in the data explained by the four factors we simply calculate H, where

$$H = \frac{\text{sum of all } h^2\text{'s}}{\text{number of variables}} \times 100$$

$$= \frac{11.61}{14} \times 100$$

$$= 83\%$$

This value is called the *common variance* explained by the factors.

To calculate the amount of variation in the data accounted for by a factor, we square each loading for a factor and add, then divide the result by the number of variables. For example, for factor 1 the value is

$$(.86)^2 + (.91)^2 + (.86)^2 + \cdots + (.90)^2 = 10.42$$

This value is called an *eigenvalue* in the vocabulary of factor analysis. Thus, the percentage of total variance explained by factor 1 is $10.42/14 = 74.4$ percent. The percentage of common variance explained by this factor is then $10.42/11.61 = 90$ percent. We note that the percentages of both common variance and total variance are presented in Table 25-2.

In order to obtain an interpretation of the results we examine the rotated factors. Table 25-3 presents one such interpretation. There the factors have been placed with high-loading variables and each given a "creative" name by the author of the study. Note that there is no unique definition of the meaning of any factor; it is up to the creativity of the researcher. Unfortunately, researchers can all too easily fool themselves with wonderful-sounding interpretations. Great care must be taken in this regard.

The presentation of factor analysis has concentrated on the nature of the input and output. There are many more issues on all respects of factor analysis not covered here. The reader should consult a more advanced reference if interested.

CLUSTER ANALYSIS

Factor analysis allows the researcher to study the structure of a set of variables or objects in relation to how their variance is explained by a set of underlying factors. Cluster analysis allows the researcher *to place variables or objects into subgroups or clusters*. These clusters *are not defined a priori* by the researcher, but are formed by the cluster analysis procedure itself. In actuality cluster

Table 25-3 Interpretation of Factors

Factor A (comforting quality)

Variable	Attribute	Varimax	Oblique
1.	Pleasant flavor	.625	.340
3.	Mellow taste	.698	.359
5.	Comforting taste	.736	.465
11.	Pure clear taste	.512	.283

Factor B (heartiness)

Variable	Attribute	Varimax	Oblique
8.	Deep distinct flavor	.742	.396
10.	Hearty flavor	.745	.380

Factor C (genuineness)

Variable	Attribute	Varimax	Oblique
2.	Sparkling taste	.524	.232
4.	Expensive taste	.541	.334
6.	Alive taste	.594	.301
7.	Tastes like real coffee	.636	.328
8.	Deep distinct flavor	.268	.323
10.	Hearty flavor	.332	.310
14.	Overall preference	.653	.387

Factor D (freshness)

Variable	Attribute	Varimax	Oblique
9.	Tastes just brewed	.621	.359
12.	Roasted taste	.670	.465
13.	Fresh taste	.698	.238

Source: Bishwa Nath Mukherjee, " A Factor Analysis of Some Qualitative Attributes of Coffee,"
Journal of Advertising Research, vol. 5, p. 37, March 1965. Used with permission.

analysis is a group of ad hoc computational procedures. Their common dimensions are:

1 They form subgroupings and assign variables or objects to these groups.
2 They take as input a matrix of associations between variables or objects; a correlation matrix is an example of one such matrix. There are clustering algorithms available that take nominal, ordinal, interval, or ratio measures in this matrix of associations as input.
3 They assume that natural clusters exist within the data.

The number and diversity of these algorithms makes a detailed presentation of cluster analysis procedures impossible in anything except a long book.

We noted that cluster analysis can be applied to either variables or objects (people, products, places, etc.). However, its major application is in the placement of objects into clusters, based upon the values these objects have on a set of variables. Thus, our input matrix will contain the measures of association between objects. This was basically the approach used in Q-type factor analysis. In fact, some researchers consider Q-factor analysis to be a form of cluster analysis.

In general, an object is assigned to a cluster in such a way that it is more associated (as measured by the appropriate measure of association in the input matrix) with the other objects in its cluster than with objects in any other cluster. At a minimum, the computer output of a cluster analysis run identifies the objects of interest by cluster. Sometimes a number of alternative groupings of objects into clusters are presented. These alternative clusters differ on the level of association within the cluster. The reseacher then selects the solution for the level of association that seems appropriate. This type of solution is called *hierarchical* because solutions are presented at many different levels of within-cluster association. For example, one may want clusters that have $r = .5$ to $.6$ for the objects within the clusters. One would then be considering r's of less than .5 to be too weak, and r's over .6 to be too stringent a requirement. Of course, once clusters are formed it is up to the researcher to give them a marketing interpretation. This, like naming factors in factor analysis, is an art and must be done with great care.

Cluster analysis has been used in marketing to do such things as develop consumer segments based upon demographic and psychographic profiles, identify test market cities, determine similar markets in various countries, and find similar groups of magazine readers to aid in media selection.

MULTIDIMENSIONAL SCALING

Overview

Multidimensional scaling encompasses a set of computational procedures that can summarize an input matrix of associations between variables or objects. Generally, its main thrust in marketing has been to examine relationships among objects—usually brands of a particular product group. These techniques take as input a matrix of relationships between objects that have an unknown underlying dimensionality. Then they determine *the minimum dimensionality of the relationships between the objects, and the position of each object on each dimension.*

Although multidimensional scaling can be used to analyze virtually any matrix of associations, its fundamental applications in marketing have been to analyze (1) consumer perceptions of the similarity of brands and (2) consumer preferences for brands. In this context, multidimensional scaling is really an extension of the unidimensional attitude scales discussed in Chapter 13 (e.g., semantic differential). Instead of positioning attitudes about brands on unidimensional scales, we can use multidimensional scaling to position brands in an n-dimensional space, where n is the minimum underlying dimensionality of the relationship. Thus, we can speak of positioning brands and preferences related to brands in a perceptual space.

There are in general three types of multidimensional scaling. These types, which relate to the nature of the input and output data, are as follows:[7]

1 *Fully metric*. These methods require intervally or ratio-scaled input measures and generate a set of relationships among objects that is also interval or ratio.

2 *Fully nonmetric*. These methods take ordinally scaled input measures and generate the rank order of each object on each dimension.

3 *Nonmetric*. These methods take ordinally scaled input measures and generate a set of relationships among the objects that is interval. That is, the distances between objects in the perceptual space have useful meaning. It is nonmetric multidimensional scaling that has obtained the most frequent marketing application.

The mathematics of nonmetric multidimensional scaling are far too complex to discuss here. What follows is an example of this technique in which the nature of the input and output will be discussed.

An Example[8]

Suppose that we wanted to measure consumer perceptions of the similarity of, and their preference for, 11 car models: (1) Ford Fairmont, (2) Mercury Zephyr, (3) Lincoln Continental, (4) Ford Thunderbird, (5) Ford Pinto, (6) Cadillac Eldorado, (7) Jaguar XJ Sedan, (8) AMC Concord, (9) Plymouth Volare, (10) Buick Le Sabre, and (11) Chevrolet Chevette.

For similarities we need to obtain from the consumers the rank order of the similarity of all 55 combinations of car models taken two at a time. In general, there are $n(n - 1)/2$ rank orders to obtain, where n is the number of objects of interest. One way to do this is to put each of the 55 combinations on a separate card. The respondents are then asked to rank-order the cards in terms of the most similar pair to the least similar pair.[9] One consumer's possible ranking of the pairs of models is given in Table 25-4. Here, for example, we see that the consumer considered cars 1 and 2 (Fairmont and Zephyr) to be the eighth most similar pair, and the Lincoln (car 3) and Cadillac (car 6) to be the most similar. Preference data could be collected by asking each consumer to simply rank-order the eleven cars from most preferred to least preferred.

Figure 25-3 illustrates the type of output generated by analyzing the similarities matrix given in Table 25-4. In this case a two-dimensional perceptual space was deemed appropriate to represent the data. We note that the positioning of the

---

[7] Paul E. Green and Frank J. Carmone, *Multidimensional Scaling* (Boston: Allyn & Bacon, 1970), pp. 10–11.

[8] This example is adapted from one presented in Green and Carmone, pp. 23–33. Basically we have updated some of the car names to reflect the late 1970s, replacing 1968 car names used in their study.

[9] This task can become difficult as the number of objects increases. A number of other procedures are available, but they are not discussed here.

Table 25-4   Rank Order of Similarities Between Pairs of Car Models

Stimuli	1	2	3	4	5	6	7	8	9	10	11
1	—	8	50	31	12	48	36	2	5	39	10
2		—	38	9	33	37	22	6	4	14	32
3			—	11	55	1	23	46	41	17	52
4				—	44	13	16	19	25	18	42
5					—	54	53	30	28	45	7
6						—	26	47	40	24	51
7							—	29	35	34	49
8								—	3	27	15
9									—	20	21
10										—	43
11											—

The rank number "1" represents the most similar pair.
Source: Paul E. Green and Frank J. Carmone, *Multidimensional Scaling* (Boston: Allyn & Bacon, 1970), p. 34.

car models with respect to each other seems to give us competitive segments. For example, the Fairmont, Zephyr, Concord, and Volare are positioned close to each other.

The preference data can be analyzed so that they are positioned within the similarities space in Figure 25-3. Each consumer would be positioned within this space. These positions are referred to as "ideal points." For example, consumer A, who likes big luxury cars, may have an ideal point near Lincoln and Cadillac. When each consumer's ideal point is positioned in the space, we can determine the size of ideal-point locations. That is, we may get clusterings of ideal points in particular locations, and this can be used to predict market shares. On Figure 25-3 the two dimensions were labeled "sportiness" and "luxuriousness." These labels, like factor labels in factor analysis, are based upon research judgment.

The questions naturally arise: (1) How do we get interval output from ordered input? (2) How does one determine the required dimensionality? We get interval output because the large number of rank-order pairs in the input matrix puts so many constraints on the positioning of objects that we find an underlying interval relationship. The dimensionality of the space is determined by calculating a goodness-of-fit measure between the input rank order and the output. This measure is called *stress*. Stress gets smaller as the number of dimensions increases. When a rule-of-thumb acceptable level is reached, the dimensionality is determined.

Marketing Applications

There are a number of possible applications of nonmetric multidimensional scaling in marketing. These include:[10]

[10] James R. Taylor, "Management Experience with Applications of Multidimensional Scaling Methods," unpublished working paper, Marketing Science Institute, Cambridge, Mass., 1970, p. 15.

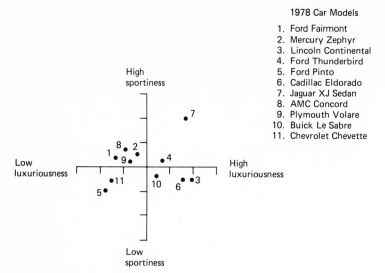

Figure 25-3   Perceptual space solution based on data in Table 25-4. [Adapted from Paul E. Green and Frank J. Carmone, *Multidimensional Scaling* (Boston: Allyn & Bacon, 1970), p. 34.]

1   The identification of salient product attributes perceived by buyers in a market.

2   The combination of attributes most preferred.

3   The products that are viewed as substitutes and those that are differentiated from one another.

4   The viable segments that exist in a market.

5   Those "holes" in a market that can support a new product venture.

The method also appears applicable to problems of product life cycle analysis, market segmentation, vendor evaluations, advertising evaluation, test marketing, salesperson and store image, brand switching research, and attitude scaling.[11]

Final Comment

This presentation of multidimensional scaling has ignored many computational issues, and it has not discussed the limitations of the technique; this is also true for our discussion of factor analysis and cluster analysis. The interested reader should therefore consult a more advanced source. We must also leave the reader with a final word of warning. All three techniques discussed in this chapter leave the researcher with major interpretation difficulties after the output is generated, and different computer programs for a technique often yield different results. Great care and skill are required in their application.

[11] Green and Carmone, op. cit., pp. 14–19.

SUMMARY

1   Dependence methods designate one or more variables as being predicted by a set of independent variables.

2   Interdependence methods do not designate any variables as being predicted by others. The interest is in the interrelationship among all the variables taken together.

3   Interdependence methods include factor analysis, cluster analysis, and multidimensional scaling.

4   Factor analysis is a procedure that takes a large number of variables or objects and searches to see whether they have a small number of factors in common which account for their intercorrelations.

5   Applications of factor analysis include data reduction, structure identification, scaling, and data transformation.

6   Factor analysis takes a correlation matrix as input. In R-factor analysis these correlations are between variables, and in Q-factor analysis these correlations are between cases or objects.

7   The factor analysis output gives the loading of each variable on each underlying factor. This output may be rotated to give either uncorrelated or correlated factors.

8   Cluster analysis places variables or objects into subgroups or clusters that are defined by the procedure. It is generally used for objects.

9   The cluster analysis input is a matrix of associations between variables or objects. These measures can be for different scale levels depending on the computer procedure.

10   The output of cluster analysis places objects in clusters or a set of alternative clusters at different levels of association.

11   Multidimensional scaling takes a matrix of relationships between objects as input, then determines the underlying dimensionality and places each object on each dimension.

12   Multidimensional scaling is generally used in marketing to measure the perception of brand similarities and preferences.

13   Nonmetric multidimensional scaling takes ordinal input measures and generates a set of relationships among the objects that is interval.

DISCUSSION QUESTIONS

1   Why is multivariate analysis becoming more used in marketing research?
2   Distinguish between dependence and interdependence methods.
3   What is the overall objective of factor analysis?
4   Describe the nature of the input and output of factor analysis.
5   What are R- and Q-type factor analyses?
6   What is the objective of cluster analyses?
7   Describe the nature of the input and output of cluster analysis.
8   What is the objective of multidimensional scaling?

9   What is nonmetric multidimensional scaling?
10 Describe the nature of the input and output of nonmetric multidimensional scaling.
11 How does one name factors, clusters, and dimensions for interdependence methods?

SUGGESTED READING

Green, Paul E., and Donald Tull, *Research for Marketing Decisions,* 3d ed. (Englewood Cliffs, N.J.: Prentice-Hall, 1975), chaps. 15 and 16. An introductory treatment of cluster analysis and multidimensional scaling.

Schuessler, Karl, *Analyzing Social Data* (Boston: Houghton Mifflin, 1971), chaps. 2 and 3. A most readable and elementary introduction to factor analysis.

Chapter 26

Multivariate Data Analysis II: Dependence Methods

This chapter is a direct follow-up to the previous one. Here we present an elementary discussion of a number of dependence methods of multivariate analysis. Again the mathematical complexities are omitted, with the emphasis being on the nature of input and output of the procedures. Each of the techniques discussed in this chapter has a number of important statistical assumptions and limitations associated with it. These assumptions and limitations are not discussed here, because of their complexity. The approach here is simply to present a brief overview of each technique. The reader who is interested in using these techniques should consult a technical specialist or a more advanced book. Again, *the techniques are extremely dangerous when used by unskilled people.*

The specific techniques we will overview are multiple regression, analysis of variance, analysis of covariance, dummy-variable multiple regression, automatic interaction detector, discriminant analysis, conjoint measurement, canonical correlation, and multivariate analysis of variance.

CLASSIFICATION OF PROCEDURES

The selection of the appropriate dependence procedure depends on (1) the number of variables that have been designated as dependent and (2) the scale levels of the dependent and independent variables. Figure 26-1 presents a flow-chart that will guide the researcher to the appropriate procedure. It is based on decision points related to the number of dependent variables designated, and on the scale level of the dependent and independent variables. We find the appropriate technique by following the flow of questions in the figure. Table 26-1 summarizes the situation where each technique is appropriate. It should be recognized that each technique has some additional statistical assumptions.

The rest of this chapter discusses each of these procedures.

MULTIPLE REGRESSION

Multiple regression is a straightforward extension of simple regression as discussed in Chapter 23. The difference is that in multiple regression the analysis is done with *more than one independent variable*. The predictive equation for a two-independent variable situation would be

$$\hat{Y}_i = a + b_1 X_1 + b_2 X_2$$

where X_1 and X_2 are the independent variables and a, b_1, and b_2 are the regression coefficients generated from our sample data. Again, we recognize that these coefficients are statistics that estimate the population parameters of the regression. We can easily generalize the equation to m independent variables. Here

$$\hat{Y}_i = a + b_1 X_1 + b_2 X_2 + \cdots + b_m X_m$$

Table 26-1 Situation Where Dependence Methods Are Appropriate

A. One Dependent Variable

Technique	Dependent variable scale level	Independent variables scale level
1 Multiple regression	Interval	Interval
2 Analysis of variance and covariance	Interval	Nominal
3 Dummy-variable multiple regression	Interval	Nominal
4 Automatic interaction detector	Interval	Nominal
5 Discriminant analysis	Nominal	Interval
6 Dummy-variable discriminant analysis	Nominal	Nominal
7 Conjoint measurement	Ordinal	Nominal

B. More Than One Dependent Variable

Technique	Dependent variables scale level	Independent variables scale level
8 Canonical correlation	Interval	Interval
9 Multivariate analysis of variance	Interval	Nominal

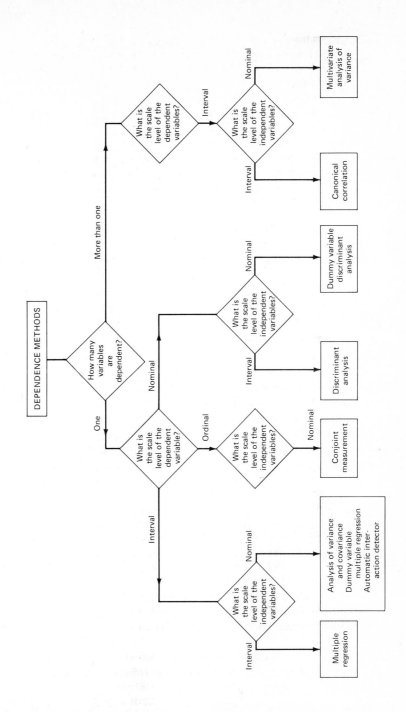

Figure 26-1 Classification of dependence methods. (Adapted from a scheme presented in Thomas C. Kinnear and James R. Taylor, "Multivariate Methods in Marketing Research: A Further Attempt at Classification," *Journal of Marketing*, vol. 35, pp. 56–59, October 1971.)

The formulas for the coefficients are too complex to present, even for a two-independent variable situation.

Multiple regression requires that both the dependent and independent variables be intervally scaled. Also, it assumes that the underlying relationship is linear, although data transformations can overcome this latter problem. Finally, our sample size must be large enough to give many observations per independent variable. The more independent variables, the larger should be the sample size.

The total variation in the dependent variable may be partitioned in exactly the same fashion as with simple regression. Specifically,

$$SS_{total} = SS_{explained} + SS_{unexplained}$$

$$\Sigma(Y_i - \overline{Y})^2 \qquad \Sigma(\hat{Y}_i - \overline{Y})^2 \qquad \Sigma(Y_i - \hat{Y}_i)^2$$

We can convert these SS to variances by dividing them by the appropriate degrees of freedom. We could then compare the explained variance with the error variance to see whether the regression as a whole has explained a significant amount of the variance in Y. We would use an F test, a detailed description of which was presented in Chapter 15. The use of the F test for simple regression was discussed in the appendix to Chapter 23.

The only difference in doing this in multiple regression as opposed to simple regression is that the degrees of freedom are different. Each independent variable requires one degree of freedom. Thus, with $n - 1$ degrees of freedom in the whole sample, the error degrees of freedom will be $n - 1 - m$, where m is the number of independent variables. The explained degrees of freedom is simply m. We may also calculate the standard error and thus the significance of each regression coefficient. Here we use a t test. In simple regression an F test on SS and a t test on the coefficient yielded identical results; in multiple regression the F test tells us whether the regression as a whole is significant, and the t tests tell us which coefficients are statistically significantly different from zero.

An Example

An example should help clarify the nature of results generated by a multiple regression program. Table 26-2 presents regression results for the following situation: (1) The dependent variable is the dollar amount of life insurance owned, (2) the independent variables are income and family size, and (3) the sample size is 15.

We see that with two independent variables the regression degrees of freedom equals 2, and with 15 cases the error degrees of freedom is $n - 1 - m = 15 - 1 - 2 = 12$. The calculated F is 162. The critical F at $\alpha = .01$ and 2 and 12 degrees of freedom is 6.93 (see Table A-5 of Appendix A). The regression clearly explains a significant amount of the variation in Y. Similarly, the critical t value for the coefficients at $\alpha = .01$ and 12 degrees of freedom is 3.055. Thus we can reject the null hypothesis that the income coefficient is zero, while we

Table 26-2 Regression Results

Source	SS	Df	Mean square	F
Regression	15,552	2	7,776	162
Error	574	12	48	
Total	16,126	14		

Variable	Coefficient	Standard error	t statistic
Constant	−1305.2		
Income	2.3	.13	18.03
Family size	−2620.8	1320.6	−1.98

Multiple R = .98205	Multiple R^2 = .96441

Source: Adapted from an example prepared by Prof. William Wrobleski, The University of Michigan.

cannot do so for the family size coefficient. Note that if we had set $\alpha = .1$, the critical t would be 1.782, and we would have concluded that the family size coefficient is significant.

The *size* and *direction* of the coefficients also have meaning. In general, a positive coefficient indicates a direct relationship between that independent variable and the dependent variable. A negative coefficient indicates an inverse relationship. The size of the coefficient indicates the amount of change in the dependent variable associated with a one-unit increase in that independent variable, given that all other independent variables remain constant. In our example, the amount of life insurance will increase by $2.30 for every $1.00 increase in income, given that family size is held constant.

The computer is also likely to generate the *multiple correlation coefficient*, R. This is the correlation coefficient between the observed Y_i and the estimated $\hat{Y}_i$'s. The closer the regression equation predictions are to the actual observations, the higher will be R. We may also calculate the *coefficient of multiple determination*, which is R^2. It is the proportion of the variation in Y explained by the regression. Alternatively, the coefficient of multiple determination may be obtained by taking the ratio $SS_{\text{explained}}$ over SS_{total}. In our example,

$$R^2 = 15,552/16,126 = .96441$$

The type of regression in our example is called *total regression*; with this type, all the independent variables are entered into the regression equation in one step. An alternative type is called *stepwise regression*; here the independent variables enter the regression equation one at a time. The variable selected to enter first is the one that explains the most variation in Y. The next variable to enter is the one that explains the greatest amount of the variation in Y after the effect of the first variable has been removed. This process continues until no significant variation remains or no variable is left that explains a significant amount of the variation.

Another point about the regression coefficients is important: The size of the coefficient does not provide a measure of its importance in the regression. In the case being studied, the smaller coefficient is the better one because the independent variables are measured in different units (people and dollars). It is possible to take the effects of units used out of the regression. We do this by means of the same principle with which we obtained unit-free measures in correlation calculations. That is, we divide the observed values' deviations from the mean by their standard deviation. We define $x°$ and $y°$ as measures of X and Y that have the units removed. In formula,

$$x° = \frac{X - \bar{X}}{s} \quad \text{and} \quad y° = \frac{Y - \bar{Y}}{s}$$

This expresses values of X and Y as a number of standard deviations. We can then directly compare regression coefficients to see their relative importance.

The applications of multiple regression in marketing are the same as for simple regression, except that the use of more independent variables allows one to specify the relationship more precisely.

ANALYSIS OF VARIANCE AND COVARIANCE

We discussed analysis of variance (ANOVA) in detail in Chapters 15 and 16. The particular ANOVA that interests us here is ANOVA with more than one independent variable—called *N-way* or *factorial ANOVA*. We note that ANOVA requires an intervally scaled dependent variable and accepts nominally scaled independent variables. Its primary application is in the analysis of experimental data.

ANOVA's close relative ANCOVA, the analysis of covariance (which we briefly discussed in Chapter 14), does warrant some discussion here. ANCOVA is appropriate in experimental situations where it is discovered after the experiment that some extraneous source of variation is contributing to the values of the dependent variable. For example, we may discover that store size has contributed to sales in an experiment we ran to test the effect of alternative coupon plans; that is, large stores automatically sell more than small stores.

A detailed example of ANCOVA would take too much space. What follows here, then, is a conceptual overview of how ANCOVA works. To use ANCOVA we must have an intervally scaled dependent variable and nominally scaled independent variables, and the variables to be controlled must be measured at an interval level. These latter variables are called *covariates*. ANCOVA essentially undertakes the following:

1 A regression is run with the covariates as independent variables (e.g., store size) and the dependent variable from the experiment as the dependent variable (sales).

2 The regression estimates, the $\hat{Y}_i$'s, are calculated for each covariate observation.

3 The estimated $\hat{Y}_i$'s are subtracted from the observed experimental data, Y_i; the result of this is a set of experimental data that has the effect of the covariates removed; we define $Y_i' = Y_i - \hat{Y}_i$, where Y_i' is a covariate-free observation.

4 ANOVA is then undertaken on the Y_i''s in a regular fashion.

In doing this one must be careful to keep the degrees of freedom straight. Since we are using regression, each covariate uses one degree of freedom. Thus, if we have k covariates, the total degrees of freedom left to do the ANOVA is $n - 1 - k$. From this adjusted number of degrees of freedom, the treatment and error degrees of freedom for ANOVA are calculated in the usual manner; if we had two covariates, one treatment with four categories, and 50 test units, the total degrees of freedom for ANOVA would be $50 - 1 - 2 = 47$. The treatment degrees of freedom would be $t - 1 = 4 - 1 = 3$, and the error would be $47 - 3 = 44$.

DUMMY-VARIABLE MULTIPLE REGRESSION

The use of regression in marketing research could be severely hampered by the fact that the independent variables must be intervally scaled. Fortunately there is a way to use nominal independent variables in a regression context. The procedure that we use is called *dummy-variable multiple regression* (DVMR). Basically, DVMR converts nominal variables into a series of binary variables that are coded 0-1. For example, suppose we wish to use the nominal variable "sex" in a regression. We could code it as follows:

Category	Code
Male	0
Female	1

The interval 0 to 1 is equal and thus acceptable to regression. Note that we have converted a two-category nominal variable into one 0-1 variable. We may extend this approach to a multicategory nominal variable. The four-category nominal variable "region of the country" could be converted to three dummy variables, X_1, X_2, and X_3 as follows:

Category	X_1	X_2	X_3
East	1	0	0
West	0	1	0
North	0	0	1
South	0	0	0

This four-category nominal variable is now converted to three 0-1 variables. In general, a k-category nominal variable converts to $k - 1$ dummy variables, because once we know whether the first $k - 1$ categories are 0 or 1, the kth category is automatically determined as 0 or 1. To create a kth dummy variable would be redundant, and in fact it would invalidate the whole regression. The choice of the category that will have all zeros is arbitrary.

To illustrate DVMR, suppose that sales of Japanese cars represents the dependent variable. The regression equation might be:

$$\hat{Y}_i = 250{,}000 + 50{,}000X_1 + 80{,}000X_2 - 6{,}000X_3$$

Note that only one of either X_1, X_2, or X_3 will take on the value 1 for any one subject, and the other two X's will be zero. The coefficients provide a measure of the effect of being from a particular region. The equations by region are:

East: $\hat{Y}_i = 250{,}000 + 50{,}000(1) = 300{,}000$
West: $\hat{Y}_i = 250{,}000 + 80{,}000(1) = 330{,}000$
North: $\hat{Y}_i = 250{,}000 - 6{,}000(1) = 244{,}000$
South: $\hat{Y}_i = 250{,}000$

We can have as many dummy variables as we need in a regression, subject to the constraint that each dummy variable uses a degree of freedom. Thus, we must have an adequate sample size.

There is a special computational version of DVMR called *multiple classification analysis* (MCA) that has obtained significant marketing application. The specific nature of this procedure, however, lies beyond the scope of this book.[1]

AUTOMATIC INTERACTION DETECTOR

The automatic interaction detector (AID) is another technique that is used with an interval dependent variable and a set of nominal independent variables. Its basic objective is to break down a total sample into a number of subgroups that are more homogeneous on the dependent variable than the sample as a whole. It does this by the repeated application of one-way ANOVA. Specifically, AID does the following:

1 It calculates the explained SS ($SS_{between}/SS_{total}$) on the dependent variable for each combination of categories for the independent variables.
2 It splits the sample into two groups based on the categories of that independent variable that explain the most SS.
3 It then repeats steps 1 and 2 for the two new groups, then splits these groups, and so on.

[1] The interested reader should see Frank M. Andrews, James N. Morgan, and John A. Sonquist, *Multiple Classification Analysis* (Ann Arbor: Institute for Social Research, The University of Michigan, 1967).

AID is primarily used in marketing to help identify market segments, and to identify variables that seem to be importantly related to the dependent variable. These variables could then be used in a DVMR analysis.

Figure 26-2 illustrates AID output.[2] This output is called an *AID tree*. The top number in each box is the sample size for that group. The lower number is the probability of a subject purchasing a nonphosphate detergent. Here the dependent variable is the likelihood of someone using a nonphosphate detergent, and the independent variables are a set of attitude measures. Group 1 is the whole sample size of 1499. We note that:

> The overall probability of a subject drawn at random from the sample using a nonphosphate laundry product was .37 (group 1's mean probability). We note that the subgroup that stated an extreme self-interest in the pollution aspects of products and who were willing to accept a moderately or more or less clean wash (group 5) had a mean probability of purchasing a nonphosphate product of .75. At the other extreme, we note that those who stated that they were less than extremely interested, and who perceived consumers to be less than very highly effective against pollution, and who thought that urging one's friends to purchase nonpollution products was not a good idea, and who were not willing to accept clothes that were any less clean (group 12), had a mean probability of purchase of .06.[3]

The major constraint for use of AID is that a large sample size (1000 plus) is needed, otherwise the subgroups become too small too soon.

DISCRIMINANT ANALYSIS

Discriminant analysis (DA) is a technique that is appropriate with a nominal dependent variable and interval independent variables. Nominal dependent variables are very common in marketing; for example, good versus bad credit risks, brand-loyal versus nonloyal consumers, different brand users, and successful versus unsuccessful salespersons. As a result of this, DA has received extensive application in marketing research.

The basic idea of DA is to find a linear combination of the independent variables that makes the mean scores across categories of the dependent variable on this linear combination maximally different. This linear combination is called the *discriminant function* (DF). In symbols,

$$DF = v_1 X_1 + v_2 X_2 + \cdots + v_m X_m$$

where X_m is the mth independent variable. The objective is to find the values for the v's that give us the required DF. The criterion used to decide when group

[2] This example is adapted from Thomas C. Kinnear and James R. Taylor, "Identifying Ecological Buying Segments Through Attitude Measurement," *Journal of Business Administration*, vol. 5, pp. 33–43, Spring 1974.
[3] Ibid., p. 49.

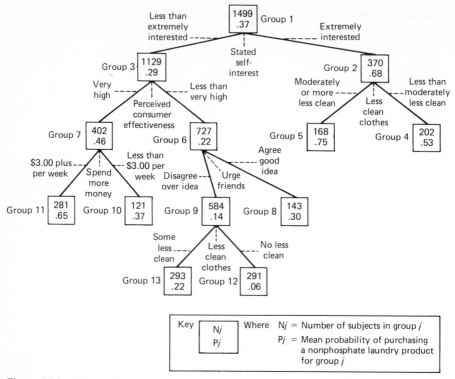

Figure 26-2 AID tree for use of nonphosphate laundry products. (Adapted from Thomas C.. Kinnear and James R. Taylor, "Identifying Ecological Buying Segments Through Attitude Measurement," *Journal of Business Administration,* vol. 5, p. 41, Spring 1974.)

means are maximally different is the familiar ANOVA F test for the differences among means. Thus, the v's are derived such that

$$F = \frac{SS_{between}}{SS_{within}}$$

is maximized.

The output of DA usually includes the values of the v's, plus what is called a *confusion matrix.* This matrix compares the category of the dependent variable that the discriminant function predicts a subject will be in with the category that the subject is actually in. Table 26-3 presents a confusion matrix for good and bad credit risks based upon a set of demographic independent variables (e.g., age, income, years in same house, etc.). Note that it is the elements on the diagonal running from top left to bottom right that give those subjects that are correctly classified by the DA. Ninety percent of subjects in this example are correctly classified. This example is for a two-category dependent variable (often called two-group). It can easily be extended to a k-group dependent variable.

Table 26-3   Confusion Matrix for Credit Risks

Actual category	Predicted category	
	Good	Bad
Good	800	40
Bad	60	100

The constraint of having to have interval independent variables is really no problem. As we did with regression, we can convert nominal independent variables to dummy variables in order to yield dummy-variable discriminant analysis (DVDA).

CONJOINT MEASUREMENT

A set of procedures that has attracted much attention of late in marketing research is conjoint measurement (CM). CM is concerned with the joint effects of two or more nominal independent variables on the ordering of a dependent variable. Thus, CM is appropriate for nominal independent variables and an ordinal dependent variable. It is in essence an analysis of variance of rank-order data. The benefit of CM is that it generates interval-level measures of the effects of the categories of the independent variables.

Its primary marketing application has been to measure the trade-offs that consumers make on product attributes, as the following example shows. Suppose we are concerned with the attributes of an airplane and that (for simplicity) only two attributes are noteworthy—price and cruising speed. Table 26-4 presents an input matrix to CM for the two attributes for one individual. Three different prices and cruising speeds are given. The entries in the matrix are the rank order of the preferences for the attribute combinations for one consumer. You can follow the trade-offs this consumer will make by following the rank order.

We shall illustrate the nature of CM by discussing how an additive version of CM could utilize the input data from Table 26-4. The basic idea is that CM develops measures of the effect of each level of each attribute such that the additive combination of these effects optimally maintains the rank order of the input preferences. Table 26-5 gives a possible result of a CM analysis of Table 26-4. Here the interval-level effects are given in parentheses. The numbers in the matrix are the various sums of the effect combinations. For example, the

Table 26-4   Rank-order Joint-effect Input Matrix

Cruising speed, mph	Price levels		
	$400,000	$600,000	$800,000
300	7	8	9
400	3	4	6
500	1	2	5

Table 26-5 Intervally Scaled Effect Measures for Attribute Levels

Cruising speed, mph	Price levels		
	$400,000 (.52)	$600,000 (.45)	$800,000 (.30)
300 (.20)	.72	.65	.50
400 (.61)	1.13	1.06	.91
500 (.75)	1.27	1.20	1.05

combination of 300 mph and $400,000 is valued at .20 + .52 = .72. Note that the interval values in the matrix perfectly maintain the input rank order. This is not always possible, but CM finds the effect measures that achieve it best.

The effect measures may be interpreted as the utility the consumer places on a particular attribute. The number of independent variables can easily be extended to more than two. Thus we can realistically use this technique to measure the total utility a consumer places on various possible attribute combinations for a product. If we did this for a sample of consumers, we could use CM to predict market share, profitability, etc., of a product offering various attribute combinations.[4]

CANONICAL CORRELATION

Canonical correlation (CC) is a technique that is occasionally used in marketing research. It is appropriate when one has both a set of intervally scaled dependent and independent variables. For example an organization might want to know how a set of attitude measures relates to a set of behaviors. Basically, CC forms one linear combination of the dependent variables and one of the independent variables. It finds the values of the coefficients of these combinations that yield the maximum correlation between the combinations.

MULTIVARIATE ANALYSIS OF VARIANCE

Multivariate analysis of variance (MANOVA) is appropriate when one has two or more intervally scaled dependent variables and one or more nominally scaled independent variables. A straightforward extension of ANOVA, it is used when the researcher in an experiment wishes to test the effects of the independent variables on a series of dependent variables. For example, sales and attitude measures may be deemed appropriate dependent variables in an experiment. MANOVA allows one to judge whether the treatments were significant on the set of dependent variables as a group, and in addition it gives an ordinary ANOVA on each one individually.

[4] For a discussion of this and other possible applications, see Paul E. Green and Vithala R. Rao, "Conjoint Measurement for Quantifying Judgmental Data," *Journal of Marketing Research*, vol. 8, pp. 355–363, August 1971.

SUMMARY

1 The choice of dependence method depends on the number of variables that have been designated as dependent and on the scale level of the dependent and independent variables.

2 Multiple regression is used with one intervally scaled dependent variable and a set of intervally scaled independent variables.

3 Analysis of variance, dummy-variable multiple regression, and the automatic interaction detector are used with one intervally scaled dependent variable and a set of nominally scaled dependent variables.

4 Discriminant analysis is used with one nominally scaled dependent variable and a set of intervally scaled independent variables.

5 Dummy-variable discriminant analysis is used with one nominally scaled dependent variable and a set of nominally scaled independent variables.

6 Conjoint measurement is used with one ordinally scaled dependent variable and a set of nominally scaled independent variables.

7 Canonical correlation is used with a set of intervally scaled dependent variables and a set of intervally scaled independent variables.

8 Multivariate analysis of variance is used with a set of intervally scaled dependent variables and a set of nominally scaled independent variables.

9 All the techniques discussed in this chapter are very complex, and in most cases a marketing research generalist would consult with a technical specialist when using them.

DISCUSSION QUESTIONS

1 How are dependence methods classified?
2 What is the coefficient of multiple determination? How is it calculated from a regression printout?
3 What does a coefficient mean in multiple regression?
4 How does ANCOVA work?
5 How are nominal independent variables handled in a regression?
6 How is AID related to ANOVA?
7 What is a discriminant function? What criterion is used to derive its coefficients?
8 How could conjoint measurements be used to predict market share?

SUGGESTED READING

This whole subject area is so diverse and complex that there is really no elementary treatment of it. Virtually all good material requires some knowledge of calculus and matrix algebra. For those willing to learn the necessary mathematics, the most readable treatment is in:

Tatsuoka, Maurice M., *Multivariate Analysis: Techniques for Educational and Psychological Research* (New York: Wiley, 1971).

Chapter 27

A Decision Theory Approach to Marketing Research

In Chapter 5 it was noted that the value of research information is related to the degree of uncertainty held by the manager and the likely benefits of marketing activity (contribution per unit, market size, and market share). The more uncertainty, or the larger the market size or market share, the more value would accrue to research information. In Chapter 5 we made no attempt to measure uncertainty or benefit. An approach to marketing research which allows the researcher to do this is called the *decision theory* or *bayesian approach*, and it constitutes the topic of this chapter.[1]

We begin with a discussion of the concept of uncertainty, noting alternative decision criteria in the face of uncertainty. The decision theory approach is then presented, with a description of the three types of analysis it allows, namely, prior, posterior, and preposterior analysis. Finally, the advantages and limitations of this approach will be discussed.

UNCERTAINTY AND DECISION CRITERIA

Marketing decisions are always made under conditions of uncertainty. Uncertainty is defined to mean that there is lack of complete knowledge about the

[1] This chapter follows an excellent discussion of this material in Joseph W. Newman, *Management Applications of Decision Theory* (New York: Harper & Row, 1971), pp. 3–27.

possible outcomes of actions and that the probabilities of the possible outcomes are not known. It is the nature of all decisions that they are made in a state of uncertainty.

In the face of uncertainty, the decision maker can adopt a number of different decision rules. Several of the rules assume that the decision maker cannot apply any probability judgments to the possible outcomes of alternative courses of action. These rules are (1) the maximin criterion, (2) the maximax criterion, (3) the minimax regret criterion, and (4) the Laplace criterion. In contrast, the decision theory approach assumes that the decision maker can assign useful probabilities to the possible outcomes of alternative courses of action. We shall now briefly discuss the first four decision criteria.

Maximin Criterion   Table 27-1 presents the payoffs associated with the various combinations of two courses of action, A_1 and A_2, with three outcomes, S_1, S_2, and S_3. The maximin criterion directs the decision maker to select the alternative that maximizes the minimum payoff. In other words, one determines the worst outcome under each alternative and selects the alternative with the largest "worst possible" outcome. In the example in Table 27-1, one would select A_1 because its minimum payoff is 15, while A_2's is 3. This criterion would be applied by a person extremely averse to taking risks.

Maximax Criterion   This reflects exactly the opposite orientation to the maximin criterion. Here one selects the alternative that maximizes the maximum payout. One would again select A_1, as its maximum payout of 115 is greater than A_2's maximum payout of 101. This criterion is relevant for the person who is most concerned about opportunity cost.

Minimax Regret Criterion   Savage[2] proposed a criterion that would take into consideration the cost of opportunity loss. To use this criterion we must convert the payoffs into opportunity losses. The maximum opportunity loss (regret) is identified for each alternative, and the alternative selected is the one with the minimum opportunity loss. Basically, we apply the maximin criterion to the opportunity loss matrix. To obtain an opportunity loss matrix from a payout matrix, we reason as follows: Suppose that, in Table 27-1, S_1 occurs. If we had selected A_1, we would have no opportunity loss, as it has the highest payout; if S_2 were selected, there would be an opportunity loss of $115 - 101 = 14$. Table 27-2 presents an opportunity loss matrix of the data in Table 27-1. In this example alternative A_2 would be selected, since its maximum regret is less than A_1's.

Laplace Criterion   The previous three criteria focus on the best or worst payouts and ignore other information in the matrix, but the Laplace criterion uses all the matrix entries. Here the decision maker assigns equal probabilities

[2] L. J. Savage, "The Theory of Statistical Decisions," *Journal of the American Statistical Association*, vol. 46, pp. 56–67, March 1951.

Table 27-1   Payout Matrix

Courses of action	Outcomes		
	S_1	S_2	S_3
A_1	115	64	15
A_2	101	80	3

to each outcome, then calculates the average value of each alternative. The alternative selected is the one with the highest average value. Here the averages are:

$$A_1: .33(115) + .33(64) + .33(15) = 64.7$$
$$A_2: .33(101) + .33(80) + .33(3)\ \ = 61.3$$

Thus, we would choose alternative A_1 on the basis of this criterion.

All four of these criteria assume that the decision maker cannot make reasoned guesses about the probability of various outcomes occurring. Clearly, however, a manager's experience and judgment are worth something in making such assessments. The decision theory approach allows a manager's subjective probability assessments to be taken into account.

THE DECISION THEORY APPROACH

To use the decision theory or bayesian approach, the decision maker must undertake the following steps:

1   Identify the objectives toward which the decision making should be directed.
2   Identify the alternative courses of action that should be considered.
3   Identify the possible events (environmental conditions) that would influence the payoff of each course of action.
4   Assign a numerical value to the payoff of each course of action, given each possible event.
5   Assign a subjective probability to the occurrence of each possible event.
6   Using the probabilities, compute the weighted average (expected value) of the payoffs assigned to each course of action.
7   Assess the exposure to both gain and loss associated with each course of action.

Table 27-2   Opportunity Loss Matrix

Courses of action	Outcomes			Maximum loss
	S_1	S_2	S_3	
A_1	0	16	0	16
A_2	14	0	12	14

Table 27-3 Payout Matrix and Subjective Probabilities

Courses of action	Outcomes and probabilities					
	S_1	$P(S_1)$	S_2	$P(S_2)$	S_3	$P(S_3)$
A_1	115	.2	64	.5	15	.3
A_2	101	.4	80	.4	3	.2

$$\text{EMV}(A_1) = 115(.2) + 64(.5) + 15(.3) = 59.5$$
$$\text{EMV}(A_2) = 101(.4) + 80(.4) + 3(.2) = 73.0$$

8 Choose among the alternative courses of action on the basis of the combination of (a) expected monetary value and (b) exposure to gain and loss that is most consistent with the decision maker's objectives and attitude toward risk;[3] i.e., convert the payouts to utility values.

The decision theory approach is then based on the belief that a decision maker can assign meaningful subjective probabilities to events or outcomes. Instead of saying, for example, "There is a good chance of S_1 occurring," the decision maker must be prepared to say "There is a .70 probability of S_1 occurring." This probability is not based on relative frequencies, as in classical statistics, but on the belief of the manager.

The two decision criteria generally used in a decision theory analysis are (1) the expected monetary value criterion and (2) the expected utility criterion.

Expected Monetary Value Criterion (EMV) According to the EMV criterion, one simply selects the alternative with the highest EMV. Table 27-3 presents the same data contained in Table 27-1, except that subjective probabilities have been assigned to the possible outcomes. Note that the decision maker has assigned different probabilities $P(S_i)$ to various outcomes depending on the alternative, and that the sum of the probabilities for outcomes of any action equals 1.0. This latter point is true because the identified outcomes must be mutually exclusive and collectively exhaustive of all possible outcomes.

The EMV of an alternative is calculated by multiplying the probability of an outcome by the value of that outcome and adding this to the probability-multiplied values associated with other outcomes. In symbols,

$$\text{EMV}(A_j) = \sum_{i=1}^{k} S_i P(S_i)$$

where A_j is the jth alternative and k is the number of possible outcomes of an alternative. Here

[3] Adapted from Newman, op. cit., pp. 6–7.

$$EMV(A_1) = \sum_{i=1}^{3} S_i P(S_i)$$
$$= 115(.2) + 64(.5) + 15(.3) = 59.5$$

For A_2 the EMV is 73.0. Since the $EMV(A_2)$ is greater than the $EMV(A_1)$, the decision maker would select A_2.

Expected Utility Value Criterion (EUV)   The EMV criterion assumes that the decision maker's utility function with respect to money is linear, but this may not be the case. For example, the utility to a small company of a $100,000 loss may be much greater than the same loss to a giant corporation. Here the differences in exposure to gain or loss are large enough to be relevant to the decision and should be incorporated into the analysis. This can be done by converting the monetary payouts to utility values,[4] a procedure which allows one explicitly to incorporate one's attitude toward risk into the analysis. One then selects the alternative with the highest EUV.

We will not make use of the EUV criterion in this chapter. All decision theory illustrations in this chapter will use the EMV criterion. We have now laid the necessary foundation to present the first type of decision theory analysis, namely, *prior analysis*, which is performed before additional information is collected.

PRIOR ANALYSIS

Prior analysis involves the application of the decision theory approach where the probabilities of outcomes are assessed on the basis of the manager's present judgments, without the benefit of additional information. Consider the situation faced by a marketing manager for a soft drink company who is considering whether to undertake a special promotion.[5] Table 27-4 represents the manager's structuring of the problem. On this table we note that (1) alternative A_1 is "run a special promotion" and alternative A_2 is "have no special promotion"; (2) the possible consumer reactions are considered to be "very favorable," "favorable," and "unfavorable"; (3) the associated probabilities of reactions are .4, .3, and .3 respectively; and (4) the associated payoffs are listed in the body of the table. The $EMV(A_1)$ is $300,000(.4) + \$100,000(.3) - \$200,000(.3) = \$90,000$. The $EMV(A_2)$ is $0. The manager would decide to run the special promotion.

Decision Trees

A decision situation can be much more complex than this example. It might have many more alternatives and possible outcomes. As an aid in understanding decision problems, we may use a decision tree. Figure 27-1 presents a decision tree for the soft drink promotion problem. Basically a graphic representation of

---

[4] For a discussion of how to do this see Robert Schlaifer, *Analysis of Decisions under Uncertainty* (New York: McGraw-Hill, 1969), pp. 140–170.
[5] Adapted from Newman, op. cit., pp. 10–13.

Table 27-4 Expected Payoffs: Soft-drink Special Promotion

Possible consumer reactions	Alternative courses of action		Probabilities of consumer reactions
	A_1	A_2	
Very favorable	$300,000	$0	.4
Favorable	100,000	0	.3
Unfavorable	−200,000	0	.3
Expected payoffs	$ 90,000	$0	1.0

Source: Joseph W. Newman, *Management Applications of Decision Theory* (New York: Harper & Row, 1971), p. 10.

the problem, it is composed of a series of nodes and branches. Decision nodes are represented by square boxes, and outcome or event nodes by circles. The decision to be made is always to the leftmost node point. Event branches then appear as they are related to the alternatives in chronological order. We note that for alternative A_1, run the special promotion, the manager has identified the same three outcomes as in Table 27-4 and has assigned the same subjective probabilities. For alternative A_2, do not run the special promotion, the manager's judgment is that it is certain no change will occur. The associated monetary value of each end point has been assigned.

The tree is solved as follows: (1) Calculate the EMV of each node, beginning with the rightmost node; (2) adopt the alternative for the branch with the highest EMV. On Figure 27-1 the EMV of each alternative is presented at the outcome nodes following each alternative. Alternatives A_1 and A_2 have EMVs of $90,000 and $0 respectively, as before. The fact that we reject alternative A_2 is indicated by the fact that we have drawn double slash marks through the A_2 branch.

A decision tree may be much more complicated than the one presented in Figure 27-1. It may have many events nodes and branches or forks in sequences and may even have a decision node in the middle of some parts of the tree. These complications really present no problem, for the same rules for solving the tree

Figure 27-1 Decision tree: soft-drink special promotion problem. [From Joseph W. Newman, *Management Applications of Decision Theory* (New York: Harper & Row, 1971), p. 13.]

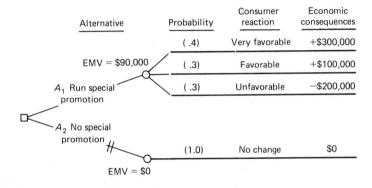

Table 27-5 Expected Payoffs under Certainity—Soft-drink Special-promotion Problem

Possible consumer reactions	Alternative courses of action		Probabilities of consumer reactions
	A_1	A_2	
Very favorable	$300,000	$0	.4
Favorable	100,000	0	.3
Unfavorable	0	0	.3
Expected payoff	$150,000	$0	1.0

Source: Joseph W. Newman, *Management Applications of Decision Theory* (New York: Harper & Row, 1971), p. 18.

apply. We just begin at the right side and work to the left. For event branches we calculate the EMVs and record them at the node, and for decision points we simply select the decision with the highest EMV.

Expected Monetary Value of Perfect Information

The structure of a prior analysis allows one to calculate the absolute theoretical limit to marketing research expenditures, known as the *expected monetary value of perfect information* (EMVPI). To calculate this value we must subtract the EMV of the decision under uncertainty from the EMV of the decision in the situation where certainty about outcomes exists. In symbols,

$$EMVPI = EMV(C) - EMV(UC)$$

where EMV(C) is the EMV with certainty and EMV(UC) is the EMV with uncertainty. The rationale for this approach is that if we were certain about outcomes, we would make the correct decision in each outcome situation. The EMV of these correct decisions represents some gain over the EMV where outcomes are uncertain. The amount of the gain is the difference between EMV(C) and EMV(UC).

For the soft drink promotion problem, we already calculated the EMV(UC) as $90,000. Table 27-5 presents the calculation of the EMV(C) for this problem, which is performed as follows: If one had perfect information that a particular outcome would occur, one would select the associated alternative with the highest payout. Thus one would select A_1 if consumer responses were known to be "very favorable" or "favorable" and A_2 if they were known to be "unfavorable." The resultant EMV(C) is then:

$$EMV(C) = \$300,000(.4) + \$100,000(.3) + \$0(.3)$$
$$= \$150,000$$

Therefore

$$EMVPI = \$150,000 - \$90,000 = \$60,000$$

Under no circumstances should the manager making these judgments be willing to spend more than $60,000 on marketing research. Marketing research information is never perfect. Many errors are likely to be in the findings, so the amount this manager should in fact be willing to spend will be substantially less than $60,000; the exact amount depends on the value of imperfect information. We will develop procedures for valuing imperfect information later in this chapter. To understand this material properly, we must first grasp certain rules of probability theory.

THE NECESSARY PROBABILITY THEORY

We begin this section on probability theory by considering a number of definitions.

Some Definitions

Conditional Probability Conditional probability is the probability assigned to an event when another event is known or assumed to have occurred. In symbols we can write $P(A/B)$, which reads "the probability of A given B." For example, one might assign a probability of .9 that a certain football team will win the big game, given that the star quarterback is not injured.

Joint Probability Joint probability is the probability that two or more events will occur. In symbols we can write $P(A$ and $B)$, which reads "the probability of A and B." For example, one might assign a probability of .2 that both the football and basketball teams will win their weekend games.

Unconditional Probability Unconditional probability is the probability assigned to an event that is independent of other events. It is also called *marginal probability*. It can be calculated by adding the probabilities of all the joint events of which it is a part. For example, if $P(A$ and $B) = .2$ and $P(A$ and $C) = .3$, then $P(A) = .5$.

The decision theory approach makes use of relationships among all these probability concepts. To apply these concepts properly we must be familiar with certain rules of probability theory.

Rules

Addition Rule The addition law states that given the two events A and B,

$$P(A \text{ or } B) = P(A) + P(B) - P(A \text{ and } B)$$

If the two events are mutually exclusive, then

$$P(A \text{ or } B) = P(A) + P(B)$$

Multiplication Rule The multiplication law states that given the two events A and B,

$$P(A \text{ and } B) = P(A/B) \cdot P(B) \tag{27-1}$$

If the two events are independent, then

$$P(A \text{ and } B) = P(A) \cdot P(B)$$

Bayes' Rule We could rearrange Equation 27-1 to yield what is called Bayes' rule, which is that

$$P(A/B) = \frac{P(A \text{ and } B)}{P(B)}$$

In words, the conditional probability of A given B is equal to the joint probability of A and B divided by the unconditional probability of B. This formula could be rewritten as

$$P(A/B) = \frac{P(A) \cdot P(B/A)}{P(A) \cdot P(B/A) + P(A') \cdot P(B/A')}$$

The numerator is simply the application of the multiplication rule for nonindependent events, and the denominator is simply the application of the fact that an unconditional or marginal probability is the sum of the joint probabilities where it occurs. In this latter formula A' represents events other than A.

We now have the necessary probability theory stated. We are ready to undertake the remaining two types of decision theory analysis.

POSTERIOR ANALYSIS

Posterior analysis requires the straightforward application of Bayes' rule; prior information is combined with additional information to provide revised probability estimates. Posterior analysis values both present and additional information. These posterior (revised) probabilities are then used to calculate a posterior $EMV(A_i)$.

An example will make this clear. Suppose that, on the basis of pretest results, we wish to revise our prior probabilities of A_1 in our soft-drink promotion problem. Table 27-6 presents the necessary information. In the first two columns of this table we have identified the three possible outcomes and their respective prior probabilities. Now suppose a pretest result on this promotion was "very favorable." To update the prior probabilities, the manager must assess the conditional probability of getting a very favorable pretest given the various possible outcomes. In symbols, the manager must assess $P(R/S_i)$, where R is the very favorable pretest. Column 3 of Table 27-6 presents one such assessment. For example, this manager has assigned a probability of .7 of getting the very favorable pretest, given that the true outcome is indeed very favorable. The joint probability of R and S_i, $P(R \text{ and } S_i)$, is obtained by multiplying columns 2

Table 27-6 An Example of Posterior Analysis

	Probabilities			
Outcome S_i (1)	Prior $P(S_i)$ (2)	Conditional* $P(R/S_i)$ (3)	Joint $P(R \text{ and } S_i)$ (4)	Posterior $P(S_i/R)$ (5)
S_1	.400	.700	.280	.757†
S_2	.300	.200	.060	.162
S_3	.300	.100	.030	.081
Totals	1.00		$P(R) = .370$	1.00

Posterior EMV(A_1) = \$300,000(.757) + \$100,000(.162) − \$200,000(.081)
= \$227,100

*R = very favorable pretest result.
†$P(S_1/R)$ = 280/.370 = .757.

and 3. This is just an application of the multiplication rule. The unconditional probability of getting a very favorable pretest, $P(R)$, is equal to the sum of all the joint probabilities where R occurs, $P(R) = .370$ in this example. The posterior probabilities are obtained by applying Bayes' rule. Here we want the $P(S_i/R)$. That is, we want the probability of various outcomes given the test results. For example, to calculate $P(S_1/R)$ we use the formula

$$P(S_1/R) = \frac{P(R \text{ and } S_1)}{P(R)}$$
$$= .280/.370 = .757$$

Thus the posterior probability of S_1 given this pretest result is .757. The probabilities of the other outcomes are calculated in a similar manner.

The posterior EMV(A_1) = \$300,000(.757) + \$100,000(.162) − \$200,000(.081) = \$227,100. Thus on the basis of the pretest the manager is able to recalculate the EMV of each alternative. At this point the EMV(C) will have changed to \$300,000(.757) + \$100,000(.162) + \$0(.081) = \$243,300. Therefore the new EMVPI = \$243,300 − \$227,100 = \$16,200. Prior to doing the pretest the EMVPI was \$60,000. This should make sense. New information has reduced the uncertainty and thus the value of additional information.

The decision theory approach may also be used to evaluate the worth of research before this research is undertaken. This type of decision theory analysis is called preposterior analysis, the topic to which we now turn our attention.

PREPOSTERIOR ANALYSIS

If one is willing to make certain probability assessments, *preposterior analysis* will allow the value of alternative research studies to be measured prior to the research being undertaken. This value is referred to as the expected monetary value of imperfect information (EMVII). In our soft-drink example we know that the EMVII must be less than $60,000, since this was the amount of the EMVPI. What follows is a simple example of how to calculate the EMVII for one specific study design. In performing this type of an analysis we must recognize that a research study will cost money; thus, we also need to calculate this expected monetary value net of the cost of the research. We define this value as the expected monetary gain of imperfect information (EMGII). In symbols,

EMGII = EMVII − cost of information

In our example, we shall also calculate the EMGII. Actually, many alternative research designs could be considered in this fashion. We would select that design with the most positive EMGII. Clearly if the EMGII were negative, we would not undertake the research.

Preposterior analysis involves the following steps:

1 List the possible research outcomes and calculate their unconditional or marginal probabilities.

2 Assume, in turn, that each of the research outcomes has been obtained. For each research outcome, (a) calculate posterior probabilities; (b) calculate the expected payoff of each course of action under consideration and select the act with the highest expected payoff; (c) multiply the expected payoff of the best course of action by the marginal probability of the research outcome.

3 Sum the products of step 2c (taken for each research outcome) to get the expected payoff of the strategy that includes ordering research before taking final action.[6]

4 Calculate the EMVII.

5 Calculate the EMGII.

6 Choose the strategy with the highest EMGII if at least one strategy has a positive EMGII; otherwise choose the strategy without research that has the highest EMV.

An example should make these steps clear. Suppose that the manager was considering undertaking a market test of the special soft-drink promotion. The cost of this test would be $3500. Figure 27-2 presents the structure of the problem in decision tree form. Note that the decision to be made is whether to market-test, and that the internal branches of the tree contain the original decision problem about whether to run the special promotion. The sequence is in chronological order. The test market decision comes first, then the test market (if it is undertaken), then the choice of decision alternatives about the promotion, then the possible outcomes of this latter decision. Also note that the prior probabilities of various outcomes are assigned to the top fork of the tree and that the EMV of the best decision without research is $90,000, as calculated in our prior analysis. Now we shall proceed to go through the steps of a preposterior analysis.

[6] Items 1–3, ibid., p. 24.

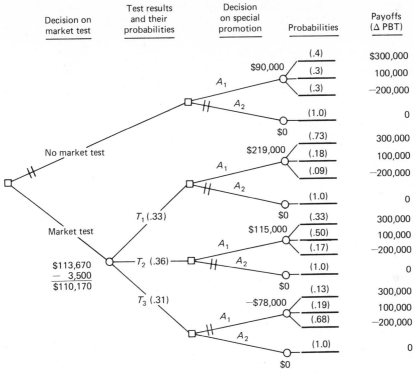

Figure 27-2 Decision tree for soft-drink special promotion problem: no market test versus market test. [Source: Joseph W. Newman, *Management Applications of Decision Theory*, (New York: Harper & Row, 1971), p. 25.]

Step 1   Three research outcomes are thought possible: a 15 percent increase in sales (T_1), a 5 percent increase in sales (T_2), and no sales increase (T_3). To obtain the marginal probabilities of T_1, T_2, and T_3, one could reason as follows: If the promotion were run as planned and received a very favorable consumer reaction, what is the probability of T_1, T_2 and T_3 occurring? This is the $P(T_i/S_1)$. One such set of assessments is given in the first line of Table 27-7. For example, we note that the conditional probability of finding T_1 given that S_1 would be found is .6. The other two lines of this table present the conditional probabilities of various test results given other possible consumer reactions, S_2 and S_3. These assessments are in essence a judgment about the ability of particular research designs to find the true situation. These $P(T_i/S_i)$'s are multiplied by the prior probabilities, $P(S_i)$, to yield joint probabilities, as found in Table 27-8. For example, $P(S_1 \text{ and } T_1) = P(S_1) \cdot P(T_1/S_1) = (.4)(.6) = .24$. The marginal probability of each T_i can be obtained by adding the joint probabilities where T_i occurs. Thus we find: $P(T_1) = .33$, $P(T_2) = .36$, and $P(T_3) = .31$. These probabilities are recorded on the decision tree in Figure 27-2.

Step 2   Next we can revise the prior probabilities of the possible outcomes

Table 27-7 Conditional Probabilities of Market Test Results

States of consumer reactions to special promotion if run as proposed	Test results		
	T_1 (+15%)	T_2 (+5%)	T_3 (±0)
S_1 (very favorable)	.6	.3	.1
S_2 (favorable)	.2	.6	.2
S_3 (unfavorable)	.1	.2	.7

Source: Joseph W. Newman, *Management Applications of Decision Theory* (New York: Harper & Row, 1971), p. 25.

given that various test results have occurred. To do this we use Bayes' rule. For example,

$$P(S_1/T_1) = \frac{P(S_1 \text{ and } T_1)}{P(T_1)} = \frac{.24}{.33} = .73$$

$$P(S_2/T_1) = .06/.33 = .18$$

$$P(S_3/T_1) = .03/.33 = .09$$

These calculations are recorded for the possible outcomes along the T_1, branch of the tree. Similar calculations are easily made for the S_i's given T_2 and T_3. These results are recorded on the decision tree. The expected payout of each alternative is recalculated using the revised probabilities. Thus the expected payoff of running T_1 is $219,000; T_2, $115,000; and T_3, − $78,000. If T_1 or T_2 were observed, we would choose A_1, but if T_3 were observed we would choose A_2. Thus the best courses of action and payoffs are $T_1 = \$219,999$, $T_2 = \$115,000$, and $T_3 = \$0$. These three best payoffs are then multiplied by their associated $P(T_i)$.

Step 3 The sum of the best outcomes, each multiplied by its respective $P(T_i)$, equals $113,670 [$219,000(.33) + $115,000(.36) + $0(.31)].

Table 27-8 Joint Probabilities of States and Market Test Results

States of consumer reactions to special promotion if run as proposed	Test results			Marginal probabilities
	T_1 (+15%)	T_2 (+5%)	T_3 (±0%)	
S_1 (very favorable)	.24	.12	.04	.4
S_2 (favorable)	.06	.18	.06	.3
S_3 (unfavorable)	.03	.06	.21	.3
Marginal probabilities	.33	.36	.31	1.00

Source: Joseph W. Newman, *Management Applications of Decision Theory* (New York: Harper & Row, 1971), p. 26.

Step 4   Now we are in a position to calculate EMVII.

$$EMVII = EMV(\text{with test}) - EMV(\text{without test})$$
$$= \$113,670 \qquad - \$90,000$$
$$= \$23,670$$

This is the absolute maximum we would be willing to pay for this research.

Step 5   The net gain of the study can also be calculated.

$$EMGII = EMVII - \text{cost of study}$$
$$= \$23,670 - \$3,500$$
$$= \$20,170$$

Step 6   Since the EMGII is positive, we would choose to do the market test. It is possible that alternative designs for this test may be possible, each having different costs and conditional probabilities, $P(T_i/S_i)$. We could calculate the EMGII for each of these, just as we have done here, and select that study with the highest EMGII. Clearly if EMGII is negative, we are better off making the decision without research.

ADVANTAGES AND LIMITATIONS

The decision theory approach has a number of advantages, including (1) the rigor of requiring the manager to structure the problem completely; (2) the rigor of having to specify the value of each outcome; (3) the ability to determine the expected value of alternatives before and after research; and (4) the ability to determine the expected value of alternative research projects before undertaking the research. These are indeed major benefits of this approach. However, we must temper these positive aspects with some strong limitations—for example, (1) the lack of knowledge among managers and researchers of the procedures of this approach; (2) the inability or unwillingness of managers to structure problems completely and identify outcomes; (3) the inability or unwillingness of managers to make the necessary conditional probability judgments; and (4) the general unwillingness of managers to expose their thinking in such an explicit manner. For the present, therefore, the decision theory approach remains a powerful theoretical tool that has obtained some usage in sophisticated organizations.[7] It is for the future to judge its long-term practical value.

[7] For some applications see Rex V. Brown, "Do Managers Find Decision Theory Useful?" *Harvard Business Review*, May–June 1970, pp. 78–89.

SUMMARY

1 In the face of uncertainty a decision maker may adopt a number of decision criteria. The decision theory approach uses the EMV or EUV criterion.

2 Prior analysis involves the selection of an alternative before any additional information is collected.

3 EMVPI = EMV(C) − EMV(UC).

4 EMVPI represents the absolute theoretical limit on research expenditures.

5 Posterior analysis involves the combining of prior information with additional information to provide revised probability estimates. The revised probability estimates are then used to calculate the EMV of each alternative.

6 Preposterior analysis allows one to measure the value of alternative research studies before undertaking the research.

7 EMVII is the measure of the value of a study.

8 EMVII = EMV(with study) − EMV(without study).

9 EMGII = EMVII − cost of study.

10 One selects the research design with the most positive EMGII. If EMGII is negative, the decision should be made without research.

DISCUSSION QUESTIONS

1 What is uncertainty?

2 What decision criteria can be applied to a decision under uncertainty? Describe each one.

3 What are the steps in the decision theory approach?

4 How is the EMVPI calculated?

5 What happens to EMVPI after research is undertaken?

6 What is posterior analysis?

7 How are prior probabilities made posterior?

8 What is preposterior analysis?

9 How is the EMVII calculated?

10 How is the EMGII calculated?

11 What criterion is used to select among alternative research designs? When is research not undertaken?

SUGGESTED READING

Newman, Joseph W., *Management Applications of Decision Theory* (New York: Harper & Row, 1971). This short book is the most readable applied book related to decision theory in marketing.

Schlaifer, Robert, *Analysis of Decisions under Uncertainty* (New York: McGraw-Hill, 1969). This book is a classic elementary mathematical treatment of all aspects of decision theory.

Glossary

Absolute frequency A measure of dispersion for nominal data, defined as the number of the total elements appearing in a given category.

Absolute precision Precision expressed in units.

Acquired source A source which has procured data from an original or primary source.

Affective component One of three main components of attitudes, concerned with a person's feelings regarding an object or phenomenon (in a marketing model, includes liking and preference stages).

Aided recall An approach to questioning which provides the respondent with cues regarding the event of interest.

Alternative forms reliability Estimating reliability by giving the respondent two forms which are judged equivalent but not identical and comparing the two measurements for degree of discrepancy in scores, as in the test-retest approach.

Alternative hypothesis A hypothesis that states a population parameter, taking on a different value from that stated in the null hypothesis.

Analysis of covariance (ANCOVA) A dependence method of multivariate data analysis appropriate for use with an intervally scaled dependent variable, nominally scaled independent variables, and one or more intervally scaled covariates; useful in assessing the effects of extraneous sources of variation in an experiment ex post facto.

Analysis of variance (ANOVA) A method of analysis used when dealing with one intervally scaled dependent variable and one or more nominally scaled independent variables; used primarily in the analysis of experiments to determine whether treatment population means are equal.

Applied research   Investigation whose aim is to assist managers in decision making.

Area sampling   A form of sequential cluster sampling which samples areas in the first $n - 1$ stages and elements in the nth stage.

Attitude   An individual's enduring perceptual, knowledge-based, evaluative, and action-oriented processes with respect to an object or phenomenon.

Attitude scaling   The various operational definitions developed for the measurement of the construct "attitude."

Automatic interaction detector (AID)   A dependence method of multivariate data analysis appropriate for use with an intervally scaled dependent variable and nominally scaled independent variables; a technique which involves the repeated application of one-way ANOVA to reduce the total sample to a number of subgroups which are more homogeneous on the dependent variable than the sample as a whole.

Balanced scale   A rating scale providing the same number of favorable and unfavorable categories.

Bar chart   A graphic presentation of magnitude in the dataset depicted by the length of various bars which have been laid out with reference to a horizontal or vertical scale.

Basic research   Investigation whose aim is to extend the boundaries of knowledge regarding some aspect of the marketing system.

Bayes' rule

$$P(A/B) = \frac{P(A \cap B)}{P(B)} = \frac{P(A) \cdot P(B/A)}{[P(A) \cdot P(B/A)] + [P(A') \cdot P(B/A')]}$$

The conditional probability of A given B equals the joint probability of A and B divided by the unconditional probability of B.

Behavioral component   One of three main components of attitudes, concerned with a person's readiness to respond behaviorally to an object or phenomenon (in a marketing model, includes intention-to-buy and purchase stages).

Bipolar adjectives   A pair of adjectives defining opposite ends of a continuum regarding some attitude or belief; used in the semantic differential scale.

Bivariate analysis   The analyses of two variables at a time.

Blocking   A method for attempting to control external effects from experiments.

Buying income method   One method of projecting the results of a test marketing program to national performance, based on income and estimated as:

$$\text{National sales estimate} = \frac{\text{total U.S. income}}{\text{test area income}} \times \text{test area sales}$$

Canonical correlation   A dependence method of multivariate data analysis appropriate for use with a set of intervally scaled dependent variables and a set of intervally scaled independent variables.

Cartoon completion   A technique in which the respondent is presented with a cartoon drawing depicting people in a situation and is asked to complete a cartoon in response to the comment of another cartoon character.

Case   A specific unit of analysis for a study, typically the respondent.

Case history   The intensive study of situations which are relevant to a particular decision problem in order to gain insight into the variables operating in the situation.

Causal research   A mode of conclusive research designed to gather evidence regarding cause-and-effect relationships.

Census A study using all available elements of a defined population.

Central-limit theorem The fundamental theorem of probability sampling. It allows one to measure sampling error, and it identifies that the sampling distribution of the mean is normal when (1) the population distribution is normal for all sample sizes and (2) the sample size increases ($n \geq 30$) for nonnormal population distributions.

Central tendency measures One type of descriptive statistics, including such measures as the mean, median, and mode.

Chi-square test A test designed for comparing a hypothesized population distribution with a distribution obtained by sampling; with nominal variables in either univariate or bivariate analysis.

Closed-ended question A question on a data collection instrument with structured answers.

Cluster analysis An interdependence multivariate data analysis technique which uses as input a matrix of associations between variables or objects; the technique forms subgroupings and assigns variables or objects to these groups.

Cluster sampling Sampling in which clusters or groups of elements are randomly selected. It is composed of two steps: (1) the population is divided into mutually exclusive and collectively exhaustive groups, and (2) a probability sample of the groups is selected.

Codebook A listing of the documentation of the coding scheme and other information regarding the variables in a dataset.

Coding In the research process, establishing categories for responses or groups of responses such that numerals can be used to represent the categories.

Coefficient of determination, r^2 The exact percentage of variation shared by two variables, obtained by squaring the correlation coefficient.

Coefficient of multiple determination In multiple regression, the proportion of the variation in Y explained by the regression, which can be calculated as $SS_{explained}/SS_{total}$.

Coefficient of variation. An expression for the standard deviation as a percentage of the mean, formally defined as $CV = S/\bar{X}$.

Cognitive component One of three main components of attitudes, concerned with a person's beliefs about some object or phenomenon (in the marketing behavioral response model, includes the awareness and knowledge stages).

Communality In factor analysis, the proportion of a variable's total variation that is involved in the factors; defined mathematically as the sum of the squared loading of a variable on all factors (h^2).

Communication method A general method of collecting data involving the questioning of respondents, either verbally or by means of written questionnaires.

Communication techniques One type of attitude measurement procedure, including such techniques as self-reports, responses to unstructured or partially structured stimuli, and performance of objective tasks, in which the measurement process is based on some sort of communicated response by the subject.

Completely randomized design (CRD) The simplest type of designed experiment; it involves only one independent variable, and the treatments are assigned to test units at random.

Computer card The basic device used for converting data to a computer-readable form; a heavy-stock paper card containing 80 columns for data input.

Conclusive research Research designed to help the decision maker evaluate courses of action and select the best one.

Concomitant variation The extent to which a cause, X, and an effect, Y, occur together or vary together as hypothesized.

Concurrent validity A method of assessing validity which involves correlating two different measurements of the same marketing phenomena which have been administered at the same point in time.

Conditional association The association between two variables conditional on one or more control variables.

Conditional probability The probability assigned to an event when another event has occurred or is assumed to have occurred; in symbols, $P(A/B)$, the probability of A given B.

Confounding variable An uncontrolled extraneous variable, the effect of which is to invalidate conclusions from an experiment.

Conjoint measurement A dependence method of multivariate data analysis appropriate for use with an ordinally scaled dependent variable and nominally scaled independent variables; essentially an analysis of variance of rank-order data which generates intervally scaled measures of the effects of the categories of the independent variables.

Consistent estimator A statistic which approaches the population parameter as sample size increases is said to be a consistent estimator.

Construct validity A means of estimating validity which relies on an understanding of the theoretical rationale underlying the obtained measurements.

Content validity Assessing validity by the subjective judgment of an expert as to the appropriateness of the measurements.

Contingency planning Specification of alternative courses of action by an organization to meet invalid planning assumptions or unanticipated changes in the situational factors.

Contrived observation An observation technique in which an artificial environment is created and the behavior of persons put in the environment is observed.

Control markets Test market cities in which a research supply house has paid retailers for a guarantee that they will carry products designated by the supply house; also known as minimarkets.

Convenience sample A sample which is selected on the basis of the convenience of the researcher.

Correlation coefficient, r A bivariate descriptive statistic, appropriate when dealing with two intervally scaled variables, which provides a measure of the linear direction and strength of the relationship between these variables.

Cross-sectional design A research design (typically associated with descriptive research) which involves taking a sample of population elements at one point in time.

Cross-tabulation table A matrix display of the categories of two nominally scaled variables, containing frequency counts of the number of subjects in each bivariate category.

Data Observations and evidence regarding some aspect of the marketing system.

Data deck The complete set of computer cards containing all the data from a given study.

Data matrix A rectangular array of data storage with n rows and m columns, where the number of rows equals the number of cases and the number of columns equals the number of variables.

Decision criteria The rules for selecting among courses of action given various data outcomes.

Decision problem A situation in which management has an objective to accomplish, two or more alternative courses of action exist which may reach the objective, and uncertainty is present regarding the best course of action.

Degrees of freedom   The number of independent observations on the variable of interest minus the number of statistics calculated.

Dependence methods   Multivariate data analysis procedures that specify a dependent variable.

Dependent variable   The presumed effect in a cause-and-effect relationship.

Depth interview   An unstructured personal interview using extensive probing in such a way that the respondent talks freely and expresses detailed beliefs and feelings on a topic.

Descriptive research   Marketing research aimed at characterizing marketing phenomena and identifying association among selected variables.

Descriptive statistics   The branch of statistics that provides researchers with summary measures for the data in samples.

Deterministic causation   The ''common-sense'' concept of causality, in which a single event (cause) always results in another event (effect).

Dichotomous question   A form of multiple-choice question which provides only two response alternatives.

Discriminant analysis   A dependence method of multivariate data analysis appropriate for use with a nominally scaled dependent variable and intervally scaled independent variables; a technique which derives a linear combination of the independent variables such that the mean scores across categories of the dependent variable on this linear combination are maximally different.

Disguised observation   Observation techniques in which the respondents are not aware that they are being observed.

Disproportionate stratified sampling   Sampling in which the overall sample size is allocated to strata on a basis disproportionate with the population sizes of the strata.

Division   A geographic unit of the Census Bureau, third highest in level of aggregation; the regions are divided into nine divisions.

Dummy-variable multiple regression   A dependence method of multivariate data analysis appropriate for use with an intervally scaled dependent variable and nominally scaled independent variables; an extension of multiple regression to less than interval data through the creation of a series of binary variables coded as 0-1.

Editing   The process of reviewing the data collection instruments to ensure maximum accuracy and unambiguity; checks for legibility, consistency, and completeness.

Effect   In ANOVA, a difference in treatments means from the grand mean.

Efficient estimator   An estimator that has the minimum variance.

Eigenvalue   In factor analysis, the amount of variation in the data accounted for by a factor.

Element   The unit in a sample about which information is sought.

Expected monetary gain of imperfect information (EMGII)   The value of a research study net of its cost. Used in decision theory; calculated as EMGII = EMVII − cost of information.

Expected monetary value criterion (EMV)   Select the alternative with the highest expected monetary value.

Expected monetary value of imperfect information (EMVII)   In marketing research terms, the measure of the value of a study; calculated as EMVII = EVM (with study) − EMV (without study).

Expected utility value criterion (EUV)   Select the alternative with the highest expected utility value; this takes into account one's attitude toward risk as well as monetary payouts.

Expected value of perfect information (EMVPI)   Equal to EMV(C) − EMV(UC); this represents the gain over expected outcomes under uncertainty and represents the absolute theoretical limit of the amount one would be willing to pay for perfect information.

Ex post facto   Searching for a cause following the observation of the effect.

Experiment   A process in which a person consciously manipulates or controls one or more independent variables and measure their effect on the dependent variable(s).

Experimental design   The specification of treatments, test units, dependent variables, and extraneous variables to be considered in an experiment.

Exploratory research   Research designed to formulate hypotheses regarding potential problems and/or opportunities present in the decision situation.

External data   Data obtained from a source other than the organization for which the research is being conducted.

External validity   The generalizability of experimental results to test units other than those used.

Extraneous variable   Any variable other than the treatments that affects the response of the test unit to the treatments.

Extreme case   A response on a variable that is so far out of the ordinary that it might represent a coding or punching error.

Factor analysis   An interdependence multivariate analysis method which takes a large number of variables or objects and attempts to find a small number of factors in common which account for their intercorrelation.

Factorial design   An experimental design useful for measuring simultaneously the effects of two or more independent variables.

Field operation   That phase of the research project which makes contact with the respondent, administers the data collection instrument, records the data, and returns the data to a central location for processing.

Fixed effects model   An ANOVA procedure in which inferences about differences among treatments administered are made, but no interpolation between treatments is made.

Focus group interview   A loosely structured interview conducted by a trained moderator simultaneously among a small number of respondents; also known as a group depth interview.

Forced scale   A rating scale which does not include a "no opinion" or "no knowledge" category and thus requires respondents to indicate a position on the attitude scale.

Grand mean   In ANOVA, the mean of all observations across all treatment groups.

Hierarchy-of-effects model   A marketing behavioral response model consisting of stages which a buyer is hypothesized to pass through, including awareness, knowledge, liking, preference, intention to buy, and purchase.

History   An extraneous variable referring to the occurrence of specific events that are external but concurrent to the experiment.

Hypothesis   A conjectural statement about the value of a variable or the relationship between two or more variables.

Independent variable   The presumed cause in a cause-and-effect relationship.

Indirect observation   Observation techniques in which some record of past behavior is used rather than observing behavior as it occurs.

Indirect scale   A self-reporting technique in which the respondent's judgments on several questions are combined in order to develop a measure of his or her position on the attitude in question.

Inferential statistics   The branch of statistics that allows researchers to make judgments concerning the population based on the results generated by samples.

Information   Data which reduce the uncertainty in a decision situation.

Instrumentation   An extraneous variable referring to changes in the calibration of the measuring instrument used or changes in the observers or scorers used.

Interaction effect   The effect (that the total effect is greater than the sum of their main effects) which occurs when the relationship between an independent variable and the dependent variable is different for different categories of another independent variable.

Interdependence methods   Multivariate data analysis methods in which no variable or variables are designated as dependent on others.

Internal data   Data that originate within the organization for which research is being conducted.

Internal validity   The extent to which experimental results are caused by the treatment variables as opposed to extraneous variables.

Interval scale   A scale of measurement in which the distances among the numbers correspond to the distances among the objects or events on the characteristic being measured; intervals between numbers are assumed to be equal.

Item nonresponse error   The refusal by the respondent to answer a question or series of questions.

Joint probability   The probability that two or more events will occur; in symbols, $P(A \cap B)$, the probability of A and B.

Judgment sample   A sample which is selected on the basis of what some expert thinks particular sampling units or elements will contribute to answering the research question at hand.

Laplace criterion   Select the alternative with the highest average value.

Latin square design   An experimental design useful for controlling and measuring the effects of two extraneous variables.

Level of confidence   The probability of not rejecting the null hypothesis when it is true, equal to $1 - \alpha$.

Levels   The categories of the independent variables in a factorial design experiment.

Likert scale   An indirect scale in which the respondent indicates the degree of agreement or disagreement with each of a series of statements; each response is subsequently numerically scored by the researcher, and a summary score for each respondent is obtained.

Line chart   A graphic presentation of magnitude in the dataset depicted by the slope of a line (or lines) which has been laid out with reference to a horizontal or vertical scale.

Longitudinal design   A research design in which a fixed sample of population elements is measured over time.

Marketing information system (MIS)   The systematic and continuous gathering, analysis, and reporting of data for decision-making purposes.

Marketing mix   Those independent variables over which the organization exerts some degree of control (product, price, place, and promotion).

Marketing research   The systematic and objective approach to the development and provision of information for the marketing management decision-making process.

Marketing research system   An information center for decision making.

Maturation   An extraneous variable concerned with changes in the experimental units that occur over time.

Maximax criterion   Select the alternative that maximizes the maximum payoff.

Maximin criterion   Select the alternative that maximizes the minimum payoff.

Mean   A measure of central tendency for interval data; the average value.

Measurement The assignment of numbers to characteristics of objects or events according to rules.

Measures of dispersion A type of descriptive statistic, including such measures as the standard deviation, coefficient of variation, interquartile range, and relative and absolute frequencies.

Mechanical observation Observation techniques involving mechanical observers in conjunction with or in place of human observers. Examples are the motion picture camera, the Audimeter, the psychogalvanometer, the eye-camera, and the pupilometer.

Median A measure of central tendency for ordinal data, defined for ungrouped data as the middle value when the data are arranged in order of magnitude.

Minimax regret criterion The alternative selected with the minimum opportunity loss.

Mixed effects model An ANOVA procedure including independent variables of both the fixed and random types.

Mode A measure of central tendency for nominal data, defined as the category which occurs with the greatest frequency.

Multidimensional scaling An interdependence multivariate data analysis method which uses as input a matrix of relationships between objects with unknown underlying dimensionality, determines the minimum dimensionality of the relationships between the objects, and positions each object on each dimension.

Multiple-choice question A question which requires the respondent to select or answer from among a list provided in the question proper or following the question.

Multiple correlation coefficient In multiple regression, the correlation coefficient between the observed Y_i and the estimated $\hat{Y}_i$'s.

Multiple regression A dependence method of multivariate data analysis appropriate for use with an intervally scaled dependent variable and intervally scaled independent variables; an extension of the simple regression technique to more than one independent variable.

Multivariate analysis The analysis of more than two variables at a time.

Multivariate analysis of variance A dependence method of multivariate data analysis appropriate for use with two or more intervally scaled dependent variables and one or more intervally scaled independent variables; the multivariate extension of ANOVA to more than one dependent variable.

Nominal scale A measurement scale in which numbers serve only as labels to identify or categorize objects or events.

Nonprobability sampling A sampling procedure in which the selection of population elements is based in part on the judgment of the researcher or field interviewer.

Nonresponse errors The differences on measures between those who respond to a survey and those who do not respond.

Nonsampling errors All the errors that may occur in the marketing research process, except the sampling error.

Null hypothesis The hypothesis which states that a population parameter takes on a particular value or set of values.

O An experimental design symbol, referring to processes of observation or measurement of the dependent variable on the test units.

Observation method A general method of collecting data from respondents in which the respondent's behavior is recorded.

Observation techniques A type of attitude measurement procedure, which includes such techniques as overt behavior and physiological reaction measurement, in which the procedure is based on observing the behavior of the subject.

Omnibus panel   A fixed sample of respondents measured on different variables over a period of time.

One-tailed test   The situation in which the alternative hypothesis is stated such that one specific direction (one tail of the possible distribution of values) is considered.

One-way ANOVA   ANOVA applied to a CRD, in which it is applied to categories of one independent variable.

Open-ended question   A question which requires respondents to provide their own answers.

Opportunity   The presence of a situation where performance can be improved by undertaking new activities.

Ordinal scale   A scale of measurement which defines the ordered relationships among objects or events.

Original source   The source which generated the data.

Overall efficiency   A relative assessment of a sampling procedure based on its statistical efficiency and cost; defined as the cost per standard error.

Paired comparison scale   A self-reporting technique presenting the respondent with two objects from a set and requiring the respondent to pick one with regard to the attitude in question.

Parameter   A summary description of a measure in the defined population.

Performance-monitoring research   Research designed to provide information about the outcomes of marketing activities.

Periodicity   In systematic sampling, a cyclical pattern within a list of elements forming the sampling frame that coincides with a multiple of the size of the sampling interval.

Pie chart   A circle divided into sections such that the size of each section corresponds to a portion of the total.

Population   The aggregate of the elements defined prior to the selection of the sample.

Posterior analysis   The combination of prior information with additional information to provide revised (posterior) probability estimates, which are then used to calculate a posterior EMV.

Power of test   The probability of rejecting a false null hypothesis, equal to $1 - \beta$.

Precision   The width of a confidence interval expressed either absolutely in units or relative to the size of the mean.

Predictive validity   A means of assessing validity which involves the ability of a measure of marketing phenomena to predict other marketing phenomena.

Preexperimental design   Experimental designs with inherent weaknesses such that questionable internal validity results.

Preposterior analysis   A method of analysis allowing the researcher to measure the value of alternative research studies prior to undertaking the research.

Pretesting   The initial testing of one or more aspects of the research design.

Prior analysis   The application of the decision theory approach when the probabilities of outcomes are assessed on the basis of present judgment, without benefit of additional information.

Probabilistic causation   The scientific concept of causality, in which one event or a series of events result in the probable occurrence of another.

Probability sampling   A sampling procedure in which each element of the population has a known chance of being selected for the sample.

Problem   Those independent variables that cause the organization's performance measures to be below objective.

Profile analysis   A method of analyzing semantic differential data, in which an arithmetic mean or median is calculated for each set of polar opposites for each object evaluated.

Programmed decisions   Decisions of a repetitive nature for which the manager's experience and judgment provide the key input.

Proportionate stratified sampling   Stratified sampling in which the number of elements drawn from each stratum is proportionate to the relative number of elements in each stratum of the population.

***Q*-type analysis**   A case-wise factor analysis.

Qualitative research   Questioning knowledgeable respondents individually or in small groups regarding the "why" of behavior.

Quantitative research   Questioning large groups of respondents regarding the "what, when, where, and how" of behavior.

Quasi experimentation   An experimental design in which the researcher has control over data collection procedures but lacks complete control over the scheduling or randomization of the treatments.

Questionnaire   A formalized schedule for collecting data from respondents.

Quota sample   A sample selected so as to match the population on some prespecified "control" characteristics.

R   An experimental design symbol, indicating that a randomizing process has been used in assigning test units and treatments.

***R*-type analysis**   A factor analysis calculated by variables.

Random-digit dialing   A telephone interviewing technique in which the sample is determined randomly through the random generation of at least some of the telephone digits.

Random effects model   An ANOVA procedure in which interpolation of results between treatments is allowed.

Random error   Bias in the measurements caused by the transient aspects of the respondent or measurement setting.

Random number list   A list of numbers that have no pattern of occurrence.

Randomized block design (RBD)   An experimental design in which test units are blocked on the basis of some external criterion variable, in such a way that scores within the blocks on the dependent variable are likely to be more homogeneous than in the absence of blocking.

Rank-order scale   A self-reporting technique in which the respondent ranks various objects with regard to the attitude in question.

Rating scale   A self-reporting scale involving ordinal, interval, or ratio scales in which the respondent indicates the position on a continuum or among ordered categories corresponding to his or her attitude; includes both graphic rating scales and verbal rating scales.

Ratio scale   A scale of measurement which has all the properties of an interval scale plus an absolute zero point.

Recognition method   Aided recall in which the actual event is presented to the respondent.

Region   A geographic unit of the Census Bureau, second highest in level of aggregation; the United States is divided into four regions.

Relative frequency   A measure of dispersion for nominal data, defined as the percentage of the total elements appearing in a given category.

Relative precision   Precision expressed as a percentage of the mean.

Reliability   The extent to which the measurement process is free from random errors.

Respondent characteristics   One of three types of data which can be obtained from respondents to forecast market behavior; this type describes respondents on demographic, socioeconomic, and psychological characteristics.

Research design   The basic plan which guides the data collection and analysis phases of the research project.

Research report   The presentation of the research findings directed to a specific audience to accomplish a specific purpose.

Response bias   An inaccurate response, resulting from such factors as respondent fatigue, boredom, desire to please, etc.

Role playing   A technique in which the respondent is presented with a verbal or visual situation and asked how the beliefs and feelings of another person relate to the situation; also known as the third-person technique.

Sales ratio method   A method of projecting the results of a test marketing program to national performance, based on sales of another brand and estimated as:

$$\text{National sales estimate} = \frac{\text{national sales of other product}}{\text{test area sales of this other product}} \times \text{test area sales of test product}$$

Sampling distribution   The distribution formed by a statistic that is calculated for each of all possible samples of a certain size from a given population.

Sampling error   The difference between the observed probability sample statistic and the population parameter.

Sampling fraction   The proportion of the number of sample elements to the number of population elements.

Sampling frame   A list of all the sampling units in the population.

Sampling interval   The size of the step between selected elements in systematic sampling; the reciprocal of the sampling fraction, i.e., N/n.

Sampling unit   The element or elements available for selection at some stage of the sampling process.

Secondary data   Published data which have been compiled for a purpose other than the present study.

Selection bias   The assignment of test units or treatment groups such that the groups differ on the dependent variable prior to the presentation of the treatments.

Semantic differential scale   A self-reporting scale requiring the respondent to evaluate an object on a seven-point rating scale bounded on each end by bipolar adjectives.

Sentence completion   A technique in which an incomplete sentence is presented to the respondent, who is asked to complete the sentence.

Share-of-market method   A method of projecting the results of a test marketing program to national performance, based on sales in the test area of the product category as a whole, and estimated as:

$$\text{National sales estimate} = \frac{\text{test area sales of new brand}}{\text{test area sales of this whole product category}} \times \text{national sales of this whole product category}$$

Significance level   The specified level of α indicating the probability of making a type I error.

Simple random sampling   A probability sampling procedure where each element has an equal chance of being selected and each combination of elements is equally likely.

Simple regression   A bivariate statistical procedure, applicable to intervally scaled variables, used to demonstrate how an independent variable is related to a dependent variable and to make predictions about scores on the dependent variable, given knowledge of the scores on the independent variable.

Simulation An incomplete representation of the marketing system designed to explicate the dynamics of the variables operating within that system.

Situational analysis The process of analyzing the past and future situation facing an organization in order to identify problems and opportunities.

Situational factors Independent variables that are not under the control of the organization.

Soloman four-group design A true experimental design which controls for both extraneous variable effects and interactive testing effects.

Split-half reliability Estimating reliability by dividing a multi-item measurement device into equivalent groups and correlating the item responses to estimate reliability.

Spurious relationship The observed relationship between variables when one does not really exist; the relationship disappears with elaboration.

SS_B In a randomized-block-design ANOVA, the blocking effect sum of squared deviations.

SS_C In a Latin-square-design ANOVA, the column effect sum of squared deviations.

SS_E In ANOVA, the sum of squared deviations related to error.

$SS_{INT(AB)}$ In a factorial-design ANOVA, the interaction effect sum of squared deviations.

SS_R In a Latin-square-design ANOVA, the row effect sum of squared deviations.

SS_T In ANOVA, the total sum of squared deviations from the grand mean.

SS_{TR} In ANOVA, the sum of squared deviations resulting from the treatments.

SS_{TRA} In a factorial-design ANOVA, the treatment A effect sum of squared deviations.

Standard deviation, s A measure of dispersion for interval data.

Standard error of the coefficient, s_b A measure of the amount of sampling error present in the determination of b in a regression equation; more precisely, the standard deviation of the sampling distribution of the regression coefficient.

Standard error of the estimate, s_{YX} The measure of the scatter of the actual Y_i values about a regression line $\hat{Y}_i$; more precisely, the standard deviation of Y_i about $\hat{Y}_i$.

Standard error of the mean The standard deviation of the sampling distribution of the mean.

Standard industrial classification (SIC code) A system of classification based on the products produced or operations performed which the federal government uses in its Census of Manufacturers.

Standard markets Test market cities in which no guarantees of retail distribution support are made; the traditional alternative to control markets.

Standard metropolitan statistical area (SMSA) A geographic unit of the Census Bureau consisting of a county or group of contiguous counties which contain at least one city of 50,000 inhabitants or more.

Stapel scale A modification of the semantic differential scale, using a unipolar 10-point ($+5$ to -5) nonverbal rating scale, designed to measure the direction and intensity of attitudes simultaneously.

Statistic A summary description of a measure in the selected sample.

Statistical efficiency Comparison of the standard errors generated by various sampling procedures.

Statistical regression The phenomenon that outliers tend to move toward a more average position over time.

Strategy   Broad principles as to how the marketing program is to operate in achieving objectives.

Stratified sampling   A two-stage probability sampling procedure in which the population is divided into mutually exclusive and collectively exhaustive strata, and a random sample is drawn from each stratum.

Study population   The aggregate of elements from which the sample is drawn.

Symptom   A condition that signals the presence of a problem or opportunity.

Syndicated source   A profit-making organization which provides standardized data to an array of clients.

Systematic error   Error that causes a constant bias in the measurements.

Systematic sampling   A type of cluster sampling in which every kth element is selected from the frame, after a random start somewhere within the first k elements, where k = sampling interval.

t **test**   A test designed for comparing the sample mean with a hypothesized mean of a population, appropriate for all sample sizes when σ is unknown; also designed for comparing the difference between two means.

Test marketing   The implementation and monitoring of a marketing program in a small subset of the target market areas for the product in question.

Test-retest reliability   Estimating reliability by repeating the measurement using the same scaling device under conditions which are judged to be very similar.

Test units   The entities in an experiment to whom the treatments are presented and whose response to the treatments is measured.

Test unit mortality   Test units' withdrawal from the experiment before completion.

Testing effect   An extraneous variable consisting of the effect on the experiment of taking a measure on the dependent variable before presenting the treatment. The *main testing effect* refers to the effect of the first measurement on the second measurement, while the *interactive testing effect* refers to the effect of the first measurement on the test unit's response to the treatment.

Thematic Apperception Test (TAT)   A projective technique using one or more pictures or cartoons depicting a situation and asking the respondent to describe what has happened or will happen as a result of the situation.

Time-series experiment   A quasi-experimental design involving a periodic measurement on the dependent variables for some test units.

Tracks   Alternate ways of processing the data from collection instruments to the computer.

Tracts   Small areas into which large cities and their adjacent areas have been divided for statistical purposes by the Census Bureau.

Traditional panel   A fixed sample measured over a period on the same variables.

Treatment   The alternatives which are manipulated and whose effects are measured in an experiment.

True experimental design   An experimental design in which all extraneous variables are eliminated or controlled.

Two-tailed test   The situation in which the alternative hypothesis is stated in such a way that both ends of the sampling distribution are considered (no specified directionality).

Type I error (α error)   The rejection of a true null hypothesis.

Type II error (β error)   The nonrejection of a false null hypothesis.

Unaided recall   A questioning approach which does not provide the respondent with cues as to the event.

Unbiased estimator   An estimator whose expected value is the parameter or population value.

Uncertainty   A lack of complete knowledge about the possible outcomes of actions, with the probabilities of the possible outcomes not known.

Unconditional probability   The probability assigned to an event that is independent of other events, also known as marginal probability.

Univariate analysis   The analysis of one variable at a time.

Unprogrammed decision   A decision involving a somewhat new, atypical situation in which a manager's experience and judgment are of limited usefulness.

Validity   The extent to which the measurement process is free from both systematic and random error.

Variable   A property that takes on different values at different times.

Variance   A measure of the dispersion of the distribution of an interval variable.

Wild codes   Codes that are not defined in the codebook for a particular variable.

Word association   A technique in which a series of words is presented to the respondent, who is to respond to each one with the first word which comes to mind.

X   An experimental design symbol, representing the exposure of a test group to an experimental treatment.

z **test**   A test designed for comparing the sample mean with a hypothesized mean of a population; it is appropriate for interval data when σ is known for any sample size, or for situations of sufficiently large sample size ($n > 30$) and σ unknown.

Zero-order association   Also known as total association, this is the original association between two variables, without controlling for any other variables (as contrasted with conditional association).

Appendix A

Table A-1 Abridged List of Random Numbers

10 09 73 25 33	76 52 01 35 35	34 67 35 48 76	80 95 90 91 17	39 29 27 49 45
37 54 20 48 05	64 89 47 42 96	24 80 52 40 37	20 63 61 04 02	00 82 29 16 65
08 42 26 89 53	19 64 50 93 03	23 20 90 25 60	15 95 33 47 64	35 08 03 36 06
90 01 90 25 29	09 37 67 07 15	38 31 13 11 65	88 67 67 43 97	04 43 62 76 59
12 80 79 99 70	80 15 73 61 47	64 03 23 66 53	98 95 11 68 77	12 17 17 68 33
66 06 57 47 17	34 07 27 08 50	36 69 73 61 70	65 81 33 98 85	11 19 92 91 70
31 06 01 08 05	45 57 18 24 06	35 30 34 26 14	86 79 90 74 39	23 40 30 97 32
85 26 97 76 02	02 05 16 56 92	68 66 57 48 18	73 05 38 52 47	18 62 38 85 79
63 57 33 21 35	05 32 54 70 48	90 55 35 75 48	28 46 82 87 09	83 49 12 55 24
73 79 64 57 53	03 52 96 47 78	35 80 83 42 82	60 93 52 03 44	35 27 38 84 35
98 52 01 77 67	14 90 56 86 07	22 10 94 05 58	60 97 09 34 33	50 50 07 39 98
11 80 50 54 31	39 80 82 77 32	50 72 56 82 48	29 40 52 42 01	52 77 56 78 51
83 45 29 96 34	06 28 89 80 83	13 74 67 00 78	18 47 54 06 10	68 71 17 78 17
88 68 54 02 00	86 50 75 84 01	36 76 66 79 51	90 36 47 64 93	29 60 91 10 62
99 59 46 73 48	87 51 76 49 69	91 82 60 89 28	93 78 56 13 68	23 47 83 41 13
65 48 11 76 74	17 46 85 09 50	58 04 77 69 74	73 03 95 71 86	40 21 81 65 44
80 12 43 56 35	17 72 70 80 15	45 31 82 23 74	21 11 57 82 53	14 38 55 37 63
74 35 09 98 17	77 40 27 72 14	43 23 60 02 10	45 52 16 42 37	96 28 60 26 55
69 91 62 68 03	66 25 22 91 48	36 93 68 72 03	76 62 11 39 90	94 40 05 64 18
09 90 32 05 05	14 22 56 85 14	46 42 75 67 88	96 29 77 88 22	54 38 21 45 98
91 49 91 45 23	68 47 92 76 86	46 16 28 35 54	94 75 08 99 23	37 08 92 00 48
80 33 69 45 98	26 94 03 08 58	70 29 73 41 35	53 14 03 33 40	42 05 08 23 41
44 10 48 19 49	85 15 74 79 54	32 97 92 65 75	57 60 04 08 81	22 22 20 64 13
12 55 07 37 42	11 10 00 20 40	12 86 07 46 97	96 64 48 94 39	28 70 72 58 15
63 60 64 93 29	16 50 53 44 84	40 21 95 25 63	43 65 17 70 82	07 20 73 17 90
61 19 69 04 46	26 45 74 77 74	51 92 43 37 29	65 39 45 95 93	42 58 26 05 27
15 47 44 52 66	95 27 07 99 53	59 36 78 38 48	82 39 61 01 18	33 21 15 94 66
94 55 72 85 73	67 89 75 43 87	54 62 24 44 31	91 19 04 25 92	92 92 74 59 73
42 48 11 62 13	97 34 40 87 21	16 86 84 87 67	03 07 11 20 59	25 70 14 66 70
23 52 37 83 17	73 20 88 98 37	68 93 59 14 16	26 25 22 96 63	05 52 28 25 62
04 49 35 24 94	75 24 63 38 24	45 86 25 10 25	61 96 27 93 35	65 33 71 24 72
00 54 99 76 54	84 05 18 81 59	96 11 96 38 96	54 69 28 23 91	23 28 72 95 29
35 96 31 53 07	26 89 80 93 54	33 35 13 54 62	77 97 45 00 24	90 10 33 93 33
59 80 80 83 91	45 42 72 68 42	83 60 94 97 00	13 02 12 48 92	78 56 52 01 06
46 05 88 52 36	01 39 09 22 86	77 28 14 40 77	93 91 08 36 47	70 61 74 29 41
32 17 90 05 97	87 37 92 52 41	05 56 70 70 07	86 74 31 71 57	85 39 41 18 38
69 23 48 14 06	20 11 74 52 04	15 95 66 00 00	18 74 39 24 23	97 11 89 63 38
19 56 54 14 30	01 75 87 53 79	40 41 92 15 85	66 67 43 68 06	84 96 28 52 07
45 15 51 49 38	19 47 60 72 46	43 66 79 45 43	59 04 79 00 33	20 82 66 95 41
94 86 43 19 94	36 16 81 08 51	34 88 88 15 53	01 54 03 54 56	05 01 45 11 76
93 08 62 48 26	45 24 02 84 04	44 99 90 88 96	39 09 47 34 07	35 44 13 18 80
33 18 51 62 32	41 94 15 09 49	89 43 54 85 81	88 69 54 19 94	37 54 87 30 43
80 95 10 04 06	96 38 27 07 74	20 15 12 33 87	25 01 62 52 98	94 62 46 11 71
79 75 24 91 40	71 96 12 82 96	69 86 10 25 91	74 85 22 05 39	00 38 75 95 79
18 63 33 25 37	98 14 50 65 71	31 01 02 46 74	05 45 56 14 27	77 93 89 19 36
74 02 94 39 02	77 55 73 22 70	97 79 01 71 19	52 52 75 80 21	80 81 45 17 48
54 17 84 56 11	80 99 33 71 43	05 33 51 29 69	56 12 71 92 55	36 04 09 03 24
11 66 44 98 83	52 07 98 48 27	59 38 17 15 39	09 97 33 34 40	88 46 12 33 56
48 32 47 79 28	81 24 96 47 10	02 29 53 68 70	32 30 75 75 46	15 02 00 99 94
69 07 49 41 38	87 63 79 19 76	35 58 40 44 01	10 51 82 16 15	01 84 87 69 38

Source: This table is reproduced with permission from tables of the RAND Corporation from *A Million Random Digits with 100,000 Normal Deviates*, New York, The Free Press, 1955.

634

Table A-2 Areas in Two Tails of the Normal Curve at Selected Values of x/σ from the Arithmetic Mean

This table shows: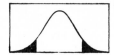

x/σ	.00	.01	.02	.03	.04	.05	.06	.07	.08	.09
0.0	1.0000	.9920	.9840	.9761	.9681	.9601	.9522	.9442	.9362	.9283
0.1	.9203	.9124	.9045	.8966	.8887	.8808	.8729	.8650	.8572	.8493
0.2	.8415	.8337	.8259	.8181	.8103	.8026	.7949	.7872	.7795	.7718
0.3	.7642	.7566	.7490	.7414	.7339	.7263	.7188	.7114	.7039	.6965
0.4	.6892	.6818	.6745	.6672	.6599	.6527	.6455	.6384	.6312	.6241
0.5	.6171	.6101	.6031	.5961	.5892	.5823	.5755	.5687	.5619	.5552
0.6	.5485	.5419	.5353	.5287	.5222	.5157	.5093	.5029	.4965	.4902
0.7	.4839	.4777	.4715	.4654	.4593	.4533	.4473	.4413	.4354	.4295
0.8	.4237	.4179	.4122	.4065	.4009	.3953	.3898	.3843	.3789	.3735
0.9	.3681	.3628	.3576	.3524	.3472	.3421	.3371	.3320	.3271	.3222
1.0	.3173	.3125	.3077	.3030	.2983	.2937	.2891	.2846	.2801	.2757
1.1	.2713	.2670	.2627	.2585	.2543	.2501	.2460	.2420	.2380	.2340
1.2	.2301	.2263	.2225	.2187	.2150	.2113	.2077	.2041	.2005	.1971
1.3	.1936	.1902	.1868	.1835	.1802	.1770	.1738	.1707	.1676	.1645
1.4	.1615	.1585	.1556	.1527	.1499	.1471	.1443	.1416	.1389	.1362
1.5	.1336	.1310	.1285	.1260	.1236	.1211	.1188	.1164	.1141	.1118
1.6	.1096	.1074	.1052	.1031	.1010	.0989	.0969	.0949	.0930	.0910
1.7	.0891	.0873	.0854	.0836	.0819	.0801	.0784	.0767	.0751	.0735
1.8	.0719	.0703	.0688	.0672	.0658	.0643	.0629	.0615	.0601	.0588
1.9	.0574	.0561	.0549	.0536	.0524	.0512	.0500	.0488	.0477	.0466
2.0	.0455	.0444	.0434	.0424	.0414	.0404	.0394	.0385	.0375	.0366
2.1	.0357	.0349	.0340	.0332	.0324	.0316	.0308	.0300	.0293	.0285
2.2	.0278	.0271	.0264	.0257	.0251	.0244	.0238	.0232	.0226	.0220
2.3	.0214	.0209	.0203	.0198	.0193	.0188	.0183	.0178	.0173	.0168
2.4	.0164	.0160	.0155	.0151	.0147	.0143	.0139	.0135	.0131	.0128
2.4	.0124	.0121	.0117	.0114	.0111	.0108	.0105	.0102	.00988	.00960
2.6	.00932	.00905	.00879	.00854	.00829	.00805	.00781	.00759	.00736	.00715
2.7	.00693	.00673	.00653	.00633	.00614	.00596	.00578	.00561	.00544	.00527
2.8	.00511	.00495	.00480	.00465	.00451	.00437	.00424	.00410	.00398	.00385
2.9	.00373	.00361	.00350	.00339	.00328	.00318	.00308	.00298	.00288	.00279

x/σ	.0	.1	.2	.3	.4	.5	.6	.7	.8	.9
3	.00270	.00194	.00137	$.0^3967$	$.0^3674$	$.0^3465$	$.0^3318$	$.0^3216$	$.0^3145$	$.0^4962$
4	$.0^4633$	$.0^4413$	$.0^4267$	$.0^4171$	$.0^4108$	$.0^5680$	$.0^5422$	$.0^5260$	$.0^5159$	$.0^6958$
5	$.0^6573$	$.0^6340$	$.0^6199$	$.0^6116$	$.0^7666$	$.0^7380$	$.0^7214$	$.0^7120$	$.0^8663$	$.0^8364$
6	$.0^8197$	$.0^8106$	$.0^9565$	$.0^9298$	$.0^9155$	$.0^{10}803$	$.0^{10}411$	$.0^{10}208$	$.0^{10}105$	$.0^{11}520$

SOURCE: This table is copyrighted by Prentice-Hall, Inc. It is reproduced by permission of Frederick E. Croxton.

Table A-3 Areas in One Tail of the Normal Curve at Selected Values of x/σ from the Arithmetic Mean

This table shows:

or

x/σ	.00	.01	.02	.03	.04	.05	.06	.07	.08	.09
0.0	.5000	.4960	.4920	.4880	.4840	.4801	.4761	.4721	.4681	.4641
0.1	.4602	.4562	.4522	.4483	.4443	.4404	.4364	.4325	.4286	.4247
0.2	.4207	.4168	.4129	.4090	.4052	.4013	.3974	.3936	.3897	.3859
0.3	.3821	.3783	.3745	.3707	.3669	.3632	.3594	.3557	.3520	.3483
0.4	.3446	.3409	.3372	.3336	.3300	.3264	.3228	.3192	.3156	.3121
0.5	.3085	.3050	.3015	.2981	.2946	.2912	.2877	.2843	.2810	.2776
0.6	.2743	.2709	.2676	.2643	.2611	.2578	.2546	.2514	.2483	.2451
0.7	.2420	.2389	.2358	.2327	.2296	.2266	.2236	.2206	.2177	.2148
0.8	.2119	.2090	.2061	.2033	.2005	.1977	.1949	.1922	.1894	.1867
0.9	.1841	.1814	.1788	.1762	.1736	.1711	.1685	.1660	.1635	.1611
1.0	.1587	.1562	.1539	.1515	.1492	.1469	.1446	.1423	.1401	.1379
1.1	.1357	.1335	.1314	.1292	.1271	.1251	.1230	.1210	.1190	.1170
1.2	.1151	.1131	.1112	.1093	.1075	.1056	.1038	.1020	.1003	.0985
1.3	.0968	.0951	.0934	.0918	.0901	.0885	.0869	.0853	.0838	.0823
1.4	.0808	.0793	.0778	.0764	.0749	.0735	.0721	.0708	.06)4	.0681
1.5	.0668	.0655	.0643	.0630	.0618	.0606	.0594	.0582	.0571	.0559
1.6	.0548	.0537	.0526	.0516	.0505	.0495	.0485	.0475	.0465	.0455
1.7	.0446	.0436	.0427	.0418	.0409	.0401	.0392	.0384	.0375	.0367
1.8	.0359	.0351	.0344	.0336	.0329	.0322	.0314	.0307	.0301	.0294
1.9	.0287	.0281	.0274	.0268	.0262	.0256	.0250	.0244	.0239	.0233
2.0	.0228	.0222	.0217	.0212	.0207	.0202	.0197	.0192	.0188	.0183
2.1	.0179	.0174	.0170	.0166	.0162	.0158	.0154	.0150	.0146	.0143
2.2	.0139	.0136	.0132	.0129	.0125	.0122	.0119	.0116	.0113	.0110
2.3	.0107	.0104	.0102	.00990	.00964	.00939	.00914	.00889	.00866	.00842
2.4	.00820	.00798	.00776	.00755	.00734	.00714	.00695	.00676	.00657	.00639
2.5	.00621	.00604	.00587	.00570	.00554	.00539	.00523	.00508	.00494	.00480
2.6	.00466	.00453	.00440	.00427	.00415	.00402	.00391	.00379	.00368	.00357
2.7	.00347	.00336	.00326	.00317	.00307	.00298	.00289	.00280	.00272	.00264
2.8	.00256	.00248	.00240	.00233	.00226	.00219	.00212	.00205	.00199	.00193
2.9	.00187	.00181	.00175	.00169	.00164	.00159	.00154	.00149	.00144	.00139

x/σ	.0	.1	.2	.3	.4	.5	.6	.7	.8	.9
3	.00135	$.0^3968$	$.0^3687$	$.0^3483$	$.0^3337$	$.0^3233$	$.0^3159$	$.0^3108$	$.0^4723$	$.0^4481$
4	$.0^4317$	$.0^4207$	$.0^4133$	$.0^5854$	$.0^5541$	$.0^5340$	$.0^5211$	$.0^5130$	$.0^6793$	$.0^6479$
5	$.0^6287$	$.0^6170$	$.0^7996$	$.0^7579$	$.0^7333$	$.0^7190$	$.0^7107$	$.0^8599$	$.0^8332$	$.0^8182$
6	$.0^9987$	$.0^9430$	$.0^9282$	$.0^9149$	$.0^{10}777$	$.0^{10}402$	$.0^{10}206$	$.0^{10}104$	$.0^{11}523$	$.0^{11}260$

SOURCE: This table is copyrighted by Prentice-Hall, Inc. It is reproduced by permission of Frederick E. Croxton.

Table A-4   Table of Critical Values of *t*

	Level of significance for two-tailed test								
Df	0.5	0.4	0.3	0.2	0.1	0.05	0.02	0.01	Df
	Level of significance for one-tailed test								
	0.25	0.20	0.15	0.10	0.05	0.025	0.01	0.005	
1	1.000	1.376	1.963	3.078	6.314	12.706	31.821	63.657	1
2	.816	1.061	1.386	1.886	2.920	4.303	6.965	9.925	2
3	.765	.978	1.250	1.638	2.353	3.182	4.541	5.841	3
4	.741	.941	1.190	1.533	2.132	2.776	3.747	4.604	4
5	.727	.920	1.156	1.476	2.105	2.571	3.365	4.032	5
6	.718	.906	1.134	1.440	1.943	2.447	3.143	3.707	6
7	.711	.896	1.119	1.415	1.895	2.365	2.998	3.499	7
8	.706	.889	1.108	1.397	1.860	2.306	2.896	3.355	8
9	.703	.883	1.100	1.383	1.833	2.262	2.821	3.250	9
10	.700	.879	1.093	1.372	1.812	2.228	2.764	3.169	10
11	.697	.876	1.088	1.363	1.796	2.201	2.718	3.106	11
12	.695	.873	1.083	1.356	1.782	2.179	2.681	3.055	12
13	.694	.870	1.079	1.350	1.771	2.160	2.650	3.012	13
14	.692	.868	1.076	1.345	1.761	2.145	2.624	2.977	14
15	.691	.866	1.074	1.341	1.753	2.131	2.602	2.947	15
16	.690	.865	1.071	1.337	1.746	2.120	2.583	2.921	16
17	.689	.863	1.069	1.333	1.740	2.110	2.567	2.898	17
18	.688	.862	1.067	1.330	1.734	2.101	2.552	2.878	18
19	.688	.861	1.066	1.328	1.729	2.093	2.539	2.861	19
20	.687	.860	1.064	1.325	1.725	2.086	2.528	2.845	20
21	.686	.859	1.063	1.323	1.721	2.080	2.518	2.831	21
22	.686	.858	1.061	1.321	1.717	2.074	2.508	2.819	22
23	.685	.858	1.060	1.319	1.714	2.069	2.500	2.807	23
24	.685	.857	1.059	1.318	1.711	2.064	2.492	2.797	24
25	.684	.856	1.058	1.316	1.708	2.060	2.485	2.787	25
26	.684	.856	1.058	1.315	1.706	2.056	2.479	2.779	26
27	.684	.855	1.057	1.314	1.703	2.052	2.473	2.771	27
28	.683	.855	1.056	1.313	1.701	2.048	2.467	2.763	28
29	.683	.854	1.055	1.311	1.699	2.045	2.462	2.756	29
30	.683	.854	1.055	1.310	1.697	2.042	2.457	2.750	30
35						2.030		2.724	35
40						2.021		2.704	40
45						2.014		2.690	45
50						2.008		2.678	50
60						2.000		2.600	60
70						1.994		2.648	70
80						1.990		2.638	80
90						1.987		2.632	90
100						1.984		2.626	100
125						1.979		2.616	125
150						1.976		2.609	150
200						1.972		2.601	200
300						1.968		2.592	300
400						1.966		2.588	400
500						1.965		2.568	500
1000						1.962		2.581	1000
∞	.67449	.84162	1.03643	1.28155	1.64485	1.95996	2.32634	2.57582	∞

SOURCE: Table C is abridged from table III of Fisher and Yates, *Statistical Tables for Biological, Agricultural and Medical Research* (Edinburgh and London: Oliver & Boyd Ltd.).   Reprinted by permission of the authors and publishers.

Table A-5 Upper Percentage Points of the F Distribution*

n	$1-\alpha$	m=1	2	3	4	5	6	7	8	9	10	12	15	20	30	60	120	∞
1	0.90	39.9	49.5	53.6	55.8	57.2	58.2	58.9	59.4	59.9	60.2	60.7	61.2	61.7	62.3	62.8	63.1	63.3
	0.95	161	200	216	225	230	234	237	239	241	242	244	246	248	250	252	253	254
	0.975	648	800	864	900	922	937	948	957	963	969	977	985	993	1,000	1,010	1,010	1,020
	0.99	4,050	5,000	5,400	5,620	5,760	5,860	5,930	5,980	6,020	6,060	6,110	6,160	6,210	6,260	6,310	6,340	6,370
	0.995	16,200	20,000	21,600	22,500	23,100	23,400	23,700	23,900	24,100	24,200	24,400	24,600	24,800	25,000	25,200	25,400	25,500
2	0.90	8.53	9.00	9.16	9.24	9.29	9.33	9.35	9.37	9.38	9.39	9.41	9.42	9.44	9.46	9.47	9.48	9.49
	0.95	18.5	19.0	19.2	19.2	19.3	19.3	19.4	19.4	19.4	19.4	19.4	19.4	19.4	19.5	19.5	19.5	19.5
	0.975	38.5	39.0	39.2	39.2	39.3	39.3	39.4	39.4	39.4	39.4	39.4	39.4	39.4	39.5	39.5	39.5	39.5
	0.99	98.5	99.0	99.2	99.2	99.3	99.3	99.4	99.4	99.4	99.4	99.4	99.4	99.4	99.5	99.5	99.5	99.5
	0.995	199	199	199	199	199	199	199	199	199	199	199	199	199	199	199	199	199
3	0.90	5.54	5.46	5.39	5.34	5.31	5.28	5.27	5.25	5.24	5.23	5.22	5.20	5.18	5.17	5.15	5.14	5.13
	0.95	10.1	9.55	9.28	9.12	9.01	8.94	8.89	8.85	8.81	8.79	8.74	8.70	8.66	8.62	8.57	8.55	8.53
	0.975	17.4	16.0	15.4	15.1	14.9	14.7	14.6	14.5	14.5	14.4	14.3	14.3	14.2	14.1	14.0	13.9	13.9
	0.99	34.1	30.8	29.5	28.7	28.2	27.9	27.7	27.5	27.3	27.2	27.1	26.9	26.7	26.5	26.3	26.2	26.1
	0.995	55.6	49.8	47.5	46.2	45.4	44.8	44.4	44.1	43.9	43.7	43.4	43.1	42.8	42.5	42.1	42.0	41.8
4	0.90	4.54	4.32	4.19	4.11	4.05	4.01	3.98	3.95	3.93	3.92	3.90	3.87	3.84	3.82	3.79	3.78	3.76
	0.95	7.71	6.94	6.59	6.39	6.26	6.16	6.09	6.04	6.00	5.96	5.91	5.86	5.80	5.75	5.69	5.66	5.63
	0.975	12.2	10.6	9.98	9.60	9.36	9.20	9.07	8.98	8.90	8.84	8.75	8.66	8.56	8.46	8.36	8.31	8.26
	0.99	21.2	18.0	16.7	16.0	15.5	15.2	15.0	14.8	14.7	14.5	14.4	14.2	14.0	13.8	13.7	13.6	13.5
	0.995	31.3	26.3	24.3	23.2	22.5	22.0	21.6	21.4	21.1	21.0	20.7	20.4	20.2	19.9	19.6	19.5	19.3
5	0.90	4.06	3.78	3.62	3.52	3.45	3.40	3.37	3.34	3.32	3.30	3.27	3.24	3.21	3.17	3.14	3.12	3.11
	0.95	6.61	5.79	5.41	5.19	5.05	4.95	4.88	4.82	4.77	4.74	4.68	4.62	4.56	4.50	4.43	4.40	4.37
	0.975	10.0	8.43	7.76	7.39	7.15	6.98	6.85	6.76	6.68	6.62	6.52	6.43	6.33	6.23	6.12	6.07	6.02
	0.99	16.3	13.3	12.1	11.4	11.0	10.7	10.5	10.3	10.2	10.1	9.89	9.72	9.55	9.38	9.20	9.11	9.02
	0.995	22.8	18.3	16.5	15.6	14.9	14.5	14.2	14.0	13.8	13.6	13.4	13.1	12.9	12.7	12.4	12.3	12.1
6	0.90	3.78	3.46	3.29	3.18	3.11	3.05	3.01	2.98	2.96	2.94	2.90	2.87	2.84	2.80	2.76	2.74	2.72
	0.95	5.99	5.14	4.76	4.53	4.39	4.28	4.21	4.15	4.10	4.06	4.00	3.94	3.87	3.81	3.74	3.70	3.67
	0.975	8.81	7.26	6.60	6.23	5.99	5.82	5.70	5.60	5.52	5.46	5.37	5.27	5.17	5.07	4.96	4.90	4.85
	0.99	13.7	10.9	9.78	9.15	8.75	8.47	8.26	8.10	7.98	7.87	7.72	7.56	7.40	7.23	7.06	6.97	6.88
	0.995	18.6	14.5	12.9	12.0	11.5	11.1	10.8	10.6	10.4	10.2	10.0	9.81	9.59	9.36	9.12	9.00	8.88
7	0.90	3.59	3.26	3.07	2.96	2.88	2.83	2.78	2.75	2.72	2.70	2.67	2.63	2.59	2.56	2.51	2.49	2.47
	0.95	5.59	4.74	4.35	4.12	3.97	3.87	3.79	3.73	3.68	3.64	3.57	3.51	3.44	3.38	3.30	3.27	3.23
	0.975	8.07	6.54	5.89	5.52	5.29	5.12	4.99	4.90	4.82	4.76	4.67	4.57	4.47	4.36	4.25	4.20	4.14
	0.99	12.2	9.55	8.45	7.85	7.46	7.19	6.99	6.84	6.72	6.62	6.47	6.31	6.16	5.99	5.82	5.74	5.65
	0.995	16.2	12.4	10.9	10.1	9.52	9.16	8.89	8.68	8.51	8.38	8.18	7.97	7.75	7.53	7.31	7.19	7.08
8	0.90	3.46	3.11	2.92	2.81	2.73	2.67	2.62	2.59	2.56	2.54	2.50	2.46	2.42	2.38	2.34	2.31	2.29
	0.95	5.32	4.46	4.07	3.84	3.69	3.58	3.50	3.44	3.39	3.35	3.28	3.22	3.15	3.08	3.01	2.97	2.93
	0.975	7.57	6.06	5.42	5.05	4.82	4.65	4.53	4.43	4.36	4.30	4.20	4.10	4.00	3.89	3.78	3.73	3.67
	0.99	11.3	8.65	7.59	7.01	6.63	6.37	6.18	6.03	5.91	5.81	5.67	5.52	5.36	5.20	5.03	4.95	4.86
	0.995	14.7	11.0	9.60	8.81	8.30	7.95	7.69	7.50	7.34	7.21	7.01	6.81	6.61	6.40	6.18	6.06	5.95

v_2	p	1	2	3	4	5	6	7	8	9	10	12	15	20	30	60	120	∞
9	0.90	3.36	3.01	2.81	2.69	2.61	2.55	2.51	2.47	2.44	2.42	2.38	2.34	2.30	2.25	2.21	2.18	2.16
	0.95	5.12	4.26	3.86	3.63	3.48	3.37	3.29	3.23	3.18	3.14	3.07	3.01	2.94	2.86	2.79	2.75	2.71
	0.975	7.21	5.71	5.08	4.72	4.48	4.32	4.20	4.10	4.03	3.96	3.87	3.77	3.67	3.56	3.45	3.39	3.33
	0.99	10.6	8.02	6.99	6.42	6.06	5.80	5.61	5.47	5.35	5.26	5.11	4.96	4.81	4.65	4.48	4.40	4.31
	0.995	13.6	10.1	8.72	7.96	7.47	7.13	6.88	6.69	6.54	6.42	6.23	6.03	5.83	5.62	5.41	5.30	5.19
10	0.90	3.29	2.92	2.73	2.61	2.52	2.46	2.41	2.38	2.35	2.32	2.28	2.24	2.20	2.15	2.11	2.08	2.06
	0.95	4.96	4.10	3.71	3.48	3.33	3.22	3.14	3.07	3.02	2.98	2.91	2.84	2.77	2.70	2.62	2.58	2.54
	0.975	6.94	5.46	4.83	4.47	4.24	4.07	3.95	3.85	3.78	3.72	3.62	3.52	3.42	3.31	3.20	3.14	3.08
	0.99	10.0	7.56	6.55	5.99	5.64	5.39	5.20	5.06	4.94	4.85	4.71	4.56	4.41	4.25	4.08	4.00	3.91
	0.995	12.8	9.43	8.08	7.34	6.87	6.54	6.30	6.12	5.97	5.85	5.66	5.47	5.27	5.07	4.86	4.75	4.64
12	0.90	3.18	2.81	2.61	2.48	2.39	2.33	2.28	2.24	2.21	2.19	2.15	2.10	2.06	2.01	1.96	1.93	1.90
	0.95	4.75	3.89	3.49	3.26	3.11	3.00	2.91	2.85	2.80	2.75	2.69	2.62	2.54	2.47	2.38	2.34	2.30
	0.975	6.55	5.10	4.47	4.12	3.89	3.73	3.61	3.51	3.44	3.37	3.28	3.18	3.07	2.96	2.85	2.79	2.72
	0.99	9.33	6.93	5.95	5.41	5.06	4.82	4.64	4.50	4.39	4.30	4.16	4.01	3.86	3.70	3.54	3.45	3.36
	0.995	11.8	8.51	7.23	6.52	6.07	5.76	5.52	5.35	5.20	5.09	4.91	4.72	4.53	4.33	4.12	4.01	3.90
15	0.90	3.07	2.70	2.49	2.36	2.27	2.21	2.16	2.12	2.09	2.06	2.02	1.97	1.92	1.87	1.82	1.79	1.76
	0.95	4.54	3.68	3.29	3.06	2.90	2.79	2.71	2.64	2.59	2.54	2.48	2.40	2.33	2.25	2.16	2.11	2.07
	0.975	6.20	4.77	4.15	3.80	3.58	3.41	3.29	3.20	3.12	3.06	2.96	2.86	2.76	2.64	2.52	2.46	2.40
	0.99	8.68	6.36	5.42	4.89	4.56	4.32	4.14	4.00	3.89	3.80	3.67	3.52	3.37	3.21	3.05	2.96	2.87
	0.995	10.8	7.70	6.48	5.80	5.37	5.07	4.85	4.67	4.54	4.42	4.25	4.07	3.88	3.69	3.48	3.37	3.26
20	0.90	2.97	2.59	2.38	2.25	2.16	2.09	2.04	2.00	1.96	1.94	1.89	1.84	1.79	1.74	1.68	1.64	1.61
	0.95	4.35	3.49	3.10	2.87	2.71	2.60	2.51	2.45	2.39	2.35	2.28	2.20	2.12	2.04	1.95	1.90	1.84
	0.975	5.87	4.46	3.86	3.51	3.29	3.13	3.01	2.91	2.84	2.77	2.68	2.57	2.46	2.35	2.22	2.16	2.09
	0.99	8.10	5.85	4.94	4.43	4.10	3.87	3.70	3.56	3.46	3.37	3.23	3.09	2.94	2.78	2.61	2.52	2.42
	0.995	9.94	6.99	5.82	5.17	4.76	4.47	4.26	4.09	3.96	3.85	3.68	3.50	3.32	3.12	2.92	2.81	2.69
30	0.90	2.88	2.49	2.28	2.14	2.05	1.98	1.93	1.88	1.85	1.82	1.77	1.72	1.67	1.61	1.54	1.50	1.46
	0.95	4.17	3.32	2.92	2.69	2.53	2.42	2.33	2.27	2.21	2.16	2.09	2.01	1.93	1.84	1.74	1.68	1.62
	0.975	5.57	4.18	3.59	3.25	3.03	2.87	2.75	2.65	2.57	2.51	2.41	2.31	2.20	2.07	1.94	1.87	1.79
	0.99	7.56	5.39	4.51	4.02	3.70	3.47	3.30	3.17	3.07	2.98	2.84	2.70	2.55	2.39	2.21	2.11	2.01
	0.995	9.18	6.35	5.24	4.62	4.23	3.95	3.74	3.58	3.45	3.34	3.18	3.01	2.82	2.63	2.42	2.30	2.18
60	0.90	2.79	2.39	2.18	2.04	1.95	1.87	1.82	1.77	1.74	1.71	1.66	1.60	1.54	1.48	1.40	1.35	1.29
	0.95	4.00	3.15	2.76	2.53	2.37	2.25	2.17	2.10	2.04	1.99	1.92	1.84	1.75	1.65	1.53	1.47	1.39
	0.975	5.29	3.93	3.34	3.01	2.79	2.63	2.51	2.41	2.33	2.27	2.17	2.06	1.94	1.82	1.67	1.58	1.48
	0.99	7.08	4.98	4.13	3.65	3.34	3.12	2.95	2.82	2.72	2.63	2.50	2.35	2.20	2.03	1.84	1.73	1.60
	0.995	8.49	5.80	4.73	4.14	3.76	3.49	3.29	3.13	3.01	2.90	2.74	2.57	2.39	2.19	1.96	1.83	1.69
120	0.90	2.75	2.35	2.13	1.99	1.90	1.82	1.77	1.72	1.68	1.65	1.60	1.54	1.48	1.41	1.32	1.26	1.19
	0.95	3.92	3.07	2.68	2.45	2.29	2.18	2.09	2.02	1.96	1.91	1.83	1.75	1.66	1.55	1.43	1.35	1.25
	0.975	5.15	3.80	3.23	2.89	2.67	2.52	2.39	2.30	2.22	2.16	2.05	1.94	1.82	1.69	1.53	1.43	1.31
	0.99	6.85	4.79	3.95	3.48	3.17	2.96	2.79	2.66	2.56	2.47	2.34	2.19	2.03	1.86	1.66	1.53	1.38
	0.995	8.18	5.54	4.50	3.92	3.55	3.28	3.09	2.93	2.81	2.71	2.54	2.37	2.19	1.98	1.75	1.61	1.43
∞	0.90	2.71	2.30	2.08	1.94	1.85	1.77	1.72	1.67	1.63	1.60	1.55	1.49	1.42	1.34	1.24	1.17	1.00
	0.95	3.84	3.00	2.60	2.37	2.21	2.10	2.01	1.94	1.88	1.83	1.75	1.67	1.57	1.46	1.32	1.22	1.00
	0.975	5.02	3.69	3.12	2.79	2.57	2.41	2.29	2.19	2.11	2.05	1.94	1.83	1.71	1.57	1.39	1.27	1.00
	0.99	6.63	4.61	3.78	3.32	3.02	2.80	2.64	2.51	2.41	2.32	2.18	2.04	1.88	1.70	1.47	1.32	1.00
	0.995	7.88	5.30	4.28	3.72	3.35	3.09	2.90	2.74	2.62	2.52	2.36	2.19	2.00	1.79	1.53	1.36	1.00

* Abridged from Maxine Merrington and Catherine M. Thompson: Tables of percentage points of the inverted beta distribution, *Biometrika*, vol. 33 (1943), pp. 73–88, and published here with the kind permission of the editor of *Biometrika*.

Table A-6 Percentage Points of the Chi-squared Distribution*

n \ 1−α	0.005	0.010	0.025	0.050	0.100	0.250	0.500	0.750	0.900	0.950	0.975	0.990	0.995
1	0.0⁴393	0.0³157	0.0³982	0.0³393	0.0158	0.102	0.455	1.32	2.71	3.84	5.02	6.63	7.88
2	0.0100	0.0201	0.0506	0.103	0.211	0.575	1.39	2.77	4.61	5.99	7.38	9.21	10.6
3	0.0717	0.115	0.216	0.352	0.584	1.21	2.37	4.11	6.25	7.81	9.35	11.3	12.8
4	0.207	0.297	0.484	0.711	1.06	1.92	3.36	5.39	7.78	9.49	11.1	13.3	14.9
5	0.412	0.554	0.831	1.15	1.61	2.67	4.35	6.63	9.24	11.1	12.8	15.1	16.7
6	0.676	0.872	1.24	1.64	2.20	3.45	5.35	7.84	10.6	12.6	14.4	16.8	18.5
7	0.989	1.24	1.69	2.17	2.83	4.25	6.35	9.04	12.0	14.1	16.0	18.5	20.3
8	1.34	1.65	2.18	2.73	3.49	5.07	7.34	10.2	13.4	15.5	17.5	20.1	22.0
9	1.73	2.09	2.70	3.33	4.17	5.90	8.34	11.4	14.7	16.9	19.0	21.7	23.6
10	2.16	2.56	3.25	3.94	4.87	6.74	9.34	12.5	16.0	18.3	20.5	23.2	25.2
11	2.60	3.05	3.82	4.57	5.58	7.58	10.3	13.7	17.3	19.7	21.9	24.7	26.8
12	3.07	3.57	4.40	5.23	6.30	8.44	11.3	14.8	18.5	21.0	23.3	26.2	28.3
13	3.57	4.11	5.01	5.89	7.04	9.30	12.3	16.0	19.8	22.4	24.7	27.7	29.8
14	4.07	4.66	5.63	6.57	7.79	10.2	13.3	17.1	21.1	23.7	26.1	29.1	31.3
15	4.60	5.23	6.26	7.26	8.55	11.0	14.3	18.2	22.3	25.0	27.5	30.6	32.8
16	5.14	5.81	6.91	7.96	9.31	11.9	15.3	19.4	23.5	26.3	28.8	32.0	34.3
17	5.70	6.41	7.56	8.67	10.1	12.8	16.3	20.5	24.8	27.6	30.2	33.4	35.7
18	6.26	7.01	8.23	9.39	10.9	13.7	17.3	21.6	26.0	28.9	31.5	34.8	37.2
19	6.84	7.63	8.91	10.1	11.7	14.6	18.3	22.7	27.2	30.1	32.9	36.2	38.6
20	7.43	8.26	9.59	10.9	12.4	15.5	19.3	23.8	28.4	31.4	34.2	37.6	40.0
21	8.03	8.90	10.3	11.6	13.2	16.3	20.3	24.9	29.6	32.7	35.5	38.9	41.4
22	8.64	9.54	11.0	12.3	14.0	17.2	21.3	26.0	30.8	33.9	36.8	40.3	42.8
23	9.26	10.2	11.7	13.1	14.8	18.1	22.3	27.1	32.0	35.2	38.1	41.6	44.2
24	9.89	10.9	12.4	13.8	15.7	19.0	23.3	28.2	33.2	36.4	39.4	43.0	45.6
25	10.5	11.5	13.1	14.6	16.5	19.9	24.3	29.3	34.4	37.7	40.6	44.3	46.9
26	11.2	12.2	13.8	15.4	17.3	20.8	25.3	30.4	35.6	38.9	41.9	45.6	48.3
27	11.8	12.9	14.6	16.2	18.1	21.7	26.3	31.5	36.7	40.1	43.2	47.0	49.6
28	12.5	13.6	15.3	16.9	18.9	22.7	27.3	32.6	37.9	41.3	44.5	48.3	51.0
29	13.1	14.3	16.0	17.7	19.8	23.6	28.3	33.7	39.1	42.6	45.7	49.6	52.3
30	13.8	15.0	16.8	18.5	20.6	24.5	29.3	34.8	40.3	43.8	47.0	50.9	53.7

* Abridged from Catherine M. Thompson: Tables of percentage points of the incomplete beta function and of the chi-square distribution, *Biometrika*, vol. 32 (1941), pp. 187–191, and published here with the kind permission of the editor of *Biometrika*.

Table A-7 The Greek Alphabet

Letters	Names	English equivalent	Letters	Names	English equivalent
A α	Alpha	a	N ν	Nu	n
B β	Beta	b	Ξ ξ	Xi	x
Γ γ	Gamma	g	O o	Omicron	o
Δ δ	Delta	d	Π π	Pi	p
E ϵ	Epsilon	e	P ρ	Rho	r
Z ζ	Zeta	z	Σ σ	Sigma	s
H η	Eta	—	T τ	Tau	t
Θ θ	Theta	—	Υ υ	Upsilon	u or y
I ι	Iota	i	Φ ϕ	Phi	—
K κ	Kappa	k	X χ	Chi	—
Λ λ	Lambda	l	Ψ ψ	Psi	—
M μ	Mu	m	Ω ω	Omega	—

Name Index

Abrams, Jack, 306*n*., 316
Achenbaum, Alvin R., 395, 396, 397*n*., 402*n*., 409
Ackoff, Russell L., 102*n*., 134*n*.
Ahl, David H., 400*n*.
Albaum, Gerald S., 304*n*., 311*n*., 502*n*.
Albers, Henry, 59*n*.
Alderson, Wroe, 18
Allvine, F. C., 440*n*.
Andrews, Frank M., 517*n*., 529, 531*n*., 556, 598*n*.
Assael, H., 436*n*., 438*n*.
Aucamp, J., 447
Auerback, Barbara K., 462*n*.
Axelrod, Myril D., 426*n*.

Babbie, Earl, 182, 183*n*., 191, 214, 231*n*., 236*n*., 245,
    498*n*., 506*n*., 511, 512*n*., 513*n*., 514
Bailey, Earl L., 60*n*., 62*n*., 64*n*.
Banks, Seymour, 335*n*., 343*n*., 344*n*., 346*n*., 351*n*.
Bass, Frank M., 3*n*.
Bayer, Allan E., 460*n*.
Bellenger, Danny N., 308*n*., 394, 395, 424*n*., 425*n*., 447
Bennett, Peter D., 120*n*.
Bent, D. H., 509*n*.
Berdy, Edwin M., 399*n*.

Bernhardt, Kenneth L., 424*n*., 425*n*., 427*n*., 447
Best, R., 311*n*.
Blackwell, R. D., 297*n*., 453*n*.
Blankenship, Al, 56
Blankertz, Donald F., 118*n*.
Bowen, J. M., 461*n*.
Boyd, Harper W., 27*n*., 32, 151*n*.
Bradford, Ernest S., 65*n*.
Britt, Stewart H., 161
Brown, Lyndon O., 32
Brown, Rex V., 617*n*.
Brunner, G. A., 437*n*.
Brunner, J. A., 437*n*.
Bursk, Edward C., 124*n*.

Cahalan, D., 439*n*.
Campbell, C., 456*n*.
Campbell, Donald T., 335*n*., 336, 343*n*., 344*n*., 345*n*.,
    350*n*., 353, 423*n*., 444*n*., 447
Caporaso, James, 343*n*., 344*n*.
Carmone, Frank J., 586*n*., 587*n*., 588*n*.
Carter, R. F., 309*n*.
Carvey, D. W., 305*n*.
Casey, R. S., 572

Subject Index